Sketches of
MARYLAND EASTERN SHOREMEN

Genealogical extracts from *Portrait and Biographical Record of the Eastern Shore of Maryland.* The original contained portraits of citizens of the past and present, together with portraits and biographies of the presidents of the United States, published by Chapman Publishing Company, New York and Chicago, 1898. Information was gathered by a corps of writers who interviewed the subjects of the biographies.

EDITED BY
F. Edward Wright

HERITAGE BOOKS
2011

HERITAGE BOOKS
AN IMPRINT OF HERITAGE BOOKS, INC.

Books, CDs, and more—Worldwide

For our listing of thousands of titles see our website at
www.HeritageBooks.com

Published 2011 by
HERITAGE BOOKS, INC.
Publishing Division
100 Railroad Ave. #104
Westminster, Maryland 21157

Originally published 1985

All rights reserved. No part of this book may be reproduced or transmitted in any form or by any means, electronic or mechanical, including photocopying, recording or by any information storage and retrieval system without written permission from the author, except for the inclusion of brief quotations in a review.

International Standard Book Numbers
Paperbound: 978-1-58549-056-1
Clothbound: 978-0-7884-8915-0

INTRODUCTION

This abbreviated version of Portrait and Biographical Record of the Eastern Shore of Maryland, offers an opportunity to the person who does not possess the original version to have access to the essential genealogy and much of the biography contained in the original work and the advantage of a complete every-name index not contained in the original.
In attempting to reduce the size of this material I have eliminated as much unnecessary wording as possible. The original contains much in the way of aggrandizing the accomplishments of the individual. I have tried to remove this while retaining some of the unique events and characterizations. Because a work such as this tends to use many of the same key words I have abbreviated a great deal. A list of the meanings is given at the end of this introduction. There is a danger in this type of editing; too much can lead to loss of clarity. Although this criticism may be inevitable to some extent I first challenge you to check the original. You may find that the original wording was also vague or unclear. I sometimes found difficulty in determining to what person the writer was referring when using a pronoun. Yet this problem can usually be resolved by reading through the entire paragraph or sketch.
It is hoped that this version will greatly improve the use of this major work as a genealogical tool. No genealogical data or family relationships have been omitted from the original. Once having found the family of interest you may nevertheless want to examine the original work for more biographical detail or in the case of many of the subjects, a portrait photograph (see below for the list of photographs in the original work). NUMBERS APPEARING IN THE MARGIN REFER TO THE ORIGINAL PAGES. Copies of the orignal versions are currently held at the libraries listed below. These are the locations of which I am aware; there are undoubtedly others.

Enoch Pratt Free Library, Baltimore
Maryland Historical Society
Queen Anne's County Free Library, Centreville
Talbot County Free Library, Easton
Cecil County Library, Elkton
Chesapeake College Library, Wye Mills
Wicoico County Library, Salisbury
Worcestor County Library, Snow Hill
Kent County Public Library, Chestertown

Adkins, Rev. Franklin B. 296
Adkins, William H. 344
Andrews, Joseph B. 452
Anthony, Joshua M. 508
Baldwin, Rev. Leonidas B. 242
Barber, Hon. Isaac A. 194

Beaven, Rev. George F. 498
Bernard, Joseph H. 458
Berry, George, H. M. D. 608
Bordley, James, M. D. 154
Bradley, Robert Dines 850
Bright, James B. 236

Carroll, William K., M. D. 488
Cecil, William H. 380
Chaplain, James S., M. D. 618
Connaway, James A., M. D. 726
Cook, John R. 386
Corkran, James, M. D. 798
Davidson, Charles F., M. D. 290
Day, Thomas 350
Deakyne, George A. 470
Deweese, William H. 548
Dirickson, James C., M. D. 260
Dixon, Hon. Robert B. 182
Dodd, James H. 356
Dodd, Thomas H. 338
Dryden, Francis H. 816
Dudley, S. C., M. D. 398
Fleming, Charles H. 762
Finley, Hon. Woodland P. 224
Fisher, T. Pliny, M. D. 404
Goldsborough, Hon. C. F. 160
Goldsborough, George R. 230
Goldsborough, G. W., M. D. 558
Haddaway, Capt. W. H. 628
Hardcastle, Gen. E. L. F. 188
Hicks, Hon. Thomas H. 134
Hill, Rev. Charles A. 362
Holmes, James H. 780
Holton, Joseph A., M. D. 278
Horsey, Thomas H. 272
Hurlock, David 744
Jackson, William P. 410
Jacobs, James K. H., M. D. 513
Kemp, Alfred 528

Kemp, J. H. C. 568
Lewis, John L. 638
Lloyd, Hon. Henry 124
McKenney, Gen. William 118
Merrick, Wiliam S. 308
Milbourne, Robert H. 428
Neavitt, Henry C. 538
Parvis, Joseph M. 368
Penington, J. Thomas 284
Phillips, James R., M. D. 648
Radcliffe, William H. 598
Reed, George R. 320
Roberts, Col. William S. 266
Rowe, Monmonier, M. D. 434
Ruth, John F. 668
Satterfield, William C. 588
Schoolfield, William M. 688
Selby, Walter O., M. D. 476
Seward, Capt. William E. 678
Shafer, Tilghman 326
Sisk, Hon. Albert W. 248
Smith, Hon. Marion D. 212
Spedden, Capt. Joseph H. 698
Thomas, Gen. Richard 176
Thompson, Walter H. 206
Travers, Hon. Levi D. 200
Trax, George H. 482
Trippe, Edward R., M. D. 866
Tull, S. Ashton 422
Williams, Jay 416
Willson, Thomas B., M. D. 332
Woodall, Capt. Andrew 166
Wright, Jesse A. 446

Abbreviations used

a.	acres	c.	circa (approximate)
AA	Anne Arundel	Capt	Captain
acad	academy	Car	Caroline (County)
admin	administration	Cath	Catholic
Agric	Agriculture	cav	cavalry
app	appointed	cem	cemetery
assist	assistant, assisting	Chas	Charles
		child.	children
assoc	associated, association	civ	civil
		Co	County or company
atty	attorney	Col	Colonel
b	born	coll	college
Bapt	Baptist	Confed	Confederate
bro(s)	brother(s)	d	died
bur	burial, buried, burying	d/o	daughter of

dau(s)	daughter(s)	N.Y.	New York
decd	deceased	Natl	National
Del	Delaware	Neb.	Neraska
dep	deputy	nee	maiden name
depart	department	nr	near
dist	district	Pa	Pennsylvania
Dnl	Daniel	PG	Prince George's
Dor	Dorchester	Phila	Philadelphia
Edw	Edward	pres	president
eld	eldest, elder	Presby	Presbyterian
Eng	England, or English	prev	previously
Episc	Episcopal	prob	probably
estab	established, establishment	prop	property
		purch	purchased
f/o	father of	QA	Queen Anne's
fam	family	Rbt	Robert
Fdk	Frederick	rep	represented, representative, represents
fol	following		
Frs	Francis (Not Frances)		
Gen	General	res	resident, resided, resides
Geo	George		
gov	governor	Rev	Revolutionary, Revolution
grad	graduate, graduate of, graduated	rgtr	register
granddau	granddaughter	s/o	son of
husb	husband	sec	secretary
Hy	Henry	sis	sister
insur	insurance	Sml	Samuel
Jas	James	Soc	Society
Jos	Joseph	Som	Somerset
Kt	Kent	subj	subject of this biography
La	Louisiana		
Lieut	Lieutenant	Talb	Talbot (County)
Luth	Lutheran	Thos	Thomas
m	married	Univ	University
m(1), m(2),	1st married, 2nd married, etc.	vet	veteran
		vice-pres	vice-president
Maj	Major	vol	volume
mbr	member	w/o	wife of
mcht	merchant	Wash	Washington
Md	Maryland	wid	widow
ME	Methodist Episcopal	Wilm	Wilmington
merc	mercantile	Wm	William
Mex	Mexican	Wor	Worcester
MP	Methodist Protestant	yr(s)	year(s)
N.J.	New Jersey		

Your comments and suggestions are welcomed.

F. Edward Wright

1. GEN. WILLIAM McKENNEY b Church Hill, QA Co Dec 5 1829; d at home in Centreville Jul 23 1897. His uncles: Thos Loraine McKenney, Sml McKenney, Rev Jas McKenney. His father: John McKenney b Kt Co Md Apr 13 1800; mcht in Wash & Georgetown (D.C.), later at Church Hill; 2nd wife was Maria Ambrose Merritt d/o Dr. John Merritt, Middletown, Del; they had 9 child., 7 d young, 2 living: subj and Anna E. w/o Peregrine Tilghman, Centreville. Their mother d young, 1837. John McKenney's father: Wm McKenney of Scotland.

Subj m Nov 25 1851 Eleanor Ridgely d/o Dr. Rbt Goldsborough; she d 1877; had 11 child., 6 living: Ella, w/o Rev Jas A. Mitchell, of Episc Church, Centreville; Maria Merritt, unmarried; Annie, w/o Dr. Jas K. Harper Jacobs, Kennedyville, Kt Co; Henrietta Goldsborough, m W. L. Holton, of Centreville Natl Bank; Wm, m Miss Madge McTeer, d/o Dr. Meteer, of Chestertown; and Harriet, unmarried. 2 yrs after death of 1st wife Gen. McKenney m Evelyn (Taylor) Wright, wid of Thos Wright and d/o Chas R. Taylor, of Balt.

2. JOHN P. AHERN b Dec 6 1859, Blackbird, Del, s/o Dennis and Ann (Alworth) Ahern, native Co Cork, Ireland. Reached maturity in Co Cork, then came to America. Dennis Ahern located in N.J.; he and wife mbrs Cath Church; had 8 child. who became adults: Mary, w/o Sml Hibbard; Patrick; Dennis, d at 37; Dnl d 26th yr; John P.; Maggie, w/o Andrew Lockerman; Eugene, and Wm A.

John P. Ahern m Sep 20 1883 Clara M. West of QA Co, had 6 child. (in order of birth): Anna Pearl, Ruby Catherine, Clara Elma, Sadie L., Mary and John H. Mr. and Mrs. Ahern are mbrs ME Church.

3. F. MARION HUNTER b Jun 28 1858 on farm c. 2 miles from Centreville. His father, Wm, and grandfather, Nathan Hunter, b Car Co; in 1857 Wm moved to QA Co, settling 6th dist, where he purch 196 a. He was mbr ME Church; d 1895. He m(1) Sarah Anne Coursey, of QA Co, who d 1879; of their 9 child. 2 are living: Sue R., w/o Edw F. Green, this co, and F. Marion. Wm Hunter m(2) Molly R. Barwick, by whom 3 child., 2 living, Zada A. and Jas Milton. F. Marion Hunter m Feb 10 1886 Mrs. Susie Harrington, d/o Geo Sparks, QA Co. Their child.: Justina, Wm W., Edw N., Margaret A.

4. COLIN F. TAYLOR b 1867 this dist whose father, Isaac Taylor, prob b this co or nr border in Del. In youth Isaac Taylor learned tanner's trade, later worked as tanner hereabouts and Balt. His ancestors from Va. He m Miss Ann Eliza Ferguson, 1 of 2 daus of Colin Ferguson, of Scotland, pastor St. Paul's parish, South, of Chestertown, principal Wash College. He d at 52; his wife d many yrs later at age 80; they had 5 child.: Chas Albert; Martha R., Mrs. E. C. Miller, of Kt Co; C. F.; Hyland Fdk, who d at 59; Sarah E. never m and d c. 51. C. A. went to Calif in early days, and made large fortune and later lost, d at age 65. H. F. was politician of Kt Co, d at 59. Colin F. Taylor m 1875 in Balt Emma Ridgley Chapman of Balt Co. Their daus: Susie C., grad state normal school of Balt; Belle Everett, at home.

5. HON. HENRY LLOYD, assoc judge, 1st judicial circuit; ex-gov of Md, res Cambridge, b Feb 21 1852. His father, Dnl Lloyd, b Talb Co Jul 1812; Welsh descent. His ancestors first settled in Va, after coming to America, later moved to Md. Edw Lloyd, was lieut U.S. navy, is 8th Edw in direct line of descent who has res in old family mansion of Wye House in Talb Co. Judge's grandfather, Edw Lloyd, was gov of Md 1809-1811, another Edw Lloyd served same position 1709-1714, under appointment of king and Lord Baltimore. Ex-gov Lloyd Lowndes also cousin of subj, and grand-nephew of 2nd Gov Lloyd.

Dnl Lloyd, father of judge, d Jan 1875. He m(1) Nov 22 1832 Miss Virginia, eld d/o Arthur Upshur, of eastern shore of Va; had 4 children, two living, Dnl and Upshur, in fertilizer business. After death of 1st wife, Mr. Lloyd m, Feb 3 1846, Kittie, eld d/o John Campbell and Mary (Steele) Henry, of this co. To them b: Mary Campbell, Kate Henry, and Henry, of sketch. Mrs. Kittie Lloyd was granddau of 1st U.S. senator, John Henry, from Eastern Shore of Md.

Judge Lloyd m Oct 18 1886 Mary Elizabeth, d/o Wm T. and Virginia A. Stepleforte, of this co. Their son, Henry Lloyd, Jr, b Oct 1888. They are mbrs of Christ Episc Church.

126   6. JOSEPH N. WHEATLEY, postmaster of Chestertown. Grandfather, Arthur Wheatley, was deputy sheriff of Kt Co. A. B. Wheatley, father of subj, b Kt Co 1813, elected sheriff Kt Co 1871; he d 1888 at home in Chestertown. He m Mary A. Ayres d/o John Ayres this co and who served War of 1812. In her fam were fol child.: Jos N.; Mrs. M. M. Sherwood, a wid; Miss Kate Wheatley, assist postmaster at Chestertown; J. C. res at Annapolis; J. F., living in Edesville, Kt Co; and W. A., res of Chestertown.

Jos N. Wheatley b Aug 23 1857 at home nr Edesville 5th dist. In 1889 he m Miss Fannie G., d/o T. W. Russell; they had: Jos N., Jr., and T. W. Russell.

127   7. SAMUEL G. FISHER, M. D. of Chestertown, elected clerk circuit court for Kt Co in 1891; b Sep 26 1831 this co, s/o Jacob Fisher. Latter b Sussex Co, Del, Dec 1796, came to this area c. 28, a physician, in general practice until 1859, register of wills, 1851-7. His bro Abram d young, and another one, Isaac, atty of Huntingdon, Pa., now decd. W/o Jacob Fisher was Mary Ann Ringgold, of this co, d/o Josias, farmer of Kt Co. Mrs. Mary Fisher d Oct 1880, in 72nd yr. Of her 8 sons and three daus only three survive. Jacob F. res in Germantown, Pa., and one sis living in Wash.

Sml G. Fisher m 1854 Miss Isabella Constable d/o John S. Constable. They are mbrs MP Church. Their child.: Ellen C. and Sml G., practices medicine Port Deposit, Md.

128   8. RICHARD HARRISON COLLINS, senior editor and one of owners and publishers of Transcript. Paternal grandfather was Salisbury Collins, of Eng, related to Lord Salisbury, distantly; came to Dor Co with parents when infant. His son, John M., father of subj, b Dor Co in 1819, but went to QA Co in early manhood; d 1892. His wife was former Jane Harrison of QA Co and d/o Capt Richard Harrison who served Rev Army; he d 1831 when Mrs. Collins was 6. She and John Collins had 5 child. of whom Wm Salisbury res QA Co, nr Centreville, and Washington Finley hardware mcht Millington, Kt Co.

Richard Harrison Collins b Spaniard's Neck, QA Co, Sep 16 1859; m Sep 14 1893 Elizabeth Harding Roberts, from N.C., d/o Stephen Chester Roberts, D. D. Their child.; youngest d; oldest son, Stephen Roberts b Jan 13 1896 and Richard Harrison, Jr., b May 12 1897; mbrs Episc Church, Chestertown.

129   9. SAMUEL MALLALIEU b Delph, Yorkshire, Eng, Mar 16 1836; came to this country when 4; s/o Thos and Mary Mallalieu, both in Delph. His father was b Sep 17 1814 and mother b 29 Dec 1813; they d on Jul 30 1896, she at 10:00 a.m. and he at 5:00; they had 11 child., of whom 6 grew to maturity. Jos b Phila May 10 1841, farmer in QA Co. Jas M. b May 21 1843 Phila, d 1887. Mary., b Oct 17 1847, Del, w/o R. H. Adams, presiding elder of East Dover dist. Annie J. b Jul 2 1849, Del, w/o Geo M. Jenkins, Trappe, Talb Co. John J. b Sep 23 1852 QA Co, atty & real estate man, Kearney, Neb. Thos Mallalieu left Eng when 25, settled in Phila 5-6 yrs, rented factory in Kt Co, Del, c. 1845 with

-2-

brother John. In March he came to this area, rented small woolen mill in QA Co, just across the river from Millington; mbr ME Church.

Samuel Mallalieu m Feb 17 1857 Julia Ann Walls, of Millington, by whom he had 5 child. Virginia w/o C. M. Johnson; Geo Hy res of Patterson, N.J., salesman for N.Y. firm; Wm Thos is home in business with father; Elwood R. is agent for Buffalo paper & twine manufactory; and Joshua Clifton with firm in New York that makes paper & twine.

10. WILLIAM A. HYLAND's father, Hy M. Hyland b 1800 nr Rock Hall, Kt Co., blacksmith trade & farming, mbr of Epis Church, d 1851, age 51. His wife, Maria Grant Hyland, of Kt Co; had 8 child. Wm A. Hyland b Mar 24 1833, left home at 16 to learn blacksmith trade; settled at Galena Jan 1855; mbr ME Church; m(1) 1861 by Rev John Allen, Mary C. Nordain, of parents in Odessa, Del. She d Apr 6 1883, survived by six child.: Harry H., mcht of N.J.; John Allen, bookkeeper of Mutual Reserve Fund Assoc of N.Y.; Annie W., w/o Herbert Price, of QA Co; Elizabeth Grant, w/o J. R. Wilson, this place; Emma E., w/o J. R. Van Zandt, agent at Sampson's railway sta; and Wm A., with father in business. Wm Hyland m(2) 1886 by Rev Geo W. Townsend, Catherine Clark, of Elkton; their son: Chester Arthur Gorman, at home. 130

11. THOMAS W. SKIRVEN's father, John T. and grandfather, Frs Skirven, farmers of Md. Former was capt of cav company of militia; he d in Kt Co. Thos Skirven's mother was Sarah Granger Gale, of Kt Co, d/o Thos Gale; mbr ME Church; she d at 55. Thos Gale was co surveyor & farmer. Her ancestors came to America in own ship, invested heavily in St. Mary's Co. John and Sarah Skirven had 5 child.: Thos W.; Mary Emma, deceased w/o David W. Hanes, Phila; Martha E., w/o Wm H. Colesberry, Phila; J. Walter, farmer in Kt Co; Washington Gale, farmer, 6th dist. Thos W. Skirven b Aug 3 1842 3rd dist; m 1866 Miss Angeline S. Bard of Brooklyn, N.Y.; their child.: Percy Granger farming in Mich.; Thos Arthur and Edmund Howe res in Chicago, where former in railroad business and latter in coal business; Chas Howard operates farm in 6th dist; Harry and Frank at home. 131

12. JOHN WILLIAM LATIMER, M. D. in practice over 20 yrs in Galena. His great-grandfather Latimer owned land here. His grandfather, John Ford Latimer, M. D., of Chas Co, in practice with Dr. Thos I. Marshall of Piscataway, Md, many yrs; in Battle of Bladensburg, War of 1812. His father came to Md from Eng with 2 bros; he settled in Chas Co, while the other two located in Va and Del, respectively. Joseph Latimer, father of subj, b Piscataway, PG Co, and there spent entire life, except period as surgeon Confederate army; he d in 66th yr. Mother of subj was Miss Anna A. Shipps, b in Berks Co, Pa., and still living, in 75th yr, at home of son, J. W. Of her 8 child., 5 d young. Jos N. B. is grad College of Physicians & Surgeons of Balt; went into father's practice nr Piscataway. James Marshall, druggist, lives in PG Co. Dr. J. W. Latimer was b Jun 6 1852, Piscataway, Md. In 1876 he m Eleanor Brewer, d/o Newton and Mary E. Brewer, of South River, AA Co. 132

13. THOMAS HOLLIDAY HICKS, ex-gov of Md and U.S. senator, b nr East New Market, 2 Sep 1798, eld s/o Henry C. and Mary (Sewell) Hicks, of English and Scotch descent respectively; mbrs ME Church. They had 13 children. Gov Hicks m(1) Ann Thompson Dor Co and m(2) Leah Raleigh, of Dor Co. After the death of latter he m Mrs. Jane Wilcox, wid of cousin, Henry Wilcox. One child living: Nannie, w/o Dr. Geo L. Hicks, Cambridge. Thos H. Hicks d Feb 13 1865 from apoplexy; funeral attended by Pres Lincoln. 135

138 14. SAMUEL BECK, M. D., b Sep 1839; practiced in Worton 1863-1879; elected clerk of court in 1879; d Feb 8 1896; s/o Horatio and Mary M. (Miller) Beck, of Kt Co. He m 1863 Miss Ellen Constable, of Kt Co; both mbrs of Episc Church. Child. living: Hallie R. w/o Allan A. Harris, local businessman; Horace W., with St. Louis Electric & Gas Lighting Co, m Nannie H., d/o late Jesse K. Hines. Mary I., unmarried. Wm W., admitted to bar in 1892. Sml is res Ft Worth, Tex. Sarah E. and Isabel S. at home. Hy C. is youngest.

139 15. ALEXANDER HARRIS s/o Thos and Henrietta (Ringgold) Harris b at Rock Hall Apr 7 1819. Father came to area from Calv Co c. 1800, purch estates called Rock Hall; estab line of packets from there to Balt. His wife d/o Maj. Wm Ringgold and Mary (Wilmer) Ringgold. Major was mbr committee of safety and correspondence during Rev war, which drew up constitution of Md.
Alexander went to Miss., became cashier Brandon Bank, returned home when financial crisis wrecked most banking of Miss., then farmed in Kt Co but when gold rush raged in Calif crossed plains from Mo. to Calif. on horseback; returned in 1859 to join B & O Railroad Co; d Balt Jun 3 1895. Alexander Harris m Nov 28 1843 Maria Louisa Spencer d/o Richard and Sophia (Gresham) Spencer. The father was descendant of English family, who came to America c. 1693, and settled first on Miles River, Talb Co. Maria L. Harris was b Feb 25 1824, at Spencer Hall, Kt Co; d Feb 15 1893. 4 child. survive her: Anna Maria, who m Dnl Chase Chapman of Balt Nov 23 1869; Emma, who Jun 3 1879 m Jas Latimer Banning, of Wilm, Del, and has 2 child., Henry Geddes and Jas Latimer; Spencer, who m, Oct 8 1879, Mary Rebecca Jones, and has 2 child., Mary Louisa and Richard Spencer; and Allan Alexander, who m Jan 25 1893, Harriet Ringgold Beck, d/o Dr. Sml Beck, and has child, Allan Beck.

140 16. WALTER BOOKER businessman of Hillsboro, Car Co, manufactured of boots & shoes for 35 yrs; settled permanently this village in 1876; s/o Marcellus and Clementine (Shepard) Booker, this state, and youngest of 4 surviving child.; 3 others have d. His 3 bros are Frs M., Thos A. and John H. The father served in Mex war of 1848, wheelwright, except for last 2 yrs of life when he farmed; d on farm nr Bridgetown, Car Co. His great grandfather, Jas Booker, lived nr Bridgetown, this co; d at 102.
Walter Booker b Bridgetown Apr 26 1846; reared there until age 16; in 1879 m Amanda M. Broadaway, of Kt Co, Del, d/o Ambrose and Ann Broadaway. Mrs. Booker d Jul 24 1895, at 51. She and husband mbrs Episc Church.

140 17. GEORGE H. MOORE served in Car Co as judge of orphans' court, postmaster of Greensboro 1888-1892; b Jun 21 1826 in Del s/o Luther and Nancy (Deshields) Moore of Del who had 5 child., 2 living, Geo and Margaret. Grandfather Solomon Moore b and lived in Del; owned large tract. Luther Moore d when Geo was 6. Geo Moore m 1849 Miss Anna M. Allen d/o Capt. John Allen of Del; mbrs ME Church; had 3 child.; 2 living, John A. and Geo C.

141 18. THOMAS B. DURDING b Rock Hall Mar 25 1864 s/o Benjamin R. Durding (rep elsewhere this vol); c. 17 he clerked general store in Edesville; 1891 obtained position B & O Railway Co, later purch drug store which he has conducted since 1893; m 1890 Miss Annie True of Kt Co and d/o Wm G. True, of Quaker's Neck; their child: Benjamin.

142 19. ENOCH GEORGE CLARK, M. D. b Kt Co Del Feb 24 1844; his father was Jas E. B. Clark, of Del, prob b in Kt Co, mbr of ME church; his mother was Sarah Moore, b Del and d Md at 44; she had 8 child.: Rachel, eld, wid of Dr. Marion

Dawson, of Ohio; John N. d 1893, at 63; Anna wid of Peter Brooks of Indianapolis, Ind; Sarah C. m Mordecai Clark and d when 40; Jas D., farmer of QA Co; David S., farmer and politician of Kt Co, Del; Enoch George; Epharim d at 12. Enoch Clark attended schools at Burlington, N.J. 2 yrs; later taught school in Del for 2 yrs, grad Univ Pa 1867, went to Ohio to practice; settled in Millington where he carried on general practice until Jan 1881 when he retired. He m Mary P. Johnson, d/o Col. Richard Johnson. (See sketch of Anthony Johnson.) Their child.: E. Carroll, E. Gilbert and Agnes (twins) and 2 child. that d in infancy. Mrs. Johnson is mbr Cath Church.

20. GEORGE MITCHELL RUSSUM, atty of Car Co, chief judge 2nd judicial circuit, 145 b Wye Mills, Talb Co, Jan 28 1834, s/o Sydenham Thorne and Sarah A. (Geo) Russum. His father, physician, b 1790, of Dor Co, moved to Wye Mills 1827, d Apr 1852. Mrs. Sarah A. Russum d/o Jos W. George, mbr of Quaker fam of QA Co, 3rd in order of birth of large family. Her older bro, Mathias, elected to state senate. Of large family of Sydenham T. and Sarah A. Russum, 2 reached adulthood, Geo M. and Rbt Polk, the latter mcht in Denton until outbreak of Civil War, when he joined Confederate army, taken sick and d in Feb 1862. Paternal great-grandfather of subj m Ann, d/o Wm Polk of Som Co. Her uncle, John Polk, was grandfather of Jas K. Polk, pres of U.S. The s/o Nathaniel and grandfather of subj, Maj. Mitchell Russum, gained title in Rev war; he m Elizabeth Whittington of Som Co.
Subj attended public schools of QA and Talb Counties. In 1848 he entered Strasburg Academy, Lancaster Pa, but left when father d. He m 1855 Mary Virginia George, d/o Dr. Enoch and Margaret (Turpin) George of QA Co and granddau of Bishop Enoch George, ME Church. She d Jun 28 1858. Judge Russum m(2) Octavia Orme George, sis of first wife. He has no children living.

21. JESSE H. USILTON, farmer 6th dist, Kt Co, s/o Lewin who was s/o Jos who 146 was s/o Jos Usilton, of Kt Co. Lewin elected to house of representatives twice. He m Harriet M. Smyth d/o Maj. Richard Smyth; 8 child. were b. Those living: Jos R., Jesse H., Lewin J., Mrs. C. V. Skirven, Mrs. Harry C. Willis and Mary S. The father d 1880 at 56. His wife d 1894 in 66th yr. Jesse H. Usilton b nr his present home Oct 5 1862 and res all his life in this co; attending Wash College at time of father's death and left college to manage farm; m 1896 Miss Annie Willis d/o Thos J. Willis of 3rd dist.

22. HENRY CLAY HENDRICKSON, b Jul 20 1853, res Millington since 1884. 147 Hendrickson family early German settlers in America. Augustine Hendrickson prob b Cecil Co. His son, Peregrine, grew to manhood in Cecil Co; as young man entered printing business, later ran general store at Warwick; then farmed in Cecil Co. Last five yrs of life retired at Middletown, Del, where he d at 68. Father of subj, Peregrine Hendrickson, Jr., b Cecil Co 1820; lived in Warwick, 4 yrs in Del, then Cecil Co, 1875 to Kt Co where he purch 230 a. nr Millington and res there until he d Jul 18 1880. He m Margaret d/o Jacob Hill, b Kt Co, Del, and now at age 70, res in Millington. Her sons, all living: Victor, farmer of 7th dist, Kt Co; Augustine, farmer 1st dist Kt Co; Jos E., commission mcht of Phila; John P., res of Phila; and Henry Clay.

23. ANTHONY H. JOHNSON s/o Col. Richard C. Johnson, of Smyrna, Del, and there 148 reared on farm until father's death; when Anthony was 12-13. Richard pursued commercial career in Miss. 8 yrs but failed in venture; returned to Kt Co, settled on part of father's estate he had inherited, nr Massey; d in 78th yr. He m Miss Agnes R. Malsberger, of old Pa German family who settled in co many

yrs ago. Prior to marriage he was Protestant but under her influence joined Cath Church. She d when 67; her child.: Mary P. w/o Dr. E. G. Clark, of Millington; Catherine M., unmarried; Anthony H. was b next; Stonewall Jackson, farmer this dist. A. H. Johnson was b on father's farm in 1st dist Kt Co, Sep 4 1856. After elementary education he attended course of study in Rock Hill College, at Ellicott City, nr Balt; m May 30 1882, Laura B. Wootters, of Richmond, Va; their child.: Richard Bradford, Mary Frances and Herman Clayton; they are mbrs Cath Church.

148 24. J. WALTER SKIRVEN, farms c. 2 miles from Chestertown, in 4th dist. See sketch of Thos W. Skirven. J. Walter b Kt Co Sep 25 1849. When father d he inherited interest in homestead, and there farmed, until Jan 1895, when he sold, moved to new purchase near by; he m Jun 20 1872 Virginia Usilton of Kt Co; their child.: Ada and Lewin, both at home. Mrs. Skirven mbr Episc Church.

149 25. HENRY R. LEWIS, atty Denton, 2 terms house of delegates; b nr Vernon, lower Kt Co, Del, Dec 15 1850; Eng ancestry. Grandfather, Stephen Lewis, b Del; mbr its legislature. Jacob F. Lewis, subject's father, b Kt Co, Del, Oct 1806; farmer; justice of peace 14 yrs; d Jan 14 1879; m Rachel, b 1806 Del, of Welsh ancestry, d/o Evan Lewis, farmer. These Lewis families not related. She d Dec 28 1878, shortly before husband. 3-day difference in ages. Hy R. Lewis educated public schools and Farmington Acad; later taught school; studied law; 1882 admitted* to bar at Dover; 2 yrs later came to Denton; carried on practice; elected state's atty Car Co 1887; m 1883 Martha J. Voss, d/o Jas Voss, farmer Kt Co, Del; had dau, Anna May; mbrs ME Church.

150 26. WILLIAM R. KAY, owns Plum Point farm, purch in 1893, s/o Sml W. Kay, b Phila, Pa, 1871, and now only child as his bro, Clarence M., decd; Eng ancestry. Sml W. s/o J. Hutchinson Kay, hardware mcht, and once clerk to mayor of Phila; d 1891. His wid still res Phila; nee Mary Webster. Wm R. Kay lived 21 yrs in Phila; m 1894 Eunice L. Gemmill, d/o old family this co; their son, named for grandfather, Sml W.; mbrs Episc Church.

150 27. EDWARD E. WOODALL, farmer 1st dist Kt Co, owns farm, formerly prop of father; b Apr 20 1857 s/o Capt. Edw B. and Elizabeth (Malsberger) Woodall. Capt Woodall of Georgetown, Md, master of sailing vessels, some owned by bro, Capt. Andrew Woodall; see sketch elsewhere this vol; wife from Pa; she d Jul 31 1867, aged 41, her child.: Jos, Fannie, Edw, Elizabeth, Lillan, Augustus, Louisa, Howard and Adele. Edw Woodall m 1885 Araminta Lynch of Galena; child.: Edw E., Jr., Mary E. and Agnes L.; mbrs Cath Church.

151 28. GEORGE E. LEARY, b Galena, Kt Co, Sep 26 1837, s/o Geo and Mary (Sims) Leary, bro of Capt Columbus Leary (see sketch and fam history, elsewhere this vol. At 12 Geo Leary began blacksmith's trade; at 18 went to Minn. with 20 other men as part of project to lay out new towns. In 1861 he returned and built sawmill at Rock Hall. He m 1862 Kt Co, Mary White of Salem N.J.; their son Elmer E., is partner with father in milling business.

152 29. ROBERT W. ADAMS, 4th generation of Adams family that has res on farm known as Maple Grove, in Dublin dist, Som Co. Philip Adams, of Eng, built log cabin on site of present family res. At his death his son, Thos, took over farm (d age c. 71). Only s/o Thos was Morris H. Adams, b 1804 on homestead and remained here, except one year, 1865-1866, spent in Princess Anne; owned 26 slaves, suffered greatly from loss of slaves and depreciation of prop

following Civil war; mbr ME Church, later Presby; d 1874, aged 72. He m Eleanor, d/o John Williams, of Del; their child.: Josephine, w/o J. D. A. Robinson, of Pocomoke City; Milton Leroy, who d aged 7; Adeline, who m Wm Ruark, of West Point, Va; Olivia, w/o Dr. I. T. Coston, of Pocomoke City; Laura, who m Thos H. Tull, both dead; Rbt W.; and Elizabeth, w/o R. J. Dryden, of Pocomoke City. Eleanor Adams d when 75. - Subj, Rbt W. Adams b 1847, educated at acad Princess Anne. In 1881 he m Rose, d/o J. M. Dryden, of Som Co; their child.: Eleanor W., Morris H. and Mary Louise.

30. JAMES BORDLEY, M. D., physician of Centreville, descended from Thos 155 Bordley, b Yorkshire, Eng, 1682, youngest s/o Stephen Bordley, a prebendary, and nephew of Rev Wm Bordley, of Westmoreland, Eng. 1694, at 12, Thos Bordley came to America. His father had prev d, leaving him to care of an older bro, Stephen Bordley, clergyman of Kt Co, Md, of limited circumstances. Going to Annapolis, qualified himself for practice of law; mbr Gen Assembly; atty general. He m(1) Rachel Beard, of Annapolis, d 1722, leaving child.: Stephen, Wm, Elizabeth and John W. Later he m Mrs.Ariana Frisby, nee Vanderheyden; their sons: Thos, Matthias and John (b 4 months after his father's death). Mr. Bordley went to London for surgical treatment; proved unsuccessful, d there Oct 11 1726.

John Bordley, doctor's great-grandfather, b Annapolis, Feb 11 1727. When 10 mother m again, went to Eng, leaving him with Col Hynson of Chestertown, whose wife was his maternal aunt. He received common school education, at 17 his bro, Stephen, who had nine years' law course in Eng, set up practice in Annapolis, asked younger bro to enter his office as a student, which he did. He m Miss Margaret Chew, who inherited considerable prop from her father, Samuel Chew of Md. They soon moved to Joppa Md. In 1753 John Bordley was app clerk of Balt Co which then included Harford Co. He held the position of judge of admiralty until the change of government in 1776. In 1770 he moved to estate (1600 a.) on Wye River left him by wife's bro, Philemon Lloyd Chew.

John Wesley Bordley s/o John Bordley m Deborah Fisher; was an extensive land owner of slaves and prop in QA and Talb Counties. Mbr Meth Church.

Subj's father, Dr Jas Bordley Sr, b 1808, grad Wash College, Chestertown; studied medicine Univ Md; had practice in Centreville until 1849; then moved to Balt. 1861-1869 res farm, known as Bordlington, QA Co, then to Centreville; there practiced until he d, Dec 1871; mbr Episc Church. A bro, Dr. Wm Wesley Bordley, was physician, d early manhood. Dr. Jas Bordley, Sr. m Miss Marcella Worthington Mummey, (b Balt, d 1865; d/o Thos Mummey, mcht of Balt).

Subj b Centreville Mar 14 1846, taken by parents 1849 to Balt, remained until 1861; entered St. John's College, Annapolis, but school closed by war; studied medicine Univ Md Balt; 1868 m Miss Henrietta M. Chamberlaine, of Cecil Co, who d within a year. 1871 he m Miss Ella F., sis of Edwin H. and John B. Brown, of Centreville; their child.: Madison Brown, grad Univ Md and now atty of Centreville; Dr. Jas, Jr., grad medical depart Univ Md 1896, now assist prof of diseases of eye and ear at Johns Hopkins Hospital; Marcello Worthington, still attending school. Dr. Bordley is mbr Episc Church.

31. WILLIAM THOMAS b and reared 3rd dist Kt Co; farmer 5th dist. C. 1680 Wm 157 Thomas left Wales, settled in Quaker's neck; descendants still live there. Jas Thomas, great-grandfather of subj, acquired 800 a. this co, thereon remained. Wm, grandfather of subj, in war of 1776, served short time; his son Wm in war of 1812. He m Eliza Pierce, of old fam of Md; records date back to 1600; had 12 child., 3 survive: Matilda, w/o Rev L. Palmer, of Conn.; Sarah E. Bacon, of St. Joseph, Mo., and Wm. The father d Sep 1854, aged 58.

Wm Thomas b Apr 9 1833, on home farm; entered Wash College; 1854 went across plains to Calif, spent 15 months there, and several months in Mo.; returning to Md; 1860 m Eleanora S. Elmes (b in Phila, Pa., d/o Lazel and Mary E. (Candler) Elmes and grew to womanhood in that state). Her mother was d/o Sml Candler of New York. Her parents were both natives of Mass.

158 32. THOMAS J. KEATING, JR, atty Centreville, b here Jan 22 1872, s/o Thos J. Keating, Sr, of American birth and Irish parentage. He had 4 bros, one of whom, Michael, postmaster of Centreville, active in public affairs until he d, 1896. Another bro, B. Palmer, atty in Centreville.

Father of subj was 5 when parents moved from Smyrna, Del, to Centreville; educated Princeton, then studied law; during war publ state's right paper, plant burned by Union soldiers 1862; state tax commissioner since 1894.

Subject's mother, Sarah F. Webster, sis of Col Webster, of Harf Co, mbr of old family there. She d 1880, leaving child.: Elizabeth; Hy Webster, grad Johns Hopkins Univ, now prof schools of Duxbury, Mass.; Frank Keating, M. D., grad medical depart Univ Md, now superintendent asylum for feebleminded children at Owings Mills; Thos J., Jr.; and Arthur B. Subj studied law Univ Md, grad 1893, same year admitted to bar, beginning practice in Centreville.

158 33. CHARLES P. GILPIN, D. D. S. b Elkton Sep 3 1856, has spent life this state, except period attended college in Phila; grad Phila Dental College 1876; 3 yrs later came to Chestertown, opened office, where he remains.

161 34. CHARLES FITZ-HUGH GOLDSBOROUGH b Shoal Creek, nr Cambridge, Dec 26 1830, s/o Chas Goldsborough, mbr congress during war of 1812, gov of Md 1818-1819; Apr 1846 entered St. John's college, Annapolis, remained there until 1848 when he began study of law in office of brother-in-law, Dnl M. Henry, later mbr congress from 1st dist; m Jun 22 1852 Charlotte A. P., youngest d/o John Campbell Henry, and granddau of John Henry, mbr continental congress, and later gov of Md. Mrs. Charlotte Augusta Page Goldsborough b Hambrooks, old family estate, Dor Co, Jun 23 1834, sis of Frs J. and Dnl M. Henry; (see elsewhere this vol), d/o John Campbell and Mary Nevitt (Steele) Henry. She was one of 12 child.; 9 attained adulthood: John Frs, Jas Winfield, Frs J., Dnl M., Ryder; Kate, who m Dnl Lloyd; Isabella E., Mrs. Thos B. Steele; Mary, who m Richard Tilghman Goldsborough; and Charlotte Augusta Page, Mrs. Goldsborough. Mrs. Goldsborgouh by marriage to subj, had 6 child., all decd.

162 35. WILLIAM W. BUSTEED, one of editors and senior proprietor of Centreville Observer, with which connected for past 34 yrs; b Jul 18 1843 Car Co, s/o Warner R. and Catherine M. (Barwick) Busteed, of Car Co. The father d Mar 1889. His wife d Dec 1859. Mr. Busteed began apprenticeship at printer's trade in Easton 1860 in office of Wm T. Rowlinson. He m Oct 6 1870 Miss Pattie, d/o Sml and Julianna Vickers. She d Sep 1891, leaving one child, Catherine, who keeps house for her father.

163 36. JAMES T. DIXON rgtr of wills Kt Co past 6 yrs. Thos P., father of subj, b 1816, Del, in childhood went to Cecil Co; in early life clerked in store, but chiefly farmer. 1851 he moved to this co, spent remainder life this co; d 1881. He was only son; bereaved of father when mere lad. He m Jane A. Shields, of Balt (she d 1879); both Cath; had 2 child.; dau d when 16. Like his father, Jas T. Dixon was only son, b this co, nr Chestertown, Sep 11 1857, reared on father's farm; pursued course of study at Wash College, returned to

farming; m 1879 Anna Craddock, of Cecil Co; their child: Nannie C., J. Thos, Genevieve and Marion A.

37. JAMES H. BAKER, fruit and stock farmer 7th dist Kt Co and mbr of legislature; descendant of early settlers of 7th (then 4th) dist; town of Bakerville (now Pomona) named in their honor. Father of subj, Frs Baker, s/o Thos, b this locality; engaged in farming and merchandising. He and wife were Quakers. He m Mary T. (Brown) Baker, descendant of Quakers. She d young, leaving son, Jas H. By subsequent marriage were 4 daus: Mrs. W. S. Maxwell, Mrs. C. H. Price and Mrs. Jos Clark. Mrs. Thos W. Tolson, decd. 163

Jas H. Baker b 4 miles south of Chestertown, nr Pomona, Dec 5 1839; attended Wash College; m(1), Sallie A. Trew, and m(2) Mary Trew, sis of former. By 1st marriage, dau Lizzie, and by 2nd, J. Hy and Mamie Trew. Both daus grad Wilm Conference Acad, Dover, Del. J. Hy grad Dickinson College, attended Md Univ Law School, admitted to bar; has practice in Balt.

38. THOMAS J. KEATING, Sr, b Smyrna, Del, May 3 1829, Episc, s/o Michael and Elizabeth J. (Palmer) Keating. The latter of old fam of QA Co and d/o Geo C. Palmer, farmer; had bro, John, who was clerk circuit court; she d 1862. Father of subj, b Co Tipperary, Ireland, came to America in early manhood; teacher; instructor in acad at Smyrna; 1834 came to QA Co, and remained, teacher in Centreville Acad, until he d 1847. He had bro, Paul, who followed him to this country, and d here, unmarried. Another bro, Wm, was lieut British army, served in India war, retired on pension. Subj grad Princeton College 1848; immediately afterward studied law and admitted to bar 1851. 164

39. CAPT. ANDREW WOODALL b Apr 24 1819 Georgetown, Kt Co, has lived here all his life. His father, Simon Woodall, b Eastern Shore of Md, came this town when young man; builder and carpenter until he d in 1851. He m Miss Frances Bagwell, b this place; d when 22, her son, Andrew, then 2. Her eld son, Edw B., d few yrs ago, aged c. 63, on his farm. - Capt. Woodall owns 25 farms, in this and Cecil Counties (8000 a.), 3 schooners, steamer and 1/3 interest in steamer Sassafras. He m 1841 Catherine Holt, of Georgetown; their child.: Emily, eldest, w/o Jas F. M. Woodall, clerk in employ of subj; Catherine m Capt John F. Wilson, of this town; Jas E., in business with father; Andrew W., mbr firm of Hopper & Woodall, in commission business in Balt; Simon R. d at 32; Sallie E., w/o Richard Lockwood. Mrs. Woodall d Jul 16 1892. 167

40. THOMAS W. ELIASON business man Chestertown, here b and reared. His great-grandfather was b Del, surgeon in war of Rev. The paternal grandfather, John Eliason, farmer, d when his children were young. Thos W. Eliason, Sr., b Kt Co, Del., 1816; 1839 moved to this state; 2 yrs later became res Chestertown, in mercantile business until 1871 when he retired; d 1893; m Susan Walker, of Kt Co, Del, d/o John Walker, mcht, who d when Mrs. Eliason was child. She became mother of 3 child. who reached maturity; she d 1883. Her son, John, grad Jefferson Medical College, entered promising career, but d early manhood. Wilbur, b Jan 31 1853, educated Yale Univ, leaving there his junior year; now farming and manufacturing; m Miss Mary C. Brown, of Chestertown; they have 6 child. Mbrs ME Church. 168

T. W. Eliason b Chestertown, Dec. 27 1843, attended Wash College, went into business with his father. Today he is pres of Kt Co Fire Insurance Co and vice-pres; one of directors of Chestertown Natl Bank; m Miss Violet B. Briscoe in Balt Jan 1881, d/o Wm Briscoe farmer of Balt area. Mr. and Mrs. Eliason have 2 child.: Thos W., Jr., and Irma. Family are mbrs ME Church.

169   41. CHARLES COX HOPPER, journalist, one of proprietors of Transcript, published each week in Chestertown. Mr. Hopper b on old homestead belonging to fam, 4 miles from Centreville, Oct 7 1860. His father, Dnl C., b same house 1816; farmer. About 12 yrs ago he retired in Centreville, but past 5 yrs res of Balt; mbr MP Church. His uncle, Judge Philemon B. Hopper, active in MP Church. Father of Dnl C., in whose honor he was christened, was farmer on old family estate above alluded to, and b thereon. Mother of subj was Evelina H. McCollister, of QA Co, still living. Her eld son, Frank W., is mbr of firm of Geo K. McGaw & Co., of Balt. Thos Ridgeley rep large Pittsburgh firm. Catherine Virginia is unmarried; lives with parents. The boyhood days of Chas C. Hopper spent on grandfather's farm. After public school he entered West Md College, later law depart Univ Md; admitted to bar of Balt city and Balt Co in 1889. 1 Jan 1890 he began publishing Transcript, which, with R. H. Collins. Oct 1894 Chas Cox Hopper m Miss E. M. T. Person of Chestertown. Their dau: Katherine Baird. Mbrs Episc Church.

169   42. WILLIAM S. MAXWELL, M. D., of Still Pond, Kt Co, b Apr 25 1851, s/o M. A. Maxwell, of Pa. M. A. Maxwell b and reared on farm nr Pleasant Grove, Lancaster Co, Pa. The Maxwells of old Celtic Stock, Scotch or Irish in remoter times. The doctor's fam came to Kt Co from Pa. in 1845, and settled on farm in 2nd dist. He farmed along with medical practice for yrs, until shortly before he d, 1885 at 66. He m Anna M. Price; their only child is subj. She was b 1822, still enjoys good health. The doctor lives with mother. Wm S. Maxwell m 1876 Annie Baker in Kennedyville of Kt Co, sis of Jas H. Baker, of Chestertown; they are Presby.

170   43. ALFRED GREEN owns and conducts a store in Centreville in which he carries dry goods, notions, boots and shoes; b Kt Co, Del, Dec 31 1858, s/o Elijah B. and Mary (Fox) Green. His father, b Kt Co, moved to QA Co c. 1871, settled nr Centreville, where he farmed until his death, in 1878. He had 7 sons and 3 daus, of whom survive: Rbt H., res farm nr Dover, Del; Barrett, res Centreville; Wm F., farmer of QA Co; Edw F., farmer this co; Alfred; Jos, farmer; Elijah B., farmer this co; and Elizabeth, w/o Wm T. Carter, hardware mcht of Centreville. Alfred Green m 1891 Miss Mary I. Hessy of Centreville, d/o late John W. Hessy; their son, Alfred Marion; they attend ME church.

171   44. W. LAIRD HENRY, editor Cambridge Chronicle; b Dec 20 1864 Cambridge; m 27 Dec 1894 Mrs. Mattie H. Henry, nee Arkins, b Talb Co; they have 1-yr old son, W. Larid, Jr. Dec 1894-Mar 1895 he rep 1st dist of Md in 53rd congress.

171   45. FREDERICK B. STAMBAUGH, decd, farmer. Ridgely area, pres of Farmers' Alliance Cannery when he d; attending loading of railway car with fruit for city market, Jul 16 1897, when accidentally killed, run over by train.
   Founder of Stambaugh fam in America was great-grandfather of subj; b Germany, early settler in Pa, where son, and his son's son, the grandfather and father of Fdk B., were b and reared, both farmers. The father, Michael, still living, mcht and farmer in St. Clair, Pa; m Miss Margaret Berkheimer, b Pa; living child.: Sarah, Jacob B., Lemmon, Della C. and Tillie.
   Fdk B. b Sep 16 1848; grew up in Bedford Co, Pa, after completing schoo;, taught about a year; ran general store at St. Clair, Pa., for c. 5 yrs, went to Clay Co, Neb., bt 250-acre farm there, returned to Pa after 1 1/2 yrs, in 1879; 1884 moved to Ridgely, aggregated farm of c. 200 a.; m Apr 16 1871 Francena Gallagher (b Bedford Co, Pa), whose father was mcht Hollidaysburg, Pa. Their child, E. Grace, student in college.

46. THOMAS ALEXANDER SMITH, ex-senator of Md, school commissioner Car Co; b   172
Greenwood, Del, Sep 3 1850, moved to Car Co at 6; leaving Denton Acad taught
school for several yrs, first in Del, then Md, later in Mich; returned to Car
Co; taught in schools of Ridgely; entered mercantile buinsess with bro here.
1876 he became local agent for Phila, Wilm & Balt Railroad, the position he
still occupies. 1878 Mr. Smith m Ada Clayton Frazer, b Detroit, Mich. Their
child.: Alice Anita, Elsie S. and Thos A., Jr; mbrs ME Church.
   Sylvester Smith, father of Thos Alexander Smith, co commissioner 2 terms
Car Co; b Del, Feb 22 1822, s/o Thos and Eliza (Hardesty) Smith, both of Del.
They had 3 children; 1 d in infancy, and Artemus is also decd. David· Smith,
father of Thos Smith, b in Del, farmer; his father was Englishman who came to
America before Rev war, and bt large tract in Del. 1852 Sylvester Smith purch
a tract nr Ridgely, where he now res. At 23 Mr. Smith m Sarah E. Gillett, of
Del; their child.: Theopolis W., Albert G. and Thos A., all m, and business
men of Ridgely. The mother d 1852, aged 28. Mr. Smith m(2) Mary Williams, of
Del. By her marriage she became mother ,of 6 child., two of whom died in
infancy; those living are: Laura, Jas H., Chas F. and Rbt D. Laura is w/o
John Siegler, lives in Ridgely, as do her bros.

47. ENOCH GEORGE, M. D., grad medical depart Univ Md Mar 1872; has practiced   173
in Denton; b on farm, Oak Grove, nr Sudlersville, QA Co, Jun 1850. His
father, Enoch George, M. D., s/o Rev Enoch George, 5th bishop ME Church of Va.
The former grad Univ Md; had practice at Sudlersville and Church Hill; 1851
elected to state senate; d 1858; he m Catherine, d/o John Boone, of Car Co,
state senator many yrs and judge of orphans' court. - Our subj, Dr. George m
1879, Eva M., d/o Wm G. Horsey, of Denton; they have 2 child. living, Enoch
and Dawson O.; one d at 17 months.

50. CAPT. JAMES P. SNOW. Over 20 yrs Capt Snow res Eastern Shore Md, owns   174
and occupies farm (250 a.) 6th dist Car Co; mbr old Del fam; has warranty deed
for old homestead in Del, handed down from father to son for nearly 200 yrs.
Capt Snow b Jun 1 1818, s/o John R. and Rachel (Pickering) Snow, of Del; other
son, John R., decd. His grandfather, Jas Snow, farmer of Del, s/o Silas Snow,
who came from Eng with 2 bros, Reuben and Elisha. Silas settled in Del; other
two went further west. During Rev he enlisted; taken prisoner by British,
later exchanged. During Civil war subj enlisted as mbr of Company F, 6th Del
Infantry; discharged 1863 as capt; 1877 came to Md; since then res farm Car
Co; Jun 1 1848, m Susan Snow (b Del), distant cousin; their child.: Rachel and
Sallie, both decd.

51. GEN. RICHARD THOMAS, businessman Easton, b Dec 18 1815, Wye Neck, QA Co,   177
where father, Richard Thomas, was b. Paternal grandfather, Col Sml W. Thomas,
b same place; officer Continental army, secret service depart. Thomas fam
founded here 1600; for generations mbrs res at Wye Neck, now scattered
throughout Va, N. C. and Md. The general's father served in war of 1812, in
battle nr Queenstown; lieut U. S. navy; once had command of a prize vessel.
Once owned 2000 a. in Talb Co; d 4 May 1816. Twice married; by 1st union 3
daus: one d young; Margaret, w/o Judge Hopper, of QA Co; and Frances E. m John
B. Spencer, of Centreville. Mr. Thomas m(2) Sarah Sparks, b nr Centreville,
QA Co, where her father, Rev Rbt Sparks, owned estate. He was early Meth
minister this state, traveled large circuit in N.J., Pa, Md., and Del., taking
6 weeks to make rounds. Mrs. Thomas d Aug 1834. The general's father d
during his infancy. - General Thomas m 29 Nov 1837 Miss Mary E. Smith, of

N.J.; 1839 disposed of store in Centreville and moved to Easton Jan 1840, where wife had an aunt living; his wife d Oct 1884; their only child who reached maturity was Anna Frances who d Nov 18921; a son d in infancy.

178   52.   DAVID STRAUGHN of Cambridge, app magistrate 1896, mbr legal profession; s/o Jas and Eliza (Willis) Straughn, of Centreville and Dor Co, respectively. Father d 1880 at 85. Mother d when son David was 7 . The latter was b Aug 19 1838 Cambridge. 'In 1863 he entered Yale Law School, grad 1865. He m 1873, Miss Annabel Bennett, d/o Chas W. Bennett of Carroll Co. No children.

179   53.   JAMES A. STEVENS, M. D. practitioner Oxford, Talb Co, b town of Wallace, Nova Scotia 1852; s/o Levi and Jane L. Stevens of Nova Scotia; at 17 he left Wallace for higher learning in Boston and Halifax Nova Scotia; '1880 grad Jefferson Medical College of Phila; in 1889 came to Oxford. He m 1880 Miss J. E. McCulley, of Chatham, New Brunswick, and 2 of 3 child. died in infancy. Alexander, their remaining son is 11. Mbrs Episc Church.

179   54.   CHARLES WESLEY CARROLL, res Dor Co, on one farm for almost half a century, Williamsburg dist, nr Hurlock. Paternal grandfather, Chas Carroll, b this co. Chas Wesley Carroll s/o Jas and Margaret (Medford) Carroll, b Jun 7 1816. The father, farmer, b this co. Rebecca, his eld dau, is wid of Stephen Andrews of Hurlock; Josiah and James are decd. Margaret wid of Shelby B. Fletcher; Geo W., youngest is decd. - Subj m Feb 1 1848 Ann C., d/o Jos Douglass, their child. who survived to mature yrs: Geo H., res of Miller, S.Dak.; Emma, w/o Silas Sparklin of Federalsburg; Jas manages old homestead; Benj F. and Fdk W., res Hurlock. Mr. and Mrs. Carroll are mbrs ME Church.

180   55.   IRVING T. MATTHEWS, cashier First Natl Bank Snow Hill, Md., s/o Ephraim and Leah (Jones) Matthews. The father was carpenter & builder in Snow Hill; he d 1842 and left two children. The mother d about 4 yrs later; she was d/o Giles Jones. Ellen A., sis of subj, was w/o Chas Parker, of Snow Hill, and d, leaving one child, Mary. - I. T. Matthews b Feb 3 1828, Snow HIll, later teaching in Union Acad this town; in 1849 m Sarah H., d/o Geo Hudson, of Snow Hill; they have one child living, Julia L., w/o John L. Robbins, this town. Eld dau, Lelia, decd, w/o Geo S. Paine. Mr. Matthews has 5 grandchildren and 2 great-grandchildren. He is mbr ME Church.

181   56.   ROBERT B. DIXON, pres Easton Natl Bank, pres Nickerson Phosphate Co Easton; descendant, 7th generation, Dixon fam in America; first mbr came here 1680 and received large tract. The Bartletts, subject's maternal ancestors, took up a grant another part of co. Both familes mbrs Soc of Friends; some land remains with descendants. Thos Bartlett, an ancestor, signer of Declaration of Independence.

James, s/o Rbt Dixon and father of subj, b Talb Co; contractor & builder Balt; at 36 returned to Eastern Shore; remained in banking and farming; d Jul 1891 at 81. He m Mary Ann, who d 1888; d/o Rbt Bartlett, owner of Bloomfield, which was included in original tract of several thousand acres taken up in 1680. Of her 12 child., fol survive: Rbt B.; Wm T., pres of Natl Exchange Bank of Balt, pres of Johns Hopkins Hospital and mbr of Dixon & Bartlett Shoe Co of Balt; Isaac H., mbr of firm of Smith, Dixon & Co., of Balt; and Mary Ann, w/o Caleb J. Moore, of Harf Co.

Rbt B. Dixon b Balt Aug 22 1834; attended Westtown Acad, (Friends school, Chester Co, Pa); Oct 30 1861, m S. Amanda, d/o Wm Lee and Abigail J. Amoss; great-great-granddau of Wm Amoss, Quaker preacher, who resigned commission in miltia to preach in Soc of Friends. At time of death, at 97, he had 300 living descendants. Child. of Mr. and Mrs. Dixon: Mary G., w/o J. K. Bartlett, Jr., firm of Shriver, Bartlett & Co, Balt; Laura L., w/o Wm T. Norris, business man Balt; Roberta B., at home; Jas, in business with father; Wm Amoss, res Balt, mbr firm Dixon, Bartlett & Co.; and Florence A., at home.

57. LEWIS C. SMITH owner of Derrickson farm past 7 yrs, 4th dist Talb Co. 184
Wm C. Smith, father of subj, s/o Clement Smith, of English extraction; both b Kt Co, Del. Wm C. was farmer; became res this co c. 1868; d 1888; mbr ME Church; m Sally Stafford in Del; she d 1853, leaving 5 child. One now decd; others are L. C.; Mary E., unmarried and living at Wye Mills; Angeline, w/o A. Wilson, of Easton; and Sally, Mrs. Wm G. Quimby, of Wye Mills.
L. C. Smith b Kt Co, Del Nov 12 1844; m Apr 25 1883 Annie Merrick at Chapel ME Church. Several yrs she was teacher and in 1897 app trustee of dist school. Their child., Mabel, Howard and Wm M.

58. WILLIAM F. RUSSELL b Chestertown Nov 7 1867, s/o T. Waters Russell, who 184
for 20 yrs was clerk of bd of co commissioners; grad Wash College 1889 and briefly attended law depart Univ Md; m Feb 1 1893 Allie E. Shuster; their child., Wm F., Jr., and Carmeta. He attends MP Church.

59. CHARLES A. CHIPLEY, general freight agent of Pa Railraod Co, in Phila, 185
Pa; res nr Easton 6 months a year, res Phila remainder of year. Chas Chipley b Alexandria, Va, Feb 2 1836; m Kate Smith De Camp at home of her father, Sidney De Camp, in Wash, D. C., Dec 3 1859. Their child.: 1 decd; Lizzie, w/o W. A. Sprell, of Ridgely Park, Pa; Chas A., Jr; and Sarah M., unmarried, at home. Great-grandfather of C. A. Chipley, Joshua Chipley, came from Eng. settled in Car Co, Md; m Miss Hunter, d/o Ezekiel Hunter, nr Boonsborough, Md; served in Rev war; his child.: Ezekiel, Joshua, Sml and Sarah. Joshua, grandfather of subj, b Car Co; m Miss Howard, of Kt Co, Del, grand-niece of General Warren. Joshua Chipley manufactured shoes, for yrs mcht in Boonsborough; his child.: Ezekiel, Jas, Sml, Sabrina, Frs, Emiline, Mahalah, Elizabeth and Mary Etta. Only survivors are Mahalah and Elizabeth. Sml, father of C. A. Chipley, b Boonsborough 1810. Early in life he went to Alexandria, Va, where he met and m Miss Bayliss Jul 4 1833. He had business in boots & shoes in Alexandria; he d Wash D. C. at old age.

60. EDWARD S. PHILLIPS, of Cambridge, elected sheriff of Dor Co 1895. His 186
father Geo W. Phillips, b this co; d here Jan 31 1890 in 70th yr; senior mbr of Geo W. Phillips & Son for yrs; m Mary J. Meekins, now in her 66th yr. Their child.: John H., Geo M., Luther, Milford, Edw S. and Oliver G., deceased. Edw S. Phillips b Jan 11 1869, Hooper's Island, where he lived for 14 yrs; elected sheriff at age 26; m May 8 1888 Miss Mary V. Truitt, of Cambridge, d/o John and Ella (Brown) Truitt; their dau: Mabel Alcora.

61. GEN. EDMUND L. F. HARDCASTLE of Talb Co, b 18 Oct 1824 Denton, Car Co. 189
His father, Edw B. Hardcastle, b same co, only s/o Aaron Hardcastle, who was eld s/o Thos Hardcastle, Castle Hall in Car Co. The father last-named was Rbt Hardcastle, of England, c. 1740 moved to that part of Car Co, then QA Co, head of navigation on Choptank River. Subject's grandfather, Thos Hardcastle, became large land owner and father of large fam; to each, except for eld son, Aaron, who prev d, he left fine estate. He was maj in Md militia and furnished supplies and recruits to army of Rev at Brandywine. A younger bro, Peter Hardcastle, was lieut in Md line in the command in south. Aaron

-13-

Hardcastle, a farmer, d in early manhood, leaving wid and son and dau. The son, Edw B., father of subj, did not receive any portion of grandfather's estate as inheritance, and therefore, entirely dependent on own efforts. When 14 worked in store in Denton, became successful mcht. He d 1843; his wife b May 2 1803; d Aug 19 1840; she was Mary Ann Lockwood d/o Caleb and Araminta (Day) Lockwood, of Del. For many yrs her father in tanning business in Whitleysburg, Md.

The general had four bros: Addison L., mcht of St. Louis, d in New York. Geo Thos in merchandising in St. Louis and Boonville, Mo. Wm R., mcht in early life in St. Louis, private in Confederate army during Civil war, d at home of subj. Aaron B. entered regular army 1855, became second lieut in 6th Regt, U.S. Infantry, now with Easton Natl Bank of Md; at outbreak of Civil war resigned from regular army; entered Confederate service as col under Sidney Johnston, served as brig-general in battle of Shiloh.

Gen. Hardcastle grad West Point, 5th in class of 1846; sent to Mexico and engaged in war there; in siege of Vera Cruz Mar 1847; resigned commission in 1856 to devote time to agricultural pursuits. He is largest land owner in Talb Co. On 29 Sep 1853 Gen. Hardcastle m Miss Sarah D. Hughlett, of Easton, who d Jul 31 1880. Their sons: Wm H., d 3; Richard d at 38; Thos H., res Denver, Colo.; Edw B., farmer; and Hughlett, pursuing medical course in Vienna Austria. The general m(2) Feb 7 1882 Margaret F. Yellot, of Balt Co, d/o Jeremiah Yellot; their child.: Yellott, Mary, Maynadier and Margaret, all at home, mbrs Episc Church.

191   62. FRANK C. MASON of Easton, manufactured carriages here; b here Feb 8 1854. His father, Wm Mason, b nr Easton 1825, s/o Jas Mason, b this co, but d when Wm was child. The latter's mother, former Miss Elizabeth Millington, b and reared same locality as her husband, d at 83, 1892. He was m twice, had dau, Mahala, by first union. She m Isaac Dixon and both d this co. Jas and Elizabeth Mason had sons, John, Wm and Jas Alexander. John, only survivor, in furniture business in Easton. Wm was 14 when he walked from home to Easton, to obtain work in carriage shop on site of large repository now owned by son. Wm d in 1879; m Mary White, of Smyrna, Del; she d in a few yrs, leaving 3 children. Clara, who d in 1877, was w/o C. R. Leonard (postmaster of Easton) and mother of 3 child. The bro, Wm P., is business man of Phila.

Completing high school this city, and year's course in business college of Phila, subj returned home, joined father's firm at 18. In 1884 Mr. Mason m Lola, d/o Thos G. Reynolds, in this place, niece of ex-Gov Reynolds of Del. Three yrs after Mrs. Lola Mason d subj m(2) Anna Erbaugh, of Carroll Co, Md; she had been teacher in Easton. Her bro, Z. C., is principal of schools of Reisterstown, Balt Co. Isaac Newton, another bro, is prof of mathematics in City College, Balt. Geo W., a third, is principal No. 15 grammar school, Balt. Dr. Irving, former teacher, a physician in Balt. Albert is in journalistic work in Pittsburg, Pa. John is on editorial staff of New Orleans Times Democrat, and McKinzie works for Northern Central Railroad in Balt. A sis, Esther, was principal of Catonsville (Md.) high school, but recently m Dr. W. S. Love, of Balt; and Effie, another sis, is teacher in schools of Orangeville, Balt Co. Mr. and Mrs. Mason have two child., Clara and Frank. He and wife are mbrs Christ Episc Church.

192   63. THOMAS W. JONES, director in Denton Natl Bank, res Ridgely; mbr of state legislature, 1882-4; s/o Dr. Wm and Emily C. (Atkinson) Jones, of Phila and Car Co, respectively; only other child decd. Dr. Wm Jones was practiced in Harrington, Del, where he res for many yrs. He d Mar 2 1896. His father,

John Jones, a physician, from Phila. The father of Mrs. Emily (Atkinson) Jones, Thos Atkinson, b Car Co, farmer. His father, Solomon Atkinson, and grandfather, Aaron Atkinson, farmers this co, the former from this locality, the latter b Scotland and settled in Md long before Rev war, in Car Co. Maternal great-grandmother of subj was Miss Kenton; subj has original land warrents dated 1683, issued to maternal ancestors. Thos W. Jones b 25 Dec 1849, Car Co; attended Dickenson Acad, Williamsport, Pa, 1 year; conducted wholesale commission store in New York City 18 yrs. Mar 20 1878 he m Martha Furman, b N.Y. in 1894, returned to Car Co. He owns about 800 a. and makes speciality of growing fruit. Their child.: Jessie, Thos Jr., and Aimee.

64. ISAAC A BARBER, business man of Easton, b 26 Jan 1852 Salem Co, N.J.; his father, John W. Barber, also b N.J. The fam have for generations been mbrs Soc of Friends. He grad Hahnemann Medical College of Phila in 1872, with M. D.; opened office in Woodstown, N.J., year later came to Easton, where for 15 yrs engaged in practice, then in milling, pres of Farmers & Merchants' Bank for 3 yrs; in 1895 elected delegate to state legislature and 1896 mbr of congress. In 1878 Dr. Barber m Miss Nellie V. Collison and to them b: Ethel, decd; Earl; Emma, decd; and Nellie. 195

65. URIAH F. SHOCKLY farmer, Coulbourn dist, Wor Co, owner of 600 a.; b same dist, Nov 8 1831 s/o Peter and Nancy (Lokey) Shockly, also b Wor Co; he is one of 12 child.; besides himself now living are Lorenzo D., Henry B., Wm J., Benjamin T. and Rebecca. His grandfather, Wm Shockly, of Wor Co, farmer & lumberman, s/o Wm Shockly, Sr., farmer this, his native co. Great-great-grand-father, Richard Shockly, of Eng, came to America prior to Rev. - Subj, Uriah F. Shockly m Dec 14 1854 Julia A. Tilghman, of Wicomico Co, d/o Joshua Tilghman; their child.:Peter S., Emily J., Joshua J. W., Uriah D. C. and Clarence L. 195

66. WILLIAM S. RICHARDSON, business man, Brinkley's dist, Som Co, owns the Vanderbilt farm (450 a. formerly owned by Cornelius Vanderbilt of N.Y.); manufactures ice cream; major planter and packer of oysters this part of Eastern Shore. Richardson fam of English origin. Subject's grandfather, Wm Richardson, b Wor Co; farmed here until his death. His son, Littleton, father of subj, b and spent whole life in Wor Co on his farm; died at 66. Mother of Wm S. Richardson was Harriet E. d/o Edw Scarborough, of Va, who owned Scarborough Castle, nr Snow Hill. Mrs. Harriet Richardson b Md and spent her girlhood in said castle; res Snow hIll with grandchildren; had 8 children; 4 surive: Matilda, Mrs. Z. P. Duffey; Asher, who owns ranch in Tex; Wm S., and Virginia, w/o F. B. Nash, of Atlantic City, N.J. 196

Wm S. Richardson b nr Snow Hill, Wor Co, 1858; at 12 went to Balt and employed in retail grocery there; at 16 traveling salesman, for tobacco house of Johnson & Davis; after c. 4 yrs he located in Shelltown, Md, where he was in business two yrs; in 1882 came to present home nr Marion Station where his chief interest is farming; in 1879 he m Miss Ella Hall Long, d/o Edwin M. Long, of Kingston; their child.: Eva L., Newman C., Ruth, Pauline, Greenfield, Harriet Agnes and Ella Caroline. He is mbr MP Church.

67. JOHN C. SUTTON, agent Blacks Station, Kt Co, Balt and Del Railroad, in whose employ since 1887; b on farm nr present res, s/o John C. Sutton, Sr. His father b nr Lynch's Kt Co, grew to manhood, and farmed there; mbr Episc Church; d 1892 at 65. - Subj, John C. Sutton m(1) Annie Spencer; 6 of 8 child. living: John C., Jr., Carrie F., Annie S., Wm C., B. S. and Geo W. Mrs. Annie 197

Sutton d c. 1876. Mr. Sutton m(2) Elizabeth Heighe; 3 of 4 child. living: J. Wilson, Susan E. and Gilpin.

197 68. NICHOLAS B. KIRBY has spent his life 5th dist, QA Co. He cultivates same farm his father settled (160 a.), overlooking waters of Eastern Bay. Nicholas Kirby b here Dec 14 1830 s/o Sml and Mary (Carville) Kirby. His father was s/o Nicholas Kirby, an Englishman, b Kent Island c. 1781; learned ship carpenter's trade, which he followed in early manhood. He and wife were parents of dau and two sons, younger son, John D., rep elsewhere this vol. Dau, Rebecca, w/o Wm H. Walters; their dau: w/o Jas McGuire, of Centreville.

After death of father management of farm and support of fam fell on subj; he cared for mother until she d yrs later. Jan 1854 Nicholas Kirby m Miss Frances (d Feb 1894), d/o Edw Hopkins, & granddau of Jas Hopkins. Their child: one died in infancy; living, Florence and Edw, res of Queenstown.

198 69. FRANK G. WRIGHTSON, Bay Hundred dist, Talb co, elected mbr of house of delegates 1897, elected clerk circuit court 1897. Wrightson fam dates back to 1650 in Md. Paternal grandfather of subj was Francis Wrightson, this dist; owned large tracts and many slaves; justice of peace many yrs; d at 56, Oct 24 1825. He was s/o Jas W., farmer, and grandson of Frs Wrightson. Wm L. Wrightson, father of subj, b Clay Neck farm, Dec 11 1813, and there spent boyhood; at 16 began serving an apprenticeship to carpenter's trade; in 1857 he app magistrate and in 1861 elected sheriff of Talb co; he d Dec 4 1897; m Miss Mary E. German, of Balt, Oct 4 1849. She d May 1 1885; her child.: subj; Dr. Jas T., physician Newark, N. J.; Mary , w/o Capt H. Thompson. Joshua G. remains on old home place; Sarah D., wid of Frank E. Caulk. - Frank G. Wrightson b Oct 28 1850, eld child.; res this dist, save when attending Calvert College; in lumber business a few months in Lancaster Co, Va. Nov 28 1877 he m Annie R. Dawson; their child. in order of birth: Minnie Lowe, Helen Dawson, Frank G., Jr, Wm V., Madge S., Geo D., Anna Marie and Jas T.

201 70. LEVI D. TRAVERS, life-long res Parsons Creek dist, assisted in founding Cambridge Natl Bank; one of its directors for past 16 yrs. Judge Travers descends from English branch of Travers family, who were aristocrats. The great-great-grandfather of judge, Hy Travers, came from Eng as school teacher and educator and became county justice; mbr colonial legislature of Md 1750-1760; col of Md militia prior to Rev. He m either here or in Eng, Elizabeth Smith, and lived to old age. His son, also named Hy, m Jane Brohawn. Owing to marriage of Travers ancestors with Goeghegan, LeCompte, Dove and Spedden families, subj is of Irish, French and Scotch extraction.

His grandfather, John C. Travers, of Taylor's Island, where he spent his life as planter, vessel builder and owner of store; d when 62. His wife was Mary (Dove) Travers. During war of 1812, when one of their vessels was captured by British fleet, she boarded British admiral's boat and persuaded him to surrender to her the boat he had captured. In her family were two sons, our subject's father and Wm D.; latter was mcht, planter and slave holder on Taylor's Island. The grandfather belonged to local militia and during war of 1812 assisted in capturing one of the British boats.

Levi D. Travers, father of subj, b on Taylor's Island, mcht, planter and money loaner; d at 46. His wife, Prudence, d/o Robert Spedden and Elizabeth (nee Taylor), the former of Scotch extraction and for yrs farmer in northern part of Dor Co. Mrs. Travers was mbr ME Church. She d at 41, leaving 7 children, of whom our subj was oldest. Martha Jane, second in family, w/o Rev John F. Chaplain, D.D., formerly of Talb Co, but now decd. Julia Ann m Rev

Benj Douglas Dashiell, minister of ME Church South for 30 yrs and a leading mbr and pres elder of Texas conference when he d, 1883. His grandfather Douglas was owner of Frederick Douglas. His son, Levi D. Dashiell, now speaker in Texas state legislature. Sophia S., Mrs. Wm Keene, d at 52 and left several child. Eliza E. is w/o Thos K. Keene, of Parsons Creek dist. Frances A. m Dr. Benj L. Smith, this dist; Wm M. who d 46, was mcht and involved in politics, although never accepting an office.

Subj b Taylor's Island Nov 21 1828; attended Dickinson College, Carlisle Pa; twice elected judge of orphans' court; app to vacancy in office of chief justice; 1893 elected mbr of legislature. Judge Travers m Eliza Jane, d/o his uncle, Wm D. Travers; had 7 child., 4 d in childhood. Levi Dickinson, only surviving son, farmer Taylor's Island; m Miss Aline F. Richardson, d/o Jas Richardson, of Dor Co. Manie Eugenia is w/o Dr. Jacob L. Noble, of Preston; and Augusta Williams is w/o Rev Dnl B. Prettyman, minister of Meth Church, now farming and in business at Taylor's Island.

71. EDWARD LUSBY, farmer, 4th dist Kt Co, b Dec 6 1864, on farm he now owns. 202 His father, John Lusby, of Kt Co; spent his life here; m Elizabeth Massilon, of Kt Co. She d aged c. 45, leaving 5 child., Wm and Clay, farmers in Kt Co; Edw; Herbert, farmer in Kt Co; and Ella E. Edw Lusby remained on old homestead until father's death, then purch interests of other heirs. He m Miss Lydia Jacobs, of Kt Co; their child.: Raymond, and Lynwood and Harry Clay, twins.

72. PAUL JONES, M. D., physician and surgeon of Wor Co, res of Snow Hill; b 203 Oct 24 1851, s/o Chas P. Jones, M. D., active in medicine at 72. The family moved to Snow Hill when Paul was 12. Paul grad Jefferson Medical College Phila in 1875; went to Horntown, Va, in 1877; spent 18 months before returning to Wor Co, settling in Stockton; m 1882, Miss Lillie Irwin, d/o A. D. Irwin, then of Phila, but now res Snow Hill. Thereafter Dr. Jones moved to Snow Hill, where he and wife, res with child., Ellen E. and Chas Irwin.

73. STEVENSON CONSTABLE, farmer of Kt Co, b Kt Co Jul 11 1839, s/o John S. 203 Constable. He had one bro, Wm R., commission mcht of Balt. He was mbr Episc Church; d Mar 26 1893; m Alice A. Reiley, of Kt Co, d/o C. M. and Clementina (Beck) Reiley and granddau of John and Sophia Beck, of this co. She is cousin of late Dr. Beck and mbr of old fam. After death of husband, Mrs. Constable moved to Chestertown, her present res. She is mbr Episc Church. Her child.: M. Blanche, res with mother; Harriet Lillian, w/o T. Arthur Skirven, with South Side Railroad, in Chicago; John Stevenson, who m Estella Stephens and res in Balt; and Horace B., who attended Wash College for 4 yrs.

74. WILLIAM H. JACKSON, mcht of Salisbury, bro of ex-Gov E. E. Jackson, mbr 204 of firm, Jackson Brothers Co, dealers in lumber. In 1891 the firm of Jackson Lumber Co of Alabama was organized, with our subj as pres. The firm owns c. 140,000 a. of timber land in that state. Wm H. Jackson b Oct 13 1839, in Wicomico(now) Co, s/o Hugh and Sarah (Humphreys) Jackson. He m(1) 1863 Miss Arabella Humphreys; they became res of Salisbury a year or so later. They have son, W. P. and dau, Mary B. The son is rep elsewhere in this vol. In 1880 Mr. Jackson m Miss Jennie Humphreys; they attend ME Church.

75. WALTER H. THOMPSON, res of Easton, b Easton Nov 28 1823, s/o Geo F. 207 Thompson, of Dublin, Ireland, who b 1809, and came to America when 14, with 2 bros, Jas, who went into business in New York, and Walter, who conducted a

mercantile establishment in Phila. In Phila Geo learned carriage-maker's trade, and later came to Car Co, where he m Miss Sarah R. Harrison, of that co. Her father d when she was quite small. Mr. Thompson then came to Easton, he conducted major carriage manufactory. He d 1828; his wife d 1870. They had 4 child.; subj is only one living. Jas d at age of 4. Rebecca was w/o Wm H. Sheppard; they had 2 sons and 2 daus. After her death Mr. Sheppard m her sis, Isabella; they had a son and dau. Both parents now decd.

Educated in Easton Acad, Walter H. Thompson clerked in dry goods store of Singleton & Talbot; Feb 18 1847 m Miss Susan A. Mills, d/o Thos Mills of Dor Co. Their children, now decd: Emily M., Susan Emma, Katie, Walter Mills and one who d in infancy. Walter Mills was preparing for ministry at Dickinson College at time of his death at 19. Susan E. became w/o Leonidas Dodson, died c. 23. The others d in early childhood. Mr. Thompson is mbr ME Church.

208   76. CHARLES LOWNDES, M. D. res Miles River, Talb Co, adjoining the Anchorage, former home of father; b at Wye House, 1st dist this co, Oct 22 1832. First rep of Lowndes family in America was Christopher Lowndes, of Eng, early settler at Georgetown, D. C. Chas Lowndes, subject's grandfather, b Georgetown; in early life moved to Balt, embarked in mercantile business. Retiring, he went to Jefferson Co, Va., where he remained until his death.

Commodore Charles Lowndes, U. S. N., father of subj, b Georgetown, in 1812, at 15, entered navy. During Mexican war he commanded the Germantown; retired 1860 at 62. Coming to Talb co, he reired to the Anchorage (1000 a. bordering on Miles River); d there Dec 1885. His wife, who d 2 yrs earlier, was Sarah Lloyd, d/o Gov Edw Lloyd and sis of Col Lloyd, of Wye House. Their child.: Chas; Sarah L., who m J. W. Bennett, of Carroll Co; Lloyd, of Annapolis; and Elizabeth, w/o J. A. Johnson, M. D., of Talb Co.

Charles Lowndes grad Princeton 1853; 2 yrs later grad medical depart Univ Md. 1856 received app as assist surgeon in navy, spent most of his service in Europe; resigning from navy 1861 he started practice in Balt, where he spent 12 yrs. 1873 he returned to home of childhood, where he has remained. In Sep 1865 he m Catherine M., d/o Wm G. Tilghman. Their oldest child and only son, Chas H. G. is assist surgeon in navy, stationed in Wash. The daus, Anna P., Sarah Scott and Mary Catherine, remain with parents.

209   77. TILGHMAN E. KELLEY, farmer 4th dist Car Co. In 18th yr he enlisted in 8th Md. Infantry at Balt, 1862, placed in Company E. His division was assigned to Army of the Potomac; in battles of the Wilderness, Cold Harbor and Appomattox; in 1891 elected co commissioner; b 1844, s/o Dennis and Mary (Harrison) Kelley, of this co. His mother was d/o Jas Harrison, of Car Co. His father d when he was 3. Returning from southern battlefields he settled for a time in Queenstown, QA Co, and in 1867 came to this co and engaged in farming. In 1868 Mr. Kelley m Miss C. I. Hollis, d/o Charles Hollis, of Del; their child.: eldest, Glencoe K. farms in this co; m Leona Patchett; (they have two children, Edith I. and Elmer); Everett C., Orlan T. and Charles H.

209   78. LEMUEL P. MITCHELL, M. D. in medical profession at Sharptown, Wicomico Co; b nr Berlin, Wor Co, Oct 14 1824, s/o Isaac Mitchell, who was b same locality, being s/o John P. Mitchell, of Scotland. Isaac Mitchell d 1829, a young man, mbr Episc Church. His wife, Sarah, d 1859; d/o Edw Henry, of Berlin dist, Wor Co; of 3 child.; 2 are living, subj and John P., of Alabama.

When a boy subj was student in schools of Berlin, Md., and Flushing, N. Y.; 1844 entered Yale College; after a year came to Berlin and commenced study of medicine with Dr. Hillard Pitts; entered medical depart Md Univ, grad 1847;

returned to Berlin, opened an office. 1855 he moved to Salma, Ala., spent 11 yrs in practice; then back to Berlin; 1877 settled in Selbyville, Sussex Co, Del, from there in 1885 to present location at Sharptown, Wicomico Co. Dr. Mitchell m Nov 29 1877 Lottie, d/o Benj Ravell, of Berlin, Md. Their child.: Lemuel L., Sidney J., Marion R. and Sallie P.

79. CAPT. WILLIAM T. BARKLEY, mbr firm of W. T. Barkley & Co., of Cambridge, 210 b Hooper's Island, Dor Co, s/o Wm Washington and Margaret (Travers) Barkley, both of this co. The Barkleys are of English ancestry. William W. was for 19 yrs carrier of mail on Hooper's Island. He d 1881 in 70th yr. The father of Margaret Travers, Benj, from Hooper's Island; once rep his community in state legislature. Mrs. Margaret Barkley lives with subj, is over 75. She has 2 child., the other, Rebecca, wid of Fabricius Leland.
    Wm T. Barkley b Oct 28 1851. When about 18 he was a "tonger" and from that he went on to dredging boats and later owner of the Bugeye, a small oyster smack. His firm owns twenty ships, including one three-masted schooner. In 1872 he m Amanda Ruark, from Hooper's Island, d/o W. T. Ruark; she d 1880 leaving 4 child.: Wm Oscar, Ellen, Thos and Clara. Later our subj m Miss Mary Louise Smith, of Balt; their child.: Geo, Jesse and LeRoy.

80. MARION DE KALB SMITH, lawyer, s/o Jas Smith, who was b Dor Co 1809. He 213 came to Kt Co 1840, d here Mar 1862. He was mbr Episc Church. His only bro, John A., was civil engineer, reared in family of his uncle, Judge John A. Smith, of N. C. As young adult he went to La from his home there in N.C., and was engaged in construction of railroads there during the rest of his life. In 1845 he d, leaving a family. The only sis, Julia, m a Mr. Carter, a farmer. She d in Car Co at 84. Mother of subj was Anne B., d/o Jesse Knock. Before her marriage with Jas Smith she was wid of Isaac Hines. She d 1892, leaving Jesse K. and John W. Hines, b of first marriage; and Thos J.; Jas J.; Julia Lucinda, now w/o John N. Dodd, of Chestertown; Sallie M., w/o Rev Walter R. Graham, D.D., of Westminister, Md; and subj of sketch.
    Marion deKalb Smith b farm nr Kennedyville, Kt Co, Md, Oct 16 1850, grad Washington College 1870, studied law under Richard Hynson. At the same time he was deputy clerk of circuit court for Kt Co under his half-brother, Jesse K. Hines; in 1883 elected state's atty, later elected to comptroller of treasury of Md; m Jun 5 1878 Miss Addie d/o John H. Burchinal of Md; their child: Marion deKalb, Jr., and Anna Burton; family mbrs ME Church.
    The great-grandfather of subj b Eng; fought in war of Rev, in the Md Line; killed in battle at Camden, S. C., same engagement in which deKalb met his death. His grandfather commanded company of Md militia and was killed at battle of Bladensburg in 1814.

81. GARRETT FOXWELL res Kt Co for yrs, farming and fruit raising; elected to 214 county treasurer 1894; b Newcastle, Del, Sep 24, 1845. His father, Tilman Foxwell, b same place; in early life was sailor, but left water and to farm. At 28 he moved from Del to Ohio and for 4 yrs cultivated a farm there, but returned to Del and spent remaining yrs in Kt Co on farm; d 1885 at 83. He m Angeline Griffin; of 5 child. 3 are living: Elizabeth, w/o David Jones; Garrett and Lydia A., wid of John H. Golt. Foxwell family long identified with Del., to which its 1st mbrs came from Great Britain, of Irish and Welsh ancestry. - Garrett Foxwell remained with father until 23, when he came to Kt Co, Md., and rented farm; since 1871 he has lived in 2nd dist; in 1875 he m Miss Kate Hudson, of Kt Co, d/o John Hudson; they have a child, Annie J.

214 82. WILLIAM J. HOPKINS, business man of Cambridge, present director of Cambridge Water Co and pres of gas company. Paternal grandfather of subj was Thos Hopkins, of Talb Co, 2nd of 4 child. of Josiah and Agnes (Redditt) Hopkins, the mother from Scotland. The others are Jos R., Edw G. and Clara E., all res of Cambridge. Clara is w/o Jos H. Sauerhoff. - Wm J. Hopkins b Nov 18 1848 Cambridge; boyhod in Cambridge; entered Cambridge Acad. Later employed in father's and uncle's (Govane Redditt) stores. He m Mar 12 1890 Miss Willie A. Mulligan, from Talb Co, d/o Geo W. Mulligan, reared in family of aunt in Cambridge. Their child: Granville B. Both are mbrs ME Church.

215 83. HOPE H. BARROLL, atty Chestertown; b Chestertown, Aug 6 1860. His ancestors were seated in Byford and Mansell Lacy Parishes, Herfordshire, England, as will appear in Rev C. J. Robinson's "Mansions and Manors of Herfordshire." In 1760 Rev Wm Barroll, descendant of Col Jas Barroll, of Cannon Frome, and grad St. John's College, Cambridge, at solicitation of venerable uncle, Rev Hugh Jones, came to Md. and succeeded him as rector of this parish until 1777, when, being unwilling to take oath of allegiance, was deprived of his living. 1761 he m Ann, d/o Alexander Williamson, of Cecil Co; their child.: Wm, Richard and Jas. Of these sons, Wm was admitted to bar of Cecil Co and 1788 settled in Chestertown; lawyer and land holder. He m Lucretia, d/o Jas Edmondson, of Talb Co; their son, Jas Edmondson Barroll, b Chestertown 1789, educated at Yale; read law in Chestertown, where he was admitted to bar in 1811. He m Henrietta Jane Hackett, whose grandfather, Gunning S. Bedford, of Del, was mbr of Continental Congress of 1776. They had 6 daus and 2 sons, of whom only one remains, John Leeds, father of subj.
   John Leeds Barroll b 1830, grad St. Mary's College, Balt, 1849; admitted to bar in 1851. In 1854 he m Elleonora Keene, d/o Thos Hopewell Horsey, of Del; he had 3 sons, John Leeds, Hopewell Horsey and Morris Keene. The eld son John Leeds Barroll, b Sep 14 1855, educated at Wash College, Chestertown. He m Maria Stocker Lewis, d/o Frs A. Lewis, of Phila, where he engaged in insurance & real estate. Their child.: Ethel, Frs L., John Leeds and Anna. The youngest son, Morris Keene Barroll, b Dec 31 1866, grad West Point 1889; now 1st lieut of 1st Artillery, Angel Island, San Francisco; m Ann Van Bokken Miller, d/o Col. Marcus P. Miller; their son, Morris Keene Barroll, b at Fort Schuyler, N. Y. Hopewell Horsey Barroll educated at St. John's College, Annapolis, grad Wash College, Chestertown. He read law under Hon. Jas Alfred Pearce and at Univ Va; admitted to bar 1883; m Feb 9 1888 Margaret Spencer Wethered, d/o John L. Wethered, of Kt Co. They attend Episc Church; their sons: Lewin Wethered, Morris Keene, Hopewell Horsey and John Wethered.

216 84. BENJAMIN B. GORDY of Parsons dist, Wicomico Co, b nr present abode, Aug 28 1823; in 1853, prior to division of co, elected commissioner of what was then Dor Co; judge of orphans' court, 1888-92. Paternal grandfather of subj, Nathan Gordy, of Del, of Eng descent. John P., father of Benj B., b this dist 1799, d 1840; m Mary Dale, b 1799 and d 1881. Of 5 child.: Benj only one left; decd: Lemuel B., John S., Jas D. and Wm G. - 1844, subj, Benj Gordy purch farm in Pittsburg dist nr town of Pittsville, and there dwelt 13 yrs; then bt farm where he has res since except 3 yrs spent in Del. In 1843 he m Sarah J. Tradder; their child.: Lemuel D. in partnership with father running farm; Mary E. A., w/o L. Sherman; John T. business man of Brooklyn, N. Y. Mr. and Mrs. Gordy mbrs MP church.

85. THOMAS KING CARROLL, M. D., physician 9th dist Dor Co, 3 times elected to 219 state legislature; b at Kingston Hall, Som Co, ancestral home, s/o ex-Gov Thos King Carroll and wife, Julia, d/o Dr. Hy Stevenson, of Balt. Ancestors came to this country c. 1640, settling 1st in Va, later Eastern Shore of Md. Doctor's grandfather, Col Hy Jas Carroll, m Miss Elizabeth Barnes King, d/o Sir Thos King, baronet of Eng, came to America to escape relig persecution; Kingston Hall built by him in 1683.

Dr. Carroll grad Univ Md at Balt 1846. Of large fam at Kingston Hall, doctor and 3 sis survive. Miss Anna Ella Carroll, prominent during Lincoln admin, called by biographer "the unrecognized member of his cabinet," was one of his sis. Those left: Mrs. Thos Cradock of Balt Co; Mrs. Dr. Bowdle and Miss Mary Hy Carroll, of Wash D. C. Dr. Carroll m Miss Margaret Handy Carroll, d/o Chas Cecilus Carroll, of St. Louis, Mo.; had fam of 10 child., of whom 3 sons and 3 daus living. Thos King d at 11; Chas Cecilius res at old homestead; Hy Stevenson d when 36; and others are Margaret H.; Victor; Vivian, druggist at Church Creek; Julia S. and Nellie T., at home; and two who d in infancy.

86. P. HOWARD HUBBARD, farmer in Talb Co, b Concord, Car Co, Mar 18 1872, s/o 220 J. P. J. Hubbard. His father, of same place came from old fam thereabouts; at time of death, Mar 4 1893, he was a director of Denton Natl Bank. He m Martha Blades (still living at 54), of same region. Her father, Isaiah Blades, farmer of Car Co. P. H. is only son in parents' family, his sis being Winnie, w/o W. R. Fountain, who manages old homestead nr Concord; and Emma S., unmarried. Subj spent first 11 yrs at his birthplace; came to farm with paretns where he res in 1883; m 22 Nov 1894 Nannie Stevens, b in Va, d/o W. W. Stevens (res of Cordova, Talb Co); their dau: Helen.

87. WILLIAM F. MAY OF Tilghmans Island, Talb Co, app postmaster of island. In 220 1869 he opened store here, selling dry goods and other items. Subject's father, Wm F., b 1794, QA Co served in War of 1812; farmed nr Church Hill; m wid of Ezekiel Godwin, nee Sarah Neavitt. He d at 47. She was b same co; mbr ME Church; she d at 63. Wm F. May b Feb 13 1841, on old homestead nr Church Hill; m 1862 Sarah Harrison, of this co, who d Jun 1864, leaving son, John T., now farming and oyster dredging. Wm F. May later m Miss Margaret A. Cummings, of the island; they had 4 child., 2 living, Sallie, at home, and Effie, w/o John T. Higgins, of Balt.

88. GEORGE M. WILSON, business man of Easton, manages mill his father bt in 221 1865. His father, Wm H. Wilson, b Car Co 1815, d 1893; m Susan A. Smith, of Car Co; she d c. 10 yrs before her husband. They had 4 child.; 3 survived: C. E. is mechanic in Denton; Mariana is w/o W. F. Griffith, of Newark, Del.

Geo M. Wilson b Jul 12 1865 Denton. He attended Friends' school in boyhood; was an infant when parents moved to this town; he m Apr 21 1891 Fannie R. Shanahan, d/o W. J. and cousin of W. E. Shanahan, of Easton. Their child, Wm Griffith, age 2; mbrs Cath Church.

89. JOHN H. GEORGE, res Car Co nr Griffin, over 30 yrs, b Kt Co, Del, Jun 23 222 1819, s/o Rbt and Elizabeth (Hopkins) George, of old Del families. Father of Rbt was John George, b and reared in Del, and farmer there. His father from Ireland, settled in Del before Rev, remained there. Father of Mrs. Elizabeth George was Col Rbt Hopkins, who served in war of 1812.

John H. George, 1 of 9 children, 4 now living. His bros, Jas H. and Thos R., res Chesterville, Pa and nr Dover, Del, respectively; only living sis, Anna E., res Wilm, Del. He opened livery estab in Smyrna, Del, which he carried on 1858-1865; enlisted in 1863, Company B, 6th Del Regt of Vol, to serve a year; never in active engagement. 1855 he m Mary E. Husbands, b and reared in Del; their 10 child.: Ella H., Rbt B.; Florence, w/o Wesley Perry, whose child. are Elva and Arthur; John L., who m Mattie Carroll, whose child. are Mary; Susie; Mary E., w/o Leonard Sheubrooks; Jos H., who m Ella Slaughter, whose child. are Paul, Evelyn and Hilda; Addie H., w/o Jas T. Clark, who has 2 boys, Stanton and Russell; Walter T.; and Anna B., w/o Roland Frampton, who has child, Bernice. Several of fam mbrs MP Church.

225   90. WOODLAND P. FINLEY, mbr state senate from QA Co, b Mar 15 1851, on farm 2nd dist where he still res. First of fam in dist was his great-grandfather, Jas Finley, an atty. Father of subj, Washington Finley, M. D., b 2nd dist, educated West Nottingham Acad and Bel Air, Harf Co; grad Univ Md 1835. Dr. Finley m(1) Sarah A. Harrison; they had 16 child.; subj and J. L. survive, latter being physician of Church Hill; other child. died young, and their mother d 1 Jan 1872. In 1873 Dr. Finley m Miss Mary E. Mason (still living). He d Aug 3 1896, buried Church Hill cemetery. - Subj educated West Nottingham Acad and school in Blair Co, Pa; m 1875 Miss Catherine O., d/o Benj Coppage; of 4 child. 2 living: Sallie M. and Jas W.

225   91. W. BRADFORD COPPER, cashier of Second Natl Bank Kt Co. His father, Joshua Copper, b here 1802, farmer and carpenter; for 35 yrs steward of almshouse; d in 1892, at 90. He m Millie Perkins, b QA Co, about 20 yrs his junior. She res Kt Co. Subj is youngest of 9 child.; living are 4 sis and 3 bros. Sml A. is business man of Savannah, Ga, and Jesse R. is farmer of Kt Co. Subj b on home farm 3 miles from Chestertown Jan 15 1863, remained at home until 14. In 1893 he m Sarah Carroll; they live in Chestertown.

226   92. CAPTAIN JOHN H. OZMON, Centreville, b Denton Jun 1 1828. Paternal grandfather spent life in Talb co, where he farmed, leaving large farm at his death which remained in family for while; had 3 sons and 5 daus, the former being Sml C., father of subj; Wm, a farmer and boatsman, who d Talb Co; and Henry, who followed the water. The grandfather was soldier in war of 1812.

Sml C. Ozmon b Talb Co Jan 1807; in bay line of steamers, Balt to Norfolk, Va; for yrs master of several vessels sailing on Chesapeake and tributaries. He d in Balt at 59; m Miss Mary Ann Willoughby, who d at home of subj 1872, at 64. Her father, Edw Willoughby, was b Eng, came to this country as soldier in English army during war of 1812, but soon deserted. He m Miss Moore, by whom he had son and 5 daus, of whom Mrs. Ozmon was eldest. The son, Wm M. Willoughby, never married. He served as clerk in county clerk's office at Denton, later went to Grand Gulf, Miss., where he was bank cashier, then to Cuba and engaged in commission business; nothing heard of him since.

Subj was only son, had 2 sis who died in childhood. As small boy he went to sea with father. In 1858 he settled in Centreville. In 1857 he m Miss Isabella Whiting, of Caracas, South America, where her father was business man. After his death her mother m his bro, with whom Mrs. Ozmon came to this country. The captain and wife became parents of 2 child.: Florence Virginia, w/o Capt Bedford Laramore, res Balt, commander of steamer St. Michael; and Jos Whiting, who m Minnie Satterfield and has 2 child.: John Harry and Jos Roger. Captain Ozmon's wife d about 13 yrs ago. He is a mbr Cath Church.

93. COLONEL EDWARD WILKINS, in fruit industry of Kt Co; b Kt Co Oct 6 1813, 227 only son. Father d when Edw was small; afterward mother m Rbt Constable. Edw sent to Mass. to attend school, but death of stepfather obliged him to return home and assume management of estate. He served as judge of orphans' court and state senator from Kt Co; col of 2nd Regt of Md militia; attended ME Church; d Dec 28 1878. He m(1) Deborah Jones; had 4 child., of whom son and 2 daus attained maturity. The son, Edw M., m Miss Mary Anna Merritt. Both daus deceased: Juliana, Mrs. Rbt S. Emory; and Maria, w/o Jas Russell, teller of Citizens' Natl Bank of Balt; Mr. and Mrs Russell d, leaving several child., living in Balt. Col Wilkins m(2) Frances Olivia Merritt of Kt Co, who d at home place Jan 20 1877. Of 5 child. 4 living: Sml Merritt Wilkins, res Chestertown; Fannie L., w/o Edw B. Jones; Frank, official in Balt custom house; and Ben N. S., who owned old homestead. Ben N. S. Wilkins b 1854, received education in Wash College and state normal at Millersville, Pa; in 1895 he moved from farm to Chestertown where he now res. He attends Episc Church. Feb 28 1877, B. N. S. Wilkins m Miss Rebecca R. Gray, d/o John R. and Margaretta Ann (Anderson) Gray. Her maternal grandfather, was Dr. Anderson. Her father's mother was sis of Commodore John Rogers and relative of Adm Raymond Rogers. The child. of Mr. and Mrs. Wilkins are Frances Olivia, Ben N. S., Helen Gray, Maude, Paul, Brayman Rogers and Maurice Gray.

94. JOSEPH R. USILTON, s/o Lewin, and grandson of Jos Usilton. The latter 228 res in Chestertown several yrs; spent life in Kt Co, as farmer. Lewin, farmer, b and reared on homestead now owned and operated our subj. He d in 1880, at 57. He m wife Harriet M. Smyth, who d in 1895, aged 64, d/o Maj. Richard Smyth; she was b and reared Kt Co; they had 8 child. (See sketch on Jesse Usilton.) - Jos R. Usilton b at Rock Point, Kt Co, Oct 5 1855 on farm. In 1881 Mr. Usilton m Mary F. Aurlock, wid of Wm T. Skirven of this co.

95. GEORGE R. GOLDSBOROUGH. The first of Goldsborough fam to settle in 231 America was Nicholas, of Dor, Eng, early settler of Kt Island, where he d and was buried. Rbt, s/o Nicholas and native of Eng, settled in Talb Co c. 1670 and purch a large tract, part of which forms estates of Myrtle Grove and Ashby. Rbt's son, Rbt, b at Ashby, had son, Judge Rbt, b same place, and for yrs judge of circuit court on Eastern Shore. Rbt Hy Goldsborough, s/o Judge Robert and father of subj, b at Myrtle Grove, Jan 4 1799, grad St. John's College 1796; in 1800 m Henrietta Maria, d/o Col Rbt Lloyd Nichols, of Talb Co; she was b on family estate, Peach Blossom, d at Myrtle Grove 1838, mother of 10 child., of whom Geo R. survives. In 1835 he was app to fill unexpired term of E. F. Chambers in the U. S. senate; he d Oct 5 1836.

Subj b Apr 11 1821; in 1848 went to sea as clerk for a captain and sailed to China, absent from home for 3 yrs. He m Jun 25 1862, Eleanor A. Rogers, of Druid Hill, Balt, mmbr of old Balt fam. Her ancestors in 1760 purch tract of 487 a., comprising Druid Hill farm, which, 100 years later, is celebrated park. They make their summer home at Ashby and winter res at No. 505 Cathedral St, Balt. Mrs. Goldsborough is great-great-granddaughter of Martha Washington and is involved in preservation of Mt. Vernon.

96. ROBERT LEE SPILMAN, decd, passed his youth in Va; last quarter century on 232 Taylor's Island, Dor Co; b Jan 7 1839 Fauquier Co, Va; when 16 employed by Hodges Brothers, wholesale dry goods mcts, Balt; in mercantile businesses, first in Millwood, Clarke Co, Va., for 5 yrs, then Augusta, Ga 4 yrs, returning to Balt in 1868. After yrs there he came to Taylor's Island and taught school for 3 yrs. He m Miss Annie Hooper Pattison Dec 27 1859, in

Cambridge, where she was b and reared. She was educated in Patapsco Institute, Ellicott City, Md. He d Dec 25 1894. She now manages farm, assisted by eld son, Hy Pattison. Nannie L., her eld dau, is w/o Wm E. Dunnock, of Balt, and next in order of birth, Rbt Lee, Jr., clerk in Balt, m Miss Julie E. Provost. Hattie Keen is w/o Wm D. Travis, mcht of Taylor's Island. Jeremiah P., clerk in Balt, m Alice Brooks. Two child. d in infancy. Jas C. H., who m Lulu Keen, is capt of schooner in Balt trade. Carrie is at home. The mother is mbr Episc Church.

233 97. WILLIAM S. WALKER, judge orphans' court, b Chestertown, where he still res, Jan 6 1832; direct Scotch descent, his grandparents, John and Christiana (Graham) Walker, b Scotland, emigrated 1799, and made settled in Chestertown; then mbrs Episc Church, but Mrs. Walker later identified with Meth. Judge's father, John W. Walker, b this town 1800, remained here until he d, at 44. He had one bro, Thos, a mcht in Millington, Kt Co. Mother of Judge Walker former Elizabeth Constable, b Kt Co, where she d 1875; d/o John and Isabella (Stevenson) Constable, the former a mbr of old fam here and a mcht. In his fam were: John S. Constable, farmer; Wm S., farmer; and Albert, lawyer, once judge of courts. Subj and two sis were only mbs of fam who attained mature years. Older sis, Mary Elizabeth, became w/o Hy W. Archer, atty of Harford Co. Younger sis, Anna Isabel, m Dr. Wm H. Gale, of Som co, now decd.
  Subj educated Wash College; grad Princeton 1851; mbr Episc Church. In 1855 m Mary Rebecca Ricaud, d/o Jas B. and Ann Elizabeth (Gordon) Ricaud, of Chestertown, her father was judge of ciructit court this dist. Their child.: eld, Anna E., w/o Walter H. Beck, of St. Louis, Mo (their child: Walter H. and Mary R). Only s/o Judge Walker is Wm S. Jr., who m Jennie Hines, in business in St. Louis. Youngest child is Cornelia Ricaud, res with parents.

234 98. GEORGE F. BACON, farmer 3rd dist Kt Co, b 1866 on farm where he res. His father, Chas Bacon, of N. J., of English descent. During early life he was sailor in coasting trade along Chesapeake Bay, in 1866 came to Kt Co, Md., where he purch farm now owned and occupied by subj. He m Rachel Mulford; their child.: Chas, res Tolchester, Md.; Mary wid of John Walraven, of Camden, N.J.; Alexander, farmer 3rd dist, Kt Co; and Geo F., youngest. Father was mbr MP Church; he d 1887 at 66. Geo F. Bacon m 1882 Miss Alice, d/o John Miller, of Kt Co; their child., Ellen and Arthur; mbrs Meth Church.

234 99. JOHN E. WILSON, lawyer of Centreville. Father, John E. Wilson, b in Christiana, Del., educated public schools and Elkton (Md.) Acad; atty Elkton area; d in 1892; m Hannah D. Broomall, of Clearfield Co, Pa., now res nr Elkton. In her fam there are: Winter L., practicing civil engineer, in Central America, connected with establishment of government boundary lines; Everett B., civil engineer, res in Lambertville, N.J., with Pa Railroad; Harry C. res with mother; Fdk at home; Bertha is trained nurse in Phila; Laurine, Mary M. and Hannah C. at home. In Elkton, subj b Nov 21 1872; educated Elkton Acad, Del College, and law depart Univ Md.; Dec 1893 admitted to bar; practiced in Elkton until Feb 1896, since then in Centreville.

237 100. JAMES BENJAMIN BRIGHT, of Kt Island. An early settler on Eastern Shore of Md was Jas Bright, prob b Eng. Estab home on Kt Island, he had 10 child. Jas, oldest male heir, grew to manhood. He d in 1875; he m Susanna Eareckson; their child.: Martha S., Mrs. Richard Cray of Kt Island; Sarah E.; John Eareckson, decd; Mary E.; Annie, w/o Jas P. Norman, res of Kt Island; Jas Benj; and Laura, w/o R. R. Kelly, of Balt. - Subj b Kt Island Sep 22 1844; m

1872 Catherine Thomas; she d Feb 28 1897; d/o Sml W. Thomas, farmer of QA Co, and granddau of Kensey Harrison, atty of Centreville, now decd. Both mbrs of ME Church; their child.: Benj Harrison; Maggie A., w/o Arthur Cockey, of Kt Island; Jas Thos, grad Dover Acad and Md Law School and atty of Centreville; Katherine F., Mary O., Loleta E. and Chas M.

101. J. THOMAS HOLLAND, JR., mbr drug firm Tucker & Holland, of Centreville, b Ruthsburg, QA Co, Oct 3 1870, of old fam of QA Co. Grandfather of subj, Wm Holland b QA Co 1798, farmer; d 1865. Subject's father, Dr. J. Thos Holland, b nr Church Hill, this co, Oct 26 1834, in 1862 grad medical depart Univ Md. For 35 years in professional practice in Ruthsburg. In 1896 he moved to Balt, where he is retired; mbr MP Church. Dr. Holland m Priscilla Atwell, b AA Co, at West River, 1840, descendant of English ancestry; d/o Jos Atwell, who d on farm in QA Co in 1864, leaving son, Geo W. Atwell, farmer on Kt Island, and daus: Mrs. Jas Scott, of Balt; Mrs. W. H. H. Hopkins, of Kt Island; Mrs. J. O. Lowery, of Balt; Mrs. Alfred Tucker, Sr., of Centreville; and Mrs. J. Thos Holland, of Balt. Dr. and Mrs. Hollland have 3 sons: youngest is Geo W., res on and cultivates old home place; eld, Jos W., grad medical depart Univ Md., assist resident physician to Md Univ Hospital in Balt. Only dau, Annie R., is student state normal school.

Reared on a farm and educated in the local schools, subj took up the study of Pharmacy under Charles H. Walters, and in 1892, after 18 months of training, he formed present partnership with Alfred Tucker, Sr.

102. WILLIAM MAXWELL WATTS, principal Still Pond schools, b on farm nr Still Pond 1874. Grandfather, Geo Watts, b Kt Co, carpenter & builder Chestertown and Still Pond. Watts family of English extraction prob descend from Isaac Watts. The grandfather served war of 1812 mbr of Judge Chambers' comp, in battle of Caulks Field; d 1830, at 52. He m(1)1 Miss Greenwood, issue decd. Fol her death he m Mary Spry, of Millington, and Wm, father of subj, is 1 of 5 child. b this union that still survives.

Wm Watts, Sr., b Chestertown 1820, reared, educated Balt, where, at 13, he began learning tailor's trade with Holzman & Hunt, whom he accompanied on their move to Bainsville, Ohio, working 4 yrs. Returning to Md he was similarly employed in Chestertown and Still Pond until 1849. In early manhood Wm Watts, Sr., m Miss Mary Jones, who d leaving dau still living, Mary R., w/o J. F. Wilson. Mr. Watts m(2) Miss Lavinia Palmatary, by whom 2 sons, Wm Maxwell, of this review, and Chas Garfield, of Chestertown. Prof Watts grad Dover Academy 1890 and Dickinson College with PH. B degree in 1893; m Nov 12 1895 Miss Jane F. Penny, of Schenectady, N. Y.; their little son: Wm M., Jr.; mbrs ME Church.

103. CHARLES HENRY BEDFORD MASSEY, M. D., decd, Kt Co; b old Massey estate Oct 4 1828, attended Newark (Del.) College, medical course Univ Md, Balt; in medical practice for few yrs, eventuallly gave attention to estate he inherited; he d Jun 11 1891; 1855 m Mary Amanda Oldham, d/o Geo W. and Susan Ann (Biddle) Oldham. Her father, b Bohemia Manor, Cecil Co, served in war of 1812, farmed in Cecil Co. Her grandfather, Col Edw Oldham, fought in Rev, mbr Soc of The Cincinnati; his father was Col Edw Oldham, Sr., of Ky, who fought in Indian wars. The family came from Eng. Child. of Dr. and Mrs. Massey: George O.; Susan E., w/o Philip A. M. Brooks, Kt Co; Chas H. B.; Herman B.; Mary Ella and Eben T. The doctor's ancestor, Peter Massey, came from Eng in 1644. He had bro, Hugh, for services rendered in rebellion of 1645 was made Lord Massey, with estates in North of Ireland. Later two other bros crossed

Atlantic and settled in Kt Co, aquiring large land grants. This prop, "Massey's Venture," comprised about 20,000 a. upper part Kt Co; here are located parts of Millington and Massey.

In 1760 a descendant, Nicholas, went to N. C. and became founder of Va and Tenn families. During Rev war Elijah Massey was officer in Md lines; he d at Fort Mifflin, where he was in command after the war. He m cousin, Elizabeth Massey; their child.: Eben T., Col. Elijah, Benjamin Franklin, Jas, Geo W., Pamelia and Caroline. Eben, who m his cousin, Emily Ann Massey, of QA Co, became father of subj. He was educated at Princeton College, N.J. and settled on estate nr Masey, where he lived and d.

Col. Elijah served on Halleck's staff in Civil war. Benjamin F., who went to Mo c. 1830, twice state senator, sec of state. Several of his children were lawyers and physicians. Jas was minister of Meth Church. Geo W. was atty in Centreville, but d young. Pamelia m her cousin, Joshua Massey, and went to Alabama. J. Albert was minister of Episc Church, d in Rochester N. Y. Addeson is atty of Memphis. Caroline d unmarried.

243   104. REV. LEONIDAS B. BALDWIN, rector St. Peter's Parish, Easton, for syrs, church known as Christ's Church. Ancestors were Congregationalists, early settlers of Milford and New Haven, Ct. Father of Rev Baldwin, Jos B., born Milford, Nov 29 1802, and when m espoused Episc faith. His wife was Cynthia Eliza, d/o Elam Bradley. Her fam dates back to founding of New Haven colony; related to Capt Bradley, who won his title in Cromwell's army, in England. Only bro of subj is Jos C., pres of New York Dye Wood Co, of New York City.

L. B. Baldwin b New Haven, Conn, Mar 5 1834, of 7th generation of Baldwins that city; grad Trinity College 1860; in 1863 m Annie M. Willard, d/o Wm D. Willard of Middletown, Ct. They had dau and son: Alice S. d Easton, in young womanhood; Jos Willard d New Hampshire on threshold of promising career.

244   105. WASHINGTON A. SMITH, M. D., of Taylor's Island, Parson's Creek dist, Dor Co; served 6 terms as mbr of house of delegates and one term in state senate; born Dec 25 1820, Jefferson Co, Va., only survivor of fam of 3 sons and 2 daus of Fdk and Mary E. (Cover) Smith. He grad Univ Md medical depart in 1844; attended Dunbar Institute in Balt, then came to Taylor's Island, since then his home. He is mbr Episc Church. In 1847 Dr. Smith m Jane L. Travers, this place; she d at 33, leaving 5 child., Chas D., M.D., of Hooper's Island; Annie F., wid of Dr. Thos J. Correll, of Balt; Virginia, wife of M. M. Dunnock, farmer this vicinity; W. Breckenridge, student medical depart Univ Md.; and Capt Sml F., who d age about 34. Dr. Smith m(2) Mrs. Martha E. Travers, d/o Benj F. Berry, of PG Co.

Fdk Smith, father of subj, from Jefferson Co, Va; d when about 72. His father, Chas Smith, of province of Lorraine, France, sub-liuet in French army during Rev there. Emigrated to Va where he lived rest of his life. He m Mary Cover, from Fdk Co, Md, who d at 70. She and husband mbrs Luth Church.

245   106. M. M. RASIN, proprietor general country store at Melitota, 3rd dist, Kt Co. Oringinal ancestor of Rasin fam in America setttled in Kt Co several immigrated from Ireland. Philip, grandfather subj, and his bro Wm served in Rev war, Wm with rank of capt. They were all farmers and business men. Delany, father of M. M. Rasin, lived in Kt Co with exception of 2 yrs in QA Co. He d 1887, at 74th. He m Mary E. Beck; they had 9 children; all but 3 still living. - M. M. Rasin b this co 1855; eldest surviving son in fam. In 1892 he bt out Mr. Wood, who owned a general store, and since then has carried on business. In 1882 he m Alphonzo Parks, d/o A. R. Parks, formerly of the

-26-

3rd dist and postmaster at Still Pond, now decd. Their children: boys, Merritt and Parks, and dau, Minnie.

107. BENJAMIN R. DURDING, postmaster at Rock Hall 1893-1897. Father, John T. Durding, b East Neck Island, Kt Co. C. 1848 he went to Balt, remained involved in manufacturing until his death. He was sharpshooter in battle of North Point, war of 1812. W/o John T. Durding was from Balt and d at 30, leaving 4 little child. They have all since d, save B. R. and Mary Ann.
    Subj b Jun 1 1830 Balt where he spent his first 10 yrs; then lived with paternal grandparents, on this side of the Chesapeake, and remained with them about 5 yrs. Returning to Balt, he learned ship joiners trade, and worked at it for while. In 1851 he settled in Rock Hall, went into carpentering and house building. He m Jul 1850 Martha H. Stephens, b this dist Jul 16 1835. Their children, in order of birth: John and Amanda, decd; Jas M.; Wm P.; Andrew Jackson Lee; Elinora; Thos B., rep in another part of this vol; Howard R., Annie and Millard, all decd. Mrs. Durding is mbr Meth Church.   245

108. CHARLES SAULSBURY b nr Anthony's Mills, nr Denton Dec 7 1812. Mother & father d when he was young; then bound out to man Del, 3 yrs. At 11 he returned to Car Co and reared in fam of John Clarke. In 1863 he became a permanent res of Talb Co. In 1881 he purch farm on which he now lives, on Boonesboro road, c. 4 miles from Trappe. In 1835 he m Sophia Rowe; they had 2 child., Lizzie, only one surviving. In 1843 he m Sarah Collins; their child.: John; Abraham; Georgiana, w/o J. M. Davis; Richard W. and Jas (d at 22). For 60 yrs Mr. Saulsbury has been mbr of Reformed Church.   246

109. ALBERT W. SISK, business man Car Co; in 1893 elected to legislature of Md; only broker in canned goods on peninsula; home and headquarters at Preston. He is youngest of fam of five child., b nr Preston Jun 11 1860; mbr ME Church; m 1884 Miss Sallie, d/o J. B. and Henrietta (Kelly) Fletcher.   249
    First known Sisk Jos Sisk, whose son David b Oct 1753; m Elizabeth Foster Aug 14 1796; their child. Jos F., grandfather of subj b Aug 2 1797; m Susan Elliott Jan 6 1820. Their child.: Thos F. b in 1820 and d in infancy; Elizabeth, b 1822; David F., b 1823 and d young; Wm, subject's father, b Mar 1825; Frs A., b 1827; Mary A., b 1829; David (second of the name), b 1831, and Susanna, b 1834. Wm Sisk believed b this co; lived here from early childhood; res few yrs Dor Co, farmed Car Co, nr Preston, most of life; m Lucetta Dean Dec 23 1845 Dor Co; their child.: Amanda, eld, w/o J. W. Kerr, this co. Susie E. next in order of birth. Jos F. and Thos J. (twins) are mchts; and Albert W. completes fam. Wm Sisk mbr ME Church; d Mar 31 1888.

110. WILLIAM M. SLAY, of Chestertown; b QA Co Aug 5 1847; belongs to Kt Co, Del fam. His father Wm Slay, bo Del 1810, farmer and mcht. He res in Md. for few yrs, returned to old home; mber of county court and later elected to rep his dist in Del legislataure. He d Apr 1885. He m Miss Louisa Onins, from Kt Co, Del; she d 1851. Of her child., eld, John O., d in prime of legal career; Mary E. and Martha, living and unmarried.   250
    In 1868 Wm M. Slay grad Yale Univ, with honors. Coming to Chestertown he was made principal of schools, pursued legal studies with bro and Geo Vickers. In Apr 1872, he admitted to bar, since then in general practice, specializing in equity cases. In Dec 1885 he m Augusta Eccleston Hynson in this city, at her home. She is d/o Richard Hynson and reared in this place.

250   111. ARTHUR EMORY SUDLER, M. D. b old homestead 1st dist QA Co. Founder of fam owned about 1000 a. this co, on which Sudlersville was located. Dr. Sudler b Feb 22 1839; at 17 pursued study of medicine in office of uncle, Dr. Wm J. Sudler, of Sudlersville, 1859 grad Jefferson Medical College Phila, returned home, where he estab his practice. He m Miss Annie R. P. Foster 1869; she d 1876. Their only child, Foster, grad Dickinson College 1894; grad medical depart Univ Pa 1896; he is now in practice here.

John Wells Emory Sudler, father of subj, b Sudlersville, Jan 11 1817; at 14 serving as clerk; remained here 2 yrs; clerked in Phila about 3 yrs; returned home, went into business with father; served 4 years as judge of orphans' court; mbr ME Church; m Apr 26 1838 Mary R., only d/o John Morling, of Wye Landing, Talb Co. She d Mar 1865, leaving 4 child.: Dr. A. E., John M., Wm Jackson and Eugenia (Mrs. S. S. Goodhand). Mr. Sudler m Jun 11 1868, Martha Virginia, d/o Thos Hopkins, of Car Co; sons: Carroll H., of Chicago; Chas H., mbr city corps of engineers of Phila; and dau, Virginia, of Phila.

251   112. JAMES McREA ROBERTSON, res Cambridge, b Nov 15 1842, nr Mardela Springs, Wicomico Co, then called Barren Creek Springs, Som Co, s/o Thos and Henrietta Elizabeth (Jones) Robertson, both decd, former d 1889, at 73, and latter d when subj was 2 1/2 years old. There were 2 child., younger being Maria Henrietta, wid of Nathaniel Dashsiell and mother of 3. She lives at Quantico, Md. The father m(2) Miss Leah Evans, of Som Co, 1 of 5 child no living, Albert, lumberman of Whaleyville, Va. Paternal grandmother of subj bore the maiden name of Dougherty. and belonged to old fam of Nanticoke Township, Wicomico Co, nr mouth of Nanticoke River.

Subj spent boyhood on farm, after which he learned carpenter's trade, and on locating at Vienna, Dor Co, in 1866, he engaged in contracting and building. While attending school in his native dist he took up study of surveying. He m Miss Mary Hester LeCompte, d/o Solomon S. and Henrietta (Nichols) LeCompte; she d 5 yrs later. In 1878 Mr. Robertson m Miss Susie C. Judson, of Troy, N. Y., sis of Dr. Harry P. Judson, dean Univ Chicago, and 2nd cousin of ex-President Cleveland. Their child.: Edgar Wallace and Gilbert Bernard. In 1885 he was elected to Md house of delegates; served as justice of peace, co surveyor, school commissioner and treasurer of Dor Co.

252   113. JACOB B. CROWDING b Newcastle Co, Del, Apr 9 1840, and spent the first 31 yrs of his life. He has spent over a quarter of a century in Kt Co, Md.

Father of subj, Geo Crowding, of Del, life-long res of Newcastle Co. His father, Jacob, b in Del., farmer on Delaware Bay. Fam of German descent with representatives in America for several generations. Geo Crowding d at age 35, in 1848. He m Anna Suthall, still living, at 80, b Newcastle Co, now living in Wilm, Del. Her child.: Mary, wid of Geo Daniels; Jacob B.; Anna, w/o Wm Bacon, of Phila; and Janet, decd w/o Sml Thomas.

When he about 31 Jacob B. Crowding came to vicinity and located upon the Debby Turner farm. In 1883 he purch the Muddy Branch homestead; mbr of the ME Church. On Oct 17 1867 he m Ruth Robinson; they had 9 child. Two d in infancy, and two when grown; surviving: Walter, Jacob B., Jr., Eddie, Ida and Chas. Walter is at Still Pond, working for father on the farm.

255   114. THOMAS F. J. RIDER, state's atty Wicomico Co; b at Wellington, on Wicomico River, nr Quantico, Som Co, (now within limits of Wicomico Co), on Feb 3 1836, s/o Chas Rider, lieut-col in Md militia and owner of large estate; in 1854 grad Wash Acad, Princess Anne; grad 1856 Jefferson College, Wash Co, Pa. In 1858 he resigned as principal of Salisbury Acad and to read law in

office of Jones & Irving, Princess Anne. In Nov 1867 chosen clerk of circuit court for new co of Wicomico. He has been elected three times to the office of state's atty. In 1873 he m Miss Josephine A. Toadvine, of Salisbury and moved to Wash, D. C., where he practiced for 5 yrs. On the death of father-in-law, Purnell Toadvine, he returned to Salisbury, where he has since res. In 1883 his wife d, leaving only dau, Mary, who grad from Melrose in 1890 and now presides over her father's home.

115. JACOB S. DENNY, mcht of Queenstown, QA Co, b here Mar 1860, s/o Jacob Tolson and Henrietta (Mowbray) Denny. Former b on western shore, boating and farming until few months of his death; he drowned Aug 1859 in Patapsco River. He m Kt Island d/o Henry Mowbray, of Balt, and was res of Kt Island many yrs. His eld son, John F., d at 18. Wm H. and Chas H. res Kt Island. In 1893 Jacob S. Denny bt stock of Wm H. Denny, his bro. In 1889 he m Miss Clara V. Bryan in Queenstown ME Church; d/o Rbt and granddau of Rbt S. Bryan, and by her marriage mother of dau, Mary Edith. 256

116. JOHN DAVID URIE, mbr Chestertown bar, state's atty Kt Co. Founder Urie fam in America was Thos; from Glasgow, Scotland, who settled in lower part of Kt Co, Md, nr Chesapeake Bay, c. 1725; mbr Church of Eng. His son John mbr same church. He operated coopering estab for yrs in Kt Co. Jas, his son, and grandfather of subj, introduced the manufacturing of woolen goods in the south. His extensive mills employed a large force of men at Urieville, Md. He d in 1856, leaving son, Jas and Wm. The latter a homoeopathic physician in Chester, Pa., until he d, summer of 1897. Jas, father of subj, d 1866, at 35, farmer; m Mary E. Kendall, left five young child. H. Frank, of Orlando, Fla., mcht; Dr. Jas W., practicing homoeopathic physician of Still Pond. Mary w/o E. L. McGinniss and now wid; Helen w/o Jas F. Hammond, of Hawthorn, Fla. John David Urie was born Kt Co, Md, Dec 18 1860, eldest son in fam. 256

John David Urie attended Wash College and studied law under late Richard Hynson, admitted to practice in 1884. In 1888 he m Lillian Baker, whose father, Chas H. Baker, mbr of Chestertown Bar. Child. living: Mary Louisa and Helen Lillian; Jas, only son, d in infancy. They are mbrs of MP Church.

117. JOHN W. CLARK, owns c. 1000 a. of farmland 6th dist Car Co; b Del about 12 miles from Dover, Mar 14 1825, s/o John and Mary (Truitt) Clark, of Del, who had fam 13 child.; all but two are living. The father and mother d at 84 and 90 yrs, respectively. The grandfather, Sml Clark, also native of Del. 257

John W. Clark m Dec 24 1846, Mary E., d/o Manlove and Magdalene (McNitt) Smith, of Del. Their child.: Rbt, living on part of father's farm; Mary M; Laura; John W., Jr., auctioneer and crier of court at Denton; Sarah M. and Anna. All are married. Parents mbrs MP Church.

118. ANDREW J. FOBLE, business man Cambridge, b here, s/o John Foble, who for yrs in manufacture of plug tobacco in Balt. The grandfather, Wm Foble, b Germany, emigrated to Balt; wounded off North Point in war of 1812, he d 2 yrs later, from injuries. John Foble moved from Balt to Cambridge 1842 and estab first plug tobacco factory on peninsula; m Elizabeth Disney, native of Dor Co, and mbr old families of AA Co; living child.: Wm T., a bookkeeper in bro's factory; J. Jas, in charge of a machine in factory; Hy D., acigar manufacuter; and A. J. Andrew Jackson Foble b Cambridge, Dec 14 1854, attended Cambridge Acad; at16 began working in father's tobacco factory. In Jan 1880 he embarked in merchandising; sold out to E. C. Hopkins in 1893 and purch shirt factory 258

-29-

owned by L. S. McNamara, of Cambridge. Andrew J. Foble m Sep 16 1880, Miss Mary E., d/o Wm Hopkins (aged 83), of Cambridge.

261 119. JAMES C. DIRICKSON, M. D., res Berlin, Wor Co, 40 years. The fam originated in Stockholm, Sweden. Paternal grandfather of doctor was Levin Dirickson, of either lower part of Del or Md. He was killed while a young man. His father, Jas, also b on peninsula, and res here all his life.
The doctor's father, Jas Dirickson, b nr Berlin, Wor Co, 1796. He owned vessels that conveyed freight to Phila and New York City. He m Henrietta, d/o Littleton Purnell; their child.: Levin L., decd; Mary I., w/o Maj Thos L. Harris of Ill.; and subj. Levin L. educated Trinity College, Hartford, Conn, and held positions in state and co.
James C. Dirickson b Berlin 1833, at 16 began study of medicine; grad Jefferson Medical College Phila 1853, began practice in Rehoboth, Som Co; 3 yrs later went to Nicaragua and was there a few months during war of 1856. The following year received app to Samoan Islands as consul and remained 3 yrs, returning home in 1860. Since then in practice in Berlin. In Oct 1865 he m Miss Eliza B. Cummins, of Smyrna, Del; they have dau, Martha Susie.

261 120. COL. F. CARROLL GOLDSBOROUGH b at Llandaff farm, Talb Co, about 3 miles southwest of Easton. His father, Matthew Tilghman Goldsborough, b same co in 1812, eld child of Col. Nicholas and Elizabeth Tench (Tilghman) Goldsborough, of Otwell, Talb Co. She was d/o Col Tench Tilghman, aid to Gen Washington in Rev war. Subject's paternal grandfather was col of militia in war of 1812; followed farming; rep co in Md legislature; mbr Episc Church; his father, Nicholas Goldsborough, also belonged. Nicholas Goldsborough b Talb Co, d when son, the colonel, was small child. His father also named Nicholas.
Matthew T. Goldsborough educated as civil engineer, followed that field 10 yrs; surveyed Roanoke & Weldon Railroad in N. C., town of Goldsborough, N.C. laid out along along that line and named in his honor; retired to his farm, where he d 1861. In early life he m Eleanor Sarah Tilghman, d/o Edward Tilghman, of QA Co, had large fortune. He was 2nd s/o Col Edw Tilghman, of Wye. Mother of subj spent last days in Balt.
Col Goldsborough, of this review, 1 of 7 child., five still living. Anna Elizabeth is w/o Col F. H. Johnson, farmer of Talb Co; Matthew Tilghman owns and operates ancestral home in Otwell, Talb co; Col next in order of birth; E. Martha res Balt; Sarah M. w/o Hy M. Smyth, Gloversville, N. Y.; Fanny Van Wyck m Wm H. Archer and d in Balt, leaving dau, Fanny (w/o Rev Peter Gray Sears, of Miss.); and Walter Gwynn d at 19.
Subj spent boyhood on old homestead, Ellenborough, grad Univ Va 1869; now owns and operates homestead; 1885 m 1st cousin, Mary Hill Goldsborough; their child.: Nicholas, Martha, Richard and Mary Hill; parents are Episc. Sub past pres American Oxford Down Assoc, trustee Md Agric College, pres Talb Co, Fair Assoc.

262 121. JAMES V. KNOTTS, M. D., physician, d 29 Aug 1893 1st dist QA Co; b nr Roseville, QA Co, Jan 9 1840, spent boyhood on farm; grad Univ Md with degree of M. D. in 1866; moved to present home in 1st dist. In 1867 Dr. Knotts m Miss Kate O. Cooper; their child.: Estella, Gurney, Jas T., Herbert, Roland, Katie E. and Mary O., all living; and Geo, decd. Subj was mbr ME Church. He was buried Templeville cemetery.

-30-

122. T. WATERS RUSSELL, of Chestertown. His grandfather, Theophilus Russell, 263
b here Aug 11 1781, s/o Wm and Ann Russell; sailor; ran packet
Balt-Chestertown; in battle of Caulks Field, war of 1812; d Apr 27 1856.
Little known re ancestry or parentage. He m 1804 Ann Tittle (b Jul 23 1787).
   John Russell, father subj, b Chestertown Jan 26 1805; in early took charge
of packet Chestertown-Balt; embarked in mercantile business; capt of rifle
militia company; served as clerk to bd of co commissioners; magistrate; d Oct
12 1875. Mother of subj, Frances George, b Balt Jul 26 1806, d Chestertown
Dec 23 1834; d/o Fdk and Elizabeth George, sis of late Jas B. George and aunt
of Isaac S. George, pres of Traders' Bank of Balt. George fam of French
Huguenot descent. Mrs. Frances (George) Russell was 2nd wife of John Russell,
who, after her death, m Elizabeth Greenwood; their child.: John Hamer, res
Winchester, QA Co; Jas Alexander; Hester Ann; Wm George, watchmaker; Lewis L.;
and Sarah L., w/o Clinton Cook, of Denton.
   T. Waters Russell, only child of father's 2nd marriage; born Chestertown
Oct 3 1833, educated Wash College; taught in Kt Co and 2 yrs in N.C.; then dep
rgstr wills, 20 yrs with J. A. Pearce; clerk to bd of co commissioners. He m
in 1862, Benanna Greenwood Frazier, d/o Wm and Elizabeth (Ridue) Frazier, of
Chestertown. Her father b Jan 14 1805, mcht tailor, d 1887. She is mother
of: Frances George, w/o Jos N. Wheatley, postmaster of Chestertown; Charlotte
R., at home; Wm F., cashier Savings Bank of Chestertown; Ann Tittle, Amy
Claudine and John Waters.

123. CAPT. CLOUDSBURY H. CLASH, Centreville, b nr St. Michael's, Talb Co, May 264
7 1828, only child of Cloudsbury and Henrietta (Matthews) Clash, the former of
Talb Co, and latter of QA Co, d/o Jos Matthews. She was 2nd wife and lived to
about 45 yrs of age; d in Aug 1849. Cloudsbury Clash, Sr., m(1) Miss
Stableford, of Talb Co; their child.: Sarah A., w/o Sml Jewell; Gerrettson,
mcht of Phila, who d when about 68; and Nathaniel, who d at home of his bro
Cloudsbury in 1895.
   Capt Clash, was 11 when fam moved to Tilghman Island, Talb Co, where they
spent 4 yrs, then moved to Milton farm, nr Easton. In Oct 1845 he shipped
aboard a schooner, and for yrs sailed Chesapeake Bay. In Apr 1854 he came to
Centreville and assumed charge of schooner Harvest. In 1858 he m Miss Sarah
Ellen Anderson, d/o Chas H. Anderson, who moved from Del to Centreville. He m
Mary Jones of Del. Their child.: Chas Nicholson, b Jul 6 1859, collector for
Deering Manufacturing Co of Chicago; Howard Tilghman, b Apr 8 1861, in lumber
business in Toledo, Oh; Fdk Hy, teacher, b Mar 29 1863, d Sep 15 1890,
educated St. John's College, m Miss Marshall, had son; Vernon, born Aug 17
1865, died Mar 5 1868; Preston Anderson, b Nov 3 1867, at home; Henrietta, b
Apr 13 1870, teacher in Centreville; Mary Elizabeth, b Jan 25 1872, w/o Rbt A.
Cairns, chief engineer in Waterbury, Ct.; Norman Matthew, b Mar 7 1875, d Aug
30 1876; Sarah Ellen, b Feb 7 1878, student normal school Balt; Evelyn, b Jan
4 1881, completes the family. Captain Clash is mbr Episc Church.

124. COL. WILLIAM SCOTT ROBERTS, of Centreville, b Jul 11 1838, eld s/o late 267
Col Lemuel Roberts, who was b Dec 1802. He farmed land for which his father,
Benj Roberts, obtained grant in 1794. It was on Clinton River Red Line, where
grandfather owned and operated mill as early as 1750. He was twice m, and by
first union had sons, Benj and Thos. The latter was a miller, but went to
sea, where he lost his life. The former, who was miller and farmer, sold his
interest in old homestead, which was inherited by father subj.

Col. Lemuel Roberts rep dist state legislature 10 yrs; d Oct 1869. Mother of subj, Mrs. Maria J. (Scott) Roberts, of Annapolis, d/o Wm Scott, of Engl, capt of a vessel. Mrs. Roberts d on old homestead QA Co 1851. Col Lemuel Roberts and wife had 8 children; 3 d early life. Benj, 2nd of fam, 1st lieut, wounded at Chancellorsville and Gettysburg, d of injuries in hospital. Maria J. w/o John McFadden, of New York; Emma V. wid of late Wm G. Temple, of Del, son of ex-Gov Wm Temple. Their only son, Rev Dr. Wm Temple, now 26, lectures to post-grad theological students in St. Vincent's Theological Seminary New York. He was student in American College in Rome for 4 yrs. His father was Protestant; he in priesthood. Finley completes Roberts fam.

Subj reared on father's farm until 1851, grad Md Military Acad, Oxford, in 1859. In 1862 he was admitted to bar. He began practice in Westminister, Carroll Co. During res in Carroll Co he edited and publ Western Md Democrat, now Westminister Advocate. In May 1864 he returned to QA Co. In 1875 he estab Centreville Record. In 1872 Col Roberts m Miss Eliza J. Dunbracco.

268   125. JOHN H. HORSEY, farmer, Car Co and extensive land holder. Great-grandfather, of Germany, settled here about middle of last century, fought in Rev war. Grandfather Nathaniel Horsey b Del. Parents of subj were Wm G. and Mary A. (Harris) Horsey, both of Del; his only sis is Eliza A., w/o Thos Garrett, farmer in Car Co. Wm G. reared in this co and was mcht of Denton; served in house of delegates and co commissioner. His wife d Jun 1853, aged 28; he later m Louisa Moore, of Del. Their daus, Eva M., decd, and Clara, w/o Geo Deakyne, co treasurer Car Co (see his sketch elsewhere this vol). Maternal grandfather of subj, Isaac Harris, native of this state, founder of ME Church located on farm owned by his grandson.

John H. Horsey b Mar 13 1848, this locality; attended St. John's College Annapolis about 1 year. On Jun 7 1876 he m Annie Pennington (b Kt Co, Md). Their child.: Wm G., Norman; Hy and Pennington, twins; Mary and Harold - all unmarried and living at home; fam attend ME Church.

268   126. WILSON MOORE TYLOR, editor Easton Gazette, purch plant 1885; b nr Denton Jun 2 1856, s/o Jonathan and Rebecca (Huyck) Tylor. His father, b Car Co 1806, d 1868; mother d 1884, 61. Paternal grandparents were Thos Tylor, of Car Co, who d 1829, aged 67, and Mary Alexander Alford, who d 1820, at 50. Maternal grandparents were Girardus and Mary (Pile) Huyck, the former in war of 1812. Great-grandparents were Petrus and Magdalena (Quackenbush) Huyck, the former a s/o Johannes and Catharine (Bevier) Huyck, who m 1739. Johannes was s/o Mayke Hoes, who in 1703 m Burger Huyck, of Kinderhook, N. Y. Burger's parents were Andries Hanse and Cathalin Lammerse (Van Valkenburg) Huyck. Andries was s/o Elizabeth Peters, who m Jan Huyck, "chieftain of the groot straat" in Nymegen, 18 Apr 1607, emigrated from Wesel to New Amsterdam, 4 May 1626. Jan was s/o Henric Huyck, mcht of Roemund, Holland.

Wilson M. has one bro, Jonathan Edw, lawyer of Balt, and one sis, Annie (Tylor) Miller, of Wash, D. C. Subj taught in Car 2 yrs and Talb Co for 5 yrs, and 3 yrs Easton, N. Y., where he was principal of Marshall Seminary on the Hudson. In 1885 he retired from teaching and purch Easton Gazette.

269   127. JOHN G. MILLS, Cambridge, editor of Democrat and News, b 6th dist Dor Co 24 Nov 1857 s/o Wm H. and Mary M. (Gootee) Mills. The father, farmer and mcht, b Eastern Shore of Va, spent greater part of life in Md, where he d 1865; the mother d Mar 1897 on old Mills homestead in Dor Co at 76.

John G. Mills 4th son and 5th child of 8 children. He taught school 7 yrs at Meekins Neck school 6th dist Dor Co, studied law, admitted to bar 1881, and engaged in practice; in 1883 purch newspaper and become editor and proprietor. In 1887 John G. Mills m Miss Mamie G. Winterbottom, d/o Harrison T. and Mary E. Winterbottom, of Cambridge. Her father, now decd, was magistrate in Cambridge. Mr. and Mrs. Mills have dau, Evelyn R. The mother is mbr Meth Church South.

128. J. HORTON KELLEY, A.B., M.D., of Locust Grove, physician and surgeon of 270 Kt Co, b Kt Co Oct 2 1850 s/o John Kelley who was b Kt Co 1795. Original emigrant from Ireland, located on Kt Island, where his son Wm, subject's grandfahter, was b. In 1780 the latter moved to Kt Co, where he owned several tracts; mbr Episc Church. The doctor's father, farmed, later conducted general store at Still Pond, where he d 1877, at 82. He m Miss Mary E. Jump; they had 6 child., of whom 4 living: Mrs. John T. Gale; Mrs. W. F. Wroth, wid; Edvina, w/o J. C. Rosebery; and Dr. J. Horton.
    The doctor was 7 when parents left farm and moved to Still Pond. He studied law under Judge Wicks, of Chestertown, admitted to bar in 1872; in practice a few years; grad from medical depart Univ Pa Mar 1881; began practice in Locust Grove. In Sep 1879 he m Miss Lillie Deringer, a granddau of inventor of Deringer pistol. She is from Del. and d/o B. M. Deringer. The doctor and wife are mbrs Episc Church.

129. THOMAS HOPEWELL HORSEY, res of Galena, born Millington, Kt Co, 1844. At 273 16 he clerked in large store New York City; in 1861 came to Galena with bro-in-law, late Wm T. Betton, for whom he clerked. In 1868 he began in business for himself. On Oct 10 1876 Mr. Horsey m Mary E. Rasin, of St. Louis, Mo. Their sons: Unit Rasin, Thos H., Hanson and Palmer Keene, all at home. Mr. Horsey d Sep 23 1893. He and wife attend Episc Church.

130. FRANKLIN H. HARPER b Kt Co, Del Nov 30 1838 s/o Chas Harper, of Del. 274
    His father, farmer and mcht of Leipsic, Del; died 1854; identified with ME Church; m Martha L. Hardcastle, of Car Co d/o Rbt Hardcastle. Her only bro, Rbt Everett Hardcastle mbr constitutional convention of Md in 1867. Wm Harper, subject's grandfather, b Del. A son of latter, Frs B. Harper, mbr of legislature of Del, and another son, Andrew, also prominent.
    Subj came to Kt Co, Md, 1858, clerked in store at Millington; went to Still Pond, 2nd dist, purch farm and opened general store; 1895 elected judge of orphans' court. A bro, E. B. Harper, pres Mutual Reserve Fund Life Insurance Assoc of New York, d Jul 2 1895. Another bro, Geo W. Harper, connected with same assoc. Third bro, Walter S., unmarried, res Phila. The sis, Mrs. Annie Davis, res on farm nr Still Pond.
    The maternal ancestors of this family, the Hardcastles, were originally from Ireland, where they owned large tracts of land. Wm Hardcastle, a great uncle, owned Castle Hall in Caroline Co.
    Judge Harper m Mrs. Martha A. E. (Webb) Merritt, wid of Thos Merritt and d/o Jos W. Webb, of Kt Co. They are mbrs ME Church. Their only surviving child, Joseph W., grad Princeton 1891, in business with father; he m Miss Lavina Baynard, their child.:Franklin and Florence Olivia.

131. ROBERT M. DAWSON, M. D. res Bolton farm Bay Hundred dist, Talb Co, since 275 1877, in practice here until 1894.
    The Dawson family originated in Eng. The first of name in Md was Ralph, who came, it is thought, direct from Eng, settling at Royal Oak, Talb Co, and owning land there and in QA Co. The doctor's grandfather, John Dawson, b Talb Co. Maj John Dawson, father of doctor, b this co, where he spent his entire

life farming. He m(1) Fannie Caulk, who d childless. Me m(2) Mary Darden, they had seven children. His third wife, Mary, d/o John Robson, of old family here. She d 1883; her husband, d 1854, at 86. Their child.: Eliza J., w/o D. L. Gold, of Wash, D. C.; Selina, decd; Luvenia Lucretia, who m Wm Stewart; and Rbt M. Parents mbrs ME Church.

Rbt M. Dawson b Mar 12 1839 at Royal Oak; attended old Md Military Acad of Oxford, Md., and Ft Edward (N.Y.) Institute; 1860 taught school at Royal Oak. At opening of war he entered Company C., Md Line Infantry, C. S. A., served for 3 yrs, in battles of Winchester, Fisher's Hill, Gettysburg and Lookout Mountain; remained through entire war, except when prisoner at Ft Del and Point Lookout. Returning home in 1865, he studied medicine under Dr. W. G. G. Wilson, of Easton, and later attended lectures at Md Univ Balt. 1869 he grad with degree of M. D., practiced Royal Oak 8 yrs; in 1877 came to Bay Hundred dist and settled on farm where he has since lived.

Mr. Dawson m 1884, Mary Kemp, d/o John Kemp who owned farm where sub res. This tract was granted to Edward Webb, who m a Miss Kemp, for yrs home of John Kemp, judge of orphans' court. Twice married, his second wife, Susan, was sis of his first, Maria Larabee. By first marriage 4 child. were b, while Mrs. Dawson is only living mbr of second fam. Mr. Kemp d 1869, at 67; wife d 1877, at 77. Dr. Dawson attends Episc Church and wife ME Church.

276 132. ALFRED TUCKER, of Centreville, well known educator of 35 yrs; Centreville, Feb 19 1839, s/o Alfred Tucker, Sr., who was b Kt Island, Oct 19 1806. Paternal grandfater, Richard Tucker, of Va, in war of 1812, as was his wife's bro, Peter Cockey. He m Susanna Cockey, of Kt Island, their sons: Alfred, father of subj; Geo W., druggist of Balt; Richard, soldier in Mexican war; and John, a mason by trade, of Kt Island, d at Greensborough.

In early life Alfred Tucker, Sr., learned brick mason's trade, which he followed until 1847, then moved to a farm; d Nov 25 1878; 1833 m Miss Emily F., d/o Capt Thos C. Dawson, and half sis of ex-Senator John F. Dawson, of Car Co. She was b 1811, d Jan 2 1875.

Subj is one of 8 child., of whom 1 d in childhood. Dr. John T., the oldest, b Aug 6 1836, grad Md Univ, physician of Church Hill; Mary never married; Geo L., b Aug 1844, farmer; Wm C., b Apr 1846, farmer and school teacher; Emily F. m Dnl Wright of Dor Co; Chas Edw, farmer, d early manhood. He had m a Miss Denney, d/o Jas Denney, of Kt Island.

Jul 1861 subj began teaching school. On 20 Nov 1866 he m Miss Susie C., d/o Jos and Mary Atwell; their child.: Alfred, who m Clara A. Long, d/o Lethy Long, who is teller in QA Natl Bank; Clarence Atwell, who grad Md Law School, and now practicing Balt; Chas E., practicing law in Centreville; and Percy, bookkeeper for firm of Wright & McKenney, hardware dealers. Mr. Tucker is mbr MP Church.

279 133. JOSEPH ALEXANDER HOLTON, M. D., physician in Centreville. Paternal grandfather, Thos Holton, b in North of Ireland, of Scotch-Irish ancestry; c. 1780 settled Chester Co, Pa; farmed until he d 1831, at 90; mbr Presby Church. In his fam were 3 sons: Wm, b 1780, founder of branch of fam now in Ky; Alexander, res Chester Co, Pa.; and Thos, doctor's father who was b Oxford, Chester Co, Pa, May 4 1799, came to Cecil Co, Md, in 1822, c. 1843 returned to birth place, where he spent remaining days on farm; d Sep 1875. He m Mary Alexander, d/o Jos Alexander, of Cecil Co, whose father was Geo, s/o Theophilus and grandson of Jas Alexander, founder of fam in this country. Geo Alexander, the doctor's great-grandfather, in Rev war, and his grandfather, Jos Alexander, in war of 1812. The latter was farmer of Cecil Co. He had one

son John, who during gold excitement went to California, nothing further heard from him. Mrs. Holton still living at 92, living with her, Hart B. Holton, in Balt Co.

Dr. Holton is 2nd in order of birth; others are: Margaret Ann, wid of Asa Warner, of Balt Co, where she res; Wm B., grad Phila medical College, in practice at time of death, age 27; John, in harness business in Wilm, Del.; Thos S. grad medical depart Univ Md., in practice in Kt Co until his death in 1881; Mary, living with mother and bro in Balt Co; Hart B., farmer and stock raiser of Balt Co, mbr of 49th congress of U. S.; and Susan, w/o Philip Owings, of Balt Co. - Subj b Jun 10 1825, Cecil Co, 7 miles from Elkton; in 1852 grad Phila College of Medicine; began practice at Landisburg, Perry Co, Pa; in Aug 1852, went to Chestertown, Kt Co, Md, and fol year to Centreville, where he has remained. In 1857 he m Miss Catherine Jane, d/o Tilghman Layton, of Sussex Co, Del. Their son Wm Layton Holton, since 19 has been teller in Centreville Natl Bank. He m 4th d/o Gen. Wm McKenney.

134. COL. OSWALD TILGHMAN, state senator from Talb Co, b Mar 7 1841, old 280 homestead, Plinhimmon, near Oxford, Talb Co. The first of the name in America was Richard Tilghman, M. D., surgeon of London, who came to Md in 1660 and settled at the Hermitage, near Queenstown, QA Co, which has remained in the possession of his descendants.

Jas, grandson of Richard, b Dec 6 1716; studied law, admitted to bar and entered in practice in Annapolis, c. 1760 moved to Phila; in 1764 chosen common councilman of Phila and fol year app secretary of land office of Pa.

Matthew, his bro, was b at the Hermitage Feb 17 1718; in 1751 elected delegate to gen assembly of Md; in 1777 retired from congress to accept position of state senator from Talb Co.

Wm, s/o Jas, b Talb Co Aug 12 1756; admitted to bar 1783. In Feb 1806 he became chief justice of state supreme court.

Tench, another s/o James, b Talb Co 25 Dec 1744; in 1781 commissioned lieut col. On the surrender of Cornwallis he was selected by Washington to bear his dispatch to congress announcing that event. After the war he settled in Balt; was in merchandising; there he d Apr 18 1786.

Lloyd, great-grandson of Matthew, b Talb Co 1816, grad U. S. Military Acad 1836, assigned to First Dragoons, but resigned to become civil engineer; principal assist engineer of Panama div of Isthmus Railraod and was engineer on southern roads until 1859; in 1861 enlisted in Confederate service, was col of 4th Ky Confederate Infantry Regt then brigadier-general. He was killed in battle of Champion Hill nr Vicksburg, Miss., May 16 1863. His sons Fdk Boyd Tilghman and Sidell Tilghman are stock brokers in New York City.

Gen. Tench Tilghman, great-grandson of Richard, and subject's father b Plinhimmon, Talb Co, Mar 25 1810. He grad West Point 1832, assigned to 4th Artillery, resigned in 1833 to farm nr Oxford. 1837-1860 he was brigadier-general of state militia. 1849-50 he was U.S. consul at Mayaguez, Porto Rico. He d Dec 22 1894.

Subj educated Md Military Acad Oxford, Md; in 1859 went to Texas; at the outbreak of Civil war enlisted in Confed service; 8th Texas Cav, or Terry's Texas Rangers. At seige of Port Hudson he was only officer of 4 in battery not killed; taken prisoner and held at Johnson's Island, Ohio 23 months. After war Col Tilghman returned to Talb Co and studied law under Chas H. Gibson; admitted to the bar; practice in Easton. He is author of "Memoir of Lieut.-Col. Tench Tilghman." Col Tilghman res Foxley Hall, Easton.

282   135. CHARLES W. SMITH, farmer and fruit grower QA Co, mbr ME Church; b Jul 9 1848 nr Marydel, Kt Co, Del, where he grew to manhood on a farm; attended normal school in Balt 2 yrs. Locating in Templeville in 1871 he served as principal of public schools 12 yrs; moved to present farm which he has operated except yrs 1884-5 when he conducted general store in Templeville; in 1891 elected judge of orphans' court. Dec 26 1871 m Miss Rachel Cahall of Kt Co, Del; their child.: Ernest F., Herman K., Wesley T. and Milton.

285   136. J. THOMAS PENINGTON, retired farmer and business man Galena, Kt Co, b Cecil Co, Apr 13 1840, s/o Edw, also b and reared that section. Edw owned many slaves and the war proved disastrous financially, which led him to Kt Co, where he rented farm remainder of life. He d at 69.
    His father, also named Edw, farmer, of Cecil Co. Fam of English descent, living on Eastern Shore for several generations. Mother of subject nee Jane Penington; her father, Rbt, of Cecil Co, farmer, in war of 1812, serving as capt of company. Mrs. Jane Penington b Cecil Co Aug 1806; she d 1875; mbr Episc Church. She left 4 sons: Wm, farmer this section; J. Thos; Hy C., res Seaford, Del., on governor's staff; and Noble E., of Westmoreland Co, Va.
    In 1871 J. Thos Penington m Annie M., d/o Geo R. and Mary E. (Duyer) Van Sant. Her father, farmer here all his life; d at 66; mbr ME Church. His father, Geo, of Kt Co, farmer; d in middle life. Mary E. (Duyer) Van Sant b Galena, d at 28; left a child, Mrs. Annie Penington, who res this immediate area all her life and who inherited from mother old Parker homestead, handed down from one generation to next since 1670, when first came into their possession. Mr. and Mrs. Penington are members of the Episc Church.

286   137. RICHARD T. CARTER, manages estate (1600 acres) of late father, res 3rd dist Car Co. His father, Col Richard C. Carter, b this co c. 1815, s/o John Carter, native this area, farmed until his death, at 50. Great-grandfather Carter came to America from Eng with 2 bros, in early days. Col R. C. Carter dealt in grain and fertilizers, d in 81st year; m Sarah E. Slaughter, d/o Thos Slaughter. She was b Del; of her 5 child only our subj remains.
    Richard T. Carter b Jul 29 1857; boyhood on father's farm; grad Dickinson Seminary 1875; cashier Denton Natl Bank; later carried on hardware and farming implement store in Denton 7 years; m Dec 8 1886, Carrie Sigler, of Patterson, N.J.; only child: Annie S., age 6. Parents mbrs ME Church.

286   138. JOHN KEMP STEVENS, atty in Denton. His great-grandfather was of Scotch-Irish descent, held c. 500 a. in 3rd dist Car Co; d when about 60. Grandfather John Stevens of Car Co, farmer. Chas Stevens, father of subj, b this co, Sep 25 1832; in boyhood moved to Camden, Del; he located on farm on Kt Island c. 1860; later moved to Talb Co and finally to Denton. In Denton he carried on drug business, then became postmaster. He d Mar 19 1896. He was mbr Episc Church; m Dec 31 1870, Miss Susan E. Kemp, b and reared in Talb Co. They had 2 sons. Chas E. b Denton Apr 5 1874, educated public school and academies of county, later attending State Agricultural College.
    J. K. Stevens b this village Mar 31 1872. At end of sophomore year at St. John's College, Annapolis, he became dep clerk in office of Col Luther H. Gadd, clerk of Car Co; admitted to bar 1894.

287   139. SAMUEL VANNORT, res Chestertown. (The sketch of bro of subj, Col. William J. Vannort, elsewhere this vol) Sml b Chestertown Aug 14 1837; spent 2 yrs in Wash College; then farmed 25 yrs. Today his three farms contain 600-700 acres. In Oct 1883 he moved to Chestertown; in 1889 elected mbr state

legislature; mbr MP Church. In 1865 he m Alletha A., d/o Jos Usilton, farmer res nr Worton. They have a dau, Julia Claire.

140. WILLIAM CAULK, M. D., retired physician, 2nd dist Talb Co. Paternal 288 grandfather was major in war of 1812, an extensive land-owner. Wm Caulk, Sr., farmer, b, and spent his entire life this d st. He was Episc; m Miss Mary E. Lamdin, of this community; she d at 38. They had 3 child. Carrie d at 27; and Mary, the younger sis, w/o H. K. George, of St. Michael's village.
Dr. Caulk b Apr 2 1845, lived on old farm c. 11 yrs; attended Easton Acad, Media Acad, Media Pa, and West River Acad; grad medical depart Univ Md 1867. Returning home he maintained practice 3 years until death of father required him to take charge of estate. In 1878 Dr. Caulk m Miss Florence A. Turner of Car Co; their child.: Wm, the eldest, res Balt, in collection business. Howard R. student in neighboring school. Florence E. at home and attending school. Mr. and Mrs. Caulk attend Episc Church.

141. CHARLES F. DAVIDSON, M. D., physician and surgeon, from old fam of QA 291 Co, b in Queenstown, Sep 29 1865, where he res. His father, Judge Geo Davidson, (whose sketch is elsewhere this vol) res in vicinity. In 1885 Chas F. Davidson entered medical depart Univ Md. where he received his M.D.; attended universities of Berlin, Germany, 12 months. He m Jun 2 1891 Miss Lolita, d/o J. P. Davidson, of this place. She is granddau of Dr. Jas Davidson, and great-granddau of Gov Wm Paca, signer of Declaration of Independence, judge of supreme court, and gov of Md. Dr. and Mrs. Davidson have a child, James P. They are mbrs Episc Church.

142. WILLIAM D. TROY, M. D., res Centrevile, b Province of Ontario, s/o an 291 Irishman, Patrick Troy, farmer. He and wife, Margaret Ryan, had 3 child.: Julia, w/o Alonzo Benedict, res County Brant, Ontario, and justice of peace; John, farmer, unmarried; and our subj. The father d some twenty years ago in Canada; the mother d Ireland.
Dr. Troy entered normal school Toronto, later Bapt College Woodstock, same province, and still later Toronto Univ. For 7-8 years he taught in public and high schools of province. Leaving Canada in 1882, he went to Chicago, where he entered Chicago Homoeopathic Medical College, from which he grad in 1884. He practiced there 11 yrs before moving to Centreville, where he has since lived and practiced medicine; in 1891 m Mrs. Annie Corinne Johnson, wid of late Andrew Johnson and d/o late Hon. Mordecai Price and Catherine Turner, his 2nd wife. Mrs. Johnson had 2 child.: A. Howard and Mary L. The family attends ME Church, though the doctor is Bapt.

143. J. FRANK HARPER, state's atty, QA Co, b Dec 23 1869 Centreville, s/o 292 John Myers Harper who was lifelong res of Centreville where he died at early age. Little known of fam history. At father's death subj was 2; adopted by Dr. R. M. Price, cousin of his father. Subj grad Western Md College 1890 and was editor-in-chief of college paper; grad law depart Univ Md, admitted to bar in Balt. In Sep 1892 he began his practice in Centreville. In 1895 he was elected state's atty. He is mbr MP Church.

144. EDWARD B. STREETS, farmer, Talb Co, b nr Greensborough, Car Co, 1820. 293 When 22 he moved to Newcastle Co, Del. and farmed. In 1856 he came to Trappe dist, Talb Co, and settled on prop where he has since remained. He is mbr Meth Church. He m 1841 Catherine Casperson (d Mar 1891). Their child.: Henrietta, Edward, Sallie, George, Dora, Maggie, Charles and Josephine..

293   145. MRS. ANNIE F. SPICER, wid of Levin J. Spicer, late of Lake dist, Dor Co, res on homestead, managed by her. She is mbr ME Church, b Taylor's Island, this co, Feb 18 1856, d/o Roger C. and Sarah (Leonard) Robinson. The father of same place, mcht and farmer, d at 56. His father, Roger Robinson, b Taylor's Island, farmer, d at 27. His father, in turn, was known as Capt Robinson, having served in war of 1812. Sarah (Leonard) Robinson was from the island, d at 52. She was mbr ME Church. Of her child.: John H., farmer this dist; Mrs. Spicer is next of fam; Roger C., drowned in childhood; Levi T., traveling salesman of Balt; Frank, blacksmith this co; Jos L., farmer of Taylor's Island; Sophia is next; Louis A. d young; Sallie A. and Mammie. E.
    Mrs. Spicer m(1) Apr 3 1876 Stewart Vickers, of her own neighborhood, farmer; he d Oct 1877, nearly 70; attended ME Church. Jas C., only child of Mr. and Mrs. Vickers, entered Randolph Macon College, at Ashland, Va, about five yrs ago, for 7 yrs' course of study. Dec 3 1878, Mrs. Vickers m Levin J. Spicer, of Taylor's Island, judge of orphans' court several yrs. To him and his 1st wife were b 6 child., of whom 3 survive, Linden T., farmer Lake dist; Mattie E.; and Jas T., oysterman. Those of the second marriage now living are Annie Luda and Levin J., at home. One d in infancy. In 1878 Mrs. Spicer moved to farm which she now manages. Mr. Spicer d Aug 3 1891 at 65.

294   147. WILLIAM HEPBRON agent for Balt & Del. branch Railroad at Lynch's P.O., 3rd dist, dealer in farm machinery. Nr his res he was b 1840, descendant of Scotch-Irish ancestors who were early settlers of Md. The farm on which Hon. Wm T. Hepbron res possessed by family mbrs over 100 yrs. Father of subj, Jas, farmer, s/o John Hepbron, b Kt Co; res there until he d 1840, at 47. He m Mary Greenwood, of Kt Co, their child.: Henrietta: Mrs. Carrow, of Balt; Jos J. and John F., decd; and Wm.
    1862 Wm Hepbron m 1862 Alphonsa Roseberry, of Kt Co. Their child.: Elizabeth; Frank; Ida, w/o E. C. Bowers; and Harry, at Still Pond. Fam attend MP Church.

297   148. REV. FRANKLIN BACHE ADKINS, rector Stephney and Spring Hill parishes, 2nd dist Wicomico Co. Rev. F. B. Adkins b nr Easton, Sep 26 1856, s/o late Dr. I. L. Adkins, of Easton; educated Easton high school, Bishop Lay's school, of Easton, and Shenandoah Valley Acad, of Winchester, Va. He was ordained a priest Nov 2 1882; m Feb 21 1889 Mary V., eld d/o Rt. Rev Wm Forbes Adams, D. D., D. C. L., bishop of Easton; their child, Mary Elizabeth, d young. Wm H. Adkins, bro of subj, is written up elsewhere this vol.

297   149. WILLIAM COLLINS, atty, retired and moved to farm, his birthplace, in Trappe dist, Talb Co; of the fourth generation bearing name of Wm. The first was born in Eng and emigrated to America, settling in Phila, but moved to Talb Co, where he farmed in Trappe dist. Next in descent was grandfather, large slave holder, extensive planter and active politician. He was b Dec 29 1816, at family res, portion of which, was built before Rev, is still in use. He d May 24 1887, at 67. May 16 1847, Wm Collins (3d) m Leah S. Griffin, of Dor Co, d/o Jas Griffin; their child: eldest, Caroline, m Feb 19 1884, Dr. S. K. Merrick, of Balt, and d Jun 17 1886; Wm, 2nd in order of birth; Frank A., 3rd child, architect, res on Long Island, m Miss Sadie L. Peck Jan 1883; Chas M., at home; Rev Hy C., youngest of fam, missionary to Ichang, China, in 1893, devoting himself to Gospel work in that country.
    Subj b Frankford farm, where he now res; student at Trappe high school; at 19 he taught school for a year. Returning to Talb Co, he became a student in

-38-

law office of Senator Gibson; remained until he admitted to bar; elected to house of delegates 1889 and in 1891. He follows the Episc belief.

150. CHARLES B. CATOR, farmer 4th dist Dor Co; operates 300 a. farm nr Taylor's Island, formerly owned by his father. Capt Wm W., father of subj b this locality Feb 1818; d 1866; a mere boy he went on board a vessel engaged in trade along Chesapeake Bay; was common sailor, later promoted to master of a ship. The mother was Mary A. Travers, d/o Thos Travers this dist, mbr Episc Church; d Apr 15 1891. Chas B. Cator is one of 5 surviving children, the others are: Thos B., res Cambridge, Md.; Sml B., in postoffice depart in Balt; Ella W., at home with her bro; and Wm W., res Balt. One child, Ida, d in infancy. Chas B. b 15 Jan 1863; m Dec 2 1891 Miss Valerie, d/o John W. Mace, this co. They have a son, Benjamin Franklin. 298

151. GEORGE W. RAUGHLEY, res Car Co, elected to state legislature 1889, b Feb 22 1838, Kt Co, Del, s/o John and Ary A. (Wilson) Raughley, of Kt co; they had 7 child., of whom Geo and 2 bros, Shadrack and Jas T., survive. Shadrack read law under Willard Saulsbury and admitted to bar at Dover, Del, 1867, but never engaged extensively in practice; he is a bachelor and makes his home with our subj. Jas T., the other bro, traveling salesman for law book firm, for 10 yrs. Rbt Raughley, a half-bro, is a son by John Raughley and his 1st wife. He is retired and lives in Dover, Del. He was a farmer and mbr of legislature of Del, and once clerk of superior court Kt Co, Del.
Grandfather of subj, Shadrack Raughley, farmer of Va, to which state his father, Hy Raughley, came from Eng, settling at Harrisonburg prior to Rev. He became owner of thousands of acres in Va. C. 1849 John Raughley bt farm now owned by subj; 3 yrs later he estab his home here, where he remained until he d in 1855. He was a farmer; register of wills in Dover for 5 yrs. 299

152. WILLARD DICKINSON, business man of Greensborough, Car Co, 5 yrs. 300
Sml Dickinson left Eng and brought material for a substantial mansion, which was erected on banks of Dickinson Bay, Talb Co, c. 1676. Great-grandfather of subj was another Sml, in direct line, b on ancestral estates called Croseadore. Gen. Solomon Dickinson, the grandfather, b Talb Co. He won his title for distinguished service in war with Mexico.
Willard Dickinson s/o Dr. Sml P. and Catherine R. (Willard) Dickinson, of Talb Co and Mass., respectively. The father grew to manhood at his birth place, grad West Point, c. 1836 grad medical depart Univ Md. He moved to Trappe, and began his practice. His elder dau, Maria W., w/o John Aiken of Greenfield Mass.; and Laura D., younger dau, res Balt.
Willard Dickinson b Trappe, Talb Co, 1854, and there spent his first 17 yrs; going then to Pittsfield Mass., he learned details of pharmacy and later located in Balt in the drug business; in 1892 he settled in Greensborough and opened drug store. He m Aug 1882 Miss Karlieb and reared in the city of Balt, d/o Chas Schnauffer. Subj and wife attend Episc Church; they have a boy, aged 4. Mrs. Dickinson's father was exiled from Germany, his native land, in 1848, on account of his political attitude toward the government. He was a journalist and managed the Baltimore Weeker for many yrs.

153. R. KYLE COLLEY, M. D., in the practice of medicine and surgery in Sudlersville; where his wife has recently opened dental office, having grad with honor at Pa College of Dental Surgery in 1897. The doctor is from Greensborough, Car Co; during childhood moved to Templeville, where he was reared; he took 4 years' course at St. John's College, Annapolis, and taught 303

school in QA Co, while between the ages of 20 & 24; grad Chicago Homeopatihic Medical College 1885, in practice in Templevile for a year and then opened office in Centreville, where he remained 5 yrs, but since 1891 has made his home in Sudlersville. Dr. Colley m Oct 11 1894, Miss Annie F. Whiteley, their child.: Mary and Ethel. Mrs. Colley b 20 Feb 1862, Templeville. She taught school 1881-1884; mbr ME Church.

303 154. LOUIS B. KEENE, mcht in town of Golden Hill, extreme southern portion of 4th dist Dor Co; in 1869 app co assessor; b Dec 10 1859, s/o Vachel J. and Mary Ann (Meekins) Keene. His mother was about 50 and his father about 10 yrs her senior when Louis was born. He attended Rock Hill College, Howard Co, two yrs; farmed until 1890 when he took up merchandising. In Feb 28 1880 he m Susie L. Mace, of Church Creek dist, their child.: eldest d in infancy; Clarence A. at home, helps his father in the work; those younger are Mary C., Bernard Louis, Edwin T., Wm Cyril, Sml Clinton and Wm Jennings Mace.

304 155. CAPT. ROBERT S. EMORY commanded vessels running Chestertown-Balt; 1854 moved to Chestertown, succeeded Capt Hiram Brown, in command of vessel Geo Washington, formed partnership with Thos Ruth as Ruth & Emory; now res 4th dist Kt Co, operates farm inherited by wife; specializes in pears. Father of subj was Wm Emory, of QA Co, farmer; d Jun 1860 on old homestead, nr Centreville, on Chester River. He m Mary Raymond, b Del, d/o Timothy Raymond; she d when middle age. - Subj b QA Co Apr 2 1832, student in Dickinson College, Carlisle, Pa 4 yrs; clerk in wholesale drug store in Pittsburgh, Pa., studying pharmacy in spare time; 1854 moved to Chestertown, made his headquarters here for 5 yrs, while in command of a boat. Jan 9 1860 he m Julia Anna, eld d/o Col Edw Wilkins, and settled on farm where since res. His wife d 1874; their child.: Edw W., farmer and fruit grower, res Quaker Neck Wharf, 4th dist; Mary Ella; Juliana and Belle, at home; and Rbt J., machinist & inventor, res Balt. Capt Emory attends ME Church.

305 156. JOHN K. CAULK, farmer of Trappe dist, Talb Co, Episc, b in old family res in 1847, s/o Jos and Mary E. (Haddaway) Caulk, of St. Michael's and Bay Hundred dists, Talb Co, respectively. Father s/o Major Caulk, in war of 1812 and b this region. Jos Caulk d 1858, at 46. His wife d 1868, in 55th year.
Subj m 1868 Miss Mary S. E., d/o Capt John H. Caulk, of St. Michael's dist, Talb Co; their child.: Jos, John, Owen, Bessie and Sallie.

305 157. THOMAS G. REYNOLDS, farmer, Goldsborough Creek, Trappe dist, Talb Co; b Dover, Del, Feb 14 1836. His bro, Rbt J. Reynolds, gov of Del, and his father, Rbt W., was regtr of wills and sheriff of Kt Co. Fam home called Golden Ridge, nr Willow Grove, 11 miles from Dover. - Subj educated mainly in Dickinson College, Carlisle, Pa. At 21 began to teach school, continuing for 2 yrs in Nottoway Co, Va. Returning to Del, he farmed until 1864, when he sold his place and purch prop in Talb Co; m 1859 Julia, d/o Dr. Jas N. Sutton, of St. George's, Del. Their child.: Lola, Jas N., Audley E., Fannie and Julia. Mrs. Julia Reynolds and all her children decd. Mr. Reynolds later m 1886 Kate Geoghegan.

306 158. THOMAS H. KIRWAN, proprietor general supply store at Lakeville, Dor Co; constable and tax collector; b 1849 s/o Thos and Mary (Dean) Kirwan. Father b and reared this part of co, farmer; res on old farm, in 79th year. His father, John Kirwan, farmer, of Eng descent, b, lived and d this dist. Mother of subj d/o John Dean, who fought in war of Rev. Child. in fam of Thomas

Kirwan; Thos H.; Fanny, w/o Edw Evans; martha, w/o J. L. Wheatley; and Benj F., mcht at Taylor's Point, this co. The mother d 1877. she and husband mbrs ME Church.

Thos H. Kirwan shipped before the mast 10 yrs, most of the time in charge of vessel; frequent trips to Balt, Phila, and Wash; 1897 opened store at Lakeville, carrying groceries, dry goods; m 1876 Laura, d/o Lorenzo Adams; their child, Walter Pattison.

159. WILLIAM S. MERRICK, business man of Trappe, for yrs in sale of drugs; b nr Trappe Jan 13 1851. His father Judge Sml B. Merrick, of St. Michael's dist, Talb Co, farmer; in coal and lumber business from 1874 until he d, Dec 1891. For 8 yrs judge of orphans' court; attended ME Church South; d at 75. Judge Merrick m(1) Miss Ann J. Seymour; they had 6 child.: 2 d in infancy. The others are Drusilla, w/o Jos Barnes, of Trappe dist; Ardilla, who m J. J. Valliant; Sml K., physician of Balt; and Wm S. Judge Merrick m(2) Mary J. Barnes; they had 2 child.: Henrietta and M. Barton. Merrick family was founded by Dnl Merrick, settler, during early part 17th century.

At 18 Wm S. Merrick began to teach school, devoting leisure hrs to study of law. In 1880 he opened drug store at present location.

160. JAMES H. CAULK, Bay Hundred dist, Talb Co, in fruit raising and oyster business. John Caulk, Scotchman, granted land between Miles River and Harris Creek, Talb Co, now owned by Chas Caulk, bro of subj. Jas, s/o John, b on this homestead, farmed here. During war of 1812 was 1 of 6 who guarded Parrott's Point at the time it was fired upon by the British. John R., s/o Jas and father of subj, b on homestead; carpenter, turned to farming and management of grist mill on Miles River; mbr ME Church; d 1876, at 67. He m Ellen Hopkins d/o Jas Hopkins; she d 1865 at 64. They had 10 child.; four living: Jas H.; Jos O., mcht in Balt; Chas K., res on old homestead; and Lida, res with Chas.

Subj b 1844 nr present res; at 16 served apprenticeship to carpenter's trade in Balt; returned to old homestead at 21, went into farming and carpentering, 1866 moved to Hopkins place, owned by mother and after her death purch the property; he m 1871 Anna R., d/o John W. McDaniel, farmer of Bay Hundred dist. Their child.: Imogen, teacher in St. Michael's school; and Walter H. The fam attend MP Church.

161. EDWARD W. GIBBONS, business man of Cambridge, Dor Co, b Balt Co, Dec 30 1859, s/o Isaiah Gibbons, iron worker, of Balt Co, and there spent his life; d at 31. He m Elizabeth Ann Young, who d at 30. Of 6 child., Edw W. Gibbons and bro John S. are only survivors of fam. Edw grew up in Balt Co and Howard Co; 1880 came to Cambridge, and learned milling; 1897 opened livery & sale stable in partnership with U. D. Hopkins. Edward W. Gibbons m Jul 30 1883 Lizzie, d/o Rbt A. LeCompte, this place; they attend Episc Church.

162. ALFRED B. TURPIN, in merchandising at Kingston, Som Co, over 3 decades. John Turpin, father of subj, of Brinkley's dist, farmer and mcht at old Kingston a while; 1843 moved to Balt and kept hotel on Camden St, d there at 44. Turpin is old fam of Som Co, of English origin. Wm Turpin, father of John Turpin, in war of 1812 and farmer this co. John Turpin m(1) Miss Susan Bell; of 5 child. 2 remain: Alfred B. and Emily, Mrs. H. Van Ausdal, of Ohio. John Turpin m(2) Mrs. Martha (Long) Mitchell; all 4 child. decd.

A. B. Turpin b Apr 17 1838 Brinkley's dist; boyhood was chiefly passed in Balt; returned to this area; served apprenticeship to carriage maker; opened general store at Carroll's corner, 5 yrs later moved to Crisfield; 1868 came to present home; Jul 1862 m Aurelia, d/o Geo H. J. Beauchamp. She d 1865, leaving 2 child., one has d; other is Cora V., w/o E. M. Brook. Mr. Turpin m(2) Elizabeth, d/o John J. Bell, of this co. Their child: Elizabeth B., Susan M., John A., Thos W. and Sidney F. Fam attend St. Mark's Episc Church.

311 163. JOHN F. DAWSON, of Car Co, school commisioner, representative and state senator; res of Greensborough, b in Centreville, Oct 5 1833, s/o Capt Thos C. and Ann (Coursey) Dawson, respectively of Talb and Car counties, sole survivor of 5 child. His father, soldier in war of 1812, d Mar 10 1840, Dor Co. Grandfather, Nicholas Dawson, farmer Talb Co; his father, Ralph Dawson, b Eng, emigrated to America prior to Rev, settled in Md. Captain Dawson, mariner, sailing a vessel Centrevile-Balt; turned to farming; d at 63.
Subj and mother came to Caro Co c. 1841; taught 4 yrs; turned to farming. 1857 m Sarah J. Delahay who was b Car Co, and d here at 29. She was distant relative of late Sml J. Tilden, of N.Y. She attended ME Church. Mr. Dawson m(2) 1868 Emma Delahay, sis of first wife, of Car Co.

312 164. HON. JOHN S. SUDLER, Fairmount dist, Som Co, mbr Md house of delegates, state fish commissioner, chairman co Democratic central committee and farmer; of 3rd generation to live on family estate. Sudler fam of Eng extraction; settled early in QA Co. Sudlersville named in their honor and from there grandfather of subj, Thos Sudler, came to this co in youth. He m Miss Nellie Waters; their child.: Wm m and left children in this co: Thos and Eleanor F. d unmarried; and Tubman was father of John S., our subj. Tubman Sudler m Elizabeth Stewart, d/o Col John Stewart, of Manokin; their child.: Sarah, w/o Thos Sudler; Elizabeth, decd; John S.; Jas E., of this co; and Thos, d young.
John S. Sudler b Jun 24 1827; m Nov 27 1861, Susan E., d/o Jas and Elizabeth (Ballard) Thompson, of Dor Co. Mrs. Sudler also descendant of Waters family. They attend Episc Church.

315 165. FINLEY ROBERTS, mbr old fam QA Co, res Centreville, b nr Sudlersville, Mar 10 1850. His father, Lemuel, b 1803 this co, and spent early life as mcht at Sudlersville, later in farming and milling. He rep dist in legislature for 6 or 8 terms at different periods, rgtr of wills, commissioner of public works for state. He d Oct 1869, at 67. He was only child of Benj Roberts, and b after father's death.
Benj Roberts purch in 1791 from Martha and Rebecca Hughes, of Pa, tract called Condon Renowned, in QA Co; later changed to "Roberts' Land Renowned."
Maria Scott, w/o Lemuel Roberts and mother of Finley Roberts, from Western Shore, and only child. She d when son Finley was 10, leaving 4 sons: W. Scott; Benj G., in Confed army, capt of company raised in QA Co, wounded at Gettysburg, d as result; Lemuel, grad Md Argicultural College, d of typhoid fever when 20; and Finley, subj.
Finley Roberts educated at West Nottingham Acad; farmed until 1888 when app rgtr of wills, vacancy caused by death of Thos A. Bryan. He m Dec 2 1875, Miss Arra Price, d/o Jas Price, of Cecil Co, mbr of old fam that co. Their child.: Lemuel, attending school New York City; and Ella, Austin, Hilda and Scott, at home. Mr. Roberts lives in Centreville, still tills farm.

316 166. WILLIAM ARMSTRONG, decd. When 18 he embarked in mercantile business in Galena. Subj b Kt Co, s/o Wm Armstrong. Wm Armstrong b Newark, Del, served

in war of 1812, carried on farm and store in Galena. He d at old age; m Sarah Medford, of Kt Co, Both mbrs Presby Church.
Subj m(1) Araminta Johnson, of Kt Co; she d young; her child. also decd: W. Josiah, d in infacny; John M.; Sarah Adalia; Araminta; and Wm. Last named m Miss Emily T. Miller and d leaving dau, Ida, w/o Rev Allison Palmer Prettyman, of Cecil Co, and mother of Raymond Allison Armstrong. Wm Armstrong m(2) Miss Elizabeth Ann W. Johnson, sis of 1st wife, mbr of Episc Church; d when 50. Her child.: Elizabeth Ann W. decd, and A. Louisa res old homestead, sole surviving rep of fam. She attends Episc Church. Her father d at 70, left her 4 farms in Kt Co and old homestead in Galena where she res.

167. M. B. NICHOLS b Balt, Sep 5 1854, s/o Patrick and Mary Nichols, who were b, reared and m in Co Mayo, Ireland, remained there until after birth of three of child. Father b 1823. 1852 he brought fam to Balt, where he worked 2 yrs in lumber yard; then a year in Car Co, and 1856 took up his res in present homestead, in Easton. Fam belonged to Cath Church. He had 5 child., of whom Wm E., 3rd son went to Birmingham, Ala., at 19, d after return to Md Jul 1893. Mary, only dau and youngest child, d Mar 30 1895. Thos C. and Hy A. in business in Easton under firm style of Nichols & Brother. 316
Subj was 2 when he came with his parents to Easton. At 14 he worked as clerk in dry goods and grocery store of J. J. Jump & Co, at $100 per year and board himself. In 1876 he embarked in business at old store as mbr of firm of Jarrell, Nichols & Cox. 1878 he m Miss Kate F., d/o Wm D. Roberts, architect and builder, judge of orphans' court. Their only child d at 1.

168. JOHN DAILY owned farms in Car Co, QA, and adjoining counties in Md and Del; co commissioner Car Co 1878 until death on Feb 21 1888; b Kt Co, Del Feb 19 1825. When a young boy he came to QA Co with John M. Downes, with whom he remained greater part of ensuing years until he was 21. Jan 21 1851 he m Miss Mary A. Nickerson, res Templeville a year, later moved to farm he had prev purch, a tract in Car Co, nr Templeville, where he d. Their child.: 1 d in infancy; Chas E.; Jos S.; Annie E., decd; John T.; Enos, d at 18; Mary, d in childhood; Mary L., d at 18; and Harry S., res old homestead. After Mr. Daily's death his wife m Sml H. Fluhartyl; she now res 1st dist QA Co. 318

169. JOHN C. HACKETT, b nr Sudlersville 1 Sep 1833, s/o Gunning Bedford and Sarah (Cacy) Hackett; left QA Co at 18, went to Kt Co; farmed; then returned QA Co, still farming; 1885 moved to Sudlersville where he entered grain business. He m Mrs. M. Cephelia Cacy, Sep 11 1856. Their child.: John C., in practice of medicine; Annie C., Blanche, Maria W. and Sml W., with West Shore Railroad. Mrs. Hackett d 1885. 318

170. GEORGE R. REED b 3rd dist Dec 6 1818, s/o Sml Reed, who came from Cecil Co to Kt when young man. Sml Reed was carpenter and builder and business man. He m wid of Rbt Ashley, whose maiden name was Hosanna Usilton. Of their child. 3 grew to maturity, Mary, Jos and Geo R., all decd. The father died when subj was small child, his mother d 1826. 321
Subj spent first 15 yrs in co, then to Wilm, Del, served apprenticeship to bricklayer's trade, 5 yrs; then worked at his calling 7 yrs in various parts of south; 1846 returned to this co and farmed; d Aug 29 1897. In 1847 George R. Reed m Frances Philena Usilton, d/o Frs and Hannah Rebecca (Lamb) Usilton, of Kt Co. Their child.: Sml Amos, of Md.; Jos Benj, of Wilm, Del; Geo Rbt, of Charleston, S. C.; Hosanna Rebecca Jones and Fannie Jenetta Jones, of Md; Kate

Gale Wenzell, of Melrose, Mass.; and Sidney Usilton Younger, of this state. Fam long identified with MP Church.

321   171.   CAPT. COLUMBUS A. LEARY, Kt Co, descendant of old American fam; b Galena, 1st dist, b Dec 6 1833. First of Leary fam of record in country is Jas Leary, prob from Ireland, owner of vessel, and c. 1730 captured by French during French war, d in prison. He m Miss Owens. Their son, Jos Leary, b Del, in Rev war, mostly in marshes; then came to Kt Co, m Miss Redgrave, d/o Abraham Redgrave; became school teacher; b 1760, d 1821, mbr Episc Church.

George Leary, s/o Jos and father of subj b 1806 Georgetown, this co; reared Georgetown, served apprenticeship as ship joiner Balt. Returning to this co he m Miss Mary Simms, of Kt Co (b 1808, d/o Wm Simms, of Kt Co, who served in the militia). She d 1871. They had 11 child., of whom Columbus A. was eldest. After him came Jos, who d at 37; Geo E., see his sketch elsewhere this vol; Hy, in charge of vessel of quartermaster's fleet during late war, then owner of several small vessels and tow-boats in Balt, where he d; Isaac, farmer this co; Susan, w/o Jas Rolison; Christiana, w/o John Blackstone, this dist; Jas, res this co; and Oregon, farmer, res this co. Mr. and Mrs. Rolison are both decd; leaving dau, Elizabeth, w/o Ralph Taylor, of Sparrow's Point. Geo Leary after his marriage carried on a cabinet making and undertaking business in Edesville, this dist, from c. 1840 until he d, Oct 13 1883; many yrs local minister in ME Church, to which his wife also mbr; he was regularly ordained minister although he held no regular charge.

Until 1850 Columbus A. Leary spent boyhood at home; then shipped on vessel Silas Richards, running Balt-San Francisco, each trip about 7 months; chief officer on Viking for trip around world, 1855-1856; purch prop nr Rock Hall and operated general store several yrs. C. 1889 sold store and has since res on farm that he had bt several yrs before. Oct 1858 he m Miss Annie Vickers, d/o Thos and Maria Vickers, of this dist; they have a dau, at home.

323   172.   CHARLES S. SMITH, mcht of Chestertown, b Chestertown May 27 1860, s/o S. Frank Smith and Mary E. Smith, of Kent Co, (see sketch of S. Franklin Smith, elsewhere this vol), one of 14 children, of whom 6 survive. He started in business of steamboating on Chesapeake, eventually lost his savings. 1888 he entered mercantile field, his store located under Voshell House; m 1888 in Balt Miss Emma N., d/o Jas and Mary E. Orem, of that city; their child.: Mary E., Ida Orem, Chas Franklin and Lurene. The parents active in MP Church.

324   173.   THOMAS R. EMORY b Centreville, on Chester River, Dec 21 1837. His father, Wm, and grandfather, Rbt Emory, b on this same farm. Founder of fam in Md came from Engl at remote date. Wm Emory, father of Thos R. Emory, was a business man; worker in Meth Church and bro of Bishop Emory, who was an officer in the denomination. Wm Emory d 1860. He was 3 times m and father of 8 child. Mother of subj was Miss Elizabeth Ruth. Her father, Rbt Ruth, in war of 1812; his bro in Rev war. Child. of Wm Emory: Rebecca, w/o Benj Perkins, of Kt Co; Rbt, of Kt Co; John, res this dist; Thos R.; Frank A., res this community; Addison, of Centreville; and Stewart Orr and Wm, both decd.

After dist schools, Thos R. Emory entered Dickinson College, Carlisle, Pa and for 2 year's course; then resumed farming. 1863 bt prop, Fairview. Feb 1862 m Miss Fanny, d/o Hy Annels Wright, of Wild Cat, QA Co. Their child.: Elizabeth, Thos, Lottie, Mary, Howard, Florence, Nellie; and Fanny and Rose, decd. Thos is farmer this neighborhood; Lottie is w/o Benj Beck, of Kt Co, and the others are living with their parents. They are mbrs Episc Church.

174. JOHN E. GEORGE, business man of QA Co, partner with brother-in-law, Jas   324
Merritt, Jr.; in business Sudlersville since 1881, dealer in fertilizers, farm
implements, lumber; b Jul 23 1859 on old home farm where father still res,
educated in common schools and under private tutors until 1878, attended
Bryant & Stratton's Business College, Balt. 1881 he and brother-in-law took
over his father's business in Sudlersville. Mr. George m 1 Nov 1881, Miss
Elvira Anderson, of Sudlersville; their child.: Elsie L., Jos M. and Madeline
M. 1893 he was elected co commissioner. He is mbr Episc Church.

175. TILGHMAN SHAFER, business man Kennedyville; b Allentown, Pa, Aug 7 1839,   327
s/o John and Theresa (Roeder) Shafer, of Pa, latter b Northampton Co. Shafer
fam of German origin, founded in Pa as early as 1750. There was b John
Shafer, Sr., subject's grandfather, large land owner and farmer nr Hellertown.
He d at 58. John Shafer, Jr., also spent life there and prev to building of
railroad engaged in teaming between Phila, Allentown and Fitchburgh, and
farmed during in early manhood. He d 1841, at 33; his child.: Tilghman, our
subj, and Elizabeth, w/o John J. Roeder, of Allentown.
   Becuase of father's early death, subj reared by maternal grandfather, Geo
Roader, who lived on farm nr Kennedyville, Kt Co, Md., where Mr. Shafer grew
to manhood. At 18 he began learning blacksmith trade, serving 3 yrs'
apprenticeship with half-brother in Harmony, Kt Co, and has continued at that
occupation. Dec 27 1861, he located in Kennedyville, taking over business of
C. B. Krusen, and 1870 embarked in wheelwright business. 8 Oct 1868 Mr.
Shafer m Miss Rachel J. Kelly, of Kt Co, d/o Wm Kelly. 2 child. b to them
both decd; wife d Mar 1872. He again m, Dec 16 1874, Miss Annie E. Parsons,
d/o Thos Parsons; they had 2 child.; one now living, Annie M. E. The second
wife d Aug 26 1877, and 2 yrs later Mr. Shafer m Miss Emma Copenhaver, of
Balt, d/o Augustus and Elizabeth Copenhaver. They had 2 child., Emma C.
stillliving. Fam attend MP Church.

176. THOMAS HENRY WILLIAMS, M. D., retired, res Cambridge; s/o Isaac F. and   328
Rebecca R. (Stuart) Williams, of Kt Co; spent boyhood in Cambridge; educated
Wash Acad, Som Co; studied medicine under Dr. Alexander H. Bayly, Cambridge,
then grad medical depart Univ Md 1848. Mar 3 1849 he was commissioned assist
surgeon U.S. Army, and stationed on frontier of Texas and Indian Territory;
served as medical director in Utah campaign. At beginning of Civil war he
resigned from U.S. Army and went to Richmond, where commissioned surgeon in
Confed Army. 1865 returned to Cambridge, but in few months moved to Richmond,
Va, to enter in drug business; c. 1870 moved to farm nr Cambridge and and then
to Cambridge. Dr. Williams m 1854 Bettie Hooper, d/o Dr. John H. and Ann C.
(Birckhead) Hooper, of Cambridge. They attend Episc Church.

177. LEVIN L. DIRICKSON, JR., of Berlin, Wor Co, b Snow Hill, Wor Co, 1860,   329
s/o Levin L. and Elizabeth Dirickson, Sr. 1882 Levin Dirickson, Jr., located
in Milton, Dell; 3 yrs later returned to Berlin; ran drug business. He had
prev studied pharmacy and passed requisite examinations in Pa and Del. 1884,
while res Milton, Del, he m Miss Annie L. Russell, at Berlin, Md. Their
child.: Helen and Conwell Foreman. They attend St. Paul's Episc Church.

178. EDWARD MIFFLIN WILKINS, farmer Kt Co, res nr Chester River until he d,   329
Nov 1881; here his wid res. He was b Apr 5 1843, on York farm, 4th dist, s/o
Col Edw Wilkins. Subj educated Wash College, and in Agricultural College of
Md. He m May 8 1866 Mary A., d/o Jos T. and Anna Rebecca (Brown) Merritt.
Her father, b 4th dist, inherited portion of Godlington manor, and there he

farmed. Her mother, b this dist, d/o Capt Hiram Brown. Mrs. Wilkins was their only child. She is mother of: Sue C., w/o Wm D. Hines, of Balt; Fannie, Jennie, Grace and Edw Mifflin (student in Md Agricultural College).

330   179. WILLIAM D. PENNINGTON, farmer 3rd dist Kt Co, b 1839, Newcastle Co. Del, of English origin, fam founded in this country c. 1750. Grandfather, Atkie Pennington b Md; his father, Fredus R. Penington, b Del. In early life latter was sailor, and as mate of a vessel went to France, being there at the time Bonaparte landed from Isle of Elba. He farmed greater part of his life, in Del; he d at 63. As lieut he served in 14th U.S. Regt during war of 1812. He m Miss Elizabeth Van Hickel, of Del, who d prev to his death, 2 of their 9 child. living: E. B., res nr Kennedyville, Md; and Wm D.
   Subj is youngest of the fam; early life spent on old homestead in Del until 18; then farmed a year in Mo., returned to Del and lived nr Delaware City; then moved to Kt Co, Md in 1868, with his bro E. B., and sis. For three yrs they res on a farm at Howells Point. 1886 Mr. Pennington purch the Grange farm (216 a.) where he now farms, raises fruit, particularly peaches, pears and berries; Dec 3 1872 m Miss Louisa Kelley; their child.: Lena, b Sep 21 1873, d Feb 26 1890; Edgar Reyland b Jul 24 1875; Wm L., b Aug 6 1877. Mrs. Pennington d Feb 25 1879. Subj then m Oct 3 1883, Miss Ella G. Sparks, of Kt Co, their child.: May G., on Jul 10 1884 and Helen Louise, on Jun 13 1886. The family attend the ME Church.

333   180. THOMAS BENNETT WILLSON, M. D., 5th dist Kt Co; b Sep 13 1843, s/o Richard Bennett Willson (see his sketch in this vol for fam history). He was reared on home farm; grad medical depart Univ Md 1866. He maintains his practice at Rees's Corners. Jan 23 1872 h m Henrietta M., d/o John Chas and Anne E. (Brooke) Willson, of 5th dist. Her father, of this dist, farmed here, d at 43, fol brief illness, caused by cold that resulted in pneumonia. His wife, Anne E. Brooke b Kt Co, now 79. Like her husband, she is mbr Cath Church. Mrs. Willson b 5th dist Nov 10 1848, and has spent her life here. She had 11 child.; 5 d in infancy; living are: Thos Bennett, Jr., assists his grandfather on latter's farm; Mary Regina, w/o B. C. Hatchison; Anna E., Julia Rena, Charlotte M. and Maude Agnes, at home.

333   181. RICHARD C. SMYTH, farmer 3rd dist, Kt Co, b nr Tolchester, Md, Feb 24 1831, s/o Richard and Caroline (Stean) Smyth, of Kt Co. His grandfather, Samuel Smyth, s/o Geo Smyth, from Eng and located in Kt Co among its earliest pioneers. Richard Smyth, Sr., in battle of Caulksfield under Captain Weeks, grandfather of Lewin Weeks; farmed old homestead where subj res. He d 1877 at 85. His wife d prev. His child.: Mary, wid of Geo S. Deal; Harriett M., decd w/o Lewin M. Usilton; Richard C., subj; and Jefferson L., decd.
   1860 Richard C. Smyth m Miss Wilmina H. Appleton, of Del, their child.: Mary C., w/o J. Raymond Bowers; Hallie E., w/o Rbt Loud; Murray, at home; Willie S., w/o Wm Edwards; and Carrie and Blanche, both at home. Fam are Methodists. Mr. Smyth was co commissioner 5 yrs.

334   182. JAMES O. DICKINSON, farmer Trappe dist, on Dickinson Bay, res Talb Co, except few yrs in Car Co. He owns 600 acres of original family homestead, old Craig farm and cattle ranch (3400 a.) in Kingman Co, Kan; b on farm where he res Oct 12 1849. His father, Sml, b same farm, was s/o Sml and grandson of Sml Dickinson, the latter an Englishman who took patented a land grant. Father of subj m Maria Goldsborough of Car Co; their child.: Sml, d 1896; Mary

A., w/o Wm Thomas; Van Ransvanselar, of Cambridge; Wm E., d 1876; John, d 1881; and Ellen, d 1893. The youngest, our subj, b and reared on homestead.

183. GUSTAVUS A. HAEFNER, M. D., physician Hurlock, Dor Co; b province of Saxe-Coburg, Germany, 1846; when 6 brought by parents to America. Father, Christian A. Haefner, b Bavaria; as young man went into prov of Saxe-Coburg where he taught; m Miss Sophia Thorman there; had five child., of whom fol grew to maturity: Caroline, Margaret, Sophia and Gustavus. Dr. Haefner crossed Atlantic 1851 and reared in Balt. His higher studies obtained in Pa College Gettysburg and 1867 grad medical depart Univ of Md. His initial practice was in Balt Co, but during war was medical cadet in Union army (in 1865); 1869 sent as physician to West Indies; after 12 months returned to U.S.; 1875 to islands again, came back 1891; since then in practice in Hurlock. 1891 he m Miss Emma B., d/o H. C. Davis, of old Eastern Shore fam. 335

184. MISS MARTHA ANDERSON, res 2nd dist QA Co, business woman, b that dist and d/o John and Martha (Holden) Anderson; father b Ireland; came to new World when young; was blacksmith, and in 1833 he located on farm where his dau now res, and there spent his remaining days. His wife d in 1857; their child.: Mary, Wm and John, all decd; Richard, retired in Church Hill; one d in infancy; Jas, decd; and Martha.
Miss Anderson educated in common schools and reared on home farm. After her mother's death she and her sis Mary took over farm which they managed for few yrs and then rented until 1876. Since then Miss Anderson has managed this farm and another one of 92 a. 335

185. GEORGE B. WESTCOTT, mcht Chestertown. Jan 1890 he succeeded his father in business. Westcott fam is among oldest of N.J. Sml Buck Westcott, grandfather of Geo B., sec to gov of N.J. and at time of death, in 1840, was clerk of Atlantic Co. Father of subj, Nicholas G., Episc, b N.J. 1815, and 1836 came to Chestertown, where he res until he d, May 15 1890. From 1847 until his demise he was in mercantile business, and sec of Mutual Fire Insur Co of Kt Co, of which an uncle had been 1st sec; m Mary, d/o Dr. Chas Tilden, of Kt Co, who d Mar 1890. They had a son, and dau, Mary L., unmarried.
George Westcott b Chestertown, Feb 20 1852. Educated Wash College, then bookkeeper in bank, and then farmed, and then succeeding father in business. 1880 he m Miss Polly, d/o Simon Wickes; their child.: Hallie R., Geo Godfrey, Edw S., Elizabeth R., Simon Wickes, Jos P., Ellen L. and Polly Wickes. 336

186. WILLIAM T. LUSBY, farmer 2nd dist, Cath, Kt Co; b Cecil Co, Feb 19 1821; remained in area until 1882, when he bt Rbt J. Lusby farm. His father, John Lusby, farmer, that co; m Sarah E. Nolan; they had 5 child.: Wm, 3rd in order of birth. Mary Ellen, eldest, is w/o Thos Lusby. Amelia decd; Jas, formerly res St. Marys Co, decd; and Rbt decd. Father of these child. d while they were young, and the mother m M. L. Wootters. Their child.: Sarah E. and Lemuel J. Mrs. Wootters d/o Thos Nolan, of Cecil Co; she d c.1870. 336

187. THOMAS H. DODD, 5th dist QA Co, owns about 1000 a.; b on father's farm 5th dist 1839. History of fam is given in sketch of his brother, James H., elsewhere this vol. Subj started as a mcht 1867, returned to farming 2 yrs later; 1872 m Annie C., d/o Frs Council, res nr Centreville. Their child.: Thos H., Jr., Ida M., Jas C., Elizabeth and Hy. 339

339 188. WILLIAM T. EVANS from old fam of Deal's Island, Som Co; b on island 1831; boatman and sea-faring man, worked at carpentering to considerable extent. Wm Evans, father of subj, after marriage came to Deal's Island and spent his whole life here; farmer, and carpenter during spare time; d at 46. His father, also named Wm Evans, was ship carpenter. Mother of subj was a Miss Sallie Kelly she m Wm Evans; by that marriage 10 child.: 2 survive: subj; and Mary C, wid of Michael Webster. Mrs. Sallie Evans d at 65.
Wm T. Evans m c. 1850 Miss Keziah, d/o Bennett Mister; of their 6 child., 2 are living: Marcellus and Eveline (w/o Wm Shores.

340 189. JAMES SETH, M. D., physician Talb co since grad Univ Md. 1865. He came to St. Michael's in 1888, carried on practice this and adjoining dist of Bay Hundred, where he formerly res. He was b Bay Hundred Jan 4 1843. His father, Alexander H. Seth of same dist, where he farmed his entire life; d at 70. For 3 terms he rep dist in state legislature. His father, Jas Seth, farmer from Bay Hundred dist and soldier of war of 1812; descendant of Jacobus Seth, from Scotland in early day.
The doctor's mother was Martha Haddaway, d/o Wm Haddaway, farmer of Bay Hundred dist. Like her husband, she was active in ME Church; she died at 70; their child.: Wm H., in mercantile business in Oxford, Md.; Jas; Jos, atty, Balt; Thos A., decd; and Sml H., cultivates homestead (in the fam since first mbr came from Scotland. Subj grad West River Classical Institute 1860; studied medicine with Dr. Tilden, of St. Michael's and later grad medical depart Univ Md; m Julia T., d/o Nicholas Orem, of Talb Co; their child.: Jas, in mercantile business Balt; Jos B., student in medicine; Rbt L., in school; Julian O.; Frank W. and Sara. He was co commissioner of schools, 1883-93.

341 190. CHARLES LAKE, b Lakeville Jan 14 1838, s/o Wm W. and Clara Lake, whose other children were: Cordelia, w/o Jas Cornell (by whom she has dau, Clara); and Cordelia, d at 7. Paternal great-grandfather of subj from Eng, founder of fam in new world. The grandfather was Maj Washington Lake. Mother of subj still living at 88; after death of 1st husband she m John S. Staplefort, their child.: Victoria, Isabella, Annie, Mary Virginia and Julia L.
Chas Lake was student 2 yrs in Cambridge Acad, and Wash College 2 1/2 yrs; went into merchandising in Lakeville, farmed and conducted a sawmill. 3 Jan 1860 he m Miss Wilhelmina Phillips, of Cambridge, d/o Richard and Mary (Applegarth) Phillips. She has one sis, Mary E., wid of Jas E. Robinson, res Cambridge; and half-sister, Laura B. Staplefort, w/o Wm T. Staplefort. Mr. and Mrs. Lake had 8 child., 4 now living: Clara S., w/o Dnl E. Dale, of Cambridge (by whom she has 2 child.; Edwin S., who m Elizabeth Mace and has 2 sons, Paul B. and Charles Reginald; Virginia Cowart and Hattie Pattison, both at home. Mr. and Mrs. Lake attend ME Church South. During war Chas Lake was postmaster at Lakeville. In 1869 he was elected co commissioner.

342 191. JUDGE JAMES ALFRED PEARCE, 1897 elected, chief justice 2nd judicial circuit. Father of subj, Hon. Jas Alfred Pearce, Sr., b Dec 14 1805, home of maternal grandfather, Dr. Elisha Cullen Dick, in Alexandria, Va, s/o Gideon and Julia (Dick) Pearce, of Kt Co, Md. His mother d when he was young; he was educated in Alexandria under oversight of grandfather; grad Princeton College 1822 at 16; studied law in Balt, admitted to bar in 1824; practiced 1 year in Cambridge; then in Sugar planting with father, in La. 3 yrs later returned to Kt Co, where he engaged in practice; mbr state legislature, U. S. House of Rep and U. S. Senate; d Dec 20 1862; 1830 m Martha J. Laird, who d 1845. Two yrs later he m Matilda C., d/o Jas Ringgold. He d Dec 20 1862.

-48-

Jas Alfred Pearce b Apr 2 1840; attended Wash College; grad Princeton College 1860; returning to Chestertown, he read law in father's office, while teaching in Wash College; 1862 entered law office of Brown & Brune, Balt; May 1 1864 admitted to bar; returned to Chestertown; state's atty 1867-75. Nov 1 1866, Judge Pearce m Eunice, eld d/o Unit Rasin, mcht of St. Louis, Mo, many yrs. His wife was Martha Hanson of Kt Co, Md, lineal descendant of John Hanson, pres Continental Congress. Judge and wife have no children.

192. WILLIAM H. ADKINS, atty Easton since 1889; director and counsel for 345 numerous companies in Easton and others. Father of subj was Isaac L. Adkins, M. D., b Milford Del., Feb 9 1823, s/o Leonard Adkins, cashier Commmercial Bank of Milford. Isaac L. was youngest of 8 children, aged 3 at time of father's death; 4 yrs employed in store owned by his bros, in Milford; went to New York, estab branch of grain commission business of Brown & Godwin, of Phila. Poor health obliged him to give up business interests. He went to Tennessee, where he studied medicine with a physician and later grad Jefferson Medical College Phila, 1848; engaged in practice in Phila, later assist surgeon in U. S. Army, sent to Ft Columbus, then to Florida and to Calif. Aug 12 1852 he m Mary E., d/o Col Wm Hughlett, of Easton, Md. Soon afterward he resigned from army and moved to Easton, where he afterward res on farm. He d May 10 1889.

By his marriage, Dr. Adkins had 6 child., of whom are living: Rev Franklin B., rector of Spring Hill Parish in Wicomico Co; Mattie H., who m Hon. W. L. Henry; M. C. from Cambridge; Wm H.; and Virginia L., w/o A. E. DeReeves, of Cambridge. Subj b at Woodland, his father's country res nr Easton, Jul 21 1862; grad Johns Hopkins Univ 1882. While in Balt he took law course in Univ of Md and studied in office of Machen & Gittings; admitted to bar and engaged in practice in Balt until 1889; then returned to Easton and has since active in law here. Oct 8 1891 he m Mary H., d/o late Mordecai M. Dawson, vice-pres Easton Natl Bank; their child: Leonard D. Mr. Adkins is Episc.

193. GEORGE C. SUTTON, D. D., Dean of Cathedral in Easton; has belonged to 346 this diocese for past 7 yrs; b Maidstone, Kent co, Eng, 1848 s/o Geo C. and Martha (Hawks) Sutton. George C. attended the common schools of dist, and arriving at maturity engaged in business a few yrs. 1871 Geo came to America, locating at first in Petersburg, Va, he reembarked in business. In his spare time he pursued higher branches of learning, especially theology; Mar 21 1877 ordained deacon and Feb 9 1881 ordained to priesthood of Episc Church; ministered to various parishes in Ky, Va and Md; 1890 placed in the Easton diocese and occupied pulpits in Kt Co; 1893 installed as Dean of Cathedral of Easton; m Miss Mary P. Stith, of Nottoway Co, Va, Apr 1875, d/o Putnam and Mary (Epes) Stith. A sister of the doctor is w/o Rev A. J. Drewitt, minister in Melbourne, Australia.

194. HON. JAMES D. ANDERSON, of Deal's Island, has spent entire life in Som 347 Co; 16 yrs Justice of Peace, later elected to state legislature. Father of subj, Levin Anderson, b Wicomico Co 1828; c. 1850 came to Deal's Island; carpenter and builder for a time. His father was Gillis Anderson, farmer of Wicomico Co; m Margaret Daniel, had 8 child., 6 living: Jas D., Levin A., Thos J., Geo A., Chas L. and Fannie, w/o Wilbur J. Thomas. Mother of fam d at 46. Subj b Deal's Island 1852; at 17 apprenticed to blacksmith's trade, and 3 yrs later into business for himself. - 1873 subj m Sarah E. Wilson, d/o Sml D. Wilson, of Deal's Island. Their children: Frank, attending school in Balt; Jas A., Barnes C. and Lizzie. He and fam mbrs ME Church.

347 195. WILLIAM P. BENSON, Talb Co, builder of ships, pres Oxford Savings Bank; b Royal Oak, Talb Co, Dec 22 1827; reared on farm; at 18 he began work in ship yard nr Easton, where he remained four yrs; 1855 built first ship at Jamaica Point; coming to Oxford 1866, formed partnership with Col Hy E. Bateman and Nathaniel Leonard in construction of ships and yachts. He later withdrew, but later still, took over entire firm.

348 196. BENJAMIN E. HARRINGTON business man of Taylor's Island, Dor Co, runs general store in Parson's Creek dist; owns 13 oyster boats; born Madison, this dist, Jul 6 1866. At 18 he taught school at Golden Hill, this dist; then in oyster busines at Cambridge in partnership with Harrington Brothers; 1895 m Miss Fannie F., d/o Benj L. Smith, of Madison; they have son, Byron E.
Paternal great-greatfather of subj, John Harrington, of Ireland, came to America in early manhood; in freighting on Chesapeake Bay, and before his death, at 80, owned several vessels; in war of 1812. His son, John, next in line of descent, also served in war, on patrol duty along the bay; b this dist; farmer and ship carpenter; mbr MP Church; d at 70. Parents of subj were John E. and Elizabeth (Jones) Harrington, both of this co. Father b this dist May 11 1824, and in youth was sailor for several yrs on the bay; operated a store and ship yard at Madison, later bt and operated farm nr Madison. He m Ann E., d/o Wm and Mary (Woolford) Thompson; 7 of their children lived to mature yrs: John Edw, physician of Balt, d at 26; Mary A. w/o Rev G. J. Smith, MP minister, in Long Island; Wm W., mcht in Madison; Frs W., clerk in revenue collector's office in Balt; Emerson, principal of seminary in Cambridge; Benj E., of this sketch, next in order of birth; Elizabeth E. at home with her father; parents mbrs MP Church.

351 197. THOMAS LOCKWOOD DAY, mbr bd of commissioners of Car Co, business man of Ridgely, where he embarked in lumber business in 1882; 6 yrs later he sold out and turned to canning and manufacture of peach baskets and berry crates.
Subject's great-grandfather, of Eng, settled in Del. Father of subj, Wm Day, b Del as was his grandfather, Rev Matthias Day, farmer and minister ME Church. Wm Day was plasterer for 10 yrs in St. Louis and New Orleans; then settled in Car Co, where he farmed; m Rebecca Roe, of Del; of 5 child. 3 living: Thos L., Emma and Wm P.
Subj b 1851 Car Co; reared on farm, remained there until 1877, entered mercantile business in Henderson, Md; burned out 9 months later; went to Phila where he worked as street car conductor; came to Ridgely 1882 and began his lumber business. 1879 he m Miss Catherine Pastorfield, of Talb Co. Of 6 child. 3 living: Beulah W., Mattie and Mabel. Fam attend ME Church.

351 198. FRANCIS NICHOLS business man 5th dist, for whom postoffice of Nichols was named; active in ME Church; 1880 elected mbr bd co commissioners; 1889 erected store building on road Fowling Creek to Federalsburg, carries dry goods, groceries, boots, and shoes. Jas, father of Frs Nichols, b 5th dist Car Co c. 1813; lived here all his life. His father, Jas Nichols, Sr., b this co; farmer. He had 5 child.: Senah m, left sons, Sml, Perry and Jas A., all this co; Rbt left 3 child.: John W., Mary, wid of Elisha Andrew, res this co, and Jas L., of Del.; Sml d unmarried; Martha, w/o Sml Stevens, had a son, Jas, res Centreville; and Elizabeth m Wm Christopher and left large fam. Jas Nichols, Jr., m Rhoda Nichols; their sons: Grenberry, who left 5 child., and Silas, who had 6 child., and Delia, w/o Enoch Covey, of Easton. After death of 1st wife James Nichols m Nellie Sullivan; their child.: Frs; Bayard;

Robinson; Wm; Amanda, Mrs. J. M. Wright, of Federalsburg; Emma, Mrs. Chas Edgell, this co; Ida, Mrs. John Scott; Ella, Mrs. Greenberry Griffith, and Anna. Subj b 1849 on partly timbered farm belonging to father 5th dist. 1872 he located nr old family homestead, cleared it of timber; now has 60 a. under tillage. He m 1872 Martha, d/o Perry D. Taylor; their sons, Clarence and Elmer (d Oct 13 1891). Mrs. Martha Nichols d Jan 27 1887, and Dec 27 1887, Mr. Nichols m her sis, Emily.

199. ROBERT K. JEFFERSON, M. D., Federalsburg, physician this locality. His father, Chas W. Jefferson, M. D., mbr medical fraternity, b Church Creek, Dor Co 1831; parents were planters; grad medical depart Univ Md, while young, and established practice in Federalsburg. He was Episc; m Caroline T., d/o Rev Rbt E. Kemp; their child.: Adelia M., Caroline, Thos O., Edith (w/o W. A. Mowbray), Rbt K., Chas W., and Geo H., of Phila. By prev marriage with her sis, Sarah Kemp, Dr. Chas Jefferson had dau, Sarah E., w/o A. P. Redhead. 352

Subj b this co 1868, reared to adult yrs here; left public schools; grad Friends' Acad, Balt; grad Univ Md with degree M. D. 1890; m 1892 Miss Roberta Davis, of Federalsburg, d/o E. F. Davis; they are active in ME Church.

200. COL. JAMES M. McCARTER, Preston; fam originated in north of Ireland. Grandfather, Arthur McArthur, b Ireland, came to America at 16; later served in Rev. By mistake in muster roll his name recorded as McCarter; afterward he went by that name. Jas Mayland McCarter b New York City 1822, s/o Sml H. and Mary Jane (Mayland) McCarter, of New York, 2nd of 6 child.; others were: Arthur, machinist of Norristown, Pa, now decd; John, decd, machinist at Norristown; Marshall, res that place; Margaret, w/o Jacob Boyer, of Montgomery Co, Pa; and Eliza, w/o Harry Bainbridge, of Phila. Parents mbrs ME Church; after birth of 2nd son moved to Phila, where father employed as machinest and builder of steam engines. Cholera plague in Phila in 1832, caused them to move to Chester Co, P.; afterward settled in Norristown, Pa, where he was employed as machinist until he d, 1834; his wife d 1864. 353

Subj attended Norristown Acad; junior preacher to Phila circuit; spring 1842 admitted on trial in Phila annual conference, 2 yrs later ordained deacon by Bishop Hedding, made elder 1846 by Bishop Morris; in Elk Ridge circuit in Pa, Delaware City, Del, Chestertown & Centreville ciructis in Md; spring of 1846 in Seaford, Del, 1847 assigned to Smyrna; then to Lancaster, Pa, West Phila, St. Paul's, Phila; West Chester; Reading; and Lebanon, Pa; served as chaplain 14th Pa Regt 1861. In 1861 received commission to raise a regt; at battle at Williamsburg, Va., Fair Oaks, Malvern Hill, Antietam, Gettysburg and Sharpsburg, still suffers from an injury; provost marshall of Car and Dor Counties until 1865. He retired from ministry 1883; m Feb 24 1846 Miss Elizabeth Kelly, of Car Co; she d Preston 1886; their child.: Mary P., d young; Jas Edw grew to manhood, in mercantile business, d at young age; surviving son, Chas H., res with father, m Dec 28 1887 Minnie Brantz, d/o Thos H. Anderson, of Talb Co; their sons, Ralph and Jas Elwood.

201. JAMES HENRY DODD, farmer QA Co, b this co 1833, s/o Hy and Anna (Phillips) Dodd, of old Md families. The grandfather of Hy was Jas H. Dodd, and grandfather of subj was also Jas, who, with son John, in war of 1812. Hy Dodd b this co Mar 31 1802; farmer; located 5th dist when young man; moved to 6th; 1843 came to dist again; had three bros: John, farmer; Thos, farmer and mcht; and Alexander, mechanic, Easton. His 1 sis, Nancy, res with Thos, neither m; both over 70 at death. Mother of subj was Anna, d/o Richard Phillips, farmer this co. She was b 1812, had 2 bros, Richard and Thos, both 357

-51-

farmers. Her only sis, Susan, 2nd w/o Hy Dodd, still living, 83rd year, at Wye Mills, Md; mother of: Elizabeth, Mrs. Washington M. Armstrong, of Wye Mills; Mary, w/o Wm F. Bailey, ex-sheriff this co, res Centreville; and Anna, w/o J. E. Bryan, of Kt Island. Hy and Anna Dodd had: Jas H.; John, b Aug 29 1835; and Thos H. (sketch appears elsewhere this vol) - Jas H. Dodd acquired old homestead year fol father's death (1873); m Dec 10 1886 Miss Mary, d/o John B. Thomas; only child d at 16 months; he and wife mbrs MP Church.

357   202. COLIN FERGUSON STAM, business man Chestertown. His father, John L. Stam, b Phila c. 1803. While young he came to this co and soon purch the business owned by B. F. Houston, c. 1850; 1867 sold out to his sons, Louis K. and Colin, and retired; d 1886, in 84th yr. He m Miss Louisa Ferguson d/o Donald Ferguson of old Kt Co fam, and descendant of political refugees active in Scottish rebellion. Great grandfather of subj educated in universities of Scotland; was 2nd pres Wash College. His bro, Colin, was teacher of English and Latin, and connected with the college. Father of John L. Stam was John Rudolf, of Germany; emigrated to U. S. prior to Rev war, in which he was an officer; later he dwelt in Phila. Only bro of Colin F. Stam, Luis, d about 10 yrs ago. - Subj b Jul 22 1846, grad Wash College 1863 with honors. Oct 9 1877 m Annie H., Roberts; their child.: Annie H., Louisa Antoinette, Lillian Roberts, John Rudolf, Donald Ferguson, Susie Roberts and Colin Ferguson, Jr. Parents are Episc. 1886 Mr. Stam erected store building and the opera house.

358   203. WILLARD C. TODD, business man Car Co, elected co commissioner 1895; of 9 child., of Bennett and Elizabeth Todd, both of this co; 3 decd, living: Frank, Ruth, Emma, Willard C., Lewis N. and Chas E. Grandfather Benj Todd b Dor Co. His father, Benj Todd, Sr, Scotchman, and in Rev war. Bennett Todd has farmed all his life where Willard C. was b; still farms, in 90th year.
Subj b Jun 6 1855; started farming c. 1879; mbr ME Church at Concord; Jan 28 1879 m Wilhelmina Willoughby; of their 7 children 3 living: Bennett, Minnie B. and Ulysses Grant.

359   204. HON. JOHN CHEEZUM BARTLETT, chief judge orphans' court; of Easton, b May 18 1839, Talb Co, at Bloomfield, res of his father, now owned by heirs of late James Dixon. Mother, Elizabeth, d/o Dnl Cheezum, of Car Co, and sis of John Cheezum, mcht of Easton. His father, Jas, was descendant of old fam of Talb Co, whose history can be traced 2 1/2 centuries. The first of the Bartlett came to co c. 1680; patented estate of several thousand acres on east side of Tred Avon River, called Ratcliffe.
Founder of fam here had sons, Jas, John and Thos; they received plantations, Bloomfield, Ratcliffe and Wakefield. Divisions and of estate make it difficult to designate ancient boundaries. Jas Dixon, who m sis of Judge Bartlett's father, res at Bloomfield until he died; homestead now occupied by his sons, Wm and Isaac. Ratcliffe was owned by Hon. R. C. Holliday, ex-secretary of state; and Wakefield was home of Thos B. Baker.
Subj of 5th generation direct descent from Thos, original settler here. At 2 his parents purch and moved to Cottage Mills, Trappe dist; where father farmed and in milling; attended public school nr Miles River Ferry with Dixon boys. At 15 sent to Friends' boarding school Balt Co (Milton Academy). Subj has 3 bros, Rbt, Jas and Edw, and 2 sis, Elizabeth, w/o Richard Kent, of Oakland, Cal., and Mary Ann, w/o Thos Wilson, of Dover, Del. His father d 1865, mother d 1893. John C. acquired farm and res there 9 yrs; mbr Soc of Friends. 1865 subj m Matilda J., d/o John Woodall, of Kt Co, Del; 1874 purch Clifton from father-in-law; their child.: Jas, b Oct 6 1866, 10 yrs employed

-52-

by Dixon, Bartlett & Co., owning interest in business; grad Univ Md Law School; while on trip south suddenly taken ill, returned home, where he d Jul 17 1893; Thos, 2nd son, employed in Easton Natl Bank; John d at 18; Geo, farmer, assists in management of homestead; Fred, cashier in Hotel Lurray, Atlantic City, and Dec took trip to South America; Pauline with her parents.

205. PROF. HENRY TONKIN, teacher; since 1868, principal of public schools of Millington; also buys and ships peaches and other fruits; surveyor; b Sep 4 1840, St. Agnes, Cornwall, Eng, native place of parents, Hy and Jane (Thomas) Tonkin. His father, mining superintendent, came to America c. 1849, in mining in Montgomery and Chester Counties, Pa; moved to N.C., became super- intendent of gold mines in Gaston, where he d 1862, at 52.; his wife d at 40, leaving child.: Hy and Emma; latter d at 15. He completed course of study at the age of 20 at Grovemont Seminary, Phoenixville, Chester Co, Pa.
    Prof. Tonkin began career in Pa, where he taught for a year; later had charge of school in QA Co 2 yrs and officiated as principal of Millington Acad; attends ME Church. He m(1) Rosamond Jennings, b Cornwall, Eng, and d Millington Feb 12 1887; Meth. Their child.: Chas Hy, bookkeeper in Middletown, Del.; Mary E., w/o Wm H. Rash, res Wilm, Del; Rosanna, w/o Sml Irwin, of Wilm, Del.; Howard J. and Arthur E., at home. 1892 Prof. Tonkin m Miss Catherine R. Moffett, of Millington; their son, Hy Moffett. 360

206. REV. CHARLES A . HILL, pastor ME Church Easton, b Centreville, Nov 30 1856; 1876 grad Dickinson College; March fol year licensed to preach and app junior pastor on Camden circuit; served in Bridgeville, Princess Anne, Kings Creek, Sassafras, Epworth, Cherry Hill, Centreville, Salsibury and then here. m 1884 Caroline, d/o late Thos C. Cruikshank, of Cecil Co, their child.: Caroline C. d at 5; Chas Westcott and Thos Cruikshank, at home. Mrs. Hill b and reared in Cecil Co. Father of subj, senior Chas Hill, b Dagsborough, Del, Feb 14 1822, not enabled to obtain a college education, admitted to Phila conference 1845. served at Cambridge, Accomac circuit, Northampton circuit, Salisbury, Snow Hill, Centreville, Easton, Smyrna, Del; Asbury Church, Wilmington; Nazareth Church, Phila; Mariners' Bethel, Phila; Port Deposit; Union, Wilmington; St. Paul's Church, Wilmington and Elkton, Md., several of which he served a second time. He m Susan, d/o Hezekiah P. Westcott; she was b Va, and still living, in 78th yr. The father d Jun 22 1892. Of their 7 child. 5 grew to maturity: Margaret, w/o Rev R. C. Jones; Anna, w/o Hy C. Downward, of Wilm, Del.; Chas A., Alexina and Mary. 363

207. ISAAC H. WRIGHT, Dor Co. His father, Isaac Wright b this co 1763, farmer, d here 1850; his child.: Wm, now of Del.; Isaac H., and John N., carrying on old home place; Celia w/o Dr. Shipley; Ann M. w/o Wm T. Vickers; and Harriet w/o Hon., Dnl Fields, of Car Co. - Subj b Northwest Fork dist, Dor Co, b Feb 18 1826; m Feb 17 1853, Miss Elizabeth S. Craft; their children, 2 decd; living: Anne, w/o Thos Lackey; Carrie, w/o Eugene Ross; May, w/o Dr. Lewis Morris; Fred, who m Miss May Houston; Hattie, Lillian P. and Harry M., at home. Both parents mbrs Episc Church. 364

208. STEWART MATHEWS spent ast 10 yrs 4th dist Kt Co, where he farmed nr Chestertown; b Newcastle Co, Del Dec 12 1840, grew to manhood on farm; 1860 settled in Kt Co, Md, where father farmed in 2nd dist; 1881 bt farm in 4th dist where he d Apr 11 1891. Jan 13 1869 he m Henrietta Sutton; their child.: Susan E.; Mary L., w/o J. W. S. Jones, of Chestertown; Jas S., Thos A., Stanley W., Herbert M., Annie S., Ettie L. and Helen M.; all res with mother 364

except 2nd dau. Mrs. Mathews b Kt Co Nov 20 1844; has spent her life here; active in ME Church.

365   209. HON. HENRY CLAY DODSON, res St. Michael's, Talb Co, rep this dist in gen assembly 3 terms and Nov 1897, elected state senator; b Oct 5 1840, in ancestral home in St. Micheal's. Over 100 yrs ancestors res on bay side. Ancestor Thos Dodson, b presumably this neghborhood, early 1700's. His son Rbt b St. Michael's; spent entire life on farm here, except period he followed the water; commissioner of village; attended ME Church; d at 66.
    Capt. Wm Dodson, s/o Rbt, and grandfather of subj, b St. Michael's 1786, sailor; during war of 1812 commanded barge under Commodore Barney; had charge of battery on Parrott's Point that repelled attack of British on that town in 1813; Meth. Father of subj, Capt Rbt A. Dodson, b and reared this place; Chesapeake Bay, owner of sailing vessels; running packet line on bay St. Michael's-Balt; postmaster St. Michel's; he m Hester A. R. Keithley (b Balt).
    At 14 subj began work in drug store in Easton; bt drug store of H. F. Byrne, St. Michael's, 1860, which he conducted until 1880; postmaster of St. Michael's until 1875; elected to gen assembly. 1861 he m Miss Maggie A. McCarty, of Easton, who d fol year; 1864 m Martha, d/o Dr. Wm B. Hahn, of Montgomery Co, Pa; of their 6 child.: 3 decd; Emma, w/o Russell S. Dawson, of Norfolk, Va; Henry Clay, Jr., with father in drug business; Hannah at home. 1894 subj and son opened drug store in St. Michael's. He is mbr ME Church.

366   210. FRANCIS J. BARNES res Som Co since 1875; on farm at Lower Trappe, Princess Anne dist, since 1893; owns large tracts Som and Wor Counties; supports ME Church. Barnes fam originated in Eng. Thos Barnes, grandfather of subj, b Wor Co; farmer; d c. 1820. Subject's father, Jas A. Barnes b Wor Co; farmer; owned general store at Pocomoke City (then known as Newtown) for 10 yrs; attended ME Church; died at 74; he m(1) Sarah A. Q. Adams, d/o Capt Mitchell Adams, who commanded a company in Mexican war. Her child., all living: Emily S., w/o W. M. Schoolfield, of Pocomoke City; Frs J.; Alfred T., of Pocomoke City; Adial P., atty Snow Hill; Mary S., wid of Sml Schoolfield; and Clarence F., res Wor Co. Mother d at 55, mbr ME Church.
    Subj b Sep 10 1839 Wor Co, grew to manhood on farm; at 23 settled on farm nr by where he farmed 9 yrs. 1875 he came to Som Co and cultivated Stewart farm, which he owns; 1893, moved to present home at Lower Trappe. He m(1) Miss Sarah A. Merrill, who d childless. He m(2) Emily, d/o Benj Langford, of Som Co, and d here at 82. She was 1 of 5 child. b to Benj Langford and Mary A. Gibbons, the others being Lizzie, now wid of Wm Passwalters; Mary A., w/o Wm Ross; Amanda J., Mrs. M. L. Porter; and Sarah E. The mother d at 61. Child. of subj and wife: Benj J., res Princess Anne dist; M. Blanche, Frank U., Emma M., Lane A. and Nettie E., with their parents.

369   211. JOSEPH M. PARVIS, Centreville, of early Del fam. Grandfather, Thos, s/o Jos Parvis; b Del 1800, farmer; owned and cultivated farm in northern part Car Co; there he d 1881. Father of subj, Jos L. Parvis b Del 1827; in early manhood school teacher, later farming and fruit raising; d Sep 1865; by 1st wife had son, Wm Parvis, employed by Chester River Steamboat Co 20 yrs. He m(2) Susan Norris, of Car Co, d/o Martin Norris (b Car Co). She is a descendant of Thos Norris, who came to America in latter 1600'-early 1700's, of 7 bros to come from Eng, all of whom settled on Western Shore except one, who estab his home Car Co. She had 2 bros, Dr. John c. Norris, physician of Phila, and Wm H. Norris, farmer of QA Co. She is 59, res Ingleside, QA Co, with son, Preston. - Subj b Mar 25 1865 Car Co on fam homestead; at 17 left

-54-

farm to clerk in store at Ingleside; 2 yrs later commenced to teach school; when 24 elected surveyor of QA Co; 1893 made clerk of bd of co commissioners.

212. EDWARDS REED BURNESTON, M. D., d Sep 12 1897 Dor Co; res Lake dist 30 yrs; postmaster of Lakesville, mbr ME Church; of Irish descent, paternal ancestors having come to Md from Ireland at an early day. Both his great grandfather and his grandfather were named Isaac. Latter spent life in Balt; one of first to use looms for weaving in state; operated large mill called the Washington Factory, where all kinds of cloth for domestic trade were manufactured. Father of doctor, Wm R. Burneston, of Balt, farmer and merchandising; d 1872 at 72; m in early manhood, Matilda, d/o Jonathan Edwards, of Balt. She d 1863, leaving 11 child.; 4 living: Hy Clay; Ellen, w/o R. H. Ridgely; Matilda; and Lucy, w/o Frederick Dutton. 369

Dr. Burneston b Jul 11 1821 Balt, and there spent boyhood; attended public schools, Abingdon Acad of Harford Co, Balt College, and Mount Hope College. 1839 he embarked in grocery business with Thos A. Norris & Son; c. 1847 began study of medicine Univ Md, grad 1850; 2 yrs later settled in Lake dist and practiced here 7 yrs, returned to Balt, joined 11th Regt of Md Volunteers as regt surgeon Jun 1864; 1867 resumed practice this dist. In 1844 he m Lucy P., d/o Geo and Mary (Miriam) Gillingham, of old Balt family; their child: Wm N., res Balt; Matilda, Mrs. Jas Webster; Lucy B., Mrs. Jas S. Wheatley; and Nellie, w/o Sml H. Woodland, of Balt; fam are mbrs ME Church.

213. ROBERT PATTON b 1833, MP, has lived entire life Car Co; m Amelia, d/o Isaiah C. Blades, business man of Car Co. Mrs. Amelia Patton d; her child.: Orlando and Emily, Mrs. John Blades. Subj m(2) Sarah E. Trice, d/o Sml Trice; she d Sep 18 1881; left 2 child., Matthew and Lydia. Fam lives at American Corner, Car Co. 370

214. CHRISTOPHER C. LLOYD, senior mbr of firm of Lloyd, Blaine & Co., of Pocomoke City, Wor Co, in drug business 41 yrs, the first to estab drug store in what was then known as Newtown, in 1856; postmaster 1857-1861; 1880 elected sheriff of co; collector of state and co taxes for 1880-1881; s/o Rbt G. and Mary Lloyd, b Lloyd Landing, Talb Co, Mar 10 1832. His father d soon thereafter, his mother moved to Trappe, where subj grew to young manhood; worked in stores of Mullikin & Dickinson, Goldsborough & Dawson, in Easton; and with Kemp & Lloyd; was in fertilizer business several yrs. 1859 he m Miss Annie G. McMaster, d/o Hon. S. S. McMaster; their child., in order of birth: Annie, w/o Wm S. Dickinson; Mollie, w/o E. B. Freeman; Sml, in fertilizer and lumber business with Mr. Freeman in Norfolk; Bertha J.; Frs J., and Edgar L., teller in Pocomoke Natl Bank; and two d in infancy. 371

215. JAMES T. SYLVESTER, farmer 3rd dist; paternal grandfather David Sylvester, farmer, b Car Co. John W., father of subj, b and reared this co, farmer and land owner; d at 58; m Sarah E. Williams; their child.: John T., Jas T., Chas H. and Sallie C. The mother, b this co, d at c. 45. Sub b Oct 1 1849, on father's old farm; Oct 2 1875 m Sarah M. Pippin, of this co, who d, leaving child, Bettie C.; Oct 1882 he m Clementine Noble; their child.: 2 decd; living: Chas W. and Martin B. The mother d Dec 6 1895; mbr ME Church. 371

216. CHRISTIAN B. KRUSEN, retired business man Still Pond, Kt Co, b Montgomery Co, Pa, 1834; of German origin, fam founded there as early as 1728, mostly farmers. Paternal grandfather of subj in Rev war; his bro, Garrett Krusen, in war of 1812. John Krusen, subject's father, of Montgomery Co, Pa, 372

mason and plasterer; m Miss Mary E. Bosbyshell; had 9 child.; living: Christian B.; Gustavus B., res Cal.; and Hy, of Kt Co, Md. The father d at home of subj 1888, at 86. - Subj b, reared and educated Montgomery Co, Pa, at 18 began learning wheelwright's and carriagemaker's trade, which he followed throughout his career; 1857 moved to Kennedyville, Md and conducted shop until 1861; fol 2 yrs in Urieville; 1864-1865 in Chestertown; 1866 came to Still Pond; added undertaking business in 1871, carrying on both until son Wm H. took charge of shops and business. Subj m 1859 Miss Mary E. Conner, of Kt Co, Del; their child.: Emma, w/o Jos Wilson, of Oxford, Pa; Mary E., w/o Hy S. Lawton; Gustavus B., undertaker Vineland, N. J.; Nellie; Virmadella, and Benj and Wm, twins, the former a res Phila; fam are mbrs ME Church.

375   217. J. H. C. LEGG, lawyer, QA Co; b Kt Island, QA Co, Jun 2 1868, s/o Wm Henry Legg (b Kt Island 1832). His father, John C. Legg, b Eng, received grant of 225 a.; owner of line of steamboats and in merchandising. Wm H. Legg, farmer, and editor Denton Journal, 1872-1876; returned to Kt Island, where he engaged in merchandising and farming. Rep in state legislature 7 terms; deputy surveyor of port of Balt; 1894 app to internal revenue office Balt. He still retains res in Centreville. He m Marietta Cook, d/o Clinton Cook, atty who served in house and senate of gen assembly. He was mbr Episc Church, d at 38. His children, Etta C., Maggie S., Clintonia and subj.
    J. H. C. Legg spent early life on Kt Island; student in Charlotte Hall, St. Mary's Co, grad Balt City College, completing a law course 1889; began practice in Balt, where he remained for 2 yrs in assoc with David Stewart; then came to Centreville, where he opened an office. 15 Apr 1896 he m Miss Caroline Eliason, d/o G. W. Eliason. Mr. Legg is mbr Episc Church.

376   218. SAMUEL L. TULL, justice of peace 33 yrs Tull's Corner, Som Co; owns tract cultivated by several generations of Tulls; b on this old homestead in 1826 and here spent his childhood. Sml Tull, father of subj, b on farm, adjoining that occupied by subj; farmer and mcht; owned several vessels carrying freight to and from West Indies. He d Balt on business trip, at 53. His father, Thos Tull, farmer of Brinkley's dist. Sml Tull m Miss Caroline Miles; they had fam of 8 children, of whom S. L. is only survivor. Mrs. Tull d at 47, mbr ME Church; her husband identified with Episc Church.
    Sml L. Tull has farmed since he arrived at man's estate. His father d when the son was an infant; the mother d c. 1835. He is mbr Episc Church. He m Miss Catherine Gunby, sis of Dr. Gunby, Nov 25 1853. They had 15 child.: 3 decd; living: Alonzo E.; S. Ashton; Edw W.; Stella K., w/o W. A. Tull; Fannie B., w/o A. Davis; Minnie, Mrs. Sml S. Horsey; Rowland; Frank H.; Gordon, state's atty and young lawyer of Princess Anne; Olive M., Mrs. R. Whittington; Carrie L., Mrs. Aden Davis, and Clifford.

376   219. MATTHEW PATTON, mbr ME Church, farmer 4th dist Car Co, b Dor Co 1806, s/o Matthew and Lydia (Barrett) Patton, of Del, 1 of 3 sons, his brothers being Rbt, d unmarried, and Barrett, who left large fam at his death. Matthew was reared in Dor Co, whence in early manhood he came to Car Co, learned trade of cabinet maker in Denton; m 1832 in Federalsburg, Martha, d/o John Rumbold, who d Car Co 1859, at 84. She was 1 of 5 child., others being: Jas B., who d Talb Co, leaving dau, Elizabeth, w/o Perry G. Stevens; Elizabeth, Leah and Mary, latter age 90. The Rumbold family is of English descent. - Subj and wife had children: Rbt, Emily, Jas B. and Lydia. Emily is wid of Dr. H. F. Willis, of Preston, has 2 children: Mary, wid of J. B. Clark, of Del; and Harry M., physician of Pocomoke City, Md. Lydia is w/o J. W. Todd, of 4th

dist. After their marriage Mr. and Mrs. Patton settled on a farm in 4th dist. Here he d 1883. She d Oct 14 1897 at home of son, Jas B.

220. GEORGE PERRY JONES, M. D., res nr East New market; 1869 opened office in East New Market, since remained; b Oct 19 1838, Wicomico Co, s/o Hon. Sml B. D. and Maria S. (Jones) Jones, former a mbr state legislataure of 1846. His maternal grandfather was Levin D. Jones. His paternal grandfather, Benj I. Jones, b Wicomico Co, contractor and builder; erected all public buildings in Princess Anne, Som Co. During war of 1812 he was commissioned officer. In his family there were: Isaac D., atty general of Md; Sarah B.; and Susan, Mrs. Algernon Dashiell, of Wicomico Co. His ancestors were Welsh. 377

Subj was only child, studied in Wash Acad; grad medical depart Univ Md 1865; m Nov 27 1867 Miss Willianana, d/o Col Geo E. Austin, of Dor Co; their child.: Sml, postmaster East New market; Bruce, Edw, Maria, Georgia and Mary.

221. CAPT. CHARLES S. CARMINE purch homestead 33 yrs ago, on Choptank River, nr Preston, Car Co 4th dist; b soon after death of father, Chas Carmine, in 1831. His mother, Sarah, d/o Wm Waddell, she had 2 sons, other being Geo, who grew to manhood here and m, went to Island of St. Thomas, West Indies, d there of malady contracted in that place; had no children. 378

At 15 subj shipped on board vessel plying the Chesapeake Bay; followed this local sailing for about 15 yrs; then purch vessel and became his own master and navigator during the 8 yrs succeeding, on frequent trips to the West Indies and to South American ports. He m 1864 Miss Mary E. Farquaharson in 1864 and settled down; their child.: eldest, Geo C., lieut in revenue service; m in Calif; Fred, 2nd son, d, leaving wid and daus, Amelia and Hilda; Emiline, only d/o captain, is w/o Edw Benson, of Pocomoke City, Md.

222. ROBERT H. JONES, owns 160 a., mbr co school bd, entire life in Som Co, res Fairmount dist, where b 1819, of 6 children of Thos and Martha (Handy) Jones. He was a child when his father d. In 1842 he m Miss Harriet Evans, who d Jul 1874. He m(2) 1875 Mrs. Elizabeth L. Tull, wid of Dr. J. Emory Tull. Their son, Rbt H., Jr., student in Johns Hopkins Univ. Mr. Jones and fam mbrs ME Church. 378

223. WILLIAM H. CECIL, of 6th dist, clerk of QA Co. The Cecil fam founded in America by Martin Cecil, of England, who settled Car Co and fought in Rev. His son, John, wounded in war of 1812. The latter's son, Martin, father of subj, b Car Co, moved to QA Co, settled on farm; m Mary, d/o Peter Pingfield, of Car Co. He d 1878; his wife d 1890; of their 8 child., living: Thos, res 3rd dist QA Co; Catherine, wid of Capt Riggins, of Centreville; Wm H.; Chas, of Queenstown; Susan, w/o W. H. Cahill, of Prices, QA Co; and Walter. 381

Wm H. Cecil b Jan 8 1840 on father's farm nr Bridgetown, Car Co; 1877 purch Royester farm (360 a.), in northern part of 6th dist, and here has farmed and raised stock, and operated sawmill; 1880 chosen co commissioner. He m(1) Marietta Hand, wid of Wm H. Holland, of QA Co, who d 1880; of her 9 child. 2 living: Hy, res Queenstown; and Bessie, at home. He m Dec 16 1890, Mary Anne Downs; they have son, William.

224. FRANCIS A. BARTLETT, postoffice address: Carmichael, QA Co, owns farm 5th dist, nr Little Wye River. For nearly 50 yrs mbr ME Church at Wye Mills; b Car Co, 1 Jan 1828, s/o Elisha and Sarah (Price) Bartlett. Other children were Mary, wid of John W. Plummer, of Talb Co; Rheuelma, w/o J. K. Skinner, of 382

Wye Mills, and Rebecca and Matthew, both d unmarried. Bartletts were settlers on Eastern Shore of Md; Dnl, grandfather of subj, b Car Co.

Subj moved to this co 1859; owns place of 30 a.; m 1852 Car Co, Martha J. Stack. After her death he m Deborah Dyott, of Kt co, Md; later m L. S. Stauffer, of Pa, their child.: Lula and Nellie, at home. Other children of subj are: Emily, w/o Wm F. Deford, of Car Co, and mother of 9 child.; Jos, res this co, who m Mary C. Cannon, and has 8 child.; Mary, w/o Wm D. Anthony, of Talb Co, and mother of 5; Hennie, d at 6; Sarah, w/o Jas H. Carter, of QA Co, and has 4 child.; Rheuelma, d in 19th yr; Frs A., Jr., farmer of QA Co, m Emma A. Draper, who have 2 little ones; and Martha, unmarried.

382 225. JACOB L. NOBLE, M. D., located in Preston 7 yrs., eld s/o Twiford S. and Ruth H. (Leverton) Noble, b Car Co Jan 6 1849. Paternal grandfather, Joshua, of Sussex Co, Del, farmer. Noble family is of Eng descent. Ruth H. d/o Jacob Leverton had 2 child.; 2nd son, Rufus, mcht Dor Co. Mrs. Noble d while boys were young; father later m Caroline Davis, their child.: Addie, w/o Rbt Jarrell, res northern part of this co; and Alexander, farmer this co. Twiford Noble b Sussex Co, Del, c. 1820, d on old homestead nr Preston 1882. He came to Md, soon after 1st marriage. He was a farmer, co commissioner of Car Co and mbr state constitutional convention of 1864.

At 18 subj entered and grad Bryan & Stratton's Business College Balt; took clerical position for a few yrs, then taught school a year or two; later app to pension depart and stationed at Indianapolis about two yrs; then principal of Preston Acad 12 months; grad medical depart Univ Md 1876. He m Miss Mamie E. Travers, d/o Judge Levi D. Travers, of Taylor's Island; their child.: Duncan L., Levi D., Ruth H., Mary E., Clara A., Inez, Maud, Wm D., Eliza J., and John W. and Jacob L., who d in infancy. Fam are mbrs ME Church.

383 226. HON. JOSEPH E. GEORGE, large land owner QA Co, 1870-1881 carried on grain and fertilizer business. Hon. Matthias George, father of Jos E., b QA Co 1801, being the s/o Jos George, farmer and mbr Soc of Friends. From his fifth year Matthias was under care of governess until he was ten, when his father and Major Massey, of Queenstown, built school house and hired a teacher. Here he completed his education. 1825 he began farming; served gen assembly, state senator and bd of co commissioners. 1824 he m Martha Elliott; their only surviving child is Jos E. 1840 he m Clarissa, d/o John Boone, of Car Co. After her death he m Mrs. Lucretia D. Hopper, d/o Thos W. Hopper, of QA Co. He d 1885, nearly 84.

Subj b 1st dist QA Co Jan 1 1830; educated Sudlersville Acad and Newark (Del) College. When 21 he took charge of farm where he had lived since 7 yrs old, and there remained for 10 yrs; then engaged in mercantile business in Sudlersville 2 1/2 yrs; purch farm (300 a.) east of Sudlersville, which he operated until 1867, when he returned to former home. Dec 1855 he m Martha L., d/o Jos Neal, of Sussex Co, Del; their child.: Jos, eldest, decd; Martha w/o Wm D. Rowe, farmer and grain mcht of Barclay; John E. res Sudlersville and mbr bd co commissioners; Annie, w/o Jas Marriet, Jr., farmer 1st dist; Edwin, of roving, unsettled disposition, not engaged in any business.

In 1872 Mr. George elected co commissioner 2 yrs; judge orphans' court to fill vacancy at death of Jas R. Sudler. Since 1878 director of Centreville Natl Bank; attends Episc Church.

384 227. W. GRASON SMITH, Williamsburg, b Dor Co 1838, res here his entire life. First Smith to locate here was his great-grandfather, Matthew Smith, emigrated Eng to America, settling in Dor Co, took up several thousand a., grew tobacco.

-58-

Next in line of descent was Matthew Smith, Jr., b nr Finchville, 1st dist, educated in England; surveyor Dor Co 42 yrs. Father of subj, Risdon L. J. Smith, b nr Finchville, Dor Co; m Hester Ann Twilly, of this co; their child.: W. Grason; Martin A., who m and at his death left 2 child.; Jas M., res Reliance, this co; and Albert H., d unmarried.

Subj, after common schools, taught school number of yrs; 1870 carried on general store in Williamsburg 1870-1878, while farming. His ancestors were mbrs Church of England, but he and fam mbrs ME Church. He m 1868 Larua V., d/o Ezekiel Williams. Of their four children, 2 living: Retta C., res Easton, and W. Harvey, in business Balt.

228. JOHN R. COOK, implement dealer, QA Co, b Kt Island Feb 3 1845, s/o John 387 and Maria J. (Walker) Cook, same place. The father, farmer, mbr Meth Church; d 1877; his wife d 1880. Of their 12 children 9 living: Virginia, w/o Chas M. Legg, of Kt Island; John R.; Jas, of Kt Island; Annie; Jos B., of Kt Island; Matilda, w/o Chas Hopkins; Everett E.; Ida M., w/o Chas Ringgold; and Rbt F. all res of Kt Island.

Until 18 John R. Cook attended schools on island; then turned to farming. At 35 he embarked in merchandising in Centreville; 15 Apr 1880 m Emma J., wid of Jacob Legg, of Kt Island, d/o John W. Perry, of Centreville; their children, Frank W. and John R., Jr.; they attend MP Church.

229. CAPT. B. FRANK LANKFORD, pres People's Bank of Som Co, Princess Anne; 387 owns a farm (530 a.) southeastern part of Princess Anne dist, his mother's birthplace, possessed by mbrs of Porter family entire century.

The captain's father, Benj Lankford b Lawsons dist 1798 and in youth learned trade of shipbuilder, which he followed in conjunction with farming. Twelve times elected to state legislature and once state senator, commissioner of public works 4 yrs. When a young man he was dep sheriff for a time. He d 1886, at 88. His father, Benj, Sr., s/o Lazarus Lankford, farmer of Som Co, where he d c. 1820.

Subject's mother, Susan, d/o John and Mary Porter; b 1806, d 1883; Presby; of her 10 child. 7 living: Hy S., res Princess Anne dist; Julia, w/o Geo W. Lankford; B. Frank; Sarah A., Mrs. Sml Miles; Mary M., wid of Rbt Miles; Susan, w/o Thos W. Taylor; and Cornelia J., w/o Wm T. Lankford.

Subj b on homestead Lawsons dist Dec 25 1827. From 16 to 20 he served apprenticeship to house carpenter, then he entered trade of ship carpenter; became engaged freighting and oyster business, acquiring 6 different vessels. 1856 he bt the Porter homestead and here he has since res. 1871 he was elected commissioner of co, then sheriff of Som Co. His family attend ME Church. He m Dec 21 1859 Amanda E., d/o Wm and Sallie (Miles) Porter; their child.: Ella, w/o Geo W. Lankford, of Mo.; Wm F.; B. Louis, U. S. N., on steamship Massachusetts; Sallie V., w/o John M. Shields, of Petosky, Mich.; and Milton S. Mrs. Lankford d 1877. Feb 16 1882, subj m Matilda A. Sudler, of Som Co, d/o Thos and Sallie J. Sudler.

230. JUDGE EDWIN S. VALLIANT b St. Michael's, Talb Co, Jul 12 1845, s/o Rigby 388 Valliant, senior mbr firm of R. Valliant & Bro, wholesale grocers of Balt; later conducted general store in St. Michael's; last days on farm in Talb Co, where he d 1858. Ancestors originally from France; left during persecution of Huguenots, going to England, whence Jean Valliant came to America, mid 1600'sth century, received patent to tract in Talb Co. Old homestead remained in fam until present generation.

During his youth Judge Valliant attended common schools and then West River Classical Institute and other private schools; 1862 joined army, becoming private in Company C., 2nd Md Infantry; in battles at Winchester, Gettysburg, Weldon Railroad, Cold Harbor, and seige of Petersburg, where captured Mar 1865; prisoner at Point Lookout until Jun 25 1865; at Gettysburg wounded in left side by gunshot; after war returned home in Talb Co, and resumed studies under private tutors. Coming to Church Hill in 1871, he began business in fertilizers, lumber and coal; sold wagons and carriages. Subj m Jan 14 1866 Miss Mary T. Faithful; of their 7 children, 5 living: Wm E., E. Stevens, Nellie, Mary and Thos R. Fam attend Episc Church. Sons, Wm E. and E. Stevens, are associated with him in business with father at Church Hill under firm name of E. S. Valliant & Sons. For 10 yrs Judge Valliant served as magistrate, 1887 elected assoc judge of orphans' court, and 1891-1895 was chief judge of same court.

389 231. ROBERT C. RICE, farmer and stock raiser, 6th distCar Co.
The Rice family came to Md from Pa, where several generations had lived. Paternal grandfather of subj was John Rice, d Aug 1855; m 1816 Margaretta Ickes, d/o Nicholas Ickes, who was owner of land on which Ickesburgh (Perry Co, Pa) now stands. From him the place took its name. Margraetta Rice d at 90, of 11 child., 6 survive her: Mrs. Susannah J. Boden, of Ickesburgh; D. I., of Duncannon, Pa.; Wm, of Bloomfield, Pa; John, of Smyrna, Del; Oliver; and Mrs. Kate E. Aldrich, of Duncannon. Subj is of nine children of John and Christina (Clark) Rice; 2 decd: John and Blanche; others are: Maggie, Luvia L., Chas J., Lila, Rebecca and Geo. The parents were from Perry Co, Pa.
Robert C. Rice b Dec 26 1857 on father's old homestead Perry Co. 1887 he became res this community, and purch farm which he now operates, 6th dist, on Choptank River; he m 1 Mar 1882 Kate L. Quillin, of Del, d/o John Quillin, res 8th dist, Car Co, farmer; their child.: Clarence, Lillian R. and Rbt J.

390 232. SOUTHEY F. MILES, retired, res Brinkley's dist, Som Co, occupying res he erected in 1897; attends the MP church. Grandfather of subj, Hy Miles, b at fam homestead on Coulbourn's Creek; d there at 40; s/o Hy Miles, Sr., who came from Scotland and settled on land grant situated between Jones' Creek and Coulbourn's Creek. Subject's father, Wm Hy Miles, b at fam home, followed the water a while; turned to farming. He d at 85; m Elizabeth, d/o Isaac Coulbourn, was Meth; he was of remarkable physique, active and robust to the last; rode horseback until shortly before he d. His wife d at 72. Of their 11 children, 4 are living: Sarah, w/o John Coulbourn; Southey F.; Luther T., res old homestead; and John Thos, of Brinkley's dist.
Subj b Apr 27 1822 at old family homestead on Coulbvourn's Creek. At 16 he began to work at oyster business, which he followed until the war. His sympathies were with the south and several times he was arrested by the Federals on account of his known opinions. He went to Va, remained there 6 months, selling goods to soldiers; prisoner in Fort McHenry 5 months; finally tried by court martial on false charge. At close of war he resumed farminig and carried on general store at Marion Station up to 1888, since which time he has lived retired. 1867 he was elected sheriff and collector of co; m Oct 1846 Miss Chritiana, d/o Wm H. Roach; their child.: Eliza J., w/o N. J. P. Tull; Adalia C., Mrs. Wm Whittington; Aurelia F.; Wm E., d 1896; Joshua W., ex-member of congress; Southey F., Jr., res old homestead; and Alonzo L., of Cambridge. The wife and mother, who d 1885, at 61, mbr MP Church.

233. JAMES M. CORKRAN, M. D., practices medicine and surgery in Centreville; 393
b Cambridge, Dor Co, Aug 14 1860, descended from old fam. His great-great-grandfather, from Eng, granted tract named Churchfield Farm. There four generations of fam were b but the prop has now passed out of the hands of the fam. Nathan Corkran, great-grandfather, farmer, lived on the old homestead, which he operated with the aid of slaves. The grandfather, Jas Corkran, also a slaveholder and owner of Churchfield Farm, served in Mexican war; d at 32.
Father of subj, Thos Corkran, b Dor Co, Mar 28 1821, farmer; res Seaford, Del where he settled 12 yrs ago; mbr ME Church; m Hester Wright, d/o Kinley Wright, of Dor Co. His father, Jos, s/o Abraham Wright, officer in Rev war. Mrs. Corkran, still living; her child.: Chas W., farmer of Mo.; Frs S., grad Glasgow College, Meth minister; d in Mo.; Mary Elizabeth, w/o Isaac Noble, broker and money loaner, of Preston; Rev Lewis P., grad Dover Conference Acad, Dover, Del, Meth minister, res Newcastle, Del; Wilbur F., grad Dover Conference Acad, presiding elder Easton dist; Thos B., farmer of Pa; Millard F., grad Univ Mdm physician Wilm, Del; Fanny, w/o Arthur Hitch, mcht Seaford, Del; David H., Meth minister at Lewis, Del, atended Dover Conference Acad, Univ Pa, grad Drew Theological Seminary; Milton W., hotel clerk in St. Louis; Adelaide, in millinery business Dover, Del; and Jas M., of this sketch.
Dr. Corkran spent his early life on farm and studied in Dover Conference Academy until 1884, grad medical depart Univ of Md 1887; came to Centreville. Jun 11 1890 he m Miss Laura S. Emory, d/o Addison Emory of Centreville; their child, Margaret Spencer, age 5. The doctor attends ME Church.

234. WILLIAM C. POWELL, Snow Hill, pres Md State Pharmaceutical Accoc; b Jun 393
24 1874, s/o Zadok and Sallie Powell, of Snow Hill; grad high school here 1892. Except for 9 months as assist teller First Natl Bank of Snow Hill, he has been in drug business since boyhood, including regular apprenticeship in pharmacy of P. D. Cottingham & Co., comprised of his uncle and father. He grad Md College of Pharmacy 1895. Since then he has been connected with the drug firm just mentioned.

235. CAPT. JAMES M. ROBERTS, farmer, postoffice address: Capitola, Wicomico 394
Co; owns homestead over 250 a.) in southern part of Tyaskin dist; runs general store and has dealt in oysters. He was b Aug 12 1838 this co, s/o Wm and Caroline (Kennerly) Roberts, both of Eastern Shore, eldest of their four child.; others: Benj O., Geo Tho and Margaret J. Grandfather Benj Roberts wb Som Co, farmer. The captain's father, farmer, d at 33.
Subj b and reared on farm, educated in district-schools; at 15 shipped on board boat which ran Wash-Ricmond, Va, 3 yrs later promoted to master; Jul 17 1860 m Olivia A. White, of Eastern Shore; their child.: Wm S., Clara, Lee J., Loretta, Olivia A., Hy W. and John B. The 4 older child are married. Olivia is proficient in drawing, teaches school in Tyaskin dist. Lee J., is mcht Oxford, Md. Hy W., unmarried, assists his father in general stroe. John B. is taking a commercial course in business college in Wilm, Del., expecting to grad in 1898. Mrs. Roberts is d/o Sml and Betsy M. (Wainwright) White, of this part of state. Of their 7 children 3 decd; remaining: Margaret E., Mrs. Roberts, Emily and Isaac. Grandfather Jas White b Eastern Shore; m Miss Elizabeth Hickman. Grandfather Joshua Wainwright. old settler of this side of bay was a farmer. Mrs. Roberts is mbr of ME Church. Subj has served as road commissioner, judge of elections, and assessor of Wicomico Co.

236. JOHN R. H. EMBERT owns and carries on homestead of about 140 acres, 5th 395
dist QA Co; b on Kt Island Mar 13 1838. Supposition that Emberts originated

in Scotland. The paternal grandfather of subj b this co. Subject's parents Wm J. and Annie (Bryan) Embert, both b this region, both decd, had large fam, of whom but 3 survive: Thos A., Wm, and John R. H.

When subj quite young his parents d, obliging him to make his way at 14; for yrs in mercantile business; m 1870 Cecilia, d/o John Kemp and Elizabeth (Bryan) Griffin. Former was s/o Capt Gwynbury Griffin, whose sailing vessel, was captured by British during war of 1812; b St. Mary's Co, Md; his father b Scotland. The capt at his death left 3 sons and 4 daus: Thos, Wm, John, Lydia, Sarah, Julia and Mary. None of his sons grow to adulthood. Subj and wife settled on homestead in 5th dist where they still res. Their child.: sons, Valentine and Cyril, d in infancy; their only surviving child, John Griffin, is 22. Many generations of Emberts mbrs Cath Church.

395   237. CAPT. GOODMAN W. BRAMBLE, capt on sailing vessels running from ports of Eastern Shore to Balt, New York City and other points, now commanding officer of police boat; owns 3 sailing vessels which ply the bay, carrying cargoes of grain and other merchandise. 1877 he purch the Sweet Prospect farm, 9th dist Dor Co, making this his home. He was b Strait dist, this co, 1837, s/o Moses Bramble, of that locality, who res in that neighborhood all his life, farming and oyster fishing; mbr ME Church; d at 70. His father, Matthew Bramble, res same section of co; owned farm there. His father, b Eng, settled in Md prior to 1776, res Straits' Desert, in southern part of co.

Capt. Moses Bramble m Adeline Willie, who d at 54, leaving several child.: Capt. Marcellus A., res where his ancestors lived, nr Straits' Desert; G. W.; Axie, w/o H. Huffman; Prediman, res Strait; Melvina, Mrs. Wm Todd; and Elisha, of Strait. The mother, mbr ME Church.

When 15, subj began life at sea; 1st 25 yrs or so spent mostly on the ocean, with home nr his birthplace, but past 20 yrs has lived at present home, farming mostly. 1877 he m Lulu Langrell, who left 3 child. when she d: Eva, w/o Arthur Stewart; Otto since decd; Alice, youngest, at home. Subj later m Sarah J. Asplen Aug 5 1879; their child.: Ida, Lulu, Ernest, Fdk, Benj Harrison and an infant son. Mrs. Bramble attends ME Church.

396   238. JOHN T. JUMP, res 6th dist, QA Co. His Jump family came to America from Eng prior to Rev and since associated with Md. Subj was magistrate 4 yrs; b Dec 10 1826, this dist, s/o Allerby and Elizabeth (Pratt) Jump, of Caroline and QA Counties, respectively.. The father, farmer and mbr Cath Church; d 1849; his wife d 1863; of their 12 child., 4 survive: Rbt, of Talb Co; John T.; Indiana, w/o Sml McCart, of Church Hill; and Julia, wid of Frank Morgan, of Queen Anne. - Subj remained at home until 20, at about which time his father d, leaving subj property. 1860 he bt Brandford and Martin place and now owns 296 a. Feb 19 1852 he m Ann Maria, d/o Jas Turner, of this dist; their child.: Alfred and Kate, both decd; he was trustee ME Church.

399   239. S. C. DUDLEY, M. D., physician of QA Co, and in drug business Church Hill.; b 7th dist, Jun 17 1843; reared on farm until 18; taught school until 1865; studied medicine; grad medical depart Univ Md 1867; clerk of courts of QA Co 1882, res Centreville until 1887; then to Church Hill, started present drug store. He m Feb 6 1873 Miss Helen Spear, of Kt Co, Md, their child.: Norman Spear, Chas Bradford, Helen Marie and Georgia Spear.

399   240. GRANVILLE E. DICKINSON, M. D., physician Som Co, in Fairmount ever since he started his practice, nearly 25 yrs ago; b Barren Creek Springs, Wicomico Co, 1855, s/o Hy J. P. and Mary A. Dickinson. The father b Pocomoke City, as

was his father, Jas T. Dickinson, a cabinet maker. Hy J. P. grad medical depart Univ Md, practiced southern part Eastern Shore. He m(1) Mary, d/o Dr. George Waller, of Barren Creek Springs; subject is their only child. After mother's death the father m Emily F. Lambden; of their children 2 grew to adult yrs: Marietta, Mrs. Chas O. Merrill, of Phila, who d Oct 1897; and Edw Hy, d unmarried. The Dickinsons are mostly mbrs Presby Church.

Subj grad medical depart Univ Pa 1874; settled in Fairmount dist, Som Co, where he began his practice. 1890 he m Miss Kate Ohlander, d/o Augustus and Louise J. Ohlander, of Sweden. Mrs. Dickinson reared in city of Montgomery, Ala., where her parents located after arrival in America, and is proficient in literature and music. They have dau, Mary Louise.

241. MARION T. MILLER, mbr firm Miller Bros, mchts of Rock Hall, b this co, 400 5th dist; mbr MP Church. Together with bro Chas, in business here since 1894; b May 29 1871, s/o Wm M. Miller, farmer and fruit grower of Kt Co, 5th dist. The father b Aug 31 1836, on farm he now owns. His father, Michael Miller, of Kent Co, capt of sloop running from landing on farm that Wm now owns, to Balt, carrying grain and produce. In later life he farmed and ran his sloop; d Jan 1837, at c. 58; served as quartermaster in war of 1812. In early days he kept tavern at Rock Hall. His wife, Harriett Legg, b Kt Co; d at 84. She and her 1st husband, Michael Miller, had 4 child., all decd but Wm M., father of Marion. She m(2) Wm Parker; they had dau, Sarah, w/o Thos W. Eades. When Michael Miller d, his son, Wm M., was five months old; he remained on farm with mother until he was 24, when he inherited his father's farm, which he has since managed. He m Miss Mollie Maslin of Kt Co, Jan 17 1861; of their 6 child., 2 d young; others: Jennie, Chas, Marion and Mollie.

242. JAMES BROWN, farmer, 2nd dist QA Co, whose farm is about 4 miles east of 401 Chestertown, where he was b 22 Aug 1838. His father, John Brown, was b same co, as was grandfather, Col Jas Brown, who was in war of 1812. John Brown was a planter of QA Co; rep in legislature one term; m Eliza G. Bonsal; their child. who reached maturity: subj; and Emma, w/o Rev Geo E. Stokes, of Balt Co. The father d 1876, at 84. - Subj, completed education Wash College, Chestertown. He owns 4 farms (c. 600 a.); director Centreville Natl Bank; m Miss Maria S. Page, of Waverly, N. Y.; of their 7 child., still living: Arthur N., res Davenport, Iowa, agent for Northwestern Life Insur Co.; Jas P., mbr Roland Park Co., of Balt; and Helen E. and Ernest B., at home. He and his wife are mbrs Episc Church of Church Hill.

243. WILLIAM H. NEWNAM, retired farmer QA Co b nr Chesterville, Kt Co, Md, May 401 4 1823; first 15 yrs were spent on home farm, then clerked in store owned by an uncle in Easton; about 10 yrs later returned to Kt co, remained about a year and then went to Kt Island; carried on a mercantile store 12 yrs; disposed of stock and purch farm in 2nd dist QA Co which he operated; 1879 moved to present home; m Dec 20 1854 Margaretta Harrison, d/o Col Sml T. Harrison, res QA Co. Of their 6 child. 4 are living: Martha w/o Ira Murphy; Harrson co commissioner from 2nd dist; and Spencer G. bookkeeper Centreville Natl Bank. Subj m(2) Jun 23 1873, Mrs. Annie H. Wright, d/o Levi L. DeFord, of Queen Anne's. He is mbr Episc Church.

244. CHARLES A. BUSTEED, business man Centreville b 31 Oct 1854, at Brick 402 Mill, three miles from Denton. When 9 yrs old he was taken by parents to Phila, where he was educated in public schools; about 17, he came to QA Co; spent 1 year nr Ruthsburg; entered the Observor office, Centreville, belonging

to his bro, W. W. Busteed; continued in printing trade in Phila until 1878; spent few months in St. Cloud and Minneapolis, Minn; returned to Centreville, as his bro offered him an interest in the Observor. Firm was known as W. W. Busteed & Brother until 1885, when former sold out. Subj was editor-in-chief until he sold his interest to Wm J. Price, Jr. Mr. Busteed now owns 4 farms (1234 a.) in QA Co. He m 3 Nov 1881 Miss Molly G., d/o Capt John Wilkinson; child.: 1 d in infancy, other, John Wilkinson, now 11. On the death of his father-in-law, Capt. John Wilkinson, Mar 1889, subj elected to succeed him as direcctor of QA Natl Bank. He is mbr ME Church.

405 245. T. PLINY FISHER, atty Denton, b Kt Co, Del, 2 miles from Sussex line, May 13 1859. His grandfather, Jabez, of same locality and s/o Richard Fisher, early settler on Eastern Shore. Richard, s/o Jabez, has headquarters in Phila, general agent of Pa for Wash Life Insur Co of N.Y. Another son, David W., farmer Sussex Co. Eldest son, Jas H., subject's father, b on home farm Delaware Co, Sep 16 1831; farmer; 1889 retired, now res Denton.

Mother of subj, Sarah Emily Smith, b Car Co; as child went to Del with father, Martin Smith, farmer, one-time tax collector for his dist, mbr MP Church. She had 2 bros: Thos J., once postmaster Harrington, Del, still res there; and Martin Bates, res old homestead in Del. Miss Smith m Jas H. Fisher Apr 21 1858; their child.: T. Pliny; Geo A., res New York; J. Ira, in Phila; and Maude, w/o T. Fred Johnson, purser of steamer Easton, operating Balt-Hillsborough.

1864 when 5, subj met with accident visiting grandfather, Martin Smith. His right hand was crushed in cane mill, as to render amputation necessary; educated in schools of Kt Co, Del, and Farmington Collegiate Institute, Del; taught school 10 yrs; 1885-86 principal of Hillsborough Acad, leisure hours in study of law with Chief Judge Geo M. Russum; Apr 1886 admitted to bar at Denton and began practice. Feb 27 1889, he m Ella, only d/o Wm E. Saulsbury, farmer of Tuckahoe Neck. They have dau, Anna, b Apr 5 1892, named for decd sister of Mrs. Fisher. Mr. Fisher is mbr MP Church.

f
405 246. JOSEPH DOWNEY, mcht Rock Hall, 5th dist, b this village nr site of present store, Jun 13 1852, s/o Wm S. and Ann E. Downey. The former, oysterman, b this co; owned small schooner; the year he d (age 38) he bt farm, intending to give up oyster business; mbr ME Church. He m Maiden Ann E. Scoon, of Kt Co, this dist, who d at 43. Their child.: Mary E., Jos, Wm T., Geo E., John W., Marion and Alice D. - Jos, eldest son of family, remained at home after father's death, to assist mother on farm. 1889 he moved to Chestertown, opened store and cannery, while running store in Rock Hall. As a result of business reverses he sold store and canning factory in Chestertown in 1895 and concentrated on business this place. Nov 1872 he m Miss Mary F. Stevens, of Balt; their child.: Geo Richard, with father in business; Annie M., Clara, Lula, Ida, Rena, Edna, Helen and an infant son; all attend ME Church; he was postmaster of Rock Hall, 1877-c.1889.

406 247. WILLIAM D. SMITH, Meth, farmer 2nd dist QA Co, co commissioner QA Co, magistrate, tax collector; b Kt Co, Apr 17 1837; student in Millington Acad, principally self educated; came to 1st dist QA Co, where he began as farmer; 1863 purch present farm in 2nd dist, where he has since res except year in mercantile pursuits; 16 Oct 1863 m Miss Fanny Walls; their child.: Emma G., Jas H., Fanny, Cora D., Wm C., Hy Earl and Ethel M.

248. GEORGE L. BRYAN, farmer 5th dist QA Co, where his ancestors lived. 407
Before settling down he traveled exetensively in the west.
  Valentine, paternal grandfather of Geo L. Bryan, of Va, came to this region in early manhood; when he d 1848, left estate of 4000 a., part on Wye Island, then known as Bordley's Island, plus 200 slaves. By 1st marriage he had 4 child.: John C., Wm I., Elizabeth and Arthur; later m Miss Ford, who became mother of Chas J., Edw and Alfred. Chas J. b Jan 1816, d Sep 1850; m Lucretia Emory, and their eldest child, subj, b Aug 10 1837; Chas Carroll, b 1839; d 1872, leaving wife and 2 child., Edw K. and Lulu, all of Balt.
  George L. Bryan reared in QA Co; at 26 m 1863, Mary H., d/o John Charles and granddau of Dr. Thos Smyth Willson, from old fam of Kt Co, Md; their child.: Kate B., Mary C., Chas, Elizabeth; Oscar, decd; Geo H., Dnl Carroll; Florence, decd; Jas B., Edna A. and Leon O.

249. SAMUEL CHASE DE KRAFFT, M. D., Episc, physician and surgeon, b Oct 19 408
1848, Wash, D. C., s/o Lieut Sml Chase and Mary Eleanor (de Krafft) Barney. The mother was left an orphan at 5, only child of Edw de Krafft, government printer and noted editor of Washington. While res D. C., at 20, subj had name changed to de Krafft, because of bequest of relative on maternal side.
  Wm Barney, progenitor of fam in America, came to this country with his uncle, when 14; parents prev d.; arrived Balt when city contained 12 houses; m Frances Holland, from Eng. One of their 14 child. was Commodore Joshua Barney, b Balt Jul 6 1759, who at 10 left school to follow the sea, much against wishes of his parents. When 14 he commanded a vessel as captain, and became one of the most prominent officers in the U. S. navy. The Memoirs of Commodore Joshua Barney were published by Gray & Brown, in Boston, in 1832, and edited by Mrs. Mary Barney, subject's grandmother, who was one of 3 daus of Judge Sml Chase, signer of Declaration of Independence, and later assoc justice of supreme court of U. S. The commodore's eldest son, Maj Wm Bedford Barney, was doctor's grandfather. His father, Lieut Sml Chase Barney, naval officer in Mexican and Seminole wars, entered the service at 14, retired 1854 with loss of hearing, contracted while thus engaged. The doctor's mother and Rear-admiral J. C. P. de Krafft, of the U. S. navy, were cousins.
  Dr. de Krafft was 1st in order of birth in fam of 2 sons and 2 daus; others: Hebe Barney, decd w/o Jas Haynes, of New York, by whom she had Hebe and Emily; Edw Barney, lawyer New York city; and Clayonia Barney, w/o Theodore K. Vogel, of Phila.
  Sub edcucated in primary schools of Wash, 1855 taken by parents to Paris, France, where he attended private school until 1861, when 13. Returning to Wash, entered Georgetown College Georgetown, D. C., studied for a year; then attended Peter White's school until 1862; then with family to Cambridge, becoming pupil under Rev Dr. Barber, who was his tutor until 1864; grad Pa Military Acad West Chester, Pa 1867. When about 20 he clerked in drug store in Wash, D. C.; grad Miami Medical College Cincinnati 1874; 1877 returned to Cambridge, where he has since engaged in practice. He m Miss Sarah·A. Parks, of Md, d/o John Parks, of Cincinnati, their child, Mary Lilley.

250. WILLIAM P. JACKSON, business man, of Salisbury, s/o Wm H. Jackson. 411
Subj is stockholder, sec and treasurer, in Jackson Brothers Co, manufacturers of box-shooks in their mills here, Nos. 1 and 2, and finishing, flooring and ceiling lumber, made in mill No. 3. He is vice-pres of Salisbury Natl Bank, vice-pres of Salisbury Shirt Co. and owns interest in lumber companies in the south, with which his father is extensively interested. (See sketch of William H. Jackson.) Subj b Salisbury Jan 1868, and completed his studies in

Conference Acad of Dover, Del. Because of ill health returned home earlier than planned; Feb 12 1890 m Miss Sallie McCombs, of Havre de Grace, Md; their children: Bell McCombs and Wm Newton. They attend ME Church of Salisbury.

412   251. WASHINGTON BEAUCHAMP, Marion Station, Som Co, has conducted general store here 11 yrs; b Princess Anne dist, Feb 1848, s/o Wm W. Beauchamp. His father, carpenter, life-long res that locality. He erected many houses and other buildings in his prime, but subsequently turned to farming. His home was nr Princess Anne, and there he d at 84. He m(1) Miss Adams and had 1 child, now decd. He m(2) Margaret Handy; of their 7 child., 5 survive: Wm T., Washington, Stephen J.; Susan, Mrs. W. T. Davis; and Elizabeth, wid of Sml Broughton. The mother d/o Levin Handy, still living, res with children.
   Subj spent 1st 26 yrs on a farm; then carpentering for 14 yrs; 1886 opened store in Marion Station; m 1882, Miss Mollie E. Horsey, d/o John C. Horsey of this co; they are mbrs Episc Church.

412   252. JOHN H. VAN GESEL, business man Denton, owner of his res and 15 other houses here, which he rents, and also a livery stable and hotel; s/o John and Priscilla (Furby) Van Gesel, of Del., where latter d 1887. The father spent early yrs as stage contractor, running all the stages on line of present railroad; later settled on farm, where he d 1860. Of his fam of 8 child., 4 still living. W. T., educated in Newark College, for a time in railroading, now magistrate in Harrington, Del. Asbury res Harrington, as does Anna M.
   Subj b nr Smyrna, Del, Mar 20 1837, where he spent boyhood; after public school opened store at Clark's Corners (now Harrington), where he was 1st mcht. During the war he made and lost a fortune. After the war he traded his prop in Del for stock of goods in Denton, where he made a new start; 6 yrs later traded store for real estate in Car Co. In 1866 he m Mary M. Macklen, of Georgetown, Del, d/o Chas Macklen, of Sussex Co. Their child, Clara, m Wm H. Anderson, has son, Eugene. Family attend Episc Church.

413   253. CAPT. STEPHEN W. DOLBEY, citizen of Eastern Shore 44-45 yrs, res Tyaskin dist, Wicomico Co. For 10 yrs after his arrival here he was chiefly interested in boating and the oyster business. He was b in Conn., Mar 9 1832, s/o Stephen and Anna (Lyons) Dolbey, also b in Conn., and had 9 children; surviving: Sml, Stephen W., Sarah and Irenous. The father of Stephen Dolbey, Sr., was b Eng, came to America prior to Rev and fought in Rev. His son, father of captain, farmer, in war of 1812. - Subj came to Md 1853; attends ME Church; 12 Feb 1855 m Henrietta Simpkins this dist, of which she is a native; their child.: in order of birth: Sarah C., Betsy Ann, Wm, John, Stephen, Hattie, Lula, Sml and one who d in infancy, unnamed.

413   254. RICHARD BENNETT WILLSON, co commissioner, judge orphans' court, res 5th dist Kt Co, b Dec 10 1817 QA Co same farm where his father was b. Here the father was reared, remaining until 1819, when he came to Kt Co to read medicine with Dr. Anderson, of Chestertown; then attended Jefferson College Phila, Pa; after graduation returned to QA Co, where he practiced with father a while. Here he married, but soon moved to this co, purch the farm that Richard Bennett now owns, which prev belonged to father of his wife. Here he d Oct 1859, at 85; practiced medicine until shortly before he d; once surgeon in state militia; he was Cath.
   Thos Bennett, father of last named and grandfather of Richard B., of QA Co, physician, educated Edinburgh, Scotland; d at old age. His father, Thos; physician, came to America from Scotland in train of Lord Baltimore, c. 1632.

Mother of subj, Maria Smyth, of Kt Co, d/o Thos Kent, of Kt Co, mcht and farmer, who carried on business in Chestertown. Gresham Smyth, maternal great-grandfather of Richard Bennett, was large importer in Chestertown. Mrs. Maria Willson d in middle life; leaving 10 child., all decd except Richard Bennett.

Subj remained at home with parents until c. 17, educated in public schools; clerked in Balt store few months, then clerked Vicksburg, Miss. 3-4 yrs, returned home to assist father in management of farm. When his father d he purch old homestead from heirs, has since res here. Oct 3 1842, Mr. Willson m Miss Ann M. Young, dau of Benjamin Young, of Kent Co, who lived near the head of the Sassafras River on a plantation. In later life he moved to Prince George's Co, where he died at the age of 50. His father, Notley Young, was born in England and came to America with his father, Benjamin, who built a large mansion in Washington, one of the famous houses of its day. He owned at one time the whole southern portion of the District of Columbia, and numbered among his friends, George Washington. Mrs. Willson's mother was, previous to her marriage, Miss Charlotte Manning, of Prince George's Co.

Mrs. Willson b in 1819, Chas Co, Md; her child.: Dr. Thos B., whose sketch appears elsewhere this vol; Wm, who d young; Milford M., farmer res this dist; Horace A., mcht at Eadesville, decd, this dist; Notley O., who assists father on farm; Julia R., w/o Jas C. Ringgold, this dist; Peter C., clerk in treasury depart Wash, D. C.; Paul Alexander, farmer res this dist, and 4 who d young. Mr. and Mrs. Wilson mbrs Cath Church.

255. JAY WILLIAMS, lawyer Salisbury, Wicomico Co, admitted to bar this co Jul 417 1884; b Som Co, 3 1/2 miles west of Salisbury, on farm now in Wicomico Co, Jun 28 1859, s/o Luther M. and Eleanor W. (Wootten) Williams, of Sussex Co, Del who became res this locality c. 1855. The father was a farmer and business man; owned 325 a. in Del. and over 425 a. this state; d at 72 in 1882. The mother d prev, in 53rd year. Of their ten child. 7 grew to maturity: Alonzo L., farmer this co; Caroline, wid of Isaac Connoly, of Delmar, Del; Martha J., w/o Louis A. Pollitt, who owns old home place in Del; Lucy E., w/o Hugh Ellingsworth, of Salisbury; Eliza C., decd, former w/o Thos C. Morris. Jas M. Episc minister, d Burlington, N.J., where rector of Burlington College, and pastor pro tem St. Paul's Episc Church Camden, N. J.; his fam now living at Nyack on the Hudson, N. Y.

Jay Williams grad St. John's College, Annapolis 1880; next enrolled Wesleyan Univ Middletown, Conn., fell ill with scarlet fever; after recovery taught school Bridgeville, Del, Crisfield, Md; Chincoteague, Va, and Port Deposit, Md; admitted to bar Jul 1884, established office in Salisbury; m Jan 30 1890 A. Blanche Catlin, d/o Alexander W. Catlin, of Wicomico Co; their son, Arthur Everett; mbrs Asbury ME Church, Salisbury.

The Williams family have been longer associated with Del than Md, originally from Eng, where many were miners. John Williams, of Cornwall, sailed from London 1736, settled in what is now Sussex Co, Del, d there 1760. He was great-great-grandfather of subj; bt large tract which was handed down, some of it still owned by direct descendants.

256. J. ALFRED GREENWOOD, principal Rock Hall city schools; teacher 32 years; 418 4 yrs in present position; b Feb 10 1846, Fairlee, this co, his father, John Greenwood, farmer, of that place. J. Alfred's father was sheriff of his co 1852-3, co commissioner c. 1854; mbr ME Church; d at 77. Wm, father of John Greenwood, b Southampton, Eng; came to this country c. 1778, settling in New

-67-

York a few yrs; then to Del where he farmed; 1804 purch farm 2nd dist this co, where he d at 84; belonged to Reed's rifle corps, took part in battle of Caulks Field, war of 1812. He m Mary Twiford, grandmother of J. Alfred Greenwood, came from Eng at early age and married here; d 1812. Of her 7 children, 6 d young. After her death her husband m Miss Adkinson, of Car Co, and they left one son, Jas W. Caroline Adkinson, mother of J. Alfred Greenwood, was from Rock Hall, Kent Co; attended ME Church; d at 54, leaving 5 children: John, res 3rd dist, politician; J. Alfred; Jas, farmer res 3rd dist; Hy, farmer 3rd dist; and Martha I., d at about 50.

At 14 subj went to Balt, clerked in general commmission store about 5 yrs; taught school Kt Co; m Jan 11 1872 Miss Mary M. Toulson, of Kt Co, d/o Thos Toulson; their child.: Clarence A., engaged at Tolchester Beach; Laura M. Hope, w/o Jos Kendall and Arthur. Mr. Greenwood was postmaster at Fairlee about 20 yrs, where he kept general store until 1894. Fam mbrs ME Church.

419 257. GEORGE C. INSLEY, Lakevile, Dor Co, s/o Elcanion Insley, farmer of Strait dist, Dor Co; m Miss Mary A. Robinson, who d 1897 at 80, surviving her husband by almost half a century. She m(2) Zebedee Todd, by whom had one son, Noah L. To her 1st marriage were b 2 sons and 2 daus. Rhoda became the w/o Andrew Insley, and Priscilla m James Todd. John H. res old home place.

Subj b Strait dist, Dor Co, 1848, commenced to dredge for oysters along the rivers near by at an early age. When about 18 he purch a sailing vessel. 1877 he bt out Thos J. Stewart, general mcht at Toddville, carried on the store 7 yrs, then opened store, containing general line of supplies, and in 1891 built a 2-story store, now occupied by his store and ware rooms; mbr ME Church; m Melissa F. Robinson, d/o Wdm J. Robinson, of Strait dist, Dor Co.

420 258. GEORGE W. GRIFFIN, farmer Talb Co, res farm (100a.) Trappe dist, owns 3 other farms; b Dor Co, nr Cambridge Feb 27 1833, reared on farm Dor Co, until 1844 when he came to Talb Co with father, Caleb Griffin, and settled in Trappe dist. In early manhood he went aboard bay vessel and for 5 yrs followed the water, returning to Trappe dist and settling on farm. 1878 he purch farm where he has since res. He m in 1865 Harriet E. Boone, of this co; their child.: Chas T., farmer res this dist; Geo N., decd; Franklin, decd; Nanie B., w/o Geo Stephens, this dist; Rbt T., decd; and Geo Linden.

420 259. JOHN L. ROBINS, of Snow Hill dist, Wor Co, farmer. Paternal grandfather, John L. Robins, farmer this co, and Jas B., father of subj, mcht Snow Hill many yrs. Subj b Feb 1 1854 Snow Hill, twin bro of Jas who d in infancy; where his father was in business. The mother was former Elizabeth Hayward, b and reared this co. Subj reared and educated in Snow Hill; when 15 sent to Wash and Lee Univ Lexington, Va. At end of one term he returned home and devoted attention to farming; now owns over 700 a. He m Dec 12 1878, Miss Julia L. Matthews of Snow Hill d/o I. T. Matthews (See sketch of Matthews family in this vol.); their sons: Thos M., grad Snow Hill schools; Jas B., both at home. Mrs. Robins is mbr ME Church of Snow Hill.

423 260. S. ASHTON TULL, postmaster Tulls Corner, Som Co, past 8 yrs; long-time mbr of firm S. L. Tull & Co., who run general store here; also mbr firm of A. E. Tull & Co., oyster planters and packers, and firm of Tull, Miles & Co., mchts and oyster packers. They own several boats and oyster vessels. - Subj b Tulls Corner, Feb 6 1856, s/o Sml L. Tull, whose sketch is elsewhere this vol. Subj m Jan 1894 Miss Sarah Mather, d/o Rev A. W. Mather, mbr Md annual conference; their child.: Margaret and Sml W. mbrs MP Church.

261. WILLIAM F. DASHIELL, Dames Quarter, located here many yrs ago; 423
conducting general store here for past 30 yrs, retired since his son took
over; mbr ME Church. His father, Wm Dashiell b soon after close of the Rev
war, in Wicomico Co; lumberman most of his life, and delt chiefly in ordinary
squared timber; d 1865 at 77; s/o Jas Dashiell, of Wicomico Co, farmer of
English extraction. Mother of subj was Margaret White; d at 65. Of her 11
child. 3 survive: Maria, wid of Wm Simkins; Peter twin brother of W. F., res
Mt. Vernon, Md. - Subj b 1833; lived at his birthplace in Wicomico Co until
about 17, came to Dames Quarter, learned carpenter's trade. He worked as
carpenter 4 yrs; turned to oyster trade; 1860 m Miss Annie White, d/o Major
White; their child.: S. Frank, carries on the store; Ida May, w/o Ernest
Kelley; and Bessie, at home. 1867 he opened his store, town having been estab
by wife's father, Major White.

262. FLOYD C. RAMSDELL, former senior editor of American Union, Denton, only 424
living mbr of large fam; b Chautauqua Co, N. Y., 1836; learned printer's trade
in office of older bro, C. P. Ramsdell. After working as journeyman printer
in Meadville, Pa, he with brother-in-law of his wife bt American Citizen plant
of his older brother. 1869 Mr. Ramsdell moved to Wyoming, Del; 1879 came to
Eastern Shore of Md., where he has since res. He and oldest son, Harry E.
Ramsdell, leased from John H. Emerson, his newspaper plant, The American
Union, of Denton, and published the paper. Mr. Ramsdell was postmaster of
Denton 4 yrs. He is 2nd of 3 bros, all in newspaper work.
   Charles P., oldest bro, with several newspapers as editor and proprietor,
one at Franklin, Pa, another at Oil City, Pa. After moving to Va he served as
mbr of house of delegates from Surry Co, later U. S. marshal for Norfolk,
Petersburg and Richmond dist, until his death.
   Hiram J. Ramsdell, younger bro of subj, was newspaper man. While young he
enlisted in Pa regt, wounded at battle of Antietam, recovered at Army Square
hospital Wash; then to St. Domingo as correspondent for New York Tribune and
with Grant commission in U. S. war vessel Tennessee; correspondent for New
York Tribune, Phila Press, Phila Times and Cincinnati Commercial; intimate
friend of Jas G. Blaine; rgtr of wills for D. C.; the appointment signed by
Pres Garfield shortly before assassinated.
   Besides the 3 bros engaged in journalistic work, the eldest son of F. C.
and two sons of C. P. Ramsdell are employed on staff of two Chicago's papers.
Harry E., managing editor of The American Union b Venango Co, Pa, Apr 1 1862
began learning the trade in Denton Journal office.
   Subj severed his connection with paper fall of 1897 and now devotes his
attention to farming and fruit growing at his home, 3 miles west of Denton.

263. FRANCIS S. LOOCKERMAN, farmer Fairmount dist, Som Co, res Som Co about 425
30 yrs. The tract of 20 a. which he owns descended to him from his mother's
side of the house, belonging to an original grant of the 17th century.
Founders of Loockerman fam, of Dutch origin, among early settlers of Del, from
whence they came into Md. Stanley B. Loockerman, grandfather of subj, was b
Dor Co. Washington C., father of subj, b Cambridge; arriving at maturity went
to Balt co; there m Miss Mary, d/o Dr. Francis Waters, minister in MP Church.
- Subj b Balt Co 1843. About 3 decades ago he came to Som Co and took charge
of farm which he still operates. 1870 he m Miss Annie Ballard, d/o Dr. R. R.
Ballard, of Fairmount dist. She, also descends from Waters family; their
child.: Sallie W. and Washington C.

426 264. WILLIAM NICHOLS EARLE WICKES b nr Fairlee, Kt Co, Jun 2 1823, 4th child of Capt Simon and Elizabeth (Blake) Wickes, who res on farm called Tulip Forest. He was educated common schools and course of study in Wash College. During this period the college buildings were destroyed by fire and the students met in a building that stood on site now occupied by res of Capt Wm D. Burchinal. Spring of 1839 Mr. Wickes went to Balt and employed by Marcus Dennison, mcht, until spring of 1845; returned to Kt Co 1845, opened store at present stand with older bro, late Siomon Wickes, under firm of Wickes & Bro. Spring of 1848 his bro withdrew and he continued alone from then until Aug 1856, when firm of Wickes & Bro. was re-established by admission of bro, Thos Stockton Wickes, as junior partner. 1866 subject withdrew, leaving business to bro, returning to firm 1878, and thereafter remained a mbr until his death. - Jun 2 1857 subj m Anne Elizabeth Wethered, d/o Peregrine and Louisa Maria (Wickes) Wethered; their children: Anne R., Lewin W.; Wm Nichols Earle, Jr, d summer of 1863; and Louisa, d 1864, at 4. Mr. Wickes d suddenly, of apoplexy, Sep 21 1895, buried St. Paul's Church.

429 265. ROBERT H. MILBOURNE, res Brinkley's dist, Som Co, estab general store in Kingston before railraod was built through town. For few yrs his son, Lewis M., managed the store, he being mbr of firm known today as R. H. Milbourne & Son; also station agent at Kingston c. 9 yrs.
Rbt H. Milbourne s/o Wm and Mary (Peyton) Milbourne, of Som Co. Father reared to maturity in Dublin dist and there farmer and dealer in lumber (mostly square lumber); d 1868, in 62nd yr. His father, Nathan, of Dublin dist, farmer; in war of 1812;; d 76th yr. Milbourne fam of Eng descent; Md branch founded by one of 2 bros. Wm and Mary Milbourne mbrs ME Church; she d at 78. Of 8 living children of Wm and Mary Milbourne subj is the eldest; others: Sml J., res Pocomoke City; Sarah, wid of Jos Stephenson; Nathan, of Crisfield; Mary, wid of Lycurgus Stephenson; Sidney F., res Crisfield; and Margaret, w/o John C. Mills, of Pocomoke City. Rbt H. b Dublin dist Apr 6 1831; 1854 opened general store Princess Anne, which he ran for 12 yrs. 1866 he located in Kingston, estab new store, and since then has carried a line of household supplies, clothing, etc. His estate (450 a.), divided into 4 farms, all in vincinity of Kingston postoffice.
Apr 1 1861 subj m Mary Wilkins, who d, leaving 1 child, Mary E., w/o John E. Gorsuch, of Balt Co. Feb 8 1865 Mr. Milbourne m Louisa, d/o Sml S. and Eleanor (Ballard) Miles; their child.: Addie, at home, and Lewis, who runs store, also in planting and dealing of oysters, mbr PE Church as are his parents.

430 266. ROBERT A. DODSON, M. D. b Balt, Jun 27 1836. (For fam record see sketch of bro, Hon., Hy Clay Dodson.) When about 2 he was brought by his parents to St. Michael's; educated public schools and under private tutor, Dr. Spencer, former profesor in Dixon College. At 19 he began to teach school, which he continued 4 yrs, while studying medicine during vacation periods; grad medical depart Univ Md 1859; returned to St. Michael's, where he remained until outbreak of late war.
Spring 1862 subj enlisted as surgeon 1st Md Cav of Union army, remained in service until Aug 1865. After war he opened an office in Balt Co; then moved to Chestertown, and res nr that place 6 yrs, in practice. On death of wife he came to St. Michael's and since then in practice this place. Jun 1865, Dr. Dodson m Miss Lucy J. Skinner, of QA Co, who d 1875, leaving child.; Rowena, w/o Prof. Chas H. Grace, of McDonogh Institute, Balt Co; and Rbt S., student

law depart Univ of Md. The doctor m(2) Miss Mary Adelaide Skinner, sis of former wife. They had daus, Lucy and Helen. Fam attend ME Church.

267. CHARLES W. CLAYVILLE, ex-sheriff of Wor Co, 2 yrs; farmer Snow Hill 430 dist, Wor Co; b Jun 31 1827, s/o Eli and Mary Clayville, of Eastern Shore and owners of extensive farm. Their other children: Emeline, Esther and Priscilla. Chas W. reared same farm which he now owns and cultivates; attended local school and later grad Snow Hill Acad; clerked in general store Salisbury 1 1/2 yrs; since then farming. - 5 Dec 1878 Mr. Clayville m Emma Smith, d/o John W. and Charlotte (Whitington) Smith, and granddau of Judge Whitington, of Del; no children; mbrs PE Church.

268. GEORGE W. MEZZICK, 2nd dist Wicomico Co, purch present res 1892; twice 431 commissioner Wicomico Co. The Mezzick family in Md many generations. Father of subj, Nelson Mezzick, of Quantico dist, Wicomico Co, in early days was ship carpenter; then farming; mbr ME Church; m Miss Susan Taylor, d/o Geo Taylor, of Rockawalking, Wicomico Co. She d, leaving 6 child., 2 living: Geo W. and Elijah T., this vicinity. Nelson Mezzick m(2) Miss Margaret Phillips; had 2 child. Fol her death, Mr. Mezzick m Margaret Venable, who has also d.

George W. Mezzick b on farm nr Quantico, Dec 2 1841; when about 14 he began farming in earnest; cultivated Farrington farm and others this dist c. 30 yrs, moving from Waters to present homestead in 1892. Nov 21 1865 he m Amelia Anderson d/o Jas Anderson, of this area. They had Herbert and Geo Marion, both young farmers this dist. Subj and wife mbrs Episc Church.

269. WILLIAM H. H. HOPKINS owns home and farm on Coxes Neck, Kt Island, 4th 432 dist QA Co; helped organize MP Church of Kt Island (dedicated in 60's); b on this island 1841; res here all his life s/o Edw and Annie (Cockey) Hopkins, the mother d/o John C. Cockey. Edw Hopkins b Kt Island c. 1804, farmer, this community. His father, Jas, settled in these parts after his move from Talb Co, where b and grown to man's estate. The Hopkins family early settlers of Md, originally from Eng. A bro of subj, Jas B., res Kt Island.

1868 W. H. H. Hopkins m Elizabeth Atwell, of this co, d/o Jos Atwell; of their 10 children, 7 d in infancy; living: E. Atwell, m and in business in New York City; Clara and Harrison. Mr. and Mrs. Hopkins are mbrs MP Church.

270. THOMAS HICKS MEDFORD cashier Dor Natl Bank, b May 28 1845, s/o Edwin E. 432 and Hersilla (Hicks) Medford. His father was mcht of East New Market at his death, 1853. They had 3 child.: Mary A., eldest, w/o Frs H. Webb, chief judge orphans' court Dor Co, now decd; Seldon P., mbr regt commanded by Col. Jas Wallace, d in camp Salisbury, 1862; and subj.

Thos Hicks Medford, upon his parents' death went to live with his uncle and namesake, ex-gov Thos H. Hicks. The gov was living on farm south of Cambridge. Subj attended acad Cambridge; enrolled St. John's College, Annapolis 2 yrs; worked as tobacconist in Balt a year; when war broke out he returned to Cambridge; clerked in general store until 1873, when he went into business for himself, purch store of late employer, Josias S. Simmons; postmaster 4 yrs; 1889 elected cashier of Dor Natl Bank. He m May 14 1873 m Miss Mary Hutchin, of Burlington, N. J. Their son, Wm H., assist bookkeeper Dor Natl Bank. They are mbrs ME Church.

271. MONMONIER ROWE, M. D., Deal's Island, descendant of Scotch fam that res 435 in Md. for generations. Paternal great-grandfather of Aberdeen, whence he

emigrated to Som Co and settled on Deal's Island, afterward farmed, served in Rev war. The grandfather, Sml Rowe, b here, farmer; d at c. 50.

Subject's father, Hon. Geo T. Rowe, spent life on Deal's Island. After following the water for a time in early yrs he turned to merchandising and carried on general store; 1867-68 co commissioner; app justice of peace by gov; elected to house of delegtes in 1877 and in 1887; d Feb 22 1891, at 60. He m Sarah E. Wallace, who d at 38, had 4 child, one now living, our subj.

Dr. Rowe b Deal's Island 1859, educated in public schools and Glenwood Institute, Howard Co; grad College of Physicians and Surgeons Balt 1881; returned to old home place; has since followed his profession. 1877 he received, through influence of Dnl M. Henry, M. C., appointment to West Point, but afterward resigned, preferring medical profession. He m Emma, d/o Geo R. and Adeline Hickman; their child.: Elizabeth Adeline and Georgia.

436   272.   GEORGE HAYWARD b and res old homestead, Snow Hill dist, Wor Co. He owns a large estate (c. 600 a.); b Feb 15 1830, s/o John E. and Margaret (Duer) Hayward, of this area. Of their 5 child. 3 decd; Geo and John E. remain. Latter is a farmer, owning the old estate in Som Co. Grandfather John Hayward of Eastern Shore, farmer. Subject's father was owner of over 100 slaves, and c. 3000 a.; commissioner this co; died in 74th yr.

Subj spent boyhood on father's farm; grad Jefferson College, Wash, Pa, 1850; read medicine a year; Oct 13 1863 m Miss Annie, d/o Rev Hy Crosdale. She was b N. Y. State; d Feb 1882, at 45. She and husband attended Episc Church; their child.: Geo, Hy C., Thos M., Wm W., Millard P., Barton L., John C., Emily F. and Annie M.

436   273.   JOHN H. SIMPERS, business man, Chestertown. Simpers is old Eastern Shore fam. John B. Simpers, grandfather of subj, of Cecil Co, farmer. He had 2 sons who attained maturity: Thos W., mbr Phila ME conference; and Hy G., father of subj. The last named b nr North East 1820, in mercantile business; also taught school; later became minister of ME Church; d 1872. He m Mary Jane Sherman; she was b Salisbury, Md, d North East at 33, leaving child.: John H.; E. W. F., business man Chestertown; Milton S., res Wilm, Del; Emma B. and Fannie W., both res Chestertown.

Subj b North East, Cecil Co, Apr 1 1849; at 17 came to Chestertown, where he clerked in store 7 yrs, and has since carried on business for himself at same stand 24 yrs; m 1873 Mary A. H. Vannort, d/o late Wm Vannort; their sons: Hy G., student College of Physicians and Surgeons Balt; Frank V., J. Raymond and Earle D. Subj attends MP Church.

437   274.   JONATHAN W. KERR. From boyhood Mr. Kerr has been interested in horticulture and it has been his chosen occupation. Apr 4 1867 he arrived in Denton, nr which place he has since res; at once embarked in nursery business; now owns over 400 a. in 3rd dist Car Co, of which 165 a. are devoted to orchard and nursery stock; making specialty of the plum. He was b York Co, Pa, Jan 23 1842, s/o Wm and Elizabeth (Gates) Kerr, of that co. He and his sisters, Sarah A. and Eliza J., only survivors of the fam of 11 children. Their grandfather, Wm Kerr, b Scotland, whence he came to America druing Rev period and settled in York Co, farmer.

Fol public school education in York Co subj taught 6 winter seasons the intervening summer months devoted to nursery business; then came to Car Co. Dec 14 1870 he m Amanda C. Sisk, d/o Wm and Lucetta Sisk, who res farm in Car Co. Of their 3 child. 2 living: Jessie V. and Sophia G. The older dau is grad Woman's College Balt, talented musician. The younger dau will grad in spring 1898 from Woman's College of Frederick. Mr. Kerr is identified with Reformed Church, while his wife is connected with ME denomination.

275. HON. PHILLIPS LEE GOLDSBOROUGH, editor, atty and politician, b Princess 438 Anne, Som Co, Aug 6 1865, 2nd of 4 living sons of Worthington and Henrietta Maria (Jones) Goldsborough, grandson of late Judge Brice Goldsborough, of court of appeals of Md, and of Hon. Sml Jones, rgtr of wills Som Co. His youth was passed principally in Dor Co and at Annapolis, Md; attended public schools of Cambridge and briefly at Episc high school of Va, nr Alexandria, when 15; then private schools in Balt.
    Before attaining majority he began study of law with late Hon. Dnl M. Henry, Jr., of Cambridge; at 21 admitted to bar of Md, and later to court of appeals of Md; then to San Francisco to act as chief clerk to his father, Worthington Goldsborough, of U. S. navy. Returning to Cambridge spring of 1890, he entered practice; elected state's atty of Dor 1891; attends Episc Church. He m 1893, Miss Ellen Showell, of Wor Co, d/o late Wm Showell. Their son, Phillips Lee, Jr.

276. JAMES L. BENNETT in the sale of general merchandise and to some extent 441 the oyster business and farming, Rock Creek, Tangier dist. The Bennett family of English descent, among early settlers of Wicomico Co. Subject's grandfather, Jas Bennett born that co, farmer; he d at 32. Father of subj, Ebenezer T. Bennett, b and reared Barren Creek dist, Wicomico Co, where he is a farmer and land owner, also in milling business; constable and deputy tax collector. The homestead where he still res is 12 miles from Salisbury and here subj b Oct 16 1849; 2nd of 7 children, others: Sophronia E., wid of Levin H. Bennett; Ebenezer T., Jr, Thos W., Gillis E., Isaac S. and Louis A. Mother of this fam was Sallie E. Taylor, d/o Levi Taylor; she is still living and mbr MP Church. - At 21 subj came to Som Co and has since res Tangier dist, postoffice address: Chance; m Miss Alice, d/o Thos Tigner, of this place; their child.: L. Atwood, atty, res Salisbury; S. Edith, w/o W. C. Todd; Bertha E. and Harley D. He attends ME Church.

277. WILLIAM A. VANE, Church Creek, Dor Co, MP, postmaster this place, cenus 441 enumerator 1880 & 1890, co commissioner and judge of orphans' court.
    Joseph T. Vane, father of subj, is 80; b nr Linkwood, Dor Co, spent c. 35 yrs there; came to Church Creek, ran wheelwright's shop c. 4 yrs, then in milling business for short time; finally located on farm where he res. His father, Allen Vane, of Linkwood, an extensive landowner and slave holder in early part of century; d about 50. His ancestor from Eng, settled nr Linkwood, and there many generations have flourished. Jos Vane was m(1) Henrietta Brinsfield, who d, leaving child.: Wm A.; Alexander, decd; and Jos H., of Golden Hill. He m(2) Mrs. Hurley; no children. After her death Jos Vane m Annie Vincent, who is still living; of their 11 child., 2 decd.
    Wm A. Vane b this co, on paternal homestead nr Linkwood, Sep 24 1839; remained at home until 18, when he began farming; 3 yrs later taught vocal music about a year; 1861-3 clerked for Thos D. Esgate; after operating general store at Church Creek 5 yrs he was burned out; since then in ship carpentering. 1862 Mr. Vane m Sarah P., d/o Capt Jas Fooks, of Dor Co; their child.: Allen P., sailor; Jas G., mcht this place; Wm B., invested in ship sailing on bay; and Floyd B., sailor, res and headquarters Church Creek. Mrs. Vane mbr ME Church.

442 278. WILLIAM W. WILLIAMSON 4th dist Car Co, of direct Welsh descent; his ancestors settled on Eastern Shore of Md many yrs ago; he was b Car Co, nr Concord, 1821, s/o Ennalls and Sarah (Fisher) Williamson, of Del, who d in early life, when subj was child. His grandfather, Elijah Williamson, of Del.
W. W. Williamson spent youth nr Preston, Car Co. He tills several hundred a.; owns mill Dor Co, carried on by son, Wm Fletcher; 1864 m Mary, d/o John H. Fletcher. Their eldest dau, Carrie, m W. T. Hassinger, and d leaving a child, Wm F. res Cabin Creek, Dor Co. Edgar is a teacher in Del. May, the youngest, is w/o Kirby Wrightson. Edgar educated in Preston Acad and Wash College. Family are mbrs ME Church.

443 279. PROF. JAMES SWANN, insur business and sec of Home Life Insur Co of Car Co; b on farm nr Ridgely, Car Co, 4 Jul 1848, s/o Jas and Mary (Chaffinch) Swann, of this co. His father b 1809 at old homestead, where he farmed; elected to local offices; d 1865 on same farm; b at old homestead, covering present site of Ridgely, land has been in possession of fam over 200 yrs.
Mother of subj d 1869, had 3 sons and 3 daus. Sarah Elizabeth d, unmarried, 1895; Wm Thos, farmer, res nr Ruthsburg, QA Co; Mary w/o Jas D. Wilson, miller and farmer in Car Co; Jas 4th in order of birth; Gilbert, farmer, res old homestead; and Henrietta d at 15.
After public school subj attended Fulton Seminary, Fulton, Del 4 yrs. At 18 he began to teach, earning means to continue education. After finishing his seminary education he taught in same institution for 2 yrs, later instructed 2 yrs, and later instructed in public schools in Car Co, also for 2 yrs a teacher in Wilm Conference Acad of Dover, Del. 1882 he became examiner, secretary and treasurer of schools of Car Co; then entered insur business. He is identified with ME Church.

444 280. JACOB WESLEY WEBSTER, res Deal's Island, retired; has passed life in Som Co, and for 35 yrs in oyster trade; 1887 app captain of a police boat, to enforce laws related to oystering; b 1833, s/o Wm J. and Mary Webster, of Deal's Island. The father lived to be over 80, the mother d at 78; mbrs ME Church. Of their 6 child. subj is eldest; others: Wm J.; Julia A., Mrs. L. L. Shores; Melissa J., w/o Hampton B. Walter; Isabel, w/o Lazarus Wilson; and Zachary W., see his sketch elsewhere this vol.
During war subj charged of being a rebel and confined in prison at Salisbury a while. He m Drusilla, d/o Jabez and Elizabeth Webster. Of their 9 living children, five older ones are sons: Benj F., Wm W., Thos J., David O. and Andrew J. Benj F. m Mary J. Horner. Melissa, eldest dau, is w/o Thos Horner. Mary E., next, is w/o David White. Catherine C. is w/o Thos Anderson. Virginia C., youngest of fam and at home. Fam attend ME Church.

444 281. JOSEPH F. SISK, in mercantile business Cordova, Talb Co, since 1882, once postmaster of the place; at first in partnership with bro, bt the latter's interest and has since conducted business alone. He was b nr Cambridge, Dor Co, Mar 3 1856, s/o Wm and Lucetta (Dean) Sisk. His father, farmer, magistrate for many yrs and assessor of his dist. From Car he moved to Dor Co in early life; where he d Mar 1887; mbr ME Church. His wife is still living at 70; their child.: Amanda, w/o J. W. Kerr, of Denton; Lizzie E.; Jos F.; Thos J. (twin borther of subj); and Alfert W., of Preston.
Subj attended high school in Preston; then taught 9 yrs in Ohio and Ill; fall 1882 he came to Md, settling in Cordova, where with twin bro he bt business of R. R. Shull. He is mbr ME Church; Jun 1 1883 m Emma Gilbert Dixon, d/o Col Geo Dixon, of Preston, who d Aug 6 1895. Of their 7 child. 5

-74-

are living: Wm, Pauline, Grace, Herman and Gilbert. Oct 20 1897 Mr. Sisk m Miss Minnie Grace Fleckenstein, d/o L. N. Fleckenstein, farmer nr Easton.

282. JESSE A. WRIGHT, business man. In 1882 he came to what is now Choptank 447 and has remained here; b nr Federalsburg, Car Co, 1856, s/o John P. and Anne (Kimmey) Wright, respectively of Dor and Car Counties, and for many yrs past res of Choptank. Paternal grandfather, Jesse Wright, s/o Constant Wright, of Eng and emigrant to Md. Subj was eldest of fam; others: Wm J., of Choptank; Walter M., res Talb Co; Oliver R., res Hurlock; Maggie A., Martin M., of Easton; and Nettie V., w/o M. M. Willey, of Choptank.
   1877 Jesse A. Wright m Miss Dora, d/o Peter Carroll; their child.: Emilene, Clarence E., Ira W., Minnie E., Dora, Alcade, Riley W. and Roland. 1882 Mr. Wright came to Choptank and built hominy factory, which he operated each winter until 1895; 1883 he added manufacture of fertilizer, which he carried on until 1887; built a factory for canning fruit, a shirt factory and a store building. Jun 1894 Mr. Wright met with a serious accident, occasioned by a boiler explosion in his shirt factory. He was so badly scalded that for 21 days he lay unconscious, and though he finally recovered, because of a crushing fracture of the limb he was left a cripple for life. This did not interfere, however, with his continued manangement of his various enterprises. He and his family mbrs ME Church.

283. CAPT. WILLIAM K. LEATHERBURY, Whitehaven, Wicomico Co, in oyster packing 448 business; owns a hotel; b 11 Dec 1858, eldest of 8 child. One is decd, others: Chas, John, Rbt L., Harry B., Hettie and Jas L. The parents were Capt James and Matilda (Wingate) Leatherbury, both of Eastern Shore. Grandfather Leaven Leatherbury b this part of Md, farmer. His father, Maj Rbt, from Eng served in Rev; settled nr town of Whitehaven, this co.
   Wm K. Leatherbury reared with his father to sea-faring life and followed the water until his 19th yr; then became captain of his own vessel and sailed on bay and ocean until 29th year; since then involved in packing and shipping oysters. Dec 7 1882 he m Lillian N. Toadvine who was b and grew to womanhood this vicinity. Their child.: Mazie, eldest, decd; Wm K., youngest, decd; Lettie and Nellie. Mr. and Mrs. Leatherbury attend ME Church.

284. HARRY A. ROE, business man Denton, b Minn., Aug 18 1857, s/o Hon. A. B. 448 and Catherine (Skirven) Roe, both of Md. His father, in building business, then with fruit industry, and for 25 yrs in canning business; 1881 elected to state senate. During the war he served as jusice of peace; for a short time he res in Minn; d on 28 Oct 1897. His wife d 1885; they had 2 sons and 2 daus. Fdk is superintendent of late father's canning factory; Blanche w/o R. W. Richards, of Greensborough; and Catherine R. m Dr. J. G. Emerson, dentist of Sao Paulo, Brazil. - Subj entered builder's trade at 19; 1887 turned to canning business. He is in partnership with J. H. Nichols, in shirt factory. He is mbr ME Church; 1878 m Sallie S., d/o Sml M. Carter, farmer res nr Denton. Their dau, Helen, age 5.

285. HARRY L. BREWINGTON, senior mbr firm of Brewington Bros, proprietors and 449 publishers of Wicomico news, a weekly printed in Salisbury. He and his bro undertook management of paper 9 yrs ago. Circulation: 1600-1700 weekly.
   Subj s/o Hy and Orinthia A. (Long) Brewington, of Wor Co, where they m. Father was dealer and manufacturer of hats Salisbury, in business until about a year before he d, 1892, at 74; once crier of the court at Wicomico Co. His wife d 1868. Of their 12 child., fol survive: Wm, Virginia, Harry L., Marion

V. and Allen. - Subj b Mar 17 1858; student of public and high schools of Salisbury; worked in office of Salisbury Advertiser as printer's "devil," worked a year in New York City for Pa Railway Co, returning to Advertiser, where he stayed until 1886. With other mbrs of fam he moved to N.Y. and obtained a position with Erie Railroad Co; formed partnership with bro, Marion V., Oct 1888, and bt Wicomico News, of this town; Feb 1881 m Julia A. Johnson, d/o Joshua Johnson, now of Jersey City, N. J., former mbr of state legislature, from Wicomico Co. Subj and wife have 2 child.: Walter J. pupil in grammar school, and Mary. The family attend Meth Church South.

450 286. HON. JOHN O. PHILLIPS, 4th dist QA Co, b and has always lived on Kt Island. The Phillips were early settlers of Md; subject's grandfather, Rbt, and father, Jas, from Talb Co. In early manhood Jas Phillips came to Kt Island and here continued as a mechanic. He m Margaret, d/o Wm Harrison; their child.: Wm H., of Dor Co; Harriet E., w/o Chas S. Day, of Balt; Sarah E., Mrs. Albert Cowman, of this island; Annie, Mrs. Wm Graves, of St. Mary's Co, decd, and John O. - Subj b 1840; teacher for nearly quarter of century on this island; 1868 m Laura Champion; their child.: Jas H., d when 17; Claiborne, student Westminister College, preparing for ministry; and Owen, youngest, at home. After his wife d Mr. Phillips m Mrs. Juliet M. Tucker, wid of Chas Tucker, and d/o late Jas Denney, of Kt Island; they have dau, Arianna Denney. 1870 Mr. Phillips was commissioned magistrate of Kt Island; 1894 served in Md house of delegates. He and his children attend MP Church.

453 287. JOSEPH B. ANDREWS, co commissioner Dor from 1891-1893, of Hurlock, b nr this village; 1894 erected his res here. He was b Apr 11 1850, s/o Stephen Andrews, whose history appears in sketch of James M. Andrews, elsewhere this vol. The mother was Rebecca, d/o Jas Carroll and sis of C. Wesley Carroll. In this co subj grew to manhood; taught school one term. Prev to marriage in 1881 he located on farm nr Cabin Creek postoffice, and remained thereon a few yrs. In addition to that farm, he owns about 700 a. within the co. About 1891 he erected a cannery for tomatoes, peas, pumpkins and peaches. Mar 1 1881 he m Mary, d/o John W. B. Todd; their child.: S. Elwwod, Grace M., A. May, Edith Estelle, Olin Ray, Elizabeth Rebecca and Mary Todd. Apr 1896, Mrs. Andrews d, mbr ME Church, as is Mr. Andrews.

453 288. JAMES A. WALLER, farmer Barren Creek dist, Wicomico Co. Three bros came from England, in colonial days, one locating in Va, one in Md and one in Del. Of descendants was Richard Waller, great-grandfather of subj, and his son, Jonathan, next in line, capt of militia company and farmer.
Geo Waller, father of subj, b Sussex Co, Del., as was his father. He d Mar 6 1896, on old homestead known as Poplar Hill, in Salisbury. He moved from Del c. 1842; commissioner of Wicomico Co in 1878; m Miss Julia Ann Waller, 2nd cousin; had fam of 8 child.; 1 d in infancy, others: Martha I., unmarried; Jonathan, of Salisbury; Adeline, w/o Chas E. Williams, nr Salisbury; Jas A.; Geo W. B., of Salisbury; Richard Lee, of Salisbury; and Julia D., w/o T. R. Jones, of Quantico, this co. The mother d fall of 1895. Geo Waller and wife were mbrs Episc Church.
Jas A. Waller b nr Delmar, Del, in Md, this co, Feb 8 1857; student Salisbury High School; bt John Crockett farm (256 a.); attends Episc Church; Jun 30 1885 m Margaret C., d/o John and Catherine Williams; child.: 1 d in infancy; surviving: Myra, Jas A., Jr., Margaret C. and Geo W.

289. CHARLES R. WALLS, judge of orphans' court since 1895, res farm 6th dist 454
QA Co, where b Mar 30 1860. Same farm purch by grandfather, Sml Walls, in
1831, known as "Tilghman's Chance" (200 a.). Later owned by Sml C. Walls,
father of subj, and now prop of his widow. The Walls fam came originally from
Scotland. The father, farmer, b on homestead; was mbr ME Church South. He d
1886, buried old family burying ground on farm. He m Mary C. Rigby, still
living QA Co 60. They had 8 child., surviving: Chas R., Florence, Fanny and
Estelle. - Judge Walls educated dist school until 18; rented farm, but
shortly after father's death assumed management of homestead. He m Nov 16
1881, Miss Elizabeth Barcus, d/o Wm Barcus, of QA Co; their child.: Chas
Oscar, Sml C., Mary E., Wm L., Mildred, Edna, Ruth, Frank and Edgar.

290. GEORGE C. MOORE res 4th dist, farmed on homestead 4th dist called 455
Moorley for 20 yrs, also deals in lime, coal, phosphate fertilizer; operates
mill nr by; school commissioner for Talb Co 4 yrs.
    Moore fam is one of oldest of Del. Luther Moore, grandfather of subj, b
Laurel, Del, in same town as Geo H., the latter's father, was b. Geo H.
retired 1885; ship-builder and mcht at Greensborough, Md, accumluated large
estate; owns several farms besides 300 a.-homestead occupied by son Geo C.;
1860-1866 rgtr of wills, later judge orphans' court of his co; mbr ME Church.
He is 71; m Annie M., d/o Capt. John Allen, of Greensborough; she is in 69th
yr. Their children : Geo C., John Allen and F. Howard. John A. is res Balt.
    Geo C. Moore b Greensborough Jan 15 1856 and after common school education
went to Wilm Conference Acad. When about 21 he took charge of farm he has
since operated, Moorley. He is mbr ME Church; Oct 17 1878 m Miss Mary A.
Brindle, d/o Rev Jas A. Brindle, of Wilmington ME Conference. Of their 8
child. 4 decd; living: Ethel B., student in Northfield (Mass.) Seminary; Harry
A., Jas A. and Geo C., Jr.

291. JAMES S. BRADLEY, owner of store on High st, Chestertown; carries staple 456
and fancy groceries. The Bradleys are an old fam of Del, connected by
marriage with Dyatts and Moores. Grandfather of subj, Thos C. Bradley, b
Newark, Newcastle Co, Del, 1801; farmer; identified with Bapt Church.
John F. Bradley, subject's father, b Newark, Del, farmer; d Jan 1893; m
Elizabeth Jane Moore (b Newcastle, Del, 1829, d 1861). She was d/o Jesse and
Eliza (Wiley) Moore, of Newcastle; her father was wheelwright. Her grand-
father, John Wiley, clerk of courts of Newcastle; he and his bro served in
Rev. His son, Rev John Wiley, rector Episc Church Cockeysville. He d Balt; a
dau, Olivia, m John Cannon, in U. S. navy. Two bros of John F. Bradley served
in Del regt during Civil war, one of whom, Wm, now res Newark, and other,
Taylor, Middletown, Del. Subject's mother had one bro, John W. Moore, farmer,
res Wilm; her child: subj; Thos, b 1858, res farm at Still Pond, Kent co;
Elyda w/o Andrew J. Calley, manufactures clothing, res Phila.
    Subj b Sep 1 1851 nr St. Georges, Newcastle Co, Del; at 15 came to Kt Co,
and entered the store of his uncle, James M. Van Dyke, who had m his mother's
sister, Olivia. After a year he came to Chestertown; 10 yrs later, he
embarked in business for himself; since Apr 1877 has carried on store of his
own; mbr Episc Church; Dec 10 1878 m Miss Josepha Davis, d/o Jas Davis, of QA
Co, decd. She d Sep 13 1880, leaving only son, Jos Arthur, now student Wash
College. Mr. Bradley m(2) Mrs. Kate Gill. June 5 1894 he m Miss Anna T.
Gill, sister-in-law of former wife and d/o Benj and Mary B. Gill, of Del.

292. JOSEPH H. BERNARD, farmer and business man, Car Co. When a youth he 459
followed carpenter's trade, assisted in erection of many buildings in this

locality; at 30 turned to farming; now owns nearly 800 a. nr Greensborough; has large canning establishment. He was b Car Co, Aug 31 1838, s/o Jos M. and Mary (Cannon) Bernard. His father, b this co, mechanic, long-time magistrate of Greensborough. Subj grew up on home place; Oct 1871 m Miss Josephine Jarrell; their child.: Mary, J. Oscar and Fanny E. In fam of which hs is mbr are three others: Mary E., wid of Wm Brindle; Catherine M.; and Rebecca, w/o late Andrew B. Roe. Mr. Bernard is of French descent; his paternal grandfather emigrated from France to Balt, where he spent remaining yrs and reared his family. Subj planned and superintendended construction of court house at Denton. He and wife are mbrs ME Church.

459 293. HON. DEMETRIUS W. NEWBURY, mcht and farmer, Woolford, Dor Co; sent to state legislature 1888; conducted general store here 20 yrs; b nr Plymouth, N.C. 1844, s/o Jos D. Newbury, of that place. He was mbr Episc Church; d 1892, aged 87. His father, Stephen Newbury, of N.J., b nr Little Egg Harbor; farmed; moved to N. C.; of Eng descent. Jos D. Newbury m Eliza Elder of New York City; of their 9 child., five survive. Edw E. S. res Elizabeth, N. J. Geo located in Seattle, Wash. Dr. Arthur res Hallettsville, Tex. Sarah is w/o Levi Blunt, of Plymouth, N. C. The mother d 1882, at 65, mbr Episc Church. Subj spent early yrs in N.C. When 17 war broke out; he enlisted Company C., Lt Artillery, under Capt Wm Badham, served during most of conflict, Confed army, artillery branch until 1864, raised new company, and commissioned its captain; captured, held prisoner 2 weeks; wounded in knee at Ft Anderson Feb 18 1865, never in active service after that. Returning home he taught in private school about 12 months, grad Balt Commercial College 1867 and came to this co, where he taught 10 yrs. 1868 Mr. Newbury m Henrietta P. Linthicum, d/o Zachariah Linthicum, of Woolford, Dor Co; their child.: Elmer L., in marine ventures in Balt; Nora, w/o W. H. Ne..(?); Eliza E.; Edith; Guy and Maud, at home. Family attend ME Church South.

460 294. JAMES BENJAMIN BROWN, contractor, builder and dealer in lumber, Cambridge, b Matthews Co, Va, Mar 20 1849, s/o Warner Brown, who was in lumber business in Va. He came to Dor Co 1853 as a lumberman in charge of a gang of men; fol year moved his family to Cambridge. He m wife Mary A. C. Newcomb of King and Queen Co, Va. Mr. Brown d 1875, at 62; his wife d Feb 1897, at 72; of their 5 child., 4 reached maturity. Geo R. m Miss Catharine W. Mowbray, of Cambridge, with subj in building and lumber business until 1882, when he turned to hardware and painting business. He d Aug 16 1897, leaving 4 child.: Drusilla A., w/o John Truett, blacksmith of Cambridge; subj, next younger; and Marion wid Wm O. Moore and res in Cambridge.

Subj came to Cambridge at 5, attended public schools and began working at shoemaker's trade when 13, at 15 began clerking in store of H. Page Ray; after 2 yrs apprenticed to Vernon C. Drain, carpenter, for whom he worked 2 yrs; employed as journeyman in Kansas City; Chicago; Wyandotte, Neb.; Balt and Annapolis. At 19 entered into partnership with older brother under name of Geo R. Brown & Bro. About 1870 the brothers purch the Austin mill and began manufacture of timber and rough lumber from native pine and oak. Subj m Jun 17 1875, Miss Laura M. Hopkins, d/o Wm Hopkins. He attends Episc Church; elected first mayor of Cambridge 1882, under the new charter.

461 295. JOSEPH A. F. NEAL, Skipton, Talb Co., for past quarter of century in lime and fertilizer; operates granary at the landing and manages small farm; b Sussex Co, Del, Sep 8 1832, was 7 when his father, Jos W., d suddenly. Latter was successful mcht and surveyor in his home dist nr Concord, Del; elected to

state legislature 1839; b 1799. He m Miss Ann D. Powell, of Del; they had 8 child. Louis W. res Skipton. Martha w/o Jos E. George, of QA Co. Wm H. res Syracuse, N. Y. Four are decd. The mother d 1873. The Neals settled in Del. in the last century.

After dist school J. A. F. Neal was sent to Pa school, then to St. Timothy Hall, Catonsville, Balt Co. At 17 he worked in a store at Wye Mills, later worked at Wye Landing; 1862, opened a store for himself at Skipton Landing, and this he managed 6 yrs; then turned to sale of lime and fertilizer. He attends Episc Church; Dec 21 1860 m Sally A. Hopkins, d/o Thos Hopkins, of this place; of their 9 child. 3 have d; remaining: Thos H., of Syracuse, N. Y.; Henrietta G., unmarried, trained nurse Balt; Jas L., traveling salesman; subj, of Oneida, N. Y.; Lucy B., unmarried; and John R. H., at home.

296. NICHOLAS WRIGHT, farmer, res Hurlock, Dor Co, res this co his entire 462 life; mbr Meth Church. Sml Wright, paternal grandfather, of Eng descent, early settler of this co, d here. Sml Wright, Jr., father of subj, of this co, m Dorcas Nicholas, from Car Co; their child.: Eleanor, Nicholas, Isaac, Margaret A., Harriet, Emily, Sml, Mary (w/o Jabez Wright) and Sarah J. - Subj b 12th dist Dor Co, Aug 1812, grew up on farm; 1837 m Mary E. Shanahan; their child.: Eliza, w/o John M. Dean, of New Market; Jas, who d and left 1 child; Margaret E., Mrs. Thos Rowins; Fannie; Thos I., of Hurlock; Ida, w/o Geo Trice, of Elwood; and Emma, Mrs. Wesley Stephens. For 40 yrs Mr. Wright res on border line of Car and Dor Counties; retired, res Hurlock 2 yrs.

297. HON. GEORGE DAVIDSON, res QA Co on farm, part of Carmichael estate, 5th 465 dist; elected co commissioner 1887, later judge of orphans' court. The Davidsons are old Md fam. 4 generations back, Geo Davidson, of Edinburgh, Scotland, came to America; located permanently in Md and his son, Geo, Jr., b Cecil Co. Next in descent was Philip T. Davidson, father of subj, from Cecil Co, b c.1807, and grew to manhood there. He then came to QA Co, and here m Miss Mary Tilghman Earle, d/o Judge Richard Tilghman Earle; child. who lived to maturity: Richard, farmer this co; Geo, Catherine T. and Susan Earle.

Subj b nr Centreville, 3rd dist, this co, Mar 2 1840, educated public schools and private acad of Centreville; in merchandising Queenstown; c. 1891 moved to farm he now tills (600 a.). While res Queenstown he m Marcella Blunt, Nov 16 1864; their sons: Chas F., physician of Queenstown (see his sketch), and Philip T., farmer this dist. For 14 yrs judge remained widower; 1884 m Sarah D., d/o Hon. R. B. Carmichael; their child.: Richard Bennett Carmichael and Mary Elizabeth. Fam attends Episc Church.

298. EDWIN L. GRIFFITH, postmaster Taylor's Island, Dor, since Aug 1897; 465 earlier inspector of customs Balt City; b AA Co, Oct 13 1838, nr town of Fair Haven, 8th dist, s/o Rbt and Elizabeth (Sutton) Griffith. The father was from Calvert Co, Md, spent most of his life in AA Co, where he owned large estate and many slaves; conducted store in town of Friendship, later he went to Balt, where he embarked in grocery and commission business. He d about two yrs after his move, in 1847, in his 49th yr. He and wife were mbrs ME Church. She was d/o Rev Lewis Sutton minister in ME Church. Mrs. Griffith d at 35, leaving 4 child.: Edwin L., eldest; Virginia decd; Rbt C., in business in Balt; and Roberta w/o Hon. Wm E. Deal, regent Univ San Francisco.

Subj entered West River Classical Institute, at about 14, where he studied for 2 yrs, then Dickinson Acad where he grad 1857; embarked in dry goods business in Balt, selling and buying on commission; returned to old homestead AA Co, and there he lived until 1866. That year he purch a farm in Taylor's

Island and has since attended to its cultivation. Since 1895 he has dwelt in the town. Feb 10 1864 he m Adeline, d/o Thos B. Travers of this co (d at 75). She is niece of Judge Levi D. Travers. Their child.: Mary Elizabeth, w/o Wm C. Travers, of this co, and Ada Roberta, at home.

299. WILLIAM G. SMYTH, of Chestertown. The Smyths are old Kt Co fam. Jefferson L., his father, s/o Richard, large land owner. The mother of subj, d 1892, was former Martha Isabelle Greenwood, b this co, d/o John Greenwood. She had 3 sons and 2 daus. Richard A. is constable at Fairlee, this co; Jefferson L. is principal of Townsend (Del) Acad, grad Wash College; Caroline Isabelle is teacher in schools of this co; Minnie M. res with sis Caroline I.

William G. Smyth b at home place in Fairlee, this co, Nov 3 1869; grad Wash College 1890; entered college of Physicians and Surgeons Balt, never completed the course; entered teacher's profession and Aug 4 1896 app school examiner. 1895 he m Lizzie M. Corey, b this co, d/o Capt. A. L. Corey. She attends Episc Church; Mr. Smyth is mbr ME Church.

300. SAMUEL P. WILSON came to Mardela Springs, Wicomico co, 1883; since then in milling and mercantile business; superintends small farm which he owns; tax collector 1890-1; 1897 elected co commissioner.

The Wilson family is of Irish origin, res in Del for generations. Father of subj, Jas, and his grandfather, Geo Wilson, b Kt Co, Del, where former was mcht and miller of Frederica and tax collector several times; mbr ME Church; d Dec 1885. His 1st wife was Sarah Wilson, who d 1856; her child.: Wm E., of Car Co; Sml P.; and Annie E., w/o Richard W. Lord, of Harrington, Del. He m(2) Susan T. d/o Geo W. Wilson, of Sussex Co, Del; she is 69, res Frederica, Del; of their 6 child., living: Susan, res with her mother; Clara, w/o Harry Dodson, of Clayton, Del.; and Frank, res Seaford, Del.

Subj b Frederica, Kent Co, Del, Jan 2 1856; after schooling entered father's flour mill; 1876 went to Ruthsburg, QA Co, spent 3 yrs in milling business; returned home, remained with father 2 yrs; then 3 yrs nr Laurel, Del and 1 year in Laruel. 1883 he moved to present res Wicomico Co; since then active in business in Mardela Springs. Nov 19 1878, he m Miss Jennie, d/o John Satterfield, of Kt Co, Md; of 2 child., one survives, Norman S.

301. EZEKIEL MARSH FORMAN. Ezekiel Forman, nephew of Gen Forman of Cecil Co, lived on Eastern Shore; his son Ezekiel T. M. Forman b Chestertown 1821, educated Wash College. Moving to QA Co, he engaged in farming, then settled in Centreville, where he followed business pursuits during the remainder of his life; once justice of peace. He favored the doctrines of PE Church. He d suddenly Jun 27 1875; had a bro, Wm H., who was father of Fdk W., Richard Carmichael, Jas Cranston and Wm H., of Balt, and of Laura Forman Grimes.

Mother of subj, F. Maria, d/o Peregrine and Harriet (Tilghman) Tilghman, b on farm known as Tilghman's Recovery, QA Co. Her child.: Peregrine T. (see sketch on another page); Hy, Wm H., Ezekiel M., Harriet of Balt, and Araminta. Subj b Centreville Jan 15 1858. At 13 he began to earn his own livelihood; in drug store of John T. Wooters, of Centreville, 8 yrs; bt interest in store of W. J. Hopper, remained with him until 1888; since then alone in business; 2 yrs mbr Centreville bd of Commissoners; pres Md State Pharmaceutical Assoc; mbr Epis Church. Apr 28 1882 he m Miss S. Catherine Earl; their child.: Peregrine, Ezekiel and Mary Earl.

302. S. KENNEDY WILSON, M. D., physician Tilghman's Island, Talb Co, b 468 Boonsborough, Wash Co, Md., Mar 29 1859; mbr Eng fam that settled early in Va. His grandfather, John Wilson, owned mercantile store in Winchester, Va.
Father of subj, Hy Beatty Wilson, M. D., b Winchester, Va, where his early life was spent; practicing physician 30 yrs at Boonsborough, where he d 1883, at 53; Episc; m Ellen E. Kennedy b Wash Co and still res there, only d/o George Scott Kennedy, land owner and miller of Boonsborough. Dr. and Mrs. Wilson had 12 child., 10 living: S. Kennedy; Hy Beatty, M. D., prof medical college Omaha; Katie, w/o John Overington, of Phila; Walter Duncan, in wholesale drug business in Omaha; Mary Louise, res Boonsborough with mother; John A., in mercantile business Cincinnati; Geo Rochester, in treasury depart of Pa Railroad Co Phila; Edith Jennings, Agnes and Jos C., at home.
After high school in Boonsborough, subj grad medical depart Univ of Md 1879; then 1 year as assist in Md hospital, returned to Boonsborough and practiced with father until death of latter; 1895 came to Tilghman's Island. He is mbr Episc Church; 1881 m Miss Cora V. Nicodemus, of Wash Co; their child.: Luther Roy; Frank Kennedy; Ethel May, d at 9 months; Harry Eugene, John Nicodemus and Margaret. Subj owns farm (134 a.) in Wash Co, with orchard of 6000 peach trees. His father-in-law, John L. Nicodemus, owns large tracts of land in Wash Co, is pres People's Natl Bank at Hagerstown, vice-pres Second Natl Bank and pres ice factory and stocking factory.

303. GEORGE A. DEAKYNE, treasurer Car Co, b Newcastle Co, Del, Sep 11 1857; 471 mbr old Del fam. His grandfather, John Deakyne, m Miss Greenwood, of Kt Co, and afterward went to Calif during gold rush of 1849; never heard of since. Father of subj, Geo A. Deakyne b nr Chestertown, Kt Co, Md, Mar 13 1819; over 10 yrs in mercantile business in Del; then settled on a farm in Newcastle Co, remaining there until 2 yrs before his death; moved to Clayton, Del, where he d Mar 1895; attended ME Church; m Elmira Redden, of Sussex Co, Del, d/o Stephen Redden. She is still living, res Clayton, Del.
Child. of Geo A. Deakyne, Sr.: Geo A., eldest; Willard D., farmer Kt Co, Del; Walter G., res QA Co; Clarence, at home; Veronica, who m Judge E. M. Phillips, of Tunkhannock, Pa.; Mary C., w/o Frank Gootee, of Smyrna, Del; Rachel G., who m Reuben Warren, proprietor of hotel at Clayton; Elva and Addie, school teachers in Newcastle, Del; and Eugene, at home.
Subj spent boyhood on farm; at 18 went to Phila; 3 yrs as clerk in commission house; then to Denton; 1882 entered county clerk's office as deputy under Col. Luther H. Gadd; 1889 elected co treasurer; 1883 m Clara Horsey, d/o Wm G. Horsey, vice-pres Denton Bank. Their child, Luther Stanley, age 10; they own several farms, res Denton.

304. EDWIN C. FIELDS, clerk circuit court Car Co, res Denton, b Newark, 472 Newcastle Co, Del, May 28 1853. Early ancestors settled in New York on coming to America. His grandfather, John Fields d N.Y. during cholera epidemic 1833, had 3 sons, of whom, Wm C., mbr congress from N.Y.; another was Meth minister in that state; and the 3rd, Dnl, father of subj, was in public affairs. B in New York City 1812, he spent early yrs as mcht there, with country home at Newark, Del. 1855, he moved to Car Co and settled on farm nr Federalsburg; elected 3 times to state senate and 1875 elected pres of that body; mbr Unitarian Church; d 1883. His wife, still living, was Harriet, d/o Isaac Wright, farmer, Dor Co; she was b and reared in that co.
Subj is eldest mbr of fam of 7 child. Others: Helen, w/o Jos Douglas, of Frederick, Md; Dnl res old homestead; John W. and Harman partners in merchandising, Zachary, La; Wm C., druggist, res Pikesville, Balt Co; Minnie,

w/o Geo C. Skirven, bookkeeper Denton Natl Bank. Subj clerk to a commmittee of U. S. house of representatives 1884; app U.S. Indian Agent at Ft Belknap, Mont. 1887; 1891 elected clerk of circuit court Car Co. 1878 Mr. Fields m Anna, d/o Capt Wm H. Watkins, of this co; their child.: Harry V., Roberta, Edwin Claude, Myra Rose and Wm Watkins. Mrs. Fields is mber ME Church.

472 305. HON. THOMAS ROMAIN STRONG owner and manager of homestead on Piney Neck, Lankford Bay, 5th dist Kt Co; fall 1875 elected co commissioner, later rgtr of wills, 1891 elected to the state legislature. Strongs are old fam in these parts, of Eng extraction. Grandfather Wm Strong b nr Chestertown; subject's father, Thos A., from this dist, farmer; d Mar 1895, in 84th yr; connected with Meth Church; m Catherine A. Eagle (b Kt Co, d at 35).

Subj b Jul 10 1841, this dist, remained with fam until about 15, clerked in general store in Chestertown; 1863 went to Balt, clerked in dry goods house; 2 yrs later in merchandising at Edesville, Kt Co, selling out to good advantage afterwards; moved to present farm, inherited by wife. 1867 he m Charlotte A. Wickes; their child.: Anna Page, Jas P., Mary Augusta, Elwood S., Martha Edna, Louisa and Wm R., all at home. Fam are mbrs Episc Church.

473 306. WILLIAM H. BARTON, pres Natl Bank of Cambridge, b Cambridge, Oct 27 1839; attended Cambridge Acad, conducted by Dr. Barber, where he pursued a course in engineering; clerked in store of Mr. Creighton; 1856 received app to naval academy at Annapolis and grad Jun 1860, and at once entered active naval service that continued for 7 yrs; ordered to Seminole, American vessel then off coast of Brazil and later participated in blockade of Charleston, where he remained until Hatteraas expedition, when he was sent to Fortress Monroe and the Potomac River; later joined the Wyoming off Pacific coast which soon not long after started on her next cruise in the Pacaific to China and Japan. On this cruise the Wyoming achieved victory over 3 Japanese warships. Fall 1863 Lieut Barton transferred to the Jamestown; May 1867 Lieut Barton resigned his commission, as lieutenant Commander, so that he might enjoy the comfort of home life. He m Miss Louisa Brown, whose father had lived in New York, in contracting and building and who erected several large custom houses for government of Chili. Mr. Barton returned with bride to Cambridge. His first wife d in 1874 and he subsequently re-married.

477 307. WALTER O. SELBY, M. D. res Rock Hall several yrs. John Parker Selby, father of subj, from Del. He read law in Phila for brief period, admitted to bar and started in legal practice in that city; later met with severe misfortune in loss of voice, obliged to give up his vocation, farmed in Va until 1860. With rumors of approaching conflict, he returned home. He did not sell his property, however, and after farming in Md a few yrs he returned to Va estates (nr Fredericksburg). Here he d about 65. He m Wilminia Beck, of Del; she still lives in old Va farm, at 73.

Subj b during parents' temporary res in Md, on farm Car Co, Mar 12 1862; when war was over, went to Va with his father; enrolled Bowling Green College, Caroline Co, Va, later Richmond College, and still later grad Balt Medical College 1888 with honors. After 2 yrs of work in Md General Hospital, he settled in Rock Hall where he practices today.

478 308. GILBERT M. SEARS, farmer and financier, d Apr 30 1890; Bay Hundred dist, Talb Co; b on bay shore Sep 14 1822, assist in management of homestead, absent from farm few yrs when at Annapolis; owns homestead (250 a.), known as Sears' Choice. 1879 Mr. Sears m Miss Susie Lambdin, d/o Wm and Catherine (Lowe)

-82-

Lambdin, of Bay Hundred. The father d 1869, in 65th yr; mother d few yrs later 1872, at 60; 4 of her child. d earlier; 4 survive: Georgia, wid of Chas Smith; Rbt L. and Harry C., farmers this locality; and Mrs. Sears. Only child of Mr. and Mrs. G. M. Sears is Bessie M., who lives with her mother. Parents of G. M. Sears were Wm and Elizabeth (Murdock) Sears; their child.: Wm H., Margaret E., Gilbert M., Amanda M., John K., Chas E. and Mary E.

309. ALEXANDER DICKSON IRWIN built whip factory at Snow Hill, styled the 478
Luray Manufacturing Co, a branch of U. S. Whip Co., of Westfield, Mass. The concern was founded here by subj as A. D. Irwin & Brother Co. He is now the manager of the enterprise. The process of manufactjuring rawhide centers for whips is done here (the process is described). Among the other business houses in which Mr. Irwin is now financially concerned is: A. D. Irwin & Brother, Phila, engaged in manufacture of cotton dress fabrics; partner in Columbia Mill in Phila. Currently A. D. Irwin is one of three councilmen of Ocean City, Md. - Subj b Oct 2 1839, Phila, and there educated and reared. His father, an Englishman, was mbr of firm of Irwin & Stinson, cloth manufacturers of Phila. He came to this country when 19. Subj m(1) Miss Lizzie Todd, in Phila. Their child.: Lillie, Blanche and Florrie. Lillie is w/o Dr. Paul Jones, of Snow Hill. Blanche m John L. Nock, formerly postmaster of Snow Hill. Florrie is Mrs. Walter Doyle, of Phila. Mr. Irwin's m(2) 1880 Miss Rose E. Truitt, of this place, and settled in Snow Hill; their child.: Alexander Dickson, Jr., Mabel and Rose.

310. W. IRVING BOWDLE junior mbr dry goods firm of Cornwell, Bowdle & Co, 479
Cambridge. 1891 they purch new stock of goods, and again entered business on Race st, where they have two story building. Subj is s/o Wm H. Bowdle, business and newspaper man of Cambridge who came from Talb at 20. Purchasing the Cambridge Democrat, he carried it on for 10 or more yrs, then founded the Cambridge Herald, and still later Cambridge Telegraph, which was sold to Col. Clement Sullivane and merged into the Chronicle. The father d 1880, when 64. His wid res with only surviving child, and is now 72.
Subj b Jun 15 1860 Cambridge. He left school in 1876 and worked for Webb & Co., Vienna, then Thos W. Anderson & Co., remaining until their failure in 1884; became partner of Z. D. Jones. 1889 Cornwell, Bowdle & Co was formed. 1894 Mr. Bowdle m Maggie, d/o T. E. Wright, their dau, Helen Louise; they are mbrs Grace ME Church South. 1893 Mr. Bowdle built res on Race st.

311. JAMES LAWRENSON BRYAN, M. D., app school examiner 1866; b Cambridge, Dor 480
Co, Aug 25 1824, of Eng descent. Founder of fam in America was grandfather of Richard Bryan, the great-grandfather of subj. Latter was father of Capt Chas Kennerley Bryan, of Cambridge, capt of artillery company, war of 1812. His son, Jas Bryan, the doctor's father, served in depart of interior; state elector 1856, mbr Md delegation that gave Lincoln the nomination over Salmon P. Chase at 1860 Repub natl convention. He m Emily Le Compte, of French descent, her ancestors fleeing France after revocation of Edict of Nantes. After death of 1st wife, Mr. Bryan m again; moved with fam to Norfolk, Va, engaged in merchandising and later went to Petersburg, Va.
Subj spent early life in Va, attended schools of Norfolk, and Petersburg; grad VMI, Lexington, 1843, taught at Petersburg Military Acad; formed company to go to Mexican war, served in that struggle as 1st lieut, discharged 1848; studied medicine Univ Md; grad Wash Univ Balt 1849; practiced medicine southern part of Dor Co 17 yrs. 1866 he estab Cambridge Military Acad and app pres school bd Dor Co; 1868 made school examiner Dor Co. He m 1852, Miss

Aurelia Pattison, of Taylor's Island, d/o Jas M. Pattison; had 11 child., 9 living: Julian L., of Staunton, Va.; D'Arcy P., of Balt; Frank Otis, res nr Cambridge; Wm L. H., of Balt; Mary Virginia, at home; Nora, w/o Edwin Dashiell, Jr., of Cambridge; Emily, of Balt; Guy Lee, of Cambridge; and Lay, of Balt. 30 yrs subj served as deacon Episc Church and assist pastor to Dr. Barber; ordained to priesthood; acting rector Dor parish.

483 312. GEORGE H. TRAX, farmer, contractor and builder 1st dist Talb Co, co commissioner since 1895. His father and grandfather both named Jacob, both of northern part of Germany; both cabinet makers; ran a large sash, door and blind factory in Allegheny Co, Pa. Jacob Trax, Jr., a young man when he landed in America, now in 78th yr; came to this co Dec 1875, settling in 4th dist, farmed about 12 yrs. Since then lived in Rochester, Pa, mbr of town council there. He m Catherine Knovershoe of Germany; she is about 73. Of their 7 children, Kate m Dan Steiner, of Monica, Pa; Geo is next in order of birth; Emma is w/o Harry Hawkins, of Beaverfh, Pa.; John res 4th dist this co; Lydia, Mrs. Hy Greenbough, of Columbus, Ohio; and Louis is with parents.

Subj b on father's farm Allegheny Co, Pa, Jun 27 1851, attended Duff's Business College Pittsburgh; at 14 found work in Cleveland in cabinet making. In Chicago, at 18 built houses and other structures; then spent 5 yrs in Cleveland. 1876 he located in 4th dist Talb Co; in contracting and building ever since. He owns Chestnut Hill farm (160 a.); mbr Episc Church Easton. May 5 1880 he m Emma Carson, d/o Alexander Carson, formerly of Norristown, Pa; their child.: Annie, Lola, Rose, Eurith, Percy, Hy, Cruitt and Emma.

484 313. THOMAS A. HUDSON res Lankford Bay, 5th dist Kt Co; b Feb 7 1828, Canadaville, 2nd dist this co, s/o John Hudson b this co, who participated in battle of Caulksfield, war of 1812, as musician in Capt Thos Wilson's cav. He d as result of an accident when he was 40. His father, farmer, also named John, b this locality, of English ancestry. Mother of subj was Henrietta Ashley in her girlhood, b and reared Kt Co, d 1849, when about 65. Of her 8 children, only Thomas A. is living, who was only a week old when his father was killed. He stayed on the farm with mother until she d.

1849 subj went to Phila, served 5 yrs' apprenticeship to carpenter's trade; returned to this co, worked at his trade along Sassafras River about a yr; rented farm a while, then purch homestead where he res. He m Miss Addie L. Usilton, of this co, Dec 18 1859; their child.: Wm J., in oyster business Kt Co; Mary Henrietta; Thos F., res Balt; Chas Hy; Walter, d age about 20; Edw, d at 19; John R., d in 12th yr; and Alfred Washington, farmer.

485 314. EDWARD T. MOORE, whose home and farm c. 2 miles from Preston, Car Co; ME. His paternal grandfather was early settler on Eastern Shore and farmer. Parents of subj were Edw T. Moore, Sr., and Emma, d/o Tilghman E. Andrews, a res East New Market, Dor Co. The senior Moore, farmer from this co, dwelt in co all his life; had one son and 3 daus: Mary, Sallie and Bessie.

Subj b parents' homestead Preston 1869. After common schools attended Preston Acad, then a commercial college, Phila. His father, somewhat of an invalid during his last yrs, not strong enough to do arduous work, and subj assumed management of the farm. 1895 he bt prop where he now res. Feb 1893 he m Amanda, youngest d/o Perry D.Taylor; their child, Effie T.

485 315. REV. ZACK H. WEBSTER, pastor ME Church Denton, b Deal's Island, Som Co, Oct 18 1858, s/o Sml and Sarah Jane (Shores) Webster. His father, Meth, of Som Co, in mercantile business there; once co commissioner; d 1880. His

-84-

grandfather was 1st of fam to settle on Deal's Island. Mother of subj d/o Lambert Shores, farmer; owned considerable land and number of slaves. She d Feb 1894; her child.: Geo, farmer Deal's Island; Zack H.; Luther, res Deal's Island, owns several vessels; Oscar C., accidentally shot and killed by schoolmate; Brazilia, wid of Geo W. Windsor, mother of large fam, with whom she lives on Deal's Island; and Indiana F., w/o Sml C. White, of Del.

Subj educated Som Co schools; at 17 went on the water, 4 yrs a mariner; after teaching 3 yrs entered ministry ME Church 1886; received into the conferenc, given charge of a church; 1 year at Quantico, 1 year at Fruitland, Md, 3 yrs at Whitesvile, Del, 2 yrs at Tangier, Va, and then Denton, where he has been for 4 yrs. Dec 6 1882 Rev Webster m Elizabeth E. Brewington, formerly of Salisbury, Md, but at time of their marriage res Som Co. Their daus: Esther, Ruth, Sarah, Ethel and Helen. Another dau, Grace d when 5.

316. THOMAS T. CORNWELL, senior mbr firm Cornwell, Bowdle & Co, Cambridge; 486 clerked as boy; now head of largest dry goods store this secton; b Hampton, Va, Oct 15 1816, 3rd of 5 child. who attained maturity; others: Joel, d Vienna, at 56, leaving 3 child., 1 living; Rosa A., wid of Ballard Venable, res Riverton, Md; John S., mcht of Vienna; and Sarah L., decd, w/o Josiah Carr, of Vienna. The father of fam, Wm Cornwell, b Long Island, N. Y., moved to Va in early manhood and there followed the mechanic's trade. In Princess Anne Co, Va, he m Johanna Ship, sis of Col John Ship. Mr. Cornwell d Wicomico Co, Md, as did his wife, who survived him many yrs; she d at 94.

When his father d, subj, at 15, made his home with bro Joel, mcht Balt and later in Vienna. He was educated in Wicomico Co, came to Cambridge, clerked in store of Col Wm Sullivane, remained nearly 4 yrs; then with Hooper C. Hicks until his store burned down and then with Frs J. Henry, where he remained until that gentleman was elected clerk of the court. Jun 1889 he formed a partnership with Mr. Bowdle and Mr. Barnett, and they have since conducted business together, having the largest store of the kind in the city. 1840 Mr.Cornwell became mbr Meth Church.

317. WILLIAM KENNEDY CARROLL, M. D., owns home and 400 a. farm land 5th dist 489 QA Co. His paternal grandfather b AA Co, and reared there. One of his sons, David, was father of subj. David b PG Co; pioneered in manufacturing of fabric known as duck, used extensively in clothing. Around 1850 he started Whitehall mills and later those of Woodberry and Mount Vernon. He m Miss Annie Ayler, of Centreville; their children who grew to maturity: Rev D. H. Carroll, D. D., pastor ME Church Balt, now pres Laurel Manufacturing Co; Albert d Balt c. 1886, left a family; Fannie, wid of John T. Timanus, manufacturer Balt; Laura D. m E. E. Shipley, of Howard Co; and Dr. Wm K.

Subj b village of Woodberry, now part of Balt, Aug 18 1851; became familiar with management of mills operated by his father; grad medical depart Univ Md with honors 1873, commenced practice in Woodberry. After 5 yrs he went to Denver, Colo, engaged in professional work three yrs or more. His father being in failing health at this time he returned to Queenstown. 3 yrs later he settled in Balt and practiced another 5 yrs. For about 10 yrs he has dwelt on homestead nr Queenstown. He m Miss Margaret Frederick May 9 1872, in Balt, d/o Jacob and Sarah (Garrett) Frederick, of Balt, now decd.

318. JOHN T. WILSON in mercantile business Mardela Springs, Barren Creek 489 Dist, Wicomico Co; b Apr 8 1846, about 2 miles from present res, s/o Levin M. and bro of L. N. Wilson, M. D., elsewhere this volume. At 18 he began to

teach school in Barren Creek dist, where he remained an instructor for 10 yrs; operated general store Mardela Springs 1876-91, when he went to Balt, embarked in cigar and tobacco business; 2 yrs later came back to Wicomico Co, and has since carried on general business. Mr. Wilson m Dec 31 1890 Miss Lizzie, d/o James W. Lard, of Dor Co; they have dau, Fannie.

490 319. JOHN C. HACKETT, M. D. physician Millington, Kt Co, here since 1894; b on farm nr this place 1857, s/o John C. and Cephelia (Woodland) Hackett. His father now retired, res Sudlersville, QA Co, for several yrs.
Subj student Millington Acad, fol dist schools; 1884 grad Jefferson Medical College, Phila, opened office Sudlersville, nr father's home; spent 9 yrs there, then 3 yrs res Crumpton, combining drug business with his profession; about 3 yrs ago came to this town. 1892 Dr. Hackett m Miss Jessie Guthrie Macbeth, of Cumberland, Md, d/o Rev Jas W. Macabeth, minister Presby Church. She had been school teacher QA Co. They attend Episc Church.

491 320. WILLIAM H. JACOBS, M. D. res Millington, Kt Co, 5 yrs. Wm H. Jacobs, Sr., from Kt Co, Del, carried on farm and mercantile business at Downs Chapel. He m(1) Miss Moore, of Del, who d; her child.: Nehemiah and Rbt. He m(2) Naomi Truitt, of Del; their child.: Geo W., Jonathan, Wm H., Jas and Jacob (twins). - Subj b 1865 Kt Co, Del, nr Downs Chapel; 1889 grad Chicago Medical College; in practice in Denton, Md 12 months; post-grad course winter of 1890 at his alma mater; fol yr estab in business in Delaware City, Del, but soon moved to this place. 1892 he m Miss Mary E. Maloney, res Newcastle Co, Del; their child.: Jas Paul, Gladys D.; Dorothy, decd; and Bernice, d at 6 weeks. Sub and wife mbrs ME Church.

491 321. THOMAS STOCKTON WICKES, Chestertown, b here Sep 2 1832. His grandfather, Simon Wickes, surveyor, Meth, officer in colonial army; d 1816. He had older bro, Jos (grandfather of Judge Wickes), and two sis, Nancy and Fannie; former m Wm Brown, land owner and res of Kt Co; latter m man from Phila. Great-grandfather of subj, Jos Wickes, b Kt Co, res on ancestral estate; which was out of fam for 49 yrs, bt back by subj in 1879.
Father of subj, Simon Wickes, b 7 miles from Chestertown, on Tulip Forest farm, 1781, farmed old homestead until 1831, retired to Chestertown, and there res until he d 1848. Because of failing health unable to manage business affairs; lost inherited estate. Fam mbrs Episc Church; he was only son; his sis: Hannah, m Capt Benj Houston, nephew of Judge Jas Houston, of U. S. Dist court Balt, and whose grandson, Rev Jas H. Eccleston, is rector Episc Church Balt; and Polly, who d unmarried.
Subject's mother, Elizabeth Blake, b QA Co, lineal descendant of Eng admiral, Geo Blake; she d 1878, at 85; her bro, Wm Blake, officer American army, stationed Ft McHenry. Subj youngest and only survivor of 9 child. Mary Hamilton, named for grandparents, Mary Freeman and Hamilton M. Blake, w/o Jas Arthur, mechanic. Simon, b 1818, farming and drug business, d 1869; his son Thos W. Wickes, druggist Chestertown. Chas Hy, b 1820; clerk Balt, went to sea; studied law, Union soldier in Civ war; d 1893, leaving dau, res Chestertown. Wm Nichols Earle Wickes, b 1823, d 1895, leaving son and dau. Isaac Freeman, b 1825, druggist Chestertown and Balt, fate unknown. Anne Rebecca, b 1827, d 1889, w/o Benj Chambers Wickes (d 1854); she later m Judge Jos A. Wickes. Elizabeth, b 1830, d unmarried 1888. One child d in infancy.
Subj educated Wash College, began business in present store; res Chestertown except 2 yrs in N.Y.; owns farm; attends Episc Church.

322. JOHN COPPAGE over 2000 a. QA Co and 1100 a. Talb Co; res 2nd dist, where he was b Oct 23 1810, s/o John and Martha (Dudley) Coppage, 2nd of 7 child.; 6 attained mature yrs; all now decd except himself and Edw E., who lives in Del. John Coppage m(1) Mary A. Nickerson (d 1846); m(2) Rebecca Taylor, of Del, by whom were 14 child., 5 living: Annie, Martha, Kate, Maggie and Enoch, farmer 2nd dist. Subj has served as co assessor, tax collector and co commissioner.

323. REV. JAMES BLACK MERRITT, D. D.   Thos Merritt, of Eng, sailed up Del River in trading vessel, called The Little Baltimore, had grant on St. John's River, Reedy Island Neck, Newcastle Co, Del; settled in Rye, Westchester Co, N. Y., before 1673, and purch "Hog-Pen Ridge" Sep 4 1680, and owned Pine Island other lands c. 1690. He was vestryman, constable, supervisor and deputy to general court. He m(2) Abigail, d/o Rbt Francis, of Wethersfield, Conn., before 1688. His children by first wife: Thos, Jos, Ephraim and Sml.

Thos Merritt 2nd, of Rye, N. Y., had son Benoni (or Benj), who m Mary ___; sold land to John Merritt, May 14 1720, at Rye; bt 200 a. at Forcorners and d 1779, intestate, on farm in Reedy Island Neck, Newcastle Co, Del, leaving wid and sons: Wm, Benj, Thos and John.

Wm Merritt, b 1726, bt Ivingo, tract of 330 a. Kt Co, Md, adjacent to Shrewsbury Episc Church; m Martha Bergin 1759 and m(2) Martha Vansant, d/o Benj Vansant, 1776. He petitioned court of Newcastle Co, Del, for sale and partition of Benj Merritt's estate, his father, who d on his estate in Reedy Island Neck, New Castle Co, Del, intestate. For yrs he was vestryman and church warden of Shrewsbury Episc Church and high sheriff of Kt Co, 1779; d at Ivingo 1793. His children: Benj, Rebecca and Mary.

Benj Merritt, b 1779, d 1832; m Patty Kerr, of Newark, Del, d/o Andrew and Martha Kerr, 1808, had child.: Wm K., Geo A., John and Adeline K.; none left descendants. He m(2) Eliza Jane, d/o John and Mary Black, of Black's Cross Roads, Kt Co, Md, where she was b Oct 3 1803. Benj Merritt in battle of Caulk's Field, war of 1812, under Captain Chambers. Child. of Benj Merritt: Thos A., Benj G., Jas Black, Sml A., Mary Ann and Caroline R.

Subj b Sep 20 1826, Ivingo, home of father and grandfather, now owned by subj; educated in common schools, 1 term at Dickinson College, and theology at Concord, N. H., admitted to Phila Meth Conference, assigned to Dover, Del 1852. Here he m Hannah Pleasanton, d/o Dr. Sml Webb and Eliza Pleasanton, Apr 10 1855, at their country res, Muddy Branch, nr Dover, Del. He served as pastor of Fredrerica, Cambridge, Easton, Centreville, Chestertown, Dover, 2nd time (1872-75), St. Paul's, Wilm, Odessa, and Middletown; present pastor of Salem and Union, Fairlee, Kt Co, Md. Subj and wife had fol child.: Margarettta Boone, b Mar 16 1856, d Nov 10 1869; Eliza Pleasanton, b 1857, m May 10 1883, to A. M. Hepbron, of Balt, and their child. are Archer Kerr and Jas Merritt; Jas Black, b 1859, physician Easton; he m Georgetta, d/o Alexander Parks, of Kt Co, Md, and their child. are Jas Black (Jay Bee) and Addie Kerr; Sml Webb, b Aug 19 1862, res Phila, m Florence Katherine, d/o Dr. Frs N. Sheppard and Amanda F. Bowker, his wife, of Kt Co, Md, Apr 10 1894.

324. THOMAS HOPKINS, ex-co commissioner of Talb Co, mcht Wye Mils and Skipton Landing, farmer on homestead which he owns 4th dist, known as Skipton farm; aged 86. Founders of this branch of Hopkins family in America mbrs Soc of Friends, from London, Eng, to Talb Co 1658; had patent to lands on Hopkins' Point, opposite Oxford. Great-grandfather of subj, Dennis Hopkins; grandfather, next in descent, was Thomas. Sml, father of subj, mcht and miller at Wye Mills; last days on farm now owned by Dr. Earl, nr Easton. He d

1836; m(1) Sarah Hart; she d 1811, leaving infant, subj; he m again soon, her sis, Martha; she d 1814; later he m Rebecca Richards, of QA Co.

Subj only survivor of father's fam, b Nov 11 1811, Wye Mils; attended dist schools until 17, worked in father's store. When father moved to Easton, subj bt his interest in old mill and the store and conducted same 1836-1841; purch Skipton farm and managed it, while running store and vessel at the landing; 1844 elected co commissioner. Jul 1834 Mr. Hopkins m Hester A. McDaniel, who d Jan 1839, left children, Sarah A. and infant, both decd. Jun 1840, he m Hester A. McDaniel, cousin of 1st wife; their child.: Jas L., at home, superintending farm; Thos, res Long Woods; Hester Ann, wid of Rev A. Manship, of Germantown, Pa; Jane B., unmarried; and Grace, w/o Lewis Osborne, of Fredericktown, Md. The mother d Nov 1854. Aug 1858 Mr. Hopkins m Martha E. McCeeney, who d 1881. Julia, her eldest child, w/o S. W. Hopkins, of Wye Mills; Benj at home; and Martha H., youngest, living with father.

495 325. BLANCHARD EMORY, JR., Centreville, b Mar 4 1855, nr village where he res, fam home being 2 miles north of this place; attended public schools and Centreville Acad; at 16 was purser on steamer Osceola, on Corsica Creek; clerked in store of S. E. Dyott Centreville, and for firm of J. Edw Bird & Co, of Balt. He then formed partnership his cousin, E. B. Emory, 1877, in fertilizer business, and later with P. H. Feddeman, and later still with Chas H. Burgess. 1891-1895 Justice of peace. Mar 1895 app postmaster Centreville. May 7 1879 he m Miss Mary Kerr, of QA Co; of their 6 children 3 remain: Alan G., Edw B. and Blanchard.

495 326. J. WILSON DAIL farmer, co commisniners of Dor Co; owns farm (200 a.) 7th dist, nr Cambridge; b Cambridge, Sep 24 1851, s/o Levin S. and Sallie E. (Wilson) Dail. The Dails were from Eng, and located in Md in colonial days. His great-grandfather, Wm Dail, b and res Dor Co, as did grandfther Thos Dail. The latter had 5 sons; Wm and Wheatley, both decd; Thos J., formerly a business man of Cambridge, now res Balt; Josiah, decd; and Levin S., father of subj, who d 1880, at 60. He m Miss Sarah E. Wilson, of Sussex Co, Del, and of 9 child. 7 lived to maturity, in order of birth: J. Wilson; Edgar, d in 27th yr; Louisa, m Ezekiel Wilson, of Sussex Co, Del, and d leaving several children; Bessie B., w/o Wm Coulburn; she d a few yrs ago,leaving 4 child.; Levin S., res Cambridge; Clara, w/o Frank Marble, of Sussex Co, Del; and Sally, teacher Cambridge Acad.

Subj m Miss Annie P. Robinson in old Episc Church nr Church Creek, Nov 14 1883, d/o Jos and Mary C. (Bowdle) Robinson; their child.: Herbert Hall and Annie Wilson; they are mbrs St. James' Parish Episc Church, of Cambridge.

496 327. HUGH DUFFEY, druggist Hillsborough, Car Co, b Phila, Aug 23 1836, s/o Roger and Eleanor (O'Neill) Duffey. His father, came to America from Ireland in youth; as a child stricken with small pox lost sight of one eye; the other became affected so that at 35 unable to attend to business; formed partnership with cousin, Hugh Duffey, in business of dyeing hats. He d Phila at 75. His wife also d in that city. Their child.: Hugh and Elizabeth.

Subject came to Md at 14; worked as farm hand; clerked in general store in Hillsborough; 1865 embarked in drug business Hillsborough. May 31 1860, he m Catharine See, b in Hillsborough d/o John and Hester S. (Shepherd) See, former from Del, and latter of Md; their child.: 5 decd, living: Roger W., Hugh C., A. Linden, Anne E. and Catharine S. Fam attend ME Church.

-88-

328. REV. GEORGE F. BEAVEN, minister St. John's Episc Church Hillsborough, 499 Car Co, 40 yrs. Great-great-grandfather of subj located Charles Co 1730 and settled on land where several subsequent generations were b. With few exceptions descendants were farmers. Great-grandfather Beaven named Blandford. His son, John, grandfather of subj, owned c. 400 a. - Subj s/o John and Anna (Pagett) Beaven, of Charles Co; 3 of their 4 child. decd. The father, business man, served in war of 1812. Subj b Oct 15 1824 on father's old homestead Chas Co, there educated and grew to maturity; grad theological seminary Nashotah, Wis. 1855. His first pastorate was in Ellicott City, Balt Co 2 yrs, then to present charge. Teacher prior to ministry for 15 yrs; co school examiner 14 yrs. 1848 Mr. Beaven m Virginia L. Waters, of Chas Co; their child.: Wordsworth Y., rector All Saints parish, Talb Co; John M., Grace A., Geo H., Mary V., Arthur R., H. Lay and J. M., mcht Hillsborough. Grace d when 37. The mother d 1881, at 48. 1885 Mr. Beaven m Mrs. Anna De Rauchbrune Wilson, nee Wilkinson,, b and reared Car Co, descendant of Rev Christopher Wilkinson, colonial clergyman of Md who grad Oxford Univ.

329. HARRY L. DODD, M. D., physician, Chestertown. Dodds are old fam of 500 Chestertown. Doctor's grandfather, John T. Dodd, d 1873, mbr MP Church and his home headquarters for visiting Meth preachers. Doctor's father, Thos S., b Chestertown, carpenter and builder, until he d, in early manhood. He m Sarah A. Lambert; she was b Chestertown, still living here. Their sons: Harry L.; Chas L., in mercantile business Chestertown; and Thos S., ex- sheriff of Kt Co. - Subj b Sep 18 1865 Chestertown; at 20 grad Wash College; 1886, commenced study of medicine, grad Hahnemann Medical College, Phila 1889. Returning to Chestertown, he opened office. He is mbr MP Church.

330. CHARLES T. RATHELL, farmer 4th dist Talb Co, postoffice address: Wye 500 Mills. His country home called Dolvin acquired at his father's death, 12 yrs ago, comprises 635 acres. Father of subj, Chas Rathell, of Del, farmer; m Miss Sarah Draper; of their 5 child., 3 d in infancy or youth, 1 survives, C. T.; his sis, Mrs. Thos Dudley, d about 5 yrs ago. The mother d 1878, and the father d 1883. - Subj b nr Easton, Feb 10 1861. When he was about 16 he began farming. Jan 28 1885 he m Miss Minnie Donaldson, of Newcastle, Pa; their child.: Chas, Warren, Mary and Donald.

331. THOMAS J. WILLIS, farmer 3rd dist; Kt Co, ME, res on homestead. In 501 early days of Md history 2 bros, John and Wm, came here from Eng, settled in Car Co. Subject's grandfather was John Willis, and 2 of his uncles were soldiers of Rev war. He served in coast defense in war of 1812; mcht in Vienna, Dor Co, revenue collector at Oxford, Md, succeeded in that office by his son Nicholas. He d 1838, when 71.
Wm B., father of Thos J. Willis, b Talb Co. When young man he made a trip to West Indies, but soon returned home. He owned a sailing vessel, and shipped freight from Oxford to Balt; managed a farm; sheriff Talb Co. He m Mary Spencer, of same co, from old fam, who had many mbrs in war of 1812, one being Col R. Spencer. Mr. Willis d 1865, aged 61. His wife d 10 yrs later at 70. Their child.; eldest, Rev Jonathan S., a Del politician, mbr 54th congress of U. S.; Alexander d in 24th yr; Margaret E., m Alexander E. Bell, and d at 33; Elizabeth m Rev J. H. Lightbourn; Thos J. next in order; Sallie B. w/o Alfred M. Moore; and Wm.
Subj b 15 Sep 1836, Talb Co, in father's farm house. When about 32 he went into Del, returned 2 yrs later to Kt Co, Md; 1870 came to this co, and 3 yrs res nr Lynch; conducted a produce and commission business 3 yrs Balt. 1878

returned to Kt Co and farmed nr Lynch; 1888 purch Jas W. Skirven farm, settling on it 1891. 1862 he m Mary E. Chaplain, of Talb Co, of old Talb fam, sis of Dr. Jas S. Chaplain, of Trappe, Talb Co; Prof. Alexander Chaplain, of Easton; and of Rev John F. Chaplain, of Phila Conference ME Church. She d Feb 14 1897 when 56. Five children left: Harry C., res nr Fairlee; Eleanor S., w/o L. J. Keyser; Annie C., who m Jesse H. Usilton (see his sketch on another page); Wm B. and May L., both at home.

502 332. GEORGE D. FREENEY, constable past 23 yrs, farmer of Quantico dist, Wicomico Co. He moved onto homestead, Bowers Hill, 25 Dec 1864; b Som Co, s/o Peter Freeney, tailor. His father, Richard, was from Ireland, Protestant. Peter Freeney m Elizabeth, d/o Geo Davis; she is in 76th yr; of their 10 child., fol survive: Geo D.; Julia, w/o John T. Phillips, of Laurel, Del; Jas C., res Va; Benj B., of Balt; Sarah M., w/o Thos C. Callaway, of Balt; and Sml W., of Spring Hill, Md. Peter Freeney, b same part of Som Co subj, d Aug 4 1896. - Subj b Dec 22 1839; at 18 he turned to farming; became owner of Bowers Hill farm 33 yrs ago; mbr MP Church. May 7 1861 he m Sarah J. Waller, d/o Jonathan Waller, of Delmar, Del. Of their 5 children 4 survive: Jas T. A., Wm J., Ernest G. and Edw D., all at home.

503 333. THOMAS P. FLETCHER elected manager of almshouse, about 5 yrs ago. This almshouse is located 1 3/4 miles north of Quantico, Wicomico Co, on farm (c. 200 a.). Father of subj, John W. Fletcher, from Som Co; d 1888. His wife was Martha, d/o Chas Rider, this dist. She d 1877; of her 7 children 4 have d. John W., Jr, and Mary lives nr Quantico. Grandfather John W. Fletcher was a tailor and conducted his business in Salisbury, Wicomico Co and Princess Anne, Som Co; once magistrate. He d 1887; mbr ME Church.
Subj b nr Quantico Oct 121 1856; attended dist school until 18; turned to farming; now owns prop in Hebron, this co, cultivates farm (about 60 a.) Quantico dist. He m 25 Dec 1885, Maggie, d/o Columbus Messick; their daus: Mildred and Rosalie. Mr. Fletcher is mbr ME Church; Mrs. Fletcher is mbr Episc Church.

503 334. THOMAS A. DUDLEY farmer 4th dist, Talb Co; past 12 yrs has cultivated Kingston farm (290 a.); commissioner of Talb Co 1894-1895; b nr the village of Matthews on his father's farm Mar 30 1853. His father, Alexander E., b on same farm as subj, 1813, s/o Thos Dudley, of this state. He d 1859 at 46. He owned 18 slaves. He m Miss Elizabeth Arringdale, of this dist; she had 2 child., one decd; she d 1867. When subj reached maturity he took charge of farm that he inherited. He farmed except when employed on steamboat, 1877-1878. Dec 3 1879 he m Lucretia, d/o Chas Rathell; managed latter's homestead; then returned to old farm; Mar 10 1885, came to Kingston, which had been left to wife by her father, who d a wealthy man (worth perhaps $75,000). Mrs. Dudley d Apr 29 1890, leaving child.: Edw A., Elizabeth R., Carroll T. and Mary L. Mr. Dudley m Aug 29 1892 Elma, d/o Hy P. Hopkins, of 4th dist.

504 335. GEORGE W. TRUITT, M. D., Parsonsburg, Wicomico Co; b here Nov 7 1854, s/o Sml P. and Eliza M. Truitt. After high school of Salisbury he taught school Dennis dist 12 yrs. Formerly he had operated a sawmill in Berlin, Wor Co, about 2 yrs. Last 2 yrs of teaching he studied medicine and grad Univ of Md, Balt, 1889; returned to old home in Parsonsburg and estab office.

505 336. EUGENE CROCHERON, business man, 20 yrs in Dor Co; fall 1876 came to Strait dist and 2 yrs later embarked in mercantile business in partnership

-90-

with grandfather, who d leaving him sole owner. 1876-1882 associated with Mr. Anderson in blacksmith's trade; has interest in oyster vessels and oyster planter. Crocheron fam of French origin. First settler to this country c. 1670, in Richmond Co, N.Y., one descendants, sheriff and another co judge. Father of subj, John H. Crocheron, s/o Nathan Crocheron, both of Richmond Co. Latter spent last his 12 yrs Bishop's Head, Md, where owner of mercantile estab; here he d 1890, at 88. The former in mercantile business and farming, still res Richmond Co, with wife, Mahala (Blake) Crocheron, where their childhood and middle age were spent; their child.: Emelie, Geo (decd), Eugene, Ophelia, Winfield, Abbie, Ella, Claudia and Irving. - Subj b 1857 Richmond Co, N.Y. Fam attend ME Church. He m 1880 Miss Tryphena Johnson, d/o Ezeikiel Johnson, their child.: Emelie S., Irving, Clarence and Eulalia.

337. SAMUEL G. WALLS b nr Sudlersville, 1st dist QA Co, Apr 27 1838, s/o Sml 505 Walls, b same farm where subj res. Here his grandfather, Jos W. Walls, res; d at 79; slave holder; in war of 1812; m Rebecca Cloake; their child.: Sml, Jos W., Hy, Joshua, Jas and John, all decd; Geo, res Wilm, Del; Sally A., decd; and Elizabeth, w/o Thos Elliott, of Sudlersville.
When subj was 17, his father d, at 55, and he remained with mother 2 yrs; worked as farm hand, by the month for 2 yrs; purch present farm 1884, located there 1892; 1862 m Miss Temperance A. Lollee; their child., in order of birth: Walter, in plumbing business Phila; Spencer, mcht Sudlersville; Geo A., operates threshing machine and clerks for bro; Jennie, decd; Elwood, farmer 1st dist, QA Co; Carrie, Arthur S. and Chas W. Subj mbr ME Church.

338. JAMES T. TRUITT, Salisbury; 1885 app dep collector internal revenue; 506 clerk circuit courts Wicomico Co; b in Wicomico Co (now), Jun 5 1849, s/o Rufus K. and Mary A. (Stanford) Truitt, respectively of Wor and Som Cos. He was 2nd of 5 child., others: Alice, Florence, Geo W. and Laura; reared in Salisbury, where father owned a store; at 14 his school days ended and he assisted in work of store. 1875 m Henrietta Griffin, of Som Co, d/o John H. Griffin. Of their three child. 2 living: Jas G., in College of Pharmacy Balt, and Raymond King. Mr. Truitt is mbr dME Church.

339. JOSHUA M. ANTHONY 3rd dist Car Co; b here May 20 1848, d Sep 12 1896. 509 In addition to farm he operated mill and general store; postmaster at Anthony, founded by him and named in his honor.
First of fam to America was subject's paternal grandfather, of England, emigrant to Car Co, where he built the mill that has since his death been operated by his descendants. Father of subj, Rbt Anthony, carried on farm pursuits and milling business. He m Elizabeth Melvin, of Md., of their 7 child. 4 living: Sarah M., Wilhelmina, Jos P. and Rbt W.
Subj reared on farm now occupied by his wid, who carried on store, mill and postoffice. Subj m Dec 23 1874 M. Ella Lowe, of Car Co d/o Esma and Margaret (Records) Lowe. Both b Del; had 3 sons and 3 daus. Her maternal grandfather was farmer and soldier in war of 1812. Her father, Esma Lowe, was farmer and sheriff Car Co. Child. of subj and wife: Bertha, Lulu and Ella, all married and res this co; Edna, Geo, Joshua M. and Anna M., at home. Mr. Anthony was mbr MP Church.

340. CHARLES BENJAMIN DOWNS has large landed interests QA Co; res village of 509 Kt Island; b Centreville, QA Co, 1832; brought to Kt Island at 2, s/o Chas and Mary Downs, former of Car Co, most of life res island, where he d 1885; carriage trimmer, with apprenticeship under Dnl Newnam, of Centreville. He m

Mary, wid of Arthur Carter and d/o Benj Tolson. Of her 1st marriage one child b, Arthur, business man Annapolis. - Subj m 1866 Miss Mary E., d/o Jas Bright; farmed until recently. Their child.: Arthur; Estella, w/o Eugene Herbert, of Stevensville; Ella and Sarah. Mrs. Downs attends ME Church.

510 341. WILLIAM P. TANNER owns farm southern part Kt Island, 4th dist QA Co; b lower part of island 1841, s/o Thos and Elizabeth (Shawn) Tanner; m c. 1877 Miss Hester A. Carter, d/o Richard Thos Carter, business man this region. Besides cultivating farm (350 a.), he attends to 1000 a. belonging to Christ Church, and another large farm for Wm S. Young, of Balt. He purch farm where he now dwells 1881. He and wife mbrs Episc Church. One John Wm Tanner, mechanic, came to America early 1600's. His son Philemon, grandfather of subj, b Kt Island; here Thos Tanner b 1806. He grew to maturity on island, m and reared fam here. His children were: Cornelius, Elizabeth, Wm P., Eliza, Susan, Emma and Ella (d unmarried). Susan is w/o Jas R. Legg, this locality; and Emma m Jas H. Cockey. Wm Tanner, an uncle of subj, never married.

510 342. GEORGE F. STERLING, of this place, conducts mercantile business at Lawsonia, Som Co, succeeded his father in business, c. 20 yrs ago. The father, Wm Sterling, b 1810; carried business this town for about 40 yrs prior; now in 88th yr; has always res in Lawsonia or vicinity, now res on farm nr where he was b; mbr Asbury ME Church. His father was John Sterling of this dist. Wm Sterling m 4 times, and by his union with mother of subj (formerly Jane Moore) had 7 child; 4 survive: Geo F.; John E.; Cornelia, w/o E. H. Prewitt; and Mary E., wid of Luther Sterling. - Subj b Jun 1847; in packing and shipping oysters; since 1877 has carried on general store here; postmaster of Crisfield. Apr 16 1874 he m Eveline Lawson, d/o John W. Lawson; their child.: Lillie, wid of Chas G. Cullin; Warren, of Crisfield Bank; Edith, John C. and Marhia. mbrs of fam attend Asbury ME Church.

511 343. BENJAMIN F. DAVIS, farmer Tyaskin dist, Wicomico Co; b Sep 1 1846; owns homestead nr Wicomico River nr Whitehaven. This branch of the Davis fam long associated with Eastern Shore of Md; supposedly of Welsh or Eng ancestry. Paternal grandfather of subj was Elzie Davis. Of 15 child. of Benj and Margaret (Price) Davis, Benjamin F. only survivor. Apr 1850 he m Miss Esther V. Harrison; of this co; their child.: Ella L., Minnis S., Sallie, Florence, Nellie, Annie, Georgia, Wm and Ola Ray.

512 344. SAMUEL OSCAR TULL mcht Kingston, Som Co, in business of planting, packing and shipping oysters; in partnership with bro, T. H. Tull, c. 15 yrs; his bro d 1882; since then subj has conducted his affairs alone. He was deputy commander of police boat 2 yrs and registration officer. Subject's father Hy T. Tull b nr Tulls Corner c. 1813; res Brinkley's dist; in farming (250 a.) and ship-building; he owned 20 slaves. He owned shipyard on Big Annemessex River and there built several schooners and large vessels for ocean transit. He and his wife mbrs MP Church. He d 1893 at 80. He m Mary D. Ballard d/o Dnl Ballard, of Fairmount. She d in 76th yr. Of her 8 children who grew to maturity, 5 survive: Elzabeth, w/o Wm G. Simmons, of Wyoming, Del; Sml O.; Annie, Mrs. Chas Mathews, of Newport News, Va; Alice, w/o Dr. F. Robertson; and Florence, Mrs. Ira N. Coulbourn, of Marion Station.

Subj b Tulls Corner, Dec 1848, spent boyhood on farm nr Kingston, the same he now owns and cultivates. Feb 1867 associated with bro, T. H., in general store in Kingston. He m Miss Sallie Elizabeth, d/o Alexander Robertson, of this locality; their child., in order of birth: Grace S., Hy R., Oscar Paul, Allen, Ruth, Rodger and Franklin. mbrs of fam attend Presby Church.

345. CAPT. JAMES E. KIRWAN business man, farmer and mcht, Kt Island; only fire insur agent and coal dealer on island; raises terrapins for market. 512
  Captain Kirwan b Balt Jun 9 1848; mbr of fam of Eng ancestors and seafaring men. His father, Capt Lamuel Kirwan b Dor Co, mostly followed the sea; d at 36; m Sophia Stallings, of Balt Co; their child: Wm H. H., chief engineer on steamer John W. Garrett, d Dec 19 1895; Lemuel, d in boyhood; Lavinia, m Martin L. Jones, of Dor Co, res Kt Island, where Mr. Jones d 1893; and Jas E., subj. - Subj spent boyhood on the water; at 16 took command of schooner Wm Banes. Later had charge of schooners Rebecca, Thos Brinkley, Julia A. Thomas, Richard Sands and Gen Rbt E. Lee; in mercantile business in village of Kt Island; depart commander of oyster navy 2 yrs. Sep 10 1867 he m Mary Rebecca, d/o Nelson Gardner, and niece of Rev Sml Gardner, preacher on Kt Island. Their children: Chas E., Sophia and Lemuel. Chas E., mcht of Chester, m Maggie, d/o Joshua Coooper, and niece of Rev J. A. Cooper.

346. HON. JESSE K. HINES, decd, legislator of Md b Nov 17 1829, nr Millington, Kt Co, s/o Isaac and Anne (Knock) Hines. Parents left farm, and moved to Balt when he was infant. There he attended private schools kept by Dr. Baxter and Jos Walker. When 14 his father d and fam returned to Kt Co. He entered mercantile house of Thos Walker, of Millington; worked for Wm F. Smyth, of same town, and for Spruance Bros, of Smyrna, Del, up to 1848, when he taught school in Morgan Creek dist, nr Chestertown. 1852 he embarked in mercantile business on his own; 1854 elected constable. After studying law under Hon. Richard Hynson, admitted to bar 1868; 1873 sent as rep to state legislature; 1874 speaker of house of Delegates. (Other details of his political life are given in this sketch.) 513
  Subj m(1) Emily Alphonsa Massey, d/o Col Elijah E. and Mary Massey. Col Massey entered army at beginning Civil war, served on Halleck's staff, rose to rank of lieut col. Child. of Mr. and Mrs. Hines: Thos L., res Balt; W. Franklin, res Chestertown; Jesse Knock, Jr., in N.J.; Isaac res Ill.; Annie and Jannie, both m and res St. Louis; and Catherine A., w/o Dr. Richard Gundry of Catonsville, Md.
  Father of Jesse Knock Hines was Isaac Hines, of Cecil Co, Md, officer of Balt Bank, chief clerk in house of delegates. His father, Isaac, in Rev war. They were Welsh people and came to Md in early days. Mother of Jesse K. Hines was descendant of Knocks who came from Scotland in early 1700's and settled in Kt Co. Today there is no one bearing that name in Kt Co.
  W. Franklin, 2nd son of subj, b Sep 19 1856; attended Wash College; when 17 entered office of Dr. Thos R. Brown, prof of surgery College of Physicians and Surgeons Balt; grad Feb 1877; since then in practice Chestertown; mber Episc Church. 1880 he m Miss Mary, d/o Wm Emory, of QA Co; their child.: Frank Brown, Jennie Emory, Chas Gilpin, Mary Alphonsa and Emory Massey.

347. LUTHER T. MILES, JR conducts general store at Marion Station, and planting and packing of oysters here. His father, Luther T. Miles. Sr., co commissioner of Som 4 terms, farmer, res on part of original tract known as Heart's Ease. He m Annie E. Handy; their child.: Ida E., w/o Chas S. Whittington; Carrie E., Mrs. E. W. Tull; Lillian H., Mrs. C. L. Gunby; and Luther T. Jr. The parents mbrs MP Church. - Subj b on farm nr present home 1867; fol common schools went to Marion Acad; at 20 embarked in business with E. W. Tull; postoffice located in their store. Subj m Miss Florence M. Hall 515

80N
1894, at home of bride's father, Hy W. Hall, of Marion Station. She was b and reared in Som Co. Their little son, Luther T. They attend MP Church.

515 348. CAPT. DANIEL FRIEL, res Queenstown, QA Co, Cath, b Phila 1841; came to this co 1854, growing to mature yrs on his father's farm. His father, John Friel, of Adams Co, Pa, s/o Dnl Friel of Irish birth. The father of Dnl Friel, Bernard, of weath and influence, built a section of turnpike between Hagerstown and Gettysburg, a contractor in general. Early in 30's the captain's father and his bro Dnl came to this co and organizaed Schuykill Lime Co. John Friel m Miss Clarke, of Phila, still living, res with her son, subj, in her 79th yr. Her childrren all living: Dnl; Thos, of Queenstown; John, of Phila; Jeannie and Katherine.

Subj left home at 20; sailed the sea 2 yrs, went to Phila, studied at nautical college, grad in navigation and nautical astronomy; as a sailor visited nearly every country; m 1871 Miss Emma J., d/o Sml Whiting, of Corsica Neck, QA Co, 1871; their son, Sml E. Whiting, of Queenstown. Mrs. Friel d May 24 1874. Dec 1875 subj m Miss Virginia Whiting, half- sister of 1st wife and d/o Wm Whiting. She d suddenly Apr 3 1896. 1869 Capt Friel dealtin grain on Wye River about 6 yrs; 1875 estab present business. He owns a wharf, granary and dwelling houses in Queenstown and schooner Wm McKenney.

516 349. LEWIN W. WICKES, lawyer Chestertown b Dec 17 1866 s/o Wm N. E. and Anne Elizabeth (Wethered) Wickes; after high school entered Wash College; 1886 enrolled Johns Hopkins Univ, returning to Chestertown spring 1887; studied law with J. A. Pearce; admitted to bar 1890. He is mbr of PE Church.

519 350. JAMES KENT HARPER JACOBS, M. D., physician, surgeon and business man Kennedyvile, Kt co; b Feb 11 1856, Centreville, QA Co, s/o Wm H. Jacobs, of same co, who spent early life in Church Hill, where the grandfather, Wm Jacobs, Sr. (b QA Co), in merchandising. Founder of fam in new world came from Eng prior to Rev war. When a young man the doctor's father went to Wilm, Del; became editor of Port Gibson Herald, Port Gibson, Miss; organized company for Mexican war, commissionied first lieut, had charge of company of Texas Rangers at battle of Monterey. On return to Centreville, Md, embarked in merchandising with Col John McKenney and son, Wm McKenney. When the col withdrew few yrs later the firm remained Jacaobs & McKenney. He was one of the original promoters of the QA & Kent Railroad, of which he was sec and treasurer. He died in retirement on his farm nr Centreville, Briarfield, at 65, Dec 23 1880. He was Episc. 17 May 1855 Wm H. Jacobs m Miss Caroline B. Harper, d/o Dr. Jas K. Harper, of Centreville, who descended from royal fam of Eng. The Browne family, of which Mrs. Jacobs was descendant, settled in Md 1720 and acquired tract at Batchelder Hoope, QA Co. Mr. and Mrs. Jacobs had 2 child.: subj and Caroline Browne, res with her brother. She was educated by private teacher at home, attended a private school in Greensborough, taught by Miss Betts, under Bishop Lay.

Subj spent boyhood on home farm nr Centreville, educated by private tutors, at acad at Centreville; grad Univ Md 1877, with degree of M. D.; opened office in Kennedyville; director of Second Natl Bank of Chestertown. He owns 2 farms (450 a.). 1892 he m Miss Nannie, d/o Gen Wm McKenney, of Centreville; their sons, Jas K. H., Jr., and Wm McKenney. The doctor, his wife, mother and sister mbrs St. Paul's Episc Church of Centreville. The Jacobs, Brownes, and Harpers all related to Kent family of Eng, of royal blood, and in whose honor Kent Co was named.

351. JAMES FASSETT DOUGHERTY, M. D., physician, Presby, Princess Anne, Som 520 Co, from old fam of southern part of Eastern Shore of Md. His father is still in business in this place. Subj b Nov 8 1869, s/o Z. Jas and Adelia (Henry) Dougherty, who had 3 child. He pursued his studies in local schools until 17; instructed under private tutor; then went into father's mercantile business; soon entered College of Physicians and Surgeons Balt, grad spring 1895; retuned to Princess Anne, into partnership with Dr. Rufus W. Dashiell.

Z. Jas Dougherty, father of subj, one of 10 child of John and Esther (Wainwright) Dougherty, of Wicomico Co. The mother d in 57th yr. The father was wealthy farmer; d 73. Z. Jas Dougherty commenced clerked in general store, Princess Anne until after war; since 1865 has conducted general supply store, 5 yrs with a partner, nearly 30 yrs alone. He m Adalie Henry, of Wor Co; child.: Jas F., Ellen Myers and Bredelle H.

352. LIEUT. HENRY COOKE TILGHMAN d some yrs ago, spent much of his life at 521 sea, lieut in U. S. navy; his health induced him to abandon seafaring life. His last yrs were spent at home Easton dist, Talb Co, where his fam still res. He was b at Hermitage QA Co 1809 s/o Richard Cooke Tilghman, of Balt and grandson of Richard Tilghman, b at Hermitage. At 15 he ran away to sea; 14 Nov 1839, m Miss Milcha M. Skinner, d/o Andrew Skinner, of Talb Co, descendant of Elder Brewster, a leader on the Mayflower. Fairview, on Miles River, granted to Skinners remained in fam of wife of Lieut Tilghman until all the child. of Andrew Skinner were m. After his marriage Lieut Tilghman settled at Riverslie, an estate (206a.) that belonged to his wife Easton dist. Here he res, until he d Feb 19 1880. He and his family attended Episc Church. He and his wife had 9 child.; living: Elizabeth, res old homestead; Louisa T., w/o Wm Carroll, Balt Co; Fannie, w/o Rbt Huff, of Balt; Sophia, who m Powell Holliday, of Key West, Fla.; Susan Tilghman, at home; and Millie M., w/o John L. Pascault, who carries on old homestead in Talb Co. Mrs. Tilghman, with her two daus and son-in-law, res at old homestead.

(History of The Hermitage is given.) In old family graveyard lies Richard Tilghman, surgeon, who d 1675, and by his side, Maria Foxley, his wife, and their child. and grandchild. unto the 3rd and 4th generation and beyond: Richard and Anna Maria Lloyd, his wife; Richard and Susanna Frisby, his wife; and again, Richard (comonly called "the colonel") and Elizabeth his wife. This last Richard was 4th of the name. Surviving his only son, he left the Hermitage to son of his sis, Mrs. Wm Cooke. This nephew, adding Tilghman to his name, became Richard Cooke-Tilghman, and founder of branch known as Cooke-Tilghmans.

At his death, these broad acres were divided among his five surviving sons: Wm, Richard, Hy, Jas and John, 2nd son, Richard Cooke-Tilghman, Jr., getting the home place. For various reasons, all parted with their patrimony, save said Richard Cooke-Tilghman, Jr. He m 1st cousin, Elizabeth Cooke Williams, and d 1879, without children, leaving the Hermitage to his wife. She d 11 yrs later, leaving it to her bro, Otho Holland Williams, the present owner, who makes it his home. Mr. Williams and his brother-in-law, Richard Cooke Tilghman the second, are grand-nephews of Col Richard Tilghman. Mr. Williams' mother, Susan Frisby Cooke, a niece of Col Tilghman, and sis of Richard Cooke, who took his uncle's name when made his heir. Their father, Wm Cooke, m Elizabeth Tilghman, sis of col, and d/o Richard and Susan Frisby Tilghman. Mr. Cooke was lawyer and res in Annapolis, where, because of his Tory proclivities, he was for a time forbidden to practice. Of English parentage, he studied law in the Temple, and among the few relics now at the Hermitage are the table and chair used by him when a student in London.

522   353. WILLIAM M. COOPER, Episc, sec Wicomico Building and Loan Assoc. and assist editor Salisbury Advertiser; b Barren Creek dist, Wicomico Co, Apr 7 1863, 2nd s/o Lambert H. and Martha Washington (Bradley) Cooper, of this co. After the common schools he entered Md Military academy at Oxford, Md, where he remained a student until 1887; assist editor Salisbury Advertiser, 1887-1892; went to Cullman, Ala.; returned to Md, spending short time in Balt as an employe on Balt Sun; went to Duluth, Minn., resumed as assist editor of Advertiser Aug 1893.

523   354. HENRY HUBBERT, business man and farmer, Dor Co; postoffice address: Williamsburg; b old homestead where he has managed since 18; b 1839, s/o Thos and Ann M. (Coey) Hubbert. The father b nr Williamsburg 1803, carpenter and cabinetmaker and ship building; later in life he turned to farming. He and wife had child: Jos, of Hurlock; Martha, who m Matthew Marine; Peter, decd; Hy; Angeline; and Irene, w/o Geo Felter. Paternal grandfather of subj was Michael Hubbert, who m Mrs. Payne, wid. He was prob a native of this co, and his land was bt by subj 1890, and on it is still standing the old mill, since rebuilt, which he erected last century. 1879 he m Mary J. Gambrill, d/o Darius Gambrill; their child.: in order of birth, Hattie, Frank H., Orra, Dorsey, Eva and Elmer.

523   355. PETER W. SULLIVAN, farmer 8th dist Car Co, b same farm house where he now res. His father, Peter Sullivan, of Car Co, farmer, m Mary Warren who was b and reared this locality; their child who attained adult age: Eliza, m Henry Culver, of this co; Tansy J., w/o Chas Smith, res nr American Corner, this dist; subj, b Jan 3 1860, fell heir to old home place about 1886 and has since managed it. Subj m Jan 6 1886 Clara Roach, d/o Hy Roach, of Seaford, Del; their child.: Harry, Nettie, Howard and Nellie.

524   356. CAPT SAMUEL M. TRAVERS, decd, res 4th dist. Capt John Travers, father of subj, of this dist, and here res. He sailed on long voyages most of each year, master of a vessel several yrs. He m Miss Geoghegan, who lived to old age.
    Subj b Jun 3 1815; at 5 his father d; at 12 yrs he shipped before the mast on a vessel of which his uncle, Sml Travers, was master; for 3 yrs the lad sailed between the chief ports along the Chesapeake Bay. When 15 he entered employ of Capt Hicks Travers, in trade along the bay; at 22 he was placed in command of vessel of Jas Hooper, of Balt, that sailed back and forth to West Indies, next 7 yrs; then worked for Scotch importer, as captain of bark Francis Partridge, in coffee trade and in hides and horns in Uruguay for 8 yrs. Later he went to St. Thomas (belonging to Denmark) and entered into partnership, in the firm Travers & Spaulding, conducting ship chandler's supply store on that island; sold out, returned to native co and bt farm on western side of mouth of Slaughter Creek (farm now owned by son Harry). Here he d Sep 2 1892. In the city of Balt the captain m Catherine A. Carpenter, who d Mar 22 1888, in 69th yr. She child: Sml C., farmer this dist; Harry, who owns old homestead, farmer and fruit grower; Wm C., farmer this dist; and Margaret E., res with bro Harry in summer and res Balt in winter. Harry Travers m Apr 27 1893 Mrs. Ella G. Phillips, of Balt.

525   357. JOHN R. NEILD, farmer Dor Co, operates old homestead 9th dist, former prop of father; house built as early as 1800. Subj reared nr Woolford; b Jul 10 1830; only survivor of fam of 12 child. of Hugh and Elizabeth (Fooks) Neild. The father b nr here, in Milton (then), Jul 3 1792; farmer and ship

builder; mcht Milton, where h d 1860, at 68; s/o Abraham Neild, who came from Eng, settled in Milton, where he owned land, and in merchandising and ship building; owned many slaves. He m 3 times; he m(1) Miss Wheeler, who d in young womanhood and left no child. After death of subject's mother, his father m Mary A. Rea. Mrs. Elizabeth Neild was a member of the ME Church.

Subj was 16 when mother d; reared and educated nr Milton (since called Woolford); grad Dickinson College, Carlisle, Pa 1852; returned home and has since farmed, also in merchandising and lumber. Feb 16 1859 Mr. Neild m Hester A. Neal (b Del); d/o Outerbridge H. Neal, of Del. Children of subj and wife: Elizabeth E., w/o W. W. Harrington; Wm H., of this place; Nicey A., w/o Jas W. Brook, Jr.; Nora Belle, decd; M. Estelle, w/o Jas Guy Vane; John R., Jr., of Taylor's Island; Bertie J., w/o Chas Asplin; Cina L., at home; Outerbridge H., Alton B. and Harry G., all at home. Fam attend ME Church.

358. WILLIAM T. ANDERSON, decd, b 24 Mar 1838, Kt Co, mbr Meth Church. His father d when he was 10; then subj res with uncle in Cecil Co. Attaining his majority he returned to Kt Co, rented farm 4th dist; here he remained; d Feb 13 1897. Nov 1867 he m Mary J. Stephens in Kt co. She was b Balt, spent 12 yrs in primary schools of that city, then moved to this locality with parents, grew to maturity on farm 3rd dist. Their child., order of birth: Emma J., Carrie S., Thos S. and Jane D. Mrs. Anderson mbr MP Church. 526

359. JOHN RICHARD BENTON, M. D. res nr Stevensville, Kt Island, in home called Medical Hill. ' In addition to general practice he is co health physician, since 1896. Earliest Benton fam mbr to locate in QA Co was doctor's grandfather, Jas Benton, of AA Co. Father of subj, Richard Benton, b on island 1814 and grew up here, farmer; m Sarah E. Bryan, d/o Sml Bryan; their child.: Geo R., d unmarried, Jul 31 1885, at 31; John R.; Jos, d Apr 17 1886, at 26, leaving only child, Geo R.; Luther B., pharmacist res Balt; Sarah C., who m Prof. Edw F. Taylor, of Va, and d May 25 1895, at 30; and Minnie, who m Prof Edw F. Taylor of Balt, 1897. 526

After common schools, subj entered state normal school Balt; taught school 3 yrs, to support medical studies; grad medical depart Univ Md 1883. Until her death, Nov 8 1896, in 71st yr, doctor's mother kept house for him. Jan 14 1897 he m Miss Alice G., d/o Jas Bateman Hopkins; she is mbr Episc Church.

360. ALFRED KEMP; spring 1897, settled on farm, Trappe dist, Talb Co; owns total of 487 a.; pres Trappe Creamery Co; b Trappe 1837, s/o Dr. Sml T. and Elizabeth (Hardcastle) Kemp, of Talb Co; at 16 began work in Ross Wynan's machine shop, Balt (15 months); clerked in store of Kemp & Lloyd, Trappe, about 2 yrs; 1860 became mbr of firm Dellehay, Kemp & Co in Trappe, fol year withdrew and moved to Bolinbroke. 1864 returning to Trappe he became mbr of mercantile firm of Mullikin & Kemp, and when partnership dissolved 1867 he continued alone. Selling out store 1870, he went to Houston, Tex.; worked in cotton house 14 months; from then until 1890 cashier of Houston & Texas Central Railroad Houston Station; returned to Trappe 1890, to retire; 1897 settled on farm. He m 1891 Mrs. Mattie H. Naylor, d/o Col. Wm R. and Lydia L. (Carter) Hughett, of Md. Their child, Sml T. 529

361. HENRY CLAY CONNAWAY, postmaster Berlin; b 1844, s/o Noah and Louisa Connaway (d/o Peter Blizzard). Parents b and reared Sussex Co, Del; after they m, moved to vicinity of Berlin, became homesick and returned to Del; well along in yrs they once more came to Berlin and settled; both d here. Of their fam Margaret m Wm P. Jones, of Del, now a wid; Edw d in childhood; Annie w/o 530

-97-

Bolivan Williams, of Berlin; Sophia w/o Jos F. Miller, of Phila. 1861 subj enlisted Company G., Md Infantry, under Capt Geo S. Merrill and Col Wm H. Purnell; company served on Eastern Shore, then joined General Banks. He served in Va campaign; in battle at Harper's Ferry, returned home late 1862, employed by army in Ga., Ala., and Tenn. He m 1872, Miss Annie T. Quillen, d/o Thos N. Quillen, of this place. Their child.: Thos N, eldest; Hy Clay, Jr.; and Louisa. Mr Connaway owns farm and prop in Berlin.

530 362. HON. HENRY PAGE, chief judge 1st judicial dist of Md, res Princess Anne, Som Co; app to present office Aug 1892, and elected Nov 1893 to position for 15 yrs, resigning his place in congress to which elected 1891. Mr. Page's name was originally John Woodland Crisfield, Jr., named after his father (see his biography elsewhere this vol). Subj b 28 Jun 1841; mother d same day; then lived in home of maternal grandmother, Mrs. Ann Page (nee Woodland) in Cambridge, until she moved to Balt, where she d in 1876, wid of Dr. Hy Page, of Rock Hall, Kt Co, Md, physician who d 1820. In accord with her desire his name changed by legislative act to Hy Page 1848. Her only son also named for his father. Subj educated in boarding school 6 yrs, West Chester, Pa; student Univ Va until outbreak of war; stationed Harper's Ferry 6 weeks. When his battalion disbanded at Charlottesville he yielded to father's plea and returned home. He read law with father; then nearly 2 yrs in office of Wm S. Waters, of Balt; admitted to bar 1864; came to Princess Anne, becoming partner of father; practiced by himself 1871-1884; then he and Joshua Miles formed co-partnership lasting until app to bench. He attends Presby Church; m Oct 1867 Miss Virginia W. Dennis, of Wor Co, d/o John W. Dennis; their children: Julia E.; Hy Page, M. D., grad Univ Pa, surgeon U. S. army; Louisa J., Ann and John, all at home.

531 363. E. A. HIMMELWRIGHT, res 7th dist QA Co, b Montgomery Co, Pa., Dec 17 1824. His father d when he was quite young; mother moved her fam to her father's home nr Spinnerville. Subj worked in grandfather's flourihg mill until 17, then farmhand until 1845; 10 Feb enlisted in marine corps at Phila; served in navy yard under Maj Edw Twiggs until Aug 1845, sent on board sloop of war John Adams, at Brooklyn navy yard, then ready to sail for Pensacola, Fla., to relieve the Falmouth; later in engagements of Tempeci and Tuxpan and bombardment of Vera Cruz; Point Isabella, then Tobasco; later to Vera Cruz. (Additional details are given on the events of Mexican campaign.) Subj discharged c. 1848, returned to Phila. He then taught school Milford Square, Bucks Co, Pa, 3 yrs; clerked in clothing store Phila for a yr; in grocery business a while, then a salsesman; continued in Phila until 1855, then to QA Co, and since 13 Apr that year at his present res; 1867-1874 taught school, but now farms. 8 Apr 1855 he m Miss Margaret A. Book; of theri 6 child., 2 living: Mary L., w/o Hiram G. Tarberton, res 7th dist QA Co; and Annie G., w/o Cooper Tarberton. The other children d in infancy. Subj mbr MP Church.

532 364. L. WESLEY BEAUCHAMP, farmer Fairmount dist, Som Co, for past 10 yrs has tilled Zell farm (purch 1887); owns c. 400 a.; raises variety of crops, deals in livestock and fertilizer; b Westover Jul 1859; s/o Levin H. and Margaret (White) Beauchamp. Father b and reared Dublin Dist, Som Co, res Westover; owned large tracts and slaves; mcht and postmaster Westover; d at 80. He and wife mbrs MP Church. The wife, d/o Tubman White, still living on old homestead nr Westover, in 67th yr; of her child., decd: Helen and Frances. Here 2 sons: subj and Oliver T. Subj m Jan 1880, Miss Grace Broughton, d/o Elijah Broughton, of Kingston; their child.: Harriet, Chas W. and Helen.

365. HON. A. LINCOLN DRYDEN, state senator from Som Co; b Fairmount dist, Som 533 Co, Feb 18 1865, s/o Littleton T. and Charlotte E. (Ford) Dryden of this co. Subj descendant of 1 of 2 bros who c. 1660 emigrated from England and settled on Eastern Shore. Littleton T. Dryden, has lived mostly on Eastern Shore; 12 yrs dep U. S. marshal, U. S. commissioner of Eastern Shore, now superintendent of bureau of emigration Balt; age over 60. First 10 yrs of subject's life in Fairmount dist, then res Crisfield, where father was in crab and oyster business. Subj attended acad here, Wash Acad, Princess Anne, and St. John's College Annapolis; grad Dickinson College, Carlisle, Pa, with honors; brifly in oyster business Grand Rapids, Mich; returned to Crisfield; 1889 elected to house of delegates; assist librarian navy depart 1890-1893. Collecting statistics for library on Civil war, he visited Europe; since then general agent for Northwestern Mutual Life Insur Co Milwaukee, Wis., Eastern Shore of Md, Del, and Va; mbr ME Church. He m Miss Effie C. Venable, of this place; their child, Ethelyn. Mrs. Dryden d/o Seth and Susan A. (Jones) Venaable, of Eastern Shore, both decd.

366. FRANCIS A. WRIGHTSON, retired, Talb Co, of Bay Hundred dist, res on 534 farm, called Chance; b 1812, s/o Frs and Mary Ann Wrightson, of Talb Co. (see sketch of Wm L. Wrightson, elsewhere this vol); c. 1828-33 carpenter's apprentice Annapolis; 1849 purch farm where he still res. 1848 he m Ellen J., d/o John Graham, of St. Michael's dist; their child.: Chas T., in canning business Easton; Wm J., of St. Michael's; Jos G., decd, traveling salesman; Mary F., w/o A. Lowe; Edw G., manages of old farm; Ada G., w/o Frank Lowe; Mattie E., w/o Capt Lloyd Tidings, of Balt; and Emma L., w/o J. E. Shannahan, of Easton, now decd. Mr. and Mrs. Wrightson mbrs MP Church. G. Edw, s/o subj b 1849, farmer; m 1892 Miss May Grace, d/o Thos E. Grace; their child.: Geo E. and May Grace.

367. GEORGE W. OWENS b 1863; of English ancestors here late 1600's. His 534 father, Geo E. Owens, of Balt, brought by parents to Kt Co. Paternal grandfather was chief engineer on S. S. Savanah. For past 30 yrs father of subj res Betterton; contractor and builder; mbr ME Church, still living, at 57; m Mary A. Browball, of Kt Co; their child.: Florence, w/o Wm Jester; subj; Mary M., w/o J. W. Smith; John S., clerk on steamer Republic, running Phila-Cape May; Jos R., cabin officer on Eicksson Line, running Balt-Phila; Annie, Harry and Howard. Subj attended common schools of Betterton; at 15 began learning carpenter's trade; since 1893 in contracting and building on his own; erected Hotel Wilmer and ME Church and steeple in Betterton. 1889 he m Miss Ida Reed, of Balt City; their child.: T. Guy and Howard C. Subj elected co commissioner 1895; mbr ME Church.

368. JAMES MARCUS WRIGHT b father's farm Dor Co, in 1855, s/o Jabez (of 535 Co) and Mary Wright. The child.: Rowena, Jas M., Rodolph, Kennely J. and Alvin and Everett, twins, and Zed. Eldest dau m Jas A. Nichols; Rodolph res Morse, Custer Co, Idaho; K. J., mcht Hurlock; Alvin res New Haven, Conn.; and Everett minister ME Church. Subj came to this co 1888, bt farm nr Federalsburg. 1877 he m Car Co, Amanda, d/o Jas Nichols; their child.: Herman, Eva, Ethel and Elsie; fam attend ME Church. Since 1894 he has owned store in Federalsburg, carrying hardware, farming implements, harness, etc. Paternal grandfather of subj named Kennely, b Dor Co; reared fam of 13 children; lived to old age.

369. RUFUS W. DASHIELL, M. D., physician Princess Anne, Som Co, b 1850 this co; at 8 his father moved to this place; student in old Wash acad of Princess Anne until 16 or 17, entered St. John's College, Annapolis, but left junior year; studied in father's office, who was physician; studied under Dr. Nathan R. Smith, Batl, his father's old preceptor; grad Balt Univ, 1872, opened office Wicomico Co; soon entered into partnership with Dr. L. W. Morris, of this place; after a year opened his own office; 1895 took a partner, Dr. James F. Dougherty. During Grant's administration app U. S. pension surgeon in Princess Anne; mbr Episc Church. 1877 he m(1) Laura Henry, of Berlin, Wor Co; she d Feb 1881, leaving child, Laura, who lives with her father. 1894 he m Cecilia, d/o Jas U. Dennis (see sketch elsewhere this vol).

Father of subj, Dr. Cadmus Dashiell, b this co; grad Univ Md; in medical practice in what is now Wicomico Co for many yrs. 1858 came to Princess Anne and soon retired, now 84. He is mbr old Green Hill Church Wicomico Co. His father, Gen Mathias Dashiell, of Som (now Wicomico) co, extensive land owner, had many slaves; served in war of 1812, later sheriff this co; m Miss Harriet Walter. She was b this co, d at 65, leaving child.: Margaret, wid of H. H. Robertson; Rufus W.; Frs H., farmer this dist; Sarah, w/o Rev O. H. Murphy, Episc minister; and Julus T., dentist of Harrisburg, Pa.

370. HENRY C. NEAVITT, business man St. Michael's dist, Talb Co; 1856 opened general store at Broad Creek Neck. 1862 app 1st postmaster here, the place named Neavitt in his honor; now owns 2 stores run by sons, Oliver K. and Alvin. Subj b Oct 7 1834, s/o Jos E. and Annie (Hunt) Neavitt, respectively of QA and Talb Cos. The former moved to neighborhood as young man and purch farm where he d in middle age; his wife d at about 65; both assoc ME Church; their child.: Julia Ann, Deborah E. and John A., decd; Mary W.; Johanna and Samuel W., decd; and subj. Jos E. Neavitt m in early life to Miss Dawson, their child.: Mary Anne, decd; other d in infancy.

After his father d subj continued to res on farm with mother, attending public schools. At 21 he clerked in store in St. Michael's (3 yrs). 1856 he opened store, he now owns. He m Miss Mary A. Neavitt, of Balt, their child.: Wm Hy, bookkeeper with Wheeler & Wilson Manufacturing Co Balt; Albert Arnold d at 5; Oliver K. and Alvin, in business with father. Mrs. Neavitt d/o Wm C. and Margaret (Kennard) Neavitt, of QA Co. Another dau S. C., m B. H. Kennard, of QA Co.

371. CHARLES COCKEY, M. D., in practice since 1866, Queenstown, QA Co, except yrs 1873-74, when res Kt island; assoc with son, B. E. Cockey in drug store in Queenstown; also health officer. Cockeys are old fam on Kt Island. Subject's father, Edw Cockey, b there (see also sketch of M. T. Cockey, elsewhere this vol); grew up on island, became farmer; m Susan d/o Hy Legg; their child.: Peter, d leaving an only dau, w/o W. T. Stevens, of Kt Island; Chas; Wm H., d leaving wife and a dau; Jas H., farming on the island; and John and Mordecai, decd. - Except when attending acad at Centrevile, subj passed boyhood on farm on Kent Island where b Jul 22 1842; grad medical depart Univ of Md 1866; came to Queenstown; fam mbrs Episc Church. Dec 1868 he m Elizabeth, d/o Dr. R. W. Eareckson, of Kt Island. Their son, Benj Earickson Cockey, m Harriet Magness, of Balt; their child, Harriet E.

372. SAMUEL EDWARD WHITMAN, editor Star Democrat Easton, b Apr 8 1855 Bradford Co, Pa, s/o Fdk S. and Jane M. (Van Saun) Whitman. Paternal grandfather, John Whitman, from Wernsheim, Wurtemberg, Germany; 1806 came to America, located Lititz, Lancaster Co, Pa, started a pottery with father and

-100-

bro, one of first ever estab this country; later moved to Dauphin Co, Pa, and while res there enlisted in U. S. army in war of 1812; contracted disease which ended his life 1826. He had come to this country with father, bro and two sis, as their prop had been confiscated during rev in their native land. Besides the father of subj he had two older sons, Geo and John, one a mcht and other a painter, both decd.

Fdk S. Whitman b Londonderry township, Dauphin Co, Pa., Nov 29 1815, and there res until adult, poor health in early life, attended German schools to some extent; in merchandising, lumbering and farming; went to New York and Maine to superintend shipping of stone for New York high bridge; later worked briefly in office of Geo Law, contractor of the bridge; then located Bradford Co, Pa, farmed until 1875, came to Easton, and until fall of 1896 followed farming and mercantile pursuits. While res of Pa he was co auditor, friend of Judge Mercur, chief justice of Pa and Judge David Wilmot. He is still living; his wife, from N.J., d Mar 6 1890, leaving child, subj. Another son, Walter, drowned Dec 19 1871, at 11. Mrs. Whitman's father, Sml Van Saun, of Holland family which originally spelled the name Van Zandt, direct descendent of Annecke Jans, original owner of Trinity Church prop in New York City.

Reared Towanda, Pa, subj educated in public schools, attended Susquehanna Collegiate Institute, preparing for Princeton College (prevented by failing health); learned printer's trade in Bradford Argus. Coming to Talb Co, he spent short time on father's farm, entered office of Easton Star, became stockholder; on consolidation with Easton Democrat 1896 continued as editor. 28 Aug 1877 he m Miss Anna L. Weston, of Talb Co, d/o Wm E. Weston, lumberman belonging of old fam of Easton; their child.: Fdk Wm, d at 1; Bertram Edw, grad Easton high school 1896, in business with father; Walter Weston, attending school; and Louise, d Sep 1896, at 7 1/2. Fam mbrs Episc Church.

373. HON. EUGENE L. DUDLEY QA Co, elected postmaster house of delegates in Annapolis 1893; 1895, elected to state legislature; b nr Crumpton, QA Co, 1850, s/o Jas P. and Mary A. (Goodhand) Dudley. Father b this co, farmer, rgtr of wills. His father was Eng, came to Md at early day, settled in this co. Jas Dudley and wife, Mary, had 9 child., subj 8th in order of birth; others: Wm C., of Talb Co; Georgia, w/o Jas B. Hackett, of Sudlers- ville; Olivia, Mrs. C. G. Lynch; Mary, w/o Cornelius Comegys, of Centreville; Dr. Chas; Jennie; Hiram G.; and Martha, Mrs. Harry McPhaley. Subj attended dist schools; now res on place long known as old Grayson homestead (224 a.)., former home of ex-Gov Grayson. 541

374. PROF. JOHN F. COPPER, educator Kt Co, res 6th dist, b Feb 6 1838, Still Pond, this co, s/o Joshua Copper, of Kt Co. Father, carpenter in younger yrs, later steward co almshouse 36 yrs, then res with son on farm 3rd dist; descendant of early fam of Md; d at 89. He m Ann Woodle (d at 45), of Kt Co; their 6 child., decd except subj and sis Phoebe, wid of Jesse Jerome. By his 2nd union no surviving children. He m(3) Mrs. Reed; their child., all living: Mary, Catherine, Mintie, Sml, Jesse and Bradford. - Subj attended public schools until 19, taught at dist school at Morgan Neck, Kt Co 2 terms, 2 yrs farm work; taught at Broad Neck, Kt Co (4 yrs); taught at Quaker Neck and Lankford; 1865 to present, teaching here. He m Miss Regina M. Jones, of Som Co; their child.: Whittier C., teacher Sassafras, Kt Co; and Anna Louisa, at home. 1871 subj purch lot nr schoolhouse and erected res, still his home. 542

375. ROGER WOOLFORD, from old fam on Eastern Shore, cashier People's Bank Som Co, Princess Anne. 1889, with father, Col Levin Woolford, organized old 542

savings bank this place, in which he was assist cashier until 1896 when he took present position. Col Levin Woolford b on old fam estate, on Manokin River nr this town. Family dates back to Roger Woolford who came to Md from Eng and held large grant. This tract, called Wappings, handed down,now owned by subj. His grandfather, John Woolford, physician, spent his life on estate, d age c. 71. Col. Levin Woolford attended old Wash Acad of Princess Anne, admitted to bar when young, but never practiced much; clerk Som Co court 1851-1869; then comptroller of Md 8 yrs; state tax commissioner which he held at death; b 1819, d Sep 30 1890; res old farm; mbr Episc Church. He m Annie E. Waters, still living, sis of Levin L. Waters (see his sketch elsewhere this vol). She has 3 child.: Elizabeth E., Lena B. and Roger.

Subj b Princess Anne, Oct 13 1851; entered Univ Va 1867; 2 yrs later became clerk in father's office of comptroller of state; returned to manage homestead; 1889 he and father formed Savings Bank of Princess Anne. He is mbr Episc Church; m Clara L. Hicks, of Va; their daus, Annie E. and Lena R.

543   376. GORDON TULL, Som Co, elected state's atty here 1896; b Jan 4 1870, s/o Sml L. Tull, of Tulls Corner, Som Co. The latter, now about 74, res many yrs at Tulls Corner, where he conducted mercantile establishment. His father, Sml, Sr., of same locality from old fam on Eastern Shore. Mother of subj, former Miss Catherine Gunby, sis of Dr. Hiram H. Gunby, of Tulls Corner. - After public schools subj grad St. John's College, Annapolis with honors Jun 1892; Sep same yr became 1st assist Princess Anne School; studied law; admitted to bar; opened office here spring 1894. He is mbr Episc Church.

544   377. STEPHENSON WHITTINGTON res Som Co b Lawson's dist 1814, res home of son, Alfred. Father of subj, Southey Whittington, farmer of Lawson's dist, mbr ME Church; m Mary Coulbourn; of their children: John, of Balt, and subj, survive. Father d at 80. - Subj farmer on old homestead, prop of father before him; c. 1839 m Jane, d/o Thos Tull; their child.: Alfred, farmer; S. Frank (see his sketch else- where this vol); Chas S.; Jos H.; Mrs. Nathan Conner; Emily C., Mrs W. A. Hayman, and 3 decd. Alfred m Miss Caroline Clayton, of Balt; their child.: Mary and Beulah. Fam attend ME Church.

544   378. HON. JAMES U. DENNIS atty Som Co, in practice at Princess Anne about 35 yrs; admitted to bar Balt 1844; b Wor (now) Co, Sep 11 1823, mbr old fam of Eastern Shore. His grandfather, Littleton Dennis, s/o Littleton, Sr., of Wor Co, farmer. Littleton, Jr. b on old homestead, a boy during Rev war. In early manhood admitted to bar, practiced in Md and Va; judge of co court; supervised of large plantation (c. 5000 a.).

Father of subj, John U. Dennis, b on old homestead 1793. He and bro only children. He inherited half an interest in estate of 5000 a., which he farmed. As a boy he attended school in Phila; no assoc with any church.

Subject's mother, Maria E. (Robertson) Dennis, b Som Co; d here at 38; d/o Geo Robertson, farmer. At her death she left 5 children; eldest was Geo. Emerson and Frank, younger brothers of subj, living in Northampton, Va, and Mary W., who m Judge E. P. Pitts, of that place, is now decd.

Subj attended Wash Acad of Princess Anne. After 3 yrs there he entered Princeton, where he grad 1842; studied law in office Wm W. Handy 2 yrs, studied in Balt 1 yr. He m(1) Cecilia Hooe, of Alexandria, Va, who d, left 3 daus: Eleanor H., wid of late Rbt F. Brattan, former mbr of congress from Som Co; Maria R., res with father; and Cecilia B., w/o Dr. Rufus W. Dashiell, of

Princess Anne. Subj m(2) Mary W. Teackle; their son, Jas T., inherited fortune at death of his mother, res Balt. Mr. Dennis is mbr Episc Church.

379. CHARLES W. WAINWRIGHT, M. D., physician, Princess Anne, b here May 11 1858; attended Wash high school; at 17 became mbr junior class Wash College, Chestertown; grad 1878 with honors, chosen to deliver valedictory address; principal of Wash grammar school this place, at 19, served 7 yrs. 1885 he entered into partnership with Dr John W. Dashiell in drug business here; same autumn became student college of Physicians and Surgeons Balt, grad 1887, with honors; since then in practice here; U. S. pension surgeon. He m Estelle, d/o late Dr. Lewis W. Morris, of Princess Anne; their child.: Frs North and Chas W., Jr. Subj and wife mbrs Presby Church. 545

Edward J. Wainwright, father of doctor, of Princess Anne, estab and conducted Somerset Herald in early manhood; still owned journal when he d at 45. His father, Jesse Wainwright, of this co, farmer on large scale; owned slaves; elder Presby Church; d nearly 60; of old Eastern Shore fam, from Eng. Mother of subj, Olivia Riggin, traces her lineage to Alexander Stuart. She was b Wicomico Co, age* now 75, mbr Presby Church res with subj. Her eldest son, Edward B., of Phila, a printer; next son, Rev L. C., minister Presby Church Lewes, Del. Rebecca J., only dau, w/o M. H. Wilson, of Phila.

380. GREENSBURY W. FREENY, M. D., in practice in Pittsville, Pittsburg dist Wicomico Co, past 30 yrs; owns farm (c. 100 a.) Pittsburg dist; b on father's farm in Wicomico (now) Co, Apr 24 1836; nr Salisbury. After dist schools he attended acad at Salisbury; studied medicine with Dr. Humphreys, Salisbury, grad medical depart Univ Md 1862; in practice in Sharptown, Som Co, few months; moved to Powellville, Wicomico Co, 1867 came to Pittsville; m Miss Ella Burbage at her home 1867. She was b and reared nr Wango, Dennis dist, this co, d/o Samson and Margaret Burbage. Their child, Lawrence, studying medicine with his father and soon expects Univ of Md. Fam mbrs MP Church. 546

381. WILLIAM H. DEWEESE, state's atty Car Co, b nr Burrsville, this co, May 9 1870, descendant of French Huguenots who fled to America when driven from France. 2 bros and a sis crossed Atlantic together, one bro settling on Eastern Shore, other bro and sis went to Pa. Hon. Wm H. Deweese, father of subj, b Del, moved to Md 1856, settled on farm Car Co; elected to legislature 1872; d Sep 20 1887; m 1877, Hester A. Smith, d/o Jas H. Smith, who was elected to state senate from Kt Co, Del; d during his term. Her 1 bro, Jas A., res Dover, Del, and another, Rbt H., res Harrington, Del. Her younger son, Dr. C. S. Deweese, grad Jefferson Medical College Apr 1895, post grad course medical depart Johns Hopkins Univ; res physician Spring Grove asylum. 549

After Camp Grove dist school, subj entered Denton Academy 1887, then normal school West Chester, Pa, left school to teach in order to secure funds to complete his studies; grad Dickinson School of Law, Carlisle, Pa, Jun 1893; Apr same yr admitted to bar Car Co; 1895 nominated state's atty and won with majority of 19 votes over Repub candidate, Rbt J. Jump. Dec 20 1893, Mr. Deweese m Natilla P. Owens, of Harrington, Del, d/o Dr. F. J. Owens, of that place. Both their child d in infancy. Mr. Deweese inclines toward Meth faith, his mother connected with MP Church and father with ME denomination.

382. PETER D. COTTINGHAM, decd, owned drug store Snow Hill, b nr this place Aug 18 1821, s/o Jonathan and Elizabeth Cottingham. His grandfather, it is said, came from Eng and settled in Wor Co prior to Rev war. Subj, one of 4 child. that attained maturity, educated principally Snow Hill Acad, at 25 549

settled here; clerked in dry goods store, then in drug business for himself; burned out 1893; built new store building; m 1853 Miss Elizabeth Parker (b Wor Co, d here 1888); their child.: Annie and Priscie, at home. Mr. Cottingham mbr ME Church, d Oct 5 1897.

550 383. HON. EDWARD T. ROE elected judge orphans' court in 1895; formerly Talb Co commissioner; res Woodland farm, 4th dist. The judge's father, Edw Roe, of this dist, farmer; once magistrate, d c. 1846; m(1) Ann Gregory, of this dist; of 6 children J. A., of Easton, and Mrs. Catherine M. Pratt, same city, surivive. He m(2) Hester Ann Pierson, of this dist, who d 1893; of their 6 child., 4 have d; remaining: Edw T. and Hettie V., Mrs. James H. Patchett, of Easton. - Subj b nr present home Dec 31 1838; fol dist schools, at 14 went into business; purch in 1879, part of old Poplar Level farm; acquired old Nabb farm 1865. He m Nov 10 1865 Mrs. Anna Shehan, of Del; their children: Maggie, d 1867; and Wm E, res 4th dist and operates father's other farm.

550 384. HON. JOHN WOODLAND CRISFIELD, (father of Judge Henry Page, whose history appears elsewhere this vol), b 1808 Kt Co, Md, attended Wash College, Chestertown; admitted to bar; located in Cambridge, few yrs; 1831-1895 in practice Som Co. He d Feb 12 1897, at 89. 1833 subj mbr legislature, congressman 1849-50 and 1861-2; pres old Eastern Shore Railroad; town of Crisfield was named for him. In last yrs identified with Presby Church. Grandfather of subj, Arthur Crisfield, came to America from Eng, settled in Kt Co, Md. His son John b and res that co, farmer; d at early age. Subj m 1836 Julia Ethelinde Page of Kt Co, Md; she d few yrs later; their sons, Judge Hy Page; and Arthur, b 1839, in congressional library Wash, D. C.

551 385. SAULSBURY HOBBS retired farmer 3rd dist Car Co; 28 Dec 1854 moved to Car Co, purch farm (184 a.), and hereon has made his home, nearly 40 yrs; elected co commissioner 1877; village of Hobbs named for him, instrumental in estab postoffice; owns over 400 a.; b 3 Jan 1818, s/o Hy and Nancy (Stevens) Hobbs, of Scotland and Del., respectively. Of 5 child. subj only survivor. Hy Hobbs, came to America in early manhood settled in Md, where he m; d when son Saulsbury was infant. The latter b and reared on farm. From ages 8-17 subj worked for neighbors; carpenter 11 yrs; Dec 17 1844 m Eleanor Lednum, of Del, d/o Wm and Mary (Stafford) Lednum, of Del. She is only survivor of 7 child. Her paternal ancestor, Ebenezer Lednum, b in Del in 1700's, farmer; his father, Thos, came to America from Eng in 1600's, located in Del, where he owned thousands of a., which he willed to his children, parts of which owned by lineal descendants; original will owned by Mrs. Hobbs. Her father, Wm, in war of 1812, and her uncle, John Lednum, minister in ME Church, and author "The Rise of Methodism in America." Mrs. Hobbs also Meth; mother of 7 child., 2 living: Judge Chas W., judge orphans' court Car Co, 1897 elected clerk of court Car Co; and Hy Clay, agent QA & Del Railroad at Hobbs.

552 386. JAMES D. NEAL farmer 3rd dist Car Co, postoffice address: Andersontown; b Car Co Jan 16 1848, s/o Wingate and Catherine (Marine) Neal, of Sussex Co, Del; their child.: 2 decd; others: Wm J., Geo R., Edw W., subj, Rhoda A., Martha J. and Mary C. Wingate Neal lived to see his children to be grown men and women; he d when 85. - Subj m Dec 16 1885 Mollie R. Green, d/o Foster and Jane (Jump) Green, of this co. She d Jul 11 1897, at 37; her child.: Allie J. and Jas O; she was mbr ME Church.

387. HON. ROBERT P. GRAHAM, state comptroller of Md, res Salisbury. 552
Col Sml A. Graham, father of subj, held a commission in Purnell Legion, Union army; after the war res Salisbury until he d; he m Louisa Collier, sis of Rbt Laird Collier, the Unitarian divine. She is still living, in 69th yr. Subj b Apr 7 1868, Wicomico, educated in Salisbury schools, Johns Hopkins Univ; grad Md Univ School of Law 1888, began law practice in Salisbury; m 1895 Caroline Dorsey, of Balt, their child: Margaret.

388. H. FILLMORE LANKFORD atty Princess Anne, Som Co; admitted to bar at 21, 553 dep clerk of co court this co, then clerk of court 6 yrs later. Subject's grandfather, Benjamin, d at 90; large land owner; served 14 terms Md legislature; commissioner of public works. Hy S., father of subj, now 75, b this co and reared on farm; in middle age turned to merchandising, a business man of Balt 25 yrs or more. 1869 he returned to this locality to manage a farm; mbr city council while res Balt, mbr house of delegates 1 term. He m Miss Mary D. Pinckard, of Northumberland, Co, Va; she d 1893, at 62, leaving child.: H. Fillmore; Clarence P., atty of Crisfield; and Marion D., w/o Benj J. Barnes, farmer this co. - Subj b Apr 21 1856 Balt; 1869 came with parents to this co; educated Wash Academy, Princess Anne and St. John's College, Annpolis. At 19 studied law under Hon. John W. Crisfield, this place, admitted to bar Oct 1877. He is pres Princess Anne Telephone Co, director Savings Bank Som Co. 1880 he m Miss Ida A. Marshall, of this town; their son, Henry, 16. Mrs. Lankford is mbr Presby Church.

389. WILFRED BATEMAN, clerk circuit court Talb Co; b Jan 17 1859, s/o late 554 Col Hy E. Bateman. He was native of Wash, D. C., has spent most of life in Easton; taught school at Bailey's Neck 1877-9; same school as taught by Chief Judge Russum in his youth. Subj studied law under preceptorship of Philip Frs Thomas; 1881 admitted to bar; examiner in chancery since the position was created; council to Democratic bd of election supervisors and council for Farmers and Merchants' Bank and Talb Savings Bank; attends Trinity Cathedral.

390. JAMES R. JONES retired; 1847-1894 res farm Kt Co; 1860 built home in 554 Millington, rents farm. Jones fam of Welsh ancestry. Grandfather of subj, Jesse Jones, b and res Del, farmer. Subject's father, Jonathan Jones, b Kt Co, Del, came to Kt Co, Md, bt old Cruikshank farm (now owned by subj), after 1 yr returned to former home in Del; returned to Kt Co, bt Knox and Quimbly farm (c. 500 a., adjoining former pasture); he raised stock and fruit; mbr ME Church South; retired at 86, d at 92. Mother of subj nee Hannah Rawlings b West Chester, Pa; of her 5 child. 3 living: Henrietta, wid of John S. Hurlock, of Kt Co; Jos R.; and Sarah M., unmarried. Subj b Kt Co, Del 1825, spent boyhood yrs on farm in Del, educated in public schools; cultivated farm owned by father, remained in Del few yrs; 1847 came to Kt Co, Md, settked and remained same farm 47 yrs; bd of co commissioners 4 yrs. Fam attend ME Church South. 1849 Mr. Jones m Miss Lydia Rees, d/o John R. Rees, of Del; their child.: Ella; Geo W. and Wm, farmers; Lucy R., Henrietta and Maggie.

391. HON. CALVIN B. TAYLOR, atty Berlin, Wor Co, recently elected to house of 555 delegates; 1891 elected co school examiner Wor Co; s/o Arthur W. and Margaret Ellen (Bowen) Taylor, of old fam of Eastern Shore and Del. Mother d/o Rbt F. and Andasia I. Bowen. Arthur W. Taylor d 1858. After his death mother res father's home, where she d, 1876. - Subj b 1857 nr Berlin, on farm on Assateague River. After public high schools of Berlin he grad Western Md College 1882, standing 2nd in his class; then principal Berlin high schools 7

yrs while studying law with Edw D. Martin, former teacher and now res Balt. 1886 he was regularly admitted to bar this co and for a few yrs in partnership with his old preceptor. Since 1892 he has conducted practice alone; 1890 estab bank in Berlin. Jul 21 1886 subj m Miss Mattie Collins, of Hannibal Mo, both mbrs Buckingham Presby Church.

556 392. HON. RANDOLPH HUMPHREYS, Episc; elected mayor Salisbury 1894 and 1896, s/o Gen Humphrey and Elizabeth (Parsons) Humphreys, both of Som Co, the former of Eng and latter of Scotch-Irish descent. His father, b 1799, d 1882, General in state militia; his wife d 1878, at 62. Of their 7 child., 3 living: subj, youngest; Lafayette, with Salisbury Natl Bank, and Eugene W., M. D., physician and surgeon Salisbury. Subj b Salisbury Apr 7 1853; student local schools until 16; worked in lumber yard and saw & planing mill owned by father; after father's death became mbr of firm Humphreys & Tilghman by purch his father's share, firm dissolved 1894; interests in manufacture of fertilizers Balt and Toadvine Lumber Co N.C.; pres bd of trade Salisbury. 1889 subj m Elizabeth, d/o John Buckner Debman, of N.C.; their daus, Florine and Mary.

559 393. GRIFFIN W. GOLDSBOROUGH, M. D., Greensborough, b Old Town, Car Co, Nov 20 1820, 4th s/o Thos H. and Maria (Thomas) Goldsborough. Fam can be traced to Goldsborough hall, York Co, England, 1057. Father of subj lawyer and planter Old Town, s/o Thos and Katherine (Fauntleroy) Goldsborough, grandson of Nicholas and Sarah (Turbutt) Goldsborough and great-grandson of Nicholas and Ann Goldsborough. Last named Nicholas, purch Old Town Jan 15 1701, was 2nd s/o Nicholas Goldsborough, who came to America from York Co, Eng 1670, settled on Kt Island. His mother was Miss Margaret Howes, of Berks Co, Eng.

Subj educated private school c. 2 miles from Old Town, later studied under Rev Hy Spencer at the Glebe of St. Michael's, Talb Co; attended Brookville Acad, Montgomery Co, and Univ Md; studied medicine under Dr. Albert White and returned to Univ of Md to grad in medicine 1858. He has practiced medicine in St. Louis, Mo, Seaford, Del, and Greensborough, Md nr Old Town, where he res; 1859 and 1875, elected to gen assembly and 1885 elected to Md senate for 4 yrs. 1860-64 active in political life of state, favoring Confederacy; met with Gen Stonewall Jackson at Harper's Ferry, planning to enter Confed army at close of legislative session. However, session broken up by Federal government. Dr. Goldsborough mbr of committee on federal relations which condemned acts of government toward Confederacy; arrested and confined in Ft Del 6 months; released on parole not to bear arms. He served as director of Md and Del Railroad (now the Del & Chesapeake Railway), 1858-1868, later elected treasurer, sec and superintendant of company.

1850 subj app capt of cav company, later adjutant gen of Eastern Shore of Volunteers. Aug 1841 he m Anne Reynolds, d/o Rev John Reynolds (Church of England), of Stoke-Newington, London, England; of 5 children, all d in childhood except Washington Elwell, and Anne Maria. Mrs. Goldsborough d May 30 1846. Subj m(2) Oct 5 1851, Angelina, d/o.Hon. Wm M. Hardcastle, of Castle Hall; no child. Anne Maria m Wm Massey, Feb 4 1864; no child. Washington Elwell Goldsborougn, lawyer, m, Jan 7 1869, Martha Pearce, d/o Wm Winder and Williamina E. C. (Goldsborough) Laird; their child.: Washington Laird, Winder Elwell, Wm Winder, Thos Alan and Martha Laird.

560 394. ELMER E. BRALY owns Braly's Brick Hotel, Cambridge, Dor Co; 3 stories high; 100 or more guests accommodated; 1897 leased Hotel Cambridge; both new and modern. Subj s/o Martin and Pheobe (Herbert) Braly, b Hagerstown, Md, May 17 1861. Grad high school 1888, studied law with Judge Stake, Hagers- town;

hotel clerk in Baldwin House, of native city; cashier Riggs House, Wash, D. C. 5 yrs. 1887 he came to Cambridge; managed Md Central Hotel, destroyed by fire 1892. When new building, known as Braly's Brick Hotel, was completed, he took charge of it. Apr 1887, subj m Miss Mary E. Cranwell, d/o Chas A. and Susan Cranwell, of Hagerstown, Md; their little girl: Helen.

395. WILLIAM J. COLEMAN, business man Kt Co; at 24 learned wheelwright's 560 trade; 1893 estab general store in Coleman, while his wife serves as postmistress; subj b 1848, Kt Co. His father, John W. Coleman, b Kt Co, of Eng origin, res nr Reese's Corners; carpenter and builder; d there 1858, at 41. He m Sarah E. Fillingen, of 5 child., 2 living: subj, and J. Thos. Subj m 1877 Miss Sarah F. Parks, d/o Alexander Parks; their child.: Jessie B. and Myrtle Effa; fam mbrs ME Church.

396. JOSEPH ENNALS MUSE CHAMBERLAINE, M. D., Easton, mbr Episc church, 561 practitioner Talb Co; b Talb Co Feb 18 1826, on farm on Choptank, 12 miles from Easton. His father, Sml Chamberlaine b Oxford Neck, Talb Co, in war of 1812 at St. Michael's, farmer; d 1828, in early manhood. His bro, Jas Lloyd Chamberlaine, farmer and slave holder Talb Co. Paternal grandparents of subj Sml and Henrietta Maria (Hollyday) Chamberlaine; maternal grandparents were Dr. W. W. and Margaret (Muse) Davis, of AA Co. The doctor's mother nee Arianna W. Davis, of Dor Co, had child.: Marian A., m a Mr. Trippe, had son, Dr. Trippe of "The Oak," Talb Co; Henrietta Maria, who m Geo Archer Thomas of Cecil Co, and has dau; Sml, farmer, who d in middle life; Wm Muse, d in Texas early part of war; Margaret Ann, who m 1st cousin, Jas W. L. Chamberlaine, now of Balt; and subj.

After father d, subj moved with mother to Easton, where she d 1835; when he 9; then lived with great-uncle, Dr. Muse, of Cambridge; educated in schools there and at Easton; grad medical depart Univ of Md; since then in practice in Easton. Jan 14 1851 he m Miss Elizabeth B., d/o Wm and Elizabeth C. (Bullitt) Hayward and granddau of Thos I. Bullitt; of their 4 child. 2 living: Elizabeth B., w/o Emmett Hayward, and Jos, farmer Dor Co. His 1st wife d Mar 2 1861. Jun 19 1866 subj m Miss S. Catherine Earle, d/o Judge Earle, of Centreville.

397. HENRY L. D. STANFORD atty, Princess Anne, Som Co; located here Jan 1895, 562 becoming partner of Joshua W. Miles (mbr of congress); supervisor of elections, of Salisbury, Md, b Oct 2 1856 s/o Isaac W. H. and Martha J. (Moore) Stanford of Wicomico Co. The father, mcht tailor, postmaster, once mbr Md legislature; d at 43; mbr ME Church. His wife d 1883, in 60th yr, leaving 4 child. Williamanna w/o Chas H. Rider, now of Wash, D. C. Mary S. w/o Richard A. Atwood, of Boston, Mass. Sml M. in commission business Omaha, Neb.

Sub attended public schools Salisbury until 12, when he went to Balt and was student in grammar school 3 yrs. At 16 he commenced clerking in law office that city; clerk in hotel Princess Anne 1876-1882; clerked with firm Washington, D. C. 6 yrs. 1888 he began reading law with Judge Henry Page and Joshua W. Miles, of this town; admitted to bar Apr 1890; opened office in Salisbury, assoc with Hon. Rbt P. Graham, now state comptroller. Since 1894 practicing in Princess Anne. He is mbr Episc Church; 1895 m Miss Marian F., d/o C. C. Waller, who is general freight and passenger agent QA Railroad Co. Subj and wife have child.: Marian Waller and Hy L. D., Jr.

398. WILLIAM E. JARRELL, farmer 1st dist Kt Co. His father, Rbt Jarrell, of 562 Car Co, farmer, d at 62; he and wife mbrs ME Church. He m Mary A. Temple (b

QA Co, d at about 60); their child.: Annie E. wid of R. J. Orrell, of Car Co; Joshua R. farmer 2nd dist same co; Rbt in canning business Car Co; Mary T. w/o M. H.Gray, of QA Co; Wesley, farmer nr Ridgely, Car Co; Louisa m W. L. Cooper, of that co; Chas L. owns old homestead; and subject.

Subj b nr Sudlersville, QA Co, Sep 8 1845, on farm; after elementary schooling, two terms in West River Acad. When about 21 he began clerking, res Greensborough, Car Co, some time. Returning home, he worked on father's farm 1 year, then moved to QA Co, where he remained 4 yrs. 1872-5 he rented farm in Kt Co, later purch the place, owned by Wm T. Spry. Besides this (235 a.) he owns 6 other tracts, in this co and QA Co (total of about 1500 a.); owns small sawmill. 1871 subj m Maggie E. Clements, of this co, their only child, W. Frank, attends Randolph College Ashland, Va. Mr. Jarrell is mbr ME Church South, Chesterville.

563 399. THOMAS STEVENSON res Lawsons dist, Som Co; ship carpenter; for a time in the oyster trade; 1871 he opened general store nr his home, began tilling part old homestead. Father of subj, Benj T. Stevenson, b Som Co 1809; spent entire life on place now occupied by son; ship carpenter, his life occupation. Under his supervision nearly 100 vessels built. Also managed his farm. He is mbr ME Church; d at 74. He m Harriet, d/o Thos Ward; of their 8 child., living: Thos, Wm J. and Benj F., who also occupy portions of old homestead. The mother connected with ME Church; she d at 72.

Subj b 1835, educated in common schools, learned trade of ship carpenter. He and fam mbrs MP Church. He m Aurinthia A. Miles, d/o John H. Miles, their child.: Lizzie M., Ira E. and Alula E., w/o W. C. Horsey, of Marion.

564 400. HON. JAMES LAWS, res Pittsburg dist, Wicomico Co, judge orphans' court; justice of peace; owns 4 farms (800 a.), in Wor Co, besides 2 farms in Dennis dist, Wicomico Co, aggregating 565 a.; store building at Pittsville and another in Salisbury, and a saw mill. 1886-1888 he carried on mercantile business at Pittsville, sold out, and 1892 retired.

Subj b Feb 3 1824 Dennis dist, Wicomico (now) Co. His father, Wm, s/o Wm, Sr., and grandson of Elijah, who was first of fam to locate in Wor Co. Subject's father b and reared Dennis dist, and there m Gertrude Duncan. He was extensive planter; owned 50 slaves worth $50,000. Their child.: subj; Margaret L., Mrs. Burbage, d 1870; Mary J., wid of Stephen L. Purnell, res Snow Hill, Wor Co; Wm L., res part of old homestead; and Catherine, Mrs. John Williams, decd. Subj educated in common and subscription schools. At 34 he left old homestead and came to Pittsburg dist. 1867 he m Sallie M. Fooks; their child.: Wm W., res Pittsville, in lumber business; Jas R. T. in mercantile business Salisbury; Mary d 1884; Ida G. wid of John Williams; Clarence, at home; John M. and Chas E. clerks in their brother's store at Salisbury; Lillian M., at home; 3 child. d in infancy.

565 401. THOMAS J. DIXON, of Som Co, res Princess Anne past 34 yrs; elected sheriff this co 1879 1 term; 1869 mbr bd of control and review; 2nd pres Som Co Savings Bank. He was b Nov 28 1821 Westover, Som Co, s/o Nathaniel and Ann (Corbin) Dixon, of this co and Virginia, respectively. The father, farmer, res this co, d at 84; his wife d at 38; of 6 children, subj only survivor. Sub educated in country school; attended Wash acad. When about 20 he engaged in mercantile pursuits at Anne Mesick, Som Co, 3 yrs; followed boating and trading on Chesapeake Bay 2 yrs or more, conducted store in Westover; began loaning money on security, holding many mortgages on real estate and other prop; now owns 7 farms in the co (2600 a.)., about 75 buiness houses and

residences in Crisfield and about 75 in Princess Anne. 1842 subj m Miss Sarah Long, of Som Co; they are mbrs ME Church.

402. EDWARD P. DAVIS elected rgtr of wills Wor Co 1897; dep 13 yrs prior to this. Father of subj is Jas E. Davis, 83. He m Elizabeth, d/o Purnell Johnson, of old fam on Eastern Shore; she d 1869, at 55. Great-grandfather of subj, Nathaniel Davis, of N. C., brought wife and fam to this co early 1700's. One of his children was Edw, the grandfather of subj. 565
With his two bros, John Porter and Wm Thos, Edw P. Davis grew to manhood. The brother Wm T. d in 23rd year. Other bro m Anna Jones, of Stockton, Md, d at 46, left child., Edw and Marguerite; he was a farmer and mechanic. Edw P. Davis b Apr 1 1843, within 4 miles of Snow Hill, on father's farm. At 17 he completed schooling and took charge of a school as a teacher; became master of wheelwright's trade; conducts Ocean View House a part of each year, (a resort located on his farm at Spence's Landing, 6 1/2 miles from Snow Hill). 1883 subj became dep under George P. Bratten, rgtr of wills, and after his death continued under succeeding registers until elected to office himself.
Subj m 1871 Mrs. Susan L. Boehm, of Cumberland, Md, wid of Louis C. Boehm, div superintendent Balt & Ohio Railroad Cumberland-Wheeling. Child. of subj and wife: Louis E., artist Snow Hill; Chas L., of Balt, with Balt, Chesapeake & Atlantic Railroad Co.; and Alice H., w/o Dr. L. S. Barnes, of Toledo, Ohio. Mr. and Mrs. Davis are mbrs All Hallows Episc Church, Snow Hill.

403. CHARLES W. CROCKETT, business man, Pocomoke City, Wor Co, in shipbuilders' trade since 13; owns large shipyard, known as Worcester & Marine Railway, employing 20 or more men; s/o Dnl J. and Sarah Crockett, b on their farm nr Princess Anne, Som Co, Jun 4 1854. At 13 he began working for his father as a ship builder; after 12 yrs went into shipyards of Young & Colbourn, this city; foreman 12 yrs. 1890 he bt half interest in the business; 1892 became sole owner. The yard constructs naphtha and steam launches, oyster boats, and various kinds of ships and vessels for coast trade, besides general line of repair. He is mbr MP Church. 1873 he m Miss Ella Brown, of Fruitland; their child: Jas, Letha and Charley. 566

404. JOHN H. C. KEMP, business man, Trappe dist, Talb Co, res here past 17 yrs; owns homestead (188 a.), and tract of 117 a., and interest in father's old farm Bay Hundred dist. Father of subj, John W. Kemp, b Balt, came to this co 1814 with his father, Thos, a shipbuilder. John Kemp purch land and moved to Wades Point; 1864 elected to state senate; co commissioner. He owned slaves; d 1881 at 69; m Miss Sally Caulk, of St. Michael's dist, Talb Co; of 12 child. surviving are: Susan E., wid of Chas Stevens, of Denton; subj; Helen D., wid of Jos T. Tunis, one of founders of Claiborne, Md; Jos O., res old homestead at Wades Point; Fannie K., w/o Jos Lowe, of Bay Hundred dist; and Chas A., farmer that dist. Wm T., assist surgeon U. S. navy, d 1864; Louisa d in 30th yr; Albert H., d at 7 and the others d in infancy. 569
Subj b on farm on Chesapeake Bay, Bay Hundred dist, Talb Co, Aug 18 1844, on Wades Point; at 16 began to follow life of a sailor; later given charge of a ship; then farmed on a place adjoining old home; then moved to that farm and to present dwelling 1880. Subj m Jan 23 1873 Esther Hopkins, of this dist; their child.: Elenor, eldest; Wm T., grad St. John's College, Annapplis, attending Columbia College N.Y.; Hester A., grad Easton High School; John H. C., Jr., youngest. Mr. and Mrs. Kemp are mbrs Episc Church.

569 405. ALBERT E. ACWORTH, 1st dist Wicomico Co, from old fam this neighborhood, of Eng ancestry. Great-grandfather of subj, Thos Acworth, b on farm 2 miles from homestead of subj, and the grandfather, Train Acworth, native of same place. Train Acworth, farmer, learned carpenter's trade when a youth, d 1853, leaving a large landed estate, to which Albert E. and his half-sister, Mrs. Dr. W. W. Robinson, of Balt, only child., fell heirs. He served in war of 1812, in defense of Balt. He m Nancy, d/o Edw Hull; she d a young woman, 1836. A bro of Train Acworth, Beacham, dep sheriff and surveyor of Som Co yrs ago. - Subj b on farm which he now owns and manages, May 26 1827; attended Salisbury Acad and acad Princess Anne; grad Princeton College 1851 with honors; studied law under T. R. Lockerman, Easton, studies interrupted by illness and death of father, 1853; abandoned legal career and attended to management of farm. 1856 he became one of the editors and proprietors of Somerset Union, and since then has contributed articles on farming to American Farmer and Md Farmer. He is mbr Episc Church. Apr 23 1855 he m Charlotte E., d/o John Dougherty, of this co.

570 406. JABEZ WRIGHT, retired farmer Hurlock, Dor Co, b this co, 12th (now) dist, Dec 31 1827, s/o Kennelly and Celia (Lewis) Wright. The father b this co Nov 14 1798, s/o Cornelius and Bethany Wright. The former was early res this co, of English-Scotch descent. Their children: Christiana, Arah Ann, Margaret Ann, Hester Ann, Lovey, Jabez, Celia, Lewis, Catherine, Minus, Bethany, Betsy Ann, Wilbur F. (d in childhood) and Abram. The mother b Sep 25 1799 d/o Abraham and Lovey Lewis.
After dist schools subj taught 2 terms; then turned to farming. Nov 7 1850 he m Mary C., d/o Sml and Dorcas (Nichols) Wright; their child.: Rhoena V., w/o Jas R. Nichols, of this co; Jas Marcus, of Federalsburg; Margaret A., d in childhood; M. Rhodolph, carrying on a ranch in Custer Co, Idaho; Kennelly J., mcht Hurlock; Alvin W., res Westville, Conn.; Everett K. (twin bro of Alvin), minister of ME Church St. Louis conference, and Zed, taking theological course in seminary Dover, Del. Fam identified with ME Church.

571 407. THOMAS K. ADREON, young business man, Deal's Island, Som Co. His ancestors, both paternal and maternal, in Balt yrs ago. On his father's side he is great-grandson of Christian Adreon, an officer in battle of North Point, war of 1812. On his mother's side he is great-grandson of Thos Kelso, millionaire of Balt. Father of subj, Harrison, s/o Wm Adreon, b and reared Balt, lawyer in Balt; served in Union army, breveted lieut col for meritorious service; postmaster at Balt 1881-85; d 1891 at 51.
Subj b Balt 1869, educated in private schools; succeeded his father in pension business; 1895 moved to Deal's Island, estab general store; now owns 2 stores; in oyster packing business. Feb 1892 he m Miss Nannie, d/o Jas T. Daniel (see his sketch elsewhere this vol). Their child, Louisa Jessie.

572 408. WILLIAM H. DASHIELL, co superintendent of schools Som Co for nearly 14 yrs; sec and treasurer co school funds; b Jan 28 1852, s/o Rev John H. Dashiell, D. D., of Salisbury. The father was reared in place of birth and educated in schools of Salisbury. After attending Dickinson College he became principal of Salisbury Acad, before he was 20; teacher in Balt several yrs; 1858 and 1859 pres Dickinson Seminary, of Wilm, Pa; entered ministry and preached ME Church in Balt Co and Pa until outbreak of war. 1862-70 he conducted large school in Balt; returned to Balt Conference and remained in ministry until 1891; retired at 70; past 6 yrs res Annapolis. He m Emily W.

Irving, sis of Hon. L. T. H. Irving, once judge of court of appeals of Md. The father of John H. was Rbt Dashiell, b Salisbury, in mercantile business for many yrs. He d when about 50.
   Subj spent early yrs in Balt; grad Dickinson College 1871 at 19; began as principal of Smyrna Acad, of Smyrna, Del; there 4 yrs; came to Princess Anne, to study law with his uncle, Judge Irving; admitted regularly to bar of this co 1875; practiced law in a measure; during 1877-1878, he was principal of high school of Crisfield, then similar position with Wash high school Princess Anne; began as co superintendent of schools in Jan 1884. He has been one of court examiners, master in chancery several yrs; mbr ME Church. He m(1) Sallie B. Upshur, of Va; she d 1886. 1893 he m Miss Ellen M. Dougherty, of this town; their dau, Emily Irving, 3 yrs old.

409. ALEXANDER C. LOWERY, Kt Island, whose ancestor, Wm, moved here from Va 573 as a young man, bt land on Coxey's Neck, still owned by fam. His dau Margaret d unmarried, but Annie m Richard Crisp, of AA Co, their children lived that locality. Parents of subj: Wm Owens and Mary Emeline (Walters) Lowery, both of this island. Father b Sep 16 1802, grew up here; farmer. He m(1) Eliza Tolson; their child.: Jos Owens, d Kt Island, leaving wid and a dau; Harriet D., decd, w/o Wm Coonsman, of Balt; and Wm S., decd. After death of 1st wife, Mr. Lowery m(2) Mary E., d/o Alexander Walters, mcht of QA Co; their child.: Alexander; Sarah Frances, d young; and Mary Ann, decd. - Subj b Jan 6 1840, on father's farm; manages homestead (175 a.), and tract adjoining village of Kt Island. Dec 11 1866 he m Maria L., d/o Sml White, of old co fam; their child.: Emma K.; Lulu, w/o Rbt Cook; she d, no child.; Elizabeth E., Claude, Florence M.; and Mary E., Wm D. and Wm A., decd.

410. VICTOR CARROLL, druggist, Church Creek, Dor Co, owns store which carries 573 drug supplies, toilet luxuries, stationery; s/o Dr. Thos King Carroll, b this dist May 5 1865, and reared at home until 16. (See sketch of father elsewhere this vol) He taught school about 14 yrs, invested saviings in drug store, and has since conducted business here.

411. CHARLES E. McSHANE, of Denton, Car Co, lawyer; b Sullivan Co, N. Y., Dec 574 10 1873, s/o Patrick H. and Catherine E. (McKenna) McShane, of N. Y.; their child.: 1 decd; subj; Mary E., Chas E., Frank P. and Catherine V. Paternal grandfather came to America from Ireland 1845, located in New York City. Grandmother, Ellen McKenna, still living. Patrick McShane was mcht at Fishkill-on-Hudson, in N.Y., also res Wurtsboro; general merchandising and lumber. 1884 he moved to Ridgely, Md.; one of its founders, opened hotel and livery, which he carried on until 1893, when he came to Denton; here he is in real estate ventures. After dist schools subj went to Phila, entered a high school there. Returning home he read law, pupil in legal depart Dickinson College, Carlisle, Pa; entered office of Judge Russum and Hon. Hy R. Lewis; 1895 regularly admitted to bar.

412. NOAH ALEXANDER HUTSON, lawyer Denton, Car Co; justice of peace 1882-96. 574 Great-grandfather of subj, on paternal side, from Germany, settled in America before Rev war. His son Jacob, subject's grandfather, captain in Rev war, of N. Y., farmer; spent last yrs in Md; he d 1812, at 58. One of his sons, John, b Md, m Catherine M. Seaman, of Pa; of their 11 child., 4 are decd; those living, in order of birth: Jacob, Frank, Kate, Wm, subj, Jas and Sallie. - Subj b May 9 1841, Georgetown, Kt Co, Md, as infant, his parents moved to Smyrna, Del, where he attended public schools; tinner; 1863 invested in a

large canning estab, until 1882; studied law; 1896 regularly admitted to bar of this co. He attends ME Church; 1863 m Ann P. Murphy, of Car Co, mbr ME Church, who d Apr 1883, at 40, left dau, Ella F. 1888 Mr. Hutson m Mary F. Horney of QA Co; their dau, Lillian A. Mrs. Hutson identified with Meth Church, d Nov 1890, aged 40. Subj m Miss Cora B. McIlvain who was b and reared in Del, 2nd cousin of Pres Harrison on mother's side.

575   413. WILLIAM H. KELLEY, business man, Locust Grove, b Balt Co 1844, s/o Amos and Susan (Hildbrandt) Kelley, fam of 11 children, 4 living. Paternal ancestors of Scotch- Irish descent. His father spent his life Balt Co, farming, nr Towson, where he d 1889, at 82.
Subj reared on home farm, attended public schools; began learning blacksmith's trade, interrupted by enlistment in Company D., 7th Md Infantry, 3 yrs. Wounded at battle of Petersburg, 4 months confined in hospital before rejoining his command; in battles of the Wilderness, Spottsylvania, Cold Harbor, South Mountain, Petersburg, Five Forks, Hatcher's Run, Chancellorsville, Fredericksburg and Appomattox. Returning home subj followed blacksmith trade; estab shop in Locust Grove, whither he moved 1870. He also works as millwright; 1896 opened a store in Locust Grove with his son Harry P., carrying hardware, farm implements, dry goods and groceries. He m Miss Ella Pennington; their child.: Henrietta E., w/o Barkley Kilburn; Grace A., w/o J. E. Sylvanius; and Harry P. Fam mbrs ME Church.

576   414. PROF. ALEXANDER CHAPLAIN, res Easton, superintendent schools Talb Co; b Trappe, Talb Co, Mar 31 1835, s/o Jas and Eliza (Stevens) Chaplain, of that locality, former b 1784, and latter b 1804. Chaplain fam of English origin, mbrs Soc of Friends, attending Third Haven Meeting House Talb Co. Maternal grand- father, John Stevens, of old fam of Talb Co, large land holder and slave owner; operated mill, conducted a bark and tan yard. In his fam were 4 sons: John, mcht and banker; Jas, shipping mcht of Phila; Wm, who d young; and Geo, farmer. Subject's father, Jas Chaplain, farming and merchandising; magistrate; d 1844; attended ME Church; in war of 1812. His widow never married again; she d 1888; their children: 1 d in childhood; John F. Chaplain, D. D., grad Dickinson College, ME minister, located in Phila, had charge in Allentown, Pa when he d; Jas Stevens grad Md Univ with M. D. degree, in practice at Trappe, Md; Sarah m Jas Robinson, mcht in Trappe, later moved to Balt, where she d; Alexander is next in order of birth; and Mary Elizabeth w/o Thos J. Willis, farmer Kt Co, Md, where she d.
Subj educated in schools of Trappe, entered Dickinson College 1851-4; taught in Trappe 5 yrs, assist teacher Easton Acad 1859-60; then taught in Trappe; elected co superintendent of schools 1868; m 1863, Miss Elma Kemp, of Trappe, who d 1869, leaving child, Maude, with her father. Subj m 1872 Miss Emily Thomas, of Dor Co; their dau, Eleanor. Subj mbr ME Church South.

579   415. CLARENCE S. HURLOCK, 1st dist Kt Co; manages farm; built canning factory at Massey 1894; cans tomatoes and peaches; owns sawmill upper part of QA Co; b 1st dist Jun 3 1851. His father, Sml Hurlock b nr Massey, this dist, Apr 12 1821; clerk in Millington, c. 1833-5; bt farm this dist and res there, tilled it until 1881; moved to farm Cecil Co, nr Cecilton, where he res. Grandfather of subj, Sml Hurlock b Del; in battle of Georgetown, war of 1812. His wife mbr of Seamans fam. Subject's mother, Mary Rebecca, d/o Benj Money; she d Oct 19 1866 at 34; Episc; her child.: 4 d in infancy; and subj. At 15 subj entered acad Smyrna, Del, remained 2 terms; then state normal school Pa; returned home Jul 1869, took up farming; manages 2 farms for father. Jan 23

-112-

1873 he m Adelaide Meginniss, of 1st dist; their child.: Mary, Sml S., Florence and Eleanor. Subj elected treasurer Kt Co 1892 and rgtr of wills .1897. He and fam mbrs Episc Church.

416. JAMES T. DANIEL in mercantile business Deal's Island, Som Co; owns farm (20a.).; owns store lower end of island, at Wenona postoffice; judge orphans' court 1876-80. Traverse Daniel, subject's father, b N.C., at 18 came to Deal's island; taught school here, later farmed; magistrate; dep collector of customs this port; mbr ME Church; d here at 81. He m Mary Wallace, who d at 78; of their 18 child.: 2 living: Mrs. Biddy Mister, wid res Balt, and subj. Wm d Oct 13 1897. Subj b 1830 Deals Island; after elementary education here; at 18 entered Dickinson College, Carlisle, Pa., student there 2 yrs; returned home and entered into business. He m(1) Louisa E. Rowe; of their 14 child.: 6 living: Nettie; Chas G.; Gertrude, w/o Arthur Andrews; and Nancy B., w/o Thos K. Adreon. Subj m(2) Elizabeth Andrews; their child.: Nellie, Clarence, Earl, Mabel, Arthur, Wm and Thos W. Fam connected with ME Church.   580

417. JOSEPH W. BROOKS owns ship yard with marine railway, on Little Choptank River, Parsons Creek dist, Dor Co; owns and operates sawmill, employing about 20 men; has built about 150 vessels. Parents of subj, John W. and Sallie (Saunders) Brooks, b Parsons Creek dist, and here d, latter at 54, and former at 35. Subj only child; b Jun 21 1832, after death of father; remained with mother until 17, when he began to work in a ship yard 4 yrs; started small ship yard in Parsons Creek, his native dist. He m Miss Louisa Tolley, of Dor Co; she d at 53, her child.: Jos W., Jr., in partnership with father; Birdie, at home; and Benj L. Subj identified with MP Church.   580

418. LOUIS KOSSUTH WARREN, miller, Cambridge, Md., b Eng Nov 6 1849. At 6 months brought to U. S. by parents, Jabez and Margaret (Webb) Warren, who located in Phila. Father, native of England, where he m. Family of 1st wife, Lydia Smith, manufactured silk goods; while she lived he was American rep with headquarters at Phila. They had 4 children, 2 living; subj of 8 child. of 2nd marriage. Fam moved from Phila to Cecil Co, Md, and after war to Car Co. Father in manufacture of brick & tile and sawmill business. 1870 he came to Cambridge, where he d. Subj assisted father, became practical miller and brick & tile maker; built brickyard in Cambridge; sold it; also in saw and grist mill business. 1895, he erected his present flouring mill in Cambridge. (Brief description of mill) He manufactures two brands of flour, hominy, cornmeal and chopped feed. Subj m Mary Elizabeth Noble, d/o Solomon Noble, of Sussex Co, Del; of their 8 child., 5 living: Louis E., Ruskin B., Gretha V., Rbt Noble and Mary Elizabeth. Subj and wife mbrs ME Church.   581

419. WILLIAM K. TRAVERS, mcht Taylor's Island, mbr old Dor fam, res chiefly Parsons Creek dist. See sketch of Judge Levi D. Travers elsewhere this vol. Subj b Parsons Creek dist; grad Dickinson College, Carlisle, Pa. When about 20 he began in mercantile business Taylor's Island; d Apr 9 1888, at 45. May 30 1865, he m Eugenia Keene, d/o Vachel J. and Mary (Meekins) Keene. Her father, of Golden Hill, Dor Co, farmer, d at 85; mbr militia, war of 1812; Cath. His father, B. J. Keene, 1 of 5 bros who came from Eng to America, settled on farm Dor Co, where he d at 80; mbr militia war of 1812. Mother of Mrs. Travers was Mary Meekins, of Dor Co, where she d at 75; d/o Dennard Meekins; he was b Scotland, settled in Dor Co in Meekins Neck (now). Mrs. Travers 3rd in order of birth of 4 child. Her bro, Sml, physician Balt; sis, Laura, w/o Dr. De Unger, of Chicago, Ill.; and Lewis B., youngest, res Golden   582

-113-

Hill. Child. of subj and wife: Wm Dove, succeeded father in management of store Taylor's Island; John Chaplin, M. D., grad Univ Md, physician Balt; Philip Lee, student at Rock Hill, Md; Nanuleita, student state normal school; and Edgar Eugene, with mother. Fam mbrs Cath Church.

582 420. W. T. H. LEE, Easton, b Broad Creek Neck, Jan 12, 1850, s/o Rbt and Milcah (Bridges) Lee, of Balt City and Talb Co, Md, respectively. Paternal grandfather, Abraham Lee, b Dor Co, of Scotch ancestry, in shoe business Balt, where he d 70. Richard Bridges, maternal grandfather, farmer, of old Talb Co fam; of his sons, Thos F. Bridges, farmer, sheriff of co. Subject's father, farmer; d when subj was young. His wife d Camden, N.J., 1896, at 65; they had 2 child.; dau, Mary, w/o Thos J. McQuary, contractor Camden, N.J.

After public schools subj attended acad Cambridge; learned carpenter's trade; contractor and builder; studied architecture in Balt, which he followed in Balt and Easton c. 12 yrs, planned bishop's res, churches and schoolhouses Talb Co; tax collector of co; dep sheriff. He m Miss Emma, oldest d/o Judge Wm Roberts, chief judge orphans' court; their child: Maude, w/o Winthrop Blakesley, of AA Co; Claude, clerk in drug store of his uncle; Dodson, at home; Hoburg, page in U. S. Senate, and Emma, 13.

583 421. ELIJAH W. WEST of old Md fam; res 4th dist Talb Co, farmer, nr Wye Mills past 5 yrs; runs steam thresher in season; his paternal grandfather, Wm, of Wicomico Co. Father, John W., b same locality, farmer; mbr ME Church. He m Ellen Nelson, who d 1876, and whose father, Eleazer Nelson, from Wicomico Co. John W. West d 1894; 3 of his 7 child. survive: Mary E., unmarried; subj and Zadockely, this co. Subj b Nov 20 1848, res old farm Wicomico Co, owned by his father. After public schools he learned carpenter's trade. 1876 he carried on store while postmaster, Cordova, Talb Co; past 20 yrs mostly farming, owns 167 a. nr Cordova; rents 264 a.; 1889-1895 trustee of co almshouse. Feb 27 1878 he m Lucinda Warner, d/o John W. Warner, of this co; their child.: Howard E., Annie G., Cora A. and Lulu E.

584 422. THOMAS QUIMBY, 4th dist Talb Co, res Powells Point farm (c. 400 a.), on Skipton River, prop of late Gen McKenney, of Centreville. Grandfather Wm Quimby and his son, Wm, Jr., were from Millington, Kt Co, Md, farmers. Latter, father of subj, taught vocal music in public schools; 1852 came to Talb Co, purch farm; app to clerkship Annapolis; while there d; led singing in local ME Church. He m Sarah Kennard, of old Del fam; their child.: 1 decd; W. G., res Wye Mills; John res QA Co; subj; Joseph and Chas, both of QA Co; and Sarah, w/o Geo Tarbutton, of this dist. The mother d 1852. Subj b Phila, Jul 28 1849; attended dist schools here until 16; learned carpenter's trade; assisted in building many dwellings and barns this part of co for 27 yrs. Feb 16 1870 he m Sarah Forman, of Del; their child d at 13 months.

584 423. HIRAM S. HALL, of Bay Hundred dist, Talb Co; res and town commissioner Jamestown, N.Y. few yrs ago; village trustee, alderman; 1886 came to Md; elected to house of delegates. He is trustee of co almshouse, mbr school bd. He was b Columbia Co, N. Y., 1830, s/o Ebenezer Hall, of Conn., who moved to N.Y. in his youth. Ebenezer was mechanic; manufactured woolen goods; d 1846, at 52; m Catherine Launt; of their 6 child., subj is youngest. The Halls of English descent; originally settled in Conn. Subj spent boyhood on farm Del Co, N.Y., student in public schools; carpenter's apprentice 3 yrs, employed at government works at West Point. 1861 he bt a factory nr Jamestown, N. Y., made wooden ware until 1886 when he came to Md and bt old Lowe farm, where he

farms and raises fruit. Mr. Hall m(1) 1852, Gertrude F. Clarke, d/o Geo G. Clarke, agent for freight co on Hudson River, res Orange Co, N. Y. Mrs. Hall d, leaving dau, Gertrude. Mr. Hall later m Miss Mary Eroe.

424. JOHN E. WILSON farmer, 6th dist Car Co, owns homestead; b Jan 19 1849 on farm nr where he res; after public schools attended St. John's College Annapolis 2 yrs. Wm Wilson, grandfather of subj, of this co, farmer. Hy Wilson, father of John E. from this co; tax collector; co commissioners; charter mbr of Natl Bank of Denton; m Susan Saulsbury, of Car Co; of their 4 child., all but subj, d in infancy. Mrs. Wilson d Mar 1 1881 at 65; the father d Sep 2 1881, in 67th year. Subj m Dec 23 1879 Ida M. Downes, b and reared this co. Their child.: Clara and Hy. Mrs. Wilson is mbr ME Church. 585

425. HON. ERNEST DOWNES, judge orphans' court Car Co 1888-1896. He and wife own over 700 a. in Car and QA Cos; res Denton. He owns mill, formerly owned by John W. Knotts, 2 1/2 miles south of Hillsborough, currently undergoing repair. Subj b this co May 10 1851, s/o Wm and Sallie R. (Ryner) Downes, of Car and Talb Cos, respectively. Their child.: 3 decd; Ryner, Anna, Stephen R., subj, Ida M., Emmett, Eldridge and Clara. The father owned over 1000 a. in QA Co; when he d in 1867, at 56; co commissioner QA Co 1860-4. His wife d in 77th yr. Grandfather Wm Downes of QA Co, extensive farmer.
Subj worked in store Henderson, Md; came to Denton, in merchandising until 1873; sold his stock and bt farm in vicinity. He is vice-pres Denton Natl Bank. Dec 12 1872, he m Josephine M. Williams, b Car Co, d/o Thos Williams, of this region; their child., in order of birth (none m): Wm, Lulu, Philip, Earnest, Jr., Hackett, Sallie, Marion and Rbt. Family attend ME Church. 586

426. WILLIAM CALVIN SATTERFIELD, business man of Eastern Shore, d Jun 18 1896; b on father's farm, Mar 9 1822, nr Farmington, Del, s/o Dnl and Mary T. Satterfield, of Del, of Scotch descent, mbrs Presby Church. After attending school he taught school few yrs; located Faulkland, Del, embarked in mercantile line, sold out few yrs later, when gold excitement of '49 broke out; went to Isthmus Panama, and from there north along California coast in a sailing vessel; mined with indifferent success; transported goods and supplies 3 yrs; retuned to Md. He m Miss Phoebe Allen, d/o Capt John Allen. He started a store in small way; owned half interest 3-masted schooner, and several other vessels some of which traded with ports in West Indies and South America; bt timberland and engaged in running sawmills and in lumbering; owned nearly 20 farms (c. 5000 a.), 28 dwelling houses in Greeensborough, in which his employes res. He was mbr Presby Church. His child.: Ida T., w/o John S. Mitchell; Clara, w/o H. L. Harper; Calvin; Minnie, w/o A. A. Christian, of Phila; Lawrence; Elizabeth, and Virginia, w/o E. C. Carter, farmer of this co. 589

Calvin Satterfield b Aug 4 1861, reared in this co, grad law depart Univ Va; office of Hon. John P. Poe, Balt, 2 yrs; in Austin, Tex. managing editor Austin Daily Statesman about 2 yrs; postoffice inspector 1887-1888, returned to assist father. Since 1895 res Greensborough, managing paternal estate with his bros; mbr Episc Church. 1886 he m Susan P. d/o Gen R. Lindsay Walker, of Richmond, Va, their child.: Rose, Phoebe, Calvin and Lindsay.

Lawrence Satterfield b Greensborough 1866, grew up in mercantile business owned by father; completed studies Swarthmore College Pa; employed by father until he went to California with Capital Packing Co; 1893 came home, assumed control of mercantile branch of father's business, now owns the same.

427. MILBOURN A. TOULSON, business, Chestertown, owner of drug store here since 1878. Paternal ancestors of subj of Eng extraction and maternal progenitors French. Paternal grandparents were Andrew, farmer, and Rachael Toulson. Maternal grandparents were John and Susan (Biscoe) Duyer, former of Kt Co, of English parentage, and in war of 1812. Thos Toulson, father of subj, has 3 bros, Philip, Jos and Jas, and 2 sis, Maria and Susan, all Quakers. Bros and sis of subject's mother: John, farmer; Jas; Dnl; Isaac, capt of vessel on the bay; Mary, twice m; Rosie, w/o Capt Skeggs; and Sarah, w/o Jonathan Crow, of Kt Co.

Father of subj b Kt Co 1812, in mercantile pursuits; he d Oct 15 1856, then making his home on a farm; associated with ME Church. He m Melcha Duyer, who was b Kt Co, Oct 15 1817, still living. Of their 10 children three d in childhood and 5 are now living. Laura Jane m Charles H. Davis and d in 1891; Catherine was first the wife of Lewis Gill and afterward m James S. Bradley, but d in 1894; John Thomas, a farmer, res in Caroline Co, where he is engaged in farming; Fannie is the wife of John Davis, of Chestertown; James H. is engaged in business in Salem, N. J.; and Mary Maria is the wife of Prof. James A. Greenwood, an instructor in the academy at Rock Hall.

The youngest member of the family is our subject, who was b in Worton, Kent Co, Md., Mar 11 1854. He received his early education in the public schools and Washington College of Chestertown. In 1873 he went to Phila and became a student in the Phila College of Pharmacy, from which he grad in 1876. For a time he clerked in that city, but in 1878 he embarked in business in Chestertown, where he has since remained. He is a member of the ME Church. In 1877 he m Sarah Isabella Bordley, of Chestertown, and five children were born to them: John Milbourn, Hallie Isabella, Mabel, William Houston and Nannie Rebecca.

428. HORATIO N. CRAWFORD, owner of homestead, Mount Pleasant, 2nd dist Wicomico Co. His father, Hy Crawford, settled in this dist 1795, from his native state, Del. He grew up in Newcastle Co, son of an Irishman. He bt Mount Pleasant early part of war of 1812; farmer; estab tannery Quantico. He m Mrs. Mary Nelson, of this co; both d 1836, mbrs Bapt Church. Of their 2 child. 1 decd. - Subj b on Mount Pleasant, Jul 13 1824, educated in dist schools and Georgetown, D. C.; started farming at 17; his farm comprises 300 a.; mbr Episc Church. Jan 15 1862 he m Elizabeth A. Phillips, d/o Johnson Phillips, of this co; of their 5 child. 2 remain: Sarah E. and Hy T. The latter assists father. A. J. Crawford, another son, d Mar 1897; a young politician, res Quantico, elected to state senate.

429. JOHN W. DASHIELL, M. D., retired, res Princess Anne, Som Co; b Jan 30 1817, this dist. His mansion, once prop of Littleton D. Teagle, one of oldest and largest houses in co. His father, Rbt K. W., native of this dist. The latter grad medical depart Univ Md, but never practiced, occupied in land interests; d when about 67. During war of 1812 he was coast guard; mbr Episc Church. His father, John Dashiell, b this dist, d at about 77; left large estate and slaves; vestryman in Episc Church. His father, Levin Dashiell, b Som Co; early settler of co; large land holder, owned many slaves; lived to be over 84. Mother of subj, former Miss Elinor Leatherbury, of this place, d 1839, at 39, leaving 8 child., 4 survive. In 16th yr subj entered Bristol College; after 3 yrs entered Kenyon College, Ohio; nearing graduation he was overcome with severe sickness; later studied medicine under Dr. Nathan R. Smith, Balt; grad medical depart Univ Md 1842; practiced Vienna, Dor Co, 2 yrs; traveled through Pa, Ohio and Va, returned and taught for short time;

1847 opened office in Princess Anne; also carried on drug store; vestryman Episc Church. 1852 he m Eliza Polk, of old fam of Eastern Shore, whose bro was Col Wm T. G. Polk. She was mbr Episc Church; d at 77, Jan 9 1897. Their child.: Rbt Kemp, mcht here until he d, nearly 40; Sarah, w/o Frs H. Dashiell, of this co; and Ella B., w/o E. O. Smith, mcht Princess Anne.

430. FRANK P. CORKRAN in merchandising 18 yrs Williamsburg, Dor Co; postmaster. Paternal great-grandfather, Jas Corkran, owned large tract. His son, John, next in descent, was sea captain, turned to farming in this co c. 1812. John Burton Corkran, father of subj b nr Williamsburg c. 85 yrs ago; taught school, later farmed, recently turned over prop to sons; prior to war owned several slaves. He m Ann L. Shyrock, of Balt; their eldest dau, Rachel, w/o John C. Corkran, of this co. Other children: Geo S.; Sarah A., Mrs. Jos H. Corkran; John R., subj, Jos B. and Edw E., who d unmarried. 593

Subj b nr this village 1852, taught in home neighborhood 7 yrs. By then he had saved enough to start a business. 1884 he m Alice M., d/o Sml D. Fairbanks, M. D., of Talb Co. Her maternal grandfather, Wm Frazier, res this co, rep to state legislature of Md for 11 terms. Children of Mr. and Mrs. Corkran: John Ellsworth and Alice Estelle.

431. GEORGE A. DEVER, whose home is named Glendale; farmer 6th dist QA Co, postoffice address: Hope; 1877-1883 assist superintendent house of correction Balt. Nov 1897 elected co commissioner QA Co to succeed Jas Benj Bright. Wm Dever, father of subj, of Churchville, Harf Co, Md, where Dever fam has res many yrs; farmer; co commisioner Harf Co. 1862 he came to this co and purch homestead (240 a.) now owned by subj; clerk of Qa Co 1887-1892. He d 1892. He m Miss Angeline Hopkins, of Harf Co; they had 4 child. Annie J. w/o Rev F. T. Tagg, of Balt. Addie, wid of John Mulligan, living in this locality. Mamie, Mrs. Jos E. Elliot, d 1875. The mother is in 75th yr. Subj b Stafford, Harf Co, Jan 19 1848, at 16 took over farm; m Apr 20 1876 Lottie M. Lucas, d/o Wm B. Lucas; their child.: Wm K. and Mamie I., both at home. 594

432. BURTON W. PARKER, business man, Car Co; owns store at American Corners; has interest in canneries here. 1893 he set up a large sawmill. He is s/o Wm and Julia (Moore) Parker, both from old fam of Del. The mother d/o Edw Moore. 4 of child. of Wm and Julia Parker grew to maturity. Jos H. and Wm still living in Del; only dau, Emily, w/o C. W. Scott, of Sussex Co, Del. The father has always res Sussex Co. - Subj b parents' homestead, Sussex Co, 1855, remained at home until 1876. Having married Annie B., d/o Thos Noble, he came to Car Co; farmed 3 yrs, then added mercantile enterprises as well; now owns 4 farms (c. 600 a.), store, and sawmill. Their child.: Lillian R., Lulu V., Wilmer B., Thos Orville and Carl A. Fam mbrs MP Church. 594

433. WILLIAM W. SEWARD, young farmer, Car Co, 7th dist, nr Ridgely; b Car Co, Sep 30 1865, s/o Joshua Seward of this co. Joshua m Ella Byns, who was b Dor Co; of their 6 child. 2 d in infancy; living: Wm, Lida, Alta and Frank. The father was a teacher few yrs, then clerk in general store, and still later farmer; now retired Ridgely. His father Wm Seward, b and reared this co. Subj educated in public schools; clerked in general store in Sudlersville, QA Co, about a year; c. 1883 returned home and located on farm which he later purch (92 a.). He m Feb 9 1887 Miss Anna Deyo, d/o Broadhead Deyo, mcht of Wallkill, N. Y. She was b and brought up N. Y. State, educated in ladies' 595

-117-

seminary in N.J. She and Mr. Seward are mbrs ME Church. Their child, Olive, about 3.

596 434. ELIAS W. WILLIAMSON descends from New England ancestors. Since 1866 he has res 3rd dist Car Co. His great-grandfather, Stephen Williamson, came from Eng in early manhood with 2 bros, to Boston; later settled in Me, prior to Rev. One of his child. was Capt Stephen Williamson, b Me. He was father of Rev Stephen Williamson, father of subj. A native of Me, he m Betsy Greenlea; of their 11 child., 3 living: Orrin, Elias W. and Manly. The father was in war of 1812; Bapt minister; d at 80. He and fam moved to Car Co 1864 and here he d. Subj b Feb 3 1823 Maine, reared on farm; became master builder; erected over 100 houses in Camden, N.J. Since 1866 he res nr Williston. Md. Nov 3 1850 he m Eliza A. Fisher, of Augusta, Me.; their child.: 2 decd; living: Addie, Allie, Chas and Wm E. Mrs. Williamson d/o John and Elmira (Davis) Fisher, of Maine. The father, carpenter and contractor, once foreman of subj. Subj and wife mbrs ME Church.

599 435. WILLIAM H. RADCLIFFE, large land owner Dor Co, has farm on Little Choptank River Cambridge dist; director in Natl Bank of Cambridge; also owns 5 other farms. He spent boyhood in Neck dist, Dor Co, where b Jan 9 1824; educated in common schools; s/o Jas and Margaret (Harris) Radcliffe; she a descendant of Beckwith family. At 21 he began work as ship carpenter, built sailing vessels nr Cornersville with his bro; after 3 yrs came to Cambridge dist, where he had a ship yard on Little Choptank River, and continued as ship builder until 1860. 1861 he traveled through the west, returned to Md, settled on farm purch in 1860. Here he res, in farming and timber business. He m May 2 1877 Miss Anna Hooper, granddau of Sml Pattison, cousin of ex-Gov Pattison of Pa. Their son: Wm H., Jr.

599 436. WILLIAM J. WOODFORD, in livery business, Centreville, b this town Feb 17 1863. His father, J. W. W., s/o Jas Woodford, clockmaker, b Elkton, Cecil Co; in early manhood moved to QA Co, May 1860. While in Elkton he clerked in store, also in Middletown and Georgetown Cross Roads. In Centreville he estab mail route and stage line; ran transfer line, and line of stages to Easton and Chestertown. 1895, he sold business to his son. 1895 J. W. W. Woodford app postmaster Centreville but opposition of Senator Gibson negated confirmation by senate. Apr 1897 Mr. Woodford app tax collector for dist. He m Annne H. Reaves, d/o Thos Reaves, of Bridgeton, N.J., granddau of Rev patriot. She is still living, now about 60. Of their 4 children, 3 living: Wm J.; Marion J., in Centreville; and Thos R., student Western Md College.
When 10 subj assisted father in business; during intervals of school he drove wagons. At 18 he hired on as a purser on river steamboat. After 6 yrs, Oct 1894, he returned home, bt livery business of John A. Scotton. Jan of fol year he bt the 'bus and stage line from his father, now runs two stage lines to Queenstown and a 'bus and transfer line in town. Dec 12 1888 he m Miss Ida Cole; their child.: John Wallace, Elmira, Wm T. and Walter E.

600 437. JOHN C. MONTAGUE owner of homestead, Juniper Hill, 4th dist Talb Co (128 a.).; ME church. Jesse Montague b Car Co, m Hettie, d/o Martin K. Ford, of Del, of their 7 child., subj 4th in order of birth. Paternal grandfather Jesse from France. Jesse Montague mbr ME Church; d 1882, wife d 5 yrs prev. Their eldest dau: Anne, wid of Geo Ross; she lives with sis Elizabeth, Mrs. Nathaniel Green, Del. Wm Hy res QA Co and Dnl in Easton. Helen, w/o Thos Hutchins, res western shore of Md. - Subj b Hazelville, Kt Co, Del, Feb 28

1838, attended local schools until c. 18; traveled in West; into farming; Feb 1860 m Emma Williams in Kt Co, Del, d/o John Williams, of Del, b and reared Kt Co. They had 6 child. 4 living: Harvey of Ridgely, Md; Correna, wid of Edw Carville, of Kt Island, mother of J. Denny, who res with grandfather; Allie w/o Harry St. Clair, of Balt; and Fannie w/o Thos P. Roe, farmer this area. Subj helped estab postoffice nr home; village bears his name.

438. JAMES W. SAULSBURY, sheriff, tax collector, co committeeman, supervisor 601 of poor house, Car Co; mbr with ME Church. Paternal grandfather, Wm Saulsbury, b and d about 80 this co. Eli, father of Jas W., of this co; in war of 1812; farmer; m Rachel Smith, who was b Kt Co, Del; subj only child.
  Subj b Aug 8 1817, this co; 1841 made tax collector, 1861 elected sheriff; 1865 elected co commissioner. Aug 7 1855 he m Ann E. Hitch, d/o Garey Hitch of this co; she d 1857; had 2 child.: 1 d in infancy; Vashti, w/o Rbt J. W. Garey, who d Apr 12 1895, at 51. Mrs. Garey res Williston. Their 6 child.: Rbt S., bookkeeper with Cochran Ice Co., of Balt; Mary E., Enoch B., V. Louise, Lena R., and Jas A. H.

439. JOSIAH S. TAYLOR b Barren Creek dist, Wicomico, Nov 8 1828, Epics, 601 farmer; owns Taylor farm (250 a.), this dist; ancestors emigrated from Eng. His father, Elias, and grandfather, Horatio Taylor, b where he now res. The former, farmer, d 1835; 9 yrs later his wife, Polly d/o°Lowdy Gosley, d: of 7 child. 3 survive: John C., of Balt; subj; and Isaac T., of Dor Co. Subj m Nov 5 1856 Hester P. Bennett, d/o Elisha Bennett, of Barren Creek dist. Of 10 child. fol survive: Nancy Virginia, w/o Geo T. Wilson, of Barren Creek dist; Mary E., w/o Perry J. Brown, of Va; Elisha S., res Balt; Letitia E., Mrs. Rbt B. Bailey; John B and Andrew J., at home; Kate M., w/o W. B. Bailey, of Mardela Springs; and Calvin M., who m Minnie Alberta Goslee, of this dist.

440. JAMES M. ANDREWS owns c. 400 a. farm land Hurlock dist Dor Co; has 02 interests in flouring mill Williamsburg, Hurlock creamery; b Jun 14 1848, eldest s/o Stephen Andrews; attended dist schools. Jan 13 1876 he m Sallie, d/o Wm Noble, of Car Co; their child.: Wm N., Carrie, Mary, Stephen, Helen and Jas E.; fam connected with ME Church. Stephen Andrews, father of subj, b 1801, res this co. His father, Medford Andrews, b Dor Co (supposedly), s/o Stephen, of Md. The latter was s/o Isaac and grandson of Maj Wm Andrews, who came from Eng in 1711, settled in eastern part of Va, moved to Eastern Shore of Md. Stephen Andrews bt timber land northern part this co, c. 500 a., cleared land for large homestead. He m Rebecca Carroll 1839; their child.: Sarah E.; Margaret M., w/o Jas H. Williams; subj, Jos B., Annie R., Stephen S.; Wm, decd; and another Stephen, who d.

441. WILLIAM F. HALL, M. D., physician Som Co; solely in drug business until 603 1885 when he began practice at Crisfield, where he owns drug store; pres Crisfield Ice Co 2 yrs; 1st pres Crisfield Bldg & Loan Assoc; b nr village of Marion, Som Co, Jan 25 1857, s/o Rbt H. and Harriet E. (Holland) Hall, of this co. His father, carpenter here, and farmer. He d at 33; in ME Church. He was s/o Richard Hall, of this co, farmer, d at 57. About 6 months after death of Rbt H. Hall his wife d, leaving 4 orphan children. Of these, John W., eldest, farmer and res old homestead at Marion; Rbt H., assists older bro on home farm; H. Emma res with William F., who is youngest of fam. Subj 3 months old when father d, and wholly orphaned by mother's death; cared for by relatives, educated in local schools; Jan 1872 came to Crisfield, clerked in drug store of Drs. Robertson and Atkinson about 8 yrs, purch Dr. Robertson's

interest; grad medical depart Univ Md 1885; began practice at Crisfield. 1886 he m Miss Maggie Carman, of Crisfield; their child.: Agnes and Cecil.

603 442. JOSPEH W. DISHAROON, business man Crisfield, grocery trade. 1897 he built the Crisfield Hotel. His father, Jos Disharoon, of French descent, native of Salisbury; farming and milling Wicomico Co, nr Salisbury; d at 45, mbr ME Church. His father, Wm W., of Salisbury, owned several large farms and many slaves. Mother subj, Sallie E., d/o Hy J. Dashiell, of Wicomico Co, farmer and slave owner; d at 83. Mrs. Sallie Disharoon, now about 60, res Phila, connected with ME Church there. Of her 11 child., 6 d in infancy; Woodland A., in advertising business N. Y.; Lawrence D. in livery business here in partnership with subj; Annie, w/o Geo W. Peirson, of Phila, auditor of Pa Railway Co; and Mary H., unmarried, res Phila.
Subj b Feb 1 1860, Wicomico Co, educated in dist schools and in Salisbury. 1878 he went to N.Y., clerked with firm of Olivit Brothers 2 yrs or more; came to Crisfield, clerked in hotel here until it burned; employed in grocery, went into business on his own. 1895 branched into wholesale trade; 1890 started livery business; built Crisfield Hotel 1897; owns many houses and oyster boats; director Bank of Crisfield. Sep 13 1883 he m Susie M., d/o Seth D. Venable, of Crisfield, (hotel man, d Jun 30 1897 whose wife, Susan A., d Feb 1894). Subject's wife mbr Meth Church.

604 443. CAPT. GEORGE TYLER res Dor Co, b Lake dist May 12 1812, d Hooper's Island 1887. When a young man he moved from Lake to Hooper's Island dist; at 15 became cook on a schooner, worked up to be master of a vessel. After marriage he bt a schooner, engaged in bay trade until sons assumed charge of boats, then retired. Subj m Caroline R. Travers, of Dor Co, of old fam of this area. She d at 70; their child.: Sarah Jane, Mrs. Sylvester T. Hall, decd; Matthew T., in oyster business and postmaster Hooper's Island; Geo W., in mercantile and oyster business here; Rbt, d at 42; Solomon, partner with brother Geo; John G., mcht Hooper's Island; Caroline, w/o Sml G. Meekins, of this place; and Elizabeth, d at 12. George W. and Solomon Tyler own largest general store on Hooper's Island and several oyster boats.

605 444. AUGUSTUS RITZEL, business man Westover, res here over 30 yrs. His father, Geo Ritzel, b Germany, grew to manhood there; c. 1849 located in Dalton Co, Pa, where he lived; stone mason; d 1893 at 73. In Germany he served regulation 7 yrs in army, became an officer. He m Miss Mary Moler, b Germany, now in 77th yr, enjoying excellent health, res Lykens, Pa, where her sons, Geo and John, res. She is mbr Cath Church. Of her 6 children Mary, who d 1895, is alone decd. Martin res this neighborhood; Chas res Chester, Pa. - Subj, eldest of fam, b 1845 province of Hesse-Darmstadt; educated in Pa, until his 15th year, worked 4 yrs with father as stone masons, went to Phila 1866, machinist 2 yrs; sent by employer to look into business interests in Westover, remained and bt lumber concern; has about 500 a. of farm land. Jul 1876 he m Elizabeth Betler, of Pottsville, Pa; their child., in order of birth: Mary, Maggie, Augustus, Jr., Annie and Edward. Family are Cath.

606 445. JOHN M. BEAVEN; po address: Hillsborough, Car Co; home in 4th dist Talb Co; mcht Hillsborough. 1891 he moved to this place and opened a store, carries dry goods, hats, shoes, etc.; runs saw and planing mill; s/o Rev Geo F. Beaven, (see his sketch elsewhere this vol). Subj b in Charles Co Jan 17 1852, brought to this locality when quite young; attended dist schools until about 18, left home and clerked in store of Mr. Holt of Hillsborough. 1883 he

went to Tunis Mills; 1884-90 he was partner in firm with Chas R. Wooters; bt out other's interest.

446. JOHN W. DOWNEY, young business man, Rock Hall, 5th dist Kt Co; owns drug store; postmaster; b Feb 19 1857, s/o Wm S. and Anne E. Scoon, of Kt Co. The father owned small schooner and purch a farm shortly before he d at 38, active in Meth Church, led singing in the choir. Their child.: Mary E., Jos (whose sketch appears elsewhere this vol), Wm T., Geo E., subj, Marion and Alice. — Subj remained on old homestead with mother until he was about 22; clerked in general store Rock Hall; employed by his bro, Jos, 10-12 yrs, dealing in general supplies. 1882 subj m Miss Mary E. Hynson, of this co; their child.: Eva, Alice and Allen; fam mbrs ME Church. 606

447. GEORGE H. BERRY, M. D., physician, res Lawson's dist; b Jun 8 1825 and reared there; educated in public schools there; 1848 he commenced study medicine under Dr. John S. McCur, of Balt; grad Wash Univ 1848, began practice this dist. He m Mrs. Mary A. J. Brown, of this area; their child.: Mary, Lucy, Rbt, carpenter, Wm T., John E., Edith and Emma. Geo d when about 38, and Jos T. decd. Paternal grandfather of subj was Rbt Berry, of Balt, pilot on Chesapeake Bay, of Eng ancestry, lived to old age; served in war of 1812; his wid received a pension. His son, Rbt, father of subj, Baltimore sea captain, d at 45. His wife, Jane, b and res Balt, d at 87. Her father, Geo Davy, came from England after Rev war. Mrs. Jane Berry mbr Bapt Church. 609

448. HON. GEORGE W. COVINGTON res of Berlin and Snow Hill. He helped incorporate Worcester Railroad, director and counsel of its successor, the Del Md & Va Railroad. 610
    Subj was 5th and youngest s/o Isaac and Amelia (Franklin) Covington, b Berlin, Wor Co, Sep 12 1838. His father d when he was 6. He was educated in Buckingham Acad; one of his teachers was Loring Johnson; deterred from entering Univ of Va by typhoid fever there; returned home, studied law under cousin, John R. Franklin. He stayed with mother and young sis until his mother's death, Aug 3 1863. 1858 he entered law depart Harvard Univ; returned home early 1859; strain on his eyes forced to abandonment of studies, received treatment from Phila oculist; principal Buckingham Acad; fol year resumed legal studies, admitted to bar, began practice in home neighborhood. Protection of mother and sis prevented service in Civil war. After death of mother he opened an office in Snow Hill. (A great amount of detail given onsupressive conditions under which subj particpated in political events during Civil war.) 1865 subj elected secretary and treasurer of bd of county school commissioners of Wor Co; 1867 elected to constitutional convention; retired to Cedar Grove farm 1871; school examiner and treasurer of co school bd 1874; res again in Snow Hill, resuming practice, 1878 he built home, the Hedges; 1880 elected to congress and 1882 re-elected. Since 1885 in private life, looking after practice and estates.
    Sep 6 1865, subj m Sallie M. D. Bishop, only d/o Geo and Louisa C. Bishop, at All Hallows Church, Snow Hill; their child.: Louisa Amelia, Geo Bishop, Harry Franklin and Arthur Dennis (d in infancy). Subj baptized at All Hallows where father had been vestryman, later attended Buckingham Presby Church, Berlin, with mother. After moving to Snow Hill he served in Makemie Memorial Church. When edifice built in honor of Frs Makemie, his cousin, Lady Kortright, of London, England, contributed substantially. A stained glass window in memory of her father, John Richardson, of Snow Hill, and former mbr

of congregation, adorns front of church. Mr. Covington and fam now worship in All Hallows Episcopal, of which wife mbr from early girlhood.

612 449. THOMAS H. CRANE, M. D. b nr Church Hill, QA Co, Feb 7 1825, s/o Dr. Jonathan and Mary (Myers) Crane, of QA Co, res Millington, Kt Co. His father, physician that area until he d; their 7 child. decd. Subj attended public school and acad; grad medical depart Univ Md 1845; in practice with father, moved to Massey, Kt Co, there 2 yrs; 1852-1887 practiced in Milling- ton; he d here 1887. Dr. Crane m(1) Ellen Massey, of Kt Co; she d leaving children: Hy M. and Edw T., both of Phila. Subj m(2) 1856, Anna E. Smith, d/o Wm F. Smith, of Va, who moved to Millington at early age, in mercantile business. He m Miss Rochester, had 1 child, Anna E. Child. of subj and wife: John A., of Phila; Jonathan, res N.Y.; and Anna M., with her mother on old homestead in Millington. Dr. Crane and fam identified with Episc Church.

613 450. JAMES FERGUSON, farmer 4th dist. His father, John, of Scotland, reared to age of 9 nr Edinburgh; emigrated with parents who settled in Albany, N.Y., 1791. John Ferguson d c. 1859; farmer Schoharie Co, N. Y., whither he had gone as adult; attended Presby Church. He m Anne Scott, Albany Co was her early home; their child.: Mary Jane, decd; Jas; and Eliza, res Fulton, N. Y.

Subj b Albany, N. Y., May 22 1823, received common school education. About 18 he returned to old home, worked for father until 1854, opened store at Fulton, N.Y., which he conducted 7 yrs; farmed next 5 yrs, then res Conn. 7 yrs. 1875 he settled on present homestead, then known as the Merrick farm (85 a.). Jun 2 1858, subj m Margaret, d/o Benj Best, of Fulton, N. Y., justice of the peace. Her maternal grandfather, Timothy Murphy, "hero of Schoharie Co," fought in Rev war with Morgan's Rigles. Julia, sis of Mrs. Ferguson, m son of ex-Gov Bouck, of N.Y., and her 2 daus, m sons of Gov Cornell. Child. of subj and wife: Chas, at home and aids on farm, and Cornelia M., teacher in public schools of N.Y.

614 451. EDWARD H. ROE, rgtr of wills Talb Co, b 28 Feb 1850, on farm about 5 miles from Easton, decandant of old fam of Eng descent, which settled here shortly after Rev war. His grandfather, Edw Roe, farmer. He had 2 sons, still living: Edw T., farmer; and Jas A., father of subj, who was b 1827, Talb Co, farmer; co assessor, crier for the courts. He is a mbr ME Church; m Martha A. Dean, of Talb Co, d/o Hy Dean. She d when subj was about 20; her child.: 2 decd; subj, eldest; Jas A., Jr., farmer Talb Co; Walter D., miller Talb Co; A. Keener, traveling salesman Balt; Mrs. Rev G. C. McSorley, Mrs. Roland Todd, Mrs. Rbt Wrightson and Miss Annie. - Subj attended Easton high school; 1 Sep 1870 he entered register's office under Tilghman N. Chance, remained with him and his successor. 1879 Mr. Roe elected rgtr, retired 1897; once farmed and cashier Farmers & Merchants Bank Easton. 1874 he m Miss Lizzie Lewis of Talb Co, school teacher. Her father, Hamilton Lewis, of Del; her only bro, T. H. Lewis, D. D., educator connected with Western Md College. Child. of subj and wife: Hamilton Lewis, law student in Rushville, Ill.; and E. Homer, Thondyke, Florence and Virginia, all attending school.

615 452. CLAYTON J. PURNELL, of Wor Co bar, recently suffered stroke which paralyzed entire left side. He is author of "The Law of Insolvency of Maryland; with Forms of Procedure." He was b on Rochester farm, nr Snow Hill, Wor Co, Jan 22 1856. His father, co commissioner, d 1889, at 65; his wid res Snow Hill, at 64; their child.: dau, Annie B., d at 11; another of same name d in infancy; Leonard D. grad in medicine Univ Md, d of typhoid fever the day he

received his diploma; subj next in order of birth; Perry W. d in 21st yr; Ella L. res with mother in Snow Hill.

When subj was 2 parents moved into Snow Hill; there and at Md Agricultural College he received his education. At 18 he entered office of clerk of court, I. T. Matthews, depy 4 yrs, reading law with Geo W. Purnell; admitted to bar at 21, examined by Judge Franklin; 1878 he opened law office in Snow Hill, active until May 24 1895 when stricken with paralysis. 1893 he was candidate for assoc judge 1st judicial circuit of Md, lost after election became deadlocked and resolved by convention (described in detail) on 5,650th ballot! Subj is a director of Md Agricultural College and vice-pres Pocomoke City Natl Bank; Presby; m 1880 Miss Ella A. d/o Dr. Edw Hubbell. Mr. Hubbell was rgtr of wills Wor Co, res of Snow Hill. Mr. and Mrs. Purnell had 3 child., 2 living: May H. and Bessie L.

453. HON. CHARLES F. HOLLAND, circuit judge 1st judicial dist of Md, Episc, b 616 Apr 3 1841 Sussex Co, Del, s/o Elisha and Louis (White) Holland, of that co. He is 3rd of 5 child.; all but one living; educated in public schools and Milton Acad, and a course at Milford; grad in 21st year, studied law in office of Judge Layton, of Georgetown, Del; 1866 admitted to bar of Del; in practice 1 year at Georgetown; 1868 came to Wicomico Co; appointed to fill unexpired term of Judge Wilson, elected fol term.

454. JAMES STEVENS CHAPLAIN, M. D., pres Trappe Savings Bank, pres of branch 619 of Balt Bldg and Loan Assoc Trappe, physician Talb Co.
1st of Chaplain family here was Frs Chaplain, from Suffolk, Eng, c. 1660, settled in Talb Co. Jun 16 1684, he bt tract from Cornelius Mulrain, on Bolinbroke Creek. He was mbr Church of England, vestryman White Marsh parish; d Aug 27 1707, his wife, Martha, d 1700.

Their only son, Jas Chaplain, b 1670, d Feb 17 1708, m Elizabeth White Feb 20 1704; their sons: Jas and Frs. The former, b Nov 17 1706, m Elizabeth Martin Jun 5, 1728, and d Feb 1776; of their 6 child., 2 were twins, Frs and Thos, b Jun 29 1731. Frs and his wife, Margaret, had two child., Frs and Jas. Frs, b Feb 16 1757, m Margaret Jenkins Jan 9 1783, and d Nov 1786. He had one son, Jas, b Nov 23 1783, who m Eliza Stevens Dec 16 1823, and d Apr 28 1844, his wife d Aug 31 1888. Their oldest child, John Frs Chaplain, D. D., mbr Phila Conference ME Church, d 1880, in 56th yr. Another son, Prof. Alexander Chaplain, sec and examiner of schools of Talb Co past 29 yrs. The 2 daus were Sarah, w/o Jas L. Robinson, d 1895; and Mary Elizabeth, Mrs. Thos J. Willis, of Kt Co, Md, who d 1897.

2nd child of Jas and Eliza (Stevens) Chaplain, Jas Stevens Chaplain, b Trappe, Talb Co, May 5 1827. After high school he entered drug store of Richard F. Hemsley Easton 1843; then chief clerk in Littlefield's drug store Balt 6 yrs; studied medicine under Dr. Thos H. Buckler (still res Balt); grad medical depart Univ Md 1854; began practice in Trappe, continued past 43 yrs. Nov 9 1854 he m Evelina, d/o Dr. Sml T. Kemp, physician Trappe; their child.: Louis, studied medicine, grad Univ Md 1877, d 2 yrs later; and Ella, d unmarried 1882. The doctor and wife attend ME Church South.

455. ALBERT E. WELSH b on farm where he lives and manages Trappe dist, Talb 620 Co, 122 a. of original homestead of the fam. The Welshes of Eng origin.
Rbt, father of subj, b on old farm 1812, and still living here. His father Wm, of this place, d when about 54. He was s/o Thos Welsh, founder of this branch of fam in Md. Child. of Wm and Sally (Harrington) Welsh: Rbt; Annie, m Abner Parrott; Mary, d in 61st yr; and Caroline, d in 31st yr. At 15 Rbt went

to Balt, learned brickmaker's trade; lived there about 10 yrs, returned to Trappe, in contracting and building many yrs. 1837 he m Margaret Jane Bagswell, who d 1891, at 72; their child.: Wm, Emmett, Thos, Ida, Ella, Rbt, subj, Chas, Margaret and 3 d in infancy. Wm and Thos, Ella (w/o John P. Holmes) and Ida are decd. Mary m Geo A. Mullican. Chas is farmer this dist. Subj b Oct 28 1854; m 1878 Miss Ella Parsons, of Oxford, their child.: Leila B., attends school West Chester, Pa; Margaret H. and Mary E., at home.

620 456. JOHN DALE, M. D., physician Princess Anne, Som Co, for over 20 yrs; surgeon for N.Y., Phila & Norfolk Railway at this point; b Oct 15 1851, Kt Co, Md, s/o Rev Wm Dale, minister MP Church, retired of poor health. He res Pocomoke City, Md, pres 1st Natl Bank there, b Wor Co, Md, entered church in early manhood; located in Chestertown area; since then res Wor Co, farmed for a while; now 75. His father, John Dale, of Wor Co; farmer; b 1801, d 1873. The Dales of English origin. Rev Dale m Miss Mary Jones, of Kt Co; she d at 32, leaving 3 children: Chas G., farmer nr Pocomoke City; subj; and Ella, w/o Wm S. McMaster, atty Princess Anne. - Subj was 5 when his mother d; soon thereafter fam moved to farm in Wor Co; he attended Western Md College; came to Princess Anne, read medicine with Drs. Morris and Briscoe; grad Bellevue Hospital and Medical College N.Y. 1874, began practice this town. Oct 2 1879 he m Miss Sallie Cook, of Phila; their child.: Richard, and Edgar, decd. Mrs. Dale is mbr Presby Church; subj on bd of trustees of the church.

621 457. HENRY BELL, res 7th dist Car Co; b this co; for many years he res of Del Co, Oh, its co commissioner, rep in Ohio state legislature. Paternal grandfather of subj, Selva Bell, came from Scotland with father, Col Wm Bell, prior to Rev war, Col Bell served in the conflict. Parents of Hy Bell were Jos and Frances (Lecompt) Bell, of Car Co; their dau, Mary A., decd. The father was a farmer; both parents mbrs ME Church.
Subj b Apr 25 1815; at 8 accompanied mother to Oh, first stopping place of any duration was village of Marion, then proceeded to Del Co, and to Green Co. Subj, then 16, purch farm (160 a.); 1840 went to Columbus, Ohio, engaged in manufacture of farm machinery; acquired extensive tracts of farm land and town prop, carried on general stores at London, Columbus, Newton and Grove City; in flour and grain business in Columbus at one time. He sold out his various Ohio enterprises 1864, settled in Seaford, Del, opened general store, built over 20 houses. He lost c. $100,000, still owns several large buildings; 1882 bt farm (162 a.) where he now lives. He attended Delaware College two yrs; mbr ME Church. May 2 1838 he m Larua Bull, of Franklin, Oh; of their 6 child. 3 survive: Frank, Katie and Amanda, all m and res Montana. Mrs. Bell d on visit to Montana. 1864 subj m Martha Clemments, of Va; their child.: Wm, Thos H., Harry (now in Ohio), Elmer, Mollie and Chas.

622 458. GILLIS T. TAYLOR b on farm where he res, Sharptown dist Wicomico Co, nr village of Riverton; owns this tract and additional 500 a. The Taylor fam res Wicomico Co several generations; of Eng descent. Levi D. Taylor, subject's father, s/o Levi, Sr., both b on same homestead. The former, farmer, owned many slaves; d 1856. He m Betsey, d/o Roger Phillips, of Del; she d 1883; of their 9 child., fol living: Gillis T.; L. C., wid res Quantico dist; Sallie E., who m E. T. Bennett, res nr old homestead; Emma, wid of John Howard; Mary H. wid of H. B. Howard; and Geo W. and Wm L., res Riverton.
Subj b Aug 28 1823, attended school, remained at home until father's death, then bt interests of other heirs and has since tilled the home place. 1885 and 1887 elected mbr bd of co commissioners. He m Feb 12 1861, Sophia, d/o

-124-

Benj Darby, of Wicomico Co; of their 6 children 4 living: Benj, res Salisbury; Levi, at home; Thos, res and works on home farm; and Martha, who m Wm F. Allen, of Salisbury, who raises strawberry plants.

459. JOHN L. CARMAN, employe of N.Y., Phila and Norfolk Railroad Co, in Crisfield, Som Co; sent there 1868 as train dispatcher; after 5 yrs app agent for this station, his present position. Subj b Jan 12 1839 Phila. His father, John L., of Phila, in contracting and building, soldier of Mexican war. His mother, Margaret, d/o Capt Jas Lee, an officer under Gen Washington in Rev war. He was carpenter and cabinet maker. On paternal side, subject's fam dates back to John and Florence Carman, of Eng birth; settled on Long Island, N.Y., c. 1630. John L. Carman m Margaret Jacobs, b and reared Phila d Phila when her children were young; 2 of her child. d in early childhood, one unnamed, other named Washington; fol survive: Mary, John L., Jr., Margaret and Ringgold. - Subj res Phila in youth; after mother's death lived in N.J. about 2 yrs; then on farm in Pa until 1862. 1863 he went to Camden, N.J., employed by railroad co., with whom employed ever since. Aug 1862 he enlisted in Company A, 124th Pa Infantry, served 9 months in Army of Potomac in Va; in battles of Antietam and Chancellorsville. He is 2nd vice-pres of Somerset Bldg & Loan Assoc of Crisfield. 1863 he m Miss Susan J. Harple, of Chester Co, Pa; their child.: Maggie, w/o Dr. W. F. Hall, of Crisfield. (See his sketch elsewhere this vol) Mary w/o Fdk Sterling, teller Crisfield Bank; John Ringgold, only son, at home, employe same railroad co as father. Subj and wife mbrs Bapt Church. 623

460. HENRY H. BALCH, proprietor and founder of Md Nautical Acad, nr Easton. Admit ages 10-17; regular academic studies in addition to nautical and military training, preparatory to U.S. Naval Acad app in army as 2nd lieut. (Curricula is described.) Subj b May 7 1856 Balt s/o Rev Lewis P. W. Balch. Rev. Balch b Va s/o Judge Stephen Balch, grad Princeton; minister Episc Church, one time rector of Christ Church Balt. He d Detroit, Mich 1875. During war he took part in securing exchange of prisoners. He m Emily, d/o Timothy Wiggin, banker of London, Eng; she d 1891; their child.: Lewis, res Albany, N.Y.; Alfred, of N.Y.; Wm, res London, Eng; Catherine, res N.Y.; subj; Adelaide, w/o Jos Coit, of St. Paul's School, Concord, N.H.; Ellen M., who m Dr. O. W. Huntington, of Newport, R.I.; Edith C., Mrs. Clifford Twombley, of Newton, Mass.; Ernest, of N.Y.; and Stephen Elliott, of Boston.
Subj educated Balt; entered Bishop's College, at Lenoxville, Quebec 1866; grad 1873; conducted cordage business N.Y.; Dec 1894, he moved to Talb Co and estab Md Nautical Acad. 1884 he went to Europe as captain with a LaCrosse team and won 15 out of 17 matches. Oct 26 1891 he m Clarissa Fleming, of WashD. C., d/o Rbt Fleming and cousin of Gen Rbt E. Lee. Their child.: Hy H., Jr. and Clarissa Anne. 623

461. THOMAS J. SHALLCROSS, farmer and business man, 2nd dist, Kt Co; b home farm, Phila Co, Pa 9 Sep 1828, s/o Jacob Shallcross, who was b Pa 1791. Fam estab in this country by 3 bros, from Eng to Pa 1704: Wm to Bucks Co; Jas to Chester Co; John to Phila Co. From John subj descends. His son Leonard was father of Thos Shallcross, subject's grandfather, who farmed in Phila Co, as did his son, Jacob. The last named m Margaret Fox, of Phila Co; of their 8 child. 4 living: Sereck, res Del; Catherine F., w/o R. W. Cochran; subj; and Frances, w/o J. K. Williams, of Del. The father was mbr Soc of Friends; overseer of almshouse in Phila. He d 1875, at 84; his wife d 1879 at 87. 624

-125-

Subj b educated in public schools of Phila Co; 1854 came to Kt Co, Md, purch part of Marshy Point land. 1863 he m Miss Jennett Gooding, of Kt Co, their child. living: Thos, b 1864, res Wilm, Del; Wm G., physician Phila; Jenett; Sereck; Emma and Lambert T., at home. 1875-1883 he was judge of orphans' court; pres bd co commissioners 1889-1895. Fam mbrs ME Church.

625 462. GORDON T. ATKINSON, M. D., druggist, Crisfield; once partner of Dr. Sml A. Robinson, now with Dr. Wm F. Hall; pres Crisfield Ice Co; owns 2 farms Som Co and houses in Crisfield; b Dec 28 1846 Dublin dist, Som Co. His father, Levin Atkinson, mbr MP church, b and reared on farm Atkinson dist, Wor Co; came to Som Co to farm inherited from great-uncle, Col Levin Pallett, who was son-in-law of Parson Sloan, wealthy Eng clergyman of Episc Church here. Levin res here until about 63; then moved to Pocomoke City, conducted tannery until he d, 1877, at 69; owned many slaves. Grandfather of subj, Maj John F. Atkinson, b Wor Co, educated Wash Acad; farmer, surveyor, builder and operator of water mills; d at 37; major in militia; s/o John Atkinson, of Eng, farmer, miller and lumberman of Md. Mother of subj, former Comfort E. Quinton, b Wor Co, d at home of subj, Crisfield, at 67, mbr MP Church. Her father, John Quinton, farmer, d when she was a child, she was taken into home of uncle, Wm Quinton, founder of MP Church Nasewango, Wor Co., nr Snow Hill. Her child.: Sallie, who m Dr. S. S. Quinn, of Pocomoke City, d there at 26; Mary, d at 17; Gordon T.; and Susan, w/o Stephen McCready, of Crisfield.

After local schools, at 17, subj entered Dickinson College, Carlisle, Pa., grad Univ Pa 1869; began and remains in practice at Crisfield. He m Julia F., d/o Wm H. Roach of Hopewell, Som Co. Subj mbr co school bd 17 yrs; assist surgeon U. S. marine hospital 5 yrs until it was abolished. He and wife mbrs MP Church.

626 463. JOHN BOON DUKES, farmer, Car Co, po address: Denton; b where he has res execept 7 yrs with mother and fam nr Denton, when he and bros attended school; tax collector 1884-1885; general assessor of co 1896. Grandfather of subj, Levi Dukes, of Car Co, b 1772, d 1824. His son, Capt Jas Dukes, father of subj b this co, capt state militia; owned c. 150 slaves and over 2000 a. nr Denton; owned vessels in which he shipped products to Balt. He d 1842, at 42. He m(1) Sarah Rhodes, of Car Co, of their 3 child. Capt Levi T. Dukes, survives, res nr Cordova. The captain m(2) Miss Mary Boon, this co; their child.: Rebecca E., J. Kent, I. Reyner and J. Boon, former state senator.

Subj b Feb 3 1840. After common schools, enrolled 2 yrs Dickerson Seminary, Williamsport, Pa; farmer; 1876-1886, he was in shipping business with late Col W. P. Downes, of Denton; reared in Cath Church. Feb 3 1864 he m Maria L. Griffith, d/o Chas and Ann (Richardson) Griffith, both b Car Co. Ann Richardson was grandchild of Col Wm Potter. Their child.: Chas G., inspector in grain depart of Mo., res Kansas City; Cora E., Maria L., Anna G. and Mabael C. Mrs. Dukes d Jul 25 1895, buried Cath Cemetery Denton.

629 464. CAPT. W. H. HADDAWAY, oyster and fish business Oxford, where he res; 1890 elected pres bd commissioners Talb Co; director natl bank; b 1844 on father's farm Broad Creek Neck, southern part St. Michael's dist. 1861-1862 enrolled in Company A, 1st Eastern Shore Infantry, in guard duty on Eastern Shore. May 11 1863 he re-enlisted in Company A, 11th Md Infantry, fought in various skirmishes in Md, in Sheridan's march through Va; discharged, Sep 29 1863; returned to Talb Co, began seafaring life, made master of a coasting vessel. He followed the water 1865-1879. 1879 he came to Oxford, in oyster business with firm of Wm T. Elliott & Co 2 yrs; continued in seafood business

with Edwin Sinclair. 1862 he m Miss Sarah C. Porter, who d 1883; their child.: Chas E., Oliver S., Rose and Susan. He m(2) 1885, Miss Mary T. Houlton; their child.: Helen D., decd; Alice, Ella, Annie and Catherine.

465. SAMUEL W. KENNERLY, of Crisfield, tax collector, dep U. S. marshal; in realty; dep warden Md penitentiary. 1888, after absence of 2 yrs, returned to Crisfield, street commissioner. Subj b May 14 1840 Wicomico (now) Co. His father, Wm Alexander Kennerly of same locality; farmer, owned large tracts, marine railway, steam sawmill and several vessels used in carrying lumber, etc, to Balt, Phila and Washington; made and lost several fortunes; d when about 56; m Elennor Wilson, who survived him by 3 yrs; she d at 58. She was reared in same neighborhood as husband; mbr Episc Church; their child.: Jas W., bailiff Salisbury; Octavia E. wid of Warren Messick, this co; and Wm L., res Harrington, Del. - Subj remained at home, in business with father until latter d, 1872; subj came to Crisfield; into lumber trade; went on his sailing vessel, the Northampton, in the Bay trade; after 2 yrs sold the ship; then public service 9 yrs; then traveling salesman for N.Y. medical co; visited N.Y., N. J., Md and Va, and finally went as far west as Lincoln, Neb. 630

466. COL. JOSEPH WICKES b Kt Co, s/o Jos and Mary (Piner) Wickes. Founder of fam in America, Maj Jos Wickes, emigrated from Eng 1650, when 30, settled on Kt Island; judge of Kt Co court 1651-56; presiding judge of court; later burgess to rep Kt Co in the assembly. 1656 he m Marie Hartwell. His son Jos, by former marriage, signer of Address of Protestants of Kt Co to King of Eng. Jos Wickes who m Mary PIner, d 1822, at 63; his wife d 1823 at 59. He left 4 child.: Thos, subj, Simon Alexander and Sarah P. Subj b Sep 2 1788; grad Wash College Chestertown, studied law under Jas Houston (later judge U.S. dist court); admitted to bar 1810, began practice in Chestertown; lieut of company of Capt Chambers at battle of Caulksfield 1814; commissioned col in militia, dep atty general of Md for Kt and Cecil Cos, until c. 1850, when he retired. Nov 20 1821, Col Wickes m Elizabeth Caroline, d/o Gen Benj Chambers and sis of Judge E. F. Chambers. Subj mbr Episc Church, one of visitors and governors of Wash College; d Jan 17 1864, leaving child.: Jos A., Peregrine L., and Sarah Augusta, Mrs. Wm H. Welsh, of Pa. Four child. d earlier: Mary Elizabeth, Mrs. Benj F. Green , of N. H.; Benj Chambers; Hester Van Bibber, who m Rev Wm Payton, of Pa; and Ezekiel Chambers. 630

467. HON. JOSEPH A. WICKES, of Chestertown, judge 2nd judicial circuit, b there Sep 27 1826, s/o Col Jos and Elizabeth C. (Chambers) Wickes; educated Wash College, Chestertown, grad Princeton 1845 with honors, studied medicine Univ Md (grad 1848); studied law under his father, admitted to bar 1852, entered into practice; m 1848 Anna Maria, d/o Wm C. Tilghman, and granddau of Richard Cook Tilghman, of QA Co. She d Apr 2 1864, leaving 5 child., living: Anna Tilghman, Hester Van Bibber and Caroline Barney. Jan 1854, he moved practice to Cumberland, Md; elected to house of delegates. After legislature adjourned, he returned to Cumberland, resumed practice. Declining health compelled him to relinquish his practice. After returning to Chestertown his health was restored; 1859 he resumed practice in Chestertown. Nov 1865 he m Anne Rebecca Wickes, d/o Col Simon Wickes. She d Oct 17 1889; her only son d in infancy; dau, Josephine Rebecca Wickes, surviving her. 1866 subj delegate to peace convention in Phila; mbr state constitutional convention 1867; circuit judge 2nd judicial court, (Cecil, Kt, QA, Car and Talb Cos); pres bd of governors and visitors Wash College. Nov 1893 he m Gladys, d/o Jos T. 631

Robinson, granddau of Maj Beverly Robinson, of Prince Williamm Co, Va; their child.: Gladys Robinson and Jos; another son d when an infant.

633 468. MILFORD PHILLIPS, business man, Cambridge, in packing and shipping oysters. His father Geo Wesley Phillips, commissioner Dor Co; dep marshal during war; d Cambridge at 69. His father, Solomon Phillips, seafaring man and s/o Benj Phillips, who operated mill upper end Hooper's Island. Geo Wesley Phillips m Mary Jane Meekins, b Hooper's Island, d/o John Meekins, of Eng descent. She is still living in old Phillips home here, in 67th yr; mbr ME Church since 15; mother of: John H., this village, oyster man; Geo M., oyster packer Cambridge; Milford; Victoria, d at 7; Edw S., sheriff this co; Oliver G., d 1893, leaving wid, former Miss Thomas, of Balt; and Luther, sailor this place. (Sketches of John H. and Edw S. Phillips, elsewhere this vol). - Subj b Apr 5 1860, Hooper's Island, on old Phillips farm; at 12 worked with oyster fishers on the bays and creeks; partner with bro, John H., a year and 3 yrs conducted mercantile business on Hooper's Island; most of his life buying, shipping and selling oysters. He m in 1881 Miss Susie E. Ruark, d/o Hy W. Ruark, of Hooper's Island; of their 7 child., 4 decd: Hattie I., Ada, Raymond and Geo H.; living: Calvert, Mary R. and John H. Mr. and Mrs. Phillips attend Zion ME Church.

634 469. JOHN C. HUTCHINSON, East New Market dist, Dor Co, eldest in fam of 5 child.; his next younger sister, Elizabeth, decd; others: Sarah A. and Emeline; only bro, Manlius P., res Car Co. His paternal grandfather from Eng; his father, Ebenezer Hutchinson, b this co, d in prime; m Miss Nancy A. Stevens. Subj b Mar 13 1817; acquired the farm after father's death; mbr ME Church; m 1840 Miss Atha Wright; she d 1890. Subj m 1893 Mrs. Louisa C. Hackett, wid of John T. Hackett, d/o Wm P. and Mary A. (Moore) Cooper, both of old Del fam. By her marriage with Mr. Hackett she had 5 child., only son, Hugh, survives.

634 470. CAPT. WILLIAM E. JOHNSON, for 10 yrs owner of Choptank Steamboat Co; resumed farming; res East New Market dist, Dor Co. The captain's father, Denwood Johnson, b Dor Co, where he still farms. He m Lottie, d/o Arthur Williams; their child: Susan; Mary; Sarah J., w/o Rbt E. Foxwell; Wm E. and Arthur H., of Balt. Subj b Dor Co, Nov 19 1847, grew up on farm, educated in neighboring schools; went on the water, soon became capt of vessel on the bay; became owner of vessel. After 10 yrs embarked in mercantile business East New Market; 1876-79 managed his store; sold out; ran Choptank steamboat line 10 yrs, being part owner. 1876 he m Miss Annie, d/o John Baker; their child.: L. Margaret, Hilda, W. Clyde, Edw B., one d in infancy.

635 471. CHARLES T. RALPH, res 3rd dist Dor Co, acquired Captain Ball Farm (600 a.) 1870; opened general store dist of Vienna 1886; runs a sawmill; store now owned by son, Wm J. Ralph. Wm Ralph, grandfather of subj, supposedly of Scotland; an early settler of Sussex Co, Del. Chas Ralph, father of subj, b and reared there Sussex Co; 2 bros, Wm and Thos, served in war of 1812. Charles Ralph, in carpentering a few yrs, then farming. He m Phyllis Calway, of Del; of their 11 child. 2 survive: subj and Mary. Wm Ellis, bro-in-law, has reached 95, living in Sussex Co, Del.

Subj b on old homestead Sussex Co, Jan 5 1824, attended neighborhood school; opened wagon and carriage manufactory Barren Creek, then Som Co, now in Wicomico Co. Dec 18 1849 he m Miss Nancy Weatherly, of old fam of Wicomico Co, d/o Jas and Elizabeth (Lowe) Weatherly, latter of Som Co. Their child.:

eldest, Wm Jas, has charge of father's store Vienna; Geo T. and Chas S. assist on old homestead; Elizabeth H. w/o Geo Bounds, of Wicomico Co; Christiana m Levin B. Weatherly, of Spring Hill, Md; and Yancey W., with firm Geo B. Kimb & Co Phila, selling horse blankets and other items since 1890.

472. PERRY DE ROCHEBRUNE TAYLOR, b Fredrick, Del, as youth brought by parents 636 to Car Co, res 4th dist this co; d Dec 12 1896; mbr Friendship ME Church; b 1819, s/o John Taylor, whose wife's maiden name was De Rochebrune. He m Elizabeth, d/o Andrew Covey; owned over 600 a.; their child.: Rbt P.; Alexine, who m Jas B. Patton, left dau, Cora; Martha, decd w/o Frs Nichols, of this co; Annie, Mrs. Jas B. Wright, of Federalsburg; Emily, Mrs. Frs Nichols; Thos, Merrill and Walter, farmers of this co; Lizzie, Mrs. Orlando Patton, of Preston; Ida, Mrs. Wm Gambrill, of this co; Mary, Mrs. Peter N. Trout; and Amanda B., Mrs. Ed T. Moore, of this co. Rbt P. Taylor, eldest s/o Perry D. Taylor b Car Co 1848. He owns homestead 4th dist; mbr ME Church; m 1875 Mrs. Mary E. Charles, d/o Madison Williams; her child. by 1st marriage: Maddison and Emma Charles. Mr. and Mrs. Taylor have son, Perry D.

473. JOHN L. LEWIS, mcht, Fairlee, Kt Co. Jas Lewis, father of John L., of 639 Kt Co; placed in charge of large farm southern part of state. He m(1) Mary E. Ayers, of Kt Co; their child.: John L. and Jas B. He m(2) Ella Schoon; their child.: Clarence N., Nellie, Wm, Frs, Fannie, Clara, Albert and Eva. Fam res on farm 6th dist. Grandfather Jas Lewis was from this co; farmer. His father, Jas, a highly educated man, left England as young man, settled permanently in this vicinity. - Subj b on farm 3rd dist 1859. When 21 he rented a farm in another part of this co; undertook carpentering work in the area. 1890 he purch general store of Rbt R. Quail, of Fairlee; also postmaster in 1893; trustee ME Church. 1881 subj m Miss Ruth Quail, of this place; their child. at home: Jas R., Hattie, Agnes Q., Raymond and Walter. Grace R. and Howard L. d in infancy.

474. CLARENCE E. COLLINS, D. D. S, dentist Crisfield, Som Co, mbr of firm 639 Ward & Collins, drug business. Father of Dr. Collins is Jacob A. Collins, of Laurel, Del, principally involved in a lumber yard and fruit farm; mbr ME Church. His father was Levi Collins, of same locality and farmer. Jacob Collins m Julia Hitch, b and reared same neighborhood as himself. They had 3 sons and 2 daus. Julia d at 42; mbr ME Church. Subj b Jan 16 1871, Laruel, Del; after public schools grad Conference Acad, Dover, Del 1891, taught school Seaford, Del, 6 months; assist superintendent Crisfield Acad 6 month; clerked with his now partner in drug store; grad Natl Institute of Pharmacy of Chicago 1895, became mbr of firm of Ward & Collins Crisfield; grad Univ Md dental depart 1897; opened his dental office here; mbr ME Church.

475. JAMES H. CULLIN, Asbury dist, Som Co, owns general store here. Father 640 of subj Jacob J. Cullin, farmer this dist; m Miss Mary A. Nelson, b and reared this locality. They have 4 child.: subj is 3rd in order of birth. Subj has spent his whole life in Asbury dist; b May 1 1859; continued in public schools until 16 or 17, then in dredging for oysters along rivers and bays near by; bt and sold oysters in wholesale quantities until 1888; now conducts mercantile business here. 1882 he m Miss Arintha J. Sterling, of this locality; they have 2 little daus, Mamie A. and Maggie.

476. ROBERT F. DUER, atty, Princess Anne; sec, treasurer and director Journal 641 Publishing Co; director of People's Bank of Som Co Princess Anne. Subj b Aug

23 1871 Princess Annne, s/o Edw F. Duer, of Som Co, mcht Princess Anne; he moved from here to Balt and engaged in business; he is 64, retired; he was postmaster for 8 yrs in Princess Anne. He m Virginia W. White, of Princess Anne, mbr Episc Church. Their child.: Edw P., in hat manufacturing business Balt; Bruce W., Virginia R., Rbt F., Hy L. and Howard S. After public schools subj grad Wash College Chestertown 1891; dep clerk circuit court Som Co, read law under Hon. Rbt F. Brattan, Princess Anne; admitted to bar 1893, sec to Congressman Brattan until latter's death, 1894; then opened office in this village.

641 477. CHARLES H. ROSE, M. D., in practice at Cordova, Talb Co, since Sep 1856; of French Huguenot fam, for generations res of Isle of Guernsey. Here Dr. John Rose, father of subj, was b and reared, settled in Md 1817; then identified himself with ME Church, now a lay preacher, while continuing his practice; d 1874 at 73. Maternal great-grandfather of subj Dnl Curtis, of London, Eng, settled in Balt 1742. Under King George III he held office of colonial justice and high sheriff. He attained the age of nearly 100 yrs. One of his daus became w/o General Lasourd, French army, and one of his sons was late Wm Curtis, of My Lady's Manor, Balt Co. Another dau w/o Richard Bennett, of Elkton, Cecil Co, and their dau Harriet m Dr. John Rose.

Subj b New Windsor, Carroll Co, Md, Mar 27 1834; after public school at Westminister, Carroll Co, he attended Balt Schools. At 14 he secured a clerkship; 3 yrs later he began to read medicine in his father's office; attended Eclectic Medical Institute Cincinnati Oh, grad Eclectic Medical College Phila 1855; came to Talb Co, went into practice; elected to house of delegates 1867; judge orphans' court 1879-87; vestryman and warden of Episc Church. May 7 1868 he m Julia E., d/o Jas H.Ridgaway, now of Va, niece of late Rev H. B.Ridgaway, connected with Northwestern Univ at Evanston, author of many religious works. Child. of subj and wife: Adela, w/o Rbt C. Morgan, of Cordova; J. H.; D. C., of Balt; Harriet and Estelle.

642 478. C. HARRY PRICE, farmer 2nd dist. The first of fam to come to Kt Co was John Hyland Price, of Sassafras Neck, Cecil Co, Md, res on fam homestead, of Stoneton, 2nd dist. There son Benj spent his life, farming. His son, Wm Hy Price, subject's father, farmed. He m Miss Rachel B. Ringgold; their child.: Rosalie M., w/o C. H. Schuyler; subj; and Maria E., w/o Dr. B. S. Roseberry. The father d 1852. Subj b at Stoneton 1848. At 18 he took over the old place. 1890 he bt the Yapp farm adjoining, and now has 550 a.; 1886 purch house in Still Pond. 1880 he m Miss Mary C. Baker, sis of Jas H. Baker; their child.: Grace R., Nannie M. and Hy Baker. Both mbrs Presby Church.

643 479. CLARENCE P. LANKFORD, atty Crisfield, Som Co res here since 1892; counsel for N.Y., Phila & Norfolk Railroad and Crisfield Ice Co, director of the latter. Subj b Balt Feb 8 1864, s/o Hy S. and Mary D. Lankford, and bro of H. Fillmore Lankford (see his sketch for history of fam in this vol). About 4, subj moved with parents to Princess Anne. After public schools he entered Wash Acad Princess Anne; grad Wash College, Chestertown, 1882.; vice-principal public schools Crisfield; dep clerk under his bro, H. Fillmore, in court house 1884-1891, read law, admitted to bar of the co 1891. Dec 12 1894 he m Miss Emily Estelle Marshall in Princess Anne. They have little dau, Priscilla P. Subj attends Presby Church.

643 480. GREENBURY TRUITT BELL, business man Williamsbury, Dor Co, practical miller; 1888 erected mill he now operates, capacity 30-40 barrels of flour a

day. His grandfather, Bose Bell, of Bermuda Islands, settled in Del, there m and reared his fam. Subject's father, Wm Bell, b Sussex Co, Del, in partnership with bro, Jos, in several vessels during his early manhood; later in milling enterprise at Gales Town, Dor Co. He m Miss Mary Truitt; they had 6 child., of whom subj is youngest. - Subj b Gales Town 1861, educated in public schools; went into milling in Sussex Co, remained until 1882, moved to Clayton, Kent Co, Del, res there about 2 yrs. 1884-1888, he ran a mill at Federalsubrg, Md, and since then has lived here. He m 1882 in Clayton, Del, Miss Susan Waples; their child.: Susan Riley, Mary E., Wm Benj; 1 d in infancy, unnamed. Mr. and Mrs. Bell mbrs ME Church.

481. JOHN M. COLSTON, from old fam of Dor Co, res here since 1740, of Eng 644 lineage, tract (226 a.) which he owns was original grant on which his ancestor settled. Subj s/o Richard and grandson of Levin Colston, both of this vicinity; farmers. The grandfather d 1832, and Richard Colston d Apr 1859, at 51. His wife, Annie W., d/o John Mace, of their 8 child., 4 survive: Levin J., John M.; Mary C., w/o Herbert Holt; and Richard J., of Car Co. The mother d at 72, Mar 23 1893. Subj b on old farm nr present home, Jan 2 1850, educated in common schools of co and N. J., where he attended school for one year. When 20 he took charge of old homestead here and carried on until 1876, when he came to this dist and bt out the interest of Dr. Wm J. Bowdle in drug store at Church Creek. He also owns the old farm. 1891 he was elected school commissioner; county commissioners, pres of the bd 2 yrs. 1882 he m Miss Adela Graham, of Church Creek, d/o John E. and Mary Graham; their daus, Elizabeth L. and Mary Anna. Fam attend ME Church Church Creek.

482. HON. ROBERT F. BRATTAN, d May 10 1894 at home Princess Anne, Som Co, at 645 49, mbr U.S. house of representatives; 1873 elected to Md senate, re-elected 1879 and 1887; trustee Wash College, director Salisbury Natl Bank. Presby. Subj b Wicomico (now), May 13 1846, s/o Jos and Elizabeth Brattan. The father, mcht and farmer; mother d/o Rbt Venables. The grandfather, Joshua Brattan, sheriff Som Co, and mbr house of delegates. The father of latter was captain in Rev war, whose wife was aunt of Pres Polk. R. F. Brattan grad 2nd Wash College Chestertown 1866, admitted to bar Jul 1867; dep rgtr of wills Som Co c. 3 yrs; Jan 1868 into partnership with Hon. James U. Dennis. Dec 1884 he m Nellie H., d/o old law partner, ex-Senator J. U. Dennis, and niece of ex-U. S. senator Dr. G. R. Dennis. Their child.: Cecilia H., Nellie Dennis and Rbt F., Jr. Mr. Brattan has one surviving bro, J. Y., of Balt; sis, w/o Dr. L. D. Collier, of Salisbury, Md.; and 5 half- sisters.

483. GEORGE LOWE, retired farmer res Salisbury dist, Wicomico Co, b nr 645 present res, Mar 4 1807; of Eng descent; his grandfather, John Lowe, came from Eng and settled in Wicomico Co, 2 bros settled in Del and Dor Co. Sml, father of subj, b on old homestead Salisbury dist, farmer; d at home place 1845; sexton Spring Hill Episc Church, same position as his father; m Ruth, d/o Wm C. Mills; she d 1864. Of 8 children subj sole survivor. After public school subj worked for father until latter's death 1845. Jan 15 1845 he m Mary Ann Bounds, of Pontico, res on inherited farm, Humphreys Chance (400 a.); he is now 90. Mrs. Lowe d Nov 12 1895, mother of 4 children living: Lizzie, w/o John Trader, of Balt; Lydia, Mrs. Whitely Woelford, of Balt; John S., res nr father's home, and Whitely, res on old homestead.

484. WILLIAM N. WILLIAMS, Car Co, farmer, owns an homestead of 400 a.; for 9 646 yrs ran general store, dealt in lumber Henderson, Md; co surveyor. Subj b

this co, Jul 20 1823, orphan at 5, taken into home of maternal grandfather, Geo Newlee. Subj only child of Richard and Elizabeth (Newlee) Williams, of Car Co. Geo Newlee likewise b this co, justice of the peace; once owned over 4000 a. in Car Co; in war of 1812; mbr ME Church; m 16 May 1844, Miss Jane L. Clendenning, of this co; of their 12 child., 7 living: Angie L.; Mary S.; Elizabeth E.; Carrie, Alcade, ticket agent in Indianapolis, Ind; Geo N., similar position in St. Jo, Tex. and Jas M., in commission business in Phila.

649 485. JAMES R. PHILLIPS, A. M., M. D., physician, Preston, Car Co; moved here fol practice at East New Market; b Dor Co 1844, s/o Jas R. and Elizabeth (Smith) Phillips; father was farmer, d mid age. In his family were 5 children, of whom Susan and Sarah d in childhood. Elizabeth m Hon. A. S. Percy, and Mary V., w/o Wm James Payne, of Dor Co. Maternal grandfather of subj was Levin Smith. Paternal grandfather, Richard Phillips, b Dor Co 1770, res Dor Co. He m(1) Miss Jones; m(2) Miss Percy, by whom a dau, Elizabeth, who m Wm Percy, and to them b dau, Sarah E., w/o Dr. Phillips. Richard Phillips s/o Edw Phillips, and prob of Eng, settled in Dor Co 1750, where he m and reared fam of child.: Sml, John, Edw, Richard, Sarah and Annie. Dr. Phillips grad Princeton College 1867; grad medical depart Univ Md 1869; same year m Miss Sarah E. Percy, and estab home in East New Market; moved to Preston; res Laurel, PG Co, Md, 1878-1884; returned to Preston. Their child.: Mary P. w/o Elbert Douglas; Elizabeth, Nellie, Jas Richard, W. Percy d at 14, and Agatha H., d in childhood. Family identified with Episc Church.

649 486. WILLIAM TRYSTRAM STEVENS, young farmer 4th dist QA Co; co commisioner 1894-5; co treasurer. Wm T. Stevens, Sr., subject's father, b Va; early history is uncertain; his parents d Va while he was a child. He went to Balt, then to Kt Island where he lived in fam of his uncle, Trystram Weedon; took his uncle's middle name; m Annie, d/o Jacob Legg, had 2 child. He d 1868, when sugbj few months old, and his dau, Georgia, d same year. The young wid later m Wm T. C. Norman; of their 3 child. only eldest survives.
Subj b locality where he dwells today, 1868; after common school education he attended Eaton-Burnett Commercial College Balt; then bookkeeper for A. J. W. Stevens, commission mcht about 4 yrs; returned to island, started in business for himself, sold out and has since farmed, owns nearly 450 acres. Jan 1892 he m Miss Catherine, d/o Peter Cockey, from Md old fam; their child.: Wm Elliot and Katherine Valerie; mbrs Meth Church Stevensville.

650 487. HON. ISAAC THOMAS COSTEN, M. D., first mayor Pocomoke City, Wor Co; 1881 elected to Md house of delegtges; s/o Wm and Rosa Costen, b on father's farm Som Co, nr Pocomoke City, Oct 10 1832. After common schools he entered Wash Acad Princess Anne, began teaching school before 21; grad Penn Medical College Phila 1857; opened office in Rehoboth, Som Co, in practice until 1863, moved to Va, nr Modest Town about 2 yrs; moved to this town 1863; trustee of high school; elder and trustee of Presby Church; owns farm (200 a.); mbr state bd Md Deaf and Dumb Asylum. 1866 Dr. Costen m Miss Olivia Adams of Som Co; their child.: Rose, Ellen, Mary, Wm A., Addie L., Olivia and Lizzie. Eldest dau, Rose, w/o Wm J. Young, of Easton, Pa., superindendent Lehigh & Newinton Railroad Co. Wm A., only son, druggist Norristown, Pa. The others at home.

488. WILLIAM F. BYRD, postmaster Crisfield, Som Co; co commissioner; b Asbury 651 (now) dist, Dec 9 1865. His father, Wm T., b same dist, oyster man and mariner; d in 57th yr; oyster inspector; mbr ME Church. His father, David Byrd, of this co; farmer; b 1804, d c. 1878; mbr ME Church. Fam descends from 1 of 2 bros who settled early in this part of Eastern Shore, from Eng. Wm T. Byrd m Mary S. Lawson, d/o Isaac Lawson, of this co. She is still living, mbr ME Church. Subj grad high school, at 16 taught in same school (1 term); 2nd assist primary depart; mcht until Feb 1895, then sold out. 1887 he m Miss Sallie, d/o Alger S. Sterling, of this co; moved to suburbs Crisfield; their child.: H. Clifton, Warren F. and Athol Lynde; mbrs ME Church.

489. GEN. BENJAMIN CHAMBERS, Kt Co, b Pa Oct 16 1749, s/o Jas and Sarah (Lee) 651 Chambers. Jun 11 1783 he m Elizabeth, d/o Ezekiel and Augusta Forman, and granddau of Thos Marsh; moved to Chestertown, Md. During war of 1812 he was brig gen; clerk of court Kt Co; d Jan 10 1816, leaving fol child.: Augusta, who m Jas Houston, judge U. S. dist Court; Thos Marsh, Ezekiel Forman, Jas David, Benj Lee, Elizabeth Caroline, who m Col Jos Wickes, and Wm Hy; 2child., Benj and Margaretta, d in lifetime of their father.

490. HON. EZEKIEL FORMAN CHAMBERS b Chestertown, Kt Co, Feb 28 1788, s/o Gen 652 Benj and Elizabeth Chambers and grandson of Ezekiel and Augustine (Marsh) Forman. His great-grandfther, Thomas Marsh, lineal descendant of Augustine Herman. He attended Wash College; studied law under Jas Houston (later U.S. dist judge); admitted to bar 1809; capt of company in battle of Caulks field, summer of 1814; officially commended by Col Reed, commanding officer. Subj m Feb 11 1817, Sarah J., d/o Maj Jas Bowers, of Kt Co; 1826 elected to U.S. senate to fill term of Edw Lloyd, resigned; re-elected 1831; 1834-1851 judge court of appeals of Md. (Further discussion given to his character and strength of judicial and legal arguments); mbr Episc Church; pres bd of visitors and governors Wash College; retired from bench 1851, resumed legal practice. He d Feb 28 1867, leaving fol child.: Jas B; Laura, who m Geo L. Davis; and Caroline, w/o Geo W. T. Perkins; 4 child. d while he was living: Elizabeth Augusta, who m Rev Dr. Jones; Sarah Maria Louise, w/o Rev Mr. Owen; Helen and Mary Clare. He was buried cemetery nr Chestertown.

491. HAMPDEN POLK DASHIELL,Princess Anne, business man, of well-known fam of 654 Eastern Shore. When about 21 he embarked in mercantile business with father, when latter retired after 6 yrs subj became manager of Manokin Steamboat Co; ran steamboat that connected with Balt steamers at Deal's Island in Tangier sound. The consolidation of other companies into Balt, Chesapeake & Atlantic Railway company forced him out of business; he then entered fire insurance, rep 8 companies. Grandfather of subj, Seth Dashiell, M. D., b on Eastern Shore, remained in medical practice; d at old age. His father was Arthur Dashiell, of Md.
Subject's father, Hampden Haynie Dashiell, b Accomac Co, Va, brought to Som Co as infant; educated in co schools and Wash Acad Princess Anne; read medicine under father;turned to business, helped organize Wilson-Small Steamboat Co. (of which he was an owner and director), later merged into Md Steamboat Co. In Princess Anne, he formed partnership with Col Wm J. G. Polk in mercantile enterprise. Civil war brought him heavy financial losses; pioneered in small fruit; 1878 sold out his mercantile establishment and 1879 elected rgtr of wills Som Co. 1894 app collector of revenue for 1st dist of Md port of Crisfield. He d Jun 15 1895, from apoplexy; mbr Episc Church.   H.

-133-

H. Dashiell was director of old Eastern Shore Railroad; director and pres Atlantic Hotel Co; helped found summer resort of Ocean City, Md; pres Mutual Fire Insur Co of Som and Wor Cos; trustee Old Washington Acad; connected with old Md Fruit Packing Co, Princess Anne. He m(1) Eleanor Kennerly, d/o Hy and Mary Kennerly, of Wicomico (now) Co. She d young, leaving son, Cassius Marion, atty at home and in fruit packing business. H. H. Dashiell m(2) Aurelia, d/o Caleb and Julia Ann Kennerly, who d 1857, leaving subj b Princess Anne, Sep 18 1856. Mr. Dashiell m(3) Elizabeth, d/o Col Wm T. G. Polk; their sons: Edwin, d in boyhood; John Woodford, railroad man in W.V.; Louis, in railroading, res in Md; and Wm Hy, farmer Som Co.

Subj educated in public schools and Wash Acad; mbr Episc Church; clerk to bd of co commissioners; first co treasurer; director People's Bank Som Co. He m Bertha Bayly Smith, d/o Dr. Chas Smith, of Northampton Co, Va.

655 492. COL. EDWARD LLOYD of Wye House. The first representative of the Lloyd fam in America was Edw Lloyd, who came to colony of Md in 1640, later surveyor general and gov under Lord Baltimore; emigrated from Wales, where another branch of fam now possesses estates on river Wye. The Colonel's great-grandfather mbr continental congress. The grandfather, pres senate of Md, mbr U. S. senate, gov of Md 1809-1811. Father was pres senate 1851-52. All named Edw, a name given to eldest son each generaton fol original settler. 8 Edw Lloyds buried fam cemetery at Wye House, 3 still living. Father of subj b Easton dist, at old homestead; took medical course in Phila, never practiced; senator from Md; 1851 mbr constitutional convention; d Aug 1861. He m Alicia, d/o Michael McBlair, mcht Balt. She d 1838, mother of 5 child., 3 living: Edw; Alice, wid of Gen Chas S. Winder, of Easton dist, killed Cedar Mountain during Civil war (grad West Point, under "Stonewall" Jackson) and Sally S., wid of David C. Trimble, s/o Gen I. R. Trimble.

Subj b Oct 22 1825 Balt; after local schools, studied at College Point, L. I., grad Princeton College 1847; before 21 elected to house of delegates, youngest mbr; captain on staff of Gen Tench Tilghman, state militia, later major on staff of Maj Gen Handy; 1849 again elected to house of delegates; retired from public life; largest slave owner in Md, owned many slaves and large tracts in Miss. War was financially disastrous, lost over $1,000,000 in prop; 1876 elected to state senate, pres of senate. He m Jun 5 1851, Mary H., d/o Chas Howard, of Balt, and granddau of John Eager Howard and Frs S. Key. Their child.: Edw, lieut in U.S. navy; C. Howard, at home; McBlair, res estate adjoining old homestead; John Eager, and DeCoursey, both res Chicago; Allice, Elizabeth and Mary, at home. Family attend Episc Church.

659 493. ROBERT DINES BRADLEY, inventor and construction engineer Car Co, mbr of old fam of Eastern Shore; through mother descends from French ancestor; b Federalsburg, this co, 1842, s/o John and Chloe A. (Dines) Bradley, His father, b Dor Co, carpenter, expert cabinet maker; his child.: Sarah, w/o J. F. Hurley, of Linchester; John W., P. M., res Linchester; Hon. Wm S., res Hurlock, Dor Co; subj; Rowena V., who m S. B. Le Count, of Vienna; and Walter M. Subj interested in hydraulics, electricity and gas. By a "cold process" he has developed from an oil a lighting system, extraordinarily safe and economic (more detail given); commissioned 1st lieut in state militia during late war, later served as captain. 1882 app to foreign steam inspection service, Balt. He m in Car Co Mary C. Noble; they have one son and 4 daus.

660 494. ALONZO R. HORSEY, mcht, director Bank of Crisfield, Som Co. (See sketch of bro, Wm P. Horsey, elsewhere this vol for fam history). Subj b Crisfield

-134-

dist, Jun 20 1855; clerked in general store Crisfield, about 2 yrs. 1876 he and bro, Wm P., opened dry goods store, operating two stores until 1895, when they combined them. 1882 Mr. Horsey m Addie C., d/o Capt Jas C. Nelson, oyster packer, res Crisfield dist; their child.: Nelsie E., Mildred L. and Alonzo R., Jr.; mbrs MP Church.

495. JAMES E. BACON, res Mardela Springs, Wicomico Co, b here, May 6 1853, 660 s/o Wm and Maria J. (Dashiell) Bacon, of Sussex Co, Del. His paternal grandfather, Henry Bacon, 1 of 3 bros who came from England, 1 settled in N. J., another went west and Hy res Sussex Co, Del. Wm Bacon, farmer, sometimes operated sawmill and in mercantile business; co commissioner. About 1842 he came to Wicomoco Co, d 1891. His wife, mbr wealthy French fam res Del, d in Wicomico Co 1886; of their 9 child., living: subj; Mary; Thos Humphreys, of Mardela Spring; and Rebecca, w/o Rbt G. Robertson, of this town.

At 21 subj began farming on prop given him by his father; a while in milling business; owns several farms (500 a.); mber MP Church. Oct 1875 he m Lizzie, d/o C. M. Wright, mbr of old fam of Barren Creek dist; of their 6 child., five living: Chas, tills home farm; Lillie, Maud, Lorenzo and Edna.

496. COL. JAMES C. NORRIS, manager Avon Hotel, erected at Easton, Mar 1891, 661 contains 56 bedrooms. The Norris fam has been in Talb Co many generations. Thos F., colonel's father, s/o Lambert Norris, b at old homestead. He assisted in maintenance MP Church Easton, of which wife was mbr. He m Mary, d/o Jas Chambers. She survived him 25 yrs; d Aug 2 1897, at 90. Of their 13 children, 5 living: Thos, res Oxford, Md.; Jas C.; Edmund W., of Hamilton, Talb Co; Kate, wid of J. B. Elliott, and res Talb Co; and Sml, mcht Easton.

Subj b Talb Co Dec 15 1835. After school he entered mercantile business Easton 10 yrs; then proprietor of old Brick Hotel Easton, until Avon Hotel built 1891; has regular boarders, including Judge Stump, who has boarded with him 30 yrs. Subj earned title of Col, serving on staff of Gov Jackson. He is identified with ME Church South. He m(1) Miss M. E. Kirby who d 1872, leaving child.:, Wm and Kate. He m(2) Helen M. Dobson, still living.

497. LOUIS N. WILSON, M. D., physician and surgeon, Mardela Springs, Wicomico 662 Co. His father, Levin M. Wilson, b nr this town, as was his father, Thos. Levin M. Wilson, farmer, elected to Md house of delegates 1856. He m Miss Elizabeth Bailey, d/o Johnston Bailey, of Del. She d 1861; her child.: Aurelia V., unmarried; John T., res this place; J. Frank, decd; Louis N.; Letitia J., w/o P. S. Pusey, of Quantico dist; Levin A., mcht this town; and Elizabeth A., w/o S. J. Brown, of Mardela Springs.

Subj b nr this village on paternal homestead, May 1 1852. After local school and at Salisbury, entered College of Physicians and Surgeons, Balt; then a year in Bellevue Medical College and Hospital New York City.

498. HON. L. H. COOPER, judge orphans' court; co commissioner; farmer; Barren 662 Creek dist, Wicomico; owned Miles' End (163 a.), since 1858. Father of subj, Levin, and grandfther, Sml Cooper, b on same farm, nr Riverton, Barren Crek dist; both famers. Levin twice m; subject's mother, Mary Walker, d 1845. Of her 5 child., 2 living: subj and Severn H., res old homestead. Subj b Oct 31 1835; left school and began work on home farm, remaining until he purch his present place 1858. Feb 8 1860 he m Martha T., d/o Wm H. Bradley. Of their 8 child. fol survive: Irving, mcht Mardela Springs; Wm M., of Salisbury; Samantha, w/o Wm T. Wilson; Philena and Chas S., at home; and Mark R., in Mardela Springs.

-135-

663 499. LEMUEL DUMBRACCO, chief dep clerk circuit court QA Co, b Dec 2 1846, AA Co; educated at Agricultural College Md Wash College this state. His father, Lemuel Dumbracco, descendant early Scotch settler of this country. His mother was Elizabeth Banning Hicks, descendant of Hicks fam Dor Co, and Bannings of Talb Co. Her parents of English extraction. Mr. Dumbracco's father served in both branches of Md legislature. - Subj came into office as dep clerk circuit court Apr 3 1871, under Jas Wooters, app clerk on death of Wm Dever, 1892; 1871-1882 chancery commissioner QA Co. Prev to move to Centreville he was in drug business Balt, then Church Hill, Md; mbr Episc Church Centreville. He m Jun 20 1872, Ella Faithful, d/o late W. E. B. Faithful, landholder and mcht of QA Co. She d May 15 1873. Mr. Dumbracco res on farm, known as Fishingham, estate of late Ward Tilghman, nr Centreville.

663 500. HON. JOSHUA WELDON MILES, atty Som Co; admitted to bar Jul 1880, began practice at Princess Anne; 1883-1887 state's atty; became partner of Judge Page (his sketch elsewhere this vol) Jan 1888; firm Page & Miles continued until withdrawal of judge 1892. Mr. Miles elected to congress 1894; became senior mbr of law firm of Miles & Stanford. Subj b on father's farm southern part Som Co Dec 9 1858, attended public schools, had private tutors; grad Western Md College 1878; studied law in legal depart Univ Md and under Judge Roberts, of Westminsister, and Dennis & Brattan, attys of Princess Anne. He is director in Som Co Savings Bank, its atty, solicitor of N.Y., Phila & Norfolk Railway Co. Feb 1884 subj m Miss Lillian M, only d/o Wm P. and Margaret A. Rider, of Princess Anne. Subj reared in MP Church, became identified with Manokin Presby Church in Princess Anne. Father of subj, Southey F. Miles, of Som Co; farmer; now retired, at 76; sheriff this co one term; collector of customs. His wife, mother of subj, former Christiana Roach, d 1885, in 62nd yr. Paternal grandfather subj, Wm Miles, of this co, d at 84; owned several large tracts and large vessels, sailing to West Indies. Father of Wm Miles, was Hy Miles, res this section; his father emigrated to Md from Eng.

664 501. ALFRED J. MOBRAY, justice of peace and real estate broker, res Vienna, Dor Co, b nr Cambridge, May 20 1836 at 9:30 A.M. Through his mother he traces his lineage in collateral line to Sir Walter Raleigh; on his father's side he is descends of John Lord Mobray, crusader of England. His grand- father, Levin, s/o Thos Mobray, b Eng; surveyor; b Dor Co, about 8 miles from Cambridge; owned large tracts of land and many slaves.

Father of subj, Levin Mobray, Jr., b on fam estate; not mbr of any church; d 1856 at old homestead. He m Leah L. d/o Hooper Raleigh, of Dor Co; she d 1844; of their 6 children, 3 living: Levin W., of Cambridge; Alfred J.; and Geo W., of Wash, D. C. Mr. Mobray m(2) Mrs. Leah J. Howard; they had one child, Mary L., decd.

Subj attended acad Cambridge. 1851 he became assist in circuit clerk's office Dor Co; read law; after 6 yrs and failing health he taught school. On death of father, he administered the estate, and farmed (1858-1865). During late war he recruited company of 100 men at Cambridge at his own expense; sheriff of co 1866-7; collector of state and co taxes for 7th and 13th districts; then resumed farm work; 1879-1885 in the office of the clerk, then farming until 1888; in navy depart 1889-1893; since then res Vienna; app justice of the peace 1896; sec and treasurer Vienna branch Mutual Protective Bldg and Loan assoc Balt City; once local preacher ME Church. Nov 14 1861 he m Laura E., d/o Dr. Robert W. Williams, physician and local preacher res Dor Co. She d Feb 14 1873; her child.: 3 decd.; surviving: Rbt W., lawyer Balt;

Laura E., w/o Thos B. Hackett, of Vienna; and Ada G., who m Jas Hampson, Jr., atty Balt.

502. JAMES McFADDIN DICK, M. D., house physician Peninsular General Hospital, 666
res Salisbury, Wicomico Co; student Columbia, (S.C.) high school; grad Univ S.C.; grad Univ Md Balt, Doctor of Medicine; served in Univ Md hospital, practiced in Free Lying-in Hospital of Balt; physician in charge of Hospital Women of Md; came to Salisbury. He is from Sumter Co, S. C., b Sep 24 1871 s/o Capt Thos H. Dick and Margaret, d/o Capt J. D. McFaddin. The father, planter, commanded company of Confed cav. His youngest son, T. M. Dick, engineer U. S. navy, grad at head of engineers naval acad 1895.

503. FRANCIS E. LOOMIS, farmer Dor Co, res East New Market dist; mbr bd of 666
control & review of assessments 1896, co commissioner; trustee of almshouse. He was b Apr 15 1850, Berkshire Co, Pittsfield, Mass., educated in Pittsfield schools. He m Miss Ellen Nichols, of Pittsfield 1870. Soon afterwards they came to this locality; purch farm (150 a.); their child.: Grace M., w/o Hon. Chas W. Hackett, and Herbert F., all mbrs Bapt Church; Herbert educated in Phila theological seminary, minister Bapt Church. Mr. Loomis is of English ancestry, s/o Marshall M. and Lucy (Frances) Loomis, of Mass.

504. JOHN F. RUTH, farmer and stock raiser, 4th dist QA Co. Parents of subj, 669
John L. and Sarah (Guessford) Ruth, of Del, m Del; moved to Md, farmed and in mercantile ventures; he now res with subj. Subj b 1st dist this co, Jan 14 1859; owns a dozen stardard bred horses and colts on his farm; about 4 yrs managed the 2 farms of Mr. Dudley, nr Queenstown; 1885 came to Kt Island, 1895 bt homestead on which he res (240 a.). 1891 he m Miss Grace M. Bryan, at home of her parents, John A. W. and Mary Bryan, Stevensville, this dist.

505. JOSEPH B. HOSSINGER, farmer 2nd dist, Kt Co. His ancestors were in Del 669
1750, originally from Germany. Jos H., father of subj, of Del, came to Md 1865, located on part of old Biddle farm until he d, 1887, at 55. He m Miss Biddel from old fam of Kt Co; she now lives at Lynch Station. Subj, 3rd name of Jos in direct line, b on homestead he now manages, Nov 15 1866; attended Wash College; assumed control of the old farm; now manages another one (total of 300 a.). 1887 he m Lillian Hepbron, d/o Lewis Hepbron, decd, of this community. Mrs. Hossinger mbr Episc Church.

506. JAMES EDWIN MORTIMER, young business man res on farm Broad Crek Neck, 670
St. Michael's dist, Talb Co; mbr state fishery force; oyster inspector St. Michael's. John Mortimer, father of subj, of Balt; in lumber trade; purch tract on Broad Creek Neck; retired there 1865; d 1890, nearly 70; Presby. His father, John, of Balt, worked in custom house; served in war of 1812. Mother of subj, former Elizabeth Chamberlain, from Balt, now 82, res with eldest son, Alexander, who manages home farm. Kate A. is 2nd of fam. Carrie is w/o Thos W. Mavitt, of this co. Lillian is w/o Jos A. Camper, of this dist. Subj b Aug 8 1857 Balt, educated in public schools; farmed until 1883, Dec 1896, came to present home, which he had purch earlier; mbr ME Church 9 yrs. He m 1885 Sarah C. Camper, of this dist, who d 1890, leaving 2 sons, John Alexander and Walter Stewart. He later m Miss Grace Burns, of St. Michael's.

507. JAMES E. LOWE, young business man, Salisbury, Wicomico Co, operates 671
livery, s/o Jackson and Maria (Palmer) Lowe, of Del. The father built first house in Lowe's Cross Roads, Sussex Co, Del, named for him. He and fam moved

to Salisbury c. 1866; he d here 1880. Subj b Lowe's Cross Roads, Feb 25 1860, attended local schools, became a blacksmith. Failing health caused him to seek a lighter occupation; entered livery business. 1881 he m Emma Collins,, residend of nr Cambridge; she d 1889; he m Feb 11 1891 Emma Anderson; their son, James E., Jr.

671 508. WALTER C. MANN res Sharptown dist, Wicomico Co, b Jan 9 1853 Federalsburg, Car Co, s/o Jos H. Mann, M. D., of Dover, Del, physician, came to Md, d 1880; also minister ME Church; m 4 times, subject's mother was Mary J., d/o Jos B. Cannon, of Laurel, Del; she d 1855, leaving 2 children, subj and Margaret, w/o S. C. Matthews, of Laurel. Subj came to Md 1871 with father to Sharptown dist; he has home nr village; in fruit and live stock business. 1885-1891 he was constable, 1883-1885 co commissioner, mbr of legislature of 1887-88, later dep fish commissioner. Mar 26 1888 he m Maggie P. Bounds, d/o Jas R. Bounds, of Quantico dist; their child.: Walter G. and Mary E.

672 509. WILLIAM T. KELLEY, owns farm, Oakland Grove, just south of Preston, Car Co. The Kelleys mbrs Soc of Friends; over 200 yrs have sent delegates to each yearly meeting. Subj descends from Sir Wm Kelley, mbr of court of St. Jas, of Whithall, Eng, 1634. About 1650 his son, Wm, of town of Kelley, Devonshire, Eng, came to Md, settled in Kt Co, 1722 one of descendants, another Wm Kelley, was living with his fam in Dor, now Car Co, nr Preston. The Kelleys worshiped 150 yrs at old Quaker meeting house still standing 4th dist. Fam coat-of-arms: "Three fluer de lis with lion rampant and crest of a sea lion holding a spike ball in its paws."
Subj b Car Co, Apr 19 1828, s/o Jonah and Hester A. (Trice) Kelley. Mother d/o Wm and Ann (Willis) Trice, and niece of Col Peter Willis, of this co, col in war of 1812. Jonah Kelley was minister in Soc of Friends. His father, Dennis, farmer, b nr Preston; m Miss Elender Perry, of Talb Co; their sons: Perry, Dennis, Jonah and Ezekiel, daus:.Elender, Mrs. Sml Fluharty; Mary, Mrs. Peter Willis; and Rebecca, never married. Great-grandfather of subj, Dennis Kelley the first, b this co, left large tracts to his children. His mother d/o noted Quaker preacher, Wm Edmondson, of England.
Subj grew to adulthood nr Linchester, Dor Co; eldest sister, Mary A., m Hon. John R. Stack , of this co; Hester A., 2nd sister, m Jas S. Bartlett, of Talb Co; Elizabeth, wid of Dr. E. E. Atkinson, of Ridgely; Jonah F. res Balt. Subj owns homestead (70 a.), and large tracts in Duval Co, Fla. He res Easton 1863-1868. He m Apr 14 1853 Julia Smith Williams at home of her parents, John and Elizabeth (Springle) Williams, of Woodford Co, Ky. The father, related to Andrew Jackson, and descendant of Sir Wm Williams, Welsh baron, extensive land owner and slave owner of Blue grass region. The grandparents of Mrs. Kelley: Dnl and Mary (Jackson) Williams and John and Elizabeth (Smith) Springle, were Va Baptists who moved from Va soon after Rev war to Ky, settling in Woodford Co and Lexingtron, respectively. Child. of subj and wife: Georgeanna, d young; Dollie Elizabeth; Julielma M.; Wm T., Jr., D. D. S., mbr Md State Bd of Dental Examiners; Lincoln Dnl, D. D.. S.; and Jonah Springle, grows fruit on homestead - all mbrs Soc of Friends. Miss Julielma has taught school in Ky and Miss Dollie has also taught. 1862 subj, in company with Hy Cockran, Frank Hubbard and John Hy Williams, met in George Mitchell Russum's office, Denton, and organized the Repub party for Car Co. Subj also writes articles for home and farm journals.

673 510. COL. JAMES E. DOUGLASS, decd, formerly res nr Preston, Car Co; b Dor Co 1820, s/o Jas and Charlotte (Wilson) Douglass, both of Car Co. He learned

carpenter's trade; co collector; app dep sheriff of his native co, 1851 made sheriff. 1854 moved to Car Co; farmer; erected sawmill, engaged in lumbering. His own homestead is just outside Preston. He served as colonel on Governor Hicks' staff. He d in 1880.

Subj m Mary C., d/o Jas Davis; 4 of 7 child. survive: Jas H., druggist and late mbr state legislature; Jos, res Frederick, Md, general agent for Derring Harvester Co; Thos H., in a manufacturing industry at Milton, Del; and Dr. Eugene, physician Balt. The mother d 1866. Later Mr. Douglass m Ann Emily, d/o Jos Mowbray, of this co; she survives him, res old homestead nr. Preston. She had prev m Steven Clement Clark, and had sons: Joshua B., editor Sussex Journal, Georgetown, Del, who d 1892; and Jos C., M. D., 1st assist physician Spring Grove (Md) Insane Asylum. Only child of Col Jas E. Douglass and wife, Ann Emily, is Stephen Elbert, b 1871. He tills over 1000 a. and carries on his parent's old homestead; educated at Oxford Military Acad, at Oxford, Md. When 19 he m Mary, d/o Dr. Jas R. Phillips, of Preston; their children, in order of birth: Percy C., Ruth and Phillips E.

511. H. LAIRD TODD, M. D., whose grandfather, Jonathan Todd, came from Eng, 674 settled in lower part Dor Co; came to this country with a bro, who settled in Del. Father of subj, Geo Todd, in boating busines in early life, but afterward (in 1812), when 18, he settled in Salisbury and embarked in general mercantile business; then retired. He d 1866, at 72. Twice married, his first union was childless; he m(2) Catherine N. Stevenson, of Snow Hill, of their 14 child. subj eldest now living. His mother b in 1800, d 1870.

Subj b Jan 29 1830; educated at Salisbury Acad; studied medicine under Dr. Nathan R. Smyth. After grad from Md Univ Balt 1851, Dr. Todd opened office at Vienna, Dor Co, soon moved practice to Salisbury, in partnership with brother, Geo W. Todd, M. D., until death of latter 1875. His son, Geo W., grad in medicine 1885 and they became partners. 1894 subj retired; m 1852 Julia A., d/o Edw Fowler, of Wicomico Co. Of their 8 child., 5 attained maturity: Harry S., mbr mercantile firm F. C. Todd & Co., of Salisbury, m Agnes Phelps, of Dor Co, they have 4 children; Lillian F., w/o S. S. Smith, of hardware firm Dorman & Smith, of Salisbury, they have 2 child.; Geo W., M. D., m Rose Wodcock, and has 2 child.; Edwin N., mcht res nr Plantersville, Ala., m Annie Vincent, of that state; Marion May, w/o Dr. Clarence L. Selover, dentist, of Cambridge.

Subj mbr bd of co commissioners 1869-1871; auditor circuit court until 1891. 1895 elected co treasurer; elder Presby Church Salisbury; his father and bro Geo W. were also elders; and another bro, W. I., holds same position.

512. RIGSBY T. WRIGHT, Cambridge; 1873 bt historic farm known as Horn's 675 Point, on Choptank River nr here; moved to Cambridge 1892; res Locust st.

Subj b Wicomico (now) Co, s/o Jos W. Wright and wife, former Sarah P. Harris, both of this co; they res Secretary; mother of subj d and buried on her 58th marriage anniversary; father still living. Of their 12 children 9 grew to maturity. Subj is eldest, b Oct 20 1839; he taught school a few yrs prior to arriving at his majority. - Subj was partner of John H. Bacon, in store on Nanticoke River 1862-8. 1871 he purch sawmill; co commissioner of Dor Co in 1881-1882. He m May 1870, Miss Edith Giles, d/o Isaac and Sarah E. (Hosea) Giles, of Laurel, Del, both decd; both connected with old families of Del; both mbrs Presby Church. Mr. Giles was a business man. Child. of subj and wife: 1 d; Hubert H., at home; Sarah G., w/o L. S. Dail, of Cambridge.

-139-

513. ALEXIS A. PASCAULT, Easton, Cath, mbr French fam. Among the officers who came with Lafayette during Rev war, was Col Louis C. Pascault. In his fam were 3 daus known as "Three Graces." One was w/o Jas Gallatin, wealthy citizen of N.Y.; the second m Columbus O'Donnell, pres Balt & Ohio Railroad; they had 3 daus: w/o Adrian Islin, of N.Y., banker on Wall st; w/o Solomon Hillen, ex-mayor of Balt; w/o Mr. Lee of Balt. Third of the "Three Graces' m General Rubell, of Paris, who came to America on staff of the bro of Napoleon Bonaparte. When Jerome Bonaparte, m Balt girl, Miss Patterson, Gen Rubell and Miss Pascault also m, latter becoming maid of honor to Madame Bonaparte.

Louis C. Pascault, s/o Col Pascault and father of subj, was b Balt 1790; and 1828 moved to QA Co, where he farmed. He d Kt Island 1885; Cath. His wife, Anne E., d/o Chas Goldsborough of Talb Co; she d 1855, 30 yrs before her husband. Of their 10 child. subj survives. He was b Sykesville, Md, nr Balt, Mar 11 1822. 1848 he moved from QA to Talb Co, where he farmed, now agent and collector; past pres town council, past pres Dover Bridge Co. Nov 9 1848, he m his cousin, Maria E. Goldsborough, d/o Hy Goldsborough, of Talb Co; of their 5 children 2 surivve: Alexander G. and Hy G., both of Easton.

514. CAPT. WILLIAM E. SEWARD, farmer Cambridge dist, Dor Co, former seafaring man, b 8th dist Mar 13 1831 s/o Levin Seward, native same locality. Levin Seward m Mary Wheatley; their child.: John H., decd; Sarah R., w/o Thos Keys, farmer 8th dist; Richard, res East Cambridge; subj; Chas H., farmer 8th dist; Jane, w/o Edw Bromwell, 8th dist; Thos, of Cambridge; Frances, w/o Alexander Greenwell; Geo, owner of schoone, res Balt; and Columbus, decd.

Subj reared on father's farm; at 20, he shipped on sailing·vessel as common sailor; soon became part owner and captain of ship; sailed the seas in command of this ship 21 yrs on Chesapeake Bay, between Balt, Norfolk and Wash; ship often loaded with pine lumber. A bachelor over 40 yrs, he m Mar 13 1873, Miss Laura Stevens, of Castle Haven, 8th dist. They began housekeeping on farm (240 a.) he had purch about a year earlier.

515. CAPT. THOMAS J. THOMPSON res on homestead QA Co; b in Dor Co 1841, educated in public schools; 1850 came with parents to Kt Island; after death of his father, in 1869, he m Mary A. Baxter, and built house he has since occupied. Their child.: Chas V.; Annie, w/o Wm Thos; Carrie; Thos E., Kirby, Howard A., and Celia M. Subj began life on the bay, as a youth, sailing from Balt and working at dredging along Eastern Shore, today engaged in tonging and oystering; owns a farm of 18 acres with fine peach orchard.

516. HON. THOMAS B. TAYLOR, Wicomico Co, in partnership with Jas E. Bacon, owns Mardela Springs and hotel. As early as 1795 a hotel was built on the grounds by Major Russum, since then visited by health seekers. The water aids digestion, valuable in treatment of chronic diseases.

Subj b nr Mardela Springs Sep 5 1823. His grandfather, Levin Taylor b Barren Creek dist, then Som Co; served in Rev with 4 bros and father, Jas, who was s/o Wm, from Eng and settled in Som Co. Thos, father of subj, b on old homestead Barren Creek dist, in war of 1812; sailor, d of yellow fever in Key West 1832. He m Eliza Smith, of Del, who d at birth of subj; she left 3 child., Ellen, who m Henry Vickers, of Balt; Uriah and Thos B.

At 19, having completed his education, subj began teaching school; after 3 yrs clerked in a store; carried on store at Mardela Springs 1850-90; then sold out and retired; surveyor; owns 5 farms (c. 1200 a.); co commissioner; mbr state legislature; mbr MP Church.

-140-

517. ARTHUR B. COCHRANE, senior mbr of firm A. B. Cochrane & Co., Crisfield, Som Co, which owns large lumber yards. They carry sash, doors, moulding; own sawmill on Pocomoke River, this co, import lumber from southern states. 681
Father of subj Jas L. Cochrane, d few yrs ago in Kt Co, Del, where he retired at 60; native of Mass., there spent early life, contracting and bldg in Mass, later N.Y. City. His father, farmer, also named Jas, of Mass.; in war of 1812; lived to 90; of Scotch extraction. Mother of subj, former Miss Mary Hallock b Eng, now in 79th yr; her children: Rbt W., res this town; Addie, w/o John W. Thawley; and Lucy, Mrs. J. Edw Cahill, of Car Co.
Subj b May 27 1862, Windham Co, Conn.; at 9 moved to Brooklyn, N. Y. with parents; after public schools, attended commercial course at Bryant & Stratton's Business College; came to Som Co; 1893 he took charge of a lumber yard and sawmill, as manager; 1893 entered into partnership with I. H. Coulbourn and George W. Long (see sketch of former this vol) in same line of business. Subj is mbr ME Church; m 1892 Miss Amy Coulbourn, d/o Jos Coulbourn, of Lawson's dist; their child.: Stanley and Ada.

518. MACKENZIE GOLDSBOROUGH, retired, res at country seat, Ammere (62 1/2 a.) 1st dist Talb Co. Father of subj, Jas N., b this co, on place known as Ottwell, s/o Nicholas Goldsborough. Jas N., farmer, vestryman Episc Church; d 1870. He m(1) Mary, d/o Commodore Kennedy, of Norfolk, Va. She d, leaving 7 child. Subj is youngest; his bros: Dr. E. K.; R. H. and A. T., all res of Wash, D. C., and sis, E. T., w/o Dr. J. H. H. Bateman, of Easton. Jas N. Goldsborough m(2) Emily Johnson; they had 4 children, living: Mrs. A. L. Sharp, of Easton; Jas N., of Pittsburg; and Miss Madge, of Easton. 681
Subj b on parents' homestead, Woodstock, this co, Nov 12 1856. After preliminary education he entered Md Agricultural College; then clerked in drug store in Easton, about 4 yrs; clerked in Centreville a like period; salesman with J. J. Thompson Balt in wholesale drug trade 1886-8; then real estate business with bro in Wash D. C.; here he met and m Miss Julia P. Fleming, of Wash, Sep 14 1888. Her mother was former Miss Lee from Va, cousin of Gen Rbt E. Lee. Her grandfather, Richard Bland Lee, was a soldier. Their child: Lee Kennedy, Philip Francis, Julia Fleming and Mary Lee.

519. PHILIP A. M. BROOKS, of early Md fam, manages portion of inherited ancestral estates. Founder of this branch was Englishman who held early grants, settled on 1400 a. 1725; prop has remained in hands of decscendants. Subj b on old homestead 1861; his father d 1862 at 25. His father, Geo C. M. Brooks, b Kt Co, res on farm now owned by subj. He possessed large estates and owned many slaves. He m Sarah Rasin, still living, res Va. Her father, McCall M. Rasin, of this co, was rep in state legislature; owned large tract and several slaves. Subj was an only child. After public schools he entered Episc high school at Alexandria, Va; finished a practical course at Md Agricultural College 1880; returned home, to manage the estates, about 700 a. He m 1883, Miss Susan E. Massey, d/o late Dr. C. H. B. Massey; their child.: Philip M. and Grace E., attending school. Fam attend Episc Church. 682

520. WILLIAM WALLACE SPENCE, cashier Talb Savings Bank, Easton, has fine tenor voice, cornet player; b Sep 20 1869 on farm 5 miles from Easton, s/o Jas McFarland Spence, who was b Dundee, Scotland, Feb 21 1829. As a young man located in Winchester, Va, went to Harford Co, Md, then to Eastern Shore; once a leading florist Wash, D. C. He d suddenly of apoplexy at home Talb Co Oct 1893. Since no Presby Church available he attended MP Church. He m Miss Martha Plummer, of QA Co, d/o Wm Plummer, farmer. She d when subj 9 days old; 683

subj youngest of 7 child.; living: Mary R; David McClellan, compositor in public printing office Wash; Jas A., carriage manufacturer Easton; and Martha M., w/o Matthew T. Plummer.
    Subj attended high school Easton, grad Northwestern Normal and Collegiate Institute Wauseon, Ohio; clerked in shoe store of R. S. Fountain, Easton; 1894 became cashier Talb Savings Bank. He m 28 Nov 1894 at res of Judge J. B. Bennett, bride's father, Mrs. Susie (Bennett) Graseley. Educated at Western Md College, she, like her husband, has musical talent, soprano soloist, performs on piano and organ; both active in MP Church. Jerome Bonaparte Bennett, Mrs. Spence's father, b Kt Co, Del 1830, of French and Eng extraction. His father, of France, first settled in Phila; d when Jerome was 7. 1842 latter moved to QA Co; then moved to Easton; large land owner; pres Talb Savings Bank; constable 1849-1855, then sheriff; judge orphans' court Talb Co 1892-6, chief judge 4 yrs; mbr Calvary MP Church. 1849 he m Miss Susan Wilcutt, of Talb Co; their only child w/o subj. His wife d 2 Apr 1897.

684   521.   CHARLES W. MEYER, business man East New Market. Subject's father, August Meyer, b Leipsic, Germany. Alone, he crossed Atlantic, settled in Balt, where he lives; there met and m Miss Mary Deal, d/o Hy Deal; of their 7 child. subj is eldest. Subj b Balt Dec 1 1860, worked for Alexander Dodd & Co, later with Bergman Manufacturing Co, chiefly as traveling salesman, selling harness. 1888 he came to East New market and went into hardware business for himself. Nov 23 1887 he m Miss Katie, d/o Rbt Wright and granddau of Wm O. Wright, of Balt; their sons: Lelan Winfield and Willie R. Mr. and Mrs. Meyer mbrs Bapt Church.

685   522.   HARRISON I. PARSONS, farmer 3rd dist Kt Co. The Parsons fam of Eng extraction. Father of subj, Isaac Parsons, b Pa; c. 1843 moved to Md, settled in Kt Co, where he purch tract (c. 1000 a.) nr Smithville; m Mary Wood, of Del, of 8 child. 4 living: Alphonza, w/o Geo R. Beck; Elizabeth, w/o Elias Walraven; subj; and Rachel A., w/o Thos Gale; the father once school commissioner, active in St. James' MP Church, d 1888, at 82. Subj b Newcastle Co, Del, nr Md state line 1841; at 2 brought to Md by father, educated in common schools of Kt Co. At 25 he took charge of father's prop, continues to farm in same neighborhood. 1866 he m Anna J., d/o Joshua Bell; of their 7 child. those living: Mary E., w/o J. E. Morris; Harry B.; Grace M., w/o John F. Clark; Wm G. and Lewis B. Subj active in St. James' MP Church.

685   523.   ALPHEUS W. NICHOLS, tills Cherry Grove farm, owns homestead called Brainard's Pasture (237 a.) 6th dist QA Co; runs steam thresher during season. John Nichols, father of subj, of Car Co, lived most of life at Gilpin's Point; ran line of boats from Gilpin's Point to Balt; active in ME Church; d 1873; married 3 times; last m Mary Webster, of Dor Co; of their 6 child., fol survive: Flora, wid of Richard Stevens, of Dor Co; Alpheus W.; Winnifred, of Dor co; and Dr. Clarence, of Balt. Subj b Dec 9 1857 Car Co, attended dist school; mbr ME Church; m Jan 18 1881 Ida, d/o Wm N. Cannon, of this neighborhood; their child.: Glendora, Lizzie, Mabel and Webster.

686   524.   GEORGE F. POOLEY, manager Salisbury Shirt Co, not native of Salisbury. Salisbury Shirt Co organized Jun 1897, plant constructed under supervision of subj. (Description of the operation is given; nothing further on subj)

686   525.   HARVEY LEE COOPER, atty Denton, b here Jun 17 1873. His father, Thos M., b Kt Co, Del, mbr of old fam of that locality. When a young man he came

to Denton, embarked in mercantile business, d here Dec 1895, survived by wife, Rachel (Green) Cooper, and their 3 sons, Alceynus, mcht Denton; Ernest G., business man this place; and Harvey Lee. Subj, 2nd of 3 sons, educated in schools of Car Co; grad St. John's College Annapolis 1894; justice of peace, 1895-6. Admitted to bar of Car Co in Oct 1895, now carries on professional practice.

526. WILLIAM M. SCHOOLFIELD manufactures baskets, crates and barrrels at Schoolfield, Barnes & Co., of Pocomoke City which employs about 250 men, women and children. Mr. Schoolfield purch plant 1887; now has small mill depart, planing depart and an engine and boiler room. Subj b and reared on farm nr Pocomoke City, where he was b; in farming and fruit growing until 1885; then came to Pocomoke City, entered sawmill business with W. J. S. Clark & Co., remaining for 19 months. 1857 he m Miss Emily S. Barnes; their child.: Elijah, eldest, in business with father; Wm, mcht Pocomoke City; Geo E. in business with father; daus, Emma, Laura, Hattie and Ella, at home. Mr. Schoolfield is mbr ME Church; once school commissioiner; owns 2 farms nr Pocomoke City. He lives in town. 689

527. R. HESTON HICKS, Kt co; conducts general store Galena; b Mar 4 1858, QA Co, nr Sudlersville, s/o Levin and Sarah Matilda (Milbourn) Hicks, of QA Co, and Del, respectively. Father b Mar 2 1820; farmer; d at 64, as result of an accident, having fallen through hay loft in his barn; active in ME Church. His father, Jas Hicks, of Car Co, farmed until middle life, when he d, leaving 2 sons, Richard and Levin. Mrs. Sarah M. Hicks b 1820, d at 68; mbr Meth Church; left child.: Jas R., res this place, blacksmith; Ella F., who m Dnl Loller, and d in her 33rd yr, leaving 2 child.; Wm T., undertaker Galena; subj; and Sml, blacksmith, res Chestertown. Subj educated local schools; clerked 4 yrs in Sudlersville and Church Hill, Md. 1881 he came to Galena, employed by T. H. Horsey 10 yrs; 1892 entered mercantile business on his own; carries dry goods, glassware, harness, groceries; postmaster; director Kt Co Savings Bank Chestertown; sec and treasurer Galena Creamery. 1894 Mr. Hicks m Emily C. Nutz, of Talb Co, d/o Dr. Eben Nutz, of Easton; only child: Helen; mbrs ME Church. Mrs. Hicks pres Christian Temperance Union Society. 689

528. CHRISTOPHER COLUMBUS WARD, M. D., from old Eastern Shore fam, in practice Crisfield, Som Co, mbr of firm Ward & Collins, owns and operates drug store here; b Pocomoke City, Wor Co, Sep 21 1863. His fam of Eng extraction. Father of subj, M. P. Ward, of Pocomoke City, now res Crisfield; contractor and builder; about 62. He m Sarah A., d/o Peter Johnson, mcht and vessel owner. At 3 subj with fam moved to Balt, educated there; at 15 he went to Phila, served apprenticeship to drug business, grad Phila College of Pharmacy 1886; res there about 10 yrs, employed as druggist, running a store of his own for a while. Selling out, he came to Crisfield and managed drug store 5 yrs or more; then took present partner; grad medical college Balt 1894; since then in medical practice here. Mar 1891 he m Miss Louisa Janvier d/o Edwin P. Janvier of Kt Co, Md; they have son, Edwin E. (See history of Edwin P. Janvier elsewhere this vol) 690

529. HON. JOHN WALTER SMITH, Snow Hill, Wor Co, business man; elected to state senate 1889, 1893 and 1897; pres of senate 1894; introduced bill, providing free school books; served on staff of Gov Henry Lloyd with rank of colonel and 1890 app to staff of Gov Jackson. Subj b Snow Hill Feb 5 1845, s/o John Walter and Charlotte (Whittington) Smith, of this town. Mother d/o 691

-143-

Judge Wm Whittington. Father of subj moved to Balt prior to birth of subj and embarked in wholesale grocery business, incurred reverses, returned to Snow Hill, where he d 1850. His wife d when subj was month old.

Subj educated in private schools and acad of Snow Hill; clerked for George S. Richardson & Bro, of this place; 1867-1870 in business on his own; became mbr of firm 1870. To their general merchandising business, lumber, grain and shipping business (owning their vessels) was added. Today his firm handles lumber from 15-20 sawmills in Wor Co and millions of feet from the south; manufactures boxshooks extensively. Col Smith is charter mbr of Surrey Lumber Co., of Surrey Co, Va; in canning business Snow Hill; The Snow Hill Flouring Mill, the oyster industry in his co; pres First Natl Bank Snow Hill and director in Del Md & Va Railway Co. Jun 1869 he m Miss Mary Frances Richardson; they res in Snow Hill.

692 530. JAMES A. WARWICK, farmer 1st dist, Som Co, b on old homestead which he now cultivates, Sep 28 1863. He and his 2 sis own 4 farms (about 600 a.), this co. Father of subj, Jas W. Warwick, of Som Co, res Princess Anne dist; farmer and justice of peace; constable in younger days. He d 1895 in 72nd year. He was s/o Josiah Warwick, supposedly, from this locality, of Eng descent. Mother of subj was former Mary G. White; she m(1) John P. Lankford; their child.: John P. and Sarah, w/o Geo Brereton, both of this co. She m Jas W. Warwick, had 6 child., 3 survive: Mary J., subj and Nancy Estelle. Their mother d 1894 in 62nd yr; mbr Meth Church. Subj unmarried; he and sisters live together in their ancestral home; they attend the ME Church.

693 531. WILLIAM S. GRACE farmer, res Talb Co, on farm nr his birthplace, Broad Creek Neck, St. Michael's dist; sheriff; mbr house of delegates; justice of peace. Subj b Mar 31 1823, s/o Skinner and Lucretia (Edgar) Grace, of this co. Former reared this neighborhood. During war of 1812 he was captured by British, sent to prison in Jamaica, West Indies. While on prison ship he was taken ill with yellow fever, but survived; earlier as youth he had sailed Chesapeake Bay. He was in merchandising and farming until just before he d, at 85. He was justice of peace, judge of orphans' court. His father, Wm S., farmer, from this co; d at 87. Subject's mother, Lucretia, d at 84th; mbr ME Church. 3 of her 5 children who grew to mature yrs living: Anne Cooper, subj and Thomas (see sketch of latter elsewhere this vol).

Subj attended dist schools; went to Balt c. 1841, worked at carpenter's trade, returned home; teacher for 10 yrs in local school and farmed; mbr ME Church; m 1856 Miss Sarah Fairbanks. She was b and reared this dist, mother of 6 child. Wm S., Jr., bookkeeper Easton Natl Bank; Sarah Olivia m Thos H. H. Blades, of St. Michael's, and d 1888, leaving child; Anna L., w/o S. D. Gemeny, of this dist; Charles H., teacher Balt Co; Arthur F., clerk in store Easton; and Edith, Mrs. Chas Fairbank, of Balt.

694 532. HON. LEVIN LITTLETON WATERS res Princess Anne, Som Co. Father of subj, Levin L. Waters, b on farm now owned by subj; d at 28. He had studied medicine, never in practice. His father, Wm, farmer of this co. Ancestor John Waters purch land here 1685, his ancestors in America some time before that. Col Edw Waters, founder of the line came from Eng to Va, in early Indian wars there; d 1628 Elisabeth City, Va; his wid later m Col Obedience Robins. Mother of subj, Eliza, d/o Jas C. Hyland, of this co. Her grandfather, Lambert Hyland, came to this locality from Cecil Co, and one of his sons, John, killed in war of 1812. Lambert Hyland s/o Stephen Hyland, rep of Cecil Co in convention in Annapolis 1774, protesting against Boston port

-144-

bill. Mrs. Eliza Waters d at 39, leaving child., Levin and Annie. The latter is wid of Levin Woolford, lawyer and state comptroller 8 yrs.

Subj b May 9 1828; 5 yrs old when his father d. When his mother d, he was 18, assumed management of farm (320 a.); educated in Wash Acad Princess Anne, Som Co; read law with bro-in-law, Mr. Woolford, 1859 admitted to bar; m 1859 Miss Lucretia, d/o Col Arnold E. Jones. Her father mbr state legislature; officer in a militia company, d at 50. His son, Arnold Elzey, was commander in Confed army, led troops at battle of Bull Run. He was promoted to general on account of his bravery and leadership at that noted engagement. As there were so many men named Jones in army he dropped his surname. The 5 children of Mrs. and Mrs. Waters are: Arnold E., mbr of banking firm Townsend, Scott & Son, of Balt; Levin L., in office Mount Vernon Manufacturing Co, of Balt; Hy Jackson, practicing law with his father; and Emily R. and Eliza W., at home.

Subj conducted newspaper here 1858-61; abandoned it on account of sympathy with southern cause. 1864 he was elected to state senate; asked to resign by Gen Lew Wallace, he refused and charge was brought against him of raising a rebel flag at his newspaper office; imprisoned 2 months, released and returned to senate. He served as clerk this co 8 yrs; mbr of commission on disputed Md and Va boundaries. 1892 he was elected again to state senate. 1867 he obtained charter for Mutual Fire Insur Co of this and Wor Cos, and made pres of same, until 1892; became sec and treasurer of co; trustee of old Wash Acad and vestryman Episc Church.

533. CAPT. JOSEPH S. HARRISON, retired bay captain, res Bay Hundred dist, Talb Co, where he owns and operates small farm; ran freight boats to Balt 40 yrs. He owns 500 a., most of which is cultivated by his sons.

A Harrison migrated from Eng to lower port of Talb Co in early history. The captain's grandfather, Thos, farmer, b Bay Hundred dist; d here at 87; in war of 1812. Levi, father of subj, b and res this dist; carpenter and farmer; identified with ME Church; d 1875 at 71. He m Anna Jones, who d at 82. Of their 11 children 4 living: subj; Elizabeth, res this dist; Wm P., res Cambridge; and Chas, this dist.

Subj b Nov 12 1828 in dist where he now res, educated in public schools; took charge of boat in which father owned interest; in partnership with A. H. Seth, he built a boat, of which he was captain 11 yrs; in freighting business 40 yrs, then retired; active in ME Church South. He m Sarah V., d/o Lawrence Cummings; she was reared by her aunt, Mary Marshall, who res with her until she d 1896, at 96. Child. of Capt and Mrs. Harrison: Mary J., w/o John L. Warner; Levina, who m John T. Howarth; Henrietta, w/o John M. Singer; Josephine, Mrs. Clinton Porter; Amelia, wid of Mark Porter; Stella, who m Capt L. E. Ford; Lewis C., in mercantile business Wittman, Talb Co; Chas P., farmer res nr old homestead; and Geo K., tills land nr his father's home.

534. JAMES C TAWES mbr of Tawes & Co., wholesale dealers in fish and crabs, Crisfield; fish commissioner of Eastern Shore with 3 deputies in charge of about 25 boats and a force of men, who propagate and protect fishing interests and seek to prevent the diminishing of supply of perch, shad and trout in the bay.

Subj b May 7 1861 Crisfield dist, Som Co, s/o Edw and Grace (Lawson) Tawes, of this dist. His father, a seafaring man, once kept small store nr Jenkin's Creek bridge, opened oyster packing house; carried on trade in oyster shells; continued in business until he d, 1890, at 70. He was town commissioner, Crisfield; active in ME Church. 1867 he estab business now owned by his sons.

Fam of which subj is mbr consisted of: next to youngest d unnamed in infancy; others: Margaret, w/o Wm H. Chelton; Noah R., of Som Co; Laura A., H. E., Arentha C., Geo W., John W., Jas C., Isaac H., Lillian and Chas L. At 15 subj began clerking in grocery owned by Thos Dougherty, of Crisfield, then worked for Edw Mauck, owner of clothing store here. Two yrs later, he embarked in grocery business, remaining in business until store burned 1882; went to Kansas City, Mo., clerked for J. C. Eaglehoff, owner of large shoe house; returned to Md, carried on grocery in Crisfield 2 months, sold out and went Hornellsville, nr Buffalo, N. Y., carried on branch of oyster businesss 3 yrs; returned home and worked with father in oyster business for a year, solicited trade in Chicago, St. Louis, and other western cities; became mbr of firm Tawes, Sterling & Co., wholesale dealers in oysters in Balt, after 2 seasons firm failed. Again he returned to Crisfield, postmaster a while; identified with ME Church. He m Margaret Croswell, of Crisfield; their child.: Margaret; Julius, who d in infancy; and Adaline.

699 535. CAPT. JOSPEH HUGH SPEDDEN, res 7th dist, Dor Co. An ancestor was granted tract 8th dist, now owned by John L. Spedden, original homestead on which was b captain's paternal grandfather, Rbt B., and his father, Rbt B., Jr. Latter m Margaret Cook; their child.: Thos, decd; Mary d at 80; Rbt, next in order of birth; Hy decd; subj; Prudence and John, decd; and Levin, farmer, St. Mary's Co, Md. Subj b on farm 8th dist Dor Co, Oct 24 1821; attended public schools a portion each year. 1838 he signed on as sailor on schooner which plied the Chesapeake Bay. At 18 he was master of a vessel, made 3 voyages to West Indies; became part owner of sailing vessel; spent 18 yrs on Chesapeake Bay. 1856 he purch home here of Wm L. Hearn; assessor of this dist. He m Jan 1 1855, Margaret Wheeler, 8th dist; their child.: Salley, elder, w/o Wm P. Beckwith, teacher in acad at East New Market; Jos H., Jr., at home. Fam identified with Episc Church Cambridge.

700 536. LOUIS LACEY BEATTY, school examiner QA Co, res Centreville. His paternal grandfather b Co Tyrone, Ireland, Oct 10 1780; immigrated to U.S. when young, settled in Newcastle Co, Del, where he m Catherine Bradford, Apr 10 1803. He d Aug 14 1859. Catherine Bradford b Newcastle Co, Del May 6 1773, d Dec 31 1831. Both buried Salem Cemetery, nr Cooch's Bridge.
Louis Hunter Beatty, father of subj, of Newcastle Co, Del, b Oct 5 1814, edcuated Newark Acad, grad Jefferson Medical College Phila, settled at Ingleside, QA Co, Md, where he practiced and farmed. Apr 1839 he m Catherine Amelia Robinson, of Denton. 1847-1849 Dr. Beatty occupied chair of obstetrics and diseases of women and children in Phila College of Medicine. He d Aug 17 1871, from injuries resulting from a fall, buried Sudlersville Cemetery. His wife, Catherine A. Robinson, b Mary 25 1822, d/o Peter and Sallie R. (Mitchell) Robinson. She is still living. Her bro, late John Mitchell Robinson, chief judge circuit court and chief justce court of appeals of Md; d Jan 1896. Louis H. Beattty and wife had fol child.: Josephine A., Sarah R., Laura, Arthur J., Louis Lacey, Ralph R., Frederic W. and Eugene Mitchell.
Subj b Ingleside, QA Co, Aug 3 1850, educated at Dickinson College, Carlisle, Pa. 1881-1886 inclusive, he was co surveyor QA Co; superintendent of public schools; treasurer and sec of co school bd; mbr state bd of education. Dec 9 1896 he m Mary Morling Sudler, d/o late J. Morling Sudler, of Sudlersvile, QA Co.

700 537. OSCAR M. PURNELL, one of the editors and proprietors of Democratic Messenger Snow Hill, b Snow Hill, Oct 20 1858, s/o Stephen D. and Mary J.

(Laws) Purnell, of this co. Former d here 1879, at 53; his wid, age 70, still res in Snow Hill. Of her 12 child., fol survive: Wm Matthew (eldest), owns ancestral estate; Stephen L., mcht Snow Hill and judge orphans court Wor Co; ; Jas L., general mananger Home Sewing Maching Co Cleveland, Oh; Oscar M.; Geo E., dentist at Guadalajara, Mexico, and sec and treasurer Jalisca Packing Co; John W., dentist in city of Mexico; and Mary K., res with her mother in Snow Hill. Another son, Ralph C., grad medical depart Univ Md 1887, at 21; Jul 26 1887, he drowned at Scott's beach. Ancestor, 1 of 3 bros, from Eng in 1600's, settled in present Wor Co with his bros.

Subj b Oct 20 1858 on farm; grad Snow HIll high school; grad Wash College 1880; read law with Upshur & Purnell, admitted to bar in 1882; practiced law until Jan 1887, when, in partnership with C. L. Vincent, he bt Democratic Messenger. Subj one of the founders of Equitable Bldg and Loan Assoc of Snow Hill, estab 1894. 1883 he m Miss Emma J., d/o Thos D. Purnell, rgtr of wills Wor Co. Their daus: Eloise and Julia; mbrs Makemie Memorial Presby Church Snow Hill.

538. FREDERICK A. ADAMS, M. D., res same estate Som Co as occupied by Adams fam during entire 19th century, Brinkley's dist (100 a.); has a practice; medical examiner for N.Y. Mutual Life Insur Co., and Heptasophs and Ancient Order of United Workmen. Subj b on home farm 1840, where his father, Jas F. Adams, b 1811. The latter, farmer, owned large farm and number of slaves; was of English ancestors who came to Som Co early day; during Civil war he was proprietor of inn at Rehobeth; after the war he went to Kansas City, embarked in live stock business, remained there until he d, at 58. He was s/o Josiah Adams, res of Som Co, farmer and slave owner, sergeant in war of 1812. Jas F. Adams m Elizabeth Wilson; she d at 58.

Subj only survivor of fam of 4 child; reared in Brinkley's dist, educated at Wash Acad, Princess Anne, in private school Balt 2 yrs. During war he remained in the south; 1865 came home, began study of medicine in Jefferson Medical College, Phila, grad 1867; returned to old home, where he began his practice. He and fam attend Episc Church. 1868 he m Sallie W., d/o Jephtha Hayman; their child.: Jas F., Gertrude E., Lucille H. and Marie H.

539. HON. THOMAS LECOMPTE, judge orphans' court 1881-1889, of old fam of Dor Co. His celebrated ancestor, Anthony LeCompte, b France, forced to flee during religious persecutions early 1600's. His estates were confiscated and he, taking refuge in Eng, took up arms against his mother county; he was knighted and given coat of arms. He m Esther Doatloan of France, whose he met in London. She too was Protestant, compelled to seek a home in a foreign land. Anthony LeComnpte, with his young wife, arrived in America 1654 and settled in Md. The property now owned by Chas Mitchell. (For further particulars of LeCompte ancestry see sketch of J. S. Shepherd.)

Subj owns part of historic farm known as Castle Haven, about 9 miles from Cambridge, nr mouth of Choptank River (100 a.); b nr Castle Haven Apr 22 1820, s/o Wm G., same place, soldier of war of 1812. Paternal grandfather of judge was Isaiah LeCompte, b, lived and d at Castle Haven. Subj grew up on old farm; mbr Episc Church. 1840 he m Miss Margaret Cook; their child.:3 d in infancy; others: Thos I., mcht this dist; Dnl H., mcht Cambridge; Sml E., mcht Hills Point and sheriff Dor Co; Mary L. w/o John L. Spedden, farmer nr Hills Point; and Margaret N., w/o Geo E. Hearn, res on farm with judge's fam.

540. ISAAC J. STREET, farmer Tyaskin dist, Wicomcio Co, owns nearly 400 a. The Streets res of Eastern Shore for several generations. Subject's father was Capt Thos Street, sailor for yrs; master of a ship that plied the Chesapeake Bay. His home and headquarters were on farm he supervised. He m Ann Williams, of Eastern Shore; of their 6 children 3 living: Thos, Isaac J. and Sallie. Subj b Nov 17 1846 on parental homestead, educated in dist schools; carried on sawmilling and farming; his fam attend ME Church. He m Miss Mary W. Catlin, of this co, Nov 17 1870; their child.: 1 d in infancy; others in order of their birth: Hattie L.; Mary A.; Amos R.; Lena A., w/o Chas Parks; and Adah L. Hattie L. is w/o Marcellus Windsor; they have son, Isaac W. and infants, Langford and Matt, with bro that d at about 3 months, were triplets. Mrs. Street d Apr 15 1884, in 15th yr of her marriage, at 35.

541. BENJAMIN S. PUSEY, 2nd dist Wicomico Co, farmer, operates sawmill. Elijah J. Pusey, father of subj, of Sussex Co, Del, m May 1846, Margaret, d/o Benj Sheppard, of Sheppardsville, Wicomico Co. She d Mar 1897. He taught school in Del several yrs; later settled in Laruel, Del; carried on store until 1855; bt farm now owned by son Benj. He res here just before he d, Apr 1878. While res Del he served in state legislature; mbr ME Church. Of their children fol living: S. E., w/o John I. Scott, of Phila, and L. H., w/o W. J. Johnson, of Salisbury; subj; and E. J. of this neighborhood. Subj b Laurel, Del Jan 23 1850; leaving school he took up farming; owns old homestead (197 a.), and 600 a. elsewhere; mbr ME Church. Feb 22 1880 he m Letitia J., d/o Levin M. Wilson; their child.: Elihu W., Mary E. and Margaret J.

542. ISAAC H. COULBOURN mbr old fam of lower peninsula; 1732 a grant of 1700 a. made to Wm Coulbourn, who founded fam in Som Co; his prop remains in hands of descendants. When Wm came from Eng, he was accompanied by bro, Isaac, whose subsequent history is unknown. Grandfather of subj, Isaac Coulbourn, b on old homestead and there he farmed; d at 82. During war of 1812 he was mbr of militia. Subject's father, Wm Coulbourn, b on home farm; mariner, owned several vessels that traded on Chesapeake Bay; retired to old homestead where he d at 82; elected to legislature 1872 & 1876; sheriff Som Co, 1 term; lieut in the old militia; suported ME Church. He m Henrietta Robinson Berry, who was b Middlesex Co, Va, Aug 18 1825, res homestead Som Co, mbr ME Church; her child.: Clara L., w/o J. W. Richardson, of Wash, D. C.: subj; Addie M., who m F. A. Gunby, farmer Som Co; and Wm R., in drug business Roanoke, Va.

Subj b Lawsons dist, Som Co, Aug 21 1852; attended Dickinson Seminary 3 yrs, took commercial course Williamsport, Pa, clerked 2 yrs in general store Crisfield; mbr of firm of Brown, Coulbourn & Co (oyster business) 1874-6; formed present co-partnership, Long, Coulbourn & Co, operating hardware store Crisfield and dealing in oysters. 1876 Mr. Coulbourn helped establish firm Coulbourn, Moore & Co., manufacturers of ice; 1892, it merged into Crisfield Ice Manufacturing Co., of which he is vice-pres and a director. He and wife assoc with MP Church. He m Jane E., d/o Wm Roach, of Som Co; their child.: Wm H., 17, medical student Univ Md; Caroline V., Hugh A. and Ethel Henrietta.

543. GEORGE L. HICKS, M. D. physician and surgeon Dor Co; office and res Mill St, Cambridge; from Alexandria, Va, b Jan 3 1839. His father was from Balt, served in battle of North Point, war of 1812. Mother was former Miss Elizabeth Bayne; of their 13 child., subj next to youngest. Subj attended St. John's Acad, Alexandria; studied Medicine; grad Columbian Univ, Wash, D. C. 1866; served in the southern army, assist to leading surgeon. After war, he

settled in Rossville, Balt Co. While there, parents came to live out their yrs. 1868 he moved to Cornersville, Dor Co, much later retired to Cambridge; pres school bd Dor Co 1869-79. Subj m Mar 8 1868 Miss Nannie Hicks, d/o ex-gov Hicks, his only surviving child. (See his sketch elsewhere this vol) She and subj have 4 sons: eldest, Thos Holliday, grad St. John's College, prof of Latin and Eng, then paymaster U.S. navy; Geo Luther, assist clinical surgeon Md Univ Hospital; Fessenden Fairfax student in Columbian Univ (medical depart), Wash, D. C.; Chaplain Galloway, age 7, at home.

544. JAMES C. JOHNSON, sheriff of Wicomico Co, res Salisbury past 2 yrs, farmed prior to that 8th dist; b 1844, s/o Jas H. and Sallie Johnson, both of Parsons dist, Wicomico Co. His grandfather, Purnell Johnson, sheriff Wor Co, descendant of early settlers on Eastern Shore. Parents of subj had 4 child.: Susan E. w/o Geo T. Parsons, farmer, once sheriff Som Co; Mrs. Parsons, decd, left no child.; Theodore P., eldest son, res Nutters dist, where he farms; Sarah J. m Jehu Parsons, farmer Som Co. Jas H. Johnson, the father, d 1856. His wife, Sallie, preceded him about 3 yrs. Subj left an orphan at 12; attended common schools and Salisbury Acad about 6 months; began farming in Nutters dist; owns tract (196 a.) there. 1873 he m Miss Margaret, d/o Jehu Parsons; their child.: Geo P., Jas N. and Ernest M. C.   706

545. HON. J. H. W. G. WEEDON, M. D., physician 2nd dist QA Co; b 4th dist QA Co, Sep 1 1836, s/o Hy and Rebecca (Legg) Weedon, who spent their lives on a farm. Of their 6 children, 2 d in infancy; Mary A. w/o Robert C. Eareckson; Rebecca, wid of Thos W.Trenchard; and Austin R., atty Centreville. Subj b on home farm, educated in private and public schools and Centreville Acad; farmed short time; read medicine with Dr. William Denny, of Kt Island; grad medical depart Univ Md 1864, remained Balt 1 year as assist resident physician to Univ Md Hospital; set up practice and farmed Kent Island. 1884 he moved his practice to Church Hill. He m Dec 14 1880 Mary R., d/o Wm S. Thompson, formerly of Kent Island, then res Kt Co. Her mother was Mary E. Groome of Easton, d/o Sml and Deborah (Morris) Groome. Dr. and Mrs. Weedon attend Episc Church. 1877 while res Kt Island, subj elected to legislature.   709

546. HARRY DAVIS, farmer Kt Co, res nr Still Pond, 2nd dist; b 1851, Sussex Co, Del. Fam founded by 5 bros from Wales, who located in Del 1650. The name Nehemiah Davis was borne by 3 generations of subject's ancestors, including his grandfather, who served in war of 1812. The father, Hy Davis, b Sussex Co, Del, on old homestead, owned by fam mbrs over 2 centuries, now owned by Miss Richards. Hy Davis res Middletown, farmer and surveyor; also transacted considerable legal business; director Natl Bank Odessa, trustee Middletown acad; state senator 1874-1878; mbr ME Church. He is now 96, res with subj Kt Co, Md, since 1892. He m Miss Catherine Riley, of Del, d/o Capt Lawrence Riley, who served in war of 1812. After her death he m Miss Riley, sis of present wife; they had sons: Lawrence R., postmaster Odessa, Del; and Geo W., res Kent Co, Md, school commissioner at time of his death. There were 3 children b of third union; subject is only one living. Subj spent boyhood on home farm, in public schools and attended Middletown Acad, Newark Acad, Pennington Seminary and Del College. He was in charge of father's farm nr Middletown 1872-1883, moved to village, where he was mbr of firm S. M. Reynolds & Co., general merchandising, 1 year; later in stove and tin business at that place 4 yrs, sold out 1888 and came to Kt Co, Md, where he purch old Dr. Kennard farm (300 a.). 1877 he m Miss Annie, sis of F. H. Harper; their child.: Walter H., Hy, Mattie and Emma. Family are Meth.   709

547. EDWIN P. JANVIER, decd, b Newcastle, Del, 1827, descendant of Peter Janvier, b in France latter 1600's, came to America, settled in Newcastle, Del. His son Thos was grandfather of subj. Subject's father, Geo Janvier, farmere, b and reared in Newcastle. He m Miss Catherine Paynter; they had 10 child., 2 living: Mary, w/o Philip White, of Phila; and Thos, of Lansdowne, Md. The father d in Newcastle.
   Subj, oldest of fam, passed his boyhood in Del, educated in Newark College; gave up study of medicine on account of poor health. 1852 he came to Kt Co, Md, purch of Lewis Wethered the Draton place, farmed remainder of his life; mbr ME Church and local preacher in Still Pond Church. He m(1) Miss Elizabeth Haman, of Del; they had 2 child., 1 living, w/o Dr. W. L. S. Murray, of Wilmington, Del. He m(2) Miss Margaret Newnan, of Balt; they had 2 sons, both decd, 3 daus, living and m. 1868 Mr. Janvier m Miss Margaret, d/o Dr. Wm and Margaret (Sutton) Gemmill, of Del; of their 9 child. Mrs. Janvier is only one living. Fol death of 1st wife Dr. Gemmill m Jane Baker, of Pa; their child.: Fdk, res Balt; and Alice, living with Mrs. Janvier. The father, physician and surgeon of Kt Co, Md, also farmed. He d 1866, at 67. His father, Capt Gemmill, of Scotland, res Newcastle, Del, where he farmed.

548. JAMES T. IRELAND, farmer 3rd dist Kt Co; owns 800 a.; carries on general mercantile store. Ireland fam of Eng extraction. Chas T., father of subj, b Kt Co, in farming and merchandising in Chestertown; taught school in dist schools a while. He m Sarah Hudson; of their 6 child., 5 living: Sarah, w/o Sml Todd; John C.; Mary, wid of Amor Campbell; Henrietta and Jas T. Both father and mother d at 65, former in 1877 and latter in 1874. Subj b 1851, Chestertown; educated in public schools; farmed; 1876 began working on land he still owns. 1879 he m Catherine Worrell, of Kt Co; their child.: Jas T., Page Worrell, Chas, M. Howard, Anna W. and Wm Bryan. Mrs. Ireland d/o Wm Page and Catherine (Tilden) Worrell, and granddau of Dr. Chas Tilden, of this co. Her sis and bros: Elizabeth, d in infancy; Elizabeth (2d), decd; Dr. Fdk; Chas; Mary C.; Maria L. and Wm, decd.

549. HON. JOHN P. NICHOLSON, fruit and grain farmer Kt Co; purch farm in 6th dist 1876. Rbt Nicholson, father of subj, b Lincolnshire, Eng, and in early manhood emigrated to U. S. Settling in Del, he m there and made his home there; then moved to Kt Co, Md, farming and fruit growing; involved in bldg Kent Co Railroad; station established named Nicholson in his honor; judge orphans' court Kt Co; connectd with MP Church. He d at 70. Mother of subj, Sarah S. Burgess, b Del, where she was reared and m; survived her husband by 11 yrs, d May 10 1897, at 74. Of her family 6 child reached mature yrs: John P., eldest; Rbt G., farmer 3rd dist; Sarah E., w/o Geo W. Hatcherson, of Chestertown; Wm T., farms 6th dist; Albert S., M. D., physician New York City; and Emma, w/o Dr. John H. Hessey, 3rd dist.
   Subj b nr St. Georges, Del, Oct 7 1844. When 5 months old his parents moved to Kt Co, Md; here he was reared on farm. When about 18 he operated a rented farm for himself, until 1876, when he purch present prop. May 21 1868 he m Jennie, d/o Wm Skirven; she d Dec 14 1876. He m(2) Jan 15 1880, Emily Gowing, of New Hampshire; their daus: Mabel G. and Florence F. 1895 Mr. Nicholson elected to house of delegates. He is identified with MP Church.

550. G. S. McCREADY, mbr of firm McCready & Nelson, Crisfield, Som Co; engaged in coast trade, sailed on vessels between New York, Sandy Hook and on the Chesapeake. 1883 he built marine railway here; constructs and repairs ships. He was b Nov 14 1837, Lawsons dist, Som Co. His father, Benj

McCready, of Wor Co, bt farm in Lawsons dist and moved there; farmed and supervised construction of many sea-going vessels; militiaman war of 1812; d in 74th year. He m Elizabeth Thomas, b this co, d at 88, mbr Asbury ME Church. Subj remained with parents and 11 bros & sis until about 18. Then lived on the water. He m(1) Miss Love Ward, of this co. She d, leaving, Edw, works in cork factory Chicago, and Rbt, atty Mathews Co, Va. Subj m(2) Miss Sidonia V. Somers, of this co, who d, leaving: John and Ira, with their bro Edward in Chicago factory. 1881 Mr. McCready m Susie, sis of Dr. Atkinson, of Crisfield. (See his sketch elsewhere this vol)

551. HON. TILGHMAN NUTTLE, mbr Md senate 1857-1861, retired mcht and farmer, 3rd dist Car Co. Subj only surviving child of Wm and Margaret (Andrews) Nuttle, of Car Co, who had 8 child. Grandfather Wm Nuttle, Sr., came from Eng. Tilghman b Oct 7 1816, spent boyhood on farm. He ran general store at Andersontown, Md 1839-49, sold out and established himself at Potter's Landing; managed a general store at Andersontown c. 1862-69; turned to farming. Jan 10 1843 he m Elizabeth Blake, who was b and grew up in this co. She d Sep 5 1868, aged 43; of their 8 child., those living: Wm, Hy, Edw E. and Sml. Mr. Nuttle is mbr ME Church. 713

552. WILLIAM J. WOOLLEN, farmer New Market dist Dor Co, reared on farm where he was b and now supervises. 1878 he joined Shiloh MP Church. Subj b Feb 21 1856, s/o John and Mary (Cheesman) Woollen. Father from Car Co, carpenter and wheelwright; d 1860; his wid m Wm Willoughby; their dau, Nettie, w/o Oliver Simpson, of N.J. Father of John Woollen also named John, of Federalsburg, Car Co; farmer and miller, d young. Mrs. Mary (Cheesman) Woollen Willoughby d/o Thos Cheesman; she and Mr. Woollen had 4 child.: Geo M., of Falls Co, Tex.; Sallie E., w/o Columbus N. Ross; subj; and Mary J., w/o Jacob Charles. Subj served as tax collector. Dec 21 1880 he m Lillie B., d/o Jas H. Cockran, of New Market; their child.: Nellie H., May, Lloyd, Katie and Grace; only son, Lloyd, d at 5. 714

553. GEORGE W. TARBUTTON, Trappe dist, Talb Co, retired, res nr Trappe; mbr MP Church. Wm, father of subj, b QA Co, came to this co in boyhood; settled in Chapel dist; in war of 1812; d 1843, at 68. He m Miss Mary Fairbanks; their child.: Jas, Wm, Nancy, John, Elizabeth, Edw, Thos, subj, Chas H., Mary E., 2 eldest d in infancy. Subj b Chapel dist Sep 27 1821; farmed until 1851; then carpenter 20 yrs; purch homestead where he res 1871. Sep 27 1849 he m Mary N. Newman; their children: Annie I., w/o John Rice, this locality; Emily J., w/o Jas C. Tarbutton, farmer this dist; and Geo B., manages homestead, m Elma M. Mullikin, had child., Geo R., Addison G. and Mary S. 715

554. ISAAC H. TAWES, of firm of Tawes & Co., b Crisfield dist, Som Co, Sep 26 1863, attended local schools; employed by L. T. Dryden & Co., wholesale oyster and fish business Crisfield c. 1880-2, as assist and partner; formed partnership with father same type business, until father d, Jan 30 1890; then bro, Jas C. purch father's interest. At 17 he united with ME Church. He is director of Crisfield Ice Manufacturing Co. He m Miss Addie B., d/o Washington S. Croswell, of Som Co, ship builder. 715

555. E. STANLEY TOADVIN, senior mbr law firm Toadvin & Bell, Salisbury, rep Wicomico Co state senate, b Salisbury, Dec 3 1848. Father, Purnell Toadvin, mcht Salisbury, d 1878, about 70. His wife, Amanda, d/o Jehu Parsons, mcht Salisbury. She d 1862, about 50. Of 5 sons and daus who attained maturity 716

subj youngest. Subj educated in public schools and Salisbury Acad; grad Princeton college 1869; student depart of law Univ Va, read law under Judge Thos A. Spence, Salisbury, admitted to bar 1872; opened law office in Salisbury. 1878 app state's atty to fill vacancy caused by resignation of Jas E. Ellegood; 1879 elected to the office; 1887 elected to state senate and re-elected in 1891. He m 1889 Miss Kate H. Tilghman, d/o Wm B. Tilghman, pres Farmers and Merchants' Bank Salisbury. Their dau: Catherine H.

716   556. HON. ROBERT F.MADDOX, elected to Md house of delegates 1887, rgtr of wills 1891. Five generations ago Lazarus Maddox, ancestor of subj, held a patent to large tract in Fairmount dist, Som Co, dated 1716, and part of this original estate has come down to Rbt F., great-great-great-grandson. His great-great-grandfather was from this co and d here 1776, and his great-grandfather, Dnl, d 1819. Grandfather Wm Maddox b this co; farmer until he d, 1823. Dnl H.Maddox, father of subj, b on old fam estate Fairmount dist 1812; carpenter in young manhood Balt; chiefly farmed; active in ME Church. He d at 65. Dnl Maddox m Susan Ballard, b 1816, d/o Dnl Ballard, sheriff this co. He d 1847, about 75. Mrs. Susan Maddox, mbr ME Church, d 1891; her child.: Dnl Jas, farmer Fairmount dist; Elizabeth, w/o Gustavus A. Maddox, of this co; Jos G., employed by railway co Balt; Geo W., mcht Manokin; Laura H., Sarah E. and Clara U., all living at old home; Rbt F.; and Wm E., manages and res on old homestead. - Subj b Sep 26 1853, Fairmount dist; attended common schools; grad St. John's College Annapolis, Md, 1876; taught school on Deal's Island; principal Fairmount Acad 6 yrs; carried on a business in Fairmount, which he gave up when elected to legislature 1887. He is mbr MP Church. Dec 22 1881 he m Mollie Lankford, from same locality. She grad Western Md College; d Aug 15 1883 at 21; mbr ME Church. Apr 17 1895 Mr. Maddox m Ella, d/o Rev S. A. Hoblitzell, of Bel Air, Md; they have son, Rbt H.

717   557. JOHN N. WRIGHT, farmer Fork dist, Dor Co, raises peaches, apples and small fruits; manufacture lumber; co school commissioner; assessor. Father of subj, Isaac Wright, m Mrs. Anne Adkins, nee Jackson. Her great-grand- father, Admiral Abner Jackson, an officer under Lord Nelson, in British navy, promoted for distinguished bravery at battle of Trafalgar. His coat of arms still possessed by some of his lineal descendants in Del. Isaac Wright b Car Co, 1761, and res same neighborhood; d 1850, at 89. He possessed 4000-5000 a. and many slaves. His father, Edw Wright, b 1712, came to America 1737, from Isle of Wight, Eng (of which he was a native), and settled in Car Co. He held extensive land grant. His 3 sons: Isaac, Jesse and Jacob; all left families in the co. Child. of Isaac and Anne Wright: Wm W., of Seaford, Del.; Isaac H., of East New Market, Md; John N.; Anne, decd, who m Wm T. Vickers, of East New Market; Celia, who m Dr. Shipley, of Del, and d, leaving one son; and Harriet P., who m Hon. Daniel M. Fields, of Car Co, who twice rep his co in the Md senate; once pres of the senate.

Subj b 1829, Maple Grove farm, where he res today. He m 1856 Rebecca C. Phillips, d/o Igrus S. and Amelia Phillips, of Del. She d Dec 7 1896. Of their children, John res Cripple Creek, Colo.; Hy M. in Aspen, Colo.; Frank in Car Co, Md; Hattie w/o C. P. Tatem, of Balt; May, at home; Lyda w/o Dr. F. H. Elder, of Phila; and Rbt Lee, at home. Mr. Wright is Episc.

718   558. COL. JAMES MARION LOWE, St. Michael's, Talb Co, s/o Wm Webb and Mary Ann (Wrightson) Lowe, b nr McDanieltown, said co, May 23 1837; attended town schools until 15, entered Md Military Acad Oxford, Md; taught school most of next 18 yrs. 1868-9 he served as co school commissioner. Subject's father d

Jan 20 1863. Subj exempted from service in Union army on account of physical disablility. His bro, Wm E. Lowe, served in Capt Wm H. Murray's company of Md Infantry. After war he and bro farmed together at old homestead until 1875. Subj m and sold his interest to bro, moved to nearby farm. There he farmed; also conveyancer and surveyor. He m Dec 16 1875 Dorcas Elizabeth, d/o John Wesley Sedgwick and Ann (Wrightson) McDaniel, the latter d/o Jas and Elizabeth (Orem) Wrightson. Col and wife mbrs MP Church. Subj served as committee clerk in Md senate 1874-6, 1880 app as col on Governor's staff; elected to legislature, 1880-90.

John Lowe, supposedly of Derby or Derbyshire fam of Lowes, Eng, m Dec 2 1700, Mary Bartlett, Quaker, d/o Thos and Mary (Goodchild) Bartlett, of Radcliffe Manor, nr Easton, Md, from Yorkshire, Eng. Mr. Lowe res Bay Side, on farm, helped found Quaker Meeting house nr McDanieltown; d 1726, surviving his wife; homestead still held by descendants. On maternal side Col Lowe descends from John and Mary Wrightson. The latter an active business woman, owning and managing many farms; closely related to Col Thos Smithman, and the Sedgwicks. She d 1740, surviving her husband 23 yrs. Great-grandfathers of subj: Ensign Jas Lowe and Col Wm Webb Haddaway (descendant of Rowland and Ursula Haddaway), served in Rev war. Earliest known ancestor on paternal side of Mrs. J. M. Lowe was Laughlin McDaniel, who d 1732; his wife: Mary Lowe McDaniel. Their grandson, John McDaniel, m Mar 30 1777, Mary d/o Jas and Elizabeth (Sedgwick) Morsell, who came here from Calvert Co. Her sis, Dorcas Sedgwick, m Joshua Johnson, of London; son Thos Johnson, gov of Md; and dau Louisa Catherine Johnson, m John Quincy Adams (later U.S. pres) Jul 26 1797. Also see sketch of Albert Lowe, elsewhere this vol.

559. CAPT. NATHAN J. COCKRAN, farmer 8th dist Car Co. Paternal grandfather Nathan Cockran, prob b this co, nr Dor Co line. Maternal grandfather, "Kiah" James, b Eng. Subj s/o Ezekiel Cockran, wheelwright and carpenter, who d early manhood. Nathan b 1826, nr present home Car Co, bound out to Capt Levin T. Dukes, sailed Balt-Phila through canal, to and from, until 17; bt 1/3 vessel; became master; c. 1869 moved to present homestead. He m 1856 Margaret, d/o Capt Dennis Wilson; fol her death m Irene Blades, d/o Isaiah C. Blades & granddau of Isaiah Blades, who res on homestead where subj res, and buried on farm. Mother of Mrs. N. J. Cockran: Milcha Todd. Capt Cockran's child.: Algy J., farmer; Anthony B., oysterman and boatman Oxford; Elmina, w/o Harry R. Merican; and Margaret I., w/o E. M. Willey, farmer 3rd dist. 719

560. JOSEPH G. HARRISON, sheriff Wor Co, and senior mbr of firm, J. G., Harrison & Sons, Berlin dist, nursery business. He was b Sussex Co, Del, Nov 15 1840, 2nd of 7 child.; others: Mahala, Eliza, Louisa, Levin and Chas H.; parents were Jos G. and Rhoda (Long) Harrison, both of Sussex Co, Del. The father, farmer, and his father, farmer, b Del. - Subj became connected with N.C. lumber trade 1881; came to this co 1883, purch a farm. He raises berries and peaches for city markets; sells young peach trees, plum trees, fruit bushes, strawberry plants and asparagus plants. His sons, Orlando and Geo A., mbrs of the firm. Subj m Apr 4 1856 Miss Catherine Collins, of Md; their children, in order of birth: Orlando, Geo A., Della C. and Achsah. The sons m and daus keep house for father; mother d Apr 15 1887, mbr ME Church. 720

561. THOMAS W. K. WHITE. White fam res Kt Island, since its first white settlement. Subj res northeastern part of island. His paternal grandfather was Walter White, b on island; his land still owned by descendants. His son, Marmaduke, father of subj, b and reared here. He d, leaving farm (200 a.) on 721

Love Point, and one east of Stevensville. He m Miss Mary Carville; their child.: Madeline, w/o Jacob Calloway, of Queenstown; subj; Fdk, decd; Catherine, w/o Perry Winchester, of Pa; Edw, Jas and Annie, all decd. Subj b 1850; managed his and 2 farms belonging to fam. He m 1876 Julia Winchester, res Kt Island; their child., in order of birth: Josephine, Bernard, Walter, Jas, Sue, Gladys and Cardinal. Subj and wife mbrs MP Church.

721 562. JOHN D. KIRBY, res 5th dist QA co, b here 1831, s/o Sml and Mary (Carville) Kirby. Paternal grandfather, Nicholas Kirby, came from Eng, m on Kt Island; res there several yrs, returned home, and there d. He had been Eng naval officer; returning he again assoc with navy. Sml Kirby, ship carpenter; then purch farm on mainland QA Co and remained; Episc, later under influence of Major Massey, joined ME Church. His child.: Rebecca, Nicholas and subj. Subj passed boyhood on homestead; sailed bay and Chester River, with Capt Sml O. Tilghman; after 3 yrs located on part of father's estate; now owns farm (over 360 a.), about 6000 peach trees. Apr 1893 he lost most of prop through fire; recovered losses. May 7 1856 he m Annie M., d/o Rasin Gale, once mbr house of delegates from Kt Co. Their child.: Lavenia; Emma and Laura, decd, and Isabel, w/o Lewis D. Senat, business man Phila.

722 563. CAPT. JOHN WILKINSON b Apr 25 1808, Mount Pleasant, nr Centreville, great-grandson of Rev Christipher Wilkinson, app by Bishop of London to St. Paul's Parish QA Co, 1709. His father was Christipher (3d), farmer QA Co, in cav in war of 1812, in battle of Queenstown; distinguished for horsemanship.
Subj m(1) Mis Louisa Glenn Feb 11 1829, she not quite 21; she d, left no child. He moved to Zanesville, Ohio; after 2 yrs returned on horseback; taught at Purnell's shops, nr Ridgely (now) about 2 yrs; took charge of school at Ruthsburg, then school at White Marsh, nr Centreville. 1839 he became dep sheriff QA Co under Thos Sutton and dep U.S. marshal; moved to Holt's Mill, Talb Co, nr Cordova (now). 1845 he formed company for Mex War, app capt, company not activated; began in mercantile business in Centreville. Jan 1849 he m Eliza, d/o Thos DeRochbrune and granddau of Matthew DeRochbrune; the latter came to QA Co from France. He d mar 13 1889, in 81st year, leaving wid and 2 daus: w/o Chas A. Busteed, other w/o John M. Perry.

722 564. JOSEPH F. SMITH, 5th dist Car Co, enlisted 67th Pa Regt of Infantry, assigned to co G, Jan 1862; served under Stanton, wounded in battles of Winchester and the Wilderness, discharged Balt 1864. Leonard Smith, father of subj, of eastern Pa; farmer and lumbering. He m Miss Rebecca Kaler, had several child. John res Thornhurst, Pa; Elizabeth w/o Solomon Sitzer; Harriet m N. Slutter; Wm, served throughout war, d leaving 2 children; Mary d unmarried; Leonard next in order of birth; and Rebecca is Mrs. John Elsworth. Philip Smith, grandfather of subj, was from Pa. Subj b Luzerne Co, Pa, Mar 28 1838, became millwright and bridge builder; carpenter until 1877, when he came to this co and bt farm (106 a.). Dec 8 1867 he m Susan Downing, d/o Jesse and Cynthia (Rosencrans) Downing, of Wilksbarre, Pa; their child.: Emma, w/o Chas Kruger, of Newark, N.J.; Jos, decd; Lilian, w/o John Kent, this dist; Lorinda, Mrs. Elmer Cohee, of Elwood; Mary, Josias, Asa and Ira.

723 565. WILLIAM P. HORSEY, mcht, Crisfield; b Mar 12 1853 Crisfield dist, Som Co. His grandfather, Edw Horsey, b Som Co; farmer, in real-estate business, owned large amount of land and slaves; d about 70. First of Horsey fam on Eastern Shore was Stephen Horsey; settled in Som Co early 1600's. Father of subj, Capt Albert R. Horsey, b Som Co 1818, reared on farm Lawsons dist; began

-154-

as sailor on ocean and bay; owned several small vessels that sailed between Som Co and Balt; turned to farming; d at 53. He m Leah, d/o Thos Nelson; he was b this co, farmer and mcht here. She is living, at 76; mbr MP Church. Of her 7 child., 3 decd. Edw, eldest, mariner, res Crisfield; Alonzo R. in partnership with subj; and Joshua, mcht Crisfield. Subj 2nd of 4 sons; attended public schools and Wash College, Chestertown; clerked 2 yrs, entered tobacco business; 1876 opened general store with bro at Crisfield; they carry clothing, dry goods, carpets, and furniture. Subj m(1) Clara L. Roach, of Crisfield, who d 1884, leaving dau, Lillian H., student Western Md College. 1893 he m Miss Edith L. Crow, of Wilm, Del; their dau, Madeline; son, Albert C., decd. Subj attends MP Church; director Savings Bank Som Co.

566. WILLIAM S. SEYMOUR, M. D., physician, Trappe, Talb Co; b on farm Talb Co, Jan 20 1871, s/o Levin S. and Matilda A. (Berridge) Seymour. He attended dist schools and high school of Trappe; clerked in drug store at Trappe 1887-90; grad Md College of Pharmacy 1892; took charge of drug store. 1893 he attended College of Physicians and Surgeons in Balt, a year; grad medical depart Univ Md 1895; then physician in Univ hospital. 1896 he began practice in Trappe. He is mbr Episc Church; manages farm of 170 a. in the dist. 724

567. JAMES A. CONNAWAY, M. D., physician, Strait dist, Dor Co; c. 1890 came to present location; b Sussex Co, Del, Jun 24 1835, s/o Levin Connaway, of Del; res nr Concord; farmer; d at 78. His father, John, farmer, b, reared and d same section of Del. Fam, from Europe, dates back to 1700 in Del, early settlers of Sussex Co. Doctor's mother, of Del, former Matilda Anderson, d at 65; 5 of 8 child. living: Jos, of Lewes, Del; Mary J., wid; Annie E.; subj; and Rebecca, w/o Thos Joseph. Subj attended Cincinnati (Ohio) Medical College. Returning home 1861, at Akron, faced with draft into army, proceeded to Wash, D. C., took position in navy depart and marine corps for 4 yrs. After war he returned home and a practice there. After father d, subj practiced in Nanticoke Point, Wicomico Co, 4 yrs, then settled on Hooper's Island. He and wife mbrs ME Church. Aug 17 1871 he m Miss Wilhelmina Winsor, d/o Philip Winsor, of Georgetown, Del; their child.: Benj, of this place; Viola, w/o Hy W. Mills; and Galen, at home. 727

568. RICHARD LEE LINTHICUM, A. M., M. D., physician a few yrs Hooper's Island, Dor Co, now Church Creek, home of his childhod; manages old homestead with bro F. P. Subj b Apr 28 1861, s/o Richard Linthicum, of Welsh descent; his ancestor migrated c. 1643, settled in AA Co. Descendants have been planters, merchants, and ship-builders. (For ancestry this fam see sketch of Benj J. Linthicum, cousin of subj, elsewhere this vol). Subject's father b on farm opposite town of Woolford (formerly Milton), Dor Co; became capt of sailing vessel at 16; shipwrecked on Spanish Main and at Cape Hatteras when a mere youth; settled down as mcht Church Creek, with investments in lumber and land. He was b 1809, d at 80; m Miss Susan A., who was b Nov 12 1820, d/o Sml Linthicum; their child.: subj; F. Percy, assists in supervision of old plantation; and Aline Estelle, decd. - Subj educated in public and grammar schools Balt and in City college, later grad Western Md College 1883, received M. D. from Jefferson Medical College Phila 1887; practiced at home for short time, then to Hooper's Island, and finally resumed his res here. His mother still living, res at old homestead. 727

728   569. THOMAS C. SELLERS res 3rd dist Dor Co on farm known as Indian Town; tax collector this dist 1885-6 and 1887-1892; trustees of co almshouse. Thos Sellers, father of subj, from area of Denton, Car Co, came here c. 1837; farmer until he d, 1890; leader in MP Church; m Elizabeth Evans, of Car Co; of their 12 child., fol survive: Jas E., of Cabin Creek, Dor Co; Mary Jane, w/o Robinson F. Dillahay, of this neighborhood; Martha, w/o John W. Gootee; subj; John F. and Martin, both of this community; Ann, w/o Thos Dunn, of this locality; and Geo W., res this co. - Subj b Fairview, Dor Co, Apr 4 1850, attended dist school during winter season; carpenter until he m. 1891 he bt homestead, Ravenswood. Dec 23 1886 he m Gertrude, d/o Zion Sollaway, of this dist; their child.: Ollie M., Eva, Mary, Nellie, Thos, Chas, Lena and Lulu (twins), Herman, Stelle and Maggie.

729   570. SAMUEL J. COOPER mcht Sharptown, Wicomico Co, where he was b Nov 6 1842; mbr of old fam of Del, relative of Gov Cooper, of Del. His father, John, s/o Wm Cooper, of Sussex Co, Del, b and reared there; ship carpenter, later farmer; official of MP Church Sharptown; moved to Md and settled in Wicomico Co, Feb 1842, res here until 1864, when he returned to Del to res on old homestead until his death, Aug 1896.
   Mother of subj, Mary Elizabeth Lynch, b Laruel, Del; now res, at 71, on old Cooper homestead in Del; of her 13 child., fol survive: Sml J.; Margaret, w/o Jas F. Bradley, of Sharptown dist; Delilah, who m M. D. Bradley; Melvina, w/o J. W. Phillips, of Wicomico Co; Levan T., res Del; Edith, wid of Jas Waller, living with mother; John, on old homestead; Susan, wid of Jas F. Lowe, of Delmar, Del; and Sallie, Mrs. Sml K. Beach, of Del.
   Subj worked on home farm; for a while a sailor. He enlisted, Sep 28, 1861, at Church Creek, Dor Co, 1st Eastern Shore Regt, U.S.A., Lockwood's Brigade, 12th Army Corps; served 37 months; in battle of Gettysburg with Army of Potomac; most service with Army of Virginia. Capt of' vessels on bay until 1869; worked in large ship yard Wilm. An accident obliged him to relinquish this; then operated steam sawmill lower Del until 1873. With cousin, Noah C. Cooper, he bt out R. T. Wright, at Sharptown, founded firm of S. J. Cooper & Co; later purch cousin's interest. Jun 17 1892 fire destroyed newly constructed store and res; he quickly rebuilt. He also has interest in several vessels that carry freight on the bay. He is connected with MP Church. Dec 1 1874 he m Rachel A., d/o Jos Phillips, of Sussex Co, Del. She d Jul 8 1886, mother of 5 child., 3 living: Jos P., young man, assists father in store; Lena E. and Mary E., at home. Sallie T., twin of Mary, d at 1; and Sml W. M. d Jul 24 1886.

730   571. THOMAS J. SAUERHOFF, in marine railway business. Began as ship carpenter; 1885 he came to Sharptown dist, Wicomico Co, purch 1/4 of marine railway of Geo K. Phillips & Co (vessels of all sizes built and repaired here). Early mbrs of Sauerhoff fam were Germans, settled in Balt. Hy, father of subj, from N.Y.; res Balt; ship carpenter, foreman large yards there; became expert marine railway builder. He m Sarah Ann Jeffreys, still living, at 78; of their 11 child., 4 living: subj, b Balt Jul 28 1852; Kate, w/o Jacob Smith, of Bethel, Del; Jos H., of Cambridge; and Wm, res Bethel, Del. Subj left school at 16 to work in saw and grist mill. Oxford, Md, became ship carpenter; moved to Bethel, Del, followed trade there 8 yrs, returned to Md, short time in Cambridge, then to Wicomico Co 1885. Jan 13 1879 he m Julia C., d/o John B. Quillen, of Bethel, Del; of their 6 child., 4 living: Maggie L., Lillian, Harry W. and Chas.

572. ALBERT LOWE, res Bay Hundred dist, Talb Co, lawyer; grad law depart Univ of Md, and admitted to bar of Talb Co; b Nov 12 1852 this dist, passed boyhood on farm nr McDanieltown; educated in neighborhood schools, acad at Locust Grove and St. Michael's acad; grad Calvert College, Carroll Co, Md 1870, taught school in Talb Co; studied law in office of Seth, Seth & Mann, of Balt, grad law depart Univ Md 1877; opened office in Easton, moved 1884 to rural res, nr his birthplace; attended MP Church. Feb 8 1882 he m Mary F., d/o ·Frs A. and Ellen J. Wrightson, rep elsewhere this work. Children of subj and wife: Reba, Seth, Mary Graham and Carroll. 730

Wm Webb Lowe, father of subj, b nr Easton Sep 7 1804, in farming and ship building, owned large estates, res nr McDanieltown; owned several slaves; 1849-1852 sheriff this co. Jun 2 1829 he m Mary Anne, d/o Frs and Mary Anne (Lowe) Wrightson; their child.: Sarah Elizabeth, Mar 19 1830, d Jul 1830; Frs Wrightson, Jun 17 1831, d May 7 1894; Ann Catherine, Aug 1 1833, d Aug 12 1834; an infant, b Aug 5 1835, d a few hrs old; Col Jas Marion, b May 23 1837, of St. Michael's, see elsewhere this vol; infant, b Feb 21 1839, d Jul 12 1839; another infant, b Jun 1 1840, d unnamed 18th of fol month; Wm E., b May 23 1841, res McDanieltown; and John Thomas, b Apr 15 1843, lives nr McDanieltown. The mother d Sep 4 1846, at 38, 2 yrs later the father m sis of first wife; Rebecca Ann Wrightson. She was b Jul 3 1821, d Jul 2 1866; their child.: Jos Lowe, b Sep 22 1849, d Feb 8 1850; Enoch L., b Dec 15 1850, d Feb 26 1855; subj; Mary Roseline, b Aug 29 1854, d Aug 30 1855; Wilber Fisk, b Oct 21 1856, d May 9 1858; an infant d unnamed. The father d Jan 20 1863, at 58. He was s/o Wrightson and Susannah (Haddaway) Lowe. The former b nr Bay Side, this dist, Jul 9 1773, d May 13 1848; the latter, by whom he had 8 child., d/o Wm Webb Haddaway.

573. WILLIAM DALE, pres 1st Natl Bank Pocomoke City res here since 1871; owns 8 farms Wor Co (1800 a.); 1871-1888 mbr co bd of school commissioners, mbr state bd of education 15 yrs; b 1 Jan 1824, only s/o John and Elizabeth (Johnson) Dale, who spent their lives on farm. He had 2 sis: Sarah A, d in infancy; and Elizabeth, Mrs. L. P. Bowland, decd. Subj attended subscription schools; grad technological seminary Franklin, Md 1845; ordained in Easton, where he held a pastorate 2 yrs; served 5 yrs at MP Church Chestertown, 4 yrs at Cambridge, another 3 yrs Chestertown; retired with ill health; farmed at Rock Hall, Kt Co, Md 9 yrs; moved to farm nr Pocomoke City; 1871 moved to this place. He m 1849 Miss Mary Jones, of Kt Co, Md; their child.: Chas D., farmer res Pocomoke City; John A., physician Princess Anne; and Ellen, w/o Wm McMaster, res Princess Anne. 731

574. JUDGE SAMUEL CHASE, signer of Declaration of Independence, b Wicomico (then Somerset) Co, Apr 17 1741, s/o Rev Thos Chase, who emigrated from Eng and settled on Eastern Shore; pastor Stepney Parish. The lady he m res on farm south side of Wicomico River, nr Green Hill. Soon after mother d, 1743, father moved to Balt; pastor St. Paul's parish Balt, guided son through classics and sciences. Subj studied law under John Hammond and John Hall of Annapolis. At 22 he was admitted to practice in co and state courts. Locating in Annapolis, he gained a reputation as a logical lawyer and able advocate. As mbr of continental congress, foreign minister, circuit and supreme judge, Judge Chase was highly successful. 732

575. JAMES N. CUMMINGS, Tilghman's Island, Bay Hundred dist, Talb Co, shipped grain and oysters to Balt in his own sailing vessels; went into partnership with W. F. May, buying and operating oyster dredges. Nicholas, father of 732

subj, from Talb Co; came to Tilghman's Island, purch farm; farming and oyster business until he d, at 56; he and wife active in ME Chuurch. He m Mary Anne Sherwood, of this area. She d about 56, leaving child.:ʼ Caroline, wid of Rbt Runnell; Jas N. and Chas A. Subj b this island Aug 19 1853, remained with mother until she d; he was 25; soon shipped as sailor on Chesapeake Bay; invested in small sailing vessel. 1879 he m Miss Lillian Cooper, d/o Rbt and Mary Cooper, who was b and reared on this island.

733 576. RICHARD T. TURNER, JR., mcht and farmer; took charge of father's store in Betterton, Kt Co. Turner fam of Eng extraction, in this country many generations. Richard T. Turner, Sr., father of subj, s/o Jos, and grandson of Jos Turner, Sr. He was b Balt 1819, remained there until 32, came to Betterton, which he founded, giving it fam name of wife. Here he continued in grain, lumber and coal business, and farming; earlier in hardware business Balt. He d here 1892, at 73; m Elizabeth Betterton, of Balt, who lives with subj; her child.: Rachel B.; subj; Jos, of N.Y.; Anna, w/o Dr. Hy Chandler, of Balt; and Wm B., of Fort Worth, Tex. Subj b Balt 1845; at 6 his fam moved to Betterton, attended public schools and boarding school in Pa. He m Martha E. Birch, of Kt Co, had 6 child. They attend meetings of Soc of Friends.

734 577. SAMUEL FRANKLIN SMITH, owns mercantile estab, Chestertown. His Smith fam founded in America by his grandfather, Nathan Smith, of Eng, who emigrated to Md; farmer. During war of 1812 he was in battle of Caulksfield. Father of subj, Sml A. Smith, b Kt Co 1805, carpenter; retired to small farm; trustee ME Church Chestertown. He d Jan 20 1870, at 65; m Elizabeth Sappington, b Kt Co, where her father, Sml Sappington, then res; he later moved to Phila. She d 1845; of her 14 child., only subj reached maturity. After she d her husband m Anna Maria Bell; of their 4 child., 3 living: Wm A., in fertilizer business Chestertown; Emma; and Lottie, w/o Hy Greenwood.

Subj b Chestertown, Oct 3 1835. After public schools, became carpenter; entered mercantile business 1870; 1890 built store room; town and school commmissioner; trustee MP Church. Dec 3 1857 he m Mary Elizabeth Chambers, of Kt Co; of their 14 child., 3 sons and 3 daus living: Chas Sappington Smith, mcht of Chestertown; Owen C., engaged in drug business Balt; Frank W., student College of Physicians and Surgeons, Balt; Hallie Chambers, w/o Amos Kelly, mbr police force Chestertown; Katie Dodd and Fannie Giles.

735 578. JOHN H. PHILLIPS, senior mbr of firm John H. Phillips & Co, oyster packers Cambridge, Md. He and Jas Wallace first oyster packers in Cambridge. Subj b Hoopers Island, Dor Co, Oct 8 1846, s/o Geo W. Phillips; grad West River Institute, AA Co 1865, then public school teacher Dor co, 1 1/2 yrs; m 26 Feb 1867, Miss Mary P. Meekins, who d 1885, leaving fol child.: Alice D., w/o L. K. Hackett, farmer Dor Co; Wm T., who m Lizzie Mobry, and d 1893, leaving 2 child.; Carrie O., w/o Milton Richardson, of Cambridge, who had 2 child.; Victoria, who m Fred Schoenewolf, mcht of Balt, and has one child; John Jay, an oyster packer of Cambridge, who m Ida Myers; and Hy H. and Edna, both at home. 1890 Mr. subj m(2) Mrs. M. Jennie Howard; they are mbrs ME Church Cambridge. Coming to Cambridge 1877, subj embarked as a groceryman; started oyster business 2 yrs later, purchasing a vessel; sold store and engaged in livery business until 1889; since then, oyster trade, exclusively.

735 579. JAMES SANGSTON SHEPHERD, present chief dep clerk circuit court Dor Co. His father: Caleb Shepherd, b Nov 19 1812, d 1878; mother: Priscilla Elizabeth (Pattison) Shepherd, b Aug 2 1826, d 1880. The father, farmer; retired c.

1859 Cambridge; constructed 1st threshing machine Dor Co. Their child.: Jas Hooper, d in infancy; Nancy Pattison, w/o Geo Bryan, of Alexandria, Va; Frank Lockwood, of Balt, who m C. Wilsie Byrn; Elizabeth Hooper, w/o Edgar Bayly, of Cambridge; subj; Robinson Cator, d in infancy; Nellie, d in infancy; Dr. J. Hooper Pattison, decd, m Helen Robinson, of Balt, also decd; Mary Caroline, decd, and Hy Pattison, res Cambridge.

Subj b Mar 28 1858, age c. 1 year when parents settled in this town, from old homestead, about 3 miles away; educated in public schools and St. John's College, Annapolis; admitted to bar 1879; practiced law Cambridge; worked in land office Annapolis; later agent Md Steamboat Co, Cambridge office. Oct 19 1881 he m Miss Elizabeth Elen, d/o Dr. Sml H. and Margaret (Ballard) Robertson, of Som Co. Mrs. Shepherd b Som Co. Their child.: Jas Lockwood, b Dec 1 1882; Helen, Oct 15 1884, and Margaret Robertson, Aug 28 1893.

These children of 9th generation removed from ancestor, Anthony LcCompte, founder of fam in Md. An old manuscript, written 1819, by two blind bros, Thos and Dnl LeCompte, in existence. A few extracts - "Anthony Le Compte, a native of the province of Picorde, in France, on the account of his being a Protestant and was turned out and his estate confiscated to the Roman clergy, which was a custom at that time; he then fled into England, and there took up arms against the King of France, being war at that time between the two nations - so joined the British Army and fought eleven years for the King of Great Britain and when the war were over his fame was so great, and for his valour had him Knighted and the title of Monsieur given to him, and a coat of arms also, which, as we have heard from our ancestors is now in the tower of London, and in the same city came across a French lady of the name of Esther Doatlan and married her there. She also was a French Protestantess and born in the province of Normandie and turned out on account of her religion. He then took shipping and came into Chesapeake Bay and settled on the Potomack River in St. Mary's county; and after hearing of the great Choptank River being a settling, he and one Horn came in a boat together and viewed the shores up to where we now live; he then took up his lands upon the bay which was afterwards called Le Compte's Bay, the tract was called the land of St. Anthony; and Horn took up the land of Horn or Horn's Point that belongs to Charles Goldsborough, the two tracts close together. He then moved his family from the Potomack and settled upon the northern side of a creek that was afterward called Le Compte's creek, and there being so few whites and they so distant apart that he was obliged to hem himself in or be cut off by the natives which however, he averted by bringing white servants with small arms, ammunition and some cannon; and when surrounded by the savages would often disperse them by firing guns of most every size and killed some at different times, which was the sole cause of his preservation, no doubt."

After detailed and lengthy record of posterity of said Anthony and Esther Le Compte, the manuscript continues: "We will now conclude by observing that Monsieur Le Compte, though he was turned out of France because of his religion and then braved the wars of France and England and in London found his lady and came and settled in America, still after this there hath arisen the most numerous family here than every man perhaps that came across the ocean; which naturally implies that he was in favour both with God and man; as some other families are extinct and gone and no one to keep up the name, while there is hundreds of people that don't bear the name of Le Compte that is as near in blood as ome that bears the name; and we that have herad and kept this intelligence are blind men too. Now Moses the first from Monsieur, was the first that lost his sight, and he had 11 children, 9 of which lost their sight, which was a great part; but since by the blind men and women marrying into other families the proportion is much less, as from more that two thirds to less than one third; and as their gifts and talents are more and greater than those that could see, both in men and women; that women of other familes are commonly more attached to them that could see; also men of other families were much attached to the women that lost their sight; in or by so many women that lost their sight marrying with other familes, is the cause of so many blind people being in their familes, Since Moses the first that lost his sight, there have been two and forty, and now in year 18.9, there is 19 living in Dor and Talb of different familes and names. Now some foolish people that thought this misfortune that befel us on the account of the wickedness of their ancestors, but how different it is from the truth, reeason and scripture. For our Lord said, 'many are the afflictions of the righteous, but out of them he will deliver them all,' for 'whom he loveth he chasteneth and scourgeth every son that he receiveth." Read the ninth chapter of John's gospel."

In tracing the lineage of James S. Shepherd, we find following from this old record: "I now come to the second son of Monsieur Le Compte, which is Moses. Moses when about eighteen or nineteen began to lose his sight and was gone at about two or three and twenty, the time hath lsot has sight, after which he married a lady by the name of Skinner (Elizabeth), the daughter of old Skinner from England, that took up the land that now owned by Joseph Byus. She by him had eleven children." (And as named, nine of the eleven were blind.) The second son, Moses, was blind, but he m "the widow" Lavina Driver, and their son, Moses the third m Elizabeth Pattison. Of their children one was Moses (the fourth) and another, Nancy. Moses m Elizabeth Woodward and their dau Nancy was b in 1759 and became the wife of Jeremiah Pattison. Their son, James Pattison, m Elizabeth Le Compte. Their son, Jeremiah Le Compte, m Ann Le Compte Hooper, and one of their children, Priscilla Elizabeth Pattison, was our subject's mother.

738 580. HON. JOHN E. TAYLOR, 10th dist Wicomico Co, elected to Md legislature. 1881-1883 commissioner of co; assessor 1895. Subj b nr site of present home 10th dist, Nov 15 1849. His father, John B. Taylor, and grandfather, Ebenezer Taylor, b same farm; the patent given to great-grandfather of subj, dated 1760. John B, who d 1883, mcht, owned large estates and interests in sailing vessels. He m(1) Mary Walker, who d 1856. Of their 5 child., subj, and his sis Sophronia, remain. The father m(2) Mrs. Rebecca Wilson, of Dor Co; their child.: Rebecca, w/o Dison Bradley, of Dor Co, and Fannie, w/o Frank Wright, of Dor Co. Subj attended commercial college Balt. At 22 he went into partnership with father in store across river in Dor Co, firm known as J. B. & J. E. Taylor. Since 1887 he has been in milling, operating his farms and running a large cannery here' mbr MP Church. He m Sep 25 1881 Miss Annie, d/o Jacob De Frain, of Pa; their child.: Alice and Fred.

738 581. JOHN RILEY ROBINSON, business man, b Middletown, Conn., Jul 13 1810; banker Columbus, Oh.; had large railroad interests. 1860, at 50, he suffered financial reverses; then interested some moneyed men of N. Y. in mining enterprises in Mexico, through which he made large fortune; sold mines to "Boss" Sheppard, late of Wash, and purch country home, Landoff, 1st dist, Talb Co. When young, he m Jane Wilkinson, of Pittsburg; of their 12 child., 4 living. 1885 he m Catherine J. Taylor, of N.Y. On mother's side he was 4th cousin to Geo Washington. He d at home Talb Co, May 9 1890.

582. SAMUEL H. WRIGHTSON, retired, res St. Michael's dist, Talb Co. His father, Thos Wrightson, shipbuilder, res this dist; in war of 1812; d about 47. Mother of subj former Miss Eliza Harrison, d/o Jos Harrison, of old fam this co. She d at 44, leaving one child, Sml (b Sep 25 1826). When Samuel's mother d, he was in teens; spent 2 yrs with an uncle, helped in farm work; sold inherited property, bt another farm, and here he farmed until 1889; sold out and since res in fam of son and dau; being nearly blind; mbr Meth Church. 1848 subj m Hester Bartlett, of this co; she d in 32nd year; left child.: Jonathan J. and Rose G., w/o John R. Dawson, of Middletown, Del. Jonathan J. Wrightson b 1857 and reared on the farm; mbr Meth Church. He m Sarah A. McQuay, of Talb Co; their child.: Albert, Wm, Laura B. and Jonathan, Jr. 739

583. JOSEPH A. ROSS, M. D., young practitioner, Talb Co. Subj and sis Lulu only child. of A. P. and Laura A. (Woodland) Ross, of Talb and Balt Cos, respectively. Subj b Apr 28, 1875, Williamsport, Pa, lived there 8 yrs. Parents moved to Trappe dist res village 1 1/2 yrs; settled on nearby farm; studied medicine under Dr. T. W. Greenley, Trappe village; grad Univ Md 1896; opened office here; serves as vaccine surgeon Trappe dist; mbr Episc Church. 740

584. ARTHUR JEDSON, proprietor sawmill 7th dist Kt Co, b nr Belfast, Me, Jul 3 1832, remained with parents until about 10, when he shipped aboard vessel sailing Atlantic coastline, as cook; later master 12 yrs. On board government vessel during Civ War, carrying stores into Va, N.C., S.C. and Ga; witnessed capture of Fort Royal. 1865 he came to Md; engaged in construction of Reese's first wharf (later known as Tolchester Beach), Kt Co; built Quaker Neck wharf; 1868 opened country store; purch small farm where he res. After 7 yrs he sold store and engaged in sawmill business. He m Miss Lydia Coombs, of Balt; their child, Arminie, w/o G. M. Hadaway, mcht 7th dist, Kt Co. 740

585. HON. GEORGE W. BISHOP, M. D. Snow Hill, Wor Co, of old fam this co; co treasurer Wor Co; b Seaside Farm, Duer's Neck, Wor Co Jun 9 1826. His father, Capt John Bishop, d when subj infant. He had followed sea for several yrs. The mother d about 12 yrs later, leaving Geo W. an orphan in care of Geo Bishop, his mother's bro. His two elder bros now decd; subj only survivor of fam. After Snow Hill high school he grad Jefferson Medical College 1848, res Sandy Hill, now called Stockton 18 yrs; m c. 1858 Cora A. Lindsay; she d 1862. Both their child. d. 1870 Dr. Bishop m Miss Z. Ellen Rowley, who d 1887. Their child. now living, in order of birth: Geo, John, Mary, Sallie, Wm, Dorinda and Chas, all at home except John, grad medical depart Univ Pa, now at Johns Hopkins Hospital Balt. Wm is student in Rock Hill College, Howard Co, Md. Mary and Sallie grad Winchester Female Seminary, and Dorothy, high school student Snow Hill. Since 1865 subj not active in profession; 1863-4 treasurer of co school fund and 1865-73 rgtr of wills; 1863-4 post-surgeon Pocomoke City; state senator 1882-4; U. S. commissioner to New Orleans Cotton Exposition of 1884-5; U.S. subtreasurer Balt 4 yrs; help organize Fidelity and Deposit Co of Md; also the old Worcester Railroad. He is a director in Del, Md & Va Railroad and director 1st Natl Bank Snow Hill; mbr All Hallows Church Snow Hill. 741

586. THOMAS H. JENKINS b and res Easton, b May 9 1859, s/o Dr. Edw Jenkins (b nr Trappe, Talb Co, 1820). Latter attended N.Y. School of Medicine under Dr. Mott, practiced Balt Co in partnership with Dr. De Coursey, now of QA Co. Subj m Miss Elizabeth Dawson, of Talb Co, and d/o Thos H. Dawson, mbr of firm Thos & Dawson which owned store acquired by subj. Fam connnected with Easton 742

Natl Bank: Edw M. Dawson, teller and M. M. Dawson, stockholder and vice-pres. Mrs. Jenkins d Apr 17 1794, left child.: Edith D., res Easton, wid of Rbt P. Gillingham, coal operator; Edw, business man and partner of subj; Elizabeth, w/o C. D. Valk, of Balt, agent for Pillsbury Mills; subj; and Mary.
Subj educated Easton high school; at 17 began clerking at store which he and bro Edw purch 1892. 8 Oct 1892 he m Miss Elizabeth Causey, of Milford, Del; their daus: Elizabeth Causey and Frances Hunter (named for Mrs. Jenkins' grandmother). Her father, P. F. Causey, in government service; his father gov of Del. Mrs. Jenkins' uncle, John W., Causey, congressman. Her sis m McBlair Lloyd, s/o Col Edw Lloyd, whose father once gov of Md. Dawson fam mbrs Soc of Friends; maternal grandmother of Mr. Jenkins was leader and often held meetings at her home; Jenkins fam were Meth. Subj mbr Episc Church.

745 587. DAVID HURLOCK, 2nd dist QA Co; b 14 Oct 1824 1st dist Kt Co, Md, nr Massey Cross Roads, s/o Sml Hurlock. At 15 he went to Kt Co, Del, worked with bro until 1847, returned to native co, took charge of his uncle John Harrington's farm, nr birthplace, until 1849; purch farm; nows owns 3 other places. He m Miss Mary Amanda Benson, of Cecil Co; their child.: Sarah, w/o Chas Palmatary, who operates grist mill Church Hill; David T., assists father at home; and Arrana, Mrs. George Tatman.

745 588. JOSEPHUS A. WRIGHT, M. D., physician, res Sharptown, Wicomico Co. Founder of this branch of Wright fam in Wicomico Co was Edw Wright, who came from Eng c. 1700, located nr Mardela Springs. Here b his son, Jacob, and grandson, Benj, grandfather of subj and who served in war of 1812. Levin W., father of subj, b old homestead; farmer and miller; d 1883; owned large number of slaves; in company with bro, Josephus, built 1st MP Church on Eastern shore 1825; once co commissioner. He m Lizzie Bradley, d/o Eli Bradley, of Del. She is in 77th yr; her paternal grandfather, Richard, d at 102. Subj one of 5 child.; 4 survive. Louisa H. w/o C. English, of Vienna, Dor Co; Levin E. res Mardela Spring, as is also John A., next younger bro; subj b Mardela Springs Aug 2 1854, attended dist schools and grad Salisbury Acad 1873; taught school in co 5 yrs; studied medicine under Dr. S. P. Dennis, of Salisbury; grad medical depart Univ Md 1881; physician and surgeon to Confed Soldiers' Home Balt 6 yrs. 1892 he estab practice here. 3 Mar 1881 he grad from college and that afternoon m Miss Jennie Holmes, d/o Rev Wm G. Holmes, minister MP Church this area. Their child.: Berkley H. and Arthur L.

746 589. GEORGE E. BIBBY d 1879. Father of subj, Hy Bibby, of Lake dist, Dor Co, ship builder, farmed to some extent, res nr birthplace; sheriff Dor Co; d c. 1860. He m Miss Sarah Graham, of Lake dist; she d 1863; of their 12 child. 4 living: John, Matthew, Frank and Jas R. The father of Hy, John Bibby, left Eng, res Lake dist, Dor co. Subj b 1833 Lake dist; began farming on his own in old home dist, and conducted general store in Golden Hill; d Jun 19 1879. 1861 he m Miss Angie Insley, d/o Jos Insley at Crapo. They had 2 sons and a dau; sole survivor: Mark Ottaway. Mrs. Bibby moved from Golden Hill to Balt shortly after death of husband. 1893 she located permanently in Cambridge; became mbr Cath Church short time after husband's death. Father of Mrs. Bibby, Jos Insley, b Dor Co, Nov 1798; m Miss Matilda Love of Va, b 26 Nov 1798 (known for her exceptionally fine penmanship). Of her 12 children, 2 living; 3 grandchildren and 10 great-grandchildren survive.

747 590. WINFIELD WEBSTER owns and operates farm (300 a.) Vienna dist, Dor Co; sells machinery, carriages and phosphate; tax collector 1895-6. Subj b May 3

1862 nr East New Market, Dor Co. His father, Sml L., and grandfather, John Webster, b same neighborhood, descendants of 1 of 2 bros who came together from England. John, farmer, left large estate; pres Dor and Del Railroad. Subj attended country schools, began farming; m Priscilla A., d/o Benj Shepard, of Berlin, Wor Co, mbr of old fam. She is living at 60; had 11 child., fol survive: John B.,traveling salesman, headquarters Balt; Noah, res Cambridge; subj; Shepard, of Cambridge; Frank, res East New Market; Chas and Roland (twins), former res East New Market, latter in Cambridge; Sml, of East New Market; and Lloyd, at home. 1884 subj moved to farm, Hoopersborough, prop of father. Subj is Bapt; m Feb 6 1885 Ida A., d/o Levin R. Moore, of Vienna dist. Of their 5 child., 3 living: Guy L., Marion and Nellie.

591. JAMES S. HARRIS. Earliest mbr of this Harris fam in America was Jas Harris, of England, settled in Talb Co c. 1700; had a grant to land here. His son, Richard S., mbr first ME conference in America, in Balt. John Harris, s/o Richard S., b Talb Co; moved to Del where he owned large tract; d there. He had son, Richard H., subject's father, b and reared in Del, but after his marriage moved to Kt Co, Md, purch farm where subj res. Richard became a pioneer in peach industry; mbr ME Church; m Matilda Shepard, of Car Co; their child.: Dr. John Harris, of Balt; subj; Mary, w/o Hy Crusen; Annie, who m Wm H. Bowers; and Catherine, Mrs. H. L. Crew. The father d Jan 1867, at 56; the mother d 1882 at 69.

Subj b 1838 Del; at 11 months fam came to Md. He was educated public schools Kt Co, Md, at 21 went to Balt, where employed 2 yrs; 1862 to Calif, where he spent 2 yrs in mining districts; 1864 returned to Kt Co, where he has since res. He owns 3 farms (700 a.), 3rd dist; once chief judge orphans' court, mbr co school bd; trustee dist schools; mbr ME Church. He m Margaret Grier, of Balt, 1866; their child.: Jas G., operates farm nr old homestead; Carson W., tills one of father's farms; Arthur L., principal Kennedyville school; and Walter, student in local school.

592. WILLIAM B. USILTON, as a boy, in 1852, entered office of Kent News as printer's "devil;" was partner with Jas H. Plummer, 30 yrs, until death of Mr. Plummer 1890. The interest then purch by son, Fred G. Usilton. Subj b Kt Co, Md Sep 26 1837, named after uncle, Wm Barger, influential Mason of Phila. Father of subj, Rbt, b Kt Co; farmer, taught school and served as magistrate; d 1850. He had two bros, Jos and Frs, former a land owner, latter a farmer. The three bros m three sis, Jos m Sarah Lamb, while Rbt m Mary Lamb. The latter survived her husband 15 yr; she d 1865.

Suj 5th in order of birth of 8 child.: Rbt, farmer and carpenter, res Smithville, Kt Co; Sml, carpenter, res Phila; Adaline, w/o Thos A. Hudson, of Kt Co; Edwin L., police lieut Phila; Wm Barger; Gustavus, mechanic, res Camden, N.J.; Albert, mechanic, res Plano, Ill.; and Washington, d Plano 1894. 1852, after common school education, subj entered composing room of Kt News, becoming its owner; co treasurer 1890-2; super- intendent Chestertown MP sunday school 30 yrs. 1862 he m Mary F., d/o Sml Frazier, mcht of Chestertown, one of 3 child., her sis and bro: Martha, w/o Milton Baker and Sml M. Frazier, both of Chestertown. Mr. and Mrs. Usilton are parents of: Miriam, w/o P. T. McFeely, furniture dealer; Fdk G., his father's partner in business; Wm B., Jr., connected with newspaper office; Clara; Milton Earl, student Hahnemann Medical College of Phila; and Louise, d Apr 1895, at 12.

593. CLARENCE L. VINCENT, newspaper man, mbr of firm Purnell & Vincent, of Snow Hill, s/o Thos H. and Caroline (Toadvine) Vincent, of Wor Co. He is a

descendant on paternal side, of French Huguenot fam that suffered persecution for religious beliefs, on revocation of Edict of Nantes were obliged to flee from France. His father in merchandising in Salisbury as mbr of firm Toadvine & Vincent, and there, Feb 5 1861, subj b. His father d c. 1868, forcing him into business at early age. At 12 he entered office of Salisbury advertiser; then compositor on paper in Dover Del 1 year; then printing offices Phila. 1883 he m Miss Virginia L. Pain, of Berlin, Wor Co, Md.; returned to newspaper work Salisbury. Jan 1887 with partner, O. M. Purnell, he purch Snow Hill Democratic Messenger. The Snow Hill Democratic Messenger founded 1867 by Col John Handy, since conducted as Democratic organ. From Col Handy it passed to Geo M. Upsher and T. H. Moore; on death of Mr. Moore interest purch by John Walter Smith; then run as leased paper until purchase by Purnell & Vincent. Subject's dau Beulah, aged 13; fam mbrs Presby Church.

750 594. CAPT. HEDGE THOMPSON, commodore Chesapeake Yacht Club, for yrs in command of oyster navy, of Longwoods, 4th dist Talb Co; b Salem, N.J. Sep 13 1834, s/o Thos and Rebecca (Johnson) Thompson, of same area; of English extraction. The father of Thos was Hedge Thompson, physician, in Rev war, native of Salem. Thomas Thompson was first a druggist, later farming. He d 1844. After attending school in N.J., at 16 began clerking at wholesale grocery store, owned by uncle, on Water st, Phila; bt Forest Landing (700 a.) 1857, his pres res; vestryman All Saints' Episc Church, Longwoods. He m(1) Miss Acksah Peterson, of N.J., who d 1865. He m(2) Mary R. Wrightson; no children by either marriage. Subject's mother d/o Wm Johnson, b and reared nr Salem, N.J.; d Jan 1887. Her father bt 1800 a. of old Lloyd estate 1845. He was accidently drowned crossing Chesapeake Bay, enroute Balt.

751 595. BENJAMIN TAYLOR, decd, former res Easton dist Talb Co; vestryman in Christ Episc Church, of Easton; b 1819, d Feb 11 1892; in merchandising Hillsborough, Caroline Co. Jun 29 1869 he m Ann E. Atkinson, d/o Thos Atkinson, of Car Co. Of their 4 child., 2 d; 2 daus remain: Ida May, w/o Jas Locke Erwin, of Burlington, N.C.; and Anna, unmarried, at home.

752 596. ZACHARY W. WEBSTER, postmaster Deal's Island, Som Co, 1882-6, mcht, farmer and market gardener; s/o Wm J. Webster, of this island. Wm J. Webster followed sea; later farmer here; d abt 81. His father, Jacob, d at 83; seafarer and farmer, of English extraction. Wm J. Webster m Mary P., d/o John Webster. Of their 10 child. fol living: Jacob W.; Wm J.; Julia, Mrs. L. L. Shores; Melissa J., Mrs. Hampton B. Walter; Isabel, Mrs. Lazarus Wilson; and subj. The mother d in 78th year; she and husband mbrs ME Church.

Subj b Deal's Island 1841; attended public school; c. 22 yrs in oyster fisheries; became owner of several vessels. Since 1875 he has managed his general store on island. He m 1867 Miss Emily J., d/o Geo A. Gibson, of this place; their child.: Wm C.; Edw Z.; John W.; Ada E., w/o John W. Horner; Sadie V. and Eugene Brown, all res the island. Fam attend ME Church.

752 597. LEVIN B. DISHAROON farmer Snow Hill dist, Wor Co; b Oct 17 1856, Wor Co. His parents, Wm and Hettie A. (Bailey) Disharoon, of Eastern Shore, had 8 child., in order of birth: Levin, Chas R., Wm A., Emory L., B. Ella, Mary A., Jas and Hy W. Their grandfather, Levin W. Disharoon, farmer of Wicomico Co; sheriff. His father res same co, owned large estates. Subj owns 150 a. and farm of 325 a.; mbr MP Church; m 20 OIct 1880 Miss Emma E. Carmean, of this area; their child.: Essie L., Lillian B., Marion B. and L. Wilson.

598. WILLIAM J. HALL, young business man, Brinkley's dist, Som Co. 6 Sep 753
1897 he lost mills in a fire but soon rebuilt them. At 18 he embarked as a
mcht; at c. 24 erected mills here; owns and manages Glendale stock farm,
raising market vegetables, for shipment to the cities. Subj b Brinkleys dist
on father's farm, Apr 19 1867, in fam of 10 child., 2 decd, others: Corinne
E., Mrs. W. E. Miles; I. Hy; Jennie; Clara, Mrs. Chas H. Speightes; Florence,
Mrs. Luther T. Miles, Jr.; Ethel and Gertrude. Feb 18 1890 Mr. Hall m Miss
Susan, d/o Lewis and Mary (Lankford) Lankford, of Fairmount dist; their
child.: Lewis and Mary; they attend Trinity MP Church.
    Father of subj, Henry W. Hall, this dist; b here 1827, s/o Richard and
Martha (Lankford) Hall, only survivor of their 8 child. Richard Hall, native
of this locality; farmer and shoe maker; mbr ME Church, his wife identified
with Presby; he d in 62 yr. Hy W. Hall was a sailor 7 yrs, began at 16; then
engaged in oyster trade; during Civil war his ships burned by Federal troops
in Virginian waters. He m Elizabeth Whittington; she d 1885.

599. DEWITT C. FOOKS, of Coulbourn dist, Wor Co, once sheriff, b this co Jun 754
2 1833. The great-great-grandfather of subj on paternal side came to Md from
Eng. His son Jesse, b on Eastern Shore, operated large estate and dealt in
lumber. His son Jas, grandfather of subj, ran a sawmill and farmed on large
scale. Subject only surviving child in fam of 3 three bros and sisters, whose
parents were Hance and Julia (Howard) Fooks, both natives of this area. The
father b 1785. Subj taught school at 18 (2 yrs), then farming; owns c. 2000
a.; m(1) Apr 1852 Miss Mary Fooks, of Wor Co. She d 1854, in 31st year. Feb
18 1857, subj m(2) Mary A. Schockley, of this co; of their 8 child., 2 decd;
remaining: Margaret A., Sallie M., Lucy B., Julie H., E. Hance and DeWitt F.
3 daus m 3 bros named Truit. Subj and wife mbrs MP Church.

600. HENRY S. MATTHEWS, business man, Oxford, Talb Co, res here; trustee of 754
high school; town commissioner; b father's farm Oxford Neck, Talb co, Sep 15
1859. His father, Dr. Alexander Matthews, b Georgetown, D. C., May 26 1826;
studied medicine with Dr. Grafton Tyler; grad Univ Md 1848; prev attended
Princeton; physician in hospital connected with univ, then private practice in
Georgetown; bt farm 3rd dist this neighborhood, where subj; estab drug store
in Oxford now carried on by his son. Dr. Tyler was vestryman Episc Church; d
Oct 1890, buried Oak Hill Cem, nr Georgetown. He m Anne Spencer, b 3rd dist
Talb Co, now res with subj. She had 2 child., other child, a son, Albert E.,
d in infancy. Subj attended grammar and high schools of this village. At 17
he entered store of Mitchell & Co., of which his father was a silent partner.
Mr. Beall purch interest of senior partner, and subj admitted to firm, Beall &
Matthews. He then bt out Mr. Beall's share. 1883 he m Susanna Harrison;
their child, Emory. Family mbrs Episc Church.

601. NATHAN J. P. TULL, mcht and truck farmer Som Co;owns general store at 755
Marion Station; superintends farm near by, raising strawberries; b nr his
present res, Jan 1843, s/o Nathan T. and Emeline B. (Parker) Tull, of this
locality. His father was large land owner; and owned number of slaves; ran
large tannery at Tulls Corner; mbr ME Church; d at 57. His wife was Meth, d
at 58. Of their 8 child. 6 living: Rev. Wm T. Tull, of Wilm, Del; Margaret
J., w/o John B. Ward; Nathan J. P.; Jos S., res nr Tulls Corner; Annie O., w/o
Isaac T.Connor, of Iowa; and John E., res Crisfield.
    At 17 subj entered Williamsport (Pa.) College; after 2 yrs taught school
Som Co 2 ys; then opened general store nr Tulls Corner, moved to Marion
Station; since 1892 tax collector for his dist; 1891-3 sheriff. 1876 he m

-165-

Miss Jennie F., eldest d/o Southey F. Miles (see his sketch elswhere this vol). Their child.: Miles, Harding P., Christiana M. and Edna J., aged respectively 20, 15, 13, and 5. Mr. Tull is a worker in MP Church.

756   602. S. FRANK WHITTINGTON, young farmer Brinkleys dist, Som Co; b Lawsons dist, this co 1858, s/o Stephenson and Jane (Tull) Whittington. His father and grandfather (the latter Southey Whittington) b and reared that dist; farmers. The grandfather d at 80. The father still living, retired.
   Subj is one of 9 child.; 6 survive; S. F. is 5th in order of birth of those living. The others: Eliza, w/o N. T. Connor; Jos H.; Chas S.; Emma C., w/o W. H. Hayman; and Alfred A., superintending old home place. The mother b this dist; mbr ME Chursh; d in 77th yr. Subj received a general education in dist schools. When 22 he purch the Cahoon farm, nr Tulls Corner; he is a mbr ME Church. Jul 29 1884 he m Sallie Adams, d/o Sml T. Adams, of this dist; their child.: Austin L. and Norman T.

757   603. CHARLES E. HENDERSON, general manager Phila and Reading Coal and Iron Co, 2nd vice-pres Phila & Reading Railroad Co, res Phila, spends a portion of each year at country home, The Rest, Easton dist, Talb Co. The estate (100j a.), formerly owned by Adm Buchanan, on Miles River, nr Easton.
   The first Henderson of this fam in America was Alexander Henderson, of Glasgow, Scotland. His son, Richard, was father of John, of Montgomery Co, Md; latter had a son, Richard, of that co, b 1801. The last named, farmer, m Elizabeth Ann Beall English, dau of David English, banker of Wash, D. C. Richard Henderson d 1860; his wife d 27 yrs later. They were parents of Sarah T., wid of Wm T. Daugherty, atty of Jefferson Co, W.V.; John, decd, civil engineer, chief engineer in charge of construction of Del. & Chesapeake Railroad; David, res Jefferson Co, W.V.; Janet, w/o John Hilleary, of Roanoke, Va.; Arianna, missionary in Brazil; Elizabeth, w/o Dr. John W. Hilleary, of Frederick Co, Md; Richard, occupies old homestead Jefferson Co, W.V.; Chas E.; Minnie, res Roanoke, Va; Geo, res Kensington, Pa; and Norman F., res state of Washington.
   Subj b at family home Jefferson C., W.V. Sep 25 1844;; attended school in Georgetown, D. C.; studied medicine at Univ of Pa (grad 1869); res physician Bayview Hospital, Balt; practiced in Martinsburg, W.V. a year; clerk to railroad agent Fort Scott, Kan.; then clerk to railroad agent Kansas City; chief clerk to general superintendent; in charge of land depart; inspector of new routes; confidential agent for buying stock and bonds of other railroad lines; then entered service of Indianapolis, Bloomington & Western Railroad, general manager 8 yrs. Res Indianapolis 10 yrs; went to Phila as general manager Phila and Reading Coal and Iron co; Dec 1 1896 app 2nd vice-pres Phila & Reading Railway. Oct 22 1879 he m Miss Ida M. Lynn, d/o Wm Lynn, once treasurer of Muskingum Co, Ohio. They have 2 sons, Chas E. and Wm L.

758   604. GEORGE ALBERT THOMPSON b homestead which he now farms East New Market dist, nr East New Market. Youngest and only survivor of several child, subj b May 24 1843, s/o Mitchell and Celia (Webster) Thompson, of this co; mbrs MP Church. The father s/o Thos Thompson, of direct English descent. Subject's bro, Thos, d young, and another bro, James M., also d after reaching maturity. A sis, Elizabeth, m Jas R. Donoho; she d at 50. Subj served as judge orphans' court 2 terms . He and fam identified with Bapt Church. Jul 2 1868 when about 25, Mr. Thompson m Sarah Olivia Hearn; their child.: Chas M., Jasper L., Annie E., Celia, Leila, Lottie, Mattie, Geo, Grace and Myra.

605. JOHN N. USILTON; went to work at 13; became bookkeeper and accountant; justice of peace; b 2nd dist Kt Co, Feb 26 1815, d Chestertown Jun 18 1885; trustee ME Church. He m Sarah M. Potter, b nr Albany, N.Y., d/o Amos and Ann M. Potter. Her maternal grandmother belonged to Lake fam on the Hudson. Her only son, John Gale Usilton, educated in military acad Chester, Pa, 3 yrs; went to Texas, met and m Miss Lucia Grover; they res on old homestead Kt Co, where he farms. He and wife have 2 child., Herbert and Clarence. 758

606. E. JAMES TULL, pres town council Pocomoke City, Wor Co, mbr bd of trustees of high school; ship building and repairing of boats since he attained majority. 25 Dec 1896-Apr 1897 he ran a passenger and freight boat, Balt-Snow Hill and intermediate points. Subj b nr Westover, Som Co, Jan 19 1850, s/o John C. and Jane Tull of Md, on paternal farm; after public school and reaching majority he came to this village; worked in ship yards of Wm J. S. Clark & Co, 6 yrs; then formed partnership Hall Bros & Co 10 yrs. 1884 he leased W. J. S. Clark ship yards, on Pocomoke River; consturcted a steamship 133 feet long, 24 feet wide and 11 feet deep; medal awarded him at Chicago World's Fair on his model of an oyster boat. He makes schooners, steamers and boats of all kind. At present he has under way a yacht for Thos Dixon, Jr., of New York City. Subj is mbr ME Church. 1870 he m Matilda McDaniels, who d 8 yrs later, leaving 4 child.: Edw, Underwood, Bertie and Bessie. Underwood and Edward working with father as ship builders. 1881 Mr. Tull m Miss Anna Ross; they have 4 daus: Mattie, Casie, Jennie and Gertrude. 759

607. JOHN S. GRIFFITH, business man, Easton, Md, b Dec 11 1852, Newark, Del, s/o David B. Griffith, of Del. At 1 year his parents moved to Kt Co, Md. David B. was mcht; later turned to farming. C. 1867 he came to Talb Co; active until shortly before his death, 1871, at 45; once co commissioner. His father from Wales, farmer, worker in Bapt Church; came to America with 2 bros, one of whom went to Calif, left large estate. Grandfather Griffith had fam of 6 sons and 1 dau. Mother of subj, Julia, d/o Dr. John and Julia Sutton. The latter d about 65; Mrs. Julia Griffith still living, res Balt. Of her 7 child. fol living: John S., eldest; Alice, w/o A. W. Woodal, Jr., of Kt Co; Ella, who m Thos Hooper, of Chesapeake City, Md.; Margaret, with her mother in Balt; Lizzie, m and res Balt; and David, of Balt, in commission business with bro-in-law. After schools of Easton, subj clerked with firm of Thompson & Kersey; in charge of the business within 6 months. 1880 he embarked in a venture of his own; he m 1877 Kate E. Lynch, of Easton, d/o Wm and Elizabeth Lynch; their dau named in honor of his mother, d an infant. Mr. and Mrs. Griffith attend Episc Church. 760

608. CHARLES H. FLEMING res 6th dist Car Co; b Feb 15 1833, Kt Co, Del, s/o Nathan and Mary (Turner). Both parents from Kent Co; had 7 child., 4 decd. Those living: Chas H., Thos L. and Sarah Elizabeth. Father of Nathan Fleming was Benniah Fleming, b Del, extensive landholder Kt Co, in war of 1812. His father, Wm Fleming, b Scotland, settled in Del prior to Rev war, in which he participated. At 22 subj went into farming. Dec 24 1854 he m Frances Powell, b and reared Del, whose grandfather, Geo Powell, veteran of war of 1812, later farmer of Kt Co, Del. Children of Mr. and Mrs. Fleming: Frances J., Mary E., Cyrenius C., Sarah M. Susan C., Wm F., Geo S., Jas W. and 1 d in infancy. Fam attend ME Church. 763

609. RILEY M. STEVENSON, chief fire depart Pocomoke City since 1892; started grist mill here 1872. Besides turning out various kinds of meal and feed, 763

-167-

mill has capacity of 50 barrels of flour per day. Subj b Snow Hill, Wor Co, Nov 22 1845, s/o Thos F. and Maria Stevenson, of Md. About 15 he became engineer on steamboat. 1865 he came to Pocomoke City and opened wood working estab, making doors, windows, blinds and moldings for house builders until 1872, when he converted a bldg into grist mill. 1872 he m Miss Bettie M. Merrill; of their 4 child., one, Willie, is decd, others: Bessie, Riley P. and Mary. Mr. Stevenson is elder and mbr Presby Church.

764 610. HON. WILLIAM D. HOPKINS served in Md house of delegates; business man Cambridge, Dor Co, his grocery in Masonic Temple. He is eldest living son in fam of 10 child.: Jos H. and Purnell J., decd. The others: Sarah E., Mrs. L. J. Stewart, of Norfolk, Va; W. D.; Laura M., w/o J. Ben Brown, architect Cambridge (see his sketch); Mary E., w/o A. J. Foble, manufacturer of this place (see his sketch elsewhere this vol); Thos J., sailor and owner of 2 vessels, res Balt; John W., mcht, res James River Va; J. Richard, partner of John W.; Edwin C., grocer Cambridge; and Annie, w/o V. L. Rea, brick manufacturer this town. Their parents were Wm and Eliza (Brooks) Hopkins. The father living in Cambridge; his wife d c. 15 yrs ago.

Subj b Apr 3 1847, reared this dist; sailor 4 yrs, but after his marriage he went into merchandising at Church Creek (c. 6 yrs), moved to Cambridge; sailed on inland waters of bay 3 yrs, turned to farming; worked in ship yards here as ship carpenter. Since 1890 he has conducted a grocery, corner of Locust and West End ave, moved to present place 1894. He is building houses in Cambridge in West End. 1896 he was elected to Md house of delegates. 1872 he m Miss Margaret P., d/o Sml Christopher, ship builder, formerly of Church Creek. They had 10 child., 5 survive: Uhlan D., mbr of firm W. D. Hopkins & son, and in livery business here; Eliza B., Addie, Arthur and Ethel. Mrs. Hopkins is mbr ME Church.

765 611. OWEN C. BLADES; farmer and fruit grower 4th dist Car Co; homestead adjoining village of Choptank; part of town built on original tract. Blades fam early settlers of Md from Eng. Grandfather Isaiah Blades b, reared and buried, on old farm owned by Captain Cockran. He left large estates to his several children; much of land still owned by fam. Parents of subj: Isaiah C. and Milcah (Todd) Blades (d/o Sml Todd). Isaiah Blades b Fowling Creek, now known as Union Grove, and there reared. Their child.: Anthony, d unmarried; Eli K., d, leaving no child.; Julia E., w/o Jas Payne, d leaving 4 child.; Irene, w/o Capt N. J. Cockran; Christina, wid of Poulson E. Hubbard; Armelia, who m Robert Patton; Martha, Mrs. J. P. J. Hubbard; subj; and Emily, w/o W. T. A. Lockerman, of Easton. Subj b Mar 13 1848 4th dist Car Co; purch farm 1884, moved here fol year. 1869 he m Miss Rhoda A. Fountain, d/o Wm and Maria (Hubbard) Fountain. Their child.: Minnie M., w/o Clarence E. Smith; Alva F., Luther L., Anah L., Elsie, Geo V. and Norman R. Fam mbrs MP Church.

765 612. PROF. M. BATES STEPHENS, examiner of schools and res Denton, b Oct 5 1862 Tuckahoe Neck, Car Co, s/o Wm B. Stephens, of Kt Co, Del. Wm B. Stephens came to Car Co 1858 and settled on farm; collector of taxes 4 yrs; d 1884; s/o Thos C. Stephens, native and res of Del. Mother of subj Sarah, d/o John Wooters, mbr of old Del fam, b Kt Co, Del, 1833, d Car Co 1878. Her child.: Jas A., in mercantile business Crisfield, Md; John W., farmer at Burrsville, Car Co; and subj. Subj educated in common schools; then Greensborough Acad 2 yrs. 1880 he entered Dickinson College, Carlisle, Pa, his stay cut short by father's death; studied on his own, then given degree A. M. by college. His

entire career devoted to teaching; once principal Greensborough schools; 1886 elected examiner of schools.

613. ROBERT W. RANDALL, East New Market, Dor Co, town commissioner here; b Cambridgeshire, Eng, Oct 22 1842, s/o Wm and Eliza (Jarvis) Randall; emigrated a young boy with parents and settled in Rochester, N. Y. There he grew to manhood. Parents d Rochester, leaving 2 sons and 5 daus, of whom subj is eldest. Others: Mary, Mrs. Harry Kemp; Eliza, Emma, Lucy, Lillie and Harry. At 19 subj enlisted in Company L., 1st N.Y. Lt Artillery, commanded by Capt John A. Reynolds, 1861 proceeded with them to Balt, spent winter. Fol spring they joined army of Potomac; at battle of Antietam he was wounded and sent to hospital; mustered out Nov 1865. Jul 4 1864 Mr. Randall m Miss Mary Throp, Muncie, Pa, a few yrs later they moved to this dist, where they res on farm 8-9 yrs. 1881 he engaged in milling here; also handles coal, lumber and shingles; recently estab roller mill; owns farm nr village. The only child of Mr. and Mrs. Randall is Ella, w/o Walter Willis, of East New Market. Parents mbrs Bapt Church. 766

614. JAMES ARTHUR SAXTON, res Dor Co, b 1845, New Market dist where he now res. Father of subj, Thos J. Saxton, b and reared Del, m sis of Wm P. Smithers, of Del. After birth of one son, Wm, and death of mother, he came to Dor Co, where he m Harriet, wid of Whiteley Beckwith and d/o Jacob Howard, latter a direct descendant of Roger Williams. Jacob Howard and John Webster, father of Sml L. Webster, m sisters, Leah and Rebecca Simmons, respectively, daus of Levin Simmons. The first husband of Mrs. Saxton had 3 child. by his marriage to her. He was a widower with 1 child. Subject's father lived in Cambridge, but Jan 1845, came to East New Market and fol year settled on farm. At 16, on death of his father, subj assumed charge of the farm. 1878 he embarked in phosphate and farming implement business. 1870 he m James Anna, d/o Capt Jas Le Compte, once citizen of the co. Their child.: Eustace P., purser on steamer Avalon; Clarence L., traveling salesman for McCormick Harvesting Machine Co; May and Thomas. Fam identified with ME Church. 767

615. HON. PHILEMON BLAKE HOPPER, state's atty 1883-96. Grandfather of subj, Judge Philemon B. Hoppper, b QA Co; mbr of bar of Centreville; judge circuit court; local minister MP Church; d 1858. Father of subj, Philemon B. Hopper, b nr Centreville 1816, educated principally in Easton high school. Entering legal profession, elected to legislature as young man; mbr MP Church; d Dec 28 1870. Mother of subj, Henrietta, d/o Dr. Rbt Goldsborough, of old QA Co fam; she d Jun 28 1878. She had son and 2 daus, latter, Mary Ann, w/o Wm E. Thompson, justice of peace Centreville; and Fannie, Mrs. Wm Harper McFeely, of Chestertown. Subj b Centreville Mar 25 1853, educated Centreville Acad. 1868-70 St. John's College at Annapolis; grad Western Md College 1874; studied law, admitted to bar 1878, private practice until 1883. 767

616. EDMUND B. PENNINGTON res farm 2nd dist Kt Co; b and reared, Del; moved to Md 1869 and settled on farm at Howell Point. 1879 he purch the Wilson farm. For fam history see sketch of W. D. Pennington. Subj b Newcastle Co, Del 1837, assisted with farm work until 20 when he went to Mo., intending to make it his home; returned to Del, manager for Wm Ryebold 9 yrs. Subj mbr Episc Church. 1870 he m Mary A. Tucker, of Balt; of their 6 child., 4 living: Marion; Edmund; Mary, w/o Geo Sutton, and Elizabeth. 768

769 617. HON. JOSEPH H. JOHNSON, Cambridge, elected to house of delegates 1877 and state senate 1887 and 1893; author of the oyster laws of Md; chairman of Chesapeake Bay tributary commission.
Johnson fam in America in 1600's, of Eng extraction. Grandfather of subj was in war of 1812, for which he built a number of privateers. Edw C., subject's father, wasleft an orphan at 9, soon afterward shipped on board a large sea schooner, captain of a vessel before he was 21; later a shipbuilder on Little Choptank, where he owned 800-900 a. of fruit land. He m(1) Amelia Ross Wallace, of Scotch descent; they had 10 child.; subj was second. All grew to maturity, 5 living: Dr. L. E. Johnson, of Wash, D. C.; Jos Hy; Susan, m and res Wash; Helen, w/o Dr. Richard Dixon, of Cambridge; and Emma, w/o Calvert Orem, of Cambridge. By 2nd marriage, Edw C. Johnson had 4 child.: Jas C., bookkeeper Natl Bank of Cambridge; Sewell, studying law under John G. Mills Cambridge; Mrs. Martha Hooper, res Cambridge; and Margaret, at home. Father of these child. d Cambridge 1883, at 75.
Subj b Oct 28 1838 Lakesville, Dor Co; attended common schools, then Dickinson College, Carlisle Pa 2 yrs; entered office of Chas F. Goldsborough, with whom he studied law; admitted to bar. 1867 he purch Dorchester News which he consoldiated with Democrat; built low income housing. 1877 he built marine railway and ship yard in Cambridge. 1882 he sold paper to John G. Mills. Oct 12 1881 he m Fannie W., d/o Rev Jacob Mann, of Va Conference; of their 4 child., 2 living, Hy and Jos Marvin. An older son, Wallace, d Aug 28 1897. Mr. Johnson is identified with Episc Church.

770 618. WILLIAM G. SMITH, D. D. S. succeeded father as dentist in Salisbury 17 yrs ago; mbr city council; b this place, Jul 30 1858, eldest of 3 child., of Dr. Wm T. and Margaret (Garrison) Smith. Father from Del, while mother from N. J., both grew up in Del. Dr. Wm T. Smith 1st dentist to locate in Salisbury, and here he engaged in practice, until shortly before his death, 1880. Subj, in partnership with bro, Dr. Edgar W. Smith, res Salisbury. The sis, M. Virginia, w/o Geo R. Collier. Subj grad Pa College of Dental Surgery 1880. His father d few months later, and he took up his practice here.

770 619. JAMES BLACK MERRRITT, M. D., Easton, b Odessa, Del, Oct 28 1858, Meth, mbr of old Eastern Shore fam. His father, Rev Jas Black Merritt, D. D., b Kt Co, Md 1826; grad Dickinson College. Entered into ministry of ME Church, mbr Wilm Conference; held pastorates in Chestertown, Centreville, Cambridge, and Wilm, Del. Subject's mother, Hannah, d/o Dr. Sml Webb, of Kt Co, Del, mbr of old fam long of that section. Her two sons are Jas Black and Sml Webb. Subj attended school in various places where fam resided; Wilm high school, later school in Pa; grad Univ of Vermont 1879. Returning to Md, he opened an practice at Hanesville, Kt Co. 1889 he came to Easton. He m Georgetta, d/o Alexander Parks, of Kt Co, Md; their child.: Jas Black and Adeline Carr.

771 620. WILLIAM H. KNOWLES, senior mbr of wholesale hardware firm, W. H. Knowles & Co, and junior mbr of firm, A. W. Robinson & Co, res Sharptown, Wicomico Co, where he was b Nov 8 1862. His first busines venture was with W. W. Selby, in 1885 as Knowles & Selby, undertakers, contractors and builders. The wholesale hardware company organized 1895, composed of W. H. Knowles and A. W. Robinson, of Sharptown, and J. Dallas Marvil, s/o ex-Gov Joshua H. Marvil, of Del. These men also bt the berry crate and basket factory, chief industry of town. It was estab earlier in 1872 by late John Robinson, whose bro, Jas, became assoc with him as John Robinson & Bro. (Information is given on plant, facilities and operation of company.)

-170-

Subj of Scotch ancestry. His father, Geo R., b Sussex Co, Del, as was his grandfather, John Knowles. The former, a sea captain, traded along coast until 1865, when vessel lost and he was drowned; he was mbr ME Church. He m Mary, d/o Alger Russell, of Riverton, Wicomico Co; she is still living, at 56. Of her three child., subj only survivor. He was edcuated in schools of Sharptown; worked in carpenter's trade at age 16 to 24, until organizing firm of Knowles & Selby. Subj is mbr of co central committee and sub-fish commissioner for Wicomico Co; mbr ME Church. Feb 4 1885 he m Lizzie E., d/o Capt J. W. Bennett, once postmaster Sharptown under Pres Harrison.

621. JOHN H. TOLSON owns over 1200 a. in lower part Kt Island; school teacher 772 3 1/2 yrs, proprietor of general store Stevensville. Subj b Kt Island, nr Stevensville 1829, s/o Benj and Ann (Legg) Tolson. His father b Kt Island c. 1784, farming nr birthplace. He and wife lived in cabin with dirt floor. His children: Mary, 1st w/o Arthur Carter and later m Chas Downs; Benj, who d, leaving fam who res QA Co; Ann, w/o Jas M. Stevens, of Kt Island; Caroline, who m Jos Bright; Elizabeth and subj (twins), former m Luther W. Bryan, of Kt Island. Tolson is old Md fam. 1864 subj m Mary Victoria, d/o Jas S. Cockey, located in Stevensville, in merchandising until 1881, when he moved to the country. He has 3 sons: J. Harry, at home; Jas Sudler, who m Miss Minnie Lowe, of Centreville; and Wm Denney.

622. ROBERT JARRELL; po address: Goldsborough, Car Co, b QA Co, Oct 23 1849; 773 owns over 1000 a.. His great-grandfather on paternal side came from Ireland and settled in America before Rev war. Grandfather Richard Jarrell b Del, farmer. Subj 1 of 11 child. of Rbt and Mary (Temnple) Jarrell, both of Car Co. Subj has interests in cannery; trustee Car Co almshouse 8 yrs; mbr ME Church South. 1877 he m Addie Noble, b this co, d/o T. S. Noble of the co. Prior to marriage Mrs. Jarrell taught school in Preston, this co; she is mbr ME Church South; d at 35, Dec 21 1891. Their child., in order of birth: Fannie C., Mary T., Rbt, Jr., T. S. Noble and Addie.

623. JOSEPH E. HENRY, business man East New Market, reared in this village; 773 went to sea at 10. Ages 13 to 19 he clerked in general store, then came to East New Market and clerked in store he now owns, learning drug business under Dr. H. W. Houston. The latter d when subj was 23; he then bt business. Oct 31 1886 Mr. Henry m Miss Nettie W., d/o Capt M. S. Fletcher. Their child.: Edith, Clarence, Frank and Edw. Mr. and Mrs. Henry mbrs ME Church.

624. HON. EDWARD E. GOSLIN, mcht, Federalsburg, Car Co, for over 2 decades 774 has carried on large mercantile estab, founded over 75 yrs ago by one of fam; auditor of public accounts of Car Co; elected to gen assembly. Goslin fam sprang from 3 bros from Eng, settling in Md. Thos coming in 1654, Mathew in 1655 and Wm in 1665. Edw R. Goslin, father of subj, b Car (now) Co, s/o Margaret, d/o Wm and Elizabeth Skinner and sis to Ann Skinner, who was grandmother of ex-Gov Rbt E. Pattison, of Pa. Edw R. Goslin m Mrs. Emily Hurst, d/o John and Rose Anna Travers, and sis of Capt Sml M. Travers, of Taylor's Island, Md, who m(1) Stephen Hurst, father of Bishop John Fletcher Hurst, of ME Church. She d Aug 2 1893, at 74. The only child of Edw R. and Emily Goslin is subj. Edw R. Goslin school commissioner Car & Dor Cos. Subj b 1855 Federalsburg; unmarried; res with father on homestead.

775 625. WILLIAM C. DUDLEY, politician Talb Co, res farm called Wye Landing, 4th dist; elected sheriff QA Co 1871; judge orphans' court of this co 1891; tax collector QA Co 1866-7; b QA Co, Aug 28, 1835, of 10 child. of Jas P. and Mary A. (Goodhand) Dudley. Former from QA Co, leader in Democratic party there; rgtr of wills of his co; d 1873. His wife, b Kt Island, QA Co, d/o Christopher Goodhand, did not long survive husband. Their eldest living child is subj; Georgia w/o Jos B. Haggart, of QA Co; others: Elizabeth, Mrs. C. G. Lynch; Dr. S. C. of Church Hill, Md; Mary M., wid of C. Comegys, of Centreville,; Hiram G., former clerk criminal court Balt and commission mcht there; Eugene L., of QA Co; Sarah Jane, unmarried, res Centreville; and Martha, Mrs. H. McFeeley, of QA Co. At 15 subj employed as clerk in native town; at 17 went to Balt, clerked in grocery estab 2 yrs; then farmed until 1871, elected sheriff; farmed nr Centrevile 10 yrs; 1883 he came to present farm, which he rents from a bro. Mr. Dudley m(1) Ann Bailey, of Del; she d Oct 1871, leaving 3 sons: Jas P., in grain business Balt; W. G., of Balt; and D. H., res nr here. Jan 1874 he m(2) Irene Coppage, of QA Co; their child.: Mary, Nellie, Hiram, Jennie and John. Mrs. Dudley d Aug 1894.

776 626. SAMUEL C. TRIPPE, M. D., physician Royal Oak, Talb Co, 20 yrs; b Island Creek Neck, Talb Co, Oct 23 1849. His father, Wm R., b this co, farmer; d at 52, mbr Episc Church. He m Marian A. Chamberlain, b and reared this co; also Episc. She d at 49, left 3 child.: John H., Missouri farmer; Sml C. and Henrietta M. At 14 subj enrolled Wash College, Chestertown. Following 4 yrs' course he taught country school, then principal grammar schools Easton; grad Univ Md, M. D. degree; practiced at asylum Bay View, Balt City, 3 months; then opened office in Oxford, Md; mbr Episc Church. 1888 he m Miss Mary L. Leoanrd, d/o Nicholas B. and Mary E. Leonard, of this co, and their child.: Marian C., Mary L., Sml C., Hy V. and Wm R.

776 627. MORDECAI T. COCKEY, Kt Island. Capt John Cockey, grandfather of subj, after career at sea, took up tract now owned by subj; d there. Here son John was b and m Frances Eareckson. Subj youngest child of fam, b 1820, 4th dist; childhood spent nr Old Point. C. 1844 he moved to farm; mbr Meth Church. 1844 he m Annie, d/o Jas Bright. She d in a few yrs, leaving no child. Later he m Miss Ida Jump; their adopted dau, Clara, w/o Chas S. Clough, and mother of: Annie C., Minnie E., Willie and Ethel V.

777 628. DAVID CLEMENTS b Kt Co, Del, 1817, s/o Joel and Margaret (Roe) Clements, both from Car Co, Md. Fam founded in America over 200 yrs ago. Father of subj moved to Del; owned c. 1000 a.; farmed and raised fruit; mbr state legislature; local minister ME Church; d at 84. Mother of subj d prev; 2 of 8 child. living, subj and Margaret A., wid of Hy Slaughter. Father m(2) Miss Elizabeth Kearns; their child.: J. Richard, decd; and John Fletcher, res Phila. Father drafted war of 1812 but furnished substitute. At 22 subj took over father's farms; 1844 came to Kt Co, Md, res on Sassafras River 6 yrs on farm now occupied by B. J. McCauley. 1850 he purch Spencer tract, where he now res, raised stock, now retired, leaving management of affairs to son. Fam attend ME Church South. 1842 he m Miss Susanna Slaughter, cousin of Hy Slaughter, founder of Slaughter Steamboat Line. Their child.: Thos, Margaret, w/o W. E. Jarrell; and Alday, attends father's business and conducts store at Crumnpton. He m Miss Frances M. Merrick; their child.: Merrick, David A., Annie, Aldie, and Ruth and Geo, twins.

629. THOMAS ATKINSON COUNCELL, M. D., young physician and surgeon, Talb Co, 778
owner of Moreland pharmacy Easton, b this place Nov 11 1872, s/o Wm H. and
Eugenia A.Councell and nephew of late Thos Atkinson and Mrs. Marion Emerson,
of Talb Co. Through father's maternal ancestors he descends from Murphy fam
that settled in Md 1784. On maternal side he descends from Harrisons of Va
and Atkinsons of N.C. His father, of Easton, postmaster 16; 1881 elected to
house of delegates; editor Easton Gazette 3 yrs; d 1890. Subj grad from
schools of Easton 1890; grad College of Physicians and Surgeons Balt 1894; res
physician Balt City Hospital and Md Hospital for Insane; returned to Easton
and began practice. 1895 he m Miss May Collier, of N. C. Their child, Thomas
Atkinson, d in infancy.

630. WILLIAM T. NICHOLSON, farmer 6th dist, Kt Co; b in dist where he lives, 778
Nov 25 1853; attended public schools; rented farm 3rd dist 6 yrs, moved to
farm 6th dist, remained 4 yrs, then to farm (belongs to father-in-law) where
res there past 16 yrs. He m Miss Sarah Lusby, d/o Josiah Lusby; their child.:
Albert Earl, Julia and Daisy. They attend MP Church.

631. JAMES H. HOLMES, decd, 4th dist Car Co, d 1895; b Car Co, Oct 17 1816; 781
identified with ME Church. He m(1) Mrs. Trice; she lived few yrs; left no
child. 1842 he m(2) Anah R. Billitor, d/o Jas and Mary (Robinson) Billitor.
Latter was d/o John Robinson, from old Md fam. Jas was s/o John Billitor, who
was b Car Co, from old Md fam. One child of Mr. and Mrs. Holmes d in infancy.
Only dau living, Annie K. H. Burnite, wid and res Easton. Mary A., decd, w/o
Thos Barrow; after his death m Wm Hughes, of Talb Co. Elizabeth, decd, w/o Wm
Taylor, of Easton.

632. ROBERT W. CLUFF res Dublin dist, Som Co, on homestead, Chestnut Ridge; 782
once judge orphans' court. Father of subj, Edw W. Cluff, of Dublin dist, b
Chestnut Ridge farm, now owned by subj; farming when he d at 34. He m
Salllie, d/o Wm Marshall; 3 child. b, 2 decdd. Mrs. Cluff mbr ME Church; d in
52nd yr. Father of Edw W. Cluff, Rbt Cluff; b Chestnut Ridge; d at 65; mbr
Episc Church. His father, Jonathan Cluff, of Scotch descent. Subj b 1830;
took charge of old farm when 23; 1857 m Miss Irena Broughton, d/o Wm S.
Broughton, farmer, once undertaker; he d at 52. He m Elizabeth Colbourn, who
survived him; she d at 69-70; they had 12 child.; living: Elizabeth, Edw, Rbt
L., Harry, Annie B., Irene, John C. and Mary E. Rbt (first born), Thos J.,
Fredric B. and Winifred N. are decd; one d at 8 and one at 5. The sons have
all left home but John C., who assists father. Family attend Episc Church.

633. JOHN H. HESSEY, M. D., physician Hanesville, of old fam Cecil Co. 782
Ancestor from Germany, date unknown. Subject's father, John H. Hessey, b
Cecil Co, res farm nr Cecilton still; tax collector 1st dist; m Laura Morgan,
same co; they had 7 child.; all decd except 2: John H.; and Ella, w/o Henry
Boulden, of Cecil Co. Parents still living. Subj b 1853 nr Cecilton on home
farm; grad Wash College, Chestertown 1876; grad College of Physicians and
Surgeons Balt 1878, with M. D. degree; opened office in Fairlee, practiced 3
yrs; 1881 moved to Hanesville, where since res; raises peaches & pears. He m
1886, Emma Nicholson, of Kt Co, d/o Rbt, sis to John P. Nicholson; their
child.: Sarah, Franklin, John and Emma Morgan. Family attend MP Church.

634. THOMAS C. WEST, b 1st dist Car Co, nr Marydel, Nov 28 1838, s/o Simeon 783
West. Simeon West, farmer, b Car Co, 1813, mbr ME Church; d 1893, at 80; his
mother wid of Capt Thos Clendening d 1848. Simeon West m(1) Margaret A.

-173-

Irons, of Kt Co, Del, d/o Titus and Mariam Irons. She d 1854; had 5 child; oldest son, Titus Irons West, res in Camden, N. J.; as also 2nd son Wm, vet Civ war; and 3rd son, S. Leslie West, M. D., grad Jefferson Medical College, physician Phila; Prof. Chas H. West, 4th son, school principal Lincoln, Ill. Subj educated locally and select school Templevile; 1860 taught at Bee Tree, Md; attended West River Classical Institute AA Co; principal acad Friendship AA Co; returned to Car Co, briefly in business Marydel; in charge of school Cold Spring, Car Co; taught at Oakland, Car Co; principal Denton Acad 8 yrs; employed at hardware of D. C. Avery & Co. Easton; teller Denton Natl bank; now cashier; mbr ME Church. He m Miss Anna, d/o Jas and Jane Pippen, of Car Co, Dec 26 1863; their son Thos K. d at 18 months.

784 635. ROBERT W. MEDFORD, collector 12th dist 8 yrs, lives nr Hurlock, on farm 12th dist; b northern part of co, Dec 12 1845, s/o Nathaniel and Rebecca (Payne) Medford. Father b nr Williamsburg, Dor Co, 1822, always res this co, farmer. His father, Nathaniel Medford, Sr., of this co, d just before his son's birth. Great-grandfather and great-great-grandfather (also named Nathaniel) b this co. Subj m 1874, Miss Sarah Harper, 9 child. b: Dora A. w/o Jas Martin Covey, of American Corners. Others: Edith, Wm, Daisy, Lovey, Nathaniel, Ottis, John and Watson. Fam attend ME Church.

784 636. WILLIAM H. CASHO Car Co; paternal grandfather, Jacob Casho, b France, became American citizen prior Rev war; fought under Gen Lafayette. In France learned baker's trade, but here farmed; lived to extreme old age. His son Isaac, father of subj, b Cecil Co, millwright and blacksmith, owned farm; in war of 1812 as lieut; m Nancy Ash, of Del; 10 child.; 6 survived: Jacob, Geo, Wm H., Jos, Eliza and Lovina. Subj b Jan 15 1833, Cecil Co, on father's farm until adult; then operated sawmill; Nov 1 1870 settled in Car Co. Today he owns 500 a., large sawmill, grist mill and basket factory; co commissioner, 1877-9. Dec 26 1866 he m Matilda E. Kennedy, of Chester Co, Pa. She was mbr ME Church; d Aug 26 1884, at 50. Nov 24 1887 he m Emma, d/o Simeon Blood, farmer from Conn. He d Aug 29 1897 at 88. Mrs. Casho b and reared Kt Co, Del; she and husb mbrs ME Church.

785 637. LEVIN J. GALE, rgtr of wills Wicomico Co. 1st public service when app to unexpired term of W. H. Farington (who was shot) as co commissioner. He lives on farm Quantico dist, west of Salisbury; b Nov 27 1837, Quantico dist, Wicomico Co, reared on father's farm; only s/o Henry and Susan (Goslee) Gale, both of that dist, now decd. Their only dau, Clara, w/o J. W. Turpin and d Quantico, leaving several child. Subj attended public schools. 1861 he m Virginia, d/o W. P. Rider, of Quantico; their child.: Wm H., farmer of Quantico dist, m Miss Collier; and Susan M., at home.

786 638. COL. PHILIP WORTHINGTON DOWNES, decd, 1st pres Denton Natl Bank, b Greensborough, Car Co, Nov 13 1837, s/o Hon. Wm H. Dones, who conducted store Greensborugh, mbr house of delegates. Subj grad Dickinson College, Carlisle, Pa 1857; studied law under Col Sml Hambleton, atty Easton. Admittted to bar 1860; carried on practice in Denton; app fish commissioner; appraiser of merchandise, port Balt, jurisdiction from Balt to gulf ports; instrumental in founding Denton Natl Bank, pres until he d, Jun 1 1895. His aged mother d 16 Jan 1895. His bros and sis: Reynor, Stephen R., Ernest, Emmett, Eldridge, Mrs. Annie Carter, Mrs. John E. Wilson and Miss Clara Downes. 1863 Col Downes m Annie Hardcastle, only child of Hon. Edw and Sallie (Dukes) Hardcastle, of

4th dist of Car Co. Her father mbr Md legislature. She is living; has 2 sons, J. Dukes, teller Denton Natl Bank, and Ormond.

639. MARION V. BREWINGTON, editor Wicomico News; junior mbr of firm Brewington Bros, who purch paper 1888. Parents of Marion V. were Hy and Orinthia (Long) Brewington (for history see sketch of Harry L., bro of subj). Father was business man this town where he lived c. 55 yrs; crier of court; d 1892; his wife preceded him c. 25 yrs. M. V. Brewingon b Salisbury 1867, of 12 child., 4 decd. After high school he worked in printing office Salisbury Advertiser with bro. Apr 1893 he m Miss Madge Fulton, of Salisbury, d/o Rev Wm Fulton, from Scotland, rector, St. Peter's Episc Church. 787

640. J. DUKES DOWNES, teller Denton Natl Bank, b Denton, Nov 19 1870, older s/o Col Philip Worthington and Annie (Hardcastle) Downes. Latter b Sep 18 1842, only d/o Edw and Sallie A. Hardcastle; latter d/o Jas Dukes. Edw Hardcasltle rep Car Co in Md legislature 1850-1. Subj attended military and naval acad at Oxford, Md, and acad in Pa. 1887 he became bookkeeper Denton Natl Bank then teller. Oct 18 1893 subj m Anna Isabel, d/o Col Jas Merrick, and granddau of Major Merrick, both of QA Co, latter a financier. Mr. Downes mbr Episc Church of Denton. 787

641. DANIEL H. COX, farmer 4th dist, Talb Co, home known as White Marsh; steward ME Church. Sml Cox, grandfather of subj, from Eng. The father, Wm A., b nr the Oakes, Talb Co, farmer; d Dec 23 1880, c. 66; m Henrietta Leonard, of Trappe dist, Talb Co; she d May 1885; they had 9 child.; 3 living: subj; Jas S., res Car Co; and J. A. mcht of Preston, same co. Subj b on farm nr present home, Jul 26 1854; attended Easton schools until 17; worked on homestead until 25; rented farm Car Co called Frazier Flats 7 yrs, then to White Marsh, belonging to father-in-law, Rbt H. Jump, who lives with fam, now 78, from QA Co. Jan 27 1879 subj m Clara E. Jump; their child.: Percy Leroy, Paul and Dalpha. Another child, Annie, is adopted. 788

642. ROBERT H. WHITTINGTON, treasurer Som Co, runs general store Marion Station, descendant, 2nd generation, of Jas Whittington, of Eng, who came to co as youth, settled in Lawsons dist, Som Co, where he d, at 85. Among his sons was Isaac, this co, farmer; active in ME Church; d at 65. Subject's mother was Sallie, d/o Wm and Sallie (Long) Coulbourn who had 12 child. Wm Coulbourń b and reared in Som Co, farmer; mbr ME Church; d at 90. His dau, Mrs. Whittington, had 10 child.; 4 living: Stephen H.; Mary, wid of Thos S. Adams; subj; and Isaac T. Like her husb and father, she was Meth; she d at 70. Subj b Som Co 1841, attended private schools here; followed carpentering 10 yrs. 1867-9 he conducted general store Crisfield, sold out and built new store at Marion Station; once in oyster business; co treasurer; trustee ME Church; m(1) d/o Smith Lankford; she d leaving 4 children, 2 living: Wm R. and Aurelia M. He m(2) Mary E. Jones, d/o Thos J. Jones, of Balt. 788

643. SAMUEL L. WEBSTER, res East New Market, business man Dor Co, owns 2 mills, at Linchester, Car Co, and at Beulah, Dor Co, fertilizer plant Cambridge and c. 2000 a., some inherited, some purch; b nr village of Vienna, Dor Co, Feb 28 1830. His father, John, b upper part of co 1800, farmer, less than average height; pres railroad co., owned several thousand a. John Webster m Rebecca, d/o Jas Simmons; their child.: Winfield, decd; subj; Elizabeth, m(1) Edw Hardcastle, m(2) Frs Turner, decd; Mary, m John Nichols; Sarah, w/o A. J. Collins; M. Augusta, m John Hurst; and Margaret, Mrs. 789

Elbridge Johnson. Paternal grandfather of subj, Thos Webster, prob from Scotland; most of life on Eastern Shore.
Nov 1 1851, subj m Miss Pricilla A. Sheppard, d/o Benj and Sarah (Lloyd) Sheppard, of Wor Co; they had 2 daus who d in infancy, and 9 sons: John B., Noah, Winfield, Sheppard, Frank, Chas, Roland, Sml and Lloyd. Sons are m and in business, except youngest, in school. Mr. Webster res northern part of co during lifetime and owner of homestead formerly belonging to grandfather, site of fam bur ground. He and wife mbrs Bapt Church.

790 644. ISAAC HARRISON MERRILL in merc busines Pocomoke City 35 yrs; past 15 yrs in men's clothing. Father of subj, Levin, s/o Levin Merrill, Sr., b Wor Co, and m Julia Barrett; they had 12 child.; attaining maturity: Hy T.; Wm J., farmer and mcht; Alfred D., farmer; Levin H., farming and merc business; John S., architect; Isaac Harrison; Sallie A., Mrs. Sml J. Lambden; Julia C., w/o Jerome B. Hall; Mary E., who m Sml J. Lambden after death of 1st wife; and Harriet, d at 18. All decd except subj. - Subj b on farm nr Pocomoke City, Oct 7 1840. At 12 became pupil in schools of Pocomoke City (6 yrs); clerked for Hargis & Dickinson 3 yrs; since 1862 in business at Pocomoke City; 10 yrs deacon Bapt Church. 1861 he m Annie Primrose, of Milford , Del; their child.: Sadie P., wid of Edw Gibbons; Annie m W. H. Walters, D. D. S., of Pocomoke City; C. Beulah, w/o E. I. Blaine, druggist this place; Minnie D., w/o John W. Ennis, subject's bookkeeper, and manager of store; Wm J. d in boyhood and Julia d in infancy; and I. Harrison, student Western Md Coll.

790 645. B. HARVEY HEARN, farmer, Wicomico Co, Salisbury dist; b nr Salisbury, Mar 31 1839, s/o Benj H. Hearn who was b on farm where subj lives. Benj Hearn, farmer and sometimes wheelwright, d 1860. Mother of subj, Betsy, d/o Thos Vincent, of Wicomico Co; d 1880; she had 11 child., 4 living: Geo, res Del; Maria, m Levin S. Gordy, of N.C.; Henrietta, wid of Sml Hopkins, and res of Pontico, this co; and subj. B. Harvey Hearn had no formal education; mbr ME Church. Dec 1 1864 he m Mary E. Hearn, d/o Thos Hearn, of Delmar, Del. Their child.: Marion E., who occupies farm nr home of parents; Edith M.; and Lillie M., w/o Irvin Twilly, of Pontico.

791 646. WILLIAM J. BARTON owns Hall Barton farm, 6th dist QA Co. Here he was b, 3rd in descent named Wm, his grandfther, Wm. A. and his father, Wm E. Latter b Car Co, as his father; farmer; mbr house of delegates; mbr ME South. He m Mary E. Chance, of Car Co, d/o Batchelder C. Chance; their child.: subj; B. C., 6th dist QA Co; Lizzie B., w/o Jacob E. Morgan, of same dist and co; and Edw A., of Phila. Subj b Sep 10 1858, attended local schools and private school at Hillsborough, until c. 20. Since then farmer; raises peaches, seed potatioes and seed wheat; breeds thoroughbred Cheshire hogs; musician. Jul 28 1885 he m Loula M., d/o Hon. C. M. Jump, of Talb Co; their child.: Loula Meta, Wm Marvin, Mary Augusta Morgan, Wm Edw and Lizzie Naomi.

791 647. ROBERT J. JUMP atty Denton, b nr Greensborough, Car Co, 2nd dist, Dec 7 1833; descends from Rev ancestors, English and Scotch lineage. 3 bros emigrated c. 1700; 1 settled at Bohemia Manor, Md, another in the south, and 3rd in Del. John Jump, subject's father, b Del 1800; at 30 came to Md, settling nr Denton, purch farm; tax collector; co sheriff; d 1847. His bro, Rbt B., fruit farmer Del. Mother of subj, Elizabeth Clements, b Del; traced lineage to Scotland. Subject's only bro, Thos Hy, d in boyhood. 5 sis living: Mollie E., res Wilm, Del; Lydia A., wid of Dr. John W. Cannaway, res

Wilm; Sarah E., wid of Wm. C.Smith, farmer res nr Easton; Louisa, res Camden, Del; and Belle C., w/o Jos E. Wilson, mcht Barclay, QA Co.

Subj educated dist schools and acad; at 13 assist office of clerk circuit court; read law with J. E. Rochester; admitted to bar 1857; clerk circuit court; 1864 elected comptroller of Md. Ensuing yrs devoted to practice of law. 1891 elected state's atty Car Co; 1896 app rgtr of wills vacated by death of Jas B. Steele; elected to office 1897. 1855 he m Laura Cochran, d/o Chas and Elizabeth (Benson) Cochran, of Del; her father mcht of Cambridge, Md. Child. of Mr. and Mrs. Jump: Elizabeth E., wid of Marion Pippin; Alexander, d at 2 yrs; Ella, decd, w/o J. N. Todd, atty; Rbt J., clerk N.Y. City; and Chas C., city editor Meriden (Conn.) Record. Subj mbr ME Church.

648. FRANK D. HARRISON, farmer 2nd dist, Talb Co, b on homestead he now cultives, 17 Apr 1854. Jos H., father of subj, b St. Michael's; bt farm where son now owns; director of Easton Natl Bank, remained with bank until he d, May 16 1888, at 71. He was s/o Jos and Mary (Harrison) Harrison, former 6th Jos in line of descent in U. S., and native of Talb Co. Jos H. m Miss Mary Jane Denney, b this area; she is in 74th yr, mother of 7 child., 3 remain. Olivia w/o Geo W. Eaater, of Va; and Kate W. w/o of Stephen Harrison, of St. Michael's and subj. 792

649. AZARIAH M. KENDALL, Kt Co, local correspondent of Kent News, contractor and builder, surveyor and agent for Kt Mutual Fire Insur Co; dist assessor and rgtr of votes 6th dist. He rep 4th generation in America, first of name coming to Kt Co from Ireland. Horace, his grandfather res here. Rev Jas Kendall, the father, b this co; carpenter, later in contracting and building, sometimes wheelwright, mbr of firm Keiser & Kendall; also local preacher ME Church; d Aug 6 1886, at 57; m Eliza Legg (still living); their child.: Azariah M.; Clara O., w/.o F. H. Ward, of Fairlee; Mrs. Perpetua Moslin; and Naomi, w/o D. P. Jones, of Chestertown. Subj eldest of fam, b Rock Hall 1854; since 21 in contracting and building; mbr Salem ME Church. He m 1879 Agnes, d/o Thos B. Bordley; their child: Alice M.; J. Thos; Cattie L.; and Clara P. and Julia Marie, twins (latter two decd). 793

650. REV. JOSEPH L. MILLS, D. D., pastor St. James' MP Church Hanesvile, since 1892. The Mills are of Dutch origin. C. 1620 Lord Pieter Wonter Van Der Miller emigrated from Holland to New Amsterdam; fam finally settled in Conn. The first to move to Eastern Shore of Md was Levin Mills, whose only son, John S., b Wor Co, and there a tanner. He m Mary A. Scott, of same co, had one son, Jos Levin. He d at 31, 1844, surviving his wife by 4 yrs, who d when her son was 11. 794

Subj b Pocomoke City, Wor Co, 1840, educated in private schools and acad, discontinued studies at 16 due to health; in cabinet making, while studying ministry under Rev Dr. J. K. Nichols. May 1860 received on probation into Md annual conference MP Church; assigned QA circuit, then Susquehanna and Talb circuit. 1862 he m Marietta Dickinson, of Pocomoke City; 2 yrs later retired from ministry; organized 1st public school Pocomoke City and principal of school, wife as assist; then pastorates: Lynchburg, Va; Salisbury, Md; Laurel, Del; Montgomery, Ala; Alexandria, Va; Frederick, Md; Washington, D. C.; Newark, N. J., Westminister, Md; 1892 to present church. 1878 degree of D. D. conferred. His child.: Frank D., Jos S., Wm P., John Bibb and Marie.

651. JOHN H. HOLLAND, Lawsons dist, farmer; built saw & grist mill. His father, John S. Holland, of Som Co; purch homestead now owned by him; in 795

-177-

battle of North Point 1814. He m Nancy Miles, d/o Wm Miles this area. She survived husb several yrs, d c. 55. Their child.: Julia Anne, John H., Geo and Eliza, all living. Subj b present farm, Apr 28 1828; at 16 boatman and oyster fisher this section, 5-6 yrs; then merc line; owns about 600 a. and 18 houses in Crisfield. He m Sarah Anne Stephenson of this area. She d Nov 1894, leaving child.: Mamie, w/o of Dr. Somers, of Crisfield, and Clara, w/o Rbt Whittington, farmer & oyster packer this co. Subj mbr ME Church.

795 652. CAPT. THOMAS W. KENDALL, sea capt, res Centreville; b Kt Co, Mar 24 1824, s/o Horace Kendall, Kt Co. Paternal grandfather b Md, of Eng descent. Father, farmer & fisherman; m Miss Nancy Woods, d/o Thos Woods, of Car Co; of their 14 child. fol living: subj; Mary, w/o Jas Urie, of Kt Co; Jos, res Kt Co; Ellen, w/o Harry Gresham, Kt Co; Arthur, of Balt City; Asa, of Kt Co; and Caroline, w/o Wm Shien, of this co. The father d 1874; mother d 1883. At 16 subj enlisted U. S. navy, served 2 yrs during Mex war, on schooner Flirt. Retured home; later owned schooner sailing from Balt to points on Eastern Shore; owns home in Centreville; mbr MP Church. He m(1) Miss Louise Vicker, who d 1852, leaving son, Thos. He m(2) May 16 1855 Miss Joseph Talor; had 6 child., 4 living: Amos, Omar, Nora and Ada. 1890 he m(3) Miss Lula Booker.

796 653. WILLIAM H. H. DASHIELL, M. D., physician Quantico, Wicomico Co. The Dashiells originated in France. Arthur Dashiell, great-grandfather of subj, of this co, farmed as did his son, Arthur, Jr. The latter, grandfather of subj, b nr Barren Creek; of his child., Edwin Dashiell was father of subj. He was b on farm nr Quantico, farmer and judge of dist court; magistrate; mbr Episc Church. A cousin of his, Julius Dahiell, prof Latin and Greek St. John's College, Annapolis. Edwin Dasshiell m(1) Harriet, d/o Thos Dashiell. She d 1848, leaving 3 child.: Esther A. E., unmarried; Henrietta, d c. 18; and subj. After 1st wife d, Edwin Dashiell m Eliza, d/o John Robinson, of Barren Creek. She d Aug 1874.
Subj b nr Quantico, Aug 2 1840, attended dist schools, and later 2 yr course in old Wash Acad, Princess Anne; then taught school, while studying medicine under Dr. Cadmus Dashiell; grad medical depart Univ Md 1865; located in Quantico; also conducted drug store. 1872 he m his cousin Susie Dashiell, who d Jul 10 1876; then m Mary Meredith; their son, Hy E. b 1883, d Feb 1884.

799 654. JAMES M. CORKRAN, M. D. physician and surgeon, Centreville, b nr Hurlock, Dor Co, Aug 14 1860. His great-great-grandfather, of Eng, acquired Churchfield farm. There 4 generations b; prop now out of hands of fam. James Corkran, great-grandfather, farmer, lived on old homestead. The grandfather, Thos Corkran, slave owner as was his father, also owned Churchfield and in Mex war; d at 32. Subject's father, Thos Corkran, b Dor Co, Mar 28 1821, farmer; now res Seaford, Del; mbr ME Church; m Hester Wright, d/o Kinley Wright, of Dor Co. His father, Jos, s/o Clementine Wright, officer in Rev war. Mrs. Corkran, still living, mother of 12 child.: Chas W., farmer of Mo; Frs S., grad Glasgow Coll, Meth minister, d Kansas City, Mo.; Mary Elizabeth, w/o Isaac Noble, of Preston Md; Rev Lewis P., grad Dover Conference Acad, of Dover, Del, Meth minister Newcastle, Del; Wilbur F., student of Dover Conference Academy and D. D. of St. John's College, presiding elder Easton dist; Thos B., farmer Pa; Millard F., grad Univ Md, physician Wilm, Del; Fanny, w/o Arthur Hitch, of Seaford, Del; David H., Meth minister Lewes, Del, attended Dover Conference Acad and Univ Pa, grad Drew Theological Seminary; Milton W., hotel clerk St. Louis; Adelaide, of Dover Del; and subj. - Subj attended public schools and Federal acad; grad at 18; taught public school 2

yrs; principal public school Lebanon, Del; grad medical depart Univ Md 1887; came to Centreville. Jun 11 1890 he m Miss Laura S. Emory, d/o Addison Emory, of Centreville. Their child: Margaret Spencer, aged 5. Subj attends ME Church.

655. JOHN S. HILL, editor and manager Peninsula Press, organ of Prohibition party, b Snow Hill, May 9 1860, s/o John J. Hill, farmer and miller (still living at 67). He m Esther A. Taylor, who d some yrs ago; by 1st marriage had 2 child.; by 2nd wife had 7 child., John S. oldest. Subj taught country schools, 1880-1885; then principal Girdle Tree grammar school, vice-principal Snow Hill high school 7 yrs, principal Oxford high school 1 yr; principal Aberdeen high school 3 yrs. 1887, formed partnership with R. J. and W. A. McAllen, of Snow Hill, subj purch Peninsula Press, taking charge Aug 1897. 1897 Mr. Hill m Miss Nannie P. Asher, d/o Wm W. Asher, of Aberdeen. 799

656. CAPT. HENRY W. RUARK, in oyster industry, res on little farm on Fishing Creek, Hooper's Island, Dor co. Jun 1 1896 app capt of police boat. He and his men (6 or more) patrol Honga River, Fishing Bay, Holland and Hooper Straits and adjacent waters. Wm. T. Ruark, father of capt, from Hooper's Island; res here; began working on bay around 12; owned ships and freight boats, transporting wood and lumber to Balt & Phila; purch farm Fishing Creek and settled down; tilled farm and conducted store; d Sep 4 1891, in 64th yr; mbr ME Church. His father, Hy, from Eastern Shore, followed sea in early life, later farming. He d age c.60. He m Rebecca T. Parker, b this area (still living at 66); mbr ME Church. 3 of her child. decd, others: Hy W.; Wm W., in oyster business Cambridge; Oliver G., oysterman this area; Thos L. local oysterman; and Cora T. Subj b Hooper's Island Sep 26 1859; at 15 went aboard oyster boat and fol busines of oyster dredging until app present position. 1880 he m Miss Lucy R. Leland, of Hoopers' Island; their child.: Nettie Ann, Wm Thos, Eugene Henry and Lucy Rebecca. 800

657. REYNOR B. DOWNES, farmer 6th dist QA Co. Founder of fam settled here over 100 yrs ago. Grandfather of subj b here; the father, Wm H. Downes, from QA Co; mbr state legislature; co commissioner Car Co; m Miss Sarah Ann Reynor, of Talb Co; their child.: Philip W. and Dr. Wm H., both decd; subj; Fannie E., decd, m Jos E. Wilson; Stephen, 6th dist QA Co; Annie, w/o E. C. Carter, of Car Co; Ernest, of Car Co; Emmett, res in west; Eldridge, res QA Co; and Clar, res Hardcastle, Balt Co. Father d Apr 1867; mother d Feb 1895. Subj b QA Co, 10 May 1844, attended public school and West River Acad; took over father's farms; 1885 rented farm (present res), belonging to bro; m Dec 1879 Miss Fannie E.Corsey, d/o Sml Corsey, of QA Co. Their child: Marshall. 801

658. BRICE W. GOLDSBOROUGH, M. D., Cambridge, b Princess Anne, Som Co, oldest s/o Worthington and Henrietta (Jones) Goldsborough; early yrs passed in area of Princess Anne and Cambridge. 1871 at 12, he entered Episc high school nr Alexandria, Va, and grad at 19; entered medical depart Univ Md; grad Univ Va 1880; post grad Univ Md 1880-1, as clinical assist, post grad Johns Hopkins Univ, chemistry and physics; went to South America, 2 yrs in Montevideo, Uruguay, assist in charity hospital and British hospital. Returning to U. S. he opened office in Cambridge, where he still res; m Miss Nannie Campbell Henry; their child.: Anna, Henrietta, Louise and Mary Campbell. Dr. Goldsborough is Episc. 801

802 659. ISAAC H. A. DULANY, Wicomico Co, b here Feb 26 1825; in merc enterprises in Fruitland 45 yrs; only child of Dennis and Anna M. (Anderson) Dulany, of Som Co. Subject's grandfather, Henry Dulany, farmer of Eastern Shore. Fam of French, Scotch, Eng and Irish extraction; protestant in religion. The father, Paul Dennis Dulany, blacksmith, reared on Eastern Shore; he d when subj was 6. The mother d 1882; d/o Isaac Anderson (large land owner). At 20 subj went to Balt, clerked 5 yrs; then clerked Wash D. C. store. Returning home 1851 he went into business; turned to milling. Dec 11 1851 he m Anna M. White; she was b and reared this co; of their 7 child., 6 living. Augustine, decd; Henry S., minister ME Church Va; Albert J. and Henry S., partners with father in merc business; John H., chief clerk in father's store; Wm P., commission business Phila; Jos, clerk New York commission house; and Maria T., former teacher, now w/o Prof. V. A. Austin, of Salina, Kan. Mr. and Mrs. Dulany and fam mbrs ME Church.

803 660. JOHN W. FLETCHER, Dor Co, b Jun 21 1848 on farm nr East New Market, 2nd dist, only child 3rd marriage of father; 3 sons by 1st: Wm M., res Cambridge; other two decd; and by 2nd: Jeremiah B. and Mrs. Mary J. Williamson, both res Car Co. Fletcher fam, of Eng origin; great-grandfather of subj, John Fletcher, from Del. The grandfather, farmer, named John, while father was John H. Fletcher. Fam mbrs Meth Church. Mother of subj former Sarah Andrews, d/o Medford Andrews who owned land at Hurlock. Subj b nr New Market, attended public schools and East New Market Acad. Jan 1 1886, left farm to res Cambridge as rgtr of wills. Feb 1869 he m Miss Susan Higgins, d/o Judge Jas Higgins, once chief judge orphans' court Dor Co. Their child.: Fred H., 26, lawyer Cambridge; and Laura, w/o Thos W. Simmons, atty Cambridge, by whom 3 child.: Harriet Ruth, Lawrence Fletcher and Mary. 1871-2 subj was tax collector 2nd & 12th dists; app to close books of J. B. Nesbitt, collector; elected sheriff, then rgtr of wills; mbr ME Church.

803 661. THOMAS W. SIMMONS, b Cambridge, where he now res Aug 17 1867, s/o Josias S. and Leah C. Simmons; attended business college Balt; position at Cambridge Natl Bank 4 yrs; then private sec to John E. Hurst, head of Hurst, Purnell & Co, proprietors of large wholesale dry goods house Balt; bookkeeper and paying teller Dor Natl Bank. While there he studied law under ex-Gov Lloyd; admitted to bar 1892; m Laura Fletcher; their child.: Harriet R., Lawrence F. and Mary.

804 662. FREDERICK H. FLETCHER, s/o John W. Fletcher (rgtr of wills), b father's estate at New Market, this co, Jan 26 1871; attended Cambridge Acad, grad Dickinson College Carlisle, Pa, 1892; taught Cambridge acad; then assist principal; admitted to bar Jul 1893; continued to teach until Jun 1896, when he entered actively into law.

804 663. S. N. SMITH, business man, Willoughby, QA Co, since Dec 1863; postmaster since 1883; agent Adams Express Co. and station agent here. He was b Apr 30 1830, Talb Co, mbr of Irish fam in Md many generations. Father, s/o of Rev soldier, b 5th dist QA Co; in battle of Slippery Hill, war of 1812; farmer 5th dist; d 1831. 7 yrs later his wife Amelia d. She was d/o Geo Grayson, of Piney Neck, QA Co, mother of 12 child.; 2 survive, subj and Richard L., of Balt. At 16 subj went to Balt; ship builder there 16 yrs, in businesss for himself 9 yrs. Returning to Talb Co he farmed; Dec 1863, moved to Willoughby, where he has operated general store. 1885-6 tax collector, also school trustee. Oct 26 1851 he m Susan L. Townsend, of Balt; their child.: Margaret A., w/o Dennis F. Rhodes; S. N., Jr, and Jas T. S. S., decd.

664. LEVI T. VOSHELL res farm 4th dist, Car Co and owns another 200 a. farm 805
Talb Co. Grandfather of subj, Wm Voshell, b Del; his father, Wm, Sr., came
there from France. The latter was s/o Obadian Voshell, whose father, Levi
Voshell, acompanied Lafayette to America and served in Rev war. Two other
bros took part in war. Subject's father in war of 1812; 3rd in line named Wm,
native of Del, where he farmed until he d, at 63. He m Anne, d/o David Lynch,
who emigrated from Eng to Del; their child.: Wm H., of Oxford; Levi T.; John
W., of McPherson Co, Kan.; Sml, res Monterey, Calif; and Ruth A., decd. After
death of Wm Voshel his wid m John Young; they had son, Rbt E., now of Easton.
Subj b 1835, Kt Co Del, reared on farm. 1860 he m Miss Frances, d/o Wm S.
Vane, who d Feb 21 1897; their child.: Wm, res Talb Co; Mary, m Harry W. Snow
and at his death left one son, Hy W. Snow; Sarah E., w/o John B. Dulin;
Ulysses G., Ira S., Levi, Frances F., Rebecca C. and Lida R. 1866 subj
located on farm nr Easton; 1892 came to Car Co, where he owns a place nr
Choptank; served in Union army 9 months, enlisted 1863 as mbr Company F, 6th
Del Infantry. He is mbr ME Church.

665. WILLIAM T. DARBY, farmer nr Riverton, Barren Creek dist, Wicomico Co, 805
where he owns old Darby homestead; b nr here Mar 20 1837, s/o John T. and
Elizabeth (Harris) Darby, of Md. John T. s/o Thos and Elizabeh (Phillips)
Darby. Father of subj farmer Wicomico Co; inherited part of tract of 1000 a.
purch by his father, much of present site of Riverton and surrounding country.
He d 1873; his wife d 6 yrs later; they had 5 child.; surviving: subj and
Salllie, w/o Capt C. R. Dashiell, res Green Hill, Wicomico Co.
At 19 subj became clerk in uncle's store at Riverton. When uncle d (1881)
he went to Balt but shortly returned to Wicomico Co and purch interests of
other heirs in home farm and res there; 1887 elected mbr bd of school
commissioners; judge of orphans' court, 1893-5; mbr MP Church. Feb 28 1880 he
m Annie B., d/o Hy C. Vickers, of Balt.; 2 of 3 child. survive: Richard J.,
student Balt schools, and Mary E.

666. VACHEL DOWNS farmer 6th dist QA Co, farm known as Hogg Harbor, willed to 806
him by grandfather, for whom named. Subj b on this farm May 12 1864, m Miss
Martie Willoughby, of Car Co, Jan 1896; their child: Arthur John.
John A. Downs, father of subj, from 5th dist this co, farmer; d 1895, at
68. He m(1) Emily, d/o John Chambers; she d May 1872; their surviving child.:
Mary G., w/o Harry Montague, of Phila; Vachel; Emma C., Mrs. W. G. Turner,
this co; Alice V., w/o Allen Cherry, of Car Co; Minnie A., unmarried;
Glenwille M., res Pa; Jessie L., at home; Norman, of Car Co; and Annie P., at
home. John A. Downs m(2) Annie Cooper; he m(3) Ellen T. Starkey.

667. OLIVER T. BEAUCHAMP, clerk Som Co court, Princess Anne. Edmund 806
Beauchamp, supposed distant relative of subj, 1st clerk of courts here. Levin
H., father of subj; farmer from Westover, Som Co; mbr MP Church; d at 81. His
father, Thos Beauchamp b this co; farmer; deputy sheriff. He d c. 70.
Subject's mother former Margaret E. White, of Fairmount dist, Som Co, now in
67th yr; mbr of church; her child.: L. Wesley, farmer nr Westover, this co;
subj; Helen A., Virginia and Frs T.; latter 3 decd. Subj b nr Westover, Som
co; farmed and connected with merchandising in Westover; then elected to
present office. In 1889 elected shriff; also postmaster of Westover. Subj m
Dec 20 1887 Miss Ida Davis, of Sheltown, this co. They have 5 child of whom 1
d about 3; living: Levin Creston, Jas Roger, Mildred and Oliver T., Jr.

807 668. WILLIAM M. FLETCHER, jeweler and watchmaker, retired, res Cambridge, Dor Co. 1872 he purch 100 a. in East Cambridge and erected houses; has sold off about 60 a.; in jewelry business here and East New Market; b this co, Mar 8 1828, s/o John H. Fletcher, farmer who d at 81. He m(1) Elizabeth Bradley, b nr Gales Town, this co and d young, leaving 3 child.: subj, Major S. and Kilby B. He m(2) Miss Bramble; their child: Jeremiah and Mary J., both res Preston, Car Co. He m(3) Sarah Andrew; their only child, John, rgtr of wills, Dor Co (see his sketch). Bros of subj, Major and Kilby, mchts, former of East New Market and latter of Cabin Creek (where he operated a mill), both now decd. Major left 2 child. and Kilby left 6 child. Subj m Apr 28 1858, Sarah C. Keene, of Taylor's Island, Dor Co, d/o Rbt B. Keene who d at 74.

808 669. McBLAIR LLOYD manager of homestead, 4th dist, Wye Heights, owned by Dr. I. R. Trimble, Balt. Subj is s/o Col Edw Lloyd, of Wye House, b there Nov 12 1862, 1st dist nr Easton. (See also sketch of Col Lloyd.) 1881 subj grad Winchester (Va) Acad, then a year at Clarkstown, W.V, as clerk. Returning to Easton he was assist station agent 5 yrs; res Balt 4 yrs, then 2 yrs in general freight office of railraod company Phila. Jan 8 1896 Mr. Lloyd m Miss Virginia B. Causey, of Milford, Del, d/o Peter F. Causey.

809 670. JOHN LEWIS RHODES, politician, QA Co, tax collector; owns old homestead on which b 1860. Rhodes fam of Irish origin, John L. being 5th generation removed from founder of fam in America. Wm Washington, father of subj, s/o Dennis and Charlotte (Hutchinson) Rhodes; b Talb Co; farmer; Cath; m Miss Sarah Matilda Long. Subj acquired paternal estate when father d Nov 1 1878. He m 1881 Mary C. Skinner, d/o Rbt C. Skinner, at St. Peter's Cath Church nr Queenstown. Their sons: Wm Washington and Lewis K. All mbrs Cath Church.

809 671. LEVIN P. WILLIAMS, farmer, nr Preston, Car Co, b here 1835. Madison Williams, father of subj, descends from old Md family; b Car Co 1810; m Ann d/o Levin Poole; their child.: Jas, decd; Levin P.; Mary, who m(1) Cannon Charles and had 2 child., after his death m Rbt P. Taylor; Ann E., Mrs. Jesse Wright, of Preston; and Lydia, Mrs. Curtis A. Wright, of Harmony, Car Co. Subj mbr ME Church; m 1860 Miss Margaret d/o Jas R. Nichols; their child.: Annie, the elder, w/o Thos Taylor, and the younger, Ella M., at home.

810 672. NATHANIEL W. COMEGYS, retired on his farm 2nd dist, Kt Co, b on place opposite, Nov 30 1825, from old fam founded here by Wm Comegys, from Germany, in 1707. The grandfather and great-grandfather also named Nathaniel and spent entire lives on farm which Mrs. Emery now owns. The father, John M. Comegys farmed in Kt Co; mbr Shrewsbury Episc Church; d 1874 at 77; m cousin, Miss Anna Comegys; their child.: subj; Hannah, wid of John F. Newman; and Anna, w/o S. R. Emery. Father mbr state militia. Subj attended Wash College. At 30 he rented one of his father's farms; later inherited part of estate at father's death. He still res on part of home farm but son John M., oversees its management. 1860 he m Miss Helen Spencer, d/o Geo W. and Margaret C. (Ringgold) Spencer. Her grandfathers were Jervis Spencer, of Kt Co, and Jervis Ringgold, of QA Co, and her ancestors came from Eng as early as 1700. Her father, farmer in Kt co, nr Galena; state rep several terms, state senator twice, sheriff 1840-4, and judge of orphans' court; d 1884, at 70; his wife d 1854, at 42. Their child.: Jervis, res of Chestertown; Charlotte, w/o Thos W. Wicks; and Laura, w/o Addison Emery, of Centreville. Mr. and Mrs. Comegys have child.: John M. and Geo S. Fam mbrs Episc Church.

673. COL. WILBUR F. JACKSON of Balt, has summer home at Castle Haven, Dor Co, on Choptank River. Here Col Jackson and fam res May-Nov each yr, with trips to Balt to look after business; remainder of yr at No. 218 West Monument st. Subj b Sep 30 1849, on farm c. 5 miles from Salisbury. 1863 moved to Salisbury; pupil in public schools until 16; worked for E. E. Jackson & Co (comprising his father, Hugh and his bros, E. E. and W. H. Jackson); 1870 admitted to firm, stayed in Salisbury 7 yrs, then head of branch in Balt until firm dissolved, 1889. Corporation of Jackson Bros Co formed 1894, he becoming a stockholder, director and vice- pres. Company has mills for sawing logs in Va and N.C.; raw material shipped to mills in Salisbury, manufactured into building products. Col Jackson became director and pres of Continental Natl Bank of Balt, and director of Fidelity Trust and Deposit Co, of Md; mbr of bd of directors of Md State Penitentiary. 1872 he m Alice P. Smith, d/o of late Thos B. Smith, of Wicomico Co; their child.: John J., and Helen, w/o Hon. Jas H. Preston, late speaker of Md legislature. 811

674. FRANCIS J. HENRY, Dor Co, whose grandfather, Hon John Henry, and Chas Carroll, of Carrollton, 1st U. S. senators of Md. His father, John Campbell Henry m Mary Nevett Steele; their child.: John Frs, lawyer Cambridge, who d 1833; Jas Winfield, physician, Cambridge and Varina, d 1893; Frs Jenkins, subj; Catharine, decd w/o Dnl Lloyd, of Cambridge; Isabela, w/o Dr. Thos Steele, of Cambridge; Mary, w/o of R. T. Goldsborough, of Cambridge; Rider, who m Miss Sutherland, niece of Gen Van Dorn of Miss., res Cambridge; Charlotte P., w/o Judge Chas Goldsborough; and Mary, who d in childhood. 812

Subj b Aug 13 1816, and reared on father's estate in Cambridge; educated at Cambridge Acad; at 17 began clerking in merc estab this town; fol yr into busines for himself. Emancipation of slaves caused him to lose c. $40,000; clerk of courts 1851-79. At beginning of war he raised company of 100 men and personally gave $1,000 for their equipment. His son, John Campbell, took charge of company, then resigned and joined Confed service. Subj believed slavery constitutional; that change required constitutional amendment and purch and liberation of negroes by U. S. government.

Mr. Henry m Aug 9 1836 Miss Williamina Elizabeth Goldsborough, youngest and posthumous d/o Rbt Goldsborough, granddau of Chas Goldsborough, of Horns Point. Their child.: Mary N., w/o John S. Spence, farmer, res Secretary, Dor Co, had 11 child.; John Campbell, manufacturer New Orleans, who m Miss Lake, has 4 child.; Annie, wid of John Steele, (murdered on streets of Cambridge c. 5 yrs ago, leaving 3 child.); Elizabeth, wid of Wm T. Goldsborough, of Balt, mother of 2 child.; Williamina, wid of Dnl S. Muse and mother of 2 daus, now living with father; Frs J., commissioner in chancery and auditor of court of Dor Co; Rbt G., lawyer, postmaster Cambridge, where he res with wife, former Miss Muse, and 5 child.; Nicholas L., paymaster in navy, now hydrographic office Wash, res with wife, former Nellie Radcliffe, of Cambridge, and 5 child.; and Hampton, farmer Dor Co, m Miss Le Compte and has 5 child. Henrys originally Presby, now attend Episc Church.

675. GEORGE W. SPURRY, farmer, 6th dist Car Co; owns 1072 a.; b Del Jan 25 1819, youngest s/o Wm and Mary (Griffin) Spurry, both from Md, who had 10 child.; subj left an orphan at 13; reared on farm in Del with few advantages; millwright 30 yrs. 1856 he bt 214 a. nr Denton, engaged in dairy business. 1843 he m Adaline Taylor, from Del. Of their 3 child. 1 survived: Mary Jane, w/o Wm E. Saulsbury, of Md. They res in Car Co, have 3 child. Fam mbrs MP Church. 1885 accident in sawmill caused injuries that proved serious. In 1889 in order to save his life his right leg amputated just above knee. 813

-183-

814 676. CAPT. W. D. BURCHINAL, Chestertown, treasurer of Kt Co; paternal ancestors came from Eng and settled, one branch in Del and another in Md. Burchinal old Del fam. Subject's grandfather school teacher in Del. The father, John Howard, of Del, mcht and dealer in real estate. Moving to Chestertown he engaged in commercial transactions many yrs; mbr ME Church; m Eliza Burton, of Del, d/o David and Eliza (Spencer) Burton, mbrs Soc of Friends. Their child.: Mary H., unmarried, res Chestertown; subj, 2nd child; Elizabeth, wid of John W. Hines, res Balt; Jos J. d soon after reaching majority; John C., decd farmer nr this place, left wife, former Miss M. M. Brown and 3 child.; Anna and Rebecca d when c. 17; J. Burton, mcht of Chestertown; and Addie, w/o Marion de Kalb Smith, whose sketch appears elsewhere this vol.

Subj b Dover, Del, Oct 4 1832; at 7 moved to farm QA Co with parents; later with father when he carried on store at head of Sassafras River. He was situated in Odessa, Del, 1844-7; res Salem, N.J 1848-9, conducting a business. Then, after short res in Millington, Kt Co, Md, to Chestertown; clerked for T. W. Eliason 4 yrs. Dec 21 1861 Mr. Burchinal enlisted in Company D, 2nd Eastern Shore Md Infantry. From 2nd Lieut promoted to adjutant of regt, and to captain. Spring 1865 app quartermaster 11th Md Infantry under Col John Johannes, served until Jul 1865. After war he retured to Chestertown and entered real estate business; customs inspector of Balt; assist cashier of customs, returning to Chestertown in 1872; back to Balt as dep collector of customs 1876; resumed farming Kt Co 1881; mbr Md senate 1883-91; surveyor of port of Balt 4 yrs; co treasurer. May 13 1868 he m Mrs. Margaret A., wid of Capt Wm H. Brown, of Chestertown; she was b and reared in Kt Co, d/o Arthuir and Juliana Merritt; she d Jun 29 1894.

817 677. FRANCIS H. DRYDEN, business man, Pocomoke City, Wor Co, in real estate, vice-pres of Natl Home-seekers Assoc; deals largely in farms in Md and Va. He was b May 13 1844, nr Pocomoke City; at 15 started clerking in Hy King's store, Princess Anne 4 yrs; came to Pocomoke City to clerk for I. H. Merrill, becoming a mbr of firm; name changed to Dickinson, Merrill & Dryden. 1879 he sold his interest and invested in fertilizers, having agencies here and in Norfolk; mbr of drug firm of Lloyd, Dryden & Blaine, Pocomoke City, 1879-95.

818 678. JAMES LATIMER BANNING, farming and fruit culture on Tred Avon River, on the farm, Avondale, Talb co; b Wilm, Del, 1848 s/o Hy Geddes Banning who was b at Avondale 1816, and Emily, d/o John Eschenburg, and granddau of Caesar A. Rodney. Hy Geddes Banning s/o Freeburn Banning, who was b 1777 and d at Avondale 1826, and Sarah, d/o Capt Hy Geddes, of U. S. navy, and granddau of Jas Latimer of Del. Freeburn Banning, U.S. naval officer, under Capt Geddes, and younger son of Jeremiah Banning of the Isthmus, older son being Rbt; there was one dau, who left descendants. Freeburn once impressed, against his will, on board British ship; opportunity offering, he secreted himself in a coil of rope on board an American vessel until at a safe distance.

"Jeremiah Banning of the Isthmus," as known, b Talb Co 1733, d c. 1797. He left short written history of his time and surroundings. For 21 yrs was sea captain, importer, shipper, mcht, crossing ocean many times to various ports; retired to Isthmus.

The Isthmus house was standing until 2-3 yrs ago. Jeremiah added the farm Avondale to his estate by purchase, not later than 1797, and it was the home of Freeburn Banning after he resigned from the navy. 1773 Jeremiah Banning retired to Isthmus. His old ivory handled sabre, used when colonel of militia in Rev still preserved. Jeremiah had 2 bros, Hy and Anthony, latter res

Chestertown. All three were sons of Jas and Jane Banning; fam tradition that Jas was 1st of name from Eng. Jane, becoming wid, m Nicholas Goldsborough, who d 1756 (presumably of small pox, judging by incidental remark in Jeremiah's old journal) made his three stepsons his heirs.

Henry Geddes Banning only surviving child of Freeburn; res Wilm, Del; pres old Bank of Del. Emily Banning, nee Eschenburg, d Sep 13 1897, victim of paralysis, pres Soc of Colonial Dames of Del. Jas Latimer Banning and John H. Banning are the two child. of above. The latter, with wife Harriet, nee Tybout, res Del.

Jas Latimer Banning and Emma, his wife, nee Harris, have two child., H. G. Banning, Jr., and J. L. Banning, Jr. Emma Banning, nee Harris, d/o Alexander Harris and Maria, nee Spencer, of Spencers whose progenitor, Jas Spencer, settled on Miles River, Talb Co, 1670, his descendants known later in Kt Co, Md.

Of other names mentioned above Caesar A. Rodney atty general in Jefferson's cabinet, later U. S. minister to Argentine Republic, d there 1824; he was nephew of Caesar Rodney, signer of Declaration of Independence; first Rodneys settled in Del 1682.

Capt. Henry Gedddes, Rev naval officer (see Cooper's Naval History), m Margaret, d/o Jas Latimer and sis of Dr. Hy Latimer, of Del, Rev army surgeon; twice U. S. senator. Jas Latimer chairman of Del delegates at convention to ratify U. S. constitution.

Rbt Banning, older s/o Jeremiah, above mentioned, b 1776, d 1845; succeeded father in occupancy of Isthmus; collector port of Oxford; mbr house of delegates, capt of militia, war of 1812. On day of death visited by friend, Sml Kennard who suddenly stricken; both lay dead in house same time. Numerous descendants, but none remain on Eastern Shore. Of his child. one survives, Miss Mary E. Banning, at Winchester, Va, whose original work in botany, describing and illustrating native fungi of Md, preserved in N. Y. State Museum.

Of Wickes fam Capt. Lambert Wickes, one of America's successful Rev seamen. (See Cooper's History.) Major Ringgold, killed in Mex war. The progenitor of Ringgolds, came to Md 1650. The Spencers and Rodneys well known Eng families.

Capt. Henry Geddes of Irish birth; spent childhood (by fam tradition) about Carlingford Bay; b 1749, educated at Trinity College, Dublin, entered English navy, then the American navy 1775; d 1833.

In fol paragraph are excerpts from journal of Jeremiah Banning. In his journal he described early days of Oxford, circumstances of Rbt Morris's death, imprisonment of Capt Banning by French privateer, Braddock's arrival in Hampton Roads, in 1755, transport of Mr. Hood, the "stamp-master,' from London to Oxford. The writer states that "there is much of interest in the old journal, but space forbids more." (even less detail in this abbreviated version.)

Capt Banning took a load of Acadians from Nova Scotia when that territory was ceded by France to England, to Wye River, and distributed them among such planters as would receive them. ... In 1761 he took passage for London on the Betsey, in Eastern Bay, off Mr. Matthew Tilghmans'...separated from convoy by gales...captured by french privateer near Western Islands... Captain Bannnig and R. Tilghman, a youth permitted to remain on Betsey... in three weeks hove to off Vigo, awaiting daylight to enter ..., the Antelope, British fifty gun ship, retook Betsey and carried her into Lisbon; here he and his young friend, Dick Tilghman, restored to liberty. 1775 Mr. Banning elected first lieut of militia company to be raised at Courthouse (Easton); In Aug elected colonel of 38th Battalion of militia... app officer of port of Oxford Apr 1788. He

-185-

was first of four to rep Talb Co to a general convention at Annapolis to ratify and confirm the Federal government, of the U.S., along with Hon. Rbt Goldsborough, Hon. Edw Lloyd and Mr. John Stevens.

823 679. HON. JOHN MITCHELL ROBINSON, chief justice of Md, mbr court of appeals (Car, Talb, QA, Kt and Cecil Counties); descends from Rev Ralph Robinson, Protestant clergyman of Eng. The first of fam settled in Del over 200 yrs ago. Judge's grandfather, Ralph Robinson, planter Sussex Co, Del; the father, Peter, planter, moved to Car Co, where he owned prop. The 2nd son b of marriage to Sarah Mitchell was subj, b Car Co Dec 6 1827. When young he accompanied mother to QA Co; edcuated Dickinson College, Carlisle, Pa, studied law in Centreville; admitted to bar at 22. 1851 app dep atty general QA Co; state's atty; 1864 elected judge circuit court; judge 3rd judicial circuit; app chief judge of court of appeals 1893 to succeed Chief Judge Richard H. Alvey. When not engaged in judicial duties he res Waverly, one of old Tilghman homesteads. He d suddenly Annapolis Jan 14 1896 at 68, at home of dau, Mrs. Lloyd, w/o of Lieut Edw Lloyd, Jr, of the navy. Funeral at St. Anne's Episc Church, Annapolis; present: gov of Md, gen assembly, civil and military officers of the state, others; bur at cemetery at Waverley. (Many tributes by officials and other persons are quoted.) - 1857 Judge Robinson m Marian, d/o Thos A. Emory, mbr old QA Co fam, s/o Gen Thos A. Emory; on maternal side granddau of ex-Gov Levin Winder, of Md, lieut colonel Rev army. Their child.: Alice, w/o Frs Gowen, of Phila; Sallie M., w/o Anthony M. Hance, of Phila; Mariana W., w/o Wm F. Fullam, of U. S. navy; Elizabeth R., whose husb, Lieut Edw Lloyd, Jr, in U. S. navy; Ralph, atty Balt; and Amy, Mrs. Edw M. McIlvain of South Bethlehem, Pa. The wid res Waverley.

825 680. GEORGE W. COVINGTON res Still Pond, Kt Co, since 1851, when he came here to clerk for uncle, Dnl Haines, in general store. 1857 he purch from G. W. Price business he has since conducted; 1867 built storeroom and dwelling house; 1871-6 carried on general merc business at Lynch. He was b Middleton, Del 1836, of Eng ancestry.

His father, Nathaniel, b Del, farmer nr Middletown; latter part of life farmed nr St. Georges; d at 56, 1853; m Maria, d/o Daniel haines, of Del; their child.: subj and Jas H., now of Va.

Subj spent boyhood in Kt, Dor and Talb Cos, educated in public schools and Newton Acad, Balt. 1859 he m Helen E. Busick, of Kt Co; their child.: E. Lester, of N.Y.; Helen M.; Irene L., w/o J. C. Alston, farmer nr Middletown, Del; Jas C., in Phila; and Ethel, who m Dr. Wm E. Banard, dentist Middletown, Del. Subj postmaster at Still Pond under Pres Buchanan, at Lynch 1871; 1869 elected mbr of co school bd; he and wife mbrs ME Chruch; she d at 45, 1886.

826 681. ISAAC T. HEARN, farmer Snow Hill dist, Wor Co, b Jan 4 1867, Wicomico Co, s/o Hon. Isaac N. and Mary H. (Hayman) Hearn, of Md. Former was mbr of state legislature; owned over 2300 a.; in lumber busines Whitesville.

Grandfather Wm Hearn from Del, carried on large farms. His father, Thos Hearn, from Del, farmer, and his father, whose name was Wm, from Eng to Md 1681, had extensive land grants. Mason-Dixon line located through his land, greater part in Md; res on Del side. He lived to old age.

Subj next to youngest of 7 child., 3 decd: Olivia E., Wm and Harriet A.; living: Cordelia, Mary, subj, and Geo E. Following dist schools subj attended schools of Salisbury; began farming, milling to some extent. Mar 27 1888 he m Jennie E. Rodney, of Sussex Co, Del; related to 3 governors. Their child.: Mary H., 8; and Isaac J., 6. Mrs. Hearn mbr ME Church.

682. CAPT. DANIEL FRIEL, farmer, res on farm known as Heathworth, 3rd dist QA Co; once captain of boat that brought lime from Pa to farmers this area; co commissioner 1 term. Captain's father, Bernard Friel, b in north of Ireland, emigrated to America c. 1823, settled in Gettysburg, Pa. Of his fam 2 sons came to Md: Capt John and Capt Dnl, both settled in QA Co. Dnl b May 16 1821, d Jun 26 1892. He m Annette De Swan; their child.: Annie, wid of Jas B. Hess, this co; and Mary, m Chas Middleton, of Phila. Subj m(2) Christiana Kavanagh; their child.: Jane Maria, w/o Harry L. Boyd; Elizabeth R., unmarried; Dnl J., of Balt; Catherine V., Mrs. John H. Stokes, of Kt Co; John A. and Elva C., at home. Maiden name of captain's wid: Rebecca Gardner.   826

683. JAMES M. H. BATEMAN, M. D., physician, Easton, Talb Co, mbr state bd of examiners. Bateman is old Md fam. Subject's father, Hy E. Bateman (b Balt 1808), descended from Wm Bateman, of AA Co. He was editor of Easton Star, later clerk court of appeals for Eastern Shore, state librarian and comptroller of state; chief of depart commerce and navigation in treasury depart Wash; mbr state constitutional convention; commissiioner of Talb Co; d Nov 30 1893. Mother of Dr. Bateman was Ariana, d/o Jas Morrell and Mary (Lowe) Hopkins. Her father descended from Jas Morrell, of Balt Co, who m Elizabeth Sedgwick. The doctor's mother d Dec 21 1871. Of her 6 child., 4 living: Jas M. H.; Hy A., assist general superintendent of Balt & Ohio Railroad relief depart at Balt; J. Frank, state's atty of Talb Co; Wilfred, of Easton, and former clerk circuit court.   827
    Subj eldest son of fam, b Easton Nov 9 1844, attended school in Wash, D. C.; grad medical depart Univ Md 1867, began his practice at Easton. Nov 7 1871 he m Miss Elizabeth T. Goldsborough, d/o Jas N. Goldsborough, of Easton. Of their 8 child., 3 living: Jas G., Elizabeth T. and Hy E.

684. CAPT. THOMAS J. WALTER, mcht and farmer, Nanticoke, Tyaskin dist; b this co, Dec 7 1841, s/o Wm and Elizabeth (Porter) Walter, both from this co and parents of 4 child.; fol living: Thos J., subj; Margaret and W. A. The father of Wm Walter named Wm, b and reared on Eastern Shore. He d c. 78. All three generations were farmers. Capt Walter gained title during five yrs on bay as sailor and master of a ship. He was judge of elections 6 yrs. May 1871 he m Mary E. Harrington, of Wicomico Co, d/o Capt. Alfred Harrington, who followed the high seas as a career. Of 4 child. b to the Walters, one child survived, Bernice.   828

685. DAVID J. HOPKINS, decd, business man, Kt Co, Del, b Kt Co, Del, Sep 1 1853, s/o John and Mary A. (Taylor) Hopkins, of Del. His grandfather, John Hopkins, Sr, b Del; farmer. Subj was one of 5 children; educated in local schools, then placed in charge of a school, which he taught 2 yrs; turned to farming; d leaving over 400 a., now managed by wid. He m Feb 15 1876, Mary Tharp, who survives him, d/o Benj and Mary E. (Fleming) Tharp, of Del, and granddau of Llewellyn Tharp, land owner in Del and also b there. Children of Mr. Hopkins and wife: Benj, John, D. Norman and Mary. Benj grad from commercial college in Wilm, Del, now bookkeeper of C. T. George, of Phila. John attends Fisk's Telegraphic School, Pa. Mr. Fisk d Feb 22 1886, at 33. Mrs. Hopkins mbr Meth Church.

686. JAMES W. HARRINGTON, farmer QA Co, po address: Roe, res homestead called Duhamel estate, 6th dist; operates sawmill. Wm, father of J. W. Harrington, b Car Co, nr Henderson, in early 1800's. His father, Philemon Harrington, from Del, became res this state 1790. His father was Englisman who emigrated 1740.   829

-187-

Wm Harrington, farmer and mbr of his church; d 1867. He m Miss Ann Mria Clements, d/o Jas Clements, of Del; she d 1879. Of her 13 child., fol living: subj; Ann Maria, Mrs. H. R. Cooper, of Wilm, Del; Geo, res Millington, Md; and Louisa, Mrs. Rbt Colgan, of Wilm. - Subj b on farm nr Henderson, Car Co, Nov 5 1825; attended dist school in winter terms; carpenter at Church Hill 12 yrs. 1858 he purch prop where he res; mbr ME Church. He m(1) Rachel Rebecca Tolson, who d May 1854, leaving 3 child. He m(2) Sarah Maria Spry, who d Sep 1858; both their children decd. Jan 23 1862 Mr. Harrington m Charlotte E.Brown, of Church Hill; they had 9 child.

830   687. THE EARLE FAMILY.   taken from old Bible; most of narrative appears in handwriting of Jas Earle (abbreviated and rearranged by this compiler).

My grandfather, Jas Earle, b Jul 25, 1631, about 10 yrs before rebellion of Ireland, d Md 24 Sep, 1684, leaving wid and many sons and daus. His wid, Rhodah Earle, afterward married and lived in Md until she d 20 Oct 1714; no child. by latter marriage. She d about 74th yr, came to Md with husb Jas Earle Nov 15 1683 and brought with them 13 child. Oldest son, John, then in the country, captain of a ship, afterward taken captive, lived in slavery some yrs, finally murdered by a couple of villains.

Michael Earle, my father, 2nd s/o Jas and Rhodah, m Sarah Stevens 14 Oct 1686; she d Mar 7 1688, leaving no child. The aforesaid Michael Earl, my father afterward on 27 Dec 1690 at Trumping Town, on Chester River, m Ann Carpenter; had 4 child.; oldest son b 27 Nov 1692, d same day. Their next were twins: Elizabeth and Jas (which Jas is myself), b Feb 17 1694, Sunday, said Elizabeth about 5 p.m, Jas about half an hour later. Fourth child b 26 Dec 1697, Sunday, named Carpenter, mother's maiden name. Aforesiad Carpenter Earle m Mary Thomas, had one son, Jos, b after said Carpenter d, Christmas Eve 1720, leaving behind him Jos, now under the care of my uncle, Jos Earle.

My sis, Elizabeth Earle, m Sep 1712 Maj Wm Turbutt and d Sep 29 1725, leaving 4 child.: Michael, Annna Maria T., Mary and Elizabeth T. My father and mother, Michael and Ann Earle, d 5 Apr 1709, of violent pleurisy which raged in QA Co; both bur in one grave at old burying place Sprigg's Point, commonly called Carpenter's Point.

Myself, 2nd s/o Michael and Ann Eajrle m Mary Tilghman, d/o Richard Tilghman, and Anna Maria, his wife, whose maiden name was LLoyd. We were m at home of Richard Tilghman, 12 Oct 1721, and lived with Richard until 19 Apr 1723, when we began housekeeping in present dwelling plantation QA Co. Our first child, Michael Earle, b Oct 19 1722. Anna Maria Earle, 2nd child, b May 1725. Richard Tilghman Earle, our 3rd child b Jul 10 1727, d Jan 17 1728. Richard Tilghman Earle, our 4th child, b Feb 10 1728. Henrietta Maria Earle, our 5th child, b Nov 26 1730. Jos Earle, our 6th child b Nov 11 1732, d next day. Jas Earle, 7th child, b Apr 21 1734.

My wife, Mary called Mary Tilghman b Aug 23 1702, d Jan 10 1736; bur on right of her two babies, Richard Tilghman and Jos Earle, who d before her. It was a violent cold day. The Rev Mr. Holt preached her funeral sermon.

I m(2) at her home, Nov 6 1738, Sarah Chetham, wid of Edw Chetham, of QA Co; her maiden name was Carp, d/o John Crapp, of Phila, at which place she was born. - (End of bible portion)

By second marriage of Jas Earle a son, Jos b after death of father. Richard Tilghman Earle settled on estate that his son, late Judge Earle, called Nedwood, and there d 1788. He m 1755 Anne, d/o Sml Chamberlain, of Talb Co. 10 children were b to them, 4 sons and 6 daus, whose mother d in Aug 1786. Judge Richard Tilghman Earle, of this fam, b Jun 23 1767, educated Wash College, Chestertown, with honors; studied law under Thos B. Hand, of

Chestertown; admitted to bar 1789. For 25 yrs he served as chief judge of 2nd judicial dist of Md, resigning because of ill health. He m Dec 4 1801, Mary Tilghman, d/o Judge Jas Tilghman, his predecessor on the bench. She d 1836; they had 14 child., 3 d in infancy. Others: Elizabeth Anne, b Oct 14 1802; Mary Maria, Oct 9 1804; Susan Frisby, Mar 5 1808; Richard Tilghman, b Apr 11 1810 and d Aug 14 1814; Henrietta Maria, b Aug 16 1812; Jas Tilghman, Dec 22 1814; Richard Tilghman, b Dec 22 1816; Sml Thomas Jul 2 1818; Sarah Catherine, b Jun 30 1820, d Sep 28 1822; Geo, b Sep 10 1821; John C., May 10 1824; and Sarah Catherine, Aug 11 1827.

Of this fam Richard m(1) Catherine Spencer and m(2) her sis, Elizabeth Spencer. Jas m(1) Ann Johns and m(2) Catherine Tilghman; their child.: Ann Johns m Wm Babcock, lawyer patent office Wash. Jas m(3) Mary F. Wright, d/o Clinton Wright. He d in 1882, leaving two sons, Jas T. and Richard T., both in school Balt. Geo was assist to Postmaster General John a. J. Creswell under Pres Grant, mbr of constitutional convention of 1867 and clerk of court of appeals of Md. He went west and bt large tracts in Wash, in minning, continuing law practice; present res Wash, D. C., practically retired.

Elizabeth, eldest d/o fam, m P. H. Feddeman; had 3 daus and 2 sons, latter being P. Henry, res N.Y. for yrs, and Richard Tilghman Feddeman, farmer and loan agent, whose 1st wife was Mrs. Clayton and his 2nd Deborah, d/o Gustavus Wright. Mary, 2nd d/o Judge Earle, m Philip Davidson, and d leaving two sons, Richard T. and Geo, and 2 daus, Catherine and Susan. Susan, 3rd d/o Judge Earle, d unmarried. Henrietta Maria became w/o Dr.David Stewart, long time druggist Balt, once state chemist; she d leaving a dau, Henrietta Maria, who m Thos Dilworth, of Port Penn, Del. Sarah Catherine, Judge Earle's youngest dau, m Dr. Jos Chamberlain, of Easton, where they now res. Dr. John C. Earle, youngest son, grad Newark (Del) Coll; once practiced in Centreville, now res Easton; he m Clara d/o Col Nicholas Goldsboro, living nr Oxford Neck.

688. PEREGRINE TILGHMAN FORMAN, business man, Centreville, dealer in hardware and farming implements. Record of Forman fam appears in sketch of subject's brother, E. M., on another page this vol. Subj b on Recovery, farm of grandfather, Peregrine Tilghman, 3rd dist QA Co, Feb 13 1853; educated in local schools. At 20 he secured employment with Wm McKenney, remained 11 yrs, 1883 he embarked in hardware business on Commerce st; firm of Chambers, Forman & Co; when partnership dissolved he continued in store adjoining his brother's drug store. 1883 he m Florence Elma, d/o Jos O. and Florence M. Rasin, of Centreville, where she d 1884. 832

689. J. LANE FINLEY, M. D., Church hill, QA Co, great-grandson of Jas Finley, lawyer who managed large plantation, had fortune in land and slaves. Washington Finley, M. D., subject's father, b 2nd dist QA Co, educated in West Nottingham acad and at Bel Air, Harford Co; instructor in languages Bel Air Coll; studied medicine under Dr. Goldsborough Centreville; grad medical depart Univ Md 1835; in practiced 10 yrs, turned to management of large real estate interests; mbr house of delegates; surveyor port of Balt; chief judge orphans' court; candidate for gov of Md; d Aug 3 1896, bur Church Hill Cem. Of large family b of his union with Sallie A. Harrison, only subj and State Senator W. P. Finley surivie. - Subj b on old homestead, 2nd dist QA Co, Dec 25 1860; attended West Nottingham Acad, 2 yrs in Princeton, grad Univ Md 1884; then professional practice in Chruch Hill. 1885 he m Miss Margaret P. Grason; of their 4 children, 3 are decd: Margaret, Helen R. and Sterett G. Richard Harrison only, survives. 835

835 690. SAMUEL THOMAS EARLE, s/o Judge Richard T. and Mary (Tilghman) Earle, spent his early yrs on farm, attended school in Bel Air. Since 1836 he has res at Melfield, which he inherited from his father. He served as judge of orphans' court 24 yrs. Judge Earle m(1) Mary U., d/o Wm Brundige, of Balt, mcht that city. They had 7 child. who attained maturity: (1) Jas T. joined 1st Md Cav in Confed army, but d during his service; (2) Wm Brundige Earle res Winton, where father b, m Louisa Stubbs, of Norfolk, Va, has 3 child.: Fannie; William B., a clerk in Centreville; and Swepson, who is in Balt. (3) Richard Tilghman, 3rd son, widower res farm nr his father. (4) Dr. Sml T., grad Agricultural College, prof Univ Md and leading surgeon of Balt; he m(1) Isabella Ringgold, mother of daus, Isabella and Rosetta; he m(2) Dinette Tyler. (5) Mary, d/o Judge Earle, m P. Henry Feddeman, late of Centrevile, now decd; they had 3 child., Ellen Douglas, Sml Earle and Henry. (6) Catherine w/o E. M. Forman. (7) Another dau, d at 22. Judge Earle m(2) Rosetta M. Brundige, sis of 1st wife.

836 691. COL. WILLIAM J. VANNORT of Chestertown. 1890 he was Republican party's nominee gov, receiving large vote, but defeated. His father, Wm, b N.J. and through his mother connected with same fam of Gen. Winfield Scott; came to Chestertown c. 1827; was carriage maker; went to Phila 1844, employed in same trade on Cherry st. Returning to Kent Co he embarked in merc and lumber business at Turner's Creek, then farmed 10 yrs, then merc and lumber business in Chestertown. 1865 he retired; d 1883. He m Catherine D. Adams, b Mercer Co, N. J.; d Chestertown Apr 1888; both identifd with MP Church.

In fam of Wm Vannort there were 5 sons and one dau, of whom one son d at 8, and Augustus d in Hanesvile, Kt Co, where he was in business. Sml, farmer, rep this dist in state legislature one term. Ezra Adams, physician in Union army, after war practiced in Hanesville. Mary A. H. is w/o J. H. Simpers, mcht of Chestertown.

Subj b Jul 9 1835 Chestertown, educated in public schools and in Phila and in Wash Coll; went into merchandising at Rising Sun. 1860 he returned to Chestertown, in busines at outbreak of Civ war; raised company to join Union army, his men consolidated with Company H, 2nd Md Infantry; commissioned second lieut. With his regt he went to Va, later at Antietam; took part in engagements in Shanandoah Valley. At Snicker's Ford wounded in right lung and left leg. From 1871-1880 he res on farm, moved to res which he built in Chestertown. Dec 27 1870 he m Mrs. Avis E. Bartholow nee Dennning, who was b in Balt. 1895 he was chairman of Md delegation to Cleveland; 1896 delegate to natl convention St. Louis.

837 692. WILLIAM C. MITCHELL, Salisbury dist, Wicomico, treasurer Salisbury Canning Co and owner of farm, Whitefield; tax collector; b on farm where he now res May 28 1859. His father, Geo T., s/o Isaac Mitchell, ancestors from Ireland, b nr Salisbury, farmer and mason, until he d 1877; identified with ME Church. He m Susan, d/o John Reddish, b Salisbury dist, d here 1896. They had 6 child., all but one living. Elizabeth, oldest of fam, unmarried. Mary A., w/o Thos W. Waller, co commissioner of Wicomico Co, res Salisbury; John S. res Balt; and Geo E., mcht Salisbury. Subj attended grammar and high schools at Salisbury; taught school 1879-91, until he fell heir to estate, Whitefield, where he now res. Nov 24 1885 he m Caroline Hastings, d/o E. S. Hastings, of Salisbury dist; their child.: Olive, Thurman, Victor and Horace.

693. WILLIAM E. BROWN, business man, Denton, b nr Bridgeville, Sussex Co, 838
Del, Dec 4 1863, s/o Dnl and Ann (Smith) Brown, of that co. His paternal
grandfather, Hy Brown, farmer, as was maternal grandfather, Wm Smith, the
latter grandson of Englishman who came to this country prior to Rev war.
Mother of subj, who d Mar 7 1890, had bros: Hy, farmer of Md; David, farmer,
Del; Dnl, soldier U. S. army, served in west; and Lacy, farmer. Subject's
father, b 1815, tanner and hatter, later farming; still res Sussex Co.
Parental fam of 8 child.: 3 decd, 2 d in childhood; Maggie E., who m H. B.
Tuthill, station agent Cambridge, Md, d Mar 7 1894; Mary W., wid of L. Q.
Smith and res Phila; Jas H., former res Ohio and Wash state, now builder &
contractor Car Co; Martha, w/o J. M. Walters, farmer res nr Seaford, Del;
Albretta, w/o J. W. Clark, Jr., of Denton; subj, youngest. Subj educated in
country schools and Bridgeville Acad; taught school 11 yrs, 1 year principal
at Selbyville, Del, 3 yrs principal Denton schools; mbr Meth Church. Since
1893 in business. 1887 he m Melissa E. Smoot, d/o Wm Smoot, farmer of Car Co.
Their dau: Jeannette.

694. EMERSON G. POLK, business man, Pocomoke City, retired; private banking 838
business; mbr Presby Church, Rehobeth, Som Co; entire life Wor Co, first 15
yrs on farm nr Pocomoke City; walked to public school in town; apprentice to
tailor's trade under his bro Wm, in Pocomoke City, 5 yrs; mcht tailor in
partnership with bro. 1897 he sold out to his son. He m(1) in 1861, Miss
Addie O. Dryden; their dau, Addie, decd at 7. 1867 he m Miss Louisa W.
Benson; their child.: Annie, m Wm Schoolfield, d 1895; Emerson W., who took
over father's business; and Carrie H. 1895 Mr. Polk m Miss L. Alma Polk.

695. CHRISTOPHER G. LYNCH res Rose Cottage, farmer 4th dist;; served Confed 839
army. Attending Centreville Acad, QA Co as war approached, at 17, enlisted
4th Md, Chesapeake Battery; under Stonewall Jackson in Richmond campaign;
captured just prior to war's end. Jas P., father of subj, from QA Co, farmer;
d 1847. He m Sarah E., d/o Christopher Goodhand, of QA Co; they had 4 child.;
she d 1880. All bros and sis of subj decd. He was b QA Co Sep 14 1844; after
war he went into farming; 1882 came to present homestead, owned by bro-in-law,
nr Wye Landing. He is mbr Episc Church. Jan 4 1867 he m Elizabeth Dudley;
their child.: J. Dudley, res Phila; Willard N., bookkeeper Phila firm; and two
younger, Harry F. and J. Holton, at home.

696. EDWIN DASHIELL, JR. business man, Cambridge, insur business, rep 13 840
companies. Edwin Dashiel, Sr, b nr New Church, Accomac Co, Va, operated farm
nr Bucktown this co. Lost much of fortune through generosity to friends and
trust in others; now res Cambridge, in 70th yr; c. 20 yrs ago sheriff this co.
He m Ellen L. Gordon, of Wicomico (now) Co, still living, also at 70. Of
their 5 child. all but one grew to maturity. Subj b Apr 13 1857, at Keene's
Ditch, Dor Co, reared on father's farm nr Bucktown, educated dist school;
clerked in general store Bucktown. Studied on his own; in charge of school at
Hills Point 2 yrs; went into sale of fertilizer, rep his business house during
season in Cambridge, traveling remainder of year as general agent in Del, Va,
Md and parts of Pa. While at Centreville one day he met a bro of Senator
Gibson, insur man and persuaded to go into that business. Jun 4 1890 he m
Nora, d/o Dr. Jas L. Bryan, res Cambridge. (See his sketch elsewhere.) Their
child.: Shirley, now 3; Jas Bryan, 17 months, and one d in infancy. Parents
mbrs Episc Church.

840 697. THE POLK FAMILY. Judge Wm Polk, assoc judge court of appeals Md and chief justice circuit court of dist, res south side of Wicomico River, above Green Hill. He was father of Ann Polk and Col Jas Polk, the latter b Som Co 1794, rgtr of wills for Som Co 1818-45. The dau w/o Herschel V. Johnson, of Ga, candidate for vice-pres on Stephen A. Douglas ticket 1860. During admin of Jas K. Polk, collector of port of Balt was Col Jas Polk. The two familes were related, grandfather of Pres Polk from Eastern Shore and bro of Judge Polk's father. Esther, d/o Jas Polk, w/o Enoch Louis Lowe, gov of Md, 1 or 2 sons distinguished actors, especially Lucius Polk, of N.Y. Mbrs of Polk fam rose to distinction in Md, N.C. and Tenn. Some think original name was Pollock and that ancestors came from north of Ireland; others believe they came from Scotland.

841 698. ELIHU WHEATLEY always res Dor Co, presently New Market dist; b northern part Dor Co 1824, s/o Wm Wheatley; little schooling; small in stature, but quick and active; currently troubled with rheumatism. He m Mary Stevens and their 4 child. lived to mature yrs. Fol death of wife, Mr. Wheatley m Jennie Stevens; they had 4 child. Mrs. Wheatley mbr ME Church.

841 699. THOMAS GALE, farmer, 3rd dist Kt Co; farmer in this are since 1867. Gale fam of Eng extraction, followers of Church of England. The first rep came to America 1694, settled in Kt Co, farmer. Thos Gale, grandfather of subj, res Still Pond Neck, owning farm, now prop of W. D. Pennington; once co surveyor. His child.: John, Jas, Martha, Sarah and Mary. Major Gale, who attained prominence in Mexican war, was cousin of the fam. John Gale, father of subj, spent life on farm Kt Co, owned Worton manor house, former prop of Boardley family nr Gale's wharf. He m(1) Leonora Sutton; of their 3 child., 1 reached maturity, subj. John m(2) Sarah A. Rasin; their child.: John and Wm R. The father was mbr of St. James' MP Church; d 1872, at 62. Subj b 1840 on farm adjoining present home; educated public schools and Wash Coll, Agric Coll nr Wash. C. 1850 his father purch Eisenberry farm, to which he moved 1867. 1873 he m Rachel Parsons, d/o Isaac Parsons; their child, Lena.

842 700. EDWARD ATKINSON POWELL, res Trappe, Talb Co, s/o Wm N. Powell, who d 1884, grandson of Howell Powell, Jr, and great-grandson of Howell Powell, of Welsh extraction, early Quaker settlers Talb Co. Subj eldest of present generation, b nr Trappe Feb 6 1851. 3 sis succeeded him, Elizabeth Needles, Hetty Anna and Sallie Kemp; all m. His mother was Sallie K. Atkinson, who d 1889. 1883 subj m Annie L. Maddin, of Wyoming, Del; their dau, Edith Needles, b 1884. Mr. Powell presently judge orphans' court Talb Co, once treasurer almshouse Talb Co; educated Westtown boarding school Pa, taught short time; bookkeeper & accountant in leading commercial house Balt City. A few yrs before father's death he returned to old homestead, took charge of father's buiness, tilled the farms, later began conducting store in Trappe.

843 701. COL. CHAUNCEY H. THOMPSON, virtually retired on homestead St. Michael's dist Talb Co. His paternal grandfather, John, private in Rev war; from Conn., lived to old age. Father of subj, Wm Thompson, from Conn., moved to Jefferson Co, N. Y., where he farmed; m Miss Mary Chapen, of N.Y.; their child.: Sarah, Wm and subj. Father and mother both d c. 84.; both connected with Congregational Church. Subj b Huntington, Conn, 1835, moved to N.Y. when a yr old; educated in public schools and private acad; in harness making until Civ war; enlisted Company A, 10th Indiana Infantry, as private; in battle of Rich Mountain received gunshot wound in right thigh; about a yr later re-entered

service as capt, having organized 5th Indiana Cav; promoted to senior major; with Burnside on eastern Tennessee campaign and Sherman in Ga; captured at Macon, Ga, in prison at Charleston. Jan 1865 promoted to Lieut Colonel. Returning home he resumed harness making, conducted retail store Logansport, Ind, about 5 yrs; in wholesale and retail harness manufacturing 7 yrs Detroit, Mich; 12 yrs Minneapolis, Minn, same business; then bt prop with plans to retire. Feb 22 1871 he m Laura E. Gresham, of New York City, d/o John Gresham, of that city, owner of sawmills and ship builder of New York and Albany. He d in 65th year. His father served in Rev war. Mother of Mrs. Thompson d at about 52. Of her 5 children only Mrs. Thompson and son, Jas, survive. Subj and wife have 4 child., 3 living: Carrie, at home; Chas H., in chemical laboratory work in N.Y.; and Edith May, at home.

702. WILLIAM W. HEARN, farmer 3rd dist, Dor Co; 1865, he purch homestead, Maple Grove (448 a.). Wm Hearn, 1st of fam to settle in America, came from Eng, and located in Dor Co, later partially on Del side when Mason-Dixon line estab. A companion of Wm Hearn in early settlement was Jordan Hairun, who had barony in Northumberland, dating back to time of King Henry I., A. D. 1100. W. W. Hearn possesses history (in book form) of Hearn family, tracing lineage to A. D. 1066, when one of fam went with Wm the Conqueror from Normandy to Eng, and annals of succeeding generations are chronicled down to Wm, emigrant to this country. Sir Wm Hearn, Knight of Maidenhead, Berks, high sheriff of London 1797, and his ancestor, Sir Richard Hearn, held the same position in 1618. Paternal grandfather of subj was Wm Hearn, mentioned above; subject's father was Josiah, 1st Hearn b in America, (of this branch at least); b Sussex Co, Del., d 1837. He m Sarah Lowe, of Del; of their 7 child., 2 survive, Benj B., of Cambridge, Md., and subj. The mother d i1848.

Subj b Sussex Co, Del, Nov 22 1824. As his father d when he was young, the lad left school early; went into cabinet and wagon making in Laurel, Del. 1 Jan 1846, he came to Vienna, in partnership with bro opened shop and carried on his trade. 1857-1865 he rented different farms in co. 1865 he settled on Maple Grove farm; 1887 assessor of this dist. He is mbr Bapt Church; m(1) Miss Mary Nichols, who d 1858; of their 4 child., only Wm R. survives, res Cambridge. Later he m Mrs. Esther Ann Robinson, who d 1895, leaving Chas B., of Balt, and Henrietta, at home. Mr. Hearn later m Miss Sophia Smith (still living).

844

703. COLLISON WADDELL, 4th dist Car Co; owns nearly 700 a. Waddell is old Md family. Paternal grandfather of subj Alexander Waddell; his parents were Wm and Nancy Waddell, the latter d/o Daniel Cheezum, of this co. Subj b this co 1810, followed the sea, 1841 settled on farm Dor Co; 4 yrs later came to Car Co, bt land nr Bethlehem, which he tilled over 50 yrs; m 1841 Henrietta, d/o Jas A. Mowbray, of Dor Co; their child.: Wm Bishop; Jas W., of Cambridge; Columbus, of Hurlock, Md.; Victoria, d when young; David F., of Felton, Del; Winfield, M., of Otterbein, Ind.; and Thos Collison and Walter Scott, of the same place. W. M. and T. C. are mchts; and W.S. is a farmer and stock raiser of that locality. - Wm Bishop Waddell, eldest s/o subj, b Dor Co, 1842, reared chiefly this co; sailed about a yr with Capt. C. S. Carmine, visiting West Indies; at Charleston, S. C., while Civ war in progress; returning home, settled on farm; constable 4th dist; then in fruit and vegetable packing business Indiana, returned to Md. He m Ella, d/o Robt K. Collison, of this co; she d about yr later; their infant son, Wm Elwood, d in infancy. He m(2) Miss Agnes H., d/o Rbt and Helene (Lauder) Laing; her parents b and m

845

Scotland. Their children: Jas M., eldest, decd; others: Ella B., Wm B., Jr., Grover S., Agnes H., Ira S., Rose M. and Walter Laing.

846 704. JOHN R. PATTISON, atty Cambridge; 1896 delegate natl convention of Democratic party; mbr Democratic state compaign committee. Father of subj, also named John R. Pattison, b nr Cambridge, Dor Co, farmer; bro of Rev Rbt H. Pattison, of ME Church serving in Md and Pa, whose son, Rbt E., former gov of Pa. The grandfather, Sml Pattison, b and res Md, s/o Jeremiah and grandson of Jacob Pattison, whose father, Jas, b Eng and came to America c. 1650, settled on James Island, Dor Co. John R. Pattison, Sr., d 1882, at 60. His wife, Mary Ann Burroughs, d 1863, when subj 3. She left 5 child.: Annie t., Hattie T., Sml S., Jas B. and subj. The father m(2) Emily De Valin, sis of Chas De Balin, of U. S. navy; their child. who attained maturity: Mary Y. and Hugh De Valin. - Subj b Jan 6 1860, 4 miles south of Cambridge; attended public schools Cambridge until 19; read law with S. T. Milburn, Cambridge, admitted to bar 1882. Prev taught school, instructor Cambridge Acad until 1887. Meantime examiner in chancery and auditor of court; elected state's atty. 1888 he m Lillian Stapleford; their son, John R., Jr.

846 705. CAPT. JOHN W. SELBY, retired sea captain, 4th dist QA Co, Kt Island. From his 12th year on high seas; built, was master of, and finally sold a many vessels. He was b Wor Co, 1837, and there educated. His father and grandfather both from Va, from old fam there, hailing from Eng a few generations ago. 1867 subj retired, settling in Sharptown, ship carpenter until 1890. Since then res 4th dist in building and contracting, and has run a sawmill. Captain Selby m(1) 1858 in Sharptown and after death of wife m Miss Taylor 1861; of their 4 child., 2 d in childhood. Chas W. is mcht of this island and John T. in business Balt. Their mother d and later subj m Margaret Burford. Their eldest child, Annie, w/o Jas W. Crouch; other child.: Jas Gordon, Hattie Washington, Mamie Ellen and Edna.

847 706. JAMES BENSON, b Jul 18 1818, d Aug 23 1890 at St. Michael's, Talb Co. His father, Chas Benson, descendant of old fam this co, b 1790, in merc pursuits, d 1864. He m Rachel, d/o Thos and Elizabeth Esgate, mbr of old fam this section, d here 1842, at 56; mbr ME Church.

Subj attended public schools; assist father in store; apprentice to uncle, Rbt Benson Balt, in shoe business, Balt. Returning home he added shoe depart to father's store; then opened store here himself; 1843 lost prop by fire; started again; because of ill health he purch farm nr St. Michael's where he regained his strength. 1867 purch estate, Maiden Point, res there until 1875, returned to St. Michael's, turned to sale of fertilizers and insur business, assisted by son, Ottis Harper. Subj mbr ME Church. Collector state and co taxes Talb Co 1862-3. 1841 he m Elizabeth, d/o Edw and Elizabeth Harrison, of this co; her father, ship builder Balt. Of their 14 child., 4 living. Subject's wife d Feb 1861; he later m Mary Ann, d/o Perry Benson, of Royal Oak, this co. She now survives him, res with son, Otis Harper, unmarried. He was b Jul 4 1866, educated public schools and business college Balt, assisted father in business until father's death, then mangaed estate; owns music store St. Michael's and agent for Montgoemry Mutual Fire Insur Co; local treasurer for Balt Bldg and Loan Assoc; mbr ME Church.

848 707. WILLIAM G. QUIMBY, farmer 4th dist, Talb Co, nr Wye Mills; from Del, of 3rd generation named Wm.; rents farm called Willton, about 1000 a.; all but 300 a. under cultivation this season; farm owned by John Coppage, QA Co. Wm

Quimby, Sr., of Kt co, carpenter; music teacher Phila public school; later led singing in ME Church; app clerkship in Annapolis 1872, d before term expired. He m(1) Mary E. Kennard, who d 1861; m(2) Anne Orrell, still living. Children by 1st marriage: Wm; John, of QA Co; Thos, whose sketch elsewhere this vol; Sarah A., wid of Geo H. Tarbutton, of Skipton; Jas and Chas, both of QA Co; and one decd. Subj b Feb 14 1845. In winter seasons he attended local dist schools until 12; then worked full time for father until 21. Jan 10 1872 he m Ella B., d/o Jas Tarbutton, of Skipton; she d May 1874. He later m Jan 12 1882, Sarah Smith, d/o Wm C. Smith, of Del; their child.: Frank, Alfred, Parker; 2 d in infancy.

708. JOSEPH H. RICHARDSON, mbr ME Church; rents farm 6th dist; owns Klund farm 6th dist in partnership with bro. Jos Richardson, Sr. mbr ME Church; m Mary Stevens of Del; of their 12 child. all but two decd; remaining: subj and Mary A., w/o Jas T. Anthony, of this co. The father d 1882; his wife d 9 yrs earlier. Subj b nr village of Star, QA Co, Apr 23 1844; res with parents until 1871 when he m Louisa Legg, who d 1879; later m Florence McCloud who d Feb 8 1897, leaving 3 daus, Viola, Inez and Agnes. By 1st marriage: Mary Lillie and Raymond.   849

709. JOHN M. PERRY res Spring Garden, old homestead in fam many generations, 3rd dist QA Co. He manages this place and deals in implements; owns threshing machine; b here Nov 1 1859. Same fam as that of famous Commodore Perry. John W., subject's father, and John, his grandfather, both b 3rd dist QA Co, farmers. John W. Perry once served as assessor; still living at 78. He m Emma C. Mackey, of Easton, Talb Co, who d 1892. Of their 12 child., 7 living: Annie E., w/o J. Elliott, of Germantown, Pa.; Emma J., Mrs. John R. Cook, of Centreville; Lillie A., m Theodore Tolson, of Kent Island; John M.; Elva, Ernest and Rose. Subj educated in local schools, later grad commercial coll Poughkeepsie, N.Y. 1887; became interested in farm implement busines. Jan 7 1883 he m Miss Addie Wilkinson, d/o Capt. John Wilkinson, rep on another page. She d Mar 23 1895, leaving child.: Ella, Emma, Bessie, John, Fannie and Isabel. Subj m(2) Feb 18 1897, Emily Josephine Stapleford, of Cambridge, of old fam connected with Pattisons.   849

710. JOHN O. MILLS, res Bishop's Head, Straits dist, Dor Co, as were several generations before him. He follows oyster trade, as did his ancestors, and operates several boats. Father of subj, Wm R. Mills, b and reared this area, oysterman; mbr ME Church; d Mar 2 1895, in 73rd year. He m Rebecca Dean; of their children 2 decd; living: Rbt P., Malachi, John O., Wm A. Angeline and Susan R. The mother res old homestead. Subj b this dist 1855, educated in public schools. He and wife mbrs ME Church. 1883 he m Jennie, d/o Z. F. and Martha J. (Bramble) Jones, of Bishop's Head; they had 5 sons and daus.   850

711. HON. THOMAS R. GREEN, sheriff Car Co, b Kt Co, Del, Dec 18 1853, s/o Jonathan S. and Elizabeth (Reed) Green, of that co. He was 2 yrs old when his father d, and 6 when his mother d. Fam consisted of 10 child; he was youngest. Fol mother's death, subj res with bro, Jas, once mbr Md legislature; attended country schools and acad at Newark, Del; employed in store at Marydel, Car Co, owned by bro, Jas. At 22 he and bro began phosphate business, continuing until subj elected to legislature 1887; elected sheriff 1895. He m in 1884, Miss Annie Smith, of Denton, d/o Jas N. Smith, mcht. She is identified with Episc Church; their child.: Elsie, Woodall and Thos.   850

852   712. HON. GEORGE M. VANSANT, res 2nd dist QA Co, mbr state legislature; s/o Joshua L. Vansant, of QA Co; 1 of 4 child., in order of birth: Geo M.; Cornelia, decd; Sadie E. and J. Frank.   Subj b 1st dist   QA Co, Jul 1 1862. Both parents d same yr; dwelt with grandparents 4 yrs; found farm work with neighbors; education interrupted and fragmentary. At 18 he obtained teacher's certificate. After teaching a term or so he clerked in an Easton store; student Wash Coll, at Chestertown 2 yrs; later taught graded school 5 yrs; bt homestead of 160 a. in 2nd dist a few yrs ago. He m 1888 Miss Julia A. McGinnis; their child.: Mary J., Edith A. and Ethel G.

852   713.   JAMES W. URIE, M. D. has   practice at Still Pond 2nd dist Kt Co; health officer of co since 1895; b 1863 Goose Hill, this co; descendant of Scotch ancestry; John Urrie, of Scotland, settled in Md latter part of 18th century and fol cooper's trade.   His descendants mostly farmers.   Subject's grandfather, Jas Urie, in general merc business, first mcht Still Pond, later moved to central part of co and founded Urieville; judge orphan' court.   Jas Urie, subject's father, b Urieville; moved to Goose Hill with father.   He estab 1st nursery in Kt Co, and carried on many yrs; superintended large farm; d 1866. He m Mary E. Kendall; their child.: Mollie, wid of E. L. McGinnis; John D; Helen E., w/o J. Hammond, of Fla; Jas W., and Frank H. res of Fla. When one year old subj taken by parents to QA Co; educated in public schools; course in Agric and Mechanical Coll of Va, and Wash College; grad Hahnemann Medical Coll 1886; opened office Still Pond; once 2nd vice-pres Md Medical Society.

853   714. EDGAR A. P. JONES, M. D., young physician, Dor Co, located in Crapo, Lake dist, past 4 yrs.   Father of subj likewise medical practitioner, Dr. Elias Jones, now of Balt; b Car Co, spent youth in Federalsburg; attended Univ Mdj. 1890 he moved to Balt, app store keeper in U. S. custom house. He is pres of proposed Cambridge & Chesapeake Railroad, to run through lower part of co. He m Mary Nichols who was reared Car Co. They had 6 children: Dr. A. C. now decd; Harvey, druggist Wingate, Dor Co; subj; and 3 daus. Jones fam of Eng descent, in Md several generations. Grandfather of subj E. Jones, of Car Co; sailor; res in native co greater part of life, later settling here.   Subj b Car Co 1872; at 3 his parent brought him to this co. After dist schools he entered Balt City Coll; grad Balt Medical College 1893; returned to Lake dist, took charge of practice of bro, A. C. in Crapo, owing to latter's serious illness.

854   715.   JOHN C. JONES, farmer 3rd dist Kt Co; b Car Co 1844, s/o Richard and Elizabeth Jones; of Eng descent; his grandfather, Wm Jones, came to Md from Eng, settled in Car Co. Little known except that he was a farmer. On this prop, nr Henderson, Richard Jones, farmed; owned large tracts and many slaves. By his marriage he became father of 13 child., 5 decd. Surviving: Marcellus, Sml T., Sarah Amanda, Eleanor, subj, Florence, A. W. and Geo M.   F. The father d 1879, at 73.   Subj attended local schools of Car Co; at 25 went to Indiana; after 3 yrs returned to Car Co, where he farmed 2 yrs. 1876 he settled in Galena, Kt Co, in merchandising 3 yrs; then carried on merc business Balt. 1885 he settled on farm where he now res. 1878 he m Sallie C. Rouse; their child.: Caddie, Elmer, Daisy, Chas and Annie. Subj m(1) Mary E. Hynson, they had 3 child.: Minnie, w/o Sml Mann; Wm, who res in Omaha, Neb.; and Mamie, res Balt. Family connected with MP Church.

716. BENJAMIN J. LINTHICUM, business man, Church Creek, Dor Co, farming, lumbering and shipbuilding; owns about 3000 a.; carried on general store here 20 yrs, sold it 1896. Paternal ancestor of subj from Wales, came to America c. 1643, settling in AA Co. The great-grandfather of our subj, Richard Linthicum, moved from AA Co to Dor Co 1775. Grandfather of subj, also Richard Linthicum, b Dor Co May 12 1780; in farming, building and management of vessels in foreign & domestic trade. Josiah, father of subj, b this area, farmer at Church Creek; had huge lumber businses. He d 1895, in 76th yr. He m Miss Dixon, had 2 child. Subj b Mar 18 1856 in old home on farm nr Church Creek. After public schools here and New York and Dover Acad, of Dover, Del; he returned home and purch general store at Church Creek 2 yrs later; operated it until 1896. 1892 he started a sawmill; mbr state legislature. 1890 he m Miss Mary E. Greene, d/o Rev Wm M. Greene, of Va; their child., in order of birth: Chas, Josiah, Wm and Hy. Family attend ME Church, though Mrs. Linthicum reared in Episc belief, in which her father is minister. 854

717. ABRAHAM R. WRIGHT, of Denton, b nr Hurlock, Dor Co, May 27 1845. His father, K. A., farmer from same co, b 1797. On his plantation were many slaves; unable to free them he gave them money to pay expenses to north; local preacher ME Church; d Dor Co 1884. The mother of subj, Sella Lewis, b Dor Co, of which her father, Abraham Lewis, was native. She attended ME Church. Subj 1 of 14 child.; 2 bros and several sis res Eastern Shore. After attending Bryant & Stratton's Business College Balt he taught school 2 yrsj; 16 yrs in merc business Car Co, then in wholesale tobacco business Balt 2 yrs. 1885 he came to Denton and engaged in business. He owns farm nr Denton;1 director in Denton Natl Bank; Meth; 1869 he m S. A. Hitch, d/o Rev Elijah Hitch, Meth minister res nr Laurel, Del; of their 4 child., a son, d at 10 months. Eldest dau, Anna O., grad Lutherville Female Seminary and has taught in St. Mary's College, St. Mary's Co. Martha Maude grad conservatory of music Phila, with high honors. V. Grace, youngest dau, attending school. 855

718. ALBERT T. LA VALLETTE, JR, seafood dealer; recently built villa, nr Crisfield, over looking Tangier Sound. Here genuine diamond backs are hatched and grown. Adjacent is large oyster planting ground, also a factory where hard crab meat is canned and hermetically sealed, and also an aritificial harbor, where buster or shedder crab is transformed into soft shell. Shipments are made from this point to almost all parts of the world. La Valllette fam known in America and France. Grandfather of subj, Rear Admiral Elie A. T. La Vallette, b May 3 1790, Va. At 10 he sailed from Phila in frigate Phila, commanded by Capt., Stephen Ducator, to make reprisals on French commerce; 1810 placed in command of a ship; 1812 app acting lieut U. S. navy. Sep 11 1814, in engagement between the British and American fleets took place, La Vallette, was only lieutenant on board flagship, Saratoga, surviving the action. (A description of this action is given.) In this action, according to Commodore MacDonough, "La Valette recognized for valor and bravery by state of Va and Congress. Among admiral's ancestors are Bron de foix La Vallette, duke of Espernon and colonel general of France, and Jean Louis De La Vallette, famous grand master of the Knights Hospitallers of St. John of Jerusalem, known for exploits against Turks in 1565.
In 1764 the admiral's grandfather, Elie A. T. La Vallette, was rgtr of prerogative office of province of Md.
Father of subj b Phila 1829, at 19 made lieut in Mex war; d 1894 in Fla, where he had gone for his health; prominent in Phila as real estate speculator; promoter of La Vallette City, N. J., named for the admiral. 856

-197-

Subj b Burlington, N.J. Sep 14 1864, lived in Phila, attended State College Pa; granted pilot's license; went to Crisfield 1887, and embarked in new industry, terrapin and crab business. The State Expermimental Station for the propagation of terrapin is under Mr. La Vallette's jurisdiction. He m Amy K. Ricketts, of London, Eng; their children: Elie A. T., Ruth, and Amy.

858 719. M. WORTHINGTON GOLDSBOROUGH s/o Hon. Brice John Golsborough, judge 1st judicial dist Md; judge appellate court, until he d, Jul 1867, at 64. He was s/o Dr. Richard Goldsborough, physician of Cambridge, who practiced medicine here from early manhood until his death, at 67. His father, Hon. Rbt Goldsborough mbr contnental congress 1776, app delegate by several conventions of Md, 1774-1776; lawyer; mbr of council of safety and mbr first constitutional convention of Md 1776. His father, Chas, was s/o Rbt and Elizabeth (Greenbury) Goldsborough, and grandson of Nicholas Goldsborough, progenitor of fam in America. Mother of subj, Leah, d/o Jas Goldsborough, of Talb Co, and Achsah (Worthington) Goldsborough, latter d/o Col. Nicholas Worthington, whose father, Thos, of AA Co, was s/o Capt John Worthington, progenitor of Worthingtons in Md. In company with bro, Zacharaiah, Capt Worthington came to America from Lancaster Co, Eng, c. 1690. Reference to Worthington fam elsewhere this vol.

Subj b Cambridge, Oct 9 1834, educated Cambridge Acad. 1850-2, he secured employment inwholesale dry goods store Balt, returned to Cambridge and embarked in farming on estate, Springfield, nr town; app assist paymaster of the navy; active service commenced about Oct 1862; 1866 promoted to paymaster; 1881-1885 fleet paymaster of South Atlantic squadron, also served as fleet paymaster in other commands (these and other postions named). During war he was present at battles of Plymouth and Little Washington, N. C., and took part in many lesser engagements in sounds of N.C. - 34 yrs active in the navy; now retired, rank of commander. 1858 he m Miss Henrietta, d/o Sml W. Jones, of Som Co. They have 4 children living: Dr. Brice W.; Phillips Lee, Dr. Martin W. and Rbt. Subj mbr of Episc Church.

859 720. GEORGE T. HOBBY, Jr., Centreville, b Mar 24 1855, Greenwich, Conn., of old fam of that state, founded 6 generations ago by 2 bros from Eng. There the great-grandfather farmed throughout life. The grandfather, Lewis H. Hobby, colonel in war of 1812, from Greenwich; grad Yale; pres Univ New York City, resigning because of failing health; retired on farm nr Greenwich, Conn, where he d of heart disease. By 1st marriage he has son, M. M. Hobby, grad Univ New York City, prof in that institution, d in retirement at Stamford, Conn. Lewis H. Hobby m(2) Miss Van Duser, of old Holland fam of Orange Co, N. Y. and Geo T. Hobby, Sr., their only son.

Geo T. Hobby, Sr, b Yonkers N. Y., 1829, educated Univ New York City; taught in that institution then went to northwestern Ohio, engaging in mercantile pursuits in Bryan; inherited father's estate, started 2 stores in Buffalo, N.Y., then came to QA Co, farming; later in bakery business Plainfield, N.J.; farming at Northport, L. I., and newspaper business in Brooklyn, where he presently lives, superintendent of Brooklyn Eagle bldg; mbr Plymouth church Brooklyn. He m Miss C. Haight, from Dutchess Co, N. Y., who was left an orphan. Her fam prominent in that co and Brooklyn. Their child.: Mary C.; subj; Howard, res Port Deposit, N. Y.; Vincent M., m and in merchandising Phila; Lewis H., baker New York State; Alvina; Edw B., connected with paper of Brooklyn, called Once A Week; and Alice.

At 11 subj accompanied parents to Ohio; education in Bryan high school; clerked in father's store; 1872 entered service of New York house, then with

Wm McKenny. 1878 he embarked in own business, later in commission business with father at Plainfield, N.J., and for while at Stanton, Va. Coming to Centreville, he worked for firm of Goden & Hall; later purch third interest and since Aug 1890, alone in the business. 6 Dec 1876 he m Miss Ada C. Gearhart, of Pa, d/o Hy L. Gearhart, who at that time was living at Hillsborough, Car Co; their child.: Geo S., in the store with father; Ada C.; Emma; Edna H.; H. L. ; Alice G.; Arthur J.; and L. E.

721. A. SYDNEY GADD, proprietor of Centreville Creamery, b 1 Oct 1861, Hillsborough, Car Co, s/o A. J. and Mary A. (Dixon) Gadd, also from that co. Father b Feb 27 1832, had common school education; carpenter; contractor and builder. Coming to QA Co 1870, he located in town of QA, then moved to Sudlersville, where he farmed until 1874; in partnership with Dr. A. D. Sudler, under name of Gadd & Sudler, embarked in canning business, canning both vegetables and fruit. 1859 A. J. Gadd moved to St. Joseph Co, Mo., where 1861 he organized a company for Confed army, but did not enter the service. Having considerable prop in this state he returned to Car Co same year; mbr legislature, with W. A. Barton and Wm H. Legg. His bro, Luther H., clerk circuit court of Car Co, state librarian, now owns Md Hotel at Annapolis, mbr of firm Gadd & Neviln. Another bro, Frank Gadd, in Confed army under Gen Price, until seriously wounded; d of consumption. Alexander Gadd, 3rd bro, in blockade service during Civ war, later farmer Talb Co.
Mother of subj d 1869, leaving 2 sons, other being Dnl L., connected with Balt & Ohio locomotive works. Her father, Capt. Dnl Dixon, sea captain; d at 83. His only son followed the water and d in early life. After death of 1st wife A. J. Gadd m Mrs. E. H. Morgan, wid of Wm Morgan; they had 2 sons: Rbt F., now a civil engineer; and Luther L., an electrical engineer. Both grad Lehigh Univ Pa.
Subj attended common schools; worked for his father. 1890 he took course in Eastman's Business College, remained with father one year; 16 Dec 1891 purch creamery in Centreville; soon built trade and enlarged his plant.

860

722. LORIN CLEVELAND NELSON, mariner, especially interested in oyster business in later yrs; now owns oyster house nr Crisfield; 1895 elected sheriff Som Co; b Aug 2 1861, present res. His father, Alonzo Nelson, of same place, followed the water, engaged in bay trade; later farmed; now 75; local preacher ME Church.
Subject's grandfather, Thos Nelson, b this neighborhood; farmer and mcht, followed the water briefly; mbr ME Chjurch; d at 70. His father, Thos, known as "King" Nelson, from Eng, he d Som Co at age c. 104; direct descendant of Lord Nelson, of Eng. Mother of subj, Sallie, d/o John Sterling, lived in this area, now 74. Her child.: Hy W. oysterman here; Chas Edw, res Crisfield, fisherman; John Allen mcht; Lorin C. d in boyhood; Wm Clarke, mariner, preacher and carpenter, and res in Crisfield; Clara J. w/o J. S. Stewart, of Sussex Co, Del; subj is 7th in order of birth; others are Martin Luther and Thos, res this area.
At 12 subj began to follow the water; engaged in bay trade, becoming owner and master of a vessel. 1891 he commenced in oyster business nr Crisfield. He is mbr ME Church; m 1887 Miss Alice Lawson, who was b Som Co; their child: Jannie, Alma Lillian and Morrison Marks, all at home. Father of Mrs. Nelson, Wm T. Lawson, decd, mbr legislature 1 term and collector of customs 28 yrs.

861

862 723. I. S. BENNETT, at 19 embarked in merchandising at Dames Quarter, Som Co; opened store Riverton, Wicomico Co; 1893 opened store Spring Grove, 1st dist, 1896 another at Sharptown. Subj b Feb 16 1859 nr present res, descendant of Eng fam. His father, E. T., grandfather, Jas, and great-grandfather, Gillis Bennet, b about same locality Wicomico Co, were farmers. The father, of Barren Creek dist, collector many terms, retired at 75. He m Sarah E., d/o Levi Taylor, same dist; she is 69. Their child.: Sophronia, w/o Levin Bennett, Mardella Spring; Jas L., res Som Co; E. T., of Mardela Springs; Thos W., res 1st dist; Gillis E., res in Sharptown; subj; and Rev Louis A., res Crisfield, Som Co. Subj attended dist schools and grammar school Salisbury. Aside from business interests he served as collector for Sharptown and first dists, and mbr bd of co commissioners. Feb 22 1890 he m Laura, d/o Levin Cooper, of Barren Creek dist. Their child.: Jas M. and Ruth H.

862 724. THOMAS E. GRACE, farmer 2nd dist, Talb Co, on Broad Creek Neck. His grandfather, Wm S. Grace, farmer this co. His son, Skinner, farmer and mcht, in war of 1812, captured by British soldiers; sent on prison ship to Jamaica, West Indies, and en route contracted yellow fever; lived through it and d at his old home this co at old age. (See sketch of subjects's bro, Wm S. Grace.) Subj b Oct 17 1841, on farm nr one he now tills. About 23 he m and settled on tract rented from mother, in Bay Hundred dist; later bt another farm and res there; 1889-90 in produce and commission business Balt, and during winters 1895-1896 kept books for contracting and building firm Balt; otherwise farming all his life. He m 1864, Miss Susan R. Preston, of Balt; their child.: Elizabeth L., d at 28; Mary Ella, d at 6; Wm Preston, farmer this dist; Susan May, w/o G. Edw Wrightson, of this co; Sml S., at home; Leonara B., youngest of family, at home. Subj mbr ME Church since 15.

863 725. REV. JACOB W. PORTER, retired minister MP Church, in Wisconsin division of North Ill. conference; 1876 gave up preaching because of throat trouble and came to Md; bt farm Bay Hundred dist, Talb Co. Since c. 1884 he has carried on sawmilling; while in Wisc superintendent of public schools, chairman dist bd of supervisors and mbr co bd. Porters are old fam of N.Y. Grandfather of subj, Alexander Porter, army officer during Rev, in charge of commissary at N.Y., retired from army at close of war. Father of subj, Amasa Porter, b Seneca Co, N. Y., blacksmith at Geneva, N. Y., later in Waterloo, N.Y.; then farmed in Erie Co, d Wisc at 69; many yrs justice of peace. He m Eliza Weatherlow, of Waterloo, N. Y.; of their 8 child., 4 living: Erastus A.; Mrs. B. F. Bull; Mrs. P. Drake, of Columbia Co, Wisc; and subj.
Subj b Erie Co, N. Y., 1830, educated in public schools and Springville Acad; employed in general store in Erie Co. 1852 he joined Genesee Conference MP Church at Batavia, N. Y. 1876 he came to Talb Co. 1852 he m Martha Calkins: their child.: Mrs. Randolph Eller; Mrs. Jas F. Flower; Mrs. W. W. Cummings, res Columbia Co, Wis; Mrs. Albert W. Fairbank; Mrs. W. O. Wrightson, Mark H. W., decd; Grace W., trained nurse; and Love C., res Md.

864 726. GEORGE MULLIKIN, farmer 6th dist QA Co, b Car Co 1 Sep 1821. Both father and grandfather were named Patrick Mullikin, and from Talb Co, while great-grandfather, from Ireland, founder of fam in America, settling in Md. Patrick Mullikin, father of subj, carpenter; d Car Co 1843; his wife d 1865. They had 7 child., subj only survivor. Subj received limited education; worked as farm hand until 21, earning $5 per month, used to support parents. 1844 he m and began farming; fol yr to QA Co, where he has since res; owns 5

farms. 17 Dec 1844 he m Miss Mary Elizabeth Satterfield; of their 4 child., Geo and John are living, in QA Co. Mr. Mullikin is mbr ME Church.

727. WILLIAM B. SPARKS owns hotel and livery at Queen Anne, QA Co; magistrate. His father, Jos B.Sparks, from 1st dist, QA Co, still res there, now in 74th yr; in custom house Balt c. 9 yrs, constable many yrs. He m Sarah Rebecca, d/o Joshua Walls, of this co, now aged 63. Their child.: Annie, Mrs. Thos Hill, of Wilm, Del; subj; John F., of 1st dist; Carrie V., w/o Andrew Brown, Jr., of Balt; Franck B., of Phila; Mary, unmarried; and Jos B., Jr. Subj b 1st dist this co, Sep 15 1851, reared to farm life, educated in common schools. 1896 he rented hotel prop which he now manages. He m(1) Sudlersville, Jan 28 1881, Miss Lucy Crossley; she d May 1887; their child.: Edith and Wm Dudley. Dec 19 1888, he m Miss A. Levenia Stevens, of Scotch descent, in Sudlersville ME Church; they are mbrs ME Church. Aug 4 1897 Mrs. Sparks received her commission as postmistress Queen Anne. 864

728. ELIJAH FREENY, res 9th dist Wicomico Co, po address: Delmar, Del, built 1st house ever put up in that town, constructed 1859, and thereafter he opened general store, sold out 2 yrs later. Founder of Freeny fam in this region, Peter Freeny, of Ireland; settled on tract granted from Lord Baltimore, now lying across line in Del, and here several generations were b, including subject's great-grandfther, John, and grandfather Joshua Freeny. John, father of subj, b on farm 2 miles from home of Elijah Freeny, in Wor Co; farmer; purch farm now owned by subj 1810. No church affiliation. He m Miss Mattie, d/o Wm Brewington, of Salisbury; of their 10 child., only Elijah, survives. Subj b on this homestead Aug 7 1823; left home after he was 20. He now cultivates about 450 a.; owns another 400 a., and several houses, stores and town prop; mbr ME Church. Jan 9 1861 he m Maria E., d/o M. Fooks, of this co, who was liberal and religious man, built a church. 7 of 9 child. b to subj and wife still living: Rosa L., Matilda M., Mary E., Harry H., of Delmar; Jas W., of this area; Hy B., of Salisbury, and Elijah E. 865

729. MAJOR T. RUARK, Straits dist, in oyster business and farming; constable. Jas Ruark, father of subj, came to Md from Eng with 3 bros, Thos, Wm and Major; prob among first settlers on Hooper's Island, this co. Jas followed the sea during most of his life and d on board a vessel, at Wash, D. C. c. 1835. He had located in Straits dist, taking up tract dated Aug 30 1820, here he made his home and headquarters. He and wife Sarah, had several child., now living: Amelia A., wid of V. Cannon, and subj. Major b Apr 28 1837, Straits dist, educated in public schools before 12, when he shipped aboard a vessel as a sailor. 1893 he met with accident, his leg being broken, forcing him to abandon active life. 1861 he enlisted Company B., 1st Eastern Shore Vol, served 3 yrs, participating in battle of Gettysburg and lesser engagements. Major Ruark m(1) Miss Laura J. Wingate, who d, leaving: Alexander W., mcht of Car co; Howard, of this place; Mrs. Wm H. Moore; Ernest L., of this town; Fdk E. (see his sketch, elsewhere this vol), Richard and Lina, at home. Major Ruark m(2) Amanda A. Jones; their child: Wilbur. Mrs. Ruark attends ME Church with mbrs of fam. 866

730. EDWARD R. TRIPPE, M. D., physician of Easton, b on farm 6 miles from that place, Talb Co, Mar 25 1840, traces ancestry back to Eng. He possesses ancient escutcheon, on which is painted and emblazoned their coat cf arms. Under the shield is inscribed: "This achievement was given unto my Lord Howard's fifth son at the seige of Boulogne. King Henry V. being there, asked 867

how they took the town and castle. Howard answered: 'I trip'd upt the walls': said his majesty: "Tripp shall be thy name and no longer Howard." James II. in his autobiography mentions Mr. Trippe and Mr Howard conjointly, aiding his escape when Duke of York from Hampton Court at time of death of Charles I. That fam res in Somersetshire and had land there many generations appears from great number of parchment deeds in possession of Dr. Trippe. The oldest dated in reign of Henry VIII, and relates to estate of East Brent.

867 731. John Tripp, Esq., of Shipham and Huntshill, Somersetshire, Gen, living in reigns of William and Mary and Anne, m twice, and by 1st wife had 2 child., John mentioned below; and Mary, who d unmarried. From his 2nd marriage are derived the Tripps of Bristol, one of whom went to Holland and acquired great wealth at Amsterdam, where a street is still called Tripp street in his honor. In Holland, his son was created Baron Tripp by Prince of Orange, and one of his descendants was in British army and served against Napoleon. John Tripp, Esq., s/o 1st marriage, became rector of Huntshill, m and had two sons, John, the heir; and Sml, who m and had large fam. Older son, John Tripp, Esq., barrister at law, dep recorder of Taunton and justice of peace for cos of Wills, Dorset, Gloucester, Devon and Somerset, m Anne, d/o Rev Jas Upton, rector of Hills Bishop, nr Tautnon; they had 4 sons and 3 daus: John mentioned below; Jas Upton m Miss Edsaver, of Fibbleworth, and had 5 child.; Jas, who m(1) Miss Ruckle and m(2) Miss Harvey; Geo; Chas Upton; Frances Upton; and Sarah Caroline, Geo m Miss Deacon and had one dau, Elizabeth Anne, who m her cousin, Rev Rbt Henry Tripp. Rbt, rector of Rewe, nr Exeter m Miss Thompson, of Kirk Deighton, and had 8 child.: Rbt Henry, Victor Albarnum, County Cornwall, who m his cousin Elizabeth Anne, dau of Geo Tripp; Wm Upton; John; Chas Upton, captain in 36th Native Infantry; Marianne; Elizabeth; Anne; and Hy, lawyer of Lincoln Inn, who res at Orchard Wyndham 50 yrs and d unmarried. Mary d unmarried. Anne m Brig. Gen. Wm Owen. Frances A. Deborah Frederica Upton d unmarried.

The oldest of above named fam, Rev John Tripp, S. T. D., rector of Spofforth and Catlin, County York, m Sarah Rurchell and d Feb 11 1814. His child. were: Geo, captain of 25th Regt of Foot, who served in Egypt under Sir Ralph Abercrombie, in battle of Abonkie, and d unmarried, Aug 21 1804; Geo, present representative of fam; Peter, lieut colonel of 98th Regt of Foot, who m Frances, d/o Mr. White, Esq., army surgeon, and had fam; John Upton, who m his cousin Sarah, d/o Jas Upton Tripp,Esq., and had fam; Harriet, who d young; Frances, who m Hy Eyre, Esq., of Robleigh Grange, Hampshire; and Elizabeth, who d numarried 1845. Rev Chas Tripp, D. D., rector of Silverton, County Devon, and justice of peace, b Apr 20 1784, and m Jun 15 1815, Frances Owen, 2nd d/o Brig. Gen. Owen, lieut colonel of 61st Regt. Their child.: Hy, b Apr 6 1816, grad Holy Orders, Fellow of Worcester Coll, Oxford; John, b Jul 21 1821, m Nov 11 1856, Eliza, eld d/o Rev Jas Gould; Chas d young; Chas Geo, of Lincoln's Inn, b Jul 1 1826; Wm Owen b May 13 1828, m Nov 27 1856, Mary Georgina, eld d/o Rev Dr. Llewellyn; Arthur Sampford b Jan 1 1831; Howard d Apr 9 1857; Frances d young; Anne m Oct 5 1850, to Rev John Hy Wise, rector of Brendon, North Devon; and Eliza m Aug 1846, Capt Rentley, of 51st Regt.

868 732. First settlement of Trippe fam in Md made by Capt Hy Trippe c. 1663, Dor Co, on or nr Todd's Point, then called Sark, Trippe's Neglect and Lindy, now part of Todd's Point farm. Tract of 50 a., patented by Frs Tripp, Jan 17 1759, on Rush River, now Harford Co, but of him nothing known. From what place Capt Hy Trippe came is not known. Capt Richard Trippe, of Avonville, Md believed fam came from French Flanders, and though one of Tripps of Bristol

emigrated to Flanders, amassed great wealth and son became Baron Tripp and was captain with Blucher at Waterloo, by his will and signature thought to have been English. Capt Hy Trippe mbr of upper house of assembly of Md, from Dor Co in 1671 and 1674. He d c. 1697-8 (his will proved Mar 28 1698), leaving wid, Elizabeth Trippe, and 5 child.: (1) Hy d 1723-4, leaving wid, Susannah Trippe, and 6 child., Hy, John, Elizabeth, Edw, Sarah and Mary. (2) John 2nd s/o Capt Hy Trippe. (3) Edw d leaving two sons, Edw, Jr., d 1756, leaving as sole heiress, Mary, who m Col Jos Ennalls; and John. (4) Wm m Miss Tate and d Apr 24 1766, at old age, leaving 5 child., mentioned below; (5) and another, Hy, d 1761. (6) Henrietta only d/o Capt Hy Trippe.

733. Children b to Wm Trippe and wife, Miss Tate: Henrietta, Elizabeth, Wm, John and Edw. Henrietta m Mr. Hughes; Elizabeth m Edw Noel, cf Castle Haven, Dor Co, and left one son and 4 daus: Edw, who m Miss Eccleston, of Dor Co, and d leaving one dau, Delia, who m Capt Barthomomew Rogers and d childless; Elizabeth, who m Rt. Rev Jas Kemp, D. D., bishop of Md, and had one son, Edw D. Kemp (judge of the orphans' court of Balt City), who m Sarah Donnell, d/o John Donnell, of Balt, and d leaving 3 daus, of whom Eliza, the oldest, d unmarried. and Sarah, the youngest, m Jas Harwood, of Balt Co, a purser in U. S. navy, and had one son, Edw; Sarah, who m Captain Cox, and had one son, Edw Noel Cox, a first lieut, later purser in U. S. navy, and whose wife was Miss Lawrence, sis of Capt. Lawrence, of the Chesapeake; Mary m Wm, s/o John and Elizabeth (Noel) Trippe mentioned below, and she had one son, John, who distinguished himself at Tripoli; and two daus, Margaret and Mary. Wm came to Talb Co and bt Avonville, formerly called Marshy Point, Canterbury Manor. He d Jun 1 1777, at 57. He m(1) Mrs. Gibson; they had one son, Jas, who m Ann Dawson and d, leaving no child. His wid afterward became w/o Levin Trippe mentioned below, killed in fight at sea during Rev, and she later m Captain Caulk or Cork and after his death m Dr. Stevenson, of Balt. After the death of 1st wife, Wm Trippe m Elizabeth Skinner, of Talb co, by whom he had 5 child. Wm d unmarried. Richard, b Jan 30 1763, d Jan 16 1849, and bur at Avonville. He m Jan 5 1794, Hariett Edmondson, who d Dec 13 of same year, at 19. She left one son, Wm , who d Sep 11 1816 in 16th year. Richard Trippe m(2) May 5 1799, Mary, d/o Col Jos and Sarah (Heron) Ennalls, of Dor Co. The colonel's 1st wife, Mary, d/o Edw Trippe, d, leaving 6 child.: Wm , Thos, Jos, John, Elizabeth and Ann. Mrs. Richard Trippe (nee Mary Ennalls) d Oct 14 1836, at 56, and bur at Avonville. By this union were 10 child.: Sarah Elizabeth b Sep 17 1800, d Jul 9 1879. She m cousin, Edw Trippe, of Todd's piont, Dor Co; they had son, Edw Richard Trippe, M. D., subj. Richard John, b Aug 22 1805, d Jun 25 1845. 20 Nov 1838 he m Sarah S. H. Hayward, of Talb Co, and to them were b 4 child. Thos Hayward, b Dec 12 1842, m Martha Mason, only d/o Rev Henry M. Mason, D. D., rector of Christ Church, Easton; Richard John, b Aug 15 1844, m Annie R. Townsend, of Talb Co; Helen b Feb 3 1841, m Hugh Hambleton, of Easton; and Mary Smythe, still living and unmarried. Edw Thos, b Feb 14 1808, d Sep 23 1843. He m Nov 30 1841, Catherine D. Bowie, who d Oct 18 1856, aged 38, leaving one son, Richard (B Sep 5 1842) , who m Sophia, d/o Hon Philip Frs Thomas, ex-gov of Md. Jos Ennalls, b Mary 6 1810, m Nov 6 1832, Elizabeth H. Darrow, of N.Y., and had 5 child.: Richard Henry; Fdk Wright, who m Mary Louisa White, of N.Y.; Jos Ennalls, Jr; Wm H. who m Florence Joy, of Newark, N.J.,, and has two child., Wm H. Jr.; and Elsie Caroline. Wm Jas, b Mary 17 1812, m Mary 23 1852, to his cousin, Elizabeth Purnell, d/o Jas Trippe, and has no child. Mary Harriett, b Feb 22 1815, m May 23 1854, Barclay Haskins, of Talb Co, who d in 1877, leaving no child. Rbt H., b Sep 6 1817, m Jun 3 1846, Eliza C. Robinson, of Newark, N. J.; has 3

child.: Rbt; Theodore; and Maggie, w/o Wm Smith, of Orange, N. J. Margaret Helen b Aug 11 1820, d Oct 8 1839. Nicholas Hammond is next. Mary Susannah, b Feb 3 1803, d Oct 25 1804. John, the 3rd s/o Wm and Elizabeth (Skinner) Trippe, m Susan Heron and has 5 child. Wm Richard m Lavinia Martin, of Talb Co, sis of late Gov Dnl Martin. She d childless and he later m Marion Chamberlaine, of same co, by whom he has 3 child: John, Henrietta and Sml C. Trippe, M. D. John Fletcher m Eleanor Condit, d/o M. T. Silas Condit, of New, N. J., and has 2 sons and 4 daus. Jas m Ann, d/o Rev Dr. Matthews, of N. Y. and has 7 sons, of whom Edw, the youngest d young; and Cuthbert. Mary Ann m Thos Oldham Martin, of Talb Co, and has no child. Edw,. b Aug 5 1765, d in infancy. Mary m Mr. Benton, of Kt Island, Md., and d Nov 21 1795, at 27 and 6 months, while on visit to Avonville and bur there. She had no child. Edw, 4th child of Wm Trippe and his wife, Miss Tate, was twice married, second union being with Sarah Byas, wid of Jos Byas, and a sis of Edw Noel, of Castle Haven. Edw has a family of 7 children, of whom Jas was a son by by his first wife. He m(1) Elizabeth Purnell, who d childless, and then m Mary Purnell, of Del, and to them were b: Jos Everitt, Sarah, Margaret and Elizabeth. Jos Everitt b Jul 18 1805, m Sarah Patterson Cross, of Balt Co, and to them were b four sons and three daus, of whom two sons Jas and Henry, d in infancy and one dau also d in infancy. The others are : Andrew Cross, b Nov 29 1839, m Nov 7 1872, Caroline Augusta McConkey, and to them were b: Jas McConkey; Andrew Noel; Sarah Patterson; and Grafton Wallace, deceased. Jos Everitt, b in 1844 m Frances, d/o Daniel Holliday, of Balt, and had one son, Holliday, since deceased. Mary Purnnell is w/o Wm Bell, of Balt City, and has no chilren. Rachel Elizabeth is unmarried. Mary Purnell m John Smith, of Dor Co, who afterward became res of Balt Co. They had two daus: Mary Elizabeth; and Anne, who d unmarried in 1878. Elizabeth Purnell m her cousin, Wm Jas Trippe, s/o Richard and Mary (Ennalls) Trippe, and has no children. John, 5th child of Wm Trippe and Miss Tate, b Apr 17 1711, and d Apr 24 1778. In 1743 he m Elizabeth Noel, b Apr 25 1729, and to them were b 21 children, of whom the following reached maturity: Amelia, Wm, Henrietta, Elizabeth, Levin, Frances, Jas, Sarah, Margaret, Harriet, John, Mary and Edw. The father left to his son Jas Todd's Point, but as he d childless it becme the property of the youngest son, Edw, who is the only male surivivor of that large farmily. Amelia, b Mar 27 1744 d Jun 17 1773. She m Col. Jas Woolford, of Dor Co, and left one son, Roger, who m a lady of that co; and a dau, who also m. Wm., b Mar 19 1746, m his cousin Mary Noel and d , leaving 3 child: Margaret, b 1755 and m Capt. John Hughes, of Som Co; Elizabeth, b Oct 20 1791, m Jas Price of Talb Co, by whom she had one dau, Mary, who became w/o Henry Hooper, of Dor Co; and John, a lieutenant in the U.S. navy. who distinguished himself at Tripoli, and commanded the U. S. brig Siren at Havana. Henrieta, b Apr 16 1748, m Colonel Birkhead, father of late Dr. Solon Birkhead, and d leaving two sons: Wm who m and Levin who d unmarried; and 4 daus. Elizabeth b Feb 17 1750, m her cousin , Basil Noel, but had no children. Levin b Mar 17 1752, m wid of his cousin Jas, son of Wm, and was killed in a naval engagement during the Rev. He left no children. His wid, Nancy Dawson, of Bayside, Talb Co, afterward m Dr. Stevenson, of Balt, who survived her. She was a famous beauty, and Dr. Trippe, of this sketch, has her medallion likeness. She was b at Avonville and d in Balt. Frances, b Sep 4 1755, m John E. Gist, of Balt Co, and had 3 child.: Wm, Henrietta and Harriett. Wm m Eliza, d/o General Eccleston, of Dor Co, and had 3 daus: Henrietta, Valeria and Margaret; and one son, John Trippe Gist, who m a lady in Fla and d not long afterward, leaving a pair of twins, who have since d. Henrietta m Mr. Creighton, of Cambridge and d 1878, leaving a fam. Valeria m Jas Chaplain, of Cambridge, Dor Co, and left one dau,

Henrietta, who m John Richard Keen, of Dor Co. Margaret m Solomon Higgins, of Dor Co, had no child. Jas, b Sep 28 1758, d Jun 13 1826. He m Jan 29 1796, cousin, Henrietta Rogers (Hennie Trippe) who was b Nov 7 1775, and d May 27 1858. They had no child. Sarah, b Mar 19 1761, d Dec 18 1794, became 2nd w/o Maj. Peter Webb, of Talb Co, and had no child. Margaret, b May 19 1762, d Mary 11 1785. She was 1st w/o Major Webb, and d leaving a dau, Margaret, who m Richard Thomas, of QA Co, lieut in U. S. navy, and had 3 daus: Margaret, who m Judge Philemon B. Hopper, of QA Co, and had 3 children, all now decd; Frances E., who m John B. Spencer, of QA Co, and d childless; and Mary, who d unmarried. Harriet, b Mary 18 1764, d Aug 1 1800. She m Wm Ennalls, of Dor Co, and left one dau, Mary, who was b May 28 1799, and m Sml Corner, of Dor Co, and d Dec 2 18701. John, b Nov 21 1765, d Mar 24 1778, unmarried. Mary, b Oct 23 1767, d Jun 4 1831. She m May 10 1796, Maj. Peter Webb, by whom she had one son, Peter Webb, who m Elizabeth Dickinson, but had no child. Mary later m Dr. Sml Dickinson, of Talb Co, and elder brother of her son's wife, and to them b a son, Sml A., who m Maria Goldsborough,, of Car Co, and had five sons and two daus, one of whom m her cousin, Wm Thomas, of AA Co.

734. Edw, father of subj, b Jan 29 1771, d Feb 2 1846. He m(1) Elizabeth Barney, d/o Moses and Sarah (Bond) Barney, of Balt; she d leaving 3 daus: Harriet Choirs, Mary Webb and Ann. He m(2) Anne Tolly Towson, dau of Gen. Wm Towson, of Balt Co, and she d childless. He m(3) distant relative, Sarah Elizabeth Trippe, d/o Richard and Mary (Ennalls) Trippe, who d leaving one son, Edw R., subj. Of children by 1st marriage both Mary Webb and Ann d unmarried. Harriet Choirs m Wm Palmer, of Balt; their child.: Edw Trippe, decd; Wm Preston; David Keener; and Elizabeth Barney, who m John Pole Fowler, of Balt, and has 2 daus, Mary Trippe and Kate Palmer. In early life the doctor's father lived in Balt; was a sea captain. Later he originated a line of travel from Balt to Phila, via Frenchtown and Newcastle; built 1st steamboat in city of Balt, part owner and captain and ran this boat (and others as the travel increased) to Frenchtown, forming southern end of that line. After P. W. & B. R. R. was built these 2 lines joined, later old line was abandoned. He later moved to old homestead at Todd's Point, where he d. 871

735. Dr. Trippe spent boyhood on home farm, attended Easton Acad, later Col of Burlington, N.J.; grad medical depart Md Univ 1862, opened an office in Easton; moved to old homestead, managed it and continued with profession until 1876, when he returned to Easton. 1864 he m Miss Melusina E. Schwartze, d/o Henry Schwartze, of Balt co; of their 7 child., 6 living: Sophia Elizabeth, who m Alexis G. Pascault, of Easton, and d leaving no child.; Edw, in coffee business in Mexico; Melusina, w/o Henry Hollyday, of Easton; Fredericka Leypold, at home; Augustus Schwartze; Henry S. and Elvino Dickinson. The doctor and fam mbrs Episc Church. 871

736. CAPT. C. C. FALLIN res Strait dist, Dor Co, on farm. About 1870 he repaired and remodeled bldg at Bishops Head and opened general store; postmaster number of yrs; Co Commissioner 1 term. Subj b Oct 8 1836, nr present home, s/o Wm and Sallie (McNamara) Fallin. His grandfather, Wm Fallin, Sr. descendant of Eng ancestors; spent his life in Dor Co. Father b on old homestead here; followed the water, employed as captain on vessel runing between Balt and Havana and S.C.; latter days spent on home farm, where he d at 64; once constable and also dep sheriff. His wife d at 80, mother of 4 child. now living: Laura M., w/o J. E. Wingate; C. C.; Virginia, who m Geo W. wingate; and Wm, of Balt. Subj educated in public schools; at 22 left home 872

and spent 10 yrs on the water in oyster business. After carrying on wholesale business he turned to farming, later merchandiising; now interested in Home Insur Co. He and fam attend ME Church. He m Angie, d/o Sml Edgar; their child.: Wade H., Wm C. and Edgar, all at home.

872 737. CHARLES W. BROHAWN, Salem, Dor Co, runs the Union Store Co here. Paternal grandfather of subj came to Md with his father from Ireland prior to Rev, and settled in 1st dist; justice of peace. Sml, father of subj, b 1st dist this co 1818, farmer; d 1881. He m Louisa Fluharty, d/o Garrison Fluharty, of Federalsburg, Car Co, aged 68, still living. 3 of her child. survive: Sml, of Cambridge; Clara H., w/o Stephen R. Le Compte; and C. W. The father mbr ME Church. Subj b on place about 2 miles from Salem, Mar 28 1870; attended common schools; at 20 placed in charge of a school, taught school in Salem and Little Mills dists 3 yrs, then in a mercantile estab. 12 Jul 1894 he m Miss Katie M. Wright, of Hurlock, Dor Co, d/o S. M. Wright of that place; their child: Oma.

873 738. WILLIAM RICHARDSON 6th dist QA Co, d May 29 1889, mbr ME Church. His father, Jos Richardson, of Eng descent, b Car Co; dwelt on farm where wid of subj now res, known as Maiden Hall. He was mbr ME Church. Subj b Jan 1 1827, nr Denton, Car Co, student in dist schools. After 18 yrs he worked for his father. 1876 he bt the farm, but rented it to tenants until 1884, then moved on it. Apr 17 1872 he m Miss Malissa Turner at Ruthsburg; she was d/o Hon. Jas Turner, of Car Co, mbr state legislature and senate. 2 child. of subj and wife living: Sarah M. and Frs A. Mrs. Richardson now manages farm.

874 739. STEPHEN P. JUMP farmer 6th dist QA Co, magistrate, res town of Queen Anne. Hy Jump, subject's father, s/o Alanby Jump, who served in Rev war. Hy from Car Co, d 1856; he and bro Rbt went to Zanesbille, Ohio, conducted cooperage. In war of 1812 he was an officer in Md brigade. Hy Jump 3 times married and by last union had 5 child.; subj only survivor. The mother, who d 1848, was Harriet, d/o Rbt Baynard, of Car Co. By his former unions Hy Jump had 14 child., one now living, Mrs. Alaxine Hopkins, of Annapolis, mother of Dep Comptroller Harry J. Hopkins. - Subj b Aug 28 1840, on farm where he now lives in 6th dist. He attended classical institute 10 months; clerked with late Wm Parrott c. 3 yrs, turned to farming. Since 1874 he has conducted a store here, and managed one at Kingston several yrs. His homestead, Pemberton Resurvey, contains 186 a. May 26 1864 he m Maggie A. Lee, d/o Wm T. Lee, of Talb Co. She was mother of 2 sons, Harry L. and Fred P. Fam identified with ME Church South. Mrs. Jump d Jun 16 1893.

874 740. H. CLAY DERINGER, retired, res Locust Grove, Md; b Del 1855, s/o M. and A. G. (Woodland) Deringer, of Phila, and Kt Co, Md., respectively. His paternal great grandfather from Germany and founder of fam in America. Hy C. Deringer, grandfather, b Easton, Pa, spent greater part of life in Phila, in manufacture of Deringer pistol, invented by him; his son, B. M. also interested in that business. The latter res nr Newcastle, Del, where he d 1878, at 49. His child.: Mrs. Wm P. Duncan; Mrs. J. H. Kelley; H. Clay; Mary N. and Woodland. Subj spent his early life in Phila, educated in public school; employed by firm of J. Jas Clark, in manufacture of Deringer revolver. Later he was in commission busines in Phila, then confidential clerk for Wm P. Duncan, Philipsburg, Pa; since 1894, retired in Locust Grove, Kt Co, Md. He m Miss Alice Hurtt, d/o W. W. Hurtt; their child.: Estalena and Wm Duncan. Parents mbrs Episc Chruch.

741. ALBERT G. TOWERS, atty Denton, Car Co. His great-grandfather, Curtis 875
Towers, farmer of Car Co; lived to 98. Grandfather Elijah Towers b and reared
this co; owned large estates; Co Commissoner. Subj 2nd child in fam of Wm F.
and Mary A. (Garey) Towers, of this area. Eldest, Lawrence B., and youngest,
Thos F. Father elected 1885 as Co Treasurer. Subj b Aug 1 1873, in this co
and educated in common schools, and enrolled as student in Denton. 1890 he
attended Md Agric Coll about 2 yrs; studied law under Hon. Rbt C. Jump 2 yrs;
then admitted to practice before courts of his co.

742. REV. THOMAS F. WALDRON, pastor Cath Church Easton, b Cincinnati, Ohio, 875
Dec 8 1866, s/o Thos J. and Margaret (Gillen) Waldron, of Ireland. Father of
subj came to America in early manhood, made brief sojourn in N. Y., moved
westward to Cincinnati, Ohio, where he was in furniture and undertaking
business; presently res Pottsville, Schuykill Co, Pa, retired. Subj educated
in Cincinnati. After his father moved to Pa he entered high school of
Pottsville; grad coll in suburbs of Phila 1885; then entered St. Mary's
Seminary, Balt; in Wilm, Del, ordained to priesthood Jul 3 1892 and received
assignment to St. Peter's that city. In fall of same yr, however, he came to
Easton, and here has remained, giving to spiritual oversight of St. Peter's
and St. Paul's having under his immediate supervision 4 churches and 5 mission
stations in Talb and Dor Cos.

743. WILLIAM H. LOPER, blacksmith Millington, Kt Co, Md; b here Apr 8 1859. 876
Since his father's death, 1894, carrying on business of his decd father. Chas
P. Loper, father of subj, b Bridgeton, N.J., and there learned blacksmith's
trade. He continued there until 1857, when he came to Millington and employed
by J. A. Edward; then purch shop owned by that gentleman and carried on trade
until shortly he d in 60th yr; co commissioner and pres of bd 2. His father,
farmer nr Bridgetown, N.J. C. P. Loper m Mary J. Huntsman who was reared in
vicinity of Bridgeton, still living. Her younger child. with her at home in
Millington: Mary E., Howard L. and Lindon.
Subj eldest in parents' fam; educated in public schools and Millington Acad.
He bt out other heirs. He and his fam attend ME Church of Millington. He m
Miss Mary E., d/o Franklin Taylor of this place; their child: Lillian.

744. RICHARD G. DUCKETT, retired business man, engaged in rural life, after 876
active career in Balt; res 3rd dist QA Co on Cedarhurst. He is related to
Ridgeley fam of Md, and to Commodore Sturett. His maternal grandfather,
Richard Giddings old settler of Balt Co, extensive hardware dealer Balt City.
Father of subj, Judson N. Duckett, from PG Co, Md, farmer; as a boy he moved
to Balt Co. He promoted fairs and cattle shows. He m Elizabeth Giddings; 1
of their 2 child. decd. Subj b nr Long Green, Balt Co, Nov 9 1827; attended
Sherwood Park school Balt Co. When 16 he obtained clerkship; 1864-92 cashier
Balt City collector's office. 1892 his health seemed in danger and he
resigned to come to his present home. He is vestryman St. Luke's Church
Church Hill. Nov 9 1853 he m Miss Josephine A. Vickery. Of their 6 child.,
Graham, Richard and Katie still at home. Mrs. Duckettt d/o Stephen Thos
Vickery and granddau of Capt Vickery, early settler of city of Balt.

745. G. WARREN MUNDY, business man Cambridge, b Rahway, N.J., Mar 10 1853, 877
during childhood taken by parents, Henry E. and Fannie C. (Crowell) Mundy, to
Newark. They spent their lives in N.J., father d at 65; mother at 75. Of
their 8 child., 5 reached maturity: J. Crowell, superintendent of public works
Newark, N. J.; Henry H. lumberman of that place; Wm B., general superintendent

of J. S. Mundy Engine Works; Jos S., manufacturer of hoisting and stationary engines in Newark; and subj.
Subj educated in public schools, later Newark Military acad. At 18 he began learning the machine business, but on account of throat trouble forced to travel in Fla. Having regained his health, he returned to Newark and soon after came to Cambridge, Md, at request of uncle, Ellwood Birdsall, who was interested in Cambridge Manufacturing Co, organized by J. W. Crowell & Co, who failed. Subj made superintendent of machinery depart, as it required an expert machinist; he installed all machinery in their plant, which comprises a barrel factory, sawmill, flour and hominy mills. Subj located in Cambridge Oct 26 1877; active in reorganizing Cambridge Ice Co company into Cambridge Water co in 1893, of which he is superintendendent. In connection with bro, Jos S. Mundy, he has become interested in water front prop at Sandy Hill, called Clinton Place, on the Choptanbk. 1881 Mr Mundy m Miss Maggie K. Applegarth, of Balt, d/o Wm Applegarth, now decd; their child.: Elizabeth, Fannie and Catharine. 1888 Mr. Mundy elected mayor of Cambridge. He organizzed first fire company known as rescue fire commpany. Clement T. Mowbery is custodian of equipment. Mr Mundy mbr Christ Episc Church High st.

878   746. HON. WILLIAM F. APPLEGARTH, business man Dor Co, owns general store at Golden Hill, and farm land in Lake dist; b Lake dist Feb 11 1842, s/o John E. Applegarth, who was b on Choptank River this co, and in boyhood accompanied family to Lake dist, settling on a farm. When about 12 his father d. He followed farming; deputy sheriff 1850-3, also assessor. 1854-5 sheriff Dor Co; res here until 1855, partnership with bro-in-law in wholesale and retail boot and shoe business Balt, res there 1857-9; sold out and returned to Lake dist. In 1865, with subj, in business latter still conducts, having purch his father's interest 1881. Retiring from business, Mr Applegarth moved to Va and purch a farm; then purch res in Martinsburg, Va and retired; d Mar 1887, at 73. 1884 he united with Cath Church.
Applegarth fam of Scotch extraction. Subject's grandfather, Wm, b Neck dist, Dor Co, farmer; d at 35. One bro, Nat Applegarth, sheriff of co. Mother of subj, Ann M. Tubman, b Hooper's Island dist, res Dor Co; d here at 79; mbr Cath Church. She m(1) John Keene, by whom she had daus: Allie and Emily A. By 2nd marriage: Wm F.; Eleanor, w/o Dr S. A. Keene; and Alpheus, who d at 7.
Subj educated in public schols of Dor Co and city of Balt, St. Charles Coll, Chas Co, Md about 3 yrs; and St. Mary's Acad, Wilm, Del, 6 months; then assist on home farm; principal of school at Golden Hill 1867-1881, turned to merchandising and management of his land; mbr legislature; m Miss E. A. Keene, of Parsons Creek dist, d/o Thos H. Keene; of their 9 child., 3 d young; others: Wm F., Anita, S. Ubert, E. Vivian, Harold and Cecil. Fam identified with Roman Cath Church.

879   747. JEROME A. DAVIS, young farmer 2nd dist Car Co; b 8 Oct 1854, Car Co, s/o Curtis and Rebecca (Price) Davis, who were b this co. Subj reared in cities of New York and Phila, when 10 went to work for commission firm; remained in same business 30 yrs, dealt in fruits and vegetables, supplying large city hotels & restaurants. On his farm he raises grain, fruit and general produce for the markets. Feb 11 1881 he m Jennie E. DeRondy, from Hoboken, N. J.; mbrs ME Church.

880 &   748. PHILIP ADDISON MORGAN, po address: Queen Anne, res 4th dist Talb Co.
919   Under admin of Pres Cleveland app special agent for depart of labor; state

-208-

weigher of cattle in Balt 1871-3. Father of subj, Philip Morgan, b nr Denton, Car Co, later settled on farm QA Co, and engaged in merchandising. 1850 he returned to Car Co; d Jan 11 1856, in faith of ME Church.. He m Miss Anne Thawley, d/o Wm Thawley, of Car Co; she d 1846; 3 of her 6 child. survive: Mary H., w/o C. M. Jump, of Talb Co; P. A. and Anne L., w/o L. T. Dukes, of Cordova, Talb Co.

Great-great-grandfather of subj, Chas Morgan, from Scotland, exiled from his country by British government because he was Roman Cath. His son, Jacob, b Talb Co, and then Chas, also b this co, nr Chapel, and finally Philip, father of P. A. The commanding officer of famous Morgan Rifles, of rev war, was ancestor of·subj, and Gen John H. Morgan, celebrated Confed officer in Civ war, also related.

Subj b Apr 20 1840, at father's homestead in QA Co. His mother d when he was 6. He attended school at West River Institute, AA Co, at outbreak of war attempted to enter Confed army, but not accepted; taught school 3 yrs, then assumed charge of another school 5 yrs; carried on farm a while. He is vestryman Episc Church; m Mrs. Joseph A. Jones d/o late Dr. L. H. Beatty of QA Co Dec 8 1897.

749. FRANCIS NATHAN SHEPPARD, M. D., res 2nd dist, Kt Co; from fam founded this country by 3 bros,: Jonadab, Jos and David Sheppard, from Eng c. 1690, settled in N.J. Jonadab settled in Antucsett, his son, Nathan Sheppard, lived and d in N.J., whose son, Nathan Shepard, b Nov 13 1734, this state, m(1) Prudence; m(2) Martha Mulford and by this marriage had Nathan, Nathaniel, Reed, Jonadab, Cave Bowen and Ruma Austin.

Nathan Sheppard b Sep 16 1788, farmer, m Rachel Cook Apr 7 1814, active in Bapt Church; d Oct 15 1859; his child.: Jos Cok, Isaac Mulford, Albert Nathan, Leander Wm, Maria Elizabeth and Theodore Warren.

Jos Cook Sheppard, subject's father, mbr ME Church; b Feb 21 1815, Salem, N.J., where he res until 1852, when he came to Md and purch a tract of c. 1300 a. in QA Co, on which he laid out village of Crumpton; he d there Feb 19 1880. Through his efforts present causeway built, connecting cos of Kt and QA. He m Elizabeth, d/o Justus Bonham, of N.J., Jul 13 1836; their child.: Justus Bonham, Frs Nathan, Jos Henry, Maria Elizabeth and Isaac Mulford.

Subj b Nov 1 1839, on old home farm, Salem Co, N.J., educated at Salem Acad and Chester Seminary, Del Co, Pa; grad Phila Coll of Dental Surgery; practice in Phila 2 yrs. 1861 he met and m Amanda Freeman, d/o Wm and Katherine Bowker; later grad Univ Pa with degree, M.D.; located in Crumpton, QA Co, 1866. In connection with practice he conducted drug store until 1876, when he purch old H. B. Slaughter homestead, known as Riverside, present res. By his 1st marriage 5 child. were b, 2 living: Florence Katherine, w/o Sml Webb Merritt, s/o Rev Jas Black Merritt, D. D., of Md; and Albert Cook, at home. In 1893 he m(2) Mary Adelaide, d/o Capt R. A. Gray, of QA Co.

750. HON. SAMUEL W. WOOLFORD, mbr state legislature, in merc business at Woolford, Church Creek dist, Dor Co. The Woolford fam originated in Eng, where Col Roger Woolford b c. 1586, d 1668; he came to Md, settling in Dor Co. He held large land grants in this and Som Co. His Som prop he gave to son John, land in Dor Co bequeathed to son Col Thos, and dau, Sarah, these 3 his only child Col Thos Woolford had 7 sons and 1 dau: Roger, Stephen, Thos, Battie, Levin, Jas, John and Nancy; to each he gave a farm. Col Stephen Woolford had 3 sons and 7 daus b to his marriage with Elizabeth Whiteley, sis of Col Whiteley, of Car Co. His son Stephen, m Nellie Jones; they had 3 sons and 4 daus: Stephen, Geo Whitefield, Hiram, Elizabeth, Mary, Sallie and Charlotte. His son, Geo Whitefield, m Eliza, d/o Col John and Mary

(Edmondson) Broughan, and they had 3 sons and 10 daus. Their eldest son, J. S. B., m Mollie Rees, of Newark, Del, and unto their union were b 5 sons and 1 dau. The oldest son, Geo Whitefield, m(1) Eva Skinner and after her death m(2) Sallie Mace. He has 3 child.: Mildred, mabel and MIles.
Ellen, d/o Geo Whitefield, m Chas Jones; they had 2 child., both decd. Mary became w/o S. B. B. Woolford, had 4 children. Stephen W. m Lydia Lowe, of Salisbury, have 2 son and 4 daus. Ella is unmarried; Frank Whitefield d at 10; Elizabeth became Mrs. Thos Mace. Geo A. Mace, s/o Thos Mace, m Phoebe Tubman; they have 5 sons and 5 daus. Mary m Wm Willis, of Church Creek, and they have 3 daus and 1 son. Edwin Mace m Annie Mills; they res Cambridge. Dr. John Mace m Della Briley, res Cambridge. Susie w/o Lewis Keene, of Golden Hill; they have 6 sons and 1 dau. Sml Whitefield d Cambridge. Eliza B. Mace is an invalid. Hannah C. Wolford m Wm Mace; they had 5 daus and 2 sons. Willie m Luther Martin; they had 2 sons and 1 dau. Sallie w/o Geo Woolford. Irving Mace, atty Cambridge. Margaret and Netie are unmarried; Chas and Elen are decd. Kate Woolford m Jhn W. Mace; they had 5 sons and 3 daus. Batie res Pittsbury, Pa, single. Benj, Harry and John S., also single, res Phila. Valeria Mace m Chas B. Cator; they have one son, Benj. Emma Woolford m Thos Adolphus Willis; they had 2 sons and 4 daus. Edgar and Willie Woolford Willis res Vicksburg; Lillie is with father in Cambridge, and others decd.
Sml Whitefield Woolford m Lillie Crawford, of Phila; they have 3 child. Lizzie V. m Ralph Rees, of Chesapeake City, Md; Sml Whitefield, Jr., law student Univ Pa; and Lillie Crawford, his twin sis, at home, their farm part of prop willed by first Woolford who came to this country, Col Roger Woolford. Benj Whiteley Woolford m Emma Skinner; they had one son, in drug business Balt. Almira Woolford m Wm Hurlock, of Cambridge; they had 3 sons and 1 dau. Willie Woolford and Ben Cator, twins, are decd; Taney Lee and Susie V. in school Cambridge. Susie L. Woolford res with her bros Sml W. and is unmarried. Sallie and Willie decd.
Geo Whitefield Woolford, father of subj major land owner Dor Co; mbr legislature; co commissioner; d 1874, at 84. Of his 14 child., before named, 4 living: Susie; Kate, wid of John A. Mace, of Phila; Sml W.; and Valeris, w/o Wm Hurlock, of Cambridge. The wife d 1765, at 65; mbr old school Bapt Church, in which husband was a deacon.
At 19 in 1856, subj clerked for Whitely, Stone & Co Balt 3 yrs; returned to Dor Co and purch business owned by bro, J. S. B.; judge of elections, 1870-2 mbr of state legislature, dist collector 7 yrs. His family attend old school Bapt Church. In addition to store he owns a farm in Church Creek dist. 1872 he m Miss Lillie Crawford, of Phila, d/o Wm H. and sis of Geo L. Crawford, atty of Phila; the have 3 child.: Lizzie V., w/o Ralph Rees, of Chesapeake city; and Sml W., Jr., and Lillie c., twins.

883 751. JOSEPH MALLALIEU, farmer, res 7th dist QA Co, b Phila, Pa May 10 1841, s/o Thos and Mary Mallalieu, both of Saddleworth, Yorkshire, Eng. Father arrived Phila Aug 1, 1839, after 6-week voyage in sailing vessel, and fol year joined by wife. During childhod of subj they located nr Smyrna, Del, where father worked in Murphey's woolen mills until 1848, he formed partnership with bro John, they operated mills until 1852. That yr Thos and John, located in upper part QA Co, rented Unicorn Woolen Mills, and purch 2 yrs later; latter d 1869, after which Mr. Malalieu conducted mill alone until he retired in Millington, 1887; he d 1896, at 82. His wife d same day, at 83, married to each other 62 1/2 yrs. They had 11 child.: Sml, res Millington; Esther, decd; subj; Jas M., d Aug 7 1887; Mary R., w/o Rev R. H. Adams; Sarah; Ann J., w/o

-210-

Geo M. Jenkins, of Talb Co; John T., res Kearney, Neb; Geo H., drowned 1861; Emily, who d 1859; and Willie, who d 1862.
 Subj was 11 when he moved with parents to QA Co; attended public schools; pursued 3-yr course Dickinson College; employed in mill until father disposed of business 1887. He then purch his present farm 7th dist QA Co, raised peaches, strawberies and other fruits. He m 1867 Miss Jemima Fogwell, of Sudlersville; they had 3 child.: Clara S.; Mary J. w/o Oscar Roe; and John F. She d Sep 30 1874 and Mr. Mallalieu m(2) 1879 Miss Sallie M. Warner, d/o Rev W. M. Warner, of Wilm Conference. Their child.: W. Warner and Nattie. Subj 1st on Rep ticket to be elected to state legislature (1881); mbr ME Church.

752. RICHARD D. HYNSON, res Kt Co, lawyer; b Poplar Neck, 8 miles below Chestertown, St. Paul's parish, Kt Co, Jan 1820; descendant of 1 of 3 bros, Richard, Thos and Geo, of Eng, early settlers of Md. His father, Maj. Thos Bowers Hynson, s/o Richard Hynson, an officer in War of 1812; from Kt Co; ancestors moved from Kt Island 1659. He m Ann, d/o Rbt Dunn.
 After local schools and acad in Pa, subj studied law with Judge John B. Eccleston, of Chestertown, cousin of his father; 1843 admitted to bar of Chestertown; opened office; he d Oct 23 1889; mbr Episc Church; mbr bd of vistors and governors of Wash Coll; director Kt Natl Bank, director B & O Railroad, director house of correction, treasurer Chestertown Railroad. 1843 he m C. L. Marsh, of Phila, d/o Elias and Mary L. (Eccleson) Marsh. Her father, from N.J., in merc business. She was sis of Judge Ecleston, under whom subj studied law; also of Sml Eccleson, archibishop Roman Cath Church. They had 7 child.: eld dau, w/o Wm L. Sly; Caroline L., unmarried; Thos C. d in infancy; Thos B., decd; Alice d in childhood; Mariana, w/o Edw Rogers, of Newcastle, Del. Youngest is Richard Dunn, b 1865, grad Wash Coll 1883, student in Bryant & Stratton's Business College Balt, grad Md Law School 1886; admitted to bar Balt, in practice Chestertown; Feb 1890 app mbr of bd directors of house of correction. He m Feb 1 1892, Emma A., d/o Jos E. Gilpin, of Kt co; their child.: Caroline Marsh, Helen Eccleson and Richard Hynson.

753. JOSEPH HUBBERT, farmer East New Market dist, Dor Co; his newly erected home in Hurlock; b nr boundary line betwen this and Car Co 1834. His boyhood spent in adjoining dist of Williamsbury, settled down as a farmer in this place. Hubberts came from Eng a few generations ago; grandfather of subj, Michael, b this co, it is supposed; he setled on farm nr Williamsburg, and there father of Jas Hubbert b. The latter, Thomas, lived and d within a mile of his of his birthplace, at 52. Subj res with parents until he attained majority, when he went to sea; after 5 yrs turned to farming; m and learned carpenter's trade, has followed this and managed his farm. He m Mary, d/o Hooper Hubbert who was b 1805 this co, s/o Michael Hubbert, d at 89. His 3 sons, bros of Mrs. Hubbert, are Thos Michael, Jr., Edw and Tilghman, only sis is Mrs. Wm Harper, of Hurlock. Only child of subj and wife is Michael. Mrs. Hubbert mbr MP Church.

754. JULIUS A. JOHNSON, M. D., physician, Easton; res at The Anchorage, on Miles River. Julius A. Johnson, Sr., b New York City, as was his father, Julius Christopher Johnson, before him. W/o Julius Christopher was one of Rockwell fam, whose ancestors landed in Plymouth colony 1826, having sailed across Atlantic in good ship Mary & John. During youth of subject's father he learned printing business; came to Easton, m and soon after became editor of Easton Gazette; postmaster several yrs; moved to Balt 1855; returned to Easton

and established the Ledger. 1881 he went to Auburn, N.Y., purch the newspaper he still conducts, The Independent, now in 72nd year.
Mother of subj, Christy S., d/o Alexander Graham, of Easton. She m 1847, d 1889, about 52. Of her children subj is eldest; others: Jannie G., w/o Wm B. Chisholm, of Auburn, N. Y.; Evelyn M., Mrs. Wm Powell, of Chicago; Lucy Rockwell; Dr. F. P. Casey, of Auburn, N. Y.; and Sophia C., w/o T. Eugene Smith, of Chicago.
Subj b Easton Jul 15 1849, attended the schools of this place; studied medicine with Dr. Richard McSherry, of Balt; grad Univ Md 1871, located in Easton; U. S. examining surgeon on pensions. Feb 4 1880 he m Elizabeth T., d/o Commodore Chas Lowndes, of Easton; their child.: C. Lowndes and Julius G. Fam attend Miles River Episc Church.

887 755. HENRY ALPHA TOWERS b Sussex Co, Del, Mar 24 1867, 4th s/o Jas H. and Elizabeth (Deen) Towers. When a small boy his parents moved on a farm nr American Corners, Car Co; educated public and private schools; 1887-91 clerked in general store of B. Gootee Stevens, Williston, Car Co, moved to Trappe, Talb Co where he keeps general store of dry goods, boots and shoes, hats, caps, carpets, groceris, building materials, farm implemtnes, fishing outfits, furniture and stoves. He attends ME Church.

887 756. CAPT. SAMUEL A. LAWSON, res 11th dist Dor Co, Co commissioner. 1876 he purch farm known as Fullersville. Subject's father, Sml Lawson, sailor in early life, farming just prior to death. He m Leah Reagan; 2 child.: 1 since decd. Father of Leah was Jeremiah Reagan, in war of 1812, b Ireland. Sml Lawson d when subj was young lad, mother d 1867. Subj b this dist Oct 9 1832, sent to school a part of each year. When 14 he went to sea and continued seafaring until 1876; captain of a vessel; in government service, during the war, in transportation of troops; owns fleet of boats for the oyster fisheries hereabout. Apr 1857 he m Miss Mary Marshall, d/o Bond P. Marshall, of this co; of their 8 child., 3 survive: Octavia E., m and res this co; Thos H., of this community; and Sarah F., unmarried and at home.

888 757. FRANCIS B. PHELPS, M. D. res nr Cambridge, on Choptank River, Cambridge dist, Dor Co; retired from army 1863; b Aug 30 1836 nr Federalsburg, Car Co. His father, Dr. Frs Philps, b nr Milford, Del, physician many yrs; mbr house of delegates; d Cambirdge Nov 1886, bur cem there. When 6 subj was brought to Cambridge; student in acad at Cambridge, later 3 yrs, at Wyoming Seminary, Luzerne Co, Pa; grad Univ Md medical deprt 1853. Opening office in Preston, Car Co, he was in practice until 1858, when he purch farm formerly owned by Gov Hicks. At opening of war in 1861 Dr. Phelps enlisted in army, commissioned surgeon of 1st Regt Eastern Shore Vol; ill health forced him to resign Dec 1 1863. He m(1) 1853 Miss Mary R. Springer; their child.: Florence, wid of Wilson Lowe; Nancy, w/o Roy Hayes; and John, res Cambridge. 1862 Dr. Phelps m(2) M. T. Houston, d/o Dr. Hy H. Houston, of East New Market. The latter b Lewes, Del, 1809, grad Univ Md 1834, practiced at Frederalsburg for a year; moved to East New Market, continued practice until just before his death, 1887; Meth; he m Mrs. T. M. LeCompte; their child: Frs H., journalist and literay man res in New York City; Sml, banker, also of that city; Susan L., w/o J. Kent Dukes, of Phila; and Mrs. Phelps. By 2nd marriage Dr. Phelps had 7 child.: Frances P., M. D., in medicine Cambridge; Agnes, w/o H. S. Todd; Tryphena, Mrs. R. V. Todd, of Berlin; Jos W., at home; W. Wallace, of Balt; May and Elsie. Fam identified with Episc Church. Dr. Phelps elected 1893 to house of delegates.

-212-

758. JAMES W. HURTT, farmer 2nd dist, Kt Co; b 1828 on farm adjoining his present place, s/o Edw Hurtt, also of Kt Co, who spent his entire life on the farm where Chas Hill now res. He m(1) Miss Rebecca Merritt, sis of Benj Merritt; they had 12 child., all decd. He m(2) 2nd cousin, Martha A. Hurtt; their child.: subj, and Dr. Edw D., of PG Co, Md. The father d 1831, about 54. Subj spent early life in Galena, attended common schools and an acad. At 18 he took charge of old homestead and 2 yrs later purch that place, bt the Marsh Point farm where he res 9 yrs, 1868 purch J. F. Woodland farm, present res; farmed and raised fruit. He m Miss Mary E., only d/o Jas Freeman Woodland; of their 10 child., 7 living: Lizzie, w/o E. T. Comegys; Alice, w/o H. C. Deringer; Florence, w/o Woodland Deringer, of Spangler, Pa; Woodland; Clifton; Dr. Harry, of Wash, D. C.; and Edwin S. Julia d Jul 28 1894 at 36; Woodland Hurtt, oldest son, res Woodland Hall, late res of Jas Freeman Woodland, his maternal grandfather. He m Miss Woodland, d/o Jas F. M. and Emma A. Woodland, and they have one child, Jas Freeman. Family connected with Episc Church. Mr. Hurtt elected to state legislature 1872. 889

759. JAMES H. McNEAL, mbr bd of co commissioners Talb Co, mbr Shannahan & Wrightson Hardware Co., of Easton, b nr this city, Oct 11 1846, s/o of Hon. Jas H. and Elizabeth (Benny) McNeal, of Talb Co. The fam of Scotch-Irish lineage. Hector McNeal, of Scotland, moved to Co Antrim, Ireland, where in 1725 his son, Archibald, was b. 1747 the latter came to Talb Co, and spent remainder of life. 889

Jas, son of Archibald, had a son, Jas Hector, who was b nr Esaton, Jan 20 1807, one of 9 child. of a poor fam. 1822 his father d, Being the eldest son he assumed responsibliity of caring for fam; employed in shoe store in Balt, failing health of mother caused him to return home; soon afterward she d.

Soon after his marriage to Elizabeth, d/o Jonathan and Mary Benn, Jas Hector McNeal embarked in merc business in Easton while carrying on large farm nr town where fam res; mbr legislature of Md; 1865 elected to state senate and re-elected; collector of the state and co charges.

Jas Hector mbr ME Church; d 25 Dec 1868; his wife d Nov 16 1870. Of their 10 child. 6 living: Sarah E., w/o P. S. Reed, of Phila; Martha V., w/o Gervas Hall, of Easton; subj; Gertrude, wid of Edwin Ball, of Phila; M. Louisa, w/o M. E. Shannahan, of Easton; and Annie R., w/o Chas T. Wrightson, of Easton. 3 child. d in infancy. Jonathan Benny, eld son, m Mary C. Valliant, of Balt, d Jun 1893. After grad Easton Acad subj clerked in hardware store in Easton 1864-6; then 4 yrs employed in dry goods store; 1869-79 dep U. S. marshal under Maj. Edw Y. Goldsborough, at Balt. 1884 he bt interest in hardware firm of Shanahan & Wrightson, of Easton; co commissioner; director Easton Gas and Electric Light Co; steward ME Church. Aug 23 he m Caroline K. Budd, d/o Hy G. Budd, of Smyrna, Del; their child.: Jas Hector and Hy G. Budd.

760. J. FRANK HEARN, owns store at Bishop's Head, Strait dist, Dor Co, also in oyster dredging and planting; magistrate several yrs; b Drawbridge dist, s/o Benj B. and Charlotte A. (Smith) Hearn, 1864, next to youngest of 10 child., 6 living. He spent early life nr Cambridge, Dor Co, educated in public schools, commercial training in Bryant & Stratton's Business Coll Balt. Leaving home, he went to Wicomico, and followed merchandising there f4 yrs. 1888 he came to this place and opened a store. He and fam attend ME Church. He m 1893 Miss henrietta G. Pritchett, d/o J. N. Pritchett; their child is Omro. 890

Benj B. Hearn, father of subj, b Sussex Co, Del, 1823, s/o Josiah and Sarah (Lowe) Hearn; of the 7 child., he and bro, WM W., of Vienna, Dor Co, remain.

The father, Josiah, from Sussex Co as were his ancestors back to c. 1700. He operated portion of old fam estate nr Laurel, Del, d at 35. His father was Wm, farmer. At age c. 17, Benj B. Hearn went to Laurel Del, 1845 became assoc in manufacture of furniture with bro. 1856 partnership dissolved and Benj Hearn continued there until 1860; farmed nr Vienna c. 14 yrs; leased homestead nr Cambridge 1874-96; now retired, in Cambridge. He and wife attend Bapt Church. She is Charlotte A., d/o Sml Smith; their surviving child.: Olevia, Mrs. Geo A. Thompson; Annie, Mrs. John O. Weeden; Wm C. and Geo E., twins; J. F. and Herbert, mcht at Lloyds, this co.

891 761. FRANK M. ECCLES, M. D., physician Oxford, Talb Co, where he suceeded in practice Dr. Eugene Douglas, now of Balt. Subj b Phila, Jan 1858, s/o Perry Eccles, of Royal Oak, Talb Co. His ancestor, Perry Benson, captain in rev and general in militia during war of 1812. Benson fam settled nr Royal Oak in 17th century. Subj taken by parents to Balt as small child; there attended coll. Later he attended Swarthmore, Del Co, Pa; read medicine for 2 yrs, and grad Coll of Physicians and Surgeon Balt 1881, and made hospital assist; res physician Bay View Asylum; took up private practice in Car Co, and from there came to Oxford. Sep 30 1886 he m Miss May C., d/o Major Sandres, of Md; their child.: Wilson C. and Frank M. Subj mbr Episc Church.

892 762. J. E. McKNETT manages his homestead, Middletown, 3rd dist Dor Co. McKnett fam of Scotch extraction. Father, Thos McKnett, b Harrington, Del, millwright, moved to Balt 1837, held an office app by gov of Md; d 1839 from Asiatic cholera; m Josephine, d/o J. Ennalls, of English descent. She was b and reared Dor Co, d 1856. Of their 7 child. subj only survivor. His great-grandfather, J. Ennalls, colonel in Rev war and received large grant in Dor Co. Subj b Balt Jun 6 1839, taken by mother to New Market dist, Dor Co, and there reared on farm. He attended public schools; taught school at ages 20-28. Dec 1 1863 he m Sarah Vincent, d/o John and Elizabeth Vincent, of this co. Of their 10 children, 1 d. John, eldest son, at home, helps on farm; Rose w/o Augustus LeCompte, overseer of co almshouse nr by; Thos res of Big Mills, Md; Rbt A. is next; May m John Bassett, of this vicinity; and Josephine, Chas, Magie and Jos are at home.

892 763. RUFUS S. NOBLE, commissioner Dor Co, business man and postmaster of Taylor's Island, in merchandising and oyster business, owner of 6 oyster boats; 3 are dredgers; elected co commissiner 1895; b nr Preston, Car Co, Dec 3 1851. His grandfather, J. Noble, from Sussex Co, Del, where he spent his life farming. It is thought that his father was b in Eng, whence he emigrated to Md.
Twiford S. Noble, subject's father, b Sussex Co, Del, moved to Car Co, where he remained until his death, at 62; delegatge to state constitutional convention and co commissioner; identified with ME Church. He m Ruth Leverton, who was b nr Preston, Car Co, and d Dor Co at 20; mbr Soc of Friends. Her father, Jacob Leverton, from Car Co, farmer there; her mother, Ruth (Hannah) Leverton active Abolitionist. Mrs. Noble d leaving 2 child., older of whom, J. L. Noble, M. D., physician at Preston.
At the time of his mother's death subj was infant; he attended public schools and Preston academy; at 19 teacher of dist school in Car Co and later in Dor Co. On his marriage he settled down as farmer nr Preston for 2 yrs, then moved to Solomon's Island, Md, where in merchandising about 3 yrs, and then came to Taylor's Island and opened the store. He m Katie B. Dewell, of Balt, d/o Col. Thos Dewell, who owned tannery in Balt, mbr of city council

there and during war was col in Union army. Mr. and Mrs. Noble had 3 child.: Twiford Sewell, student Dover Acad, at Dover, Del; Fannie L. and Marie, at home. Fam connected with ME Church.

THE GOLDSBOROUGH FAMILY

764. Nicholas Goldsborough, progenitor of the Goldsborough family of MD, b 1640-1641, at Malcon Regis, nr Weymouth, in Co of Dorset, Eng, and m, 1659, Margaret Howes, only d/o Abraham Howes, s/o Wm Howes, of Newbury, Co of Berks, Eng. He had 3 child: Rbt, b Advent Sunday, 1660, at Blandford, Dorset Co, Eng, d Christmas day, 1746; Nicholas d 1705; and Judith. Nicholas Goldsborough left Eng 1669, went to Barbadoes, thence to New England, and finally, 1670, settled on Kt Island where he d; buried on plantation of Tobias Wells. His wife survived him and m 1672 Geo Robins, of Talb Co, and had son, Thos who m twice. He m (1) February 3, 1696, Susannah Vaughan, and had son, Geo. He m (2) Elizabeth Standley; their child: Thos b Oct 11 1705; Wm and John, twins, b Dec 22 1709; Elizabeth; Lambert; and Standley, who m Jan 6 1742, Sarah Goldsborough. Thomas Robins d Dec 29 1721. Rbt Goldsborough of Ashby, Talb Co, Md (s/o Nicholas and Margaret Howes Goldsborough) came to Md 1678 and m Sep 2 1697, Elizabeth Greenbury, d/o Col Nicholas and Ann Greenbury, of Greenbury Point, nr Annapolis. She was b Sep 23 1678, AA Co, d Mar 2 1719, and had child: Ann, b Jul 13 1698, d Feb 24 1708; Elizabeth, b Feb 13 1700, d Jan 17 1708; Mary, b Dec 14 1702, d Jan 15 1742; Rbt, b Feb 17 1704, d Apr 30 1777; Nicholas, twin b/o Rbt, b Feb 17 1704, d Nov 14 1757; Chas, b Jun 26 1707, d Jul 4 1767; Wm, b Jul 6 1709, d Sep 1760; John, b Oct 12 1711, d Jan 18 1778; Greenbury, b Nov 16 1713, d Feb 2 1715; Howes, b Nov 14 1715, d Mar 30 1746; a second Greenbury, b Nov 13 1717, d Nov 20 1717; a third Greenbury, b Nov 19 1718, d 3 hrs after birth.

765. Mary Goldsborough, d/o Rbt and Elizabeth Greenbury Goldsborough, m M. Mooney, their child: Mary, Elizabeth and Anna Keziah. Mary Mooney, d/o Mary Goldsborough Mooney, m Jun 16 1751, Thos Sherwood; their son, Maj Hugh, m Dec 10 1795, Elizabeth, d/o Richard Tilghman. Ann Keziah Mooney, d/o Mary Goldsborough Mooney, m Dec 8 1763, Dnl Feddeman, their child: Mary, b Jun 29 1766; Annie, b Apr 19 1768; and Dnl, b Jan 9 1770, d Feb 25 1832. Dnl Feddeman, s/o Dnl and Ann Keziah Mooney Feddeman, m Mar 16 1794, Rebecca Sherwood Wrightson, who d Oct 15 1842; their child: Mary Mooney, b Feb 3 1795; Ann Keziah, b Feb 13 1797; Richard, b May 8 1800; Elizabeth, b Jan 8 1805; Mary, b May 8 1807; Jane Maynadier, b May 27 1809; Emma, b Dec 18 1811; Philemon Hy, b Aug 3 1814; Dnl Maynadier, b Jan 24 1817, who m Apr 27 1865, Alice Colbert; and Dorothy, b Feb 4 1819.

Ann Keziah Feddeman, d/o Dnl and Rebecca Sherwood Wrightson Feddeman, m Nov 25 1813, Philemon Williamson Hemsley, their child: Philemon Feddeman, b Sep 8 1814, d young; Martha Ann, b Dec 23 1815, who m Alexander Lackey; Philemon Feddeman, b Oct 1 1817, who m Mary Hambleton; and Richard Feddeman, b Jul 19 1819, d Apr 1854. Philemon (Philip) Hy Feddeman, s/o Dnl and Rebecca Wrightson Feddeman, m Nov 25 1840, Ann Matilda Groome, d/o Sml and Deborah Morris Groome, had one son, Morris Groome. Sml Groome s/o Chas and Sarah Kennard Groome. Chas Groome, rgtr Chester Parish, Kt Co Md, s/o Sml and Margaret Groome. The last-named Sml Groome church warden St. Paul's Parish, Kt Co, Md in 1726.

766. Rbt Goldsborough, s/o Rbt and Elizabeth Greenbury Goldsborough, m (1) Nov 5 1739 Sarah Nicols, d/o Rev Hy Nicols, rector of St. Michael's Parish, Talb Co, had one son, Rbt, b Nov 8 1740, d 1798. Mrs. Sarah Nicols Goldsborough d Sat, Nov 15 1740. He m (2) Jul 8 1742, Mrs. Mary Ann Turbutt Robins, wid of John Robins, atty, who d 1739, and d/o Foster and Bridget Turbutt; she d Aug 29 1794.

Rbt Goldsborough and second wife had child: Elizabeth, b Apr 29 1745, d Apr 29 1748; Howes, b Sep 14 1747, d Jan 30 1797; Wm, b Mar 17 1750, d Jan 23 1801; and Mary Ann Turbutt, b Oct 21 1752, d unmarried April 18 1811.

Rbt Goldsborough of Myrtle Grove, s/o Rbt and his first wife, m Sep 22 1768, Mary Emerson Trippe, youngest d/o Henry Trippe, of Dor Co, and their child: Rbt, b Mar 21 1771, d Apr 1 following; Rbt Hy, b Feb 17 1774, d Sep 18 1777; Elizabeth, b Jul 30 1776, d Aug 14 1798, and a second Rbt Henry, b Jan 4 1779, d Oct 5 1836.

Elizabeth Goldsborough, d/o Rbt and Mary Emerson Trippe Goldsborough, m Sep 22 1793, Gov Chas Goldsborough, their child: Elizabeth Greenbury and Ann Maria.

767. Hon Rbt Hy Goldsborough, s/o Rbt and Mary Emerson Trippe Goldsborough, U.S. Senator May 21 1813-Dec 21 1819, m Jan 16 1800, Henrietta Maria Nicols, d/o Col Rbt Lloyd Nicols and wife, Susannah Robins Chamberlaine Nicols, their child: Rbt Wm, b Oct 18 1800; Wm, b Apr 20 1802; Chas Hy, b Apr 12 1804; Susan Elizabeth, b Jan 4 1806, who m Mr. Collidge of Boston, and d Jan 14 1838; Mary Caroline, b Nov 11 1808; Henrietta Maria, b Jan 31 1811; John McDowell, b Oct 4 1813; Mary McDowell; Eliza, b Sep 19 1815; and Geo Robins, b Apr 11 1821. Col Rbt Lloyd Nicols was s/o Jeremiah Nicols and Deborah Lloyd. Deborah Lloyd d/o Jas Lloyd and Ann Grundy. Susannah Robins Chamberlaine, when she m, Aug 1775, Col Rbt Lloyd Nicols, was wid of Thos Chamberlaine. She was d/o George Robins and Henrietta Maria Tilghman, who m Apr 22 1721. Henrietta Maria Tilghman d/o Richard and Ann Maria Lloyd Tilghman of the Hermitage.

768. Howes Goldsborough, s/o Rbt and his second wife, Mary Ann Turbutt Robins Goldsborough, m Nov 16 1773, Rebecca Goldsborough, d/o Rbt and Sarah Yerbury Goldsborough, their child: Sarah, b Oct 5 1774; Rbt, b Mar 6 1776, d Dec 5 1777; Mary Ann, b Feb 23 1778; Charles, b Jun 4 1779, d Aug 13 1824; Rbt Yerbury, b Jan 24 1782; Hy Turbutt, b Dec 11 1783, d Feb 2 1785; Wm Henry, b May 6 1785, d Aug 14 1842; Ann, b May 11 1787, who m May 30 1810, Chas Louis Pascault, s/o the Marquis de Poleon, of Balt, and d Dec 24 1855; Howes, b Mar 11 1789, who m Maria Ward; Rebecca, b Nov 25 1790, d Sep 1792; Elizabeth, b Feb 8 1791, d Feb 19 1791; and Hy, b Feb 16 1792, d 1832.

Sarah Goldsborough, d/o Howes and Rebecca Goldsborough, m Mar 25 1802, Dr. Sml Y. Keene, their child: John Hy and Mary Ann, who m ---Hollingsworth.

Mary Ann Goldsborough, d/o Howes and Rebecca Goldsborough, m Mar 4 1804, Dr. Tristram Thomas, of Easton, Md, their child: Juliana, b Dec 20 1804; and Rbt T. Goldsborough, who m Mar 1831, Mary Isabella Willson, d/o Jas and Mary Jacob Willson.

Charles Goldsborough, s/o Howes and Rebecca Goldsborough, m Nov 2 1802, Sarah Keene, b Dec 16 1789, d Nov 26 1819, d/o Vachel Keene who was s/o Rev Samuel Keene, of Talbot, their child: Howes, Eleanor; Charles, b Jun 1 1807; Saml and Sarah.

Hy Goldsborough, s/o Howes and Rebecca Goldsborough, m (1) Apr 24 1817, Eliza Ann Thomas, of QA, who d Aug 24 1817; (2) Susannah Shippley, and had two sons and a dau; (3) May 18 1823, Annie Keene, who d Jun 9 1824; and (4) Nov 15 1825, Margaret Tilghman, d/o Jas Tilghman, s/o Jas Tilghman, of Phila.

769. Mrs. Margaret Tilghman Goldsborough survived her hus, m Jun 22 1817, John Goldsborough, s/o John and Caroline Goldsborough, of Four Square.
   Nicholas Goldsborough, s/o Rbt and Elizabeth Greenbury Goldsborough, and twin bro of Rbt, m Apr 7 1746, Mrs. Jane Banning, wid of Jas Banning, and d Nov 14 1756. Having no child of his own he adopted those of his wife, and in his will, dated Oct 20 1756, left them his prop. His adopted child.: Jeremiah, Hy and Anthony Banning.
   Chas Goldsborough, s/o Rbt and Elizabeth Greenbury Goldsborough, m (1) Jul 18 1730, Elizabeth Ennalls, s/o Col Jos Ennalls, their child.: Elizabeth Greenbury, b Jul 4 1731, who m Wm Ennalls, s/o said Col Jos Ennalls; and Rbt, b Dec 3 1733, d Dec 20 1788. He m (2) Aug 2 1739, Elizabeth Dickinson, half sister of John Dickinson of Phila., and had one son, Chas, b Apr 2 1740.
   Hon Rbt Goldsborough, barrister, s/o Chas and Elizabeth Ennalls Goldsborough, m in Eng Mar 27 1755, Sarah Yerbury, d/o Richard Yerbury, of Bassing-Hall street, London, who d Dec 20 1788, in Cambridge, their child: Chas, b Dec 19 1755, d Dec 29 1758; Rebecca, b Jul 4 1757, d Jun 26 1802, m Nov 16 1773, Howes Goldsborough; Sarah, b Oct 11 1758, m Hy Ennalls of Dor Co, and d Apr 21 1822, sine prole; Elizabeth, b June 3 1760, d Nov 6 1827; Chas, b Nov 21 1761, d Jun 1801; Wm, b Aug 5 1762, d May 22 1826; John, b Dec 16 1763, d May 10 1767; Rbt, b 1766, drowned 1791; Richard, b Aug 13 1768; Rachel, b Dec 10 1769, m Horatio Ridout of AA Co, left son, John Ridout; John, b Oct 28 1772, d Oct 1788; and Howes, b Feb 18 1775, m Mary Rogers.

770. Elizabeth Goldsborough, d/o Hon Rbt and Sarah Yerbury Goldsborough, m Dr. Jas Sykes of Del, their child: Jas, b 1794; Wm, b 1798; Alfred, b 1801, and Anna Matilda, b 1805, d 1812.
   Chas Goldsborough, Horn's Point, s/o Hon Rbt and Sarah Yerbury Goldsborough, m (1) Williamima Smith, d/o Dr. Wm Smith of Phila., their child: Rbt, b 1785, d 1817; Wm, b 1787, d 1812, and Sarah Yerbury, b 1789, who m Gov Chas Goldsborough. He m (2) Elizabeth Greenbury Goldsborough, d/o John and Caroline Goldsborough, who d Apr 7 1797. He m (3) Mrs. Anna McKeel Stevens, had son, Chas, of Lewistown, Del. She survived him and m Dr. Alward White of Cambridge, Md, and had child: John and Dr. Alward McKeel.
   Rev. Wm Smith, D.D., last principal of celebrated free school at Chestertown; then 1st principal Wash College nr Chestertown; later provost of Univ Pa.

771. Rbt Goldsborough, s/o Charles and Williamima Smith Goldsborough, m Mary Nixon of Dover, Del, who survived him and m Gardiner Bailey of Cambridge.
   Wm Goldsborough, s/o Hon Rbt and Sarah Yerbury Goldsborough, m Nov 8 1792, Sarah Worthington, d/o Nicholas Worthington of AA Co, and in 1795 moved to Frederick Co and purch estate, Richfield. He d Frederick City May 26 1826, in 63rd yr. His child: Wm, b 1793, d 1813; Nicholas Worthington, b 1795; Dr. Edw Yerbury, b Dec 5 1797, d Nov 14 1850; Dr. Chas Hy, b Feb 14 1800, d Aug 17 1862; Dr. Leander W., b May 21 1804; and Catherine, b Mar 25 1807, m Nov 15 1827, Thos Duckett of Prince George, their child: Richard and Allen Buoy.
   Dr. Edw Yerbury Goldsborough, s/o Wm and Sarah Worthington Goldsborough, m Nov 21 1826, Margaret Schley, d/o John and Mary Schley, their child: Mary Catherine; Wm, b Nov 29 1830, d May 14 1853; Eliza Margaret, b Feb 25 1833; d Aug 25 1834; John; Edw, b Feb 28 183-, d Mar 18 1839; Edw Yerbury; Rbt Henry;

and a second Eliza Margaret, b Apr 10 1845, d Aug 15 1845. Mrs. Margaret Schley Goldsborough d Dec 28 1876, in 73rd yr.

Dr. John Goldsborough, s/o Dr. Edw Yerbury and Margaret Schley Goldsborough, m Dec 1863, Julianna Strider, their child: John Schley and Edward Yerbury, twins, and Julianna.

Edw Yerbury Goldsborough, U.S. marshal (1876) in Balt, s/o Dr. Edward Yerbury and Margaret Schley Goldsborough, m Jun 10 1874, Amy Ralston Auld (a grand-niece of Hon Salmon P. Chase, late U.S. chief justice) d/o Rbt and Jane Chase Auld of Ohio.

897 772. Dr. Charles Henry Goldsborough, s/o Wm and Sarah Worthington Goldsborough, m Nov 24 1836, Amelia Poe, their child: Catherine Duckett, who m Dec 27 1866, Prof. Alfred M. Mayer, the distinguished chemist, and d May 2 1868; Chas Worthington; Sarah Worthington, b Apr 6 1848, d Dec 10 1868; Josephine, who m Jan 17 1871, Lewis Trail, and d Nov 17 1871; and Amelia.

Dr. Chas Worthington Goldsborough, s/o Dr. Chas Henry and Amelia Poe Goldsborough, m Nov 9 1866, Henrietta Bedinger Lee, d/o Edmond J. Lee of Va, their child: Chas, Edmond Lee, Catherine Duckett, Edw Lee and Nelson Poe.

Dr. Leander W. Goldsborough, s/o Wm and Sarah Worthington Goldsborough, m 1830, Sarah Duncan, their child: Maj Wm (C.S.A.), Dr. Charles, Leander, Lewis, Eugene and Alice.

Catherine Goldsborough, d/o Wm and Sarah Worthington Goldsborough, m Nov 15 1827, Thos Duckett of PG Co Md, their child: Sarah; Richard, who m Miss Warring; and Allen Bowie.

Dr. Richard Goldsborough, s/o Hon Rbt and Sarah Yerbury Goldsborough, m Achsah Worthington, their child: Catherine, b 1794, who m James B. Patterson and afterward Lisle R. Robinson of Winchester, Va; Richard Yerbury, b 1796; Rbt, b 1797, d 1809; Sarah, b 1799, who m Ephraim Gaither of Mont Co; Nicholas, b 1800, who m Jane Edelin; Brice John, b 1803, who m Leah Goldsborough, d/o James Goldsborough, and had two sons, Richard and Worthington; Elizabeth, b 1805; Chas and Wm, twins, b 1808; and Matilda.

897 773. Chas Goldsborough of Horn's Point, s/o Chas and his second wife, Elizabeth Dickinson Goldsborough, m Anna Maria Tilghman, d/o Wm and Margaret Lloyd Tilghman of Groces, thier child: Chas, b Jul 15 1765; and Wm Tilghman, b Dec 1766, and d 1787, sine prole.

Hon Chas Goldsborough, b Jul 15 1765, d Dec 13 1834, of Hunting Creek, s/o Chas and Anna Maria Tilghman Goldsborough, was gov of Md 1818, m (1) Sep 22 1793, Elizabeth Goldsborough, d/o Judge Rbt Goldsborough of Myrtle Grove, Talb Co, their child: Elizabeth Greenbury, b 1794, and Anna Maria Sarah, b Nov 15 1796, who m Jan 10 1814, Wm Hy Fitzhugh, of Va. He m (2) May 22 1804, Sarah Yerbury Goldsborough, d/o Chas Goldsborough of Horn's Point, the eldest s/o Chas Goldsborough of Cambridge, their child: Chas Yerbury, b Feb 1805, d 1807; John McDowell, b Aug 22 1806, d Aug 24 1807; Wm Tilghman, b Mar 5 1808, d Jan 23 1876; Geo Washington, b Jan 20 1810, d Sep 27 1812; Chas McDowell, b Oct 27 1811, d May 24 1815; Williamina Elizabeth Cadwalader, b Mar 30 1813, d Feb 9 1865; Rbt Henry, b Dec 31 1814, d Sep 9 1819; Mary Tilghman; Wm Henry Fitzhugh, b Aug 15 1818, d Oct 9 1819; Caroline; Rbt Fitzhugh, b Aug 28 1822, d Sep 20 1824; Sarah Yerbury, b aug 31 1824, d Jul 26 1825; Richard Tilghman and Henrietta Maria, b Aug 29 1828, d; and Chas Fitzhugh.

Elizabeth Greenbury Goldsborough, d/o Gov Chas and his first wife, m Oct 30 1828, Hon John Leeds Kerr of Easton, Md. She m in Balt in 1870, at age 80. She d Feb 1874. Their child: Elizabeth Goldsborough, Chas Goldsborough and Edw Leeds.

774. Hon Chas Goldsborough Kerr of Balt, s/o the Hon John Leeds and Elizabeth 898
Greenbury Goldsborough Kerr, m Apr 25 1867, Ella Johnson, d/o Hon Reverdy
Johnson, lawyer, statesman and diplomatist, their child: Mary Bowie, Ella
Johnson and Chas Goldsborough.
    Hon Reverdy Johnson of Balt, b Annapolis, May 21 1796, s/o Chancellor
John Johnson, d suddenly Feb 10 1876, from effects of accidental fall while
walking in dusk of evening on grounds of the executive mansion, Annapolis.
    Hon John Leeds Kerr, f/o Hon Chas Goldsborough Kerr, and s/o David Kerr,
who came from Scotland while a young man, settled in Falmouth, Va on
Rappahannock River. Then he came to Md and m in Annapolis Mrs. Hammond, who
soon d, leaving no child. He later settled in Talb Co, Md and m Rachael Leeds
Bozman, d/o John Leeds Bozman, historian of Md, and had several children, one
of whom was Hon John Leeds Kerr. David Kerr held many prominent positions,
mbr Md legislature 1793.
    Hon John Leeds Kerr rep in house of delegates and senate of Md, 3 times
in house of reps, and mbr U.S. senate Jan 5 1841 - Mar 4 1843. He m (1) Apr 8
1801, Sarah Hollyday Chamberlaine, d/o Sml and Henrietta Maria Hollyday
Chamberlaine of Talb, their child: John Bozman, Rev Sml C., David, Sophia,
who m Mr. Leigh; Henrietta Maria, who m Gen Tench Tilghman; and Rachael Ann,
who m Wm H. Done. He m (2) Elizabeth Greenbury Goldsborough.

775. Hon Wm Tilghman Goldsborough b Mar 5 1808, d Jan 23 1876, of Horn's 899
Point, Dor Co, s/o Gov Chas and Sarah Yerbury Goldsborough, m Oct 26 1837,
Mary Ellen Lloyd, d/o Col Edw Lloyd, of Wye House, Talb, and Sara Scott Murray
Lloyd, and had child: Chas, Wm Tilghman; Edw Lloyd, b Dec 15 1843, d Mar 29
1861; Ellen Lloyd, Fitzhugh, Nannie Lloyd; Sallie Murray, b Jan 27 1855, d Dec
6 1856; Richard Tilghman, Alice Lloyd and Mary Lee.
    Hon Wm Tilghman Goldsborough d at his res, No. 130 Cathedral street,
Balt, Sun, Jan 23 1876, buried 11 o'clock Jan 26 1876 Greenmount Cem. He was
6 feet, 4 inches in height, served in Md senate and 1847 candidate of Whig
party for gov, but defeated by a small majority by Hon Philip Francis Thomas;
1850 again elected to state senate. 1860-61 he was mbr of peace convention in
Washington. 1867 he rep his co in constitutional convention of Md.
    Chas Goldsborough, s/o Hon Wm Tilghman and Mary Ellen Lloyd Goldsborough,
m Nov 7 1865, Mary C. Galt of Va; their child.: Mary C., Ellen Lloyd, Chas,
Wm Fitzhugh and Rbt Galt.

776. Williamina Elizabeth Cadwalader Goldsborough, d/o Gov Chas and Sarah 899
Yerbury Goldsborough, m Jun 1837, Wm Laird, their child: Winder, b Oct 1838,
d a soldier in Confed army; Wm Hy, who m Miss Packard; Martha, who m
Washington Elwell Goldsborough; and Philip.
    Mary Tilghman Goldsborough, d/o Gov Chas and Sarah Yerbury Goldsborough,
m Wm Goldsborough of Myrtle Grove, their child: Susan, Rbt, Wm, Charles and
Mary.
    Caroline Goldsborough, d/o Gov Chas and Sarah Yerbury Goldsborough, m
Philip Pembleton Dandridge of Va, their child: Mary Lee, Nannie, Lillie,
Philip, Chas, Wm and Caroline.
    Henrietta Maria Goldsborough, d/o Gov Chas and Sarah Yerbury
Goldsborough, m Danl Henry of Dor Co.
    Richard Tilghman Goldsborough, s/o Gov Chas and Sarah Yerbury
Goldsborough, m Mary Henry s/o Danl Henry.
    Chas Fitzhugh Goldsborough, s/o Gov Chas and Sarah Yerbury Goldsborough,
m Charlotte Henry, sis of Dnl Henry, their child.: Charlotte, Chas, Dnl and
Sterling.

Wm Goldsborough, s/o Rbt and Elizabeth Greenbury Goldsborough, m 1734 Elizabeth Robins, d/o Thos Robins, who d Dec 29 1721, s/o Geo Robins, who d May 12 1677. Geo Robins came to America, settled in Talb Co, Md 1670, on tract of 1000 a. originally patented to Job Nutt and called "Job's Content" adjacent to Capt Miles Cook's patent for "Cook's Hope." This homestead later called "Peach Blossom" because of peach and other trees planted there by Geo Robins, s/o Thos, who being sent to Eng for commercial training, formed a life-long friendship with Peter Collison, then world-renowned naturalist and botanist. Wm and Elizabeth Robins Goldsborough's child: Greenbury, Henrietta Maria, Wm; and Elizabeth, b Jul 28 1743. Wm Goldsborough m (2) Sep 2 1747, Mrs. Henrietta Maria Tilghman Robins, wid of Geo Robins who d Dec 6 1742; She was b Aug 18 1707, d/o Richard Tilghman, second of the Hermitage, and d Nov 7 1771. Wm Goldsborough d 1760.

900 777. John Goldsborough of Four Square, Talb, s/o Rbt and Elizabeth Greenbury Goldsborough, m Oct 31 1733, Ann Turbutt, b Apr 29 1715, d/o Foster Turbutt and Bridget, his wife. Foster Turbutt, clerk of Talb Co for years, b Nov 15 1679, s/o Michael Turbutt and wife Sarah. Michael Turbutt, justice of Talb 1688, d 1696. Foster Turbutt d Feb 21 1720. Bridget Turbutt d Oct 18 1719. Child of John and Ann Turbutt Goldsborough: Elizabeth, b Jan 22 1735; Rbt, b Feb 1735, d Jan 2 1770; John, b Mar 26 1740, d Nov 18 1803; Greenbury, b Apr 22 1742, d Feb 19 1829; Chas, b Jun 16 1744, m Ann Tilghman, d/o Edw Tilghman, and was accidentally killed by a gun in 1774; Anna, b Jan 2 1751, m Vincent Loockerman of Dover, Del and d May 15 1781, leaving a dau Susan Hall Lockerman, who m Mr. Stoops; Henrietta Maria, b Dec 6 1752; Mary, b Oct 19 1755, d Mar 20 1796; and Capt Wm of Rev army, who was b Jun 2 1759, d Dec 22 1794, sine prole. Mrs. Ann Turbutt Goldsborough d Nov 11 1766, age 51.
John Goldsborough m (2) Mrs. Mary Skinner Loockerman, wid of John, s/o Jacob Loockerman, who d 1732 and had 2 child: Ann, who m Arthur Emory of QA Co, who left a dau Mary, who m Perry Wilmer; and Rbt.
Elizabeth Goldsborough, d/o John and Ann Turbutt Goldsborough m (1) John Campbell, their child: Ann, d young; and Margaret. She m (2) Benton Staunton of Car Co. She m (3) Richard Kennard who d 1796. She d Mar 20 1796.
Margaret Campbell, d/o John and Elizabeth Goldsborough Campbell, m Hon John Henry, gov of Md in 1797, and d 1789, leaving two sons, John Campbell, who m Miss Steele; and Francis Jenkings.

900 778. John Goldsborough of Four Square, s/o John and Ann Turbutt Goldsborough, who m Oct 26 1762, Caroline Goldsborough, d/o Howes and Rosanna Piper Goldsborough, their child: John, b May 7 1767, d Aug 12 1840; Howes, b Nov 20 1771, d Oct 20 1804; Rbt, b Apr 5 1775, who m Sarah Potter of Phila., and d Apr 16 1811; Elizabeth Greenbury, b Apr 5 1775, who m Chas s/o Hon Rbt and Sarah Yerbury Goldsborough who d Apr 7 1797; Chas Washington, b Apr 18 1777, d Dec 14 1843; Horatio, b Dec 26 1788, d Dec 16 1812; and Matthew and Saml, twins, b Jun 1 1784, d in infancy. John Goldsborough was dep commissary Dor Co under provincial government; after Rev was rgtr of wills.
John Goldsborough, son of John and Caroline Goldsborough of Four Square, m Jan 24 1797, Anna Maria Chamberlaine, their child: John b 1797; Henrietta Maria b Oct 16 1798, d Oct 13 1799; John Chamberlaine, b Sep 22 1800; and a second Henrietta Maria, b Nov 2, 1805, d Aug 17 1826; Saml Chamberlaine, b 1807, d Sep 17 1828; Elizabeth Greenbury, b Jan 1 1803, d Dec 1 1860; Rbt Lloyd, b Aug 26 1810; Jas Kemp, b Feb 14 1813, drowned in Treadavon Creek and buried Apr 21 1864; Marion Caroline, b Jan 31 1815; and Hy Hollyday, b Jun 22

1817. He m (2) Nov 28 1837, Mrs. Margaret Goldsborough, the wid and fourth w/o Henry, s/o Howes and Rebecca Goldsborough.

779. Sml Chamberlaine, who m Jan 15 1772, Henrietta Maria Hollyday, f/o Anna Maria Chamberlaine above mentioned, was b Aug 23 1742, s/o Samuel Chamberlaine of Plain Dealing, Talb Co, who was b May 17 1697, settled at Oxford, Talb 1814, and was s/o Thos Chamberlaine, b 1658, and his first wife, Ann Penketh, whose child: Thos, John, Saml, Mary and Esther. 901

Sml Chamberlaine, Plain Dealing m (1) Mary Ungle, d/o Rbt Ungle, who d sine prole, and he m (2) Jan 22 1729, Henrietta Maria Lloyd, d/o Col James Lloyd and Ann Grundy, d/o Rbt Grundy. He d Apr 30 1773, and his wife d Mar 29 1748. Their child: Thos, b May 25 1731, m Oct 1 1761, Susannah Robins, d/o Geo Robins and Henrietta Maria Tilghman; Jas Lloyd, b Oct 11 1732, who m Apr 16 1757, Henrietta Maria Robins, s/o his bro Thomas' wife; Ann, b Oct 23 1734, m Richard Tilghman Earle, QA Co; Henrietta Maria, b Mar 21 1736, d May 17 1737; a second Henrietta Maria, b Oct 28 1739, m May 21 1760, Wm Nicols; Sml, b Aug 23 1742, and Rbt Lloyd, b Sep 14 1745, d Jul 27 1756.

Sml Chamberlaine, s/o Sml and Henrietta Maria Lloyd Chamberlaine, m Jan 15 1772, Henrietta Maria Hollyday, d/o Hy and Anna Maria Robins Hollyday, their child: Anna Maria, who m Jan 24 1797; John Goldsborough of Easton; Lloyd; May; Sarah Hollyday, who m Hon John Leeds Kerr Apr 8 1801; Harriett Rebecca, who m Hon Levin Gale of Cecil Co; Sml; Jas Lloyd of Bondfield, who m Anna Maria Hammond, d/o Nicholas Hammond, distinguished lawyer of Talb Co, and his wife, Rebecca Hollyday, d/o Hy and Anna Maria Robins Hollyday; and Hy, of Richmond Hill, who m Henrietta Gale, d/o Hon George Gale, mbr of 1st congress held under constitution of U.S. Hy Chamberlaine d Dec 30 1863, on visit to nephew, Jas Lloyd Chamberlaine, of Island Creek Neck, in Talb.

780. John Chamberlaine Goldsborough, s/o John and Anna Maria Chamberlaine Goldsborough, m Apr 3 1827, Eliza Bishop Emory, d/o Chas and Frances Bishop Emory. Frances Bishop Emory d/o Wm Bishop of Greenbury Point farm, nr Annapolis. Their child: John, Chas Emory, Henrietta Maria, b Mar 7 1833, d Apr 11 1847; Hy Chamberlaine; Sml Chamberlaine, b Jun 15 1839, d Jul 2 1844, and Frs Emory, b Jul 5 1843. 901

Rbt Lloyd Goldsborough, s/o John and Anna Maria Chamberlaine Goldsborough, m Oct 1836, Fannie Miller, d/o Alexander Miller of Phila, their child.: Alexander Miller, John, Alfred, Wm Miller and Hy Chamberlaine.

Marion Caroline Goldsborough, c/o John and Anna Maria Chamberlaine Goldsborough, m Jun 6 1837, Dr. Alward McKell White (s/o Alward White and Mrs. Anna McKell Goldsborough White, who was wid and 3rd wife of Chas Goldsborough of Horn's Point, whose maiden name was Anna McKell, and whose 1st hus was John Stevens, and was 2nd wife of Dr. Alward McKell White. His 1st wife was Miss Warfield, d/o Rev Mr. Lot Warfield of Easton) and their child: Anna Maria, b Mar 31 1838, d Sep 29 1839; Henrietta Maria, m Hy Chamberlaine; Sally, John Goldsborough, Alward, Anna Maria, Fannie and Chas.

781. Hon Henry Hollyday Goldsborough, s/o John and Anna Maria Chamberlaine Goldsborough, has been a prominent politician. 1862 he was commandant of military post nr Easton, Md with rank of brig-gen, had command of militia of Eastern Shore of Md called into service of the U.S. 1863 he was comptroller of treasury of Md; 1874 app U.S. appraiser of merchandise port of Balt. He m Jan 25 1853, Anna Maria Kennard, d/o Sml Thomas and Elizabeth Thomas Kennard (d/o Wm Dorson Thomas); their child: Hy Hollyday, b Nov 8 1853, d Jul 20 1854; Sml Kennard, b Oct 31 1855, d Jul 30 1866; Louis Piper, Anna Maria, 902

Elizabeth Kennard, Mary Hammond, Chas Carroll and John Whittingham, b Jul 15 1868, d Jul 31 1868. Anna Maria Kennard d Jul 31 1868, and he m (2) Jun 1 1871, Kate Haley Cadwell of Lynn, Mass, d/o Dnl and Mary Lord Cadwell (Mary Lord Cadwell d/o Capt John Lord and his w, Lucy Perkins of Ipswich, Mass) and their child: Kate; Hy Cadwell, b Aug 3 1873, d Aug 30 1874; and Anita.

Howes Goldsborough, s/o John and Caroline Goldsborough, m Mary McCallmont of Newcastle, Del who was b 1774, and d Mar 14 1821; their child: Francis McCallmont, d; Rbt, d; Ann Caroline (who m May 1824, Dr. Nicholas Hammond, s/o Nicholas and Rebecca Hammond, d leaving child: Nicholas, Chas, Jas and Mary G.) and Chas Howes.

902 782. Chas Washington Goldsborough, s/o John and Caroline Goldsborough, m August 28 1802, Catherine Roberts of Phila and had child: Caroline, b Jan 9 1804; Louis Maledhardes, b Feb 18 1805; Chas Hy, b Dec 22 1806; John Roberts, b July 2 1809, who m Mary Pennington of Phila; and Hugh Allen, b Aug 17 1813, who m Mrs. Ellen K. Lesslie.

Caroline Goldsborough, d/o Chas Washington and Catherine Roberts Goldsborough, m Oct 6 1825, John Lane Gardner, U.S.A., and thier child: Elizabeth Greenbury, Caroline Goldsborough, Catherine Frances and Henry W.

Admiral Malesherbes Goldsborough, U.S.N., s/o Chas Washington and Catherine Roberts Goldsborough, m Nov 1 1831, Elizabeth G. Wirt, d/o Hon Wm and Elizabeth Wirt, their child: Wm Wirt, Louis Malesherbes and Elizabeth Wirt.

Henrietta Maria Goldsborough, d/o John and Ann Turbutt Goldsborough, m Philip Francis, s/o Tench Francis (clerk of Talb Co 1726-1734) and Elizabeth Turbutt, and their child: John, who was lost at sea, and Maria.

Foster Turbutt and wife Bridget had child: Mary, b Jan 15 1703; Sarah, b Dec 2 1706, who m Nicholas Goldsborough; Elizabeth, b Mar 17 1708, who m Dec 29 1724, Tench Francis; Mary Anne, b Jul 13 1711, who m Feb 9 1730, John Robins and afterward Rbt Goldsborough; Mary, b Sep 9 1713, who m Edw Tilghman; Ann, B Apr 29 1715, who m Oct 31 1733, John Goldsborough; Rachel, b 1718, who m May 8 1735, Thos Bullen.

903 783. Maria Francis, d/o Philip and Henrietta Maria Goldsborough Francis, m 1809 Dr. Tristram Thomas, their child: Philip Francis, b Sep 24 1810; Chas, b Nov 30 1812; Henrietta Maria, b Jul 8 1815; Ellen Francis, b May 25 1817; Mary Morre and Ann.

Hon Philip Francis Thomas, s/o Dr. Tristram and Maria Francis Thomas, succeeded Hon Thomas G. Pratt as gov of Md in 1847 and was sec of the treasury in administration of President Buchanan.

Mary Goldsborough, d/o John and Ann Turbutt Goldsborough, m Jan 1775, Benedict Brice, s/o John and Sarah Frisby Brice, had a dau, Sarah Goldsborough, b Aug 10 1776, who m Andrew Price. Benedict Brice d 1786 and she m Dr. James Cooke, d Mar 20 1796, leaving two child: Sarah Loockerman, b Dec 28 1790, and Mary Elizabeth b Mar 1 1793. Dr. Jas Cooke d 1794.

Susan Loockerman Cooke, d/o Dr. Jas and Mary Goldsborough Brice Cooke, m Greenbury Turbutt, their child: James Edw, Anna Maria and Saml.

Mary Elizabeth Cooke, d/o Dr. James and Mary Goldsborough Brice Cooke, m Jan 1828 Jeremiah Mulliken, their son: Arthur Cooke.

Dr. Rbt Goldsborough of Centreville, QA Co, Md, s/o John and Mary Skinner Loockerman Goldsborough, m Mrs. Henrietta Nicholson Bracco, wid of Dr. John Bracco, d/o Jos and Mary Nicholson of Kent, and left one son, Rbt.

Rbt Goldsborough, s/o Dr. Rbt and Henrietta Nicholson Bracco Goldsborough, m Eleanora Dall Lux, d/o Darby and Mary Lux, their child: Rbt,

John, Jos Nicholson; Henrietta, who m Philemon Hopper; Ellen Ridgley, Edw Ridgley, Mary Nicholson, Jacob Loockerman, Wm Lux, Thos Hy, Mary Rebecca, Anna Maria and Frs Spencer.

784. Howes Goldsborough, s/o Rbt and Elizabeth Greenbury Goldsborough, m 903 Rosanna Piper, d/o Protestant Episc clergyman, Rev Michael Piper and Rosanna B. Piper, and had dau, Caroline, who m Oct 26 1762, her cousin, John Goldsborough, s/o John and Ann Turbutt Goldsborough, and d Mar 10 1816. Howes Goldsborough d Mar 30 1746, his wid, Rosanna Piper Goldsborough, m 1747 James Auld. In 1765 they moved to Halifax, Halifax Co, N.C. Their child: James b Oct 14 1747, d Jun 30 1851; Anne, b Dec 26 1749, d unmarried Mar 1 1822; John, b May 30 1752 (who m Aug 17 1775, Elizabeth Shurlock, d Dec 28 1796, and had child: Elizabeth, b May 291776; Jas Sherwood, b Jan 15 1778, d in Alabama i1827; Hy W., b 1781; Elizabeth, b Mar 1 1783, m Jas Graves and d 1803; Sarah, b 1785, d 1788; Chas, b Dec 13 1787, d Jan 30 1797; Alexander, b Sep 6 1789, d 1822; Sarah Shurlock, b Dec 25 1792, m May 1811, Dr. Jas Bogle); Rosanna, b Dec 2 1754 (who m Jul 31 1776, an Englishman, Hy Wm Harrington of S.C., d Oct 13 1828, their child: Rosanna, b Feb 2 1778, m Jan 21 1800, Rbt Troy and d Mar 30 1838; Henrietta, b Oct 29 1779, d Sep 16 1780; Hy W., b Mar 14 1782, d Mar 23 1792; Jas Auld, b Aug 11 1785, m Dec 28 1808, Eleanor Willson, d/o John Willson; she d Sep 12 1843; he d Mar 21 1834; Henrietta, b Jan 24 1788, d Oct 2 1791; Michael, b Dec 5 1790, d Jan 3 1794; Hy Williams, b Jul 5 1793; Harriett, b Nov 22 1795, m Feb 15 1815, Beld Wm String, killed in a duel May 27 1815; and Caroline, b Nov 8 1798, m Dec 2 1821, Otter Chambers, and d Apr 10 1829); Michael Auld, b Mar 3 1757, d Sep 18 1788 (he m Sidney Fields and left a son, John Fields, who m Mary Jackson, their child: Rosamond, Elizabeth, Michael, Susan, Jas and Sidney); Mary, b Oct 14 1761, d Oct 25 1837 (who m (1) May 22 1794, Hartwell Ayre, their child: Michael, b 1795, d 1796 and Hy Wm, b May 6 1797, d Aug 4 1839; (2) she m Jas Blakeney); Elizabeth, b Nov 11 1764, d Dec 30 1847; and Jas, b N.C. Nov 30 1766, d Jan 21 1770. All child of Jas and Rosanna Piper Goldsborough Auld, except last, b Dor Co.

785. Nicholas Goldsborough s/o Nicholas and Margaret Howes Goldsborough, was 904 deputy sheriff of Talb Co in 1689, under Sml Withers, and justice of co court several yrs before he d, 1705. His first wife, Ann Goldsborough had child: Nicholas b 1687, d Sep 1766; Rachel, who m Mar 30 1712, Sml Turbutt, and Rbt. His second wife, Elizabeth, in her will dated Dec 6 1708, mentions her two daus, Mary and Elizabeth, who appear to have been child. of her former hus.
Nicholas Goldsborough, s/o Nicholas and Ann Goldsborough, m Jan 25 1721, Mrs. Sarah Jolly Turbutt, wid of Sml Turbutt, and d/o Peter Jolly and had child.: Ann, b Feb 8 1722, who m Edw Oldham, s/o John Oldham, who was grandfather of late Gen Dnl Martin and late Edw Martin; Sarah, b Dec 26 1724, m Jan 6 1742, Standley Robins, who d 1749, leaving a son Standley, who m Mary Greene; Nicholas, b Jan 3 1726; Thos b Feb 24 1728, d Mar 1793; Rachel, Rbt, Foster, Elizabeth, Bridget and Mary, b May 1 1741, d Oct 11 1812.
Nicholas Goldsborough, s/o Nicholas and Sarah Jolly Turbutt Goldsborough, m Mary Thomas (d/o Wm Thomas and Elizabeth Allen, who were m May 11 1732), d May 31 1777, and had child: Nicholas, b Feb 25 1759, who m 1787 Sarah Harrison, and d May 6 1788, leaving son, Col Nicholas, of Otwell, b Jun 30 1787, m apr 25 1801; Elizabeth Tench Tilghman, d/o Col Tench Tilghman; Jas; Elizabeth, who m Thos Coward; Mary who d unmarried in 1821; Anna, who m Feb 25 1765, and became 2nd w/o John Singleton, whose 1st wife was Bridget Goldsborough. John Singleton d March 15 1819.

-223-

904 786. Col Nicholas Goldsborough of Otwell, Talb, s/o Nicholas and Mary Thomas Goldsborough, m Apr 25 1801, Elizabeth Tench Tilghman, d/o Col Tench Tilghman (see Tilghman) and had child: Matthew Tilghman (who m Eleanor Sarah Tilghman, d/o Edw and Anna Maria Tilghman); Jas Nicholas; Tench; Richard Hy; Ann Margaretta (who m Hy Hollyday); Anna Maria; Sally; Clara (who m Dr. John Chas Earle) and Mary.

James Goldsborough, s/o Nicholas and Mary Thomas Goldsborough, lived at "Boston" in Talb Co. He m(1) Miss Elbert. He m(2) June 20 1789, Ann Martin, d/o Thos and Mary Ennalls Martin, their child: Mary, b Jun 27 1790, d Sep 3 1828; Jane, b Aug 1 1799, m Nicholas Thomas, and d May 1856; Ann, b Feb 17 1804, d May 15 1856; Leah, b Jun 26 1806, m Brice John Goldsborough; Martin, b Jan 20 1808, who m Ann Hayward of Cambridge, Md; Elizabeth, b Jun 5 1812, m Wm F. Rudestine; and Tench. He m(3) Margaret Patterson, and d Mar 1 1827.

Thomas Goldsborough, s/o Nicholas and Sarah Jolly Turbutt Goldsborough, m Catherine Fauntleroy of Va, niece of Gen Geo Washington, and had child: Thos, who m Oct 2 1801, Maria Thomas, d/o Hon Jas Thomas of Annapolis; Sarah Fauntleroy, who m 1808, Dr. John Barnett; Griffin; and Catherine, who m Jun 3 1798, Dr. Nathaniel Potter of Balt. Thos Goldsborough d Mar 1793.

905 787. Rachel Goldsborough, d/o Nicholas and Sarah Jolly Turbutt Goldsborough, m May 4 1768, Rev John Barclay, rector St. Peter's Church, Talb, who d Sep 13 1772, s/o David and Christina Barclay of King-card Co, Scotland, and had a dau Sarah, b Aug 1 1771, who m Oct 23 1788, Jos Haskins, cashier branch bank of Farmers' Bank of Md at Easton, Md and had child: Barclay, who m 1842, Elizabeth Robins Hayward, and (2) Mary Trippe, d/o Richard Trippe of Baylies Neck; Anna, who m John Bowie, and had child: Jos Haskins; Louisa Emily, who m Chas P. Craig; Isabell Dallas, and Josephine Haskins, who m 1854 Thos Smyth Hayward (she was his 2nd wife) their child: Henrietta Maria Robins, Elizabeth Haskins, Wm, Thos Smyth and Dallas Bowie.

Thos Smyth Hayward s/o Thos Hayward who was b Oct 8 1771, and m May 12 1795, Mary Smyth of Kent Co, d Jul 1838, s/o Wm Hayward of Locust Griove, in Baylies Neck, Talb, who m Nov 29 1760, Margaret Robins, d/o Geo and Henrietta Maria Tilghman Robins. Jos Haskins s/o Capt Wm Haskins and Sarah, d/o Rev Thos and Elizabeth Airey.

Foster Goldsborough, s/o Nicholas and Sarah Jolly Turbutt Goldsborough, m Rachel Bruff of Car Co, had son Foster who m Miss Potter, s/o Col Wm Potter, and had child.: Thos and Sophia.

Bridget Goldsborough, d/o Nicholas and Sarah Jolly Turbutt Goldsborough, m Feb 14 1774, and was 1st wife of John Singleton, who was b Dec 28 1750, at Whitehaven, Eng.

905 788. JAMES H. PHILLIPS, mcht Crapo, Dor Co, owns general store; carries line for country trade and boatmen; makes and repairs sails; b Lake dist Nov 1865, s/o Sml T. Phillips, of this locality; he has been in farming and oyster dredging since boyhood; now living nr Crapo on farm; in 66th yr. His father, Gabriel Phillips, of Eng origin. Sml T. Phillips and 1st wife, Eliza E., had 12 child.; 6 living: Benj T., Wm F., Jas H., Chas W., Sml Edw and Rufus. Mother mbr ME Church. Sml T. Phillips m(2) Emeline Harper, still living. Subj lived on old homestead, going to school for few terms; 3 yrs on sailing vesel on bay; at 16 he bt boat for himself, and up to 1894 he sailed it on bays and rivers of this shore. 1889 he m Cora A., d/o Jos Wroten, of Wroten's Island; their child: Lula E.

789. EDWIN P. SPARKS, St. Michael's Talb Co; mbr ME Church; justice of peace; 906 constable in 1884; b Sep 12 1849. His father was Oliver P. Sparks, of same place, b Jul 31 1821. He was reared and educated here, learned carpenter's trade and cabinet making; employed in these lines, later adding undertaker's business; sheriff 1858-9 and 1864-5 and once mbr state legislature; identified with MP church; of English extraction; his father, Walter Sparks, b Balt Co, and located in this town as a young man. Maiden name of mother of subj was Mary A. Kemp, d/o Jos Kemp, of St. Michael's and ship builder. He attained rank of col in war of 1812; active in ME Church. Mrs. Sparks, now in 74th year, had fol child.: Marion J., subj, Isabella, Louisa, Alice, and 2 d in infancy. Subj attended school in village and assisted father; went into partnership with father until his father d. Then subj purch interests of other heirs. 1861 he m Miss Kate, d/o Wm Harrison, of this place; their child: Lillian, at home.

790. ROBERT G. NICHOLSON, owns Little Grove nurseries, 3rd dist, Kt Co, nr 907 Chestertown. 40 a. are planted in peaches, 2500 trees. He purch farm in 1877. His res was burned to the ground 1892. Two yrs later creamery and ice plant that he owned and operated in Chestertown also burned down; he has since rebuilt ice plant. History of Nicholson fam appears in sketch of John P. Nicholson, on another page. Subj b 3rd dist Kt Co Nov 5 1846, educated in the common schools. At 21 he embarked in nursery business with father, making a specialty of peaches; after 6 yrs his father retired, and he continued on home farm 4 yrs. 1877 he bt present farm and planted the trees. He is steward of Meth Church. He m Laura A. Lusby, d/o Josiah Lusby, farmer; she was active in MP Church, b Feb 26 1853, d Nov 28 1890. Their child.: Rbt Josiah, law student of Balt; Harry Bates, Horace W., Bessie Morton, Mary, Walter Lusby, Chas Burgess and Nellie.

791. P. T. POTTS, village of Hope, 6th dist, QA Co, has carried on general 907 merc business and postmaster of the place; magistrate, dist accessor; also tax collector; b Roe, nr Hope, same dist, s/o John and Emily (Courcey) Potts, of 6th dist. His father, s/o John Potts, Sr, of Eng, farmer; mbr ME Church; d 1880; his wife d 1846. Of 5 child. 4 reached maturity: Jas W., of Crumpton, this co; subj ; Mary E., single, res Phila; and John E. John Potts m(2) Mary Embert, of Car Co, who d 1870; of her 2 child., 1 survives, Geo W., res N.J. At 17 subj discontinued schooling and began to work on the farm for his father; later carpentering, 6 yrs. 1872 he opened general store at Hope; mbr MP Church. Jan 6 1880 he m Margaret M., d/o Warren Busteed, of Car Co. Of 5 child. b to them, 2 survive, Mifflin G. and Rbt H.

792. D. C. KIRBY owns general store Trappe, Talb Co, carries boots, 908 provisions, shoes, dry goods, hardware, farm machiner and fertilizers; b May 28 1868 and reared on farm in Trappe dist, nr Kirby's wharf. At 16 he attended Md Military School at Oxford; worked in wholesale grocery house in Birmingham, Ala, 7 yrs; entered into partnership with J. F. Clark of this place. He is mbr of ME Church.

793. GEORGE L. BRYAN, farmer 5th dist, QA Co. In early yrs he traveled in 908 the west. Valentine, paternal grandfather of Geo L. Bryan, of Va, came to this region in early manhood; d 1848, leaving estate of 4000 a. on Wye Island, and c. 200 slaves. By 1st marriage he had: John C., Wm I., Elizabeth and Arthur. Later he m Miss Ford; their child.: Chas J., Edw and Alfred. Chas J. b Jan 1816, d Sep 1850; m Lucretia Emory, and their eld child, subj, b 1837;

-225-

Chas Carroll, b 1839, d 1872, leaving wife and 2 child., Edw K. and Lulu, all res Balt. Subj reared to maturity QA Co; m 1863, Mary H. d/o John Charles and granddau of Dr. Thos Smyth Willson, of Kt Co, Md. They began life together on farm still owned by subj. Their child: Kat B., Mary C., Chas, Elizabeth, Oscar, Geo H., Dnl Carroll, Florence, Jas B., Edna A. and Leon O.

909 794. JOSEPH M. PARKER b on farm where he res, Parson dist, Wicomico Co; agent for sewing machines; sells pianos and organs, fertilizer. Father of subj Levin Parker, farmer, s/o John W. Parker, both of this co. Levin Parker d in 78th yr; m Miss Brewington, by whom 6 child.; 3 surivve. John W., Jr., is farmer of this dist. Lizzie is wid of E. Walston. Subj b Sep 15 1847, educated in public cschools; attended Salisbury high school 2 yrs after age of 21; placed in charge of a school, taught 6 yrs; returned to old farm. 1877 he m Miss R. A. Fooks; 1 child d; 8 living; they attend ME Church.

910 795. THOMAS Y. FRANKLIN, M. D. of Berlin, Wor Co, mbr of Md legislature, co school examiner, sec and treasurer; b here Jul 1860, s/o Littleton Purnell and Sarah E. Franklin, of 5 child., of whom he is eldest; Emily P., d unmarried; Wm C., res Balt; Mary I. and Louisa R. live with subj. After high school in Berlin he attended medical depart Univ Va; grad Jefferson Medical Coll 1883; returned home and purch drug store which he has since conducted.
Littleton Purnell Franklin, subject's father, b this co; elder in Presby Church, mbr Md house of delegates; d 1888. His grandfather, Isaac Franklin m Martha, d/o Wm Iranshire, of Eng, then res in Wor (now) Co. He left one child (Martha, just mentioned). She became mother of Sallie, w/o Dr. Rbt Purnell; Hy, subject's grandfather; Mrs. Amelia Covington; Mrs. Milcah Spence; Louisa, w/o John Richardson (one of whose children became Lady Cartwright); and Mary, w/o Dr. Jas Purnell, who had child.: Thos Isaac and Littleton Purnell (both grad Yale, the latter at 18).

910 796. GEORGE ALFRED COX business man upper Fairmount dist, Som Co, s/o Elijah Cox (still living in this co), Som 1854. After public school he attended course in an acad; in business for himself since 1882; worked for firm of Miles, Avery & Co., then bt out firm and had paid off debt when store was burned by an incendiary. He now has fine modern building. He m 1882, Miss Susie E. Miles, d/o Dnl Miles; their child.: Richard Allen and Elsie Merrill. Parents are mbrs ME Church.

911 797. EDWIN W. SPEAR, res Milllington, b here Aug 15 1841; of Irish descent; his paternal grandfather emigrated from Ireland in early manhood and settled prob in Del. Father of subj, Jas Spear, b and reared on farm in Del, moved to Kt Co, Md when young, spent remainder of life here on farm; conducted general store in Millington; d at 74. He m Elizabeth of Del; she d at 75, leaving 7 child., 4 survive. Subj attended public school; when 21 enlisted in Confed army, 1st Md Cav under Col Brown,, served until close of war; spent most of war in Va; captured on Rapidan River and held prisoner c. 6 months; at Beaver Dam horse shot out from under him. After war he returned to Millington and farmed until 1887; then rented his place and moved to village; proprietor of Millington roller mills since 1892; mbr ME Church. He m Lucy Hurtt, of Millinigton; their child.: Jas Edwin, farmer; L. R.; Franklin Lee; Emily E.; Edna J. and Esther, all at home.

913 798. JAMES E. McDANIEL formerly in drug business, now owns farm Talb Co, Bay Hundred dist; mbr bd of Co school commissioners; general assessor of co; b Oct

-226-

14 1834, of Irish origin. His grandfather, Jas M., of Bay Hundred dist, ran wheelwright and blacksmith shop; owned serveral farms around McDanieltown (named in his honor). Father of subj, John W. S. McDaniel, b this co, mcht and farmer at McDanieltown; judge orphans' court, res farm now occupied by subj; here he d 1863, at 56; he m(1) Sarah, d/o Jas Wrightson; of their 4 child., 1 d in infacny. Others: Jas E.; Mrs. M. A. Bunsfield, of Royal Oak; and Mrs. G. E. Booth, living nr Matthews. He m(2) Ann Wrightson, sis of 1st; had 8 child.: Lewis A., in dairy business, Balt Co; Dorcas E., w/o Col J. M. Lowe; Anna, w/o J. H. Caulk; Mary M., decd, former w/o Capt Collison; Alice, res St. Michael's, this co; Mary V., w/o J. E. Wadkins; Wm R., prof Wesminister (Md) Coll; and Frank W., killed on railroad in WV at 25.

After attending public schools of McDanieltonw, subj taught school in Talb Co 6 yrs; grad coll of pharmacy Balt 1863; opened drug store on corner of Chas and Mulberry st, Balt in partnership with another. 1870 he returned to Talb Co and settled on home farm. Feb 5 1873 he m Mary C. Hopkins, d/o Solomon S. Hopkins, of Trappe dist, Talb Co. She d May 4 1890, leaving child., John S. and Mary L. Fam attend Episc Church.

799. FREDERICK E. RUARK, busines man Bishop'6 Head, Strait dist, Dor Co, b this vicinity 1870, s/o Major T. Ruark, whose history is elsewhere this vol. He worked in oyster banks 8 yrs, in charge of oyster boat much of this time. 1892 he entered into partnership with bro, Alexander W., and opened general store in Bishop's Head. 914

800. EDWARD THOMAS WHALEY in business 55 yrs. His father, Capt Peter Whaley, b 1779, descendant of Judge Edw Whaley, early settler of Eastern Shore of Md. Father of Capt. Peter was Seth Whaley. The captain was master on sailing vessels running from New York to Phila, later farmed. He m Elizabeth, d/o Abisha Davis; of their 7 child., Jas, eldest, decd; Hester A. w/o Dr. Gillis; Seth M. res Va; Mary m John S. Timmons; Maria K. m Zadoc Puarnell, subj is next, and Peter is youngest. Subj b 1829, Presby; m 1869 Mary C., d/o John W. Jones, nr Snow Hill; their child.: John W. and Florence, (w/o Jas P. Dale, and mother of twin girls, Mary and Virginia). 914

801. WILLIAM WYATT BARBER, B. A., b Cambridge, whose father was rector of Christ Protestant Episc Church Cambridge. Subj is senior master in Greek in St. Mark's Acad, Southboro, Mass. Dr. Theodore P. Barber b Brattleboro, Vt, grad Yale Coll 1841 with honors, taught for several yr, then entered ministry. His first charge was at Laurel, Md; founded St. Philip's Church, then Cambridge Church 1850 where he continued until he d at 71. He m Miss Anne E. Hooper, still res Cambridge at 60. 915

Prof. W. W. Barber b Nov 5 1865, youngest of 5 child.; Philip, Dora and Sidney, d in childhood. His only surviving bro, Hy A., 1st lieut in U.S. army, stationed Port De Quesne, Utah. He m Miss Inez Smith, d/o Capt Smith, U.S.A. Prof. Barber spent boyhood in Cambridge; at 15 entered St. James' grammar school nr Hagerstown, grad Trinity Coll in Hartford, Conn. 1888 and offered chair of Greek which he occupies; vestryman and warden St. Mark's Episc Church Southboro, Mass. Jul 26 1892 he m Miss Florence H. Harmon, d/o Dr. Geo Harmon, of Cambridge; their child.: Theodore P. and Geo Harmon.

802. EDWARD B. EMORY farmer and stock raiser, on peninsula between Chester and Corsica River, 3rd dist, QA Co; farm known as Poplar Grove stock farm. 916

Grandfather of subj, Col Thos Emory, b on Poplar Grove farm, officer in war of 1812; farmer, raised trotting horses and short horn cattle; mbr state senate; sent by state with Geo Peaboyd, to Eng, to sell state bonds. John R. Emory, subject's father, b at Poplar Grove farm, farmer of QA Co. One of his sons, Gen. W. H. Emory, served in Union army in Civil war under Gen. Butler at New Orleans; retired as col 5th U.S. Cav; breveted brigadier of U. S. army. At 20 John R. Emory app in U. S. army; served during Florida war; returned to homestead to manage prop, his father having d. John R. Emory d 1880; m Alice G. Bourke; their child.: subj; John R., res Wash D. C.; Alice G. and Mrs. Harry Wilmer. The father was trustee Episc Church.

Subj b on place where he now res, Sep 29 1849; grad Univ Va 1869; settled on farm owned by father, which he later inherited. Jun 5 1877 he m Miss Henrietta, d/o Lloyd T. and Edw T., Jr. (Prize race horses are described)

917 803. ALONZO R. TODD, M. D., Cambridge, b Easton, 1852, s/o Peter Todd. Father farmed brifly, contractor and builder remainder of career; d 1876 at 66. He m(1) Miss Fairbanks, who d leaving 5 child. He m(2) Miss Sallie Coon, d/o Hy Coon, of Hill's Point; of their child. only subj survives. Peter Todd mbr ME Church. Subj spent boyhhod on father's farm Talb Co, and in Cambridge; went to Phila at 18 to learn drug business; grad Jefferson Medical Coll, Phila 1879, opened practice in Millington, Kt Co; thence to Balt 1892 wher he engaged in practice, until he came to this place. He is mbr ME Church; he m Miss Margaret Hazzard, of Seafaord, Del; their child.: Lucinda H., Anna R. and Alonzo E.

917 804. FRANCIS A. PORTER retired farmer Car Co, 3rd dist, nr Burrsville; enlisted Sep 1861 Cambridge, assigned to Company F, 1st Regt Eastern Shore Vol; in battle of Gettysburg; discharged 1864; b Balt Apr 14 1840, s/o Frs A., Sr., and Margaret B. (Terrell) Porter, both of this state. Their other child., in order of birth: Mary E., Margaret B., Geo C., Theophilis W., Ricahrd C., and Arlington T. Paternal grandfather was John Porter, of Del, farmer. Frs A. Porter, Sr. mcht in Milford, Del, and later in Burrsville, Md. Subj was child when brought by parents to Car Co, where he was reared and educated; started in business Burrsville 1860, interrupted by war. Afterward he operated general store 4 yrs but sinice 1868 he has farmed. May 6 1867 he m Mary F. Thawley; she was b and reared Car Co, mbr ME Church; she d at 32; of her 4 child. only Mary A. survives. Later Mr. Porter m Mary L. Raughley, of this co; their child.: Lida, Nettie M., Lyman R. and 2 decd.

918 805. SAMUEL E. JUMP succeeded his father in busines in town of Matthews, Talb Co. He was b nr Mount Vernon, Som Co, Jul 16 1869. After public schools he attended Phila Business College; then bookkeeper in commission house Phila, but, on acccount of illness resigned and returned home 1888. Next a clerkship in a statistical depart of Balt custom house, then inspector of customs; he then came to Matthews.

Three Jump bros came to America from Eng, one locating in Del, and the other two in Kt and Car Cos, Md. The great-great-grandfather of subj, Maj. John Jump, in war of 1812. His son, named John also, res Car Co, as also did his son, Ed P. The latter in commission business Balt and after Civ war was dep internal revenue collector for QA Co. He attended M E Church; d Jul 1885; m Miss Elizabeth Lewis, of Del, d/o Dr.F. Lewis and niece of Gov Thorpe, and related to Gov Flemming of WV. She d 3-4 months before her husb.

John Jump, father of subj, b Dec 20 1844, and after he completed school began teaching; later operated farm in Del; then 7 yrs in commission business in partnership with father in Balt; 20 yrs he carried on store in Matthews, after buying out C. P. Matthews, original owner; tax collector 2 yrs, pres of bd of trustees of co almshouse. Jul 28 1867 he m Mary E., d/o Sml Graham of Del; of their 4 child., 2 survive, Sml E. and Mary E.

806. THOMAS L. COULBORN. Fam dates back to Col Wm Coulburne, who emigrated 919 from Scotland to Md; took up a tract known as Pomford's tract. Subj b Som Co, on old homestead nr Hopewell 1826, s/o Jas C., likewise b and reared same farm. Jas C. d 1837; subj then under guardian. His father left him half interest in farm in Brinkley's dist, where he now lives; raises fruit, vegetables, and in oyster business. He m(1) Elizabeth Adams, d/o Sampson Adams; she d young, leaving no child. He m(2) Caroline C., d/o Jas Briggs, of WV; she d c. 1877. 2 yrs later he m S. Elizabeth Connor, of this vicinity, d/o Nathan C. Connor; their child.: Harry B., Thos P., Geo C. and Carrie; fam attends ME Church.

808. BERNARD J. McCAULEY, farmer 2nd dist, Kt Co; b Phila 1843, s/o Dennis 920 McCauley, b Ireland, of Scotch-Irish ancestry. Great-grandfather, Dennis McCauley, Sr., lived in Ireland; grandfather, Bernard McCauley, emigrated at an early day and took up res Phila 1816. His son Dennis, subject's father, about 14 when he came to America. He res Phila until 1851, in coal and lime business; sold out, came to Kt Co, Md, purch Palmer farm; returned to Phila, shipped flour to South America; 1880 came to Kt Co; owned 7 farms this area; d here 25 Dec 1889, at 76. He m Miss Mary Gallagher, from Ireland, who had come to America when a young girl; she d 1887, at 74. Only 2 of their 5 child. living: subj; and Edwin D., bookkeeper Camden Iron Works Camden, N.J.
Subj educated in public schools of Phila, came to Kt Co, Md at 8, attended schools here. Attended Mount St. Mary's Coll, Frederick Co, 1856-60; 3 yrs later took charge of father's farm; 7 Jan 1864 m Miss Ella A., d/o Simon and Ann Woodall, of Georgetown, Md; 9 of 13 child. living: Dennis J., who m Eva Jarman, d/o J. W. Jarman, has 4 child; Nellie E.., Lester B., Agnes and Granville; Frs A., m Nannie Laney and has 2 child.; Bernard R., m Alice M. Holmes of Boyden, WV, has 3 child.; Jerome H., M. Augustus and Geo H.; and Cecelia, Frs A., Holle Genevieve, Theresa, Andrew W. and Simon H., all at home. Fam are Cath.

809. TILGHMAN E. KELLEY, farmer 4th dist Car Co. At 18 he enlisted in 8th Md 921 Infantry, at Balt, 1862, placed in Company E. His division assigned to Army of Potomac; participated in battles of wilderness, Cold Harbor and Appomattox. Has served as general assessor Car Co; co commisisoner. He was b 1844 s/o Dennis and Mary (Harmon) Kelley, both of this co, and the latter d/o Jas Harrison, also of Car Co. Subject's father d when he was 3. He was reared on a farm and obtained common school education. After the war he settled in Queenstown, QA Co, 1867 came to this co, and engaged in farming. He bt present farm 1885. 1868 he m Miss C. I. Hollis d/o Chas Hollis, of Del; they have 4 sons: eldest, Glencoe K., farmer this co; he m Leona Patchett; their child.: Edith I. and Elmer. Other child. of subj: Everett C., Orlan T. and Chas H.

810. SAMUEL S. C. BARNES, res 1st dist of Som Co since 1892, when he became 922 owner of tract of 150 a. In addition to farming he runs two steam threshers and hay baler. He was b Green Hill, Md, 1852 s/o Isaac T. Barnes. Up to age 32 he farmed exclusively; 1884 he opened general store in Green Hill and continued to conduct busines there for 12 yrs. A few yrs ago he bt Beverly farm in this dist and res there. He is mbr Presby Church; he m Mollie D., d/o Geo Howith, Brinkley's dist. The have 2 sons, Sml S. and Joshua E.

INDEX (to Paragraph numbers)

ACWORTH Albert E. 405; Beacham 405; Charlotte E. 405; Nancy 405; Thomas 405; Train 405
ADAMS Adeline 29; Catherine D. 691; Eleanor W. 29; Elizabeth 29; 538; 806; Frederick A. 538; Gertrude E. 538; James F. 538; Jilton Leroy 29; John Quincy 558; Josephine 29; Josiah 538; Laura 29, 158; Lorenzo 158; Louisa Catherine 558; Lucille H. 538; Marie H. 538; Mary 642; Mary Louise 29; Mary R. 751; Mary V. 148; Miss 251; Mitchell 210; Morris H. 29; Olivia 29, 487; Philip 29; R. H. 9, 751; Robert W. 29; Sallie 602; Sallie W. 538; Sampson 806; Samuel T. 602; Sarah A.Q. 210; Thomas 29; Thomas S. 642; William Forbes 148
ADKINS Franklin B. 192; Franklin Bache 148; I. L. 148; Isaac L. 192; Leonard 192; Leonard D. 192; M.C. 192; Mary E. 192; Mary Elizabeth 148; Mary H. 192; Mary V. 148; Mattie H. 192; Mrs. Anne 557; Virginia L. 192; William H. 148; 192
ADKINSON Miss 256
ADREON Christian 407; Harrison 407; Louisa Jessie 407; Nancy B. 416; Nannie 407; Thomas K. 407; Thomas K. 416; William 407
AHERN Ann (Alworth) 2; Anna Pearl 2; Clara Elma 2; Dennis 2; Eugene 2; John H. 2; John P. 2; Mary 2; Patrick 2; Ruby Catherine 2; Sadie L. 2; William A. 2
AIKEN John 152; Maria W. 152
AIREY Elizabeth 787; Sarah 787; Thomas 787
ALDRICH Kate E. 231
ALEXANDER George 133; John 133; Joseph 133; Mary 133; Theophilus 133
ALFORD Mary Alexander 126
ALLEN Anna M. 17; Annie M. 290; Elizabeth 785; John 10, 17, 290, 426; Martha 458; Phoebe 426; William F. 458
ALSTON Irene L. 680; J. C. 680
ALVEY Richard H. 679
AMOSS Abigail J. 56; S. Amanda 56; William 56; William Lee 56
ANDERSON Amelia 268; Anna M. 659; Barnes C. 194; Catherine C. 280; Charles H. 123; Charles L. 194; Dr. 93, 254; Elvira 174; Emma 507; Eugene 252; Fannie 194; Frank 194; George A. 194; Gillis 194; Isaac 659; James 184, 268; James A. 194; James D. 194; John 184; Levin 194; Levin A. 194; Lizzie 194; Martha (Holden) 184; Martha 184; Mary 184; Matilda 567; Minnie Brantz 200; Richard 184; Sarah Ellen 123; Thomas 280; Thomas H. 200; Thomas J. 194; Thomas W. & Co 310; William 184; William H. 252
ANDREW Elisha 198; Mary 198; Sarah 668
ANDREWS A. May 287; Annie R. 440; Arthur 416; Carrie 440; Edith Estelle 287; Elizabeth 416; Elizabeth Rebecca 287; Emma 314; Gertrude 416; Grace M. 287; Helen 440; Isaac 440; James E. 440; James M. 287, 440; Joseph B. 287, 440; Margaret 551; Margaret M. 440; Mary 287, 440; Mary Todd 287; Medford 440, 660; Olin Ray 287, 440; Rebecca 440; S. Elwood 287; Sallie 440; Sarah 660; Sarah E.; Stephen 54, 287, 440; Stephen S. 440; Tilghman E. 314; William 440; William N. 440
ANTHONY Anna M. 339; Bertha 339; Edna 339; Elizabeth 339; Ella 339; George 339; James T. 708; Joseph P. 339; Joshua M. 339; Lulu 339; M. Ella 339; Mary 224; Mary A. 708; Robert 339; Robert W. 339; Sarah M. 339; Wilhelmina 339; William D. 224
APPLEGARTH Alpheus 746; Anita 746; Ann M. 746; Cecil 746; E. A. 746; E. Vivian 746; Eleanor 746; Harold 746; John E. 746; Maggie K. 745; Nat 746; S. Ubert 746; William 745, 746; William F. 746; Wilmina H. 181
ARCHER Fanny 120; Henry W. 97; Mary Elizabeth 97; Walter Gwynn 120; William H. 120
ARKINS Mattie H. 44
ARMSTRONG A. Louisa 166; Araminta 166; Elizabeth 201; Elizabeth Ann W. 166; Ida 166; John M. 166; Mrs. Washington M. 201; Raymond Allison 166; Sarah Adalia 166; W. Josiah 166; William 166
ARRINGDALE Elizabeth 334
ASH Nancy 636
ASHBY 95
ASHER Nannie P. 655; Wm W. 655

ASHLEY Henrietta 313; Robert 170
ASPLEN Sarah J. 237
ATKINSON Aaron 63; Ann E. 595; Comfort E. 462; Dr. 441, 550; E. E. 509; Elizabeth 509; Family 629; Gordon T. 462; John F. 462; Julia F. 462; Levin 462; Mary 462; Sallie 462; Sallie K. 700; Solomon 63; Susan 462; Susie 550; Thomas 63, 595, 629
ATWELL Elizabeth 269; George W. 101; Joseph 101, 132, 269; Mary 132; Priscilla 101; Susie C. 132
ATWOOD Mary S. 397; Richard A. 397
AULD Alexander 784; Amy Ralston 771; Anne 784; Charles 784; Elizabeth 784; Henry W. 784; James 784; James Sherwood 784; Jane Chase 771; John 784; John Fields 784; Mary 784; Mary Jackson 784; Michael 784; Robert 771; Rosamond 784; Rosanna 784; Rosanna Piper Goldsborough 784; Sarah 784; Sarah Shurlock 784; Sidney 784; Susan 784
AURLOCK Mary F. 94
AUSTIN Maria T. 659; V. A. 659; Willianana 220
AYERS Mary E. 473
AYLER Annie 317
AYRE Hartwell 784; Henry Wm 784; Mary 784; Michael 784
AYRES John 6; Mary A. 6

BABCOCK Ann Johns 687; Wm 687
BACON Alexander 98; Alice 98; Anna 113; Arthur 98; Charles 98, 495; Edna 495; Ellen 98; George F. 98; Henry 495; James E. 495, 516; John H. 512; Lillie 495; Lizzie 495; Lorenzo 495; Maria J. (Dashiell) 495; Mary 98, 495; Maud 495; Rebecca 495; Thomas Hunphreys 495; William 113, 495
BADHAM William 293
BAGSWELL Margaret Jane 455
BAGWELL Frances 39
BAILEY Ann 625; Elizabeth 497; Gardiner 771; Hettie A. 597; Johnston 497; Kate M. 439; Letitia E. 439; Mary 201; Mary Nixon Goldsborough 771; Robert B. 439; W. B. 439; William F. 201
BAINBRIDGE Eliza 200; Harry 200
BAKER Annie 42, 470; Charles H. 116; Francis 37; J. Henry 37; James H. 37, 42, 478; Jane 547; John 470; Lillian 116; Lizzie 37; Mamie Trew 37; Martha 592; Mary C. 478; Mary T. (Brown) 37; Milton 592; Thomas 37; Thomas B. 204
BALCH Adelaide 460; Alfred 460; Catherine 460; Clarissa 460; Clarissa Anne 460; Edith C. 460; Ellen M. 460; Emily 460; Ernest 460; Henry H. 460; Henry H., Jr. 460; Lewis 460; Lewis P. W. 460; Stephen 460; Stephen Elliott 460; William 460
BALDWIN Alice S. 104; Annie M. 104; Cynthia Eliza 104; Joseph B. 104; Joseph C. 104; Joseph Willard 104; Leonidas B. 104
BALL Edwin 759; Farm 471; Gertrude 759
BALLARD Daniel 344, 556; Margaret 579; Mary D. 344; Susan 556
BALTIMORE Lord 103
BANARD Ethel 680; William E. 680
BANKS General 361
BANNING Anthony 678, 769; Emily 678; Emma 678; Freeburn 678; Harriet 678; Henry 678, 769; Henry Geddes 15, 678; James 678, 769; James Latimer 15, 678; Jane 678; Jeremiah 678, 769; John H. 678; Mary E. 678; Mrs. Jane 769; Robert 678; Sarah 678
BARBER Anne E. 801; Dora 801; Earl 64; Emma 64; Ethel 64; Florence H. 801; George Harmon 801; Henry A. 801; Inez 801; Isaac A. 64; John W. 64; Nellie 64; Philip 801; Sidney 801; Theodore P. 801; William Wyatt 801
BARCLAY Christina 787; David 787; John 787; Rachel 787; Sarah 787
BARCUS Elizabeth 289; William 289
BARD Angeline S. 11
BARGER Wm. 592
BARKELY Clara 79; Ellen 79; George 79; Jesse 79; LeRoy 79; Margaret (Travers) 79; Rebecca 79; Thomas 79; William Oscar 79; William T. 79; William Washington 79
BARNES Adial P. 210; Alfred T. 210; Alice H. 402; Benjamin J. 210, 388; Clarence F. 210; Drusilla 159; Emily 210; Emily S. 526; Emma M. 210; Francis J. 210; Frank U. 210; Isaac T. 810; James A. 210; Joseph 159; Joshua E. 810; L. S. 402; Lane A. 210; M. Blanche 210; Marion D. 388; Mary J. 159; Mary S. 210; Mollie D. 810; Nettie E. 210; Samuel S. 810; Samuel

INDEX (to paragraph numbers)

S. C. 810; Sara A.Q. 210; Sarah A. 210; Thomas 210
BARNETT John 786; Sarah Fauntleroy 786
BARNEY Clayonia 249; Commodore 209; Edward 249; Elizabeth 734; Hebe 249; Joshua 249; Mary 249; Mary Eleanor (de Krafft) 249; Moses 734; Samuel Chase 249; Samuel Chase de Krafft 249; Sarah (Bond) 734; William 249; William Bedford 249
BARRETT Julia 644
BARROLL Anna 83; Ethel 83; Francis L. 83; Hope H. 83; Hopewell Horsey 83; James 83; James Edmondson 83; John Leeds 83; John Wethered 83; Lewin Wethered 83; Morris Keene 83; William 83
BARROW Mary A. 631; Thomas 631
BARTHOLOW Mrs Avis E. 691
BARTLETT Daniel 224; Deborah 224; Edward 204; Elisha 224; Elizabeth 204; Emily 224; Emma A. 224; Francis A. 224; Fred 204; George 204; Hennie 224; Hester 582; Hester A. 509; James 204; James S. 509; John 204; John Cheezum 204; Joseph 224; L.S. 224; Lula 224; Martha 224; Martha J. 224; Mary (Goodchild) 558; Mary 224, 558; Mary Ann 56, 204; Matilda J. 204; Matthew 224; Nellie 224; Pauline 204; Rebecca 224; Rheuelma 224; Robert 56, 204; Sarah (Price) 224; Sarah 224; Thomas 56, 204, 558
BARTON B. C. 646; Edward A. 646; Lizzie B. 646; Lizzie Naomi 646; Louisa 306; Loula M. 646; Loula Meta 646; Mary Augusta Morgan 646; Mary E. 646; W. A. 721, 646; William E. 646; William Edward 646; William H. 306; William J. 646; William Marvin 646
BARWICK Molly R. 3
BASSETT John 762; May 762
BATCHELDER Hooper 350
BATEMAN Ariana 683; E. T. 518; Elizabeth 683; Elizabeth T. 683; H. H. 518; Henry A. 683; Henry E. 195, 389, 683; J. Frank 683; James G. 683; James M. H. 683; Wilfred 389; 683; William 683
BAXTER Dr. 346; Mary A. 515
BAYLISS Miss 59
BAYLY Alexander H. 176; Edgar 579; Elizabeth Hooper 579

BAYNARD Harriet 739; Lavina 130; Robert 739
BAYNE Elizabeth 543
BEACH Mrs. Samuel K. 570; Sallie 570
BEALL Mr. 600
BEARD Rachel 30
BEATTY Arthur J. 536; Catherine 536; Catherine Amelia 536; Eugene Mitchell 536; Frederic W. 536; Josephine A. 536, 807; L. H. 807; Laura 536; Louis Hunter 536; Louis Lacey 536; Mary Morling 536; Ralph R. 536; Sarah R. 536
BEAUCHAMP Aurelia 162; Charles W. 364; Edmund 667; Elizabeth 251; Frances 364; Francis T. 667; George H.J. 162; Harriet 364; Helen 364; Helen A. 667; Ida 667; James Roger 667; L. Wesley 364, 667; Levin Crreston 667; Levin H. 364, 667; Margaret (White) 364; Margaret 251; Margaret E. 667; Mildred 667; Mollie E. 251; Oliver T. 364, 667; Oliver T. Jr 667; Stephen J. 251; Susan 251; Thomas 667; Virginia 667; Washington 251; William T. 251; William W. 251
BEAVEN Anna (Pagett) 328; Anna D. 445; Anna De Rauchbrune 328; Arthur R. 328, 445; Blandford 328; G. F. 328; George F. 328, 445; George H. 328, 445 Grace A. 328; 445; H. Lay 328, 445; J. M. 328; John 328; John M. 328, 445; Mary V. 328, 445; Mr. 748, 807; Thomas C. 445; Virginia L. 328, 445; Wordsworth Y. 328, 445
BECK Alphonza 52; 2 Anna E. 97; Benjamin 173; Dr. 73; Samuel 15; George R. 522; Hallie R. 14; Harriet Ringgold 15; Henry C. 14; Horace W. 14; Horatio 14; Isabel S. 14; John 73; Lottie 173; Mary E. 106; Mary I. 14; Mary M. (Miller) 14; Mary R. 97; Samuel 14; Sarah E. 14; Sophia 73; Walter H. 97; William W. 14; Wilminia 307
BECKWITH Harriet 614; Salley 535; Whiteley 614; William P. 535
BEDFORD Gunning S. 83
BELL --- 555; Alexander E. 331; Amanda 457; Anna J. 522; Anna Maria 577; Bose 480; Charles 457; Elizabeth 162; Elmer 457; Frances (Lecompt) 457; Frank 457; Greenbury Truitt 480; Harry 457; John J. 162; Joseph 457, 480; Joshua 522; Katie 457; Laura Bull 457;

-232-

Margaret E. 331; Martha 457; Mary 480;
Mary A. 457; Mary E. 480; Mary
Purnnell 733; Mollie 457; Selva 457;
Susan 162, 480; Susan Riley 480;
Thomas H. 457; William 457, 480, 773;
William Benjamin 480;
BENEDICT Alonzo 142; Julia 142
BENN Elizabeth 759; Jonathan 759;
Mary 759
BENNETT Annabel 52; Charles W. 52; E.
T. 458, 723; Elisha 439; Gillis 723;
Gillis E. 723; Harriet 477; Hester P.
439; I. S. 723; J. B. 520; J. W. 76,
620; James 723; James L. 723; James M.
723; Jerome Bonaparte 520; Laura 723;
Levin 723; Lizzie E. 620; Louis A.
723; Richard 254, 477; Ruth H. 723;
Sallie E. 458; Sarah E. 723; Sophronia
723; Susie 520; Thomas 254; Thomas W.
723
BENSON Amanda 587; Charles 706;
Edward 221; Elizabeth 647, 706;
Emiline 221; James 706; Louisa W. 694;
Mary Ann 706; Ottis Harper 706; Perry
706, 761; Rachel 706; Robert 706;
William P. 195
BENTON Alice G. 359; George R. 359;
James 359; John R. 359; John Richard
359; Joseph 359; Luther B. 359; Mary
733; Minnie 359; Mr. 733; Richard
359; Sarah C. 359; Sarah E. 359
BERGIN Martha 323
BERKHEIMER Margaret 45
BERNARD Catherine M. 292; Fanny E.
292; J. Oscar 292; Joseph H. 292;
Joseph M. 292; Josephine 292; Mary
(Cannon) 292; Mary 292; Mary E. 292;
Rebecca 292
BERRIDGE Matilda A. 556
BERRY Benjamin F. 105; Edith 447;
Emma 447; George H. 447; Henrietta
Robinson 542; Jane 447; John E. 447;
Joseph T. 447; Lucy 447; Mary 447;
Mary A. J. 447; Robert 447; William T.
447
BEST Benjamin 450; Julia 450;
Margaret 450
BETLER Elizabeth 444
BETTERTON Elizabeth 576
BETTON William T. 129
BETTS Miss 350
BEVERLY Farm 810
BIBBY Angie 589; Frank 589; George
E. 589; Henry 589; James R. 589;

John 589; Mark Ottaway 589; Matthew
589; Sarah 589
BIDDEL Miss 505
BIDDLE farm 505
BILLITOR Anah R. 631; Jas 631; Mary
(Robinson) 631
BIRCH Martha E. 576
BIRD J. Edward 325
BIRDSALL Ellwood 745
BIRKHEAD Colonel 733; Henrieta 733;
Levin 733; Solon 733; Wm 733
BISCOE Susan 427
BISHOP Sallie 585; Charles 585; Cora
A. 585; Dorinda 585; George 448;
George W. 585; John 585; Louisa C.
448; Mary 585; Sallie M. D. 448;
William 585, 780; Z. Ellen 585
BLACK Eliza Jane 323; John 323; Mary
323
BLACKSTONE Christiana 171; John 171
BLADES Alva F. 611; Amelia 213; Anah
L. 611; Anthony 611; Armelia 611;
Christina 611; Eli K. 611; Elsie 611;
Emily 213, 611; George V. 611; Irene
559, 611; Isaiah 86, 611; Isaiah C.
213, 559, 611; John 213; Julia E. 611;
Luther L. 611; Martha 86, 611; Milcah
(Todd) 611; Minnie M. 611; Norman R.
611; Owen C. 611; Rhoda A. 611; Sarah
Olivia 531; Thomas H. H. 531
BLAINE --- 677; C. Beulah 644; E. I.
644
BLAKE Elizabeth 321; 551; George 321;
Hamilton M. 321; Mahala 336; William
321
BLAKENEY James 784; Mary 784
BLAKESLEY Maude 420; Winthrop 420
BLIZZARD Louisa 361; Peter 361
BLOOD Emma 636; Simeon 636
BLOOMFIELD 204; 56
BLUNT Levi 293; Marcella 297
BOARDLEY family 699
BODEN Susannah J. 231
BOEHM Alice H. 402; Charles L. 402;
Louis C. 402; Louis E. 402; Susan 402
BOGLE James 784; Sarah Shurlock 784
BOHEMIA Manor 103
BOLTON Farm 131
BONAPARTE Jerome 513; Madame 513;
Napoleon 513
BONHAM Elizabeth 749; Justus 749
BONSAL Eliza G. 242
BOOK Margaret A. 363
BOOKER Clementine (Shepard) 16;
Francis M. 16; James 16; John H. 16;

INDEX (to paragraph numbers)

Lula 652; Marcellus 16; Thomas A. 16; Walter 16
BOON Mary 463
BOONE Catherine 47; Clarissa 226; John 226; John 47
BORDLEY Agnes 649; James Sr 30; James Jr. 30; William Wesley 30; Elizabeth 30; James 30; John 30; John W. 30; John Wesley 30; Madison Brown 30; Marcello Worthington 30; Matthias 30; Sarah Isabella 427; Stephen 30; Thomas 30; Thomas B. 649; William 30
BORDY John S. 84
BOSBYSHELL Mary E. 216
BOTH Mrs. G. E. 798
BOUCK Gov. 450; Julia 450
BOULDEN Ella 633; Henry 633
BOUNDS Elizabeth H. 471; George 471; Helen Louise 310; James R. 508; Maggie 310; Maggie P. 508; Mary Ann 483; W. Irving 310; William H. 310
BOURKE Alice G. 802
BOWDLE Mary C. 326; Mrs. Dr. 85; William L. 481
BOWEN Andasia I. 391; Margret Ellen 391; Robert F. 391; Annie 591; E. C. 147; Ida 147; J. Raymond 181; James 490; Mary C. 181; Sarah J. 490; William H. 591
BOWIE Anna 787; Catherine D. 733; Isabell Dallas 787; John 787; Joseph Haskins 787; Josephine Haskins 787; Louisa Emily 787
BOWKER Amanda F. 323; Amanda Freeman 749; Katherine 749; Wm 749
BOWLAND Elizabeth 573; Mrs. L. P. 573
BOYD Harry L. 682; Jane Maria 682
BOYER Jacob 200; Margaret 200
BOZMAN John Leeds 774; Rachael Leeds 774
BRABLE Sarah J. 237
BRACCO Henrietta Nicholson 783; John 783
BRADFORD Catherine 536
BRADLEY Anna T. 291; Catherine 427; Chloe A. (Dines) 493; Cynthia Eliza 104; Delilah 570; Dison 580; Elam 104; Eli 588; Elizabeth 668; Elizabeth Jane 291; Elyda 291; James F. 570; James S. 291, 427; John 493; John F. 291; John W. 493; Joseph Arthur 291; Josepha 291; Kate 291; Lizzie 588; M. D. 570; Margaret 570; Martha T. 498; Martha Washington 353; Mary C. 493;

P. M. 493; Rebecca 580; Richard 588; Robert Dines 493; Rowena V. 493; Sarah 493; Taylor 291; Thomas 291; Thomas C. 291; Walter M. 493; William 291; William H. 498; William S. 493
BRAINARD's Pasture 523
BRALY Elmer E. 394; Helen 394; Martin 394; Mary E. 394; Pheobe (Herbert) 394
BRAMBLE Alice 237; Benjamin Harrison 237; Elisha 237; Ernest 237; Eva 237; Frederick 237; G. W. 237; Goodman W. 237; Ida 237; Lulu 237; Marcellus A. 237; Matthew 237; Melvina 237; Miss 668; Moses 237; Otto 237; Prediman 237; Zxie 237
BRANTZ Minnie 200
BRATTAN Cecilia H. 482; Eleanor H. 378; Elizabeth 482; George P. 402; J. Y. 482; Joseph 482; Joshua 482; Nellie Dennis 482; Nellie H. 482; Robert F. 378, 476, 482; Robert F. Jr. 482
BRERETON George 530; Sarah 530
BREWER Eleanor 12; Mary E. 12; Newton 12
BREWINGTON Elizabeth E. 315; Harry L. 369; Henry 639; Madge 639; Marion V. 639; Mattie 728; Miss 794; Orinthia (Long) 639; William 728
BREWSTER Elder 352
BRICE Benedict 783; John 783; Mary Goldsborough 783; Sarah Frisby 783; Sarah Goldsborough 783
BRIDGES Milcah 420; Richard 420; Thomas F. 420
BRIGGS Caroline C. 806; Jas 806
BRIGHT Annie 100; 627; Benjamin Harrison 100; Caroline 621; Charles M. 100; James 100, 340; James Benjamin 100, 431; James Thomas 100; Jas 627; John Eareckson 100; Joseph 621; Katherine F. 100; Laura 100; Loleta E. 100; Maggie A. 100; Martha S. 100; Mary E. 100; Mary E. 340; Mary O. 100; Sarah E. 100
BRILEY Della 750
BRINDLE William 292
BRISCOE Dr. 456; Violet B. 40; William 40
BROADAWAY Amanda M. 16; Ambrose 16; Ann 16
BROHAWN Charles W. 737; Clara H. 737; Jan 70; Katie M. 737; Louisa 737; Oma 737; Sml 737

-234-

BROMWELL Edward 514; Jane 514
BROOK Cora V. 162; E. M. 162; James W. Jr. 357; Nicey A. 357
BROOKE Anne E. 180; Alice 96; Benjamin L. 417; Birdie 417; Eliza 610; George C. M. 519; Grace E. 519; John W. 417; Joseph W. 417; Joseph W., Jr. 417; Louisa 417; Peter 19; Philip A. 519; Philip A. M. 103; Philip M. 519; Sallie (Saunders) 417; Sarah 519; Susan E. 103, 519
BROOMALL Hannah D. 99
BROUGHAN Eliza 750; John 750; Mary (Edmondson) 750
BROUGHTON Elijah 364; Elizabeth 251; Grace 364; Irena 632; Samuel 251; Wm S. 632
BROWBALL Mary A. 367
BROWN & BRUNE 191
BROWN & GODWIN 192
BROWN Albretta 693; Andrew, Jr. 727; Ann (Smith) 693; Annie 694; Arthur N. 242; Carrie V. 727; Catharine W. 294; Charlotte E. 686; Daniel 693; Drusilla A. 294; Edwin H. 30; Elizabeth A. 497; Ella 403; Ella F. 30; Emma 242; Ernest B. 242; George R. 294; Helen E. 242; Henry 693; Hiram 155, 178; J. Ben 610; James 242; James Benjamin 294; James P. 242; Jas H. 693; Jeannette 693; John 242; John B. 30; Laura M. 294; 610; Louisa Brown 306; M. M. 676; Maggie E. 693; Maria S. 242; Marion 294; Martha 693; Mary A. C. 294; Mary C. 40; Mary E. 439; Mary W. 693; Melissa E. 693; Mrs. Margaret A. 676; Mrs. Mary A. J. 447; Nancy 321; Perry J. 439; S. J. 497; Thomas R. 346; Warner 292; William 321; William E. 693; William H. 676
BROWNE family 350
BRUFF Rachel 787
BRUNDIGE Mary U. 690; Rosetta M. 690
BRYAN Alfred 248, 793; Anna 201; Arthur 248, 793; Charles 248, 793; Charles Carroll 248, 793; Charles J. 248, 793; Charles Kennerley 311; Clara V. 115; D'Arcy P. 311; Daniel Carroll 248, 793; Edna A. 248, 793; Edw 248, 793; Edward K. 248, 793; Elizabeth 248, 621, 793; Emily 311; Florence 248, 793; Frank Otis 311; Geo H. 793; Geo L. 793; George 579; George H. 248; George L. 248; Grace M. 504; Guy Lee 311; J. E. 201; James 311; James B. 248, 793; James L. 696; James Lawrenson 311; John A. W. 504; John C. 248, 793; Julian L. 311; Kat B. 793; Kate B. 248; Lay 311; Leon O. 248; Leonar O. 793; Lucretia 248, 793; Lulu 248, 793; Luther W. 621; Mary 504; Mary C. 248, 793; Mary H. 248, 793; Mary Virginia 311; Nancy Pattison 579; Nora 311, 696; Oscar 248, 793; Richard 311; Robert S. 115; Samuel 359; Sarah E. 359; Thomas A. 165; Valentine 248; 793; William I. 248, 793; William L. H. 311
BUCHANAN Admiral 603; President 119
BUCKLER Thomas H. 454
BUDD Caroline K. 759; Henry G. 759
BULL Laura 457; Mrs. B. F. 725
BULLEN Rachel 782; Thomas 782
BULLITT Elizabeth C. 396; Thomas I. 396
BUNSFIELD Mrs. M. A. 798
BURBAGE Ella 380; Margaret 380; Margaret L. 400; Samson 380
BURCHINAL Addie 80, 676; Anna 676; Eliza 676; Elizabeth 676; J. Burton 676; John C. 676; John H. 80; John Howard 676; Jos J. 676; M. M. 676; Margaret A. 676; Mary H. 676; Rebecca 676; W. D. 676
BURFORD Margaret 705
BURGESS Charles H. 325; Sarah S. 549
BURNESTON Edwards Reed 212; Ellen 212; Henry Clay 212; Isaac 212; Lucy 212; Lucy P. 212; Matilda 212; Nellie 212; William N. 212; William R. 212
BURNITE Annie K. H. 631
BURNS Grace 506
BURROUGHS Mary Ann 704
BURTON David 676; Eliza (Spencer) 676; Eliza 676
BUSICK Helen E. 680
BUSTEED Catherine 35; Catherine M. (Barwick) 35; Charles A. 244; Margaret M. 791; Molly G. 244; Pattie 35; W.W. 244; Warner R. 35; Warren 791; William W. 35
BYAS Jos 733; Sarah 733
BYNS Ella 433
BYRD Athol Lynde 488; David 488; H. Clifton 488; Mary S. 488; Sallie 488; Warren F. 488; William F. 488; William T. 488
BYRN Wilsie 579
BYRNE H.F. 209
BYUS Joseph 579

INDEX (to paragraph numbers)

CACY M. Cephelia 169
CADWELL Danl 781; Kate Haley 781; Mary Lord 781
CAHALL Rachel 135
CAHILL Lucy 517
CAHILL Mrs. J. Edward 517; Susan 223; W.H. 223
CAHOON farm 602
CAIRNS Mary Elizabeth 123; Robert A. 123
CALKINS Martha 725
CALLAWAY Sarah M. 332; Thomas C. 332
CALLEY Andrew J. 291; Elyda 291
CALLOWAY Jacob 561; Madeline 561
CALWAY Phyllis 471
CAMPBELL Amor 548; Ann 777; Elizabeth 777; Elizabeth Goldsborough 777; John 777; Kittie 5; Margaret 777; Mary 548
CAMPER Joseph A. 506; Lillian 506; Sarah C. 506
CANDLER Samuel 31
CANNAWAY John W. 647; Lydia A. 647
CANNON Amelia A. 729; Ida 523; John 291; Joseph B. 508; Mary C. 224; Mary J. 508; Olivia 291; V. 729; William N. 523
CARMAN Florence 459; John L. 459; John Ringgold 459; Maggie 441, 459; Margaret 459; Mary 459; Ringgold 459; Susan J. 459; Washington 459
CARMEAN Emma E. 597
CARMICHAEL R. B. 297; Sarah D. 297
CARMINE Amelia 221; C. S. 703; Charles 221; Charles S. 221; Emiline 221; Fred 221; George C. 221; Hilda 221; Mary E. 221; Sarah 221
CARPENTER Ann 687; Catherine A. 356
CARR Josiah 316; Sarah L. 316
CARROLL Albert 317; Ann C. 54; Anna Ella 85; Annie 317; Benjamin F. 54; C. Wesley 287; Charles 54, 674; Charles Cecilius 85; Charles Wesley 54; D. H. 317; David 317; Dora 282; Emma 54; Fannie 317; Frederick W. 54; George H. 54; George W. 54; Henry James 85; Henry Stevenson 85; James 54; Josiah 54; Julia 85; Julia S. 85; Laura D. 317; Louisa T. 352; Margaret (Medford) 54; Margaret 54, 317; Margaret H. 85; Margaret Handy 85; Mary Henry 85; Mattie 89; Nellie T. 85; Peter 282; Rebecca 54, 287, 440; Sarah 91; Thomas King 85, 410; Victor 85, 410; Vivian 85; William 352; William K. 317; William Kennedy 317
CARROW Mrs. 147
CARSON Alexander 312; Emma 312; Annie 638, 657; Annie S. 137; Arthur 340, 621; E. C. 426; E. C. 657; Hester A. 341; James H. 224; John 137; Julia 80; Lydia L. 360; Mary 340; 621; Mr. 80; R.C. 137; Richard C. 137; Richard T. 137; Richard Thomas 341; Sallie S. 284; Samuel M. 284; Sarah 224; Virginia 426; William T. 43
CARTWRIGHT Lady 795
CARVILLE 561; Correna 437; Edward 437; J. Denny 437; Mary 562
CASHO Ash 636; Eliza 636; Emma 636; Isaac 636; Jacob 636; Joseph 636; Lovina 636; Matilda E. 636; William H. 636
CASPERSON Catherine 144
CASTLE Hall 61; Haven 539
CATLIN A. Blanche 255; Alexander W. 255; Mary W. 540
CATOR Benjamin 750; Benjamin Franklin 150; Charles B. 150, 750; Ella W. 150; Ida 150; Samuel B. 150; Thomas B. 150; Valeria 750; Valerie 150; William W. 150
CAULK Anna 798; Anna R. 160; Bessie 156; Capt. 733; Carrie 140; Charles 160; Charles K. 160; Fannie 131; Frank E. 69; Florence E. 140; Howard R. 140; Imogen 160; J. H. 798; James 160; James H. 160; John 156, 160; John H. 156; John K. 156; John R. 160; Joseph 156; Joseph O. 160; Lida 160; Mary 140; Mary E. 156; Mary S. E. 156; Owen 156; Sallie 156; Sally 404; Sarah D. 69; Walter H. 160; William 140; William Sr. 140
CAUSEY Elizabeth 586; John W. 586; P. F. 586; Peter F. 669; Virginia B. 669
CECIL Catherine 223; Charles 223; John 223; Marietta 223; Martin 223; Mary 223; Mary Anne 223; Susan 223; Thomas 223; Walter 223; William 223; William H. 223
CHAMBERLAIN Anne 687; Elizabeth 506; Jos 687; Marian A. 626; Sarah Catherine 687
CHAMBERLAINE Ann 779; Ann Penketh 779; Anna Maria 778, 779; Arianna W. 396; Elizabeth B. 396; Esther

-236-

779; Harriett Rebecca 779; Henrietta M. 30; Henrietta Maria (Hollyday) 396; Henrietta Maria 396, Henrietta Maria 779, 780; Henrietta Maria Hollyday 774; Henrietta Maria Lloyd 779, Henrietta Maria R. 779; Henry 779, 780; James Lloyd 396, 779; James W. L. 396; John 779; John Goldsborough 779; Joseph 396; Joseph Ennals Muse 396; Lloyd 779; Margaret Ann 396; Marian A. 396; Marion 733; Mary 779; Mary Ungle 779; May 779; Robert Lloyd 779; S. Catherine 396; Samuel 396, 774, 779; 396; Sarah Hollyday 774, 779; Samuel 779; Susannah Robins 767; Thomas 767, 779; William Muse 396
CHAMBERS --- 688; Augusta 489; Benjamin 466, Benjamin 489, 490; Benjamin Lee 489; Capt. 323, 466; Caroline 490, 784; E. F. 95, 466; Elizabeth 489; 490; 577; Elizabeth Augusta 490; Elizabeth C. 467; Elizabeth Caroline 466; 489; Emily 666; Ezekiel Forman 489, 490; Helen 490; James 489, 496; James B. 490; James David 489; John 666; Judge 102; Laura 490; Margaretta 489; Mary 496; Mary Clare 490; Otter 784; Sarah (Lee) 489; Sarah J. 490; Sarah Maria Louise 490; Thomas Marsh 489; William Henry 489
CHAMPION Laura 286
CHANCE Batchelder C. 646; Mary E. 646
CHANDLER Anna 576; Henry 576
CHAPEN Mary 701
CHAPLAIN Alexander 331, 414, 454; Eleanor 414; Eliza (Stevens) 414; 454; Elizabeth 454; Ella 454; Elma 414; Emily 414; Evelina 454; Francis 454; Henrietta 733, James 414; James S. 331; James Stevens 414; 454; James 733; John F. 70, 331, 414; John Francis 454; Louis 454; Margaret 454; Martha 454; Mary E. 331; Mary Elizabeth 414; 454; Maude 414; Sarah 414, 454; Thomas 454; Valeria 733
CHAPMAN Daniel Chase 15; Emma Ridgley 4
CHARLES Cannon 671; Emma 472; Jacob 552; Maddison 472; Mary 671; Mary J. 552; Mrs. Mary E. 472
CHASE Salmon P. 771; Samuel 249, Thomas 574;
CHEESMAN Mary 552; Thomas 552

CHEEZUM Daniel 204; 703; Elizabeth 204; John 204; Nancy 703
CHELTON Margaret 534; William H. 534
CHERRY Alice V. 666; Allen 666; Grove 523
CHETHAM Edw 687; Sarah 687
CHEW Lloyd Philemon 30; Margaret 30; Samuel 30
CHIPLEY Charles A. 59; Charles A. Jr 59; Elizabeth 59; Emiline 59; Ezekiel 59; Francis 59; James 59; Joshua 59; Lizzie 59; Mahalah 59; Mary Etta 59; Sabrina 59; Samuel 59; Sarah 59; Sarah M. 59
CHISHOLM Jannie G. 754, Wm B. 754
CHOPTANK Steamboat Co. 470
CHRISTIAN A. A. 426; Minnie 426
CHRISTOPHER Elizabeth 198; Samuel 610; William 198
CLARK Addie H. 89; Agnes 19; Albretta 693; Ann Emily 510; Anna 19, 117; Catherine 10; David S. 19; E. Carroll 19; E. Gilbert 19; E.G. 23; Enoch 19; Enoch George 19; Epharim 19; Grace M. 522; J. F. 792; J. James 740; J. W. Jr. 693; J.B. 219; James D. 19; James E.B. 19; James T. 89; John 117; John F. 522; John N. 19; John W. 117; John W. Jr. 117; Joseph C. 510; Joshua B. 510; Laura 117; Mary (Truitt) 117; Mary 219; Mary E. 117; Mary M. 117; Mary P. 23; Mordecai 19; Mrs. Joseph 37; Rachel 19; Robert 117; Russell 89; Samuel 117; Sarah C. 19; Sarah M. 117; Stanton 89; Steven Clement 510; W. J. S. 526; William J. S. 606
CLARKE George G. 423; Gertrude F. 423; John 108; Miss 348
CLASH Charles Nicholson 123; Cloudsbury H. 123; Evelyn 123; Frederick Henry 123; Gerrettson 123; Henrietta (Matthews) 123; Henrietta 123; Howard Tilghman 123; Mary Elizabeth 123; Nathaniel 123; Norman Matthew 123; Preston Anderson 123; Sarah A. 123; Sarah Ellen 123; Vernon 123
CLAY Henry 558
CLAYTON Caroline 377; Mrs. 687
CLAYVILLE Charles W. 267; Eli 267; Emeline 267; Emma 267; Esther 267; Mary 267; Priscilla 267
CLEMENTS Alday 628; Aldie 628; Anna Maria 686; Annie 628; David 628;

INDEX (to paragraph numbers)

David A. 628; Elizabeth 628; 647;
Frances M. 628; George 628; J.
Richard 628; Jas 686; Joel 628; John
Fletcher 628; Maggie E. 398;
Margaret (Roe) 628; Margaret 628;
Margaret A. 628; Merrick 628; Ruth
628; Susanna 628; Thomas 628
CLEMMENTS Martha 457
CLENDENING Thos 634
CLENDENNING JANE L. 484
CLEVELAND President 87, 112
CLIFTON 204
CLOAKE Rebecca 337
CLOUGH Annie C. 627; Charles S. 627;
Clara 627; Ethel V. 627; Minnie E.
627; Willie 627
CLUFF 632; Annie B. 632; Edward 632;
Edward W. 632; Elizabeth 632; Frederic
B. 632; Harry 632; Irena 632; John C.
632; Jonathan 632; Mary E. 632; Robert
632; Robert L. 632; Robert W. 632;
Thomas J. 632; Winifred N. 632
COADE John 466
COCHRAN Catherine F. 461; Chas 647;
Elizabeth (Benson) 647; Laura 647;
R. W. 461
COCHRANE Ada 517; Addie 517; Amy
517; Arthur B. 517; James L. 517;
Lucy 517; Mary 517; Robert W. 517;
Stanley 517
COCKEY Annie 627; Arthur 100; B. E.
371; Benjamin Earickson 371; Catherine
486; Charles 371; Clara 627; Edward
371; Elizabeth 371; Frances 627;
Harriet 371; Harriet E. 371; Ida 627;
James H. 341, 371; James S. 621; John
371, 627; John C. 269; M. T. 371;
Maggie A. 100; Mordecai 371; 627;
Peter 132; 371; 486; Susan 371;
Susanna 132; Victoria 621; William H.
371
COCKRAN Algy J. 559; Anthony B. 559;
Capt. 611; Elmina 559; Ezekiel 559;
Henry 509; Irene 559; 611; James H.
552; Lillie B. 552; Margaret 559;
Margaret I. 559; N. J. 611; Nathan J.
559
COEY Ann M. 354
COHEE Lorinda 564; Mrs. Elmer 564
COIT Adelaide 460; Joseph 460
COLBERT Alice 765
COLBOURN --- 403; Elizabeth 632
COLE Ida 436

COLEMAN J. Thomas 394; Jessie B. 394;
John W. 394; Myrtle Effa 394; Sarah
E. 394; William J. 394
COLESBERRY William H. 11
COLGAN Louisa 686; Mrs. Rbt 686
COLINS Salisbury 8
COLLEY Annie F. 153; Ethel 153; Mary
153; R. Kyle 153
COLLIDGE Mr. 767; Susan Elizabeth 767
COLLIER George R. 618; L. D. 482;
Louisa 387; M. Virginia 618; May
629; Miss 637; Robert Laird 387
COLLINS A. J. 643; Caroline 149;
Catherine 560; Charles M. 149;
Clarence E. 474; Emma 507; Frank A.
149; Henry C. 149; Jacob A. 474;
John M. 8; Julia 474; Levi 474; Mattie
391; R. H. 41; Richard Harrison 8;
Richard Harrison Jr. 8; Sarah 108,
643; Stephen Roberts 8; Washington
Finley 8; William 149; William
Salisbury 8
COLLISON Capt. 798; Ella 703; Mary
M. 798; Nellie V. 64; Peter 776;
Robert K. 703
COLSTON Adela 481; Annie W. 481;
Elizabeth L. 481; John M. 481; Levin
481; Levin J. 481; Mary Anna 481; Mary
C. 481; Richard 481; Richard J. 481
COMEGYS Anna 672; C. 625; Cornelius
373; E. T. 758; George S. 672; Hannah
672; Helen 672; John M. 672; Lizzie
758; Mary 373; Mary M. 625; Nathaniel
W. 672; William 672
CONDIT Eleanor 733; T. Silas 733
CONDON Renowned 165
CONNAWAY Annie 361; Annie E. 567;
Annie T.361; Benjamin 567; Edward 361;
Galen 567; Henry Clay 361; Henry Clay,
Jr. 361; James A. 567; John 567;
Joseph 567; Levin 567; Louisa 361;
Margaret 361; Mary J. 567; Matilda
567; Noah 361; Rebecca 567; Sophia
361; Thomas N. 361; Viola 567;
Wilhelmina 567
CONNER Mary E. 216; Mrs. Nathan 377
CONNOLY Caroline 255; Isaac 255
CONNOR Annie O. 601; Eliza 602;
Isaac T. 601; N. T. 602; Nathan C.
806; S. Elizabeth 806
CONSTABLE Albert 97; Elizabeth 97;
Ellen 14; Harriet Lillian 73; Horace
B. 73; Isabella (Stevenson) 97;
Isabella 7; John 97; John S. 7,

73, 97; John Stevenson 73; M. Blanche 73; Robert 93; Stevenson 73; William R. 73; William S. 97
COOK Annie 228; Clinton 122; 217; Emma J. 228, 709; Everett E. 228; Frank W. 228; Ida M. 228; James 228; John 228; John R. 228; John R. Jr. 228; Joseph B. 228; Lulu 409; Margaret 535, 539; Maria J. (Walker) 228; Marietta 217; Matilda 228; Miles 776; Mrs. John R. 709; Rachel 749; Robert 409; Robert F. 228; Sallie 456; Sarah L. 122; Virginia 228
COOKE Elizabeth 352; Fannie 352; James 783; Louisa T. 352; Mary Elizabeth 783; Mary Goldsborough Brice 783; Milcha M. 352; Millie M. 352; Mrs. William 352; Sarah Loockerman 783; Sophia 352; Susan Frisby 352; Susan Lockerman 783; Susan Loockerman 783; Susan Tilghman 352
COOKE-TILGHMAN Henry 352; James 352; John 352; Richard 352; William 352
COOMBS Lydia 584
COON Hy 803; Sallie 803
COONSMAN Harriet D. 409; William 409
COOPER Alceynus 525; Ann Maria 686; Annie 666; Charles S. 498; Delilah 570; Edith 570; Ernest G. 525; Gov. 570; H. R. 686; Harvey Lee 525; Irving 498; J. A. 345; John 560, 570; Joseph P. 570; Joshua 345; Kate O. 121; L. H. 498; Lambert H. 353; Laura 723; Lena E. 570; Levan T. 570; Levin 498, 723; Lillian 575; Louisa 398; Maggie 345; Margaret 570; Mark R. 498; Martha T. 498; Martha Washington (Bradley) 353; Mary 498, 575; Mary A. (Moore) 469; Mary E. 570; Mary Elizabeth 570; Melvina 570; Noah C. 570; Philena 498; Rachel (Green) 525; Rachel A. 570; Robert 575; Sallie 570; Sallie T. 570; Samantha 498; Samuel 498; Samuel J. 570; Samuel W. M. 570; Severn H. 498; Susan 570; Thomas M. 525; W. L. 398; William 570; William M. 353, 498; William P. 469
COOPAGE Irene 625
COPENHAVER Augustus 175; Elizabeth 175; Emma 175
COPPAGE Annie 322; Benjamin 90; Catherine O. 90; Edward E. 322; Enoch 322; John 322, 707; Kate 322;

Maggie 322; Martha (Dudley) 322; Martha 322; Mary A. 322; Rebecca 322
COPPER Ann 374; Anna Louisa 374; Bradford 374; Catherine 374; Jesse 374; Jesse R. 91; John F. 374; Joshua 91, 374; Mary 374; Mintie 374; Phoebe 374; Regina M. 374; Samuel 374; W. Bradford 91; Whittier C. 374
CORBIN Ann 401
COREY A. L. 299; Lizzie M. 299
CORK Capt 733
CORKRAN Adelaide 233, 654; Alice Estelle 430; Alice M. 430; Ann L. 430; Charles W. 233; 654; David H. 233; 654; Edward E. 430; Fanny 233, 654; Francis S. 233, 654; Frank P. 430; George S. 430; Hester 233, 654; James 233, 430, 654; James M. 233, 654; John 430; John Burton 430; John C. 430; John Ellsworth 430; John R. 430; Joseph B. 430; Joseph H. 430; Laura S. 654; Lewis P. 233, 654; Margaret Spencer 233; 654; Mary Elizabeth 233; 654; Millard F. 654; Millard R. 233; Milton W. 233, 654; Nathan 233; Rachel 430; Sarah A. 430; Thomas 233; Thomas B. 233, 654; Thomas 654; Wilbur F. 233, 654
CORNELL Cordelia 190; Gov. 450
CORNER Mary 733; Sml 733
CORNWALLIS 61
CORNWELL Joel 316; Johanna 316; John S. 316; Rosa A. 316; Sarah L. 316; Thomas T. 316; William 316
CORNWELL, BBOWDLE& CO 310
CORRELL Annie F. 105; Thomas J. 105
CORSEY Fannie E. 657; Sml 657
COS Susie E. 796
COSTEN Addie L. 487; Ellen 487; Isaac Thomas 487; Lizzie 487; Mary 487; Olivia 487; Rosa 487; William 487; William A. 487
COSTON I.T. Coston 29
COTTINGHAM Annie 382; Elizabeth 382; Jonathan 382; P.D. 234; Peter D. 382; Priscie 382
COULBORN Caroline c. 806; Carrie 806; Elizabeth 806; Geo C. 806; Harry B. 806; Jas C. 806; S. Elizabeth 806; Thomas L. 806; Thos P. 806
COULBOURN Addie M. 542; Amy 517; Caroline V. 542; Clara L. 542; Elizabeth 232; Ethel Henrietta 542; Florence 344; Henrietta Robinson

INDEX (to paragraph numbers)

Berry 542; Hugh A. 542; I. H. 517; Ira N. 344; Isaac 232; Isaac H. 542; Jane E. 542; John 232; Joseph 517; Mary 377; Sallie (Long) 642; Sallie 642; Sarah 232; William 542, 642; William H. 542; William R. 542;
COULBURN Bessie B. 326; William 326
COULBURNE Wm 806
COUNCELL Eugenia A. 629; May 629; Thomas Atkinson 629; Wm H. 629
COUNCIL Annie C. 187; Francis 187
COURSEY Sarah Anne 3
COVER Mary 105
COVEY Andrew 472; Delia 198; Dora A. 635; Elizabeth 472; James Martin 635
COVINGTON Amelia (Franklin) 448; Amelia 795; Arthur Dennis 448; E. Lester 680; Ethel 680; George Bishop 448; George W. 448, 680; Harry Franklin 448; Helen E. 680; Helen M. 680; Irene L. 680; Isaac 448; James C. 680; James H. 680; Louisa Amelia 448; Maria 680; Nathaniel 680; Sallie M. D. 448
COWARD Elizabeth 785; Thomas 785
COWMAN Mrs. Altert 286
COX Annie 641; Captain 733; Clara E. 641; Dalpha 641; Daniel H. 641; Edward Noel 733; Elijah 796; Elsie Merrill 796; George Alfred 796; Henrietta 641; J. A. 641; James 687; James S. 641; Paul 641; Percy Leroy 641; Richard Allen 796; Sarah 733; Samuel 641; William A. 641
CRADOCK Mrs. Thomas 85
CRAFFOCK Anna 36
CRAFT Elizabeth S. 207
CRAIG Chas P. 787; farm 182; Louisa Emily 787
CRANE Anna E. 449; Anna M. 449; Edward T. 449; Ellen M. 449; Henry M. 449; John A. 449; Jonathan 449; Mary (Myers) 449; Thomas H. 449
CRANWELL Charles A. 394; Mary E. 394; Susan 394
CRAPP John 687; Sarah 687
CRAWFORD A. J. 428; Elizabeth A. 428; Geo L. 750; Henry 428; Henry T. 428; Horatio N. 428; Lillie 750; Mary 428; Sarah E. 428; Wm H. 750
CRAY Martha S. 100
CREIGHTON Henrietta 733; Mr. 306, 733
CRESWELL John A. J. 687
CREW Catherine 591; H. L. 591

CRISFIELD Arthur 384; John 384; John W. 388; John Woodland 384; John Woodland Jr. 362; Julia Ethelinde Page 384
CRISP Annie 409; Richard 409
CROCHERON Abbie 336; Clarence 336; Claudia 336; Ella 336; Emelie 336; Emelie S. 336; Eugene 336; Eulalia 336; George 336; Irving 336; John H. 336; Mahala (Blake) 336; Nathan 336; Ophelia 336; Tryphena 336; Winfield 336
CROCKETT 403; Charley 403; Daniel J. 403; Ella 403; James 403; Letha 403; Sarah 403
CROSDALE Annie 272; Henry 272
CROSS Sarah Patterson 733
CROSSLEY Lucy 727
CROSWELL Addie B. 554; Margaret 534; Washington S. 554
CROUCH Annie 705; Jas W. 705
CROW Edith L. 565; Jonathan 427; Sarah 427
CROWDING Anna 113; Charles 113; Eddie 113; George 113; Ida 113; Jacob 113; Jacob B. 113; Jacob B. Jr. 113; Janet 113; Mary 113; Walter 113
CROWELL J. W. 745
CRUIKSHANK Caroline 206; farm 390; Thomas C. 206
CRUSEN Henry 591; Mary 591
CULLIN Arintha J. 475; Charles G. 342; Jacob J. 475; James H. 475; Lillian 342; Maggie 475; Mamie A. 475; Mary A. 475
CULVER Eliza 355; Henry 355
CUMMINGS Caroline 575; Charles A. 575; James N. 575; Lawrence 533; Lillian 575; Margaret A. 87; Mary ann 575; Mrs. W. W. 725; Nicholas 575; Sarah V. 533
CUMMINS Eliza B. 119
CURTIS Daniel 477; William 477

DAHLGREN John A. 306
DAIL Annie P. 326; Annie Wilson 326; Bessie B. 326; Clara 326; Edgar 326; Herbert Hall 326; J. Wilson 326; Josiah 326; L. S. 512; Levin S. 326; Louisa 326; Sallie E. 326; Sally 326; Sarah E. 326; Sarah G. 512; Thomas J. 326; Wheatley 326; William 326

DAILEY Joseph S. 168; Annie E. 168; Charles E. 168; Enos 168; Harry S. 168; John 168; John T. 168; Mary 168; Mary L. 168
DALE Charles D. 573; Charles G. 456; Charles Reginald 190; Clara S. 190; Daniel E. 190; Edgar 456; Edwin S. 190; Elizabeth (Johnson) 573; Elizabeth 573; Ella 456; Ellen 573; Florence 800; James P. 800; John 456, 573; John A. 573; Mary 84, 456, 573, 800; Paul B. 190; Richard 456; Sallie 456; Sarah A. 573; Virginia 800; William 456, 573
DANDRIDGE Caroline 776; Chas 776; Lillie 776; Mary Lee 776; Nannie 776; Philip 776; Philip Pembleton 776; William 776
DANIEL Arthur 416; Biddy 416; Charles G. 416; Clarence 416; Earl 416; Elizabeth 416; Gertrude 416; James T. 407, 416; Louisa E. 416; Mabel 416; Margaret 194; Mary 416; Nancy B. 416; Nannie 407; Nellie 416; Thomas W. 416; Traverse 416; William 416
DANIELS George 113; Mary 113
DARBY Annie B. 665; Benjamin 458; Elizabeth (Harris) 665; Elizabeth (Phillips) 665; John T. 665; Mary E. 665; Richard J. 665; Sallie 665; Sophia 458; Thos 665; Wm T. 665
DARDEN Mary 131
DARROW Elizabeth H. 733
DASHIELL Algernon 220; Annie 261; Arthur 491, 653; Aurelia 491; Benjamin Douglas 70; Bertha Bayly 491; Bessie 261; C. R. 665; Cadmus 369, 653; Cassius Marion 491; Cecilia 369; Cecilia B. 378; Douglas 70; Edwin 491, 653; Edwin Jr. 311; 696; Edwin Sr 696; Eleanor 491; Elinor 429; Eliza 429, 653; Elizabeth 491; Ella B. 429; Ellen L. 696; Ellen M. 408; Emily Irving 408; Emily W. 408; Esther A. E. 653; Francis H. 369, 429; Hampden Haynie 491; Hampden P. 491; Hampden Polk 491; Harriet 369, 653; Henrietta 653; Henry E. 653; Henry J. 442; Ida May 261; James 261; James Bryan 696; John 429; John H. 408;John W. 379, 429; John Woodford 491;Julius 653; Julus T. 369; Laura 369; Levi D. 70; Levin 429; Louis 491; Margaret 261; 369; Maria 261; Maria Henrietta 112; Maria J. 495; Mary 653; Mathias 369; Nathaniel 112; Nora 311, 696; Peter 261; Robert 408; Robert K. W. 429; Robert Kemp 429; Rufus W. 351, 378; S. Frank 261; Sallie 665; Sallie B. 408; Sallie E. 442; Sarah 369, 429; Seth 491; Shirley 696; Susan 220; Susie 653; Thomas 653; W.F. 261; William 261; William F. 261; William H. 408; William Henry 491; William H. H. 653
DAUGHERTY Sarah T. 603; William T. 603
DAVIDSON Catherine 687; Catherine T. 297; Charles F. 141, 297; George 141, 297, 687; J. P. 141; James 141; James P. 141; Lolita 141; Marcella 297; Mary 687; Mary Elizabeth 297; Mary Tilghman 297; Philip 687; Philip T. 297; Richard 297; Richard Bennett Carmichael 297; Richard T. 687; Sarah D. 297; Susan 687; Susan Earle 297
DAVIS A. 218; Abisha 800; Aden 218; Anna 402; Annie 130, 343, 546; Arianna W. 396; Benjamin 343; Benjamin F. 343; Caroline 225; Carrie L. 218; Catherine 546; Charles H. 427; Curtis 747; E.F. 199; Edward 402; Edward P. 402; Elizabeth 332, 402, 800; Ella L. 343; Elmira 434; Elzie 343; Emma 546; Emma B. 183; Esther V. 343; Fannie 427; Fannie B. 218; Florence 343; George L. 490; George W. 546; Georgia 343; Georgiana 108; H.C. 183; Harry 546; Henry 546; Ida 667; J.M. 108; James 291, 510; James E. 402; Jefferson 492; Jennie E. 747; Jerome A. 747; John 427; John Porter 402; Josepha 291; Laura 490; Laura Jane 427; Lawrence R. 546; Margaret (Muse) 396; Margaret (Price) 343; Marguerite 402; Mary C. 510; Mattie 546; Minnie S. 343; Nathaniel 402; Nehemiah 546; Nellie 343; Ola Ray 343; Rebecca (Price) 747; Roberta 199; Sallie 343; Susan 251; Susan L. 402; W. W. 396; W.T. 251; Walter H. 546; William 343; William Thomas 402
DAVY George 447; Jane 447
DAWSON --- 214; Ann (Coursey) 163; Ann 733; Annie R. 69; Marion 19; Edward M. 586; Eliza J. 131; Elizabeth 586; Emily F. 132; John 131; John F. 132, 163; John R. 582; Luvenia Lucretia 131; M. M. 586; Mary

INDEX (to paragraph numbers)

H. 192; Miss 370; Mordecai M. 192;
Mrs. 131; Nancy 733; Nicholas 163;
Ralph 131, 163; Robert M. 131; Rose
G. 582; Russell S. 209; Selina 131;
Thomas C. 132, 163; Thomas H. 586
DAY Beulah W. 197; Charles S. 286;
Emma 197; Harriet E. 286; Mabel 197;
Matthias 197; Mattie 197; Thomas L.
197; Thomas Lockwood 197; William 197;
William P. 197
De CAMP Kate Smith 59; Sidney 59
De COURSEY Dr. 586
De FRAIN Annie 580; Jacob 580
de KRAAFT Mary Lilley 249; Edward 249;
Krafft J.C.P. 249; Samuel Chase 249;
Sarah A. 249
De POLEON Marquis 768
De SWAN Annette 682
De UNGER Dr. 419; Laura 419
De VALIN Chas 704; Emily 704
DEACON Miss 731
DEAKYNE Addie 303; Clara 125, 303;
Clarence 303; Elmira 303; Elva 303;
Eugene 303; George 125; George A. 303;
John 303; Luther Stanley 303; Mary C.
303; Rachel G. 303; Veronica 303;
Walter G. 303; Williard D. 303
DEAL George S. 181; Henry 521; Mary
181, 521; Roberta 298; William D. 298
DEAN Eliza 296; Henry 451; John 158;
John M. 296; Lucetta 109; Martha A.
451; Mary 158; Rebecca 710
DEBMAN Elizabeth 392; John Buckner 392
DeFORD Annie 243; Emily 224; Levi L.
243; William F. 224
DELAHAY Emma 163; Sarah J. 163
DELLEHAY --- 360
DENBY --- 558
DENNEY James 132, 286; Mary Jane 648;
Miss 132
DENNING Avis E. 691
DENNIS Cecilia 369, 378; Cecilia B.
378; Eleanor H. 378; Emerson 378;
Frank 378; G. R. 482; James T. 378;
James U. 369, 378, 482; John W. 362;
Littleton 378; Maria E. (Robertson)
378; Maria R. 378; Mary W. 378; Nellie
H. 482; S. P. 588; Virginia W. 362
DENNISON Marcus 264
DENNY Charles H. 115; Henrietta
(Mowbray) 115; Jacob S. 115; Jacob
Tolson 115; John F. 115; Mary Edith
115; William 545; William H. 115
DERBYSHIRE family of Lowes 558

DeREEVES A. E. 192; Virginia L. 192
DERINGER A. G. (Woodland) 740; Alice
740, 758; B. M. 128, 740; Estalena
740; Florence 758; H. C. 758; H. Clay
740; Henry C. 740; Lillie 128; M. 740;
Mary N. 740; William DUNCAN 740;
Woodland 740, 758
DeROCHBRUNE Eliza 563; Matthew 563;
Thomas 563
DeRONDY Jennie E. 747
DERRICKSON farm 57
DEVER Addie 431; Angeline 431; Annie
J. 431; George A. 431; Lottie M. 431;
Mamie 431; Mamie I. 431; William 431,
499; William K. 431
DeWEESE C. S. 381; Hester A. 381;
James A. 381; Natilla P. 381; Robert
H. 381; William H. 381
DEWELL Katie B. 763; Kattie 763; Thos
763
DEYO Anna 433; Broadhead 433
DICK Elisha Cullen 191; James McFaddin
502; Margaret 502; T. M. 502; Thomas
H. 502
DICKINSON --- 214, 644, 677; Annie
214; Catherine R. 152; Edward Henry
240; Elizabeth 733, 769; Ellen 182;
Emily F. 240; Granville E. 240; Henry
J. P. 240; James O. 182; James T. 240;
John 182, 769; Karlie 152; Kate 240;
Laura D. 152; Maria 733; Maria W. 152;
Marietta 240, 650; Mary 240, 733; Mary
A. 182, 240; Mary Louise 240; Samuel
152, 182, 733; Samuel A. 733; Samuel
P. 152; Van Ransvanselar 182; Willard
152; William E. 182; William S. 214
DILLAHAY Mary Jane 569; Robinson F.
569
DILWORTH Henrietta Maria 687; Thomas
687
DIRCKSON Conwell Foreman 177;
Elizabeth 177; Helen 177; Levin L. Jr
177
DIRICKSON Henrietta 119; James C. 119;
Levin 119; Levin L. 119; Martha Susie
119; Mary I. 119
DISHAROON Annie 442; B. Ella 597;
Charles R. 597; Emma E. 597; Emory L.
597; Essie L. 597; Henry W. 597;
Hettie A. (Bailey) 597; James 597;
Joseph 442; Joseph W. 442; L. Wilson
597; Lawrence D. 442; Levin B. 597;
Levin W. 597; Lillian B. 597; Marion
B. 597; Mary A. 597; Mary H. 442;

Sallie E. 442; Susie M. 442; William 597; William A. 597; William W. 442; Woodland A. 442
DISNEY Elizabeth 118
DIXON & Bartlett Shoe Co 56
DIXON, Bartlett & Co. 204
DIXON Ann (Corbin) 401; Daniel 721; Emma Gilbert 281; Florence A. 56; Genevieve 36; George 281; Helen 617; Isaac 62, 204; Isaac H. 56; J. Thomas 36; J. K. Bartlett Jr 56; James 56, 204; James T. 36; Laura L. 56; Marion A. 36; Mary Ann 56; Mary G. 56; Miss 716; Nannie C. 36; Nathaniel 401; Richard 617; Robert B. 56; Roberta B. 56; S. Amanda 56; Sarah 401; Thomas J. 401; Thomas Jr. 606; Thomas P. 36; William 204; William Amoss 56; William T. 56
DOATLAN Esther 579
DOATLOAN Esther 539
DOBSON Helen M. 496
DODD Alexander 201; Anna (Phillips) 201; Anna 201; Annie C. 187; Charles L. 329; Elizabeth 187, 201; Harry L. 329; Henry 187, 201; Ida M. 187; James C. 187; James H. 187, 201; James Henry 201; John 201; John N. 80; John T. 329; Lucinda 80; Mary 201; Nancy 201; Sarah A. 329; Susan 201; Thomas 201; Thomas H. 187, 201; Thomas H. Jr. 187; Thomas S. 329
DODSON Adelaide 266; Clara 300; Emma 209; Hannah 209; Harry 300; Helen 266; Henry Clay 209; 266; Leonidas 75; Lucy 266; Lucy J. 266; Martha 209; Robert 209; Robert A. 209, 266; Rowena 266; Susan E. 75; Thomas 209; William 209
DOLBEY Anna (Lyons) 253; Betsy Ann 253; Hattie 253; Henrietta 253; Irenous 253; John 253; Lula 253; Samuel 253; Sarah 253; Sarah C. 253; Stephen 253; Stephen W. 253; William 253
DOLVIN --- 330
DONALDSON Minnie 330
DONE Rachael Ann 774; Wm H. 774
DONNELL John 733; Sarah 733
DONOHO Elizbeth 604; James R. 604
DORSEY Caroline 387
DOUGHERTY--- 112; A. James 351; Adelia (Henry) 351; Bredelle H. 351; Charlotte E. 405; Ellen M. 408; Ellen Myers 351; Esther (Wainwright) 351;
James F. 351, 369; James Fassett 351; John 351, 405; Thomas 534; Z. James 351
DOUGLAS Elbert 485; Eugene 761; Frederick 70; Helen 304; Joseph 304
DOUGLASS Ann C. 54; Ann Emily 510; Charlotte (Wilson) 510; Eugene 510; James E. 510; James H. 510; Joseph 54, 510; Mary 510; Mary C. 510; Mary P. 485; Percy C. 510; Phillips E. 510; Ruth 510; Stephen Elbert 510; Thomas H. 510
DOWNES Anna 425; Anna Isabel 640; Annie (Hardcastle) 640; Annie 638; 657; Clara 425, 638, 657; Earnest, Jr. 425; Eldridge 425, 638, 657; Emmett 425, 657; Emmnett 638; Ernest 425, 638, 657; Fannie E. 657; Hackett 425; Ida M. 424; J. Dukes 638; 640; John M. 168; Josephine M. 425; Lulu 425; Marion 425; Marshall 657; Ormond 638; Philip 425; Philip W. 657; Philip Worthington 638, 640; Reynor 638; Reynor B. 657; Robert 425; Ryner 425; Sallie 425; Sallie R. (Ryner) 425; Sarah Ann 657; Stephen 657; Stephen R. 425, 638; W. P. 463; William 425; William H. 638, 657
DOWNEY Alice 446; Alice D. 246; Allen 446; Ann E. 246; Anne E. 446; Annie M. 246; Edna 246; Eva 446; George E. 246, 446; George Richard 246; Helen 246; Ida 246; John W. 246, 446; Joseph 246, 446; Lula 246; Maiden Ann E. 246; Marion 246, 446; Mary E. 246, 446; Mary F. 246; Rena 246; William 446; William S. 246, 446; William T. 246, 446
DOWNING Cynthia (Rosencrans) 564; Jesse 564; Susan 564
DOWNS Alice V. 666; Annie 666; Annie P. 666; Arthur 340; Arthur John 666; Charles 340, 621; Charles Benjamin 340; Ella 340; Ellen T. 666; Emily 666; Emma C. 666; Estella 340; Glenville M. 666; Jessie L. 666; John A. 666; Martie 666; Mary 340, 621; Mary Anne 223; Mary E. 340; Mary G. 666; Minnie A. 666; Norman 666; Sarah 340; Vachel 666
DOWNWARD Anna 206; Henry C. 206
DOYLE Florrie 309; Walter 309
DRAIN Vernon C. 294.
DRAKE Mrs. P. 725

INDEX (to paragraph numbers)

DRAPER Emma A. 224; Sarah 330
Draton place 547
DREWITT A. J. 193
DRIVER Lavina 579
Druid Hill Farm 95
DRYDEN A. Lincoln 365; Addie O. 694; Charlotte E. (Ford) 365; Effie C. 365; Ethelyn 365; Francis 677; J.M. 29; L. T. 554; Littleton T. 365; R.J. 29; Rose 29
DUCATOR Stephen 718
DUCKETT Allen Bowie 772; Allen Buoy 771; Catherine 771, 772; Catherine Goldsborough 772; Graham 744; Josephine A. 744; Judson N. 744; Katie 744; Richard 744, 771, 772; Richard G. 744; Sarah 772; Thomas 771, 772
DUDLEY Alexander E. 334; Ann 625; Carroll T. 334; Charles 373; Charles Bradford 239; D. H. 625; Edward A. 334; Elizabeth 334, 625, 695; Elizabeth R. 334; Elma 334; Eugene L. 373, 625; Georgia 373, 625; Georgia Spear 239; Helen 239; Helen Marie 239; Hiram 625; Hiram G. 373, 625; Irene 625; James P. 373; James P. 625; Jennie 373, 625; John 625; Lucretia 334; Martha 322, 373, 625; Mary 373, 625; Mary A. (Goodhand) 373, 625; Mary L. 334; Mary M. 625; Mr. 504; Mrs. Thomas 330; Nellie 625; Norman Spear 239; Olivia 373; S. C. 239, 625; Sarah Jane 625; Thomas A. 334; W. G. 625; William C. 373, 625
DUER Bruce W. 476; Edward F. 476; Edward P. 476; Henry L. 476; Howard S. 476; Robert F. 476; Virginia R. 476; Virginia W. 476
DUFFEY A. Linden 327; Anne E. 327; Catharine S. 327; Eleanor (O'Neill) 327; Elizabeth 327; Hugh 327; Hugh C. 327; Mrs. Z.P. 66; Roger 327; Roger W. 327
DUHAMEL Estate 686
DUKES Anna G. 463; Anne L. 748; Charles G. 463; Cora E. 463; I. Reyner 463; J. Boon 463; J. Kent 463, 757; James 463, 640; John Boon 463; L. T. 748; Levi 463; Levi T. 463; Levin T. 559; Mabel C. 463; Maria L. 463; Mary 463; Rebecca E. 463; Sallie A. 640; Sarah 463; Susan L. 757
DULANY Albert J. 659; Anna M. (Anderson) 659; Anna M. 659; Augustine 659; Dennis 659; Henry 659; Henry S. 659; Isaac H. A. 659; John H. 659; Joseph 659; Maria T. 659; Paul Dennis 659; William P. 659
DULIN John B. 664; Sarah E. 664
DUMBRACCO Elizabeth Banning 499; Ella 499; Lemuel 499
DUNBRACCO Eliza J. 124
DUNCAN Gertrude 400; Mrs. William P. 740; Sarah 772; William P. 740
DUNN Ann 569, 752; Robert 752; Thomas 569
DUNNOCK M. M. 105; Nannie L. 96; Virginia 105; William E. 96
DURDING Amanda 107; Andrew Jackson Lee 107; Annie 107; B. R. 107; Benjamin 18; Benjamin R. 18, 107; Ellinora 107; Howard R. 107; James M. 107; John 107; John T. 107; Mary Ann 107; Millard 107; Thomas B. 18, 107; William P. 107
DUTTON Frederick 212; Lucy 212
DUYER Daniel 427; James 427; John 427; Mary 427; Melcha 427; Rosie 427; Sarah 427; Susan (Biscoe) 427
DYATT --- 291
DYOTT Deborah 224; S. E. 325

EADES Sarah 241; Thomas W. 241
EAGLE Catherine A. 305
EAGLEHOFF J. C. 534
EARECKSON Elizabeth 371; Frances 627; Mary A. 545; R. W. 371; Robert C. 545; Susanna 100
EARL Dr. 324; S. Catherine 301
EARLE Ann 687, 779; Ann Johns 687; Anna Maria 687; Anne 687; Carpenter 687; Catherine 687, 690; Clara 687, 786; Deborah 687; Dinette 690; Elizabeth 687; Elizabeth Anne 687; Earle Family 687; Fannie 690; George 687; Henrietta Maria 687; Isabella 690; James 687; James T. 687, 690; John 687; John C. 687; John Charles 786; Joseph 687; Judge 396; Louisa 690; Mary (Tilghman 690; Mary 687, 690; Mary F. 687; Mary Maria 687; Mary Tilghman 297; Mary U. 690; Michael 687; Rhodah 687; Richard T. 687, 690; Richard Tilghman 297, 687, 779; Rosetta 690; Rosetta M. 690; S. Catherine 396; Samuel T. 690; Samuel Thomas 687, 690; Sarah 687; Sarah Catherine 687; Susan Frisby 687;

Swepson 690; William B. 690; William Brundige 690
EASTER Geo W. 648; Olivia 648
ECCLES Frank M. 761; May C. 761; Perry 761; Wilson C. 761
ECCLESON Judge 752; Samuel 752
ECCLESTON Eliza 733; General 733; James H. 321; John B. 752; Miss 733
EDELIN Jane 772
EDGAR Angie 736; Lucretia 531; Samuel 736
EDGELL Emma 198; Mrs. Charles 198
EDMONDSON Harriett 733; James 83; Lucretia 83; William 509
EDSAVER Miss 731
EDWARD J. A. 743; Willie S. 181
EDWARDS Jonathan 212; Matilda 212; William 181
EISENBERRY farm 699
ELBERT Miss 786
ELDER Eliza 293; F. H. 557; Lyda 557
ELIASON Caroline 217; G.W. 217; Irma 40; John 40; T. W. 676; Thomas W. 40; Thomas W. Jr. 40; Thomas W. Sr. 40; Wilbur 40
ELLEGOOD James E. 555
ELLER Mrs. Randolph 725
ELLINGSWORTH Hugh 255; Lucy E. 255
ELLIOT Mamie 431; Mrs. Joseph E. 431
ELLIOTT Annie E. 709; Elizabeth 337; J. 709; J. B. 496; Kate 496; Martha 226; Susan 109; Thomas 337; William T. 464
ELLIS William 471
ELMES Eleanora S. 31; Lazel 31; Mary E. (Chandler) 31
ELSWORTH Mrs. John 564; Rebecca 564
ELZEY Arnold 532
EMBERT Annie (Bryan) 236; Cecilia 236; Cyril 236; John Griffin 236; John R. H. 236; Mary 791; Thomas A. 236; Valentine 236; William 236; William J. 236
EMERSON Catherine R. 284; J. G. 284; John H. 262; Marion 629
EMERY Addison 672; Anna 672; Laura 672; Mrs. 672; S. R. 672
EMORY Addison 173, 233, 654; Alan G. 325; Alice G. 802; Ann 777; Arthur 777; Belle 155; Bishop 173; Blanchard 325; Charles 780; E. B. 325; Edward B. 325, 802; Edward T. Jr. 802; Edward W. 155; Eliza Bishop 780; Elizabeth 173; Fanny 173; Florence 173; Frances Bishop 780; Frank A. 173; Henrietta 802; Henrietta T. 802; Howard 173; John 173; John R. 802; Juliana 93, 155; Laura S. 233, 654; Lottie 173; Lucretia 248, 793; Marian 679; Mary 173, 325, 346, 777; Mary Ella 155; Nellie 173; Rebecca 173; Robert 173; Robert J. 155; Robert S. 93, 155; Rose 173; Stewart Orr 173; Thomas 173, 802; Thomas A. 679; Thomas R. 173; W. H. 802; William 155, 173, 346
ENGLISH C. 588; David 603; Elizabeth Ann Beall 603; Louisa H. 588
ENNALLS Elizabeth 769; Elizabeth Greenbury 769; Harriet 733; Henry 769; J. 762; Joseph 732, 733, 769; Josephine 762; Mary 732, 733; Sarah (Heron) 733; Sarah 769; William 733, 769
ENNIS John W. 644; Minnie D. 644
ERBAUGH Albert 62; Anna 62; Dr Irving 62; Effie 62; Esther 62; George W. 62; Isaac Newton 62; John 62; McKinzie 62; Z. C. 62
EROE Mary 423
ERWIN Ida May 595; James Locke 595
ESCHENBURG Emily 678; John 678
ESGATE Elizabeth 706; Rachel 706; Thomas D. 277; Thomas 706
EVANS Edward 158; Elizabeth 569; Eveline 188; Harriet 222; Keziah 188; Leah 112; Marcellus 188; Mary C. 188; William T. 188
EYRE Frances 731; Henry 731

FAIRBANK Mrs. Albert W. 725
FAIRBANKS Alice M. 430; Edith 531; Mary 553; Miss 803; Mrs. Charles; Samuel D. 430; Sarah 531
FAITHFUL Ella 499; Mary T. 230; W. E. B. 499
FALLIN Angie 736; C. C. 736; Edgar 736; Laura M. 736; Sallie (McNamara) 736; Virginia 736; Wade H. 736; William 736; William C. 736; William Sr. 736
FARINGTON W. H. 637
FARQUAHARSON Mary E. 221
FEDDEMAN Alice 765; Ann Keziah 765; Ann Matilda 765; Annie 765; Daniel 765; Daniel Maynadier 765; Dorothy 765; Elizabeth 687, 765; Ellen Douglas 690; Emma 765; Henry 690; Jane Maynadier 765; Mary 690, 765; Mary

INDEX (to paragraph numbers)

Mooney 765; P. H. 325, 687; P. Henry 687, 690; Philemon (Philip) 765; Philemon (Philip) Henry 765; Philemon Henry 765; Rebecca Sherwood 765; Rebecca Sherwood Wrightson 765; Rebecca Wrightson 765; Richard 765; Richard Tilghman 687
FELTER George 354; Irene 354
FERGUSON Ann Eliza 4; Anne 450; Charles 450; Colin 4; Cornelia M. 450; Donald 202; Eliza 450; James 450; John 450; Louisa 202; Margaret 450; Mary Jane 450
FIELDS Anna 304; Daniel 207; Daniel 304; Daniel M. 557; Edwin C. 304; Edwin Claude 304; Harman 304; Harriet 207, 304; Harriet P. 557; Harry V. 304; Helen 304; John 304; John W. 304; Minnie 304; Myra Rose 304; Roberta 304; Sidney 784; William C. 304; William Watkins 304
FILLINGEN Sarah E. 394
FINELY Margaret 689; W. P. 689
FINLEY Catherine O. 90; Helen R. 689; J. L. 90; J. Lane 689; James 90, 689; Finley James W. 90; Margaret P. 689; Richard Harrison 689; Sallie A. 689; Sallie M. 90; Sterett G. 689; Washington 90, 689; Woodland P. 90
FISHER Abram 7; Anna 245; David W. 245; Deborah 30; Eliza A. 434; Ella 245; Ellen C. 7; Elmira (Davis) 434; George A. 245; Isaac 7; J. Ira 245; Jabez 245; Jacob 7; Jacob F. 7; James H. 245; John 434; Maude 245; Richard 245; Samuel G. 7; Sarah 278; Sarah Emily 245; T. Pliny 245
FITZHUGH Anna Maria Sarah 773; William Henry 773
FLECKENSTEIN L. N. 281; Minnie 281
FLEMING Benniah 608; Charles H. 608; Clarissa 460; Cyrenius C. 608; Frances 608; Frances J. 608; George S. 608; James W. 608; Julia P. 518; Mary (Turner) 608; Mary E. 608; Nathan 608; Robert 460; Sarah Elizabeth 608; Sarah M. 608; Susan C. 608; Thomas L. 608; William 608; William F. 608
FLEMMING Gov 805
FLETCHER Elizabeth 668; Fred H. 660; Frederick H. 662; Henrietta (Kelly) 109; J. B. 109; Jeremiah 668; Jeremiah B. 660; John 660, 668, 733; John H. 278, 660, 668; John W. 333, 660, 662; John W. Jr. 333; Kilby B. 668; Laura 660, 661; M. S. 623; Maggie 333; Major S. 668; Margaret 54; Martha 333; Mary 278, 333; Mary J. 660, 668; Mildred 333; Nettie W. 623; Rosalie 333; Sallie 109; Sarah 660, 668; Sarah C. 668; Shelby B. 54; Susan 660; Thomas P. 333; William 278; William M. 660, 668
FLOWER Mrs. Jas F. 725
FLUHARTY Elender 509; Garrison 737; Louisa 737; Samuel H. 168
FOBLE A. J. 118, 610; Andrew J. 118; Andrew Jackson 118; Henry D. 118; J. James 118; John 118; Mary E. 118, 610; William 118; William T. 118
FOGWELL Jemima 751
FOOKS Dewitt C. 599; DeWitt F. 599; E. Hance 599; Elizabeth 357; Hance 599; James 277, 599; Jesse 599; Julia (Howard) 599; Julie H. 599; Lucy B. 599; M. 728; Margaret A. 599; Maria E. 728; Mary 599; Mary A. 599; R. A. 794; Sallie M. 400, 599; Sarah P. 277
FORD Charlotte E. 365; Hettie 437; L. E. 533; Martin K. 437; Miss 248, 793; Stella 533
FORMAN Araminta 301; Augusta 489; Augustine (Marsh) 490; Catherine 690; Forman E. M. 688, 690; Elizabeth 489; Ezekiel 301, 489, 490; Ezekiel M. 301; Ezekiel Marsh 301; Ezekiel T. M. 301; Florence Elma 688; Frederick W. 301; General 301; Hariet 301; Henry 301; James Cranston 301; Laura 301; Mary Earl 301; Peregrine 301; Peregrine T. 301; Peregrine Tilghman 688; Richard Carmichael 301; S. Catherine 301; Sarah 422; William H. 301
FOSTER Annie R.P. 111; Elizabeth 109
FOUNTAIN Maria (Hubbard) 611; R. S. 520; Rhoda A. 611; W. R. 86; Winnie 86; William 611
FOWLER Elizabeth Barney 734; John Pole 734; Julia A. 511; Kate Palmer 734; Mary Trippe 734
FOX Margaret 461
FOXLEY Maria 352
FOXWELL Annie J. 81; Garrett 81; Robert E. 470; Sarah J. 470; Tilman 81
FRAMPTON Anna B. 89; Bernice 89; Roland 89
FRANCES Lucy 503

FRANCIS Abigail 323; Elizabeth 782; Henrietta Maria Goldsborough 783; John 782; Maria 782, 783; Philip 782, 783; Robert 323; Tench 782
FRANK Marble 326
FRANKFORD Farm 149
FRANKLIN Amelia 448; Emily P. 795; Henry 795; Isaac 795; John R. 448; Judge 452; Littleton Purnell 795; Louisa 795; Luisa R. 795; Martha 795; Mary 795; Mary I. 795; Sallie 795; Sarah E. 795; Thomas Y. 795; William C. 795
FRAZER Ada Clayton 46
FRAZIER Benanna Greenwood 122; Elizabeth (Ridue) 122; Martha 592; Samuel 592; Samuel M. 592; William 122, 430
FREDERICK Jacob 317; Margaret 317; Sarah 317
FREEMAN Amanda 749; E. B. 214; Mollie 214
FREENEY Benjamin B. 332; Edward D. 332; Elizabeth 332; Ernest G. 332; George D. 332; James C. 332; T. A. 332; Julia 332; Peter 332; Richard 332; Samuel W. 332; Sarah J. 332; Sarah M. 332; William J. 332
FREENY Elijah 728; Elijah E. 728; Greensbury W. 380; Harry H. 728; Henry B. 728; James W. 728; John 728; Joshua 728; Lawrence 380; Maria E. 728; Mary E. 728; Matilda M. 728; Mattie 728; Peter 728; Rosa L. 728
FRIEL Annette 682; Annie 682; Bernard 348, 682; Catherine V. 682; Christiana 682; Daniel 348, 682; Daniel J. 682; Elizabeth R. 682; Elva C. 682; Emma J. 348; Jane Maria 682; Jeannie 348; John 348, 682; John A. 682; Katherine 348; Mary 682; Rebecca 682; Samuel E. Whiting 348; Thomas 348; Virginia 348
FRISBY Ariana 30; Susanna 352
FULLAM Mariana W. 679; William F. 679
FULTON Madge 639; William 639
FURMAN Martha 63

GADD A. J. 721; A. Sydney 721; Alexander 721; Daniel L. 721; E. H. Morgan 721; Frank 721; Luther H. 138, 303, 721; Luther L. 721; Mary A. (Dixon) 721; Robert F. 721

GAITHER Ephraim 772; Ephraim 772; Sarah 772
GALE Anna Isabel 97; Annie M. 562; Clara 637; George 779; Granger Sarah 11; Harriett Rebecca 779; Henrietta 779; Henry 637; J. Walter 11; James 699; John 699; Lena 699; Leonora 699; Levin 779; Levin J. 637; Martha 699; Martha E. 11; Mary 699; Mary Emma 11; Mrs. John T. 128; Rachel 699; Rachel A. 522; Rasin 562; Sarah 699; Sarah A. 699; Susan (Goslee) 637; Susan M. 637; Thomas 11, 522, 699; Thomas W. 11; Virginia 637; Washington 11; William H. 97, 637; William R. 699
GALLAGHER Francena 45; Mary 808
GALLATIN James 513
GALT Mary C. 775
GAMBRILL Darius 354; Ida 472; Mary J. 354; Mrs. William 472
GARDNER Caroline G. 782; Caroline Goldsborough 782; Catherine Frances 782; Elizabeth Greenbury 782; Henry W. 782; John Lane 782; Mary Rebecca 345; Nelson 345; Rebecca 682; Samuel 345
GAREY Enoch B. 438; J. W. 438; James A. H. 438; Lena R. 438; Mary E. 438; Robert S. 438; V. Louise 438; Vashti 438
GARRETT Eliza A. 125; Sarah 317; Thomas 125
GARRISON Margaret 618
GEARHART Ada C. 720; Henry L. 720
GEDDES Henry 678; Margaret 678; Sarah 678
GEMENY Anna L. 531; S. D. 531
GEMMILL Alice 547; Eunice L. 26; Frederick 547; Jane 547; Margaret (Sutton) 547; Margaret 547; William 547
GEOGHEGAN --- 70; Kate 157; Miss 356
GEORGE Addie H. 89; Anna B. 89; Anna E. 89; Annie 226; C. T. 685; Clarissa 226; Dawson O. 47; Dr. Enoch 20; Edwin 226; Elizabeth (Hopkins) 89; Elizabeth 122; Elizabeth 89; Ella H. 89; Elsie L. 174; Enoch 20, 47; Evelyn 89; Florence 89; Frances 122; Frederick 122; H. K. 140; Hilda 89; Isaac S. 122; James B. 122; James H. 89; John E. 174, 226; John H. 89; John L. 89; Joseph 226; Joseph E. 226, 295; Joseph H. 89; Joseph M. 174; Joseph W. 20; Lucretia D. 226; Madeline M. 174;

INDEX (to paragraph numbers)

Margaret (Turpin) 20; Martha 226, 295; Martha L. 226; Mary 89; Mary E. 89; Mary Virginia 20; Mathias 20; Matthias 226; Octavia Orme 20; Paul 89; Robert 89; Robert B. 89; Susie 89; Thomas R. 89; Walter T. 89
GERMAN Mary E. 69
GIBBONS Edward 644; Edward W. 161; Elizabeth Ann 161; Isaiah 161; John S. 161; Lizzie 161; Mary A. 210; Sadie P. 644
GIBSON Charles H. 134; Emily J. 596; George A. 596; Mrs. 733; Senator 149, 436, 696
GIDDINGS Elizabeth 744; Richard 744
GILES Edith 512; Isaac 512; Sarah E. (Hosea) 512
GILL Anna T. 291; Benjamin 291; Catherine 427; Kate 291; Lewis 427; Mary B. 291
GILLETT Sarah E. 46
GILLINGHAM Edith D. 586; George 212; Lucy P. 212; Mary (Miriam) 212; Robert P. 586
GILLIS Dr. 800; Hester A. 800
GILPIN Charles P. 33; Emma A. 752; Joseph E. 752
GIST Eliza 733; Frances 733; Harriett 733; Henrietta 733; John E. 733; John Trippe 733; Margaret 733; Valeria 733; William 733
Glendale farm 598
GLENN Louisa 563
GODEN --- 720
Godlington Manor 178
GODWIN Ezekiel 87
GOLD D.L. 131; Eliza J. 131
GOLDSBORO Clara 687; Nicholas 687
GOLDSBOROUGH --- 214, 764, 773; A. L. 518; Achsah (Worthington) 719; Achsah 772; Alexander Miller 780; Alfred 780; Alice 772; Alice Lloyd 775; Amelia 772; Amelia Poe 772; Amy Ralston 771; Angelina 393; Anita 781 Goldsborough Ann 393, 764, 768, 777, 782, 785, 786; Ann Caroline 781; Ann Hayward 786; Ann Margaretta 786; Ann Maria 766; Ann Martin 786; Ann Tilghman 777; Ann Turbutt 777, 778, 782, 783, 784; Anna 658, 777, 785; Anna Elizabeth 120; Anna Maria 773, 778, 781, 783, 786; Anna Maria Chamberlaine 780; 781; Anna Maria Kennard 781; Anna Maria Sarah 773;

Anna Mckell Stevens 780; Anne 393; Anne E. 513; Anne Maria 393; Annie Keene 768; Brice 275; Brice John 719, 772, 786; Brice W. 658, 719; Bridget 785, 787; Caroline 769, 770, 773, 776, 778, 781, 782, 784; Catherine 771, 772, 782, 786; Catherine Duckett 772; Catherine Roberts 782; Charles 34, 513, 579, 674, 719, 764, 766, 768, 769, 770, 771, 772, 773, 775, 776, 777, 778, 780; Charles Carroll 781; Charles Emory 780, Charles F. 617; Charles Fitzhugh 34, 773, 776; Charles Henry 767, 771, 772, 782; Charles Howes 781; Charles McDowell 773; Charles Washington 778, 782; Charles Worthington 772; Charles Yerbury 773; Charlotte 776; Charlotte August Page 34; Charlotte P. 674; Clara 786; Daniel 776; Dr. 689; Dr. Robert 1; E. K. 518; E. Martha 120; E. T. 518; Edmond Lee 772; Edward 771; Edward Lee 772; Edward Lloyd 775; Edward Ridgley 783; Edward Y. 759; Edward Yerbury 771; Eleanor 768; Eleanora Dall Lux 783; Eliza 767; Eliza Ann 768; Eliza Bishop 780; Eliza Margaret 771; Elizabeth (Greenbury) 719; Elizabeth 674, 764, 765, 766, 768, 770, 772, 773, 776, 777, 784, 785, 786; Elizabeth Dickinson 769, 773; Elizabeth Ennalls 769; Elizabeth G. 782; Elizabeth Greenbury 764, 765, 766, 769, 770, 773, 774, 776, 777, 778, 784; Elizabeth Kennard 781; Elizabeth R. 776; Elizabeth T. 683; Elizabeth Tench (Tilghman) 120; Elizabeth Tench 785; Elizabeth Wirt 782; Ellen 275; Ellen K. 782; Ellen Lloyd 775; Ellen Ridgley 783; Emily 518; Goldsborough estate 581; Eugene 7721; F. Carroll 120; Goldsborough Family 764; Fannie 780; Fitzhugh 775; Foster 785, 787; Francis Emory 780; Francis McCallmont 781; Francis Spencer 783; George R. 95; George Robins 767; George Washington 773; Greenbury 764, 776, 777; Griffin 786; Griffin W. 393; Henrietta (Jones) 658; Henrietta 1, 615, 658, 719, 783; Henrietta Bedinger 772; Henrietta Maria (Jones) 275; Henrietta Maria 95, 767, 773, 776, 777, 778, 780, 782; Henrietta Maria Tilghman Robins;

-248-

GOLDSBOROUGH (continued)
Henrietta Nicholson Bracco 783; Henry 513, 768, 778; Henry Cadwell 781; Henry Chamberlaine 780; Henry Hollyday 778, 781; Henry Turbutt 768; Horatio 778; Howes 764, 766, 768, 769, 778, 781, 784; Hugh Allen 782; Jacob Loockerman 783; James 719, 772, 785, 786; James Kemp 778; James N. 518, 683; James Nicholas 786; Jane 678, 772, 786; Jane Banning 769; John 764, 769, 770, 771, 777, 778, 780, 781, 782, 783, 784; John Chamberlaine 778, 780; John McDowell 767, 773; John Roberts 782; John Schley 771; John Whittingham 781; Joseph Nicholson 783; Josephine 772; Judith 764; Julia Fleming 518; Julia P. 518; Julianna 771; Kate 781; Kate Haley 781; Katherine (Fauntleroy 393; Leah 719, 772, 786; Leander 772; Leander W. 771, 772; Lee Kennedy 518; Lewis 772; Louis Malesherbes 782; Louis Piper 781; Louise 658; M. Worthington 719; Mackenzie 518; Madge 518; Malesherbes 782; Margaret 393, 764, 768, 778; Margaret Howes 764, 784; Margaret Patterson 786; Margaret Schley 771; Margaret Tilghman 769; Maria (Thomas) 393; Maria 182, 733, 768, 786; Maria E. 513; Marion Caroline 778, 780; Martha 120, 393, 776; Martha Laird 393; Martin 786; Martin W. 719; Mary 518, 674, 765, 776, 777, 783, 785, 786; Mary Ann 768; Mary Ann Turbutt 766; Mary Ann Turbutt Robins 766, 768; Mary Anne 782; Mary C. 775; Mary Campbell 658; Mary Caroline 767; Mary Catherine 771; Mary Ellen 775; Mary Ellen Lloyd 775; Mary Emerson 766; Mary Emerson Trippe 766, 767; Mary Hammond 781; Mary Hill 120; Mary Isabella 768; Mary Lee 518, Lee 775; Mary M. 781; Mary McDowell 767; Mary Nicholson 783; Mary Nixon 771; Mary P. 782; Mary Rebecca 783; Mary Rogers 769; Mary Skinner 777; Mary Skinner Loockerman 783; Mary Thomas 785, 786; Mary Tilghman 773, 776; Matilda 772; Matthew 778; Matthew T. 120; Matthew Tilghman 120, 786; Nannie Campbell 658; Nannie Lloyd 775; Nelson Poe 772; Nicholas 95, 120, 393, 518, 678, 719, 764, 769, 772, 782, 784, 785, 786, 787; Nicholas Worthington 771; Philip Francis 518; Phillips Lee 275, 719; Phillips Lee, Jr. 275; R. H. 518; R. T. 674; Rachel 769, 784, 785, 787; Robert 674, 678, 719, 764, 765, 766, 767, 768, 769, 770, 771, 772, 773, 776, 777, 778, 781, 782, 783, 784, 785; Robert Fitzhugh 773; Robert Galt 775; Robert Henry 766, 767, 771, 773; Robert Lloyd 778, 780; Robert T. 768; Robert William 767; Robert Yerbury 768; Rebecca 768, 769, 778; Goldsborough Richard 120, 719, 769, 772; Richard Henry 786; Richard Tilghman 34, 773, 775; Richard Yerbury 772; Robert 95, 615; Robert Henry 95; Rosanna Piper 778, 784; Sallie Murray 775; Sally 786; Samuel 768, 778; Samuel Chamberlaine 778; Samuel Kennard 781; Sara M. 120; Sarah (Turbutt) 393; Sarah 764, 766, 768, 769, 771, 772, 785; Sarah Duncan 772; Sarah Fauntleroy 786; Sarah Jolly Turbutt 785, 786, 787; Sarah Potter 778; Sarah T. 782; Sarah Worthington 771, 772; Sarah Yerbury 768, 769, 770, 771, 772, 773, 775, 776, 778; Sophia 787; Sterling 776; Susan 776; Susan Elizabeth 767; Susannah 768; Tench 786; Thomas 393, 785, 786, 787; Thomas Alan 393; Thomas H. 393; Thomas Henry 783; Washington Elwell 393, 776; Washington Laird 393; William Winder 393; Williamima 770; Williamima Smith 771; Williamina E. C. 393; Williamina Elizabeth 674; Williamina Elizabeth Cadwalader 776; Winder Elwell 393; William 764, 766, 767, 769, 770, 771, 772, 776, 777; William Fitzhugh 775; William Henry 768; William Henry Fitzhugh 773; William Lux 783; William Miller 780; William T. 674; William Tilghman 773, 775; William Wirt 782; Worthington 275, 658, 772
GOLT John H. 81; Lydia A. 81
GOODCHILD Mary 558
GOODHAND Christopher 625, 695; Eugenia 111; Mary A. 373, 625; Mrs. S.S. 111; Sarah E. 695
GOODING Jennett 461
GOOTEE Frank 303; John W. 569; Martha 569; Mary C. 303
GORDON Ellen L. 696
GORDY Benjamin B. 84; James D. 84; John P. 84; John T. 84; Lemuel B. 84;

INDEX (to paragraph numbers)

Lemuel D. 84; Levin S. 645; Maria 645; Mary E. A. 84; Nathan 84; William G. 84
GORSUCH John E. 265; Mary E. 265
GOSLEE Minnie Alberta 439; Susan 637
GOSLEY Lowdy 439; Polly 439
GOSLIN Edward E. 624; Emily 624; Margaret 624; Matthew 624; Thomas 624; William 624
GOULD Eliza 731; James 731
GOWEN Alice 679; Francis 679
GOWING Emily 549
GRACE Anna L. 531; Anne Cooper 531; Arthur F. 531; Charles H. 266, 531; Edith 531; Elizabeth L. 724; Leonara B. 724; Lucretia (Edgar) 531; Mary Ella 724; May 366; Rowena 266; Samuel 724; Grace Sarah 531; Sarah Olivia 531; Skinner 531, 724; Susan May 724; Susan R. 724; Thomas 531; Thomas E. 366, 724; William Preston 724; Grace William S. 531, 724; William S. Jr. 531
GRAHAM Adela 481; Alexander 754; Caroline 387; Christy S. 754; Ellen J. 366; John 366; John E. 481; Louisa 387; Margaret 387; Mary 481; Mary E. 805; Robert P. 387; Sallie M. 80; Samuel A. 387; Sarah 589; Walter R. 80
GRASELEY Susie (Bennett) 520
GRASON Margaret P. 689
GRAVES Annie 286; Elizabeth 784; James 784; William 286
GRAY John R. 93; M. H. 398; Margaretta Ann (Anderson) 93; Mary Adelaide 749; Mary T. 398; R. A. 749; Rebecca R. 93
GRAYSON Amelia 663; George 663; Governor 373
GREEN Alfred 43; Alfred Marion 43; Annie 711; Barrett 43; Edward F. 3, 43; Elijah B. 43; Elizabeth (Reed) 711; Elizabeth 43, 437; Elsie 711; Foster 386; James 711; Jane (Jump) 386; Jonathan S. 711; Joseph 43; Mary (Fox) 43; Mary Elizabeth 466; Mollie R. 386; Mrs. Benjamin F. 466; Nathaniel 437; Rachel 525; Robert H. 43; Sue R. 3; Thomas 711; Thomas R. 711; William F. 43; Woodall 711
GREENBOUGH Henry 312; Lydia 312
GREENBURY Ann 764; Elizabeth 764; Nicholas 764
GREENE Mary 785; Mary E. 716; William M. 716

GREENLEA Betsy 434
GREENLEY T. W. 583
GREENWELL Alexander 514; Frances 514
GREENWOOD Arthur 256; Caroline 256; Clarence A. 256; Elizabeth 122; Henry 577; J. Alfred 256; James 256; James A. 427; James W. 256; John 256, 299; Laura M. Hope 256; Lottie 577; Martha I. 256; Martha Isabelle 299; Mary 147, 256; Mary M. 256; Mary Maria 427; Miss 102, 303; William 256
GREENY Ella 380
GREGORY Ann 383
GRESHAM Ellen 652; Harry 652; James 701; John 701; Laura E. 701
GRIER Margaret 591
GRIFFIN Angeline 81, Caleb 258; Charles T. 258; Elizabeth (Bryan) 236; Franklin 258; George Linden 258; George N. 258; George W. 258; Gwynbury 236; Harriet E. 258; Henrietta 338; James 149; John 236; John H. 338; Julia 236; Leah S. 149; Lydia 236; Mary 236, 675; Nanie B. 258; Robert T. 258; Sarah 236
GRIFFITH Ada Roberta 298; Adeline 298; Alice 607; Ann (Richardson) 463; Charles 463; David 607; David B. 607; Edwin L. 298; Elizabeth (Sutton) 298; Ella 198, 607; John 236; John S. 607; Julia 607; Kate E. 607; Lizzie 607; Margaret 607; Maria L. 463; Mariana 88; Mary Elizabeth 298; Mrs. Greenberry 198; Robert 298; Robert C. 298; Roberta 298; Virginia 298; W. F. 88; William 236
GRIMES Laura Forman 301
GROOME Ann Matilda 765; Charles 765; Deborah (Morris) 545; Deborah Morris 765; Margaret 765; Mary E. 545; Morris 765; Samuel 545, 765; Sarah Kennard 765
GROVER Lucia 605
GRUNDY Ann 767, 779; Robert 779
GUESSFORD Sarah 504
GUNBY Addie M. 542; Catherine 218, 376; Dr. 218; F. A. 542; Hiram H. 376; Mrs. C. L. 347
GUNDRY Catherine A. 346; Richard 346

HACKETT Alice D. 578; Annie C. 169; Blanche 169; Cephelia (Woodland) 319; Charles W. 503; Georgia 373; Grace M.

503; Gunning Bedford 169; Henrietta Jane 83; Hugh 469; James B. 373; Jessie Guthrie 319; John C. 169, 319; John T. 469; L. K. 578; Laura E. 501; Louisa C. 469; Maria W. 169; Samuel W. 169; Sarah (Cacy) 169; Thomas B. 501
HADAWAY Arminie 584; G. M. 584
HADDAWAY Alice 464; Annie 464; Catherine 464; Charles E. 464; Ella 464; Helen D. 464; Martha 189; Mary E. 156; Mary T. 464; Oliver S. 464; Rose 464; Rowland 558; Sarah C. 464; Susan 464; Susannah 572; Ursula 558; W. H. 464; William 189; William Webb 558, 572
HAEFNER Caroline 183; Christian A. 183; Emma B. 183; Gustavus A. 183; Margaret 183; Sophia 183
HAGGART Georgia 625; Joseph B. 625
HAHN Martha 209; William B. 209
HAIGHT C. 720
HAINES Daniel 680; Maria 680
HAIRUN Jordan 702
HALL --- 720; Agnes 441; Hall Brothers 606; Catherine 423; Cecil 441; Clara 598; Corinne E. 598; Dr. 393; Ebenezer 423; Elizabeth 598; Ethel 598; Florence 598; Florence M. 347; Gertrude 598; Gertrude F. 423; Gervas 759; H. Emma 441; Harriet E. (Holland) 441; Henry W. 347, 598; Hiram s. 423; I. Henry 598; Jennie 598; Jerome B. 644; John 574; John W. 441; Julia C. 644; Maggie 441, 459; Martha (Lankford) 598; Martha V. 759; Mary 423; Richard 441, 598; Robert H. 441; Sarah Jane 443; Susan 598; Sylvester T. 443; W. F. 459; William F. 441, 462; William J. 598
HALLECK ----346
HALLOCK Mary 517
HAMAN Elizabeth 547
HAMBLETON Helen 733; Hugh 733; Mary 765; Samuel 638
HAMMOND Ann Caroline 781; Anna Maria 779; Charles 781; Helen 116; Helen E. 713; J. 713; James 781; James F. 116; John 574; Mary G. 781; Mrs. 774; Nicholas 779, 781; Rebecca 781; Rebecca Hollyday 779
HAMPSON Ada G. 501; James Jr. 501
HANCE Anthony M. 679; Sallie M. 679
HAND Bessie 223; Marietta 223; Thomas B. 687

HANDY Annie E. 347; John 593; Levin 251; Maj. Gen. 492; Margaret 251; William W. 378
HANES David W. 11
HANSE Andries 126
HANSON John 191; Martha 191
HARDCASTLE Aaron 61; Aaron B. 61; Addison L. 61; Angelina 393; Annie 638, 640; Edmund L.F. 61; Edward 638, 640, 643; Edward B. 61; Elizabeth 360, 643; George Thomas 61; Hughlett 61; Margaret 61; Martha L. 130; Mary 61; Maynadier 61; Peter 61; Richard 61; Robert 61, 130; Robert Everett 130; Sallie (Dukes) 638; Sallie A. 640; Thomas 61; Thomas H. 61; William 130; William H. 61; William M. 393; Yellott 61
HARGIS --- 644
HARMON Florence H. 801; Geo 801
HARPER --- 350; Andrew 130; Annie 546; Caroline B. 350; Charles 130; Clara 426; E. B. 130; Emeline 788; F. H. 546; Florence Olivia 130; Francis B. 130; Franklin 130; Franklin H. 130; George W. 130; H. L. 426; J. Frank 143; James K. 350; John Myers 143; Joseph W. 130; Mrs. Wm 753; Sarah 635; Walter S. 130; William 130
HARPLE Susan J. 459
HARRINGTON Alfred 684; Ann Maria 686; Benjamin E. 196; Harrington Brothers 196; Byron E. 196; Caroline 784; Charlotte E. 686; Eleanor Willson 784; Elizabeth (Jones) 196; Elizabeth E. 196, 357; Emerson 196; Fannie F. 196; Francis W. 196; George 686; Harriett 784; Henrietta 784; Henry W. 784; Henry William 784; James Auld 784; James W. 686; John 196, 587; John E. 196; John Edward 196; Louisa 686; Mary A. 196; Mary E. 684; Michael 784; Philemon 686; Rachel Rebecca 686; Rosanna 784; Rosanna Auld 784; Sally 455; Sarah Maria 686; Susie 3; W. W. 357; William 686; William W. 196
HARRIS Alexander 15, 678; Allan A. 14; Allan Alexander 15; Allan Beck 15; Anna Maria 15; Annie 591; Arthur L. 591; Carson W. 591; Catherine 591; Elizabeth 665; Emma 15, 678; Henrietta (Ringgold) 15; Isaac 125; James G. 591; James S. 591; John 591; Margaret 435, 591; Maria 678; Maria L. 15; Mary

INDEX (to paragraph numbers)

591; Mary I. 119; Mary Louisa 15;
Matilda 591; Richard H. 591; Richard
S. 591; Richard Spencer 15; Sarah P.
512; Spencer 15; Thomas 15; Thomas L.
119; Walter 591
HARRISON Achsah 560; Amelia 533; Anna
533; Catherine 560; Charles 533;
Charles H. 560; Charles P. 533; Della
C. 560; Edward 706; Eliza 560, 582;
Elizabeth 533, 706; Esther V. 343;
Harrison family 629; Frank D. 648;
George A. 560; George K. 533;
Henrietta 533; James 76, 809; Jane 8;
Joseph 582, 648; Joseph G. 560; Joseph
H. 648; Joseph S. 533; Josephine 533;
Kate 789; Kate W. 648; Kensey 100;
Levi 533; Levin 560; Levina 533; Lewis
C. 533; Louisa 560; Mahala 560;
Margaret 286; Margaretta 243; Mary
(Harrison) 648; Mary J. 533; Mary Jane
648; Olivia 648; Orlando 560; Pres.
32, 412; Rhoda (Long) 560; Richard 8;
Sallie A. 689; Samuel T. 243; Sarah
87, 785; Sarah A. 90; Sarah R. 75;
Sarah V. 533; Stella 533; Stephen 648;
Susanna 600; Thomas 533; William 286,
789; William P. 533
HART Martha 324; Sarah 324
HARTWELL Marie 466
HARVEY Miss 731
HARWOOD Edward 733; James 733; Sarah
733
HASKINS Anna 787; Barclay 733, 787;
Elizabeth Robins 787; Joseph 787; Mary
787; Mary Harriett 733; Sarah 787;
William 787
HASSINGER Carrie 278; W. T. 278;
William F. 278
HASTINGS Caroline 692; E. S. 692
HATCHERSON George W. 549; Sarah E. 549
HATCHISON B.C. 180; Mary Regina 180
HAWKINS Emma 312; Harry 312
HAYES Nancy 757; Roy 757
HAYMAN Emily C. 377; Emma C. 602;
Jephtha 538; Mary H. 681; Sallie W.
538; W. A. 377; W. H. 602
HAYNES Emily 249; Hebe 249; James 249
HAYWARD Ann 786; Annie 272; Annie M.
272; Barton L. 272; Dallas Bowie 787;
Elizabeth 259; Elizabeth B. 396;
Elizabeth C. (Bullitt) 396; Elizabeth
Haskins 787; Elizabeth Robins 787;
Emily F. 272; Emmett 396; George 272;
Henrietta Maria Robins 787; Henry C.

272; John 272; John C. 272; John E.
272; Josephine Haskins 787; Margaret
(Duer) 272; Millard P. 272; Sarah S.
H. 733; Thomas 787; Thomas M. 272;
Thomas Smyth 787; William 396, 787;
William W. 272
HAZZARD Margaret 803
HEARN Annie 760; B. Harvey 645;
Benjamin B. 702, 760; Benjamin H. 645;
Betsy 645; Charles B. 702; Charlotte
A. (Smith) 760; Charlotte A. 760;
Cordelia 681; Esther Ann Robinson 702;
George 645; George E. 539, 681, 760;
Harriet A. 681; Henrietta 645, 702;
Henrietta G. 760; Herbert 760; Isaac
J. 681; Isaac N. 681; Isaac T. 681; J.
F. 760; J. Frank 760; Jennie E. 681;
Josiah 702, 760; Margaret N. 539;
Maria 645; Mary 681, 702; Mary H.
(Hayman) 681; Mary H. 681; Olevia 760;
Olivia E. 681; Omro 760; Richard 702;
Sarah (Lowe) 760; Sarah 702; Sarah
Olivia 604; Sophia 702; Thomas 681;
William 681, 760; William C. 760;
William L. 535; William R. 702;
William W. 702, 760
Heart's Ease 347
HEDDING Bishop 200
HEIGHE Elizabeth 67
HEMSLEY Martha Ann 765; Mary 765;
Philemon Feddeman 765; Philemon
Williamson 765; Richard F. 454;
Richard Feddeman 765
HENDERSON Alecander 603; Arianna 603;
Charles E. 603; David 603; Elizabeth
603; George 603; Ida M. 603; Janet
603; John 603; Minnie 603; Norman F.
603; Richard 603; Sarah T. 603;
William L. 603
HENDRICKSON Augustine 22; Henry Clay
22; John P. 22; Joseph E. 22;
Peregrine 22; Peregrine Jr. 22; Victor
22
HENRY Adalie 351; Adelia 351; Annie
674; Catharine 674; Charlotte 776;
Charlotte A. P. 34; Charlotte P. 674;
Clarence 623; Daniel 776; Daniel M.
34, 271, 275; Daniel M. Ryder 34;
Edith 623; Edward 78; 623; Elizabeth
674; Francis J. 34, 316, 674; Francis
Jenkings 777; Frank 623; Hampton 674;
Henrietta Maria 776; Isabela 674;
Isabella E. 34; James Winfield 34,
674; John 5, 34, 674, 777; John

-252-

Campbell 34, 674, 777; John Francis 34, 674; Joseph E. 623; Kate 34; Laura 36?; Margaret Campbell 777; Mary (Steele) 5; Mary 34, 674, 776; Mary N. 674; Mary Nevett 674; Mary Nevitt (Steele) 34; Matie H. 44; Mattie H. 192; Nannie Campbell 658; Nellie 674; Nettie W. 623; Nicholas L. 674; Robert G. 674; Rider 674; Sarah 78; Varina 674; W. L. 192; W. Laird 44; W. Laird Jr. 44; Williamina 674; Williamina Elizabeth 674
HEPBRON A. M. 323; Archer Kerr 323; Eliza Pleasanton 323; Elizabeth 147; Frank 147; Harry 147; Henrietta 147; Ida 147; James 147; James Merritt 323; John F. 147; Joseph J. 147; Lewis 505; Lillian 505; William 147; William T. 147
HERBERT Estella 340; Eugene 340; Pheobe 394
HERMAN Augustine 490
Hermitage 134, 352
HERON Susan 733
HESS Annie 682; Jas B. 682
HESSEY Ella 633; Emma 549, 633; Emma Morgan 633; Franklin 633; John 633; John H. 549, 633; Sarah 633
HESSY John W. 43; Mary I. 43
HIBBARD Mary 2; Samuel 2
HICKMAN Adeline 271; Elizabeth 235; Emma 271; George R. 271
HICKS William T. 527; Chaplain Galloway 543; Clara L. 375; Elizabeth 543; Elizabeth Banning 499; Ella F. 527; Emily C. 527; Fessenden Fairfax 543; George L. 13, George L. 543; George Luther 543; Gov. 13, 510, 543, 757; Helen 527; Henry C. 13; Hooper C. 316; James 527; James R. 527; Levin 527; Mary (Sewell) 13; Nannie 13, 543; R. Heston 527; Richard 527; Samuel 527; Sarah Matilda (Milbourn) 527; Thomas H. 270; Thomas Holliday 13, 543
HIGGINS Effie 87; James 660; John 87; Margaret 733; Solomon 733; Susan 660
HILDBRANDT Susan 413
HILL Alexina 206; Anna 206; Annie 727; Caroline 206; Caroline C. 206; Charles 206, 758; Charles A. 206; Charles Westcott 206; Esther A. 655; Jacob 22; John J. 655; John S. 655; Margaret 22, 206; Mary 206; Mrs. Thos 727; Nannie P. 655; Susan 206; Thomas Cruikshank 206
HILLEARY Elizabeth 603; Janet 603; John 603; John W. 603
HILLEN Solomon 513
HIMMELWRIGHT Annie G. 363; E. A. 363; Margaret A. 363; Mary L. 363
HINES Anne (Knock) 346; Annie 346; Catherine A. 346; Charles Gilpin 346; Elizabeth 676; Emily Alphonsa 346; Emory Massey 346; Frank Brown 346; Isaac 346; Isaac 80, 346; Jannie 346; Jennie 97; Jennie Emory 346; Jesse K. 14, 80, 346; Jesse Knock Jr. 346; John W. 80, 676; Mary 346; Mary Alphonsa 346; Nannie H. 14; Sue C. 178; Thomas L. 346; W. Franklin 346; William D. 178
HITCH Ann E. 438; Arthur 233, 654; Elijah 717; Fanny 233; Fanny 654; Garey 438; Julia 474; S. A. 717
HOBBS Charles W. 385; Eleanor 385; Henry 385; Henry Clay 385; Nancy (Stevens) 385; Saulsbury 385
HOBBY Ada C. 720; Alice 720; Alice G. 720; Alvina 720; Arthur J. 720; C. 720; Edna H. 720; Edward B. 720; Emma 720; George S. 720; George T. 720; George T. Sr. 720; H. L. 720; Howard 720; L. E. 720; Lewis H. 720; M. M. 720; Mary C. 720; Vincent M. 720
HOBLITZELL Ella 556; S. A. 556
HODGES Brothers 96
HOES Mayke 126
Hog-Pen Ridge 323
HOLLAND Annie R. 101; Charles F. 453; Clara 651; Elisha 453; Eliza 651; Frances 249; George 651; George W. 101; Harriet E. 441; Henry 223; J. Thomas Jr. 101; John H. 651; John S. 651; Joseph W. 101; Julia Anne 651; Louisa (White) 453; Mamie 651; Mrs. J. Thomas 101; Nancy 651; Sarah Anne 651; William 101; William H. 223
HOLLIDAY Daniel 733; Frances 733; Powell 352; R.C. 204; Sophia 352
HOLLINGSWORTH --- 768; Mary Ann 768
HOLLIS C. I. 809; C.I. (Miss) 77; Charles 77, 809
HOLLYDAY Ann Margaretta 786; Anna Maria Robins 779; Henrietta Maria 779; Henry 735, 779, 786; Maria 396; Melusina 735; Rebecca 779

INDEX (to paragraph numbers)

HOLMES Alice M. 808; Anah R. 631; Annie K. H. 631; Elizabeth 631; Ella 455; James H. 631; Jennie 588; John P. 455; Mary A. 631; William G. 588
HOLT Catherine 39; Herbert 481; Mary C. 481; Mr. 445, 687
HOLTON Alexander 133; Catherine Jane 133; Hart B. 133; John 133; Joseph Alexander 133; Margaret Ann 133; Mary 133; Susan 133; Thomas 133; Thomas 133; Thomas S. 133; W. L. 1; William 133; William B. 133; William Layton 133
HOLZMAN & Hunt 102
HOOD Mr. 678
HOOE Cecilia 378
HOOPER Ann C. (Birckhead) 176; Ann LeCompte 579; Anna 435; Anne E. 801; Bettie 176; Ella 607; Henry 733; James 356; John H. 176; Lucretia D. 226; Martha 617; Mary 733; Thomas 607
Hoopersborough farm 590
HOPKINS Addie 610; Agnes 82; Alaxine 739; Alice G. 359; Angeline 431; Annie (Cockey) 269; Annie 610; Ariana 683; Arthur 610; Benjamin 324, 685; Charles 228; Clara 269; Clara E. 82; D. Norman 685; David J. 685; Dennis 324; E. Atwell 269; E. C. 118; Edward 68, 269; Edward G. 82; Edwin C. 610; Eliza (Brooks) 610; Eliza B. 610; Elizabeth 269; Ellen 160; Elma 334; Esther 404; Ethel 610; Frances 68; Grace 324; Granville B. 82; Harrison 269; Harry J. 739; Henrietta 645; Henry P. 334; Hester A. 324; Hester Ann 324; J. Richard 610; James 68, 160, 269; James B. 269; James Bateman 359; James L. 324; James Morell 683; Jane B. 324; John 685; John W. 610; Joseph H. 610; Joseph R. 82; Josiah 82; Julia 324; Laura M. 294, 610; Margaret P. 610; Martha 324; Martha E. 324; Martha H. 324; Martha Virginia 111; Mary (Lowe) 683; Mary 685; Mary A. (Taylor) 685; Mary C. 798; Mary E. 118, 610; Matilda 228; Mrs. W.H.H. 101; Purnell J. 610; Rebecca 324; Robert 89; S. W. 324; Sally A. 295; Samuel 324, 645; Sara 324; Sarah A. 324; Sarah E. 610; Solomon S. 798; Thomas 82, 111, 295, 324; Thomas J. 610; U. D. 161; Unlan D. 610; W. D. 610; William 118, 294,
610; William D. 610; William H. H. 269; William J. 82
HOPPER --- 783; Catherine Virginia 41; Charles Cox 41; Daniel C. 41; Fannie 615; Frank W. 41; Henrietta 615, 783; Judge 51; Margaret 733; Philemon B. 41, 733; Philemon Blake 615; Ridgeley Thomas 41; Thomas W. 226; W. J. 301; Hooper & Woodall 39
HORN --- 579
Horn's Point 512
HORNER Ada E. 596; John W. 596; Mary J. 280; Melissa 280; Thomas 280
HORNEY Mary f. 412
HORSEY Addie C. 494; Albert C. 565; Albert R. 565; Alonzo R. 494, 565; Alonzo R., Jr. 494; Alula E. 399; Clara 125, 303; Clara L. 565; Edith L. 565; Edward 565; Eliza A. 125; Elleonora Keene 83; Eva M. 47, 125; Hanson 129; Harold 125; Henry 125; John C. 251; John H. 125; Joshua 565; Leah 565; Lillian H. 565; Madeline 565; Mary 125; Mary A. (Harris) 125; Mildred L. 494; Minnie 218; Mollie E. 251; Nathaniel 125; Nelsie E. 494; Norman 125; Palmer Keene 129; Pennington 125; Samuel S. 218; Stephen 565; T. H. 527; Thomas H. 129; Thomas Hopewell 129; Unit Rasin 129; W. C. 399; William G. 47, 125, 303; William P. 494, 565
HOSEA Sarah E. 512
HOSSINGER Joseph B. 505; Joseph H. 505; Lillian 505
HOULTON Mary T. 464
HOUSTON Augusta 489; B. F. 202; Benjamin 321; H. W. 623; Hannah 321; Henry H. 757; James 321, 466, 489, 490; M. T. 757; May 207
HOWARD Charles 492; Emma 458; H. B. 458; Harriet 614; Jacob 614; John 458; John Eager 492; Julia 599; Leah 614; Leah J. 501; Mary H. 458, 492; Miss 59; Mrs. M. Jennie 578
HOWARTH John T. 533; Levina 533
HOWES Abraham 764; Margaret 393, 764; William 764
HOWITH Geo 810; Mollie D. 810
HUBBARD Christina 611; Emma S. 86; Frank 509; Helen 86; J. P. J. 86, 611; Maria 611; Martha 611; P. Howard 86; Poulson E. 611; Winnie 86
HUBBELL Edward 452; Ella A. 452

-254-

HUBBERT Angeline 354; Ann M. (Coey) 354; Dorsey 354; Edward 753; Elmer 354; Eva 354; Frank H. 354; Hattie 354; Henry 354; Hooper 753; Irene 354; James 753; Joseph 354, 753; Martha 354; Mary 753; Mary J. 354; Michael 354; Michael 753; Orra 354; Peter 354; Thomas 354; Thomas 753; Thomas Michael, Jr. 753; Tilghman 753
HUBERT Joseph 752
HUDSON Adaline 592; Addie L. 313; Alfred Washington 313; Charles Henry 313; Edward 313; George 55; Henrietta 313; John 81; John R. 313; Kate 81; Mary Henrietta 313; Sarah 548; Sarah H. 55; Thomas A. 313, 592; Thomas F. 313; Walter 313; William J. 313
HUFF Fannie 352; Robert 352
HUFFMAN Axie 237; H. 237
HUGHES Henrietta 733; John 733; Margaret 733; Martha 165; Mary A. 631; Mr. 733; Rebecca 165; William 631
HUGHETT Lydia L. (Carter) 360; Mattie H. 360; William R. 360
HUGHLETT Mary E. 192; Sarah D. 61; William 192
HULL Edward 405; Nancy 405
Humphreys Chance 483
HUMPHREYS Arabella 74; Dr. 380; Elizabeth (Parsons) 392; Elizabeth 392; Eugene W. 392; Florine 392; Humphrey 392; Jennie 74; Lafayette 392; Mary 392; Randolph 392
HUNT Annie 370
HUNTER Edward N. 3; Ezekiel 59; F. Marion 3; James Milton 3; Justina 3; Margaret A. 3; Marion F. 3; Miss 59; Nathan 3; William 3; William W. 3; Zada A. 3
HUNTINGTON O. W. 460
HUNTSMAN Mary J. 743
HURLEY J. F. 493; Mrs. 277; Sarah 493
HURLOCK Willie Woolford 750; Adelaide 415; Almira 750; Amanda 587; Arrana 587; Ben Cator 750; Clarence S. 415; David 587; David T. 587; Eleanor 415; Florence 415; Henrietta 390; John S. 390; Mary 415; Mary Rebecca 415; Samuel 415, 587; Samuel S. 415; Sarah 587; Susie V. 750; Taney Lee 750; Valeria 750; William 750
HURST John 643John E. 661; John Fletcher 624; M. Augusta 643; Mrs. Emily 624; Stephen 624

HURTT Alice 740; Alice 758; Clifton 758; Edward 758; Edward D. 758; Edwin S. 758; Florence 758; Harry 758; James W. 758; James Freeman 758; Jas W. 758; Julia 758; Lizzie 758; Lucy 797; Martha A. 758; Mary E. 758; Rebecca 758; W. W. 740; Woodland 758
HUSBANDS Mary E. 89
HUTCHIN Mary 270
HUTCHINS Helen 437; Thomas 437
HUTCHINSON Atha 469; Charlotte 670; Ebenezer 469; Elizabeth 469; Emeline 469; John C. 469; Louisa C. 469; Manlius P. 469; Nancy A. 469; Sarah A. 469
HUTSON Ann P. 412; Catherine M. 412; Cora B. 412; Ella F. 412; Frank 412; Jacob 412; James 412; John 412; Kate 412; Lillian A. 412; Mary F. 412; N. Alexander 412; Noah Alexander 412; Sallie 412; William 412
HUYCK Burger 126; Cathalin Lammerse (Van Valkenburg) 126; Catharine (Bevier) 126; Girardus 126; Henric 126; Jan 126; Johannes 126; Magdalena (Quackenbush) 126; Mary (Pile) 126; Petrus 126
HYLAND Annie W. 10; Chester Arthur Gorman 10; Eliza 532; Elizabeth Grant 10; Emma E. 10; Harry H. 10; Henry M. 10; James C. 532; John 532; John Allen 10; Lambert 532; Maria Grant 10; Stephen 532; William A. 10
HYNSON Alice 752; Ann 752; Augusta Eccleston 110; C. L. 752; Caroline L. 752; Caroline Marsh 752; Col 30; Emma A. 752; George 752; Helen Eccleson 752; Mariana 752; Mary E. 446, 715; Richard 80, 110, 116, 346, 752; Richard D. 752; Richard Dunn 752; Thomas 752; Thomas B. 752; Thos Bowers 752; Thos C. 752

ICKES Margaretta 231; Nicholas 231
INSLEY Andrew 257; Angie 589; Elcanion 257; George C. 257; John H. 257; Joseph 589; Mary A. 257; Matilda 589; Melissa F. 257; Rhoda 257
IRANSHIRE Martha 795; William 795
IRELAND Anna W. 548; Charles 548; Charles T. 548; Henrietta 548; James T. 548; John C. 548; M. Howard 548; Mary 548; Page Worrell 548; Sarah 548; William Bryan 548

INDEX (to paragraph numbers)

IRONS Margaret A. 634; Mariam 634; Titus 634
IRVING Emily W. 408; Judge 408; T. H. 408
Irwin & Stinson 309
IRWIN A. D. & Brother 309; A. D. 72; Alexander Dickson 309; Alexander Dickson Jr. 309; Blanche 309; Florrie 309; Lillie 72, 309; Lizzie 309; Mabel 309; Rosanna 205; Rose 309; Rose E. 309; Samuel 205
ISLIN Adrian 513

J. J. Jump & Co. 167
JACKSON Abner 557; Alice P. 673; Andrew 509; Anne 557; Bell McCombs 250; Jackson Brothers Co 74; E. E. 74, 529; 673; Gov. 496; Helen 673; Hugh 673; Hugh 74; John J. 673; Mary 509; Mary 784; Mary B. 74; Sallie 250; Sarah (Humphreys) 74; Stonewall 393; W. H. 673; W. P. 74; Wilbur F. 673; William H. 74, 250; William Newton 250; William P. 250
JACOBS Annie 1; Bernice 320; Caroline B. 350; Caroline Browne 350; Dorothy 320; Dr. James K. Harper 1; George W. 320; Gladys D. 320; Jacob 320; James 320; James Kent Harper 350; James Paul 320; Jonathan 320; Lydia 71; Margaret 459; Mary E. 320; Naomi 320; Nehemiah 320; Robert 320; William 350; William H. 320; William Sr. 350
JAMES "Kiah" 559; Cornell 190; McGuire 68
JANS Annecke 372
JANVIER --- 547; Edwin P. 528, 547; Elizabeth 547; George 547; Louisa 528; Margaret 547; Mary 547; Thomas 547
JARMAN Eva 808; J. W. 808
JARRELL Addie 225, 622; Annie E. 398; Charles L. 398; Fannie C. 622; Josephine 291; Joshua R. 398; Louisa 398; Maggie E. 398; Margaret 628; Mary (Temple) 622; Mary A. 398; Mary T. 398, 622; Richard 622; Robert 225, 398, 622; Robert, Jr. 622; T. S. Noble 622; W. Frank 398; Wesley 398; William E. 398
Jarrell, Nichols & Cox 167
JARVIS Eliza 613

JEDSON Arminie 584; Arthur 584; Lydia 584
JEFFERSON Adelia M. 199; Caroline 199; Caroline T. 199; Charles W. 199; Edith 199; George H. 199; Robert K. 199; Roberta 199; Sarah E. 199; Thomas O. 199
JEFFREYS Sarah Ann 571; Ann J. 751; Edith D. 586; Edward 586; Elizabeth 586; Elizabeth Causey 586; Frances Hunter 586; George M. 9, 751; Mary 586; Thomas H. 586
JENNINGS Rosamond 205
JEROME Jesse 374; Phoebe 374
JESTER Florence 367; William 367
JEWELL Samuel 123; Sarah A. 123
JOHANNES John 676
JOHNS Ann 687
JOHNSON & Davis 66
JOHNSON Amelia Ross 617; Andrew 142; Ann 697; Anna Elizabeth 120; Annie 470; Annie Corinne 142; Anthony 19; Anthony H. 23; Araminta 166; Arthur H. 470; C. Lowndes 754; Catherine M. 23; Christy S. 754; Denwood 470; Dorcas 558; Edward B. 470; Edward C. 617; Elizabeth 402, 573; Elizabeth Ann W. 166; Elizabeth T. 754; Ella 774; Emily 518; Emma 617; Ernest M. C. 544; Evelyn M. 754; Ezeikiel 336; F. H. 120; F. P. Casey 754; Fannie W. 617; George P. 544; Helen 617; Henry 617; Herman Clayton 23; Herschel V. 697; Hilda 470; J. A. 76; James C. 544; 617; James H. 544; James N. 544; Jannie G. 754; John 774; Joseph H. 617; Joseph Marvin 617; Joshua 285, 558; Julia A. 285; Julius A. 754; Julius Christopher 754; Julius G. 754; L. E. 617; L. H. 541; L. Margaret 470; Loring 448; Lottie 470; Louisa Catherine 558; Lucy Rockwell 754; Margaret 544, 617, 643; Martha 617; Mary 470; Mary Frances 23; Mary P. 19; Maude 245; Mrs. Elbridge 643; Peter 528; Purnell 402, 544; Rebecca 594; Reverdy 774; Richard 19; Richard Bradford 23; Richard C. 23; Sallie 544; Sarah A. 528; Sarah J. 470, 544; Sewell 617; Sophia C. 754; Stonewall Jackson 23; Susan 470, 617; Susan E. 544; T. Fred 245; Theodore P. 544; Thomas 558; Tryphena 336; Virginia 9;

-256-

W. Clyde 470; W. J. 541; Wallace 617;
William 594; William E. 470
JOHNSTON Sidney 61
JOLLY Peter 785
JONES & Irving 114
JONES A. C. 714; A. W. 715; Aimee 63;
Amanda A. 729; Anna 402, 533; Annie
715; Arnold E. 532; Benjamin I. 220;
Caddie 715; Charles 715, 750; Charles
Irwin 72; Charles P. 72; D. P. 649;
Daisy 715; David 81; Deborah 93; Dr.
490; E. 714; Edgar A. P. 714; Edward
220; Edward B. 93; Eleanor 715; Elias
714; Elizabeth 81, 715; Elizabeth
Augusta 490; Elizabeth L. 222; Ella
390; Ellen 750; Ellen E. 72; Elmer
715; Emily C. (Atkinson) 63; Fannie
Jenetta 170; Fannie L. 93; Florence
715; George M. F. 715; George Perry
220; George W. 390; Georgia 220; Giles
55; Hannah 390; Harriet 222; Harvey
714; Henrietta 390, 658, 719; Hosanna
Rebecca 170; Hugh 83; Isaac D. 220; J.
W. S. 208; James R. 390; Jennie 710;
Jesse 390; Jessie 63; John 63; John C.
715; John W. 800; Jonathan 390; Joseph
R. 390; Josephine A. 807; Julia D.
288; Lavinia 345; Levin D. 220; Lillie
309; Lucretia 532; Lucy R. 390; Lydia
390; Maggie 390; Mamie 715; Marcellus
715; Margaret 206; Margaret M. 361;
Maria S. (Jones) 220; Martha (Handy)
222; Martha J. (Bramble) 710; Martin
L. 345; Mary 102, 123, 220, 456, 573,
714; Mary C. 800; Mary E. 642, 715;
Mary L. 208; Mary Rebecca 15; Minnie
715; Miss 485; Naomi 649; Nellie 750;
Paul 72, 309; R.C. 206; Regina M. 374;
Richard 715; Robert H. 222; Robert H.
Jr. 222; Sallie C. 715; Samuel 220,
275; Samuel B. D. 220; Samuel T. 715;
Samuel W. 719; Sarah Amanda 715; Sarah
B. 220; Sarah M. 390; Susan 220; Susan
A. 365; T. R. 288; Thomas 222; Thomas
J. 642; Thomas Jr. 63; Thomas W. 63;
William 63, 390, 715; William P. 361;
Willianana 220; Z. D. 310; Z. F. 710
JOSEPH Rebecca 567; Thomas 567
JOY Florence 733
JUDSON Harry P. 112; Susie C. 112
JUMP Alanby 739; Alexander 647; Alfred
238; Allerby 238; Ann Maria 238; Belle
C. 647; C. M. 646, 748, Charles
C. 647; Clara E. 641; Edward P. 805;
Elizabeth (Pratt) 238; Elizabeth 647;
Elizabeth E. 647; Ella 647; Fred P.
739; Harriet 739; Harry L. 739; Henry
739; Ida 627; Indiana 238; Jane 386;
John 647, 805; John T. 238; Julia 238;
Kate 238; Laura 647; Louisa 647; Loula
M. 646; Lydia A. 647; Maggie A. 739;
Mary E. 128, 805; Mary H. 748,
Mollie E. 647; Robert 238, 739; Robert
B. 647; Robert C. 741; Robert H. 641;
Robert J. 381, 647; Samuel E. 805;
Sarah E. 647; Stephen P. 739; Thomas
Henry 647

KALER Rebecca 564
KAVANAGH Christiana 682
KAY Clarence M. 26; J. Hutchinson 26;
Samuel W. 26; William R. 26
KEARNS Elizabeth 628
KEATING Arthur B. 32; B. Palmer 32;
Elizabeth 32; Elizabeth J. (Palmer)
38; Frank 32; Henry Webster 32;
Michael 32, 38; Paul 38; Thomas J. Jr
32; Thomas J. Sr 32, 38; William 38
KEEN Henrietta 733; John Richard 733;
Lulu 96
KEENE Allie 746; Ann M. 746; Annie
768; B. J. 419; Bernard Louis 154;
Clarence A. 154; E. A. 746; Edwin T.
154; Eleanor 746; Eliza E. 70; Emily
A. 746; Eugenia 419; John 746; John
Henry 768; Lewis 750; Louis B. 154;
Mary (Meekins) 419; Mary Ann 154, 768;
Mary C. 154; Mrs. William 70; Robert
B. 668; S. A. 746; Saml Y. 768; Samuel
768; Samuel Clinton 154; Sarah 768;
Sarah C. 668; Susie 750; Susie L. 154;
Thomas K. 70; Thomas H. 746; Vachel
768; Vachel J. 154, 419; William Cyril
154; William Jennings Mace 154
KEISER --- 649
KEITHLEY Hester A. R. 209
KELLEY Amos 413; C. I. 809; Charles H.
77, 809; Dennis 77, 509, 809; Dollie
Elizabeth 509; Edith I. 77, 809;
Edvina 128; Elender 509; Elizabeth
509; Ella 413; Elmer 77, 809; Ernest
261; Everett C. 77, 809; Ezekiel 509;
Georgeanna 509; Glencoe K. 77, 809;
Grace A. 413; Harry P. 413; Henrietta
E. 413; Hester A. (Trice) 509; Hester
A. 509; Ida May 261; J. Horton 128;
John 128; Jonah 509; Jonah F. 509;
Joseph Springle 509; Julia Smith 509;

INDEX (to paragraph numbers)

Julielma M. 509; Leona 809; Lincoln Daniel 509; Louisa 179; Mary (Harmon) 809; Mary (Harrison) 77; Mary 509; Mary A. 509; Mrs. J. H. 740; Orlan T. 77, 809; Perry 509; Rebecca 509; Sir William 509; Susan (Hildbrandt) 413; Tilghman E. 77, 809; William 128, 509; William H. 413; William T. 509; William T., Jr. 509
KELLY Amos 577; Elizabeth 200; Hallie Chambers 577; J. Horton 128; Laura 100; R. R. 100; Rachel J. 175; Sallie 188; William 175
KELSO Thomas 407
KEMP --- 214; Albert H. 404; Alfred 360; Caroline T. 199; Cecilia 236; Charles A. 404; Edward D. 733; Elenor 404; Eliza 733; Elizabeth (Hardcastle) 360; Elizabeth 733; Elma 414; Esther 404; Evelina 454; Fannie K. 404; Harry 613; Helen D. 404; Hester A. 404; James 733; John 131, 236; John H. C. 404; John H. C. Jr. 404; John W. 404; Joseph 789; Joseph O. 404; Louisa 404; Mary 131, 613; Mary A. 789; Mattie H. 360; Miss 131; Robert E. 199; Sally 404; Samuel T. 360, 454; Sarah 199; 733; Susan 131; Susan E. 138, 404; Thomas 404; William T. 404
Kemp--- 360
KENDALL Ada 652; Agnes 649; Alice M. 649; Amos 652; Arthur 652; Asa 652; Azariah 649; Caroline 652; Cattie L. 649; Clara O. 649; Clara P. 649; Eliza 649; Ellen 652; Horace 649, 652; J. Thomas 649; James 649; Joseph 256, 652; Julia Marie 649; Laura M. Hope 256; Louise 652; Lula 652; Mary 652; Mary E. 116, 713; Nancy 652; Naomi 649; Nora 652; Omar 652; Perpetua 649; Thomas W. 652
KENNARD Anna Maria 781; B. H. 370; Dr. 546; Elizabeth 777; Elizabeth Thomas 781; Margaret 370; Mary E. 707; Richard 777; S. C. 370; Samuel 678; Samuel Thomas 781; Sarah 422
KENNEDY Commodore 518; Ellen E. 302; George Scott 302; Mary 518; Matilda E. 636
KENNELY --- 368
KENNERLY Aurelia 491; Caleb 491; Eleanor 491; Elennor 465; Henry 491; James W. 465; Julia Ann 491; Mary 491;

Octavia E. 465; Samuel W. 465; William Alexander 465; William L. 465
KENT --- 350; Elizabeth 204; John 564; Lilian 564; Maria Smyth 254; Richard 204; Thomas 254
KENTON Miss 63
KER Patty 323
KERR Amanda 281; Amanda C. 274; Andrew 323; Charles Goldsborough 773, 774; David 774; Edward Leeds 773; Eliza J. 274; Elizabeth (Gates) 274; Elizabeth Goldsborough 773; Elizabeth Greenbury Goldsborough 773, 774; Ella 774; Ella Johnson 774; Henrietta Maria 774; J. W. 109, 281; Jessie V. 274; John Bozman 774; John Leeds 773, 774; John Leeds 779; Jonathan W. 274; Martha 323; Mary 325; Mary Bowie 774; Rachael Ann 774; Rachael Leeds 774; Samuel C. 774; Sarah A. 274; Sarah Hollyday 774; Sarah Hollyday 779; Sophia 774; Sophia G. 274; William 274
KERSEY 607
KEY Francis S. 492
KEYS Mary R. 514; Thomas 514
KEYSER Eleanor S. 331; L. J. 331
KILBURN Barkley 413; Henrietta E. 413
KIMB George B. 471
KING Elizabeth Barnes 85; Henry 677; Thomas 85
Kingston Hall 85
KIRBY Annie M. 562; D. C. 792; Edward 68; Emma 562; Florence 68; Frances 68; Isabel 562; John D. 68, 562; Laura 562; Lavenia 562; M. E. (Miss) 496; Mary (Carville) 68, 562; Nicholas 68, 562; Nicholas B. 68; Rebecca 68, 562; Samuel 68, 562
KIRK James 543
KIRWAN Benjamin F. 158; Charles E. 345; Fanny 158; James E. 345; John 158; Lamuel 345; Lavinia 345; Lemuel 345; Maggie 345; Martha 158; Mary 158; Mary Rebecca 345; Sophia 345; Thmas 158; Thomas H. 158; William H. H. 345
Klund Farm 708
KNOCK Anne 346; Anne B. 80; Jesse 80
KNOTTS Estella 121; George 121; Gurney 121; Herbert 121; James T. 121; James V. 121; Katie E. 121; Mary O. 121; Roland 121
KNOVERSHOE Catherine 312

-258-

KNOWLES George R. 620; John 620; Lizzie E. 620; Mary 620; William H. 620
Knox farm 390
KORTRIGHT Lady 448
KRUGER Charles 564; Emma 564
KRUSEN Benjamin 216; C. B. 175; Christian B. 216; Emma 216; Garrett 216; Gustavus B. 216; Henry 216; John 216; Mary E. 216; Nellie 216; Virmadella 216; William 216; William H. 216
La VALLETTE Albert T. Jr. 718; Amy 718; Amy K. 718; Bron de foix 718; Elie A. T. 718; Jean Louis De 718; Ruth 718
LACKEY Alexander 765; Anne 207; Martha Ann 765; Thomas 207
LAING Agnes H. 703; Helene (Lauder) 703; Robert 703
LAIRD Martha 776; Martha J. 191; Philip 776; William Winder 393; Williamina E. C. (Goldsborough) 39; Williamina Elizabeth Cadwalader 77; Winder 776; William 776; William Henry 776
LAKE --- 605; Charles 190; Clara 190; Clara S. 190; Cordelia 190; Hattie Pattison 190; Miss 674; Virginia Cowart 190; Washington 190; William W. 190
LAMB Mary 592; Sarah 592
LAMBDEN Emily F. 240; Mary E. 644; Mrs. Samuel J. 644; Sallie A. 644; Samuel J. 644
LAMBDIN Catherine (Lowe) 308; Mary E. 140; Susie 308; William 308
LAMBERT Sarah A. 329
LANDFORD B. Frank 229; George W. 229
LANDOFF 581
LANEY Nannie 808
LANGFORD Benjamin 210; Emily 210; Lizzie 210; Mary A. G. 210; Sarah E. 210
LANGRELL Lulu 237
LANKFORD Amanda E. 229; B. Louis 229; B. Frank 229; Benjamin 229, 388; Benjamin Sr. 229; Clarence P. 388, 479; Cornelia J. 229; Ella 229; Emily Estelle 479; George W. 229; H. Fillmore 388, 479; Henry 388; Henry S. 229, 388, 479; Ida A. 388; John P. 530; Julia 229; Lazarus 229; Lewis 598; Marion D. 388; Martha 598; Mary (Lankford) 598; Mary D. 388, 479; Mary G. 530; Mary M. 229; Matilda A. 229; Milton S. 229; Mollie 556; Priscilla P. 479; Sallie V. 229; Sarah 530; Sarah A. 229; Smith 642; Susan 229, 598; William F. 229; William T. 229
LARABEE Maria 131; Susan 131
LARAMORE Bedford 92; Florence Virginia 92
LARD James W. 318; Lizzie 318
LASOURD Gen. 477
LATIMER Henry 678; J. W. 12; James 678; James Marshall 12; John Ford 12; John William 12; Joseph 12; Joseph N. B. 12; Margaret 678
LAUNT Catherine 423
LAW George 372
LAWRENCE Capt. 733; Miss 733
LAWS Catherine 400; Charles E. 400; Clarence 400; Elijah 400; Gertrude 400; Ida G. 400; James 400; James R. T. 400; John M. 400; Lillian M. 400; Margaret L. 400; Mary 400; Mary J. 400, 537; Sallie M. 400; William 400; William L. 400; William W. 400
LAWSON Alice 722; Eveline 342; Grace 534; Isaac 488; John W. 342; Leah 756; Mary 756; Mary S. 488; Octavia E. 756; Samuel 756; Samuel L. 756; Sarah F. 756; Thomas H. 756; William T. 722
LAWTON Henry S. 216; Mary E. 216
LAY Bishop 350
LAYTON Catherine Jane 133; Judge 453; Tilghman 133
Le COMPTE Clara H. 737; Stephen R. 737
Le COUNT Rowena V. 493; S. B. 493
LEARY Christiana 171; Columbus 28; Columbus A. 171; Elmer E. 28; George 28, 171; George E. 28, 171; Henry 171; Isaac 171; James 171; Joseph 171; Mary (Sims) 28; Mary 171; Oregon 171; Susan 171
LEATHERBURG Charles 283; Elinor 429; Harry B. 283; Hettie 283; James 283; James L. 283; John 283; Leaven 283; Lettie 283; Lillian N. 283; Matilda (Wingate) 283; Mazie 283; Nellie 283; Robert 283; Robert L. 283; William K. 283
LeCOMPT Frances 457
LeCompte --- 70
LeCOMPTE Ann LeCompte 579; Anthony 539, 579; Augustus 762; Daniel 579;

INDEX (to paragraph numbers)

Daniel H. 539; Elizabeth 579; Emily 311; Esther 539, 579; Henrietta (Nichols) 112; Isaiah 539; James 614; James Anna 614; Jeremiah 579; Lavina 579; Lizzie 161; Margaret 539; Margaret N. 539; Mary Hester 112; Mary L. 539; Miss 674; Moses 579; Mrs. T. M. 757; Nancy 579; Priscilla Elizabeth Pattison 57; Robert A. 161; Rose 762; Samuel E. 539; Solomon S. 112; Thomas 539, 579; Thomas I. 539; William G. 539
LEDNUM Ebenezer 385; Eleanor 385; John 385; Mary (Stafford) 385; Thomas 385; William 385
LEE Abraham 420; Claude 420; Dodson 420; Edmond J. 772; Emma 420; Henrietta Bedinger 772; Hoburg 420; James 459; Maggie A. 739; Margaret 459; Mary 420; Maude 420; Milcah (Bridges) 420; Miss 518; Mr. 513; Richard Bland 518; Robert 410; Robert E. 460; Sarah 489; W. T. H. 420; William T. 739
LEGG Ann 621; Annie 486; Caroline 217; Clintonia 217; Eliza 649; Emma J. 228; Etta C. 217; Harriett 241; Henry 371; J. H. C. 217; Jacob 228, 486; James R. 341; John C. 217; Louisa 708; Maggie S. 217; Marietta 217; Rebecca 545; Susan 341, 371; Virginia 228; William H. 721; William Henry 217
LEIGH Mr. 774; Sophia 774
LELAND Fabricius 79; Lucy R. 656; Rebecca 79
LEONARD C.R. 62; Clara 62; Henrietta 641; Mary E. 626; Mary L. 626; Nathaniel 195; Nicholas B. 626
LESSLIE Ellen K. 782
LEVERTON Jacob 225; Jacob 763; Ruth (Hannah) 763; Ruth 763; Ruth H. 225
LEWES Elizabeth 805
LEWIS Abraham 406, 717; Agnes Q. 473; Albert 473; Anna May 25; Celia 406; Clara 473; Clarence N. 473; Ella 473; Eva 473; Evan 25; F. 805; Fannie 473; Francis 473; Francis A. 83; Grace R. 473; Hamilton 451; Hattie 473; Henry R. 25, 411; Howard L. 473; Jacob F. 25; James 473; James B. 473; James R. 473; John L. 473; Lizzie 451; Lovey 406; Maria Stocker 83; Mary E. 473; Nellie 473; Rachel 25; Raymond 473;

Ruth 473; Sella 717; Stephen 25; T. H. 451; Walter 473; William 473
LIGHTBOURN Elizabeth 331; J. H. 331
LINDSAY Cora A. 585
LINTHICUM Aline Estelle 568; Benjamin J. 568, 716; Charles 716; F. P. 568; F. Percy 568; Henrietta P. 293; Henry 716; Josiah 716; Mary E. 716; Richard 568, 716; Richard Lee 568; Samuel 568; Susan A. 568; William 716; Zachariah 293
LLANDAFF Farm 120
LLEWELLYN Mary Georgina 731; Rev Dr. 731
LLOYD --- 214, 677; Alice 492; Alicia 492; Ann 767; Ann Grundy 779; Anna Maria 352, 687; Annie 214; Annie G. 214; Bertha J. 214; C. Howard 492; Catharine 674; Christopher C. 214; Col 76; Daniel 5, 34, 674; Deborah 767; DeCoursey 492; Edgar L. 214; Edward 5, 76, 490, 492, 586, 669, 678, 775; Edward Jr. 679; Elizabeth 492; Elizabeth R. 679; Francis J. 214; Governor 5, 661; Henrietta Maria 779; Henry 5, 529; Henry Jr. 5; James 767, 779; John Eager 492; Kate Henry 5; Kittie 5; Mary 214, 492; Mary Campbell 5; Mary Ellen 775; Mary H. 492; McBlair 492, 586, 669; Mollie 214; Mrs. 679; Robert G. 214; Sally S. 492; Sara Scott Murray 775; Sarah 76; Upshur 5; Virginia B. 669
Lloyd, Blaine & Co. 214
LLOYD Estate 594
LOCKERMAN Andrew 2; Emily 611; Maggie 2; Susan Hall 777; T. R. 405; W. T. A. 611
LOCKWOOD Araminta (Day) 61; Caleb 61; Gen. 532; Mary Ann 61; Richard 39
LOE Emma 507; James E. Jr. 507
LOLLEE Temperance A. 337
LOLLER Daniel 527; Ella F. 527
LONG Clara A. 132; Edwin M. 66; Ella Hall 66; George W. 517; Lethy 132; Mr. 542; Orinthia 639; Rhoda 560; Sallie 642; Sarah 401; Sarah Matilda 670
LOOCKERMAN Anna 777; Annie 263; Francis S. 263; Jacob 777; John 777; Mary 263; Mary Skinner 777; Sallie W. 263; Stanley B. 2631 Vincent 777; Washington C. 263

-260-

LOOMIS Ellen 503; Francis E. 503; Grace M. 503; Herbert F. 503; Lucy (Frances) 503; Marshall M. 503
LOPER Charles P. 743; Howard L. 743; Lillian 743; Lindon 743; Mary E. 743; Mary J. 743; William H. 743
LORD Annie E. 300; John 781; Lucy 781; Richard W. 300
LOUD Hallie E. 181; Robert 181
LOVE Dr. W. S. 62; Matilda 589
LOWE A. 366; Ada G. 366; Albert 558, 572; Ann Catherine 572; Carroll 572; Dorcas 798; Dorcas Elizabeth 558; Enoch 572; Enoch Louis 697; Esma 339; Esther 697; Fannie K. 404; Lowe farm 423; Florence 757; Francis Wrightson 572; Frank 366; George 483; J. M. 798; Jackson 507; James 558; James E. 507; James F. 570; James Marion 558, 572; John 483, 558; John S. 483; John Thomas 572; Joseph 404, 572; Lydia 750; M. Ella 339; Margaret (Records) 339; Maria (Palmer) 507; Mary 558; Mary Ann (Wrightson) 558; Mary Ann 483; Mary Anne 572; Mary F. 366, 572; Mary Graham 572; Mary Roseline 572; Minnie 621; Reba 572; Ruth 483; Samuel 483; Sarah 702; Sarah Elizabeth 572; Seth 572; Susan 570; Susannah (Haddaway) 572; Whitely 483; Wilber Fisk 572; William E. 558, 572; William Webb 558. 572; Wilson 757; Wrightson 572
LOWELL Elizabeth 471
LOWERY Alexander C. 409; Annie 409; Claude 409; Eliza 409; Elizabeth E. 409; Emma K. 409; Florence M. 409; Harriet D. 409; Joseph Owens 409; Lulu 409; Margaret 409; Maria L. 409; Mary Ann 409; Mary E. 409; Mary Emeline (Walters) 409; Mrs. J.O. 101; Sarah Frances 409; William 409; William A. 409; William D. 409; William Owens 409; William S. 409
LOWNDES Anna P. 76; Catherine M. 76; Charles 76, 754; Charles H. G. 76; Christopher 76; Elizabeth 76; Elizabeth T. 754; Lloyd 5, 76; Mary Catherine 76; Sarah L. 76; Sarah Scott 76
LUCAS Lottie M. 431; William B. 431
LUSBY Amelia 186; Clay 71; Edward 71; Ella E. 71; Harry Clay 71; Herbert 71; James 186; John 71, 186; Josiah 630, 790; Laura A. 790; Lynwood 71; Mary Ellen 186; Raymond 71; Robert 186; Robert J. 186; Sarah 630; William 71; William T. 186
LUX Darby 783; Eleanora Dall 783; Mary 783
LYNCH Anne 654; Araminta 27; C. G. 373; Christopher G. 695; David 664; Elizabeth 607, 625, 695; Harry F. 695; J. Dudley 695; J. Holton 695; James P. 695; Kate E. 607; Mary Elizabeth 570; Mrs. C. G. 625; Olivia 373; Sarah E. 695; Willard N. 695; William 607
LYNN Ida M. 603; William 603

MacBETH James W. 319; Jessie Guthrie 319
MACE ---750; Annie 750; Annie W. 481; Benjamin 750; Charles 750; Della 750; Edwin 750; Elen 750; Eliza B. 750; Elizabeth 190, 750; George A. 750; Hannah C. 750; Harry 750; Irving 750; John 481; 750; John A. 750; John S. 750; John W. 150, 750; Kate 750; Margaret 750; Netie 750; Phoebe 750; Susie L. 154; Thomas 750; Valeria 750; Valerie 150; William 750; Willie 750
MACHEN & Gittings 192
MACKEY Emma C. 709
MACKLEN Charles 252; Mary M. 252
MADDOX Clara U. 556; Daniel 556; Daniel James 556; Elizabeth 556; Ella 556; George W. 556; Gustavus A. 556; Joseph G. 556; Laura H. 556; Lazarus 556; Mollie 556; Robert F. 556; Robert H. 556; Sarah E. 556; Susan 556; William 556; William E. 556
MAGNESS Harriet 371
Maiden Point 706
MAKEMIE Francis 448
MALLALIEU Ann J. 751; Annie J. 9; Clara S. 751; Elwood R. 9; Emily 751; Esther 751; George H. 751; George Henry 9; James M. 9, 751; Jemima 751; John 9, 751; John F. 751; John J. 9; John T. 751; Joseph 9, 751; Joshua Clifton 9; Mary 9, 751; Mary J. 751; Mary R. 751; Nettie 751; Salie M. 751; Samuel 9, 751; Sarah 751; Thomas 9, 751; W. M. Warner 751; William Thomas 9; Willie 751
MALONEY Mary E. 320
MALSBERGER Agnes R. 23; Elizabeth 27

INDEX (to paragraph numbers)

MANN Fannie W. 617; Jacob 617; Joseph H. 508; Maggie P. 508; Margaret 508; Mary E. 508; Mary J. 508; Minnie 715; Samuel 715; Walter C. 508; Walter G. 508
MANNING Charlotte 254
MANSHIP A. 324; Hester Ann 324
Maple Grove farm 557
MARBLE Clara 326
MARINE Catherine 386; Martha 354; Matthew 354
MARRIET Annie 226; James Jr. 226
MARSH C. L. 752; Elias 752; Mary (Eccleson) 752; Thomas 489, 490
MARSHALL Bond P. 756; Dr. Thomas I. 12; Emily Estelle 479; Ida A. 388; Mary 533, 756; Miss 123; Sallie 632; William 632
MARTIN Ann 786; Daniel 733, 785; Edward 785; Edward D. 371; Elizabeth 454; Lavinia 733; Luther 750; Mary Ann 733; Mary Ennalls 786; Thomas 786; Thomas Oldham 733; Willie 750
MARVIL J. Dallas 620; Joshua H. 620
Maryland Steamboat Co. 491
MASLIN Mollie 241
MASON Clara 62; Frank 62; Frank C. 62; Henry M. 733; James 62; James Alexander 62; John 62; Lola 62; Mahala 62; Martha 733; Mary E. 90; William 62; William P., 62
MASSEY Addeson 103; Anne Marie 393; Benjamin Franklin 103; C. H. B. 519; Caroline 103; Charles H. B. 103; Charles Henry Bedford 103; Eben T. 103; Elijah 103; Elijah E. 346; Elizabeth 103; Ellen 449; Emily Alphonsa 346; Emily Ann 103; George O. 103; George W. 103; Herman B. 103; Hugh 103; James 103; Joshua 103; Lord 103; Major 226, 562; Mary 346; Mary Ella 103; Nicholas 103; Pamelia 103; Peter 103; Susan E. 103, 519; William 393
Massey's Venture 103
MASSILTON Elizabeth 71
MATHER A. W. 260; Sarah 260
MATHEWS Annie 344; Annie S. 208; Charles 344; Ettie L. 208; Helen M. 208; Henrietta 208; Herbert M. 208; James 208; Mary L. 208; Stanley W. 208; Stewart 208; Susan E. 208; Thomas A. 208

MATTHEWS Albert E. 600; Alexander 600; Ann 733; Anne 600; Ellan A. 55; Emory 600; Ephraim 55; Henry S. 600; I. T. 259, 452; Irving T. 55; Joseph 123; Julia L. 55, 259; Leah 55; Lelia 55; Margaret 508; Rev Dr. 733; S. C. 508; Sarah H. 55; Susanna 600
MAUCK Edward 534
MAVITT Carrie 506; Thomas W. 506
MAXWELL M.A. 42; Mrs. W.W. 37; William S. 42
MAY Effie 87; John T. 87; Sallie 87; W. F. 575; William F. 87
MAYER Alfred M. 772; Catherine Duckett 772
McALLEN R. J. 655; W. A. 655
McARTHUR Arthur 200
McBLAIR Alicia 492; Michael 492
McCALLMONT Mary 781
McCART Indiana 238; Samuel 238
McCARTER Arthur 200; Charles H. 200; Eliza 200; Elizabeth 200; James Edward 200; James Elwood 200; James M. 200; John 200; Margaret 200; Marshall 200; Mary Jane (Mayland) 200; Mary P. 200; Minnie 200; Ralph 200; Samuel H. 200
McCARTY Maggie A. 209
McCAULEY Agnes 808; Andrew W. 808; B. J. 628; Bernard J. 808; Bernard R. 808; Cecelia 808; Dennis 808; Dennis J. 808; Edwin D. 808; Ella A. 808; Francis A. 808; George H. 808; Granville 808; Holle Genevieve 808; Jerome H. 808; Lester B. 808; M. Augustus 808; Mary 808; Nellie E. 808; Simon H. 808; Theresa 808
McCEENEY Martha E. 324
McCLOUD Florence 708
McCOLLISTER Evelina H. 41
McCOMBS Sallie 250
McCONKEY Caroline Augusta 733
McCREADY Benjamin 550; Edward 550; Elizabeth 550; G. S. 550; Ira 550; John 550; Love 550; Robert 550; Sidonia V. 550; Stephen 462; Susan 462; Susie 550
McCULLEY J.E. 53
McCUR John S. 447
McDANIEL Alice 798; Ann (Wrightson) 558; Ann 798; Anna 798; Anna R. 160; Dorcas E. 798; Dorcas Elizabeth 558; Frank W. 798; Hester A. 324; James E. 798; James M. 798; John 558; John S. 798; John W. 160; John W. S. 798;

-262-

Laughlin 558; Lewis A. 798; Mary 558; Mary L. 798; Mary Lowe 558; Mary M. 798; Mary V. 798; Sarah 798; Wesley Sedgwick 558; William R. 798
McDANIELS Matilda 606
McFADDEN John 124; Maria J. 124
McFADDIN J. D. 502; Margaret 502
McFEELEY H. 625; Martha 625
McFEELY Miriam 592; Mrs. William Harper 615; P. T. 592
McGAW George K & Co. 41
McGINNIS E. L. 713; Julia A. 712; Mollie 713
McGINNISS E.L. 116; Mary 116
McILVAIN --- 679; Cora B. 412; Edward M. 679
McKELL Anna 780
McKENNA Catherine E. 411; Ellen 411
McKENNEY Eleanor Ridgely 1; General 422; John 1, 350; Nannie 350; Rev James 1; Samuel 1; Thomas Loraine 1; William 1, 133, 350, 688
McKENNY Wm 320
McKNETT Chas 762; J. E. 762; John 762; Joseph 762; Josephine 762; Magie 762; May 762; Robert A. 762; Rose 762; Sarah 762; Thomas 762
McMASTER Annie G. 214; Ella 456; Ellen 573; S.S. 214; William 573; William S. 456
McNAMARA L.S. 118
McNEAL Annie R. 759; Archibald 759; Caroline K. 759; Elizabeth (Benny) 759; Elizabeth 759; Gertrude 759; Hector 759; Henry G. Budd 759; James 759; James H. 759; James Hector 759; Jonathan Benny 759; M. Luisa 759; Martha V. 759; Mary C. 759; Sarah E. 759
McPHALEY Harry 373; Martha 373
McQUARY Mary 420; Thomas J. 420
McQUAY Sarah A. 582
McSHANE Catherine E. (McKenna) 411; Catherine V. 411; Charles E. 411; Frank P. 411; Mary E. 411; Patrick H. 411
McSHERRY Richard 754
McSORLEY Mrs. Rev. G. C. 451
McTEER Dr 1; Madge 1
MEDFORD Daisy 635; Dora A. 635; Edith 635; Edwin E. 270; Hersilla (Hicks) 270; John 635; Lovey 635; Mary 270; Mary A. 270; Nathaniel 635; Ottis 635; Rebecca (Payne) 635; Robert W. 635;
Sarah 166, 635; Seldon P. 270; Thomas Hicks 270; Watson 635; William 635; William H. 270
MEEKINS Caroline 443; Dennard 419; John 468; Laura 419; Lewis B. 419; Mary 419; Mary Ann 154; Mary J. 60; Mary Jane 468; Mary P. 578; Samuel 419; Samuel G. 443
MEGINNISS Adelaide 415
MELVIN Elizabeth 339
MERCUR Judge 372
MEREDITH Mary 653
MERICAN Elmina 559; Harry R. 559
MERRICK Anna Isabel 640; Annie 57; Ardilla 159; Caroline 149; Daniel 159; Drusilla 159; Frances M. 628; Henrietta 159; James 640; M. Barton 159; Maj. 640; S. K. 149; Samuel B. 159; Samuel K. 159; William S. 159
MERRILL --- 677; Alfred D. 644; Annie 644; Bettie M. 609; C. Beulah 644; Charles O. 240; George S. 361; Harriet 644; Henry T. 644; I. H. 677; I. Harrison 644; Isaac Harrison 644; John S. 644; Julia 644; Julia C. 644; Levin 644; Levin H. 644; Marietta 240; Mary E. 644; Minnie D. 644; Sadie P. 644; Sallie A. 644; Sarah A. 210; William J. 644
MERRITT Abigail 323; Addie Kerr 323; Adeline Carr 619; Adeline K. 323; Anna Rebecca (Brown) 178; Arthur 676; Benjamin 323, 758; Benjamin G. 323; Benoni 323; Caroline R. 323; Eliza Jane 323; Eliza Pleasanton 323; Ephraim 323; Florence Katherine 323, 749; Frances Olivia 93; George A. 323; Georgetta 323, 619; Hannah 323, 619; Harriet 1; James Black 323, 619, 749; James Jr. 174; Jay Bee 323; John 1, 323; Joseph 323; Joseph T. 178; Juliana 676; Margaret A. 676; Margaretta Boone 323; Maria 1; Maria Ambrose 1; Martha 323; Martha A. E. (Webb) 130; Mary 323; Mary A. 178; Mary Ann 323; Mary Anna 93; Patty 323; Rebecca 323, 758; Samuel 323; Samuel A. 323; Samuel Webb 323, 619, 749; Thomas 130, 323; Thomas A. 323; William 1, 323; William K. 323
MESSICK Columbus 333; Maggie 333; Octavia E. 465; Warren 465

-263-

INDEX (to paragraph numbers)

MEYER August 521; Charles W. 521; Katie 521; Lelan Winfield 521; Mary 521; Willie R. 521
MEZZICK Amelia 268; Elijah T. 268; George Marion 268; George W. 268; Herbert 268; Margaret 268; Nelson 268; Susan 268
MIDDLETON Chas 682; Mary 682
MILBOURN Sarah Matilda 527
MILBOURNE Addie 265; Lewis 265; Lewis M. 265; Louisa 265; Margaret 265; Mary (Peyton) 265; Mary 265; Mary E. 265; Nathan 265; Robert H. 265; Samuel J. 265; Sarah 265; Sidney F. 265; William 265
MILBURN S. T. 704
MILES ---- 347; Adalia C. 232; Alonzo L. 232; Annie E. 347; Aurelia F. 232; Aurinthia A. 399; Caroline 218; Carrie E. 347; Christiana 232, 500; Corinne E. 598; Daniel 796; Eda E. 347; Eleanor (Ballard) 265; Eliza J. 232; Elizabeth 232; Florence 598; Florence M. 347; Henry 232, 500; Henry Sr. 232; Jennie F. 601; John H. 399; John Thomas 232; Joshua 362, 397; Joshua W. 232, 397; Joshua Weldon 500; Lillian H. 347; Lillian M. 500; Louisa 265; Luther T. 232, 598; Luther T. Jr. 347; Mary M. 229; Mrs. Samuel 229; Nancy 651; Robert 229; Samuel S. 265; Sarah 232; Sarah A. 229; Southey F. 232, 500, 601; Southey F., Jr. 232; Susie E. 796; W. E. 598; William 500, 651; William E. 232; William Henry 232
MILLER Alexander 780; Alice 98; Ann Van Bokken 83; Annie (Tylor) 126; Charles 241; Emily T. 166; Fannie 780; Harriett 241; Jennie 241; John 98; Joseph F. 361; Marcus P. 83; Marion 241; Marion T. 241; Michael 241; Mollie 241; Mrs. E. C. 4; Pieter Wonter Van Der 650; Sophia 361; William M. 241
MILLINGTON Elizabeth 62
MILLS Angeline 710; Annie 750; Evelyn R. 127; Frank D. 650; Henry W. 567; Jennie 710; John Bibb 650; John C. 265; John G. 127, 617; John O. 710; John S. 650; Joseph L. 650; Joseph Levin 650; Joseph S. 650; Levin 650; Malachi 710; Margaret 265; Marie 650; Marietta 650; Mary A. 650; Mary M. 127; Robert P. 710; Rebecca 710; Ruth 483; Susan 710; Susan A. 75; Thomas 75; Viola 567; William A. 710; William C. 483; William H. 127; William P. 650; William R. 710
MISTER Bennett 188; Biddy 416; Keziah 188
MITCHELL Caroline 692; Charles 539; Elizabeth 692; Ella 1; George E. 692; George T. 692; Horace 692; Ida T. 426; Isaac 78, 692; John P. 78; John S. 426, 692; Lemuel L. 78; Lemuel P. 78; Lottie 78; Marion R. 78; Martha (Long) 162; Mary A. 692; Olive 692; Rev James A. 1; Sallie P. 78; Sallie R. 536; Sarah 78, 679; Sidney J. 78; Thurman 692; Victor 692; William C. 692
MOBRAY Ada G. 501; Alfred J. 501; George W. 501; John Lord 501; Laura E. 501; Leah J. 501; Leah L. 501; Levin 501; Levin W. 501; Levin, Jr. 501; Mary L. 501; Robert W. 501; Thomas 501
MOBRY Lizzie 578
MOFFETT Catherine R. 205
MOLER Mary 444
MONEY Benjamin 415; Mary Rebecca 415
MONTAGUE Allie 437; Anne 437; Correna 437; Daniel 437; Elizabeth 437; Emma 437; Fannie 437; Harry 666; Harvey 437; Helen 437; Hettie 437; Jesse 437; John C. 437; Mary G. 666; William Henry 437
MOONEY Anna Keziah 765; Elizabeth 765; M. 765; Mary 765; Mary Goldsborough 765
MOORE Alfred M. 331; Amanda 314; Amanda B. 472; Annie M. 290; Bessie 314; Caleb J. 56; Edward 432; Edward T. 314; Effie T. 314; Eliza (Wiley) 291; Elizabeth Jane 291; Emma 314; Ethel B. 290; F. Howard 290; George 17; George C. 17, 290; George C. Jr. 290; George H. 17, 290; Harry A. 290; Ida A. 590; James A. 290; Jane 342; Jesse 291; John A. 17; John Allen 290; John W. 291; Julia 432; Levin R. 590; Louisa 125; Luther 17, 290; Margaret 17; Marion 294; Martha J. 397; Mary 314; Mary A. 290, 469; Mary Ann 56; Miss 92, 320; Mrs. E T.,472; Mrs. William H. 729; Nancy (Deshields) 17; Sallie 314; Sallie B. 331; Sarah 19; Solomon 17; T. H. 593; William O. 294

MORGAN Adela 477; Anne 748; Anne L. 748; Charles 748; Frank 238; Jacob 748; Jacob E. 646; John H. 748; Julia 238; Laura 633; Lizzie B. 646; Mary H. 748; Mrs. E. H. 721; P. A. 748; Philip 748; Philip Addison 748; Robert C. 477; William 721
MORLING John 111; Mary R. 111
MORRELL James 683
MORRIS Bishop 200; Deborah 545; Dr. 456; Eliza C. 255; Estelle 379; J. E. 522; L. W. 369; Lewis 207; Lewis W. 379; Mary E. 522; May 207; Robert 678; Thomas C. 255
MORSELL Elizabeth (Sedgwick) Morsell 558; James 558; Mary 558
MORTIMER Alexander 506; Carrie 506; Elizabeth 506; Grace 506; James Edwin 506; John 506; John Alexander 506; Kate A. 506; Lillian 506; Sarah C. 506; Walter Stewart 506
MOSLIN Perpetua 649
MOTT Dr. 586
Mount Pleasant 428
MOWBERY Clement T. 745
MOWBRAY Ann Emily 510; Catharine W. 294; Edith 199; Henrietta 703; Henry 115; James A. 703; Joseph 510; W. A. 199
MULFORD Martha 749; Rachel 98
MULLICAN 214; George A. 455; Mary 455
MULLIGAN Addie 431; George W. 82; John 431; Willie A. 82
MULLIKEN Arthur Cooke 783; Jeremiah 783; Mary Elizabeth 783
MULLIKIN --- 360; Elma M. 553; George 726; John 726; Mary Elizabeth 726; Patrick 726
MULRAIN Cornelius 454
MUMMEY Marcella Worthington 30; Thomas 30
MUNDY Catharine 745; Elizabeth 745; Fannie 745; Fannie C. (Crowell) 745; G. Warren 745; Henry E. 745; Henry H. 745; J. Crowell 745; J. S. 745; Joseph S. 745; Maggie K. 745; William B. 745
MURPHY Ann P. 412; Murphy family 629; Ira 243; Martha 243; O. H. 369; Sarah 369; Timothy 450
MURRAY W. L. S. 547; William H. 558
MUSE Daniel S. 674; Dr. 396; Miss 674; Williamina 674
MYERS Ida 578; Mary 449

NADDIN Annie L. 700
NASH Virginia 66
NAYLOR Mattie H. 360
NE (?) W. H. 293
NEAL Allie J. 386; Ann D. 295; Catherine (Marine) 386; Edward W. 386; George R. 386; Henrietta G. 295; Hester A. 357; J. A. F. 295; James D. 386; James L. 295; James O. 386; John R. H. 295; Joseph 226; Joseph A. F. 295; Joseph W. 295; Louis W. 295; Lucy B. 295; Martha 295; Martha J. 386; Martha L. 226; Mary C. 386; Mollie R. 386; Outerbridge H. 357; Rhoda A. 386; Sally A. 295; Thomas H. 295; William H. 295; William J. 386; Wingate 386
NEAVITT Albert Arnold 370; Alvin 370; Annie (Hunt) 370; Deborah E. 370; Henry C. 370; Johanna 370; John A. 370; Joseph E. 370; Julia Ann 370; Margaret (Kennard) 370; Mary A. 370; Mary Anne 370; Mary W. 370; Oliver K. 370; Samuel W. 370; Sarah 87; William Henry 370; William C. 370
NEILD Abraham 357; Alton B. 357; Bertie J. 357; Cina L. 357; Elizabeth (Fooks) 357; Elizabeth 357; Elizabeth E. 357; Harry G. 357; Hester A. 357; Hugh 357; John R. 357; John R., Jr. 357; M. Estelle 357; Mary A. 357; Nicey A. 357; Nora Belle 357; Outerbridge H. 357; William H. 357
NELSON "King" 722; --- 550; Addie C. 494; Alice 722; Alma Lillian 722; Charles Edward 722; Clara J. 722; Eleazer 421; Ellen 421; Henry W. 722; James C. 494; Jannie 722; John Allen 722; Leah 565; Lord 557, 722; Lorin C. 722; Lorin Cleveland 722; Martin Luther 722; Mary 428; Mary A. 475; Morrison Marks 722; Sallie 722; Thomas 565, 722; William Clarke 722
NEVILN --- 721
NEWBURY Arthur 293; Demetrius W. 293; Edith 293; Edward E. S. 293; Eliza 293; Eliza E. 293; Elmer L. 293; George 293; Guy 293; Henrietta P. 293; Joseph D. 293; Maud 293; Nora 293; Sarah 293; Stephen 293
NEWCOMB Mary A. C. 294
NEWLEE Elizabeth 484; George 484
NEWMAN Hannah 672; John F. 672; Mary N. 553

INDEX (to paragraph numbers)

NEWNAM Daniel 340; Margaretta 243; Martha 243; Spencer G. 243; William H. 243
NEWNAN Margaret 547
NICHOLAS Dorcas 296
NICHOLS & Brother 167; Alpheus W. 523; Amanda 198, 368; Anna 198; Bayard 198; Clarence 198, 523; Delia 198; Dorcas 406; Élla 198; Ellen 503; Elmer 198; Emily 198; Emma 198; Flora 523; Francis 198, 472; Glendora 523; Grenberry 198; Henrietta Maria 95; Henry A. 167; Ida 198, 523; J. H. 284; J. K. 650; James 198, 368; James A. 198, 368; James L. 198; James R. 406, 671; John 523, 643; John W. 198; Kate F. 167; Lizzie 523; M. B. 167; Mabel 523; Margaret 671; Martha 472; Mary 167, 198, 523, 643, 702, 714; Nellie 198; Patrick 167; Perry 198; Rhoda 198; Rhoena V. 406; Robert 198; Robert Lloyd 95; Robinson 198; Samuel 198; Sarah 766; Senah 198; Silas 198; Thomas C. 167; Webster 523; William 198; William E. 167; Winnifred 523
NICHOLSON Albert Earl 630; Albert S. 549; Bessie Morton 790; Charles Burgess 790; Daisy 630; Emily 549; Emma 549, 633; Florence F. 549; Harry Bates 790; Horace W. 790; Jennie 549; John P. 549, 633, 790; Joseph 783; Julia 630; Mabel G. 549; Mary 783, 790; Nellie 790; ; Robert 549, 633; Robert G. 549, 790; Robert Josiah 790; Sarah 630; Sarah E. 549; Sarah S. 549; Walter Lusby 790; William T. 549, 630
NICKERSON Mary A. 168, 322
Nickerson Phosphate Co. 56
NICODEMUS Cora V. 302; John L. 302
NICOLS Deborah Lloyd 767; Henrietta Maria 767, 779; Henry 766; Jeremiah 767; Robert Lloyd 767; Sarah 766; Susannah Robins Chamberlaine 767; William 779
Niles' End 498
NIXON Mary 771
NOBLE Addie 225, 622; Alexander 225; Annie B. 432; Caroline 225; Clara A. 225; Clementine 215; Duncan L. 225; Eliza J. 225; Elizabeth 418; Fannie L. 763; Inez 225; Isaac 233, 654; J. 763; J. L. 763; Jacob L. 70, 225; John W. 225; Joshua 225; Katie B. 763; Levi D. 225; Mamie E. 225; Manie Eugenia 70;

Marie 763; Mary C. 493; Mary E. 225; Mary Elizabeth 233, 654; Maud 225; Rufus 225; Rufus S. 763; Ruth 763; Ruth H. (Leverton) 225; Ruth H. 225; Sallie 440; Solomon 418; T. S. 622; Thomas 432; Twiford S. 225, 763; Twiford Sewell 763; William 440; William D. 225
NOCK Blanche 309; John L. 309
NOEL Basil 733; Edward 733; Elizabeth 733; Mary 733; Sarah 733
NOLAN Sarah E. 186
NORDAIN Mary C. 10
NORMAN Annie 100, 486; James P. 100; William T. C. 486
NORRIS Edmund W. 496; Helen M. 496; James C. 496; John C. 211; Kate 496; Lambert 496; Laura L. 56; Martin 211; Mary 496; Mrs. M. E. 496; Samuel 496; Susan 211; Thomas 211, 496; Thomas A. & Son 212; Thomas F. 496; William 496; William H. 211; William T. 56
NUTT Job 776
NUTTLE Edward E. 551; Elizabeth 551; Henry 551; Margaret (Andrews) 551; Samuel 551; Tilghman 551; William 551; William Sr. 551
NUTZ Eben 527; Emily C. 527

O'DONNELL Columbus 513
O'NEILL Eleanor 327
Ocean View House 402
OHLANDER Augustus 240; Kate 240; Louise J. 240
OLDHAM Ann 785; Edward 103, 785; George W. 103; John 785; Mary Amanda 103; Susan Ann (Biddle) 103
ONINS Louisa 110
OREM Calvert 617; Emma 617; Emma N. 172; James 172; Julia T. 189; Mary E. 172; Nicholas 189
ORRELL Anne 707; Annie E. 398; R. J. 398
OSBORNE Grace 324; Lewis 324
OVERINGTON John 302; Katie 302
OWEN Anne 731; Brig. Gen. 731; Frances 731; Rev 490; Sarah Maria Louise 490; William 731
OWENS Annie 367 F. J. 381; Florence 367; George E. 367; George W. 367; Harry 367; Howard 367; Howard C. 367; Ida 367; John S. 367; Joseph R. 367; Mary A. 367; Mary M. 367; Miss 171; Natilla P. 381; T. Guy 367

OWINGS Philip 133; Susan 133
OZMON Florence Virginia 92; Henry 92; John H. 92; John Harry 92; Joseph Roger 92; Joseph Whiting 92; Samuel C. 92; William 92

PACA William 141
PACKARD Miss 776
PAGE Ann 362; Henry 362, 384, 397; John 362; Judge 500; Julia E. 362; Julia Ethelinde 384; Louisa J. 362; Maria S. 242; Virginia W. 362
PAGETT Anna 328
PAIN Virginia L. 593
PAINE George S. 55; Lelia 55
PALLETT Levin 462
PALMATARY Charles 587; Lavinia 102; Sarah 587
PALMER David Keener 734; Edward Trippe 734; Elizabeth Barney 734; George C. 38; Harriet Choirs 734; John 38; Rev L. 31; William 734; William Preston 734
PARKER Annie B. 432; Burton W. 432; Carl A. 432; Charles 55; Elizabeth 382; Ellen A. 55; Emeline B. 601; Emily 432; Parker Homestead 136; John W. 794; John W. Jr. 794; Joseph H. 432; Joseph M. 794; Julia (Moore) 432; Levin 794; Lillian R. 432; Lizzie 794; Lulu V. 432; R. A. 794; Rebecca T. 656; Sarah 241; Sir Peter 102; Thomas Orville 432; William 241, 432; Wilmer B. 432
PARKS A.R. 106; Alexander 323, 394, 619; Alphonzo 106; Charles 540; Georgetta 323, 619; John 249; Lena A. 540; Sarah A. 249; Sarah R. 394
PARROTT Abner 455; Annie 455; William 739
PARSONS Alphonza 522; Amanda 555; Anna J. 522; Annie E. 175; Elizabeth 392, 522; Ella 455; George T. 544; Grace M. 522; Harrison I. 522; Harry B. 522; Isaac 699; Jehu 544, 555; Lewis B. 522; Margaret 544; Mary 522; Mary E. 522; Rachel 699; Rachel A. 522; Sarah J. 544; Susan E. 544; Thomas 175; William G. 522
PARVIS Joseph 211; Joseph L. 211; Joseph M. 211; Preston 211; Thomas 211; William 211
PASCAULT Alexander G. 513; Alexis A. 513; Alexis G. 735; Ann 768; Anne E. 513; Charles Louis 768; Henry G. 513; John L. 352; Louis C. 513; Maria E. 513; Millie M. 352; Sophia Elizabeth 735
PASONS Isaac 522
PASSWALTERS Lizzie 210; William 210
PASTORFIELD Catherine 197
PATCHETT Edith I. 77; Hettie V. 383; James H. 383; Leona 77, 809
PATTERSON Catherine 772; James B. 772; Margaret 786; Miss 513
PATTISON Annie Hooper 96; Annie T. 704; Aurelia 311; Elizabeth 579; Emily 704; Gov. 435; Hattie T. 704; Hugh De Valin 704; Jacob 704; James 579, 704; James B. 704; James M. 311; Jeremiah 579, 704; John R. 704; John R. Jr. 704; Lillian 704; Mary Ann 704; Mary Y. 704; Nancy 579; Robert E. 624, 704; Robert H. 704; Samuel 435, 704; Samuel S. 704
PATTON Alexine 472; Amelia 213; Armelia 611; Barrett 219; Cora 472; Emily 213, 219, 472; James B. 219, 472; Lizzie 472; Lydia (Barrett) 219; Lydia 213, 219; Martha 219; Matthew 213, 219; Orlando 213, 472; Robert 213, 219, 611; Sarah E. 213
PAYNE James 611; Julia E. 611; Mary V. 485; Mrs. 354; William James 485
PAYNTER Catherine 547
PAYTON Hester Van bibber 466; William 466
PEARCE Eunice 191; Gideon 191; J. A. 122, 349; James Alfred 83, 191; Julia (Dick) 191; Martha 393
PEARSON E.M.T. 41
PECK Sadie L. 149
PEIRSON Annie 442; George W. 442
PELPS Florence 757; Mary R. 757
PENINGTON Annie M. 136; Edward 136; Fredus R. 179; Henry C. 136; J. Thomas 136; Jane 136; Noble E. 136; Robert 136; William 136
PENKETH Ann 779
PENNINGTON Annie 125; Atkie 179; E. B. 179; Edgar Reyland 179; Edmund 616; Edmund B. 616; Elizabeth 616; Ella 413; Helen Louise 179; Lena B. 179; Marion 616; Mary 616, 782; Mary A. 616; May G. 179; W. D. 616, 699; William D. 179; William L. 179
PENNY Jane F. 102

INDEX (to paragraph numbers)

PERCY Miss 485; A. S. 485; Elizabeth 485; Sarah E. 485; William 485
PERKINS Benjamin 173; Caroline 490; George W. T. 490; Lucy 781; Millie 91; Rebecca 173
PERRY Addie 709; Annie E. 709; Arthur 89; Bessie 709; Commodore 709; Elender 509; Ella 709; Elva 89, 709; Emily Josephine 709; Emma 709; Emma C. 709; Emma J. 709; Ernest 709; Fannie 709; Florence 89; Isabel 709; John 709; John M. 563, 709; John W. 228; Lillie A. 709; Rose 709; Wesley 89
PETERS Elizabeth 126
PETERSON Acksah 594
PHELPS Agnes 511, 757; Elsie 757; Frances P. 757; Francis 757; Francis B. 757; Francis H. 757; John 757; Joseph W. 757; M. T. 757; May 757; Nancy 757; Samuel 757; Susan L. 757; T. M. 757; Tryphena 757; W. Wallace 757
PHILLIPS Ada 468; Agatha H. 485; Alice D. 578; Amelia 557; Anna 201; Annie 286, 485; Arianna Denney 286; Benjamin 468; Benjamin T. 788; Betsey 458; Calvert 468; Carrie O. 578; Charles W. 788; Claiborne 286; Cora A. 788; E. M. 303; Edna 578; Edward 485; Edward S. 60, 468; Eliza E. 788; Elizabeth (Smith) 485; Elizabeth 485, 665; Elizabeth A. 428; Ella G. 356; Gabriel 788; George H. 468; George K. 571; George M. 60, 468; George W. 60, 578; George Wesley 468; Harriet E. 286; Hattie I. 468; Henry H. 578; Ida 578; Igrus S. 557; J. W. 757; James 286; James H. 286, 788; James R. 485, 510; James Richard 485; John 485; John H. 60, 468, 578; John Jay 578; John O. 286; John T. 332; Johnson 428; Joseph 570; Julia 332; Juliet M. 286; Laura 286; Lizzie 578; Lula E. 788; Luther 60, 468; M. Jennie 578; Mabel Alcora 60; Margaret 268; Mary (Applegarth) 190; Mary 510; Mary Jane 468; Mary P. 485, 578; Mary R. 468; Mary V. 485; Melvina 570; Milford 60, 468; Nellie 485; Oliver G. 60, 468; Owen 286; Rachel A. 570; Raymond 468; Rebecca C. 557; Richard 190, 201, 485; Robert 286; Roger 458; Rufus 788; Samuel 485; Samuel Edward 788; Samuel T. 788; Sarah 485; Sarah E. 485; Solomon 468;
Susan 201; Susan 485; Susie E. 468; Thomas 201; Veronica 303; Victoria 468, 578; W. Percy 485; Wilhelmina 190; William F. 788; William H. 286; William T. 578
PIERCE Eliza 31; Franklin 363
PIERSON Hester Ann 383
PINCKARD Mary d. 388
PINDER Mary 466
PINGFIELD Mary 223; Peter 223
PIPER Michael 784; Rosanna 784; Rosanna B. 784
PIPPEN Anna 634; JAMES 634; Jane 634
PIPPIN Elizabeth E. 647; Marion 647; Sarah M. 215
PITTS E. P. 378; Hillard 78; Mary W. 378
PLEASANTON Eliza 323; Hannah 323; Samuel Webb 323
PLUMBER William 520
PLUMMER James H. 592; John W. 224; Martha 520; Martha M. 520; Mary 224; Matthew T. 520
POE Amelia 772; John P. 426
POLEON Marquis de 768
POLK Addie O. 694; Ann 20; 697; Carrie H. 694; Eliza 429; Elizabeth 491; Emerson G. 694; Emerson W. 694; Esther 697; Polk Family 697; James 697; James K. 20, 697; John 20; L. Alma 694; Louisa W. 694; Lucius 697; 20, 694, 697; J. G. 491; T. G. 429, 491
POLLITT Louis A. 255; Martha J. 255
POLLOCK --- 697
POOLE Ann 671; Levin 671
POOLEY George F. 524
PORTA Amasa 725
PORTER --- 229; Alexander 725; Amanda E. 229; Amanda J. 210; Amelia 533; Arlington T. 804; Eliza 725; Elizabeth 684; Erastus A. 725; Francis A. 804; George C. 804; Grace W. 725; Jacob W. 725; John 229, 804; Josephine 533; Lida 804; Love C. 725; Lyman R. 804; M. L. 210; Margaret B. (Terrell) 804; Margaret B. 804; Mark 533; Mark H. W. 725; Martha 725; Mary 229; Mary A. 804; Mary E. 804; Mrs. Clinton 533; Nettie M. 804; Richard C. 804; Sallie (Miles) 229; Sarah C. 464; Susan 229; Theophilis W. 804; William 229
POTTER Amos 605; Ann M. 605; Dr. 393; Miss 787; Sarah 778; Sarah M. 605; William 463, 787

POTTS Emily (Courcey) 791; George W. 791; James W. 791; John 791; John E. 791; John Sr. 791; Margaret M. 791; Mary 791; Mary E. 791; Mifflin G. 791; P. T. 791; Robert H. 791
POWELL Ann D. 295; Annie L. 700; Edith Needles 700; Edward Atkinson 700; Elizabedt Needles 700; Evelyn M. 754; Frances 608; George 608; Hetty Anna 700; Howell 700; Howell Jr. 700; Mrs. William 754; Sallie 234; Sallie K. 700; Sallie Kemp 700; William C. 234; William N. 700; Zadok 234
PRATT Catherine M. 383; Thomas G. 783
PRESTON Helen 673; James H. 673; Susan R. 724
PRETTYMAN Allison Palmer 166; Augusta Williams 70; Daniel B. 70; Ida 166
PREWITT Cornelia 342; E. H. 342
PRICE Andrew 783; Anna M. 42; Arra 165; Benjamin 478; C. Harry 478; Elizabeth 733; G. W. 680; Grace R. 478; Henry Baker 478; Herbert 10; James 165, 733; John Hyland 478; Margaret 343; Maria E. 478; Mary 733; Mary C. 478; Mordecai 142; Mrs. C.H. 37; Nannie M. 478; R. M. 143; Rachel B. 478; Rosalie M. 478; Sarah 783; William Henry 478; William J. Jr. 244
PRIMROSE Annie 644
PRITCHETT Henrietta G. 760; J. N. 760
PROVOST Julie E. 96
PURNELL --- 593; Annie B. 452; Bessie L. 452; Clayton J. 452; Elizabeth 733; Ella A. 452; Ella L. 452; Eloise 537; Emma J. 537; George E. 537; George W. 452; Henrietta 119; James 795; James L. 537; John W. 537; Julia 537; Leonard D. 452; Littleton 119, 795; Mary 733, 795; Mary J. (Laws) 537; Mary J. 400; Mary K. 537; May H. 452; O. M. 593; Oscar M. 537; Perry W. 452; Ralph C. 537; Robert 795; Sallie 795; Stephen D. 537; Stephen L. 400, 537; Thomas D. 537; Thomas Isaac 795; William H. 361; William Matthew 537; Zadoc 800
PUSEY Benjamin S. 541; E. J. 541; Elihu W. 541; Elijah J. 541; L. H. 541; Letitia J. 497, 541; Margaret 541; Margaret J. 541; Mary E. 541; P. S. 497; S. E. 541

QUAIL Robert R. 473; Ruth 473

QUILLEN Annie T. 361; John B. 571; Julia C. 571; Thomas N. 361
QUILLIN John 231; Kate L. 231
QUIMBLY farm 390
QUIMBY Alfred 707; Anne 707; Charles 422, 707; Ella B. 707; Frank 707; James 707; John 422, 707; Joseph 422; Mary E. 707; Mrs. William G. 57; Parker 707; Sally 57; Sarah 422, 707; Sarah A. 707; Thomas 422, 707; W. G. 422; William 422; William Jr. 422; William G. 707
QUINN S. S. 462; Sallie 462
QUINTON Comfort E. 462; John 462; William 462

RADCLIFFE Anna 435; James 435; Margaret (Harris) 435; Nellie 674; William H. 435; William H. Jr. 435
RALEIGH Hooper 501; Leah 13; Leah L. 501; Sir Walter 501
RALPH Charles 471; Charles T. 471; Mary 471; Nancy 471; Phyllis 471; Thomas 471; William 471; William J. 471
RAMSDELL C. P. 262; Charles P. 262; Floyd C. 262; Harry E. 262; Hiram J. 262
RANDALL Eliza (Jarvis) 613; Eliza 613; Ella 613; Emma 613; Harry 613; Lillie 613; Lucy 613; Mary 613; Robert W. 613; William 613
RASH Mary E. 205; William H. 205
RASIN Delany 106; Eunice 191; Florence Elma 688; Florence M. 688; Joseph O. 688; M. M. 106; Mary E. 129; McCall M. 519; Merritt 106; Minnie 106; Parks 106; Philip 106; Sarah 519; Sarah A. 699; Unit 191; William 106
RATCLIFFE 204
RATHELL Charles 330, 334; Charles T. 330; Donald 330; Lucretia 334; Mary 330; Minnie 330; Sarah 330; Warren 330
RAUGHLEY Ary A. 151; George W. 151; Henry 151; James T. 151; John 151; Mary L. 804; Robert 151; Shadrack 151
RAVELL Benjamin 78; Lottie 78
RAWLINGS Hannah 390
RAY H. Page 294
RAYMOND Mary 155; Timothy 155
REA Annie 610; Mary A. 357; V. L. 610
REAGAN Jeremiah 756; Leah 756
REAVES Anne H. 436; Thomas 436
RECORDS Margaret 339

INDEX (to paragraph numbers)

REDDEN Elmira 303; Stephen 303
REDDISH John 692; Susan 692
REDDITT Agnes 82
REDGRAVE Abraham 171; Miss 171
REDHEAD A.P. 199; Sarah E. 199
REED Col. 490; George 170; George R. 170; George Robert 170; Ida 367; Joseph 170; Joseph Benjamin 170; Mary 170; Mrs. 374; P. S. 759; Samuel 170; Samuel Amos 170; Sarah E. 759; Sidney Usilton Younger 170
REES John R. 390; Lizzie V. 750; Lydia 390; Mollie 750; Ralph 750
REILEY Alice A. 73; C.M. 73; Clementina (Beck) 73
RENTLEY Capt. 731; Eliza 731
REYNOLDS Anne 393; Audley E. 157; Fannie 157; James N 157; John 393; John A. 613; Julia 157; Lola 62, 157; Robert J. 157; Robert W. 157; S. M. 546; Thomas G. 157
REYNOR Sarah Ann 657
RHODES Charlotte (Hutchinson) 670; Dennis 670; Dennis F. 663; John Lewis 670; Lewis K. 670; Margaret A. 663; Mary C. 670; Sarah 463; Sarah Matilda 670; William Washington 670
RICAUD Ann Elizabeth (Gordon) 97; James B. 97; Mary Rebecca 97
RICE Annie I. 553; Blanche 231; Charles J. 231; Christiana (Clark) 231; Clarence 231; D. I. 231; George 231; John 231, 553; Kate E. 231; Kate L. 231; Lila 231; Lillian R. 231; Luvia L. 231; Maggie 231; Margaretta 231; Oliver 231; Rebecca 231; Robert C. 231; Robert J. 231; Susannah J. 231; William 231
RICHARDS Blanche 284; Miss 546; R. W. 284; Rebecca 324; Silas 171
RICHARDSON Agnes 708; Aline F. 70; Ann 463; Asher 66; Carrie O. 578; Clara L. 542; Ella Caroline 66; Eva L. 66; Florence 708; Francis A. 738; George 297; George S. 529; Greenfield 66; Harriet Agnes 66; Inez 708; J. W. 542; James 70; John 448, 795; Joseph 738; Joseph H. 708; Littleton 66; Louisa 708, 795; Malissa 738; Mary 708; Mary A. 708; Mary Frances 529; Mary Lillie 708; Matilda 66; Milton 578; Newman C. 66; Pauline 66; Raymond 708; Ruth 66; Sarah M. 738; Viola 708; William 66, 738; William S. 66

RICKETTS Amy K. 718
RIDER Charles 114, 333; Charles H. 397; Linnian M. 500; Margaret A. 500; Martha 333; Mary 114; Thomas F.J. 114; Virginia 637; W. P. 637; William P. 500; Williamanna 397
RIDGAWAY H. B. 477; James H. 477; Julia E. 477
RIDGELEY Family 744; Ellen 212; R.H. 212
RIDOUT Horatio 769; John 769; Rachel 769
RIGBY Mary C. 289
RIGGIN Olivia 379
RIGGINS Captain 223; Catherine 223
RILEY Catherine 546; Lawrence 546; Miss 546
RINGGOLD --- 678; Charles 228; Ida M. 228; Isabella 690; James 191; James C. 254; Jervis 672; Josias 7; Julia R. 254; Major 678; Margaret C. 672; Mary (Wilmer) 15; Mary Ann 7; Matilda C. 191; Rachel B. 478; William 15
RITZEL Annie 444; Augustus 444; Augustus Jr. 444; Charles 444; Edward 444; Elizabeth 444; George 444; John 444; Maggie 444; Martin 444; Mary 444
ROACH Christiana 232, 500; Clara 355; Clara L. 565; Henry 355; Jane E. 542; Julia F. 462; William 542; William H. 232, 462
ROADER George 175
ROBBINS John L. 55; Julia L. 55
ROBERTS Annie H. 202; Austin 165; Benjamin 124, 165, 235; Benjamin G. 165; Benjamin O. 235; Caroline (Kennerly) 235; Catherine 782; Clara 235; Elizabeth Harding 8; Ella 165; Emma 420; Emma V. 124; Finley 124, 165; George Thomas 235; Henry W. 235; Hilda 165; James M. 235; John B. 235; Judge 500; Kate F. 167; Lee J. 235; Lemuel 124, 165; Loretta 235; Margaret J. 235; Maria J. (Scott) 124; Maria J. 124; Olivia A. 235; Scott 165; Stephen Chester 8; Thomas 124; W. Scott 165; William 235, 420; William D. 167; William S. 235; William Scott 124
ROBERTSON Albert 112; Alexander 344; Alice 344; Dr. 441; Edgar Wallace 112; Elizabeth Elen 579; George 378; Gilbert Bernard 112; H. H. 369; Henrietta Elizabeth (Jones)112; James McRea 112; Margaret (Ballard) 579;

Margaret 369; Maria E. 378; Maria Henrietta 112; Rebecca 495; Robert G. 495; Sallie Elizabeth 344; Samuel H. 579; Thomas 112
ROBINS Elizabeth 259, 764, 776; George 764, 767, 776, 779, 787; Henrietta Maria 779; Henrietta Maria Tilghman 767, 776, 787; James B. 259; John 764, 766, 782; John L. 259; Julia L. 259; Lambert 764; Margaret 787; Mary Ann Turbutt 766; Mary Anne 782; Mrs. Mary Ann Turbutt 766; Obedience 532; Sarah 764, 785; Standley 764, 785; Susannah 764, 767, 779; Thomas 764, 776; Thomas M. 259; William 764
ROBINSON A. W. 620; Alice 679; Amy 679; Annie P. 326; Beverly 467; Catherine 772; Catherine Amelia 536; Catherine J. 581; Eliza 653; Eliza C. 733; Elizabeth R. 679; Frank 145; Gladys 467; Helen 579; J. D. A. 29; James 414, 620; James E. 190; James L. 454; Jane 581; John 620, 631, 653; John H. 145; John Mitchell 536, 679; John Riley 581; Joseph 326; Joseph L. 145; Joseph T. 467; Levi T. 145; Lisle R. 772; Lisle R. 772; Louis A. 145; Mammie E. 145; Marian 679; Mariana W. 679; Mary 631; Mary A. 257; Mary C. 326; Mary E. 190; Melissa F. 257; Mrs. Dr. W. W. 405; Mrs. Esther Ann 702; Peter 536, 679; Ralph 679; Rev C. J. 83; Roger C. 145; Ruth 113; Sallie A. 145; Sallie M. 679; Sallie R. (Mitchell) 536; Samuel A. 462; Sarah (Leonard) 145; Sarah 414, 454, 679; Sophia 145; William J. 257
ROBSON John 131; Mary 131
ROCHESTER J. E. 647; Miss 449
ROCKWELL family 753
RODNEY Caesar 678; Caesar A. 678; Jennie E. 681
ROE A. B. 284; A. Keener 451; Andrew B. 291; Ann 383; Anna 383; Annie 451; Blanche 284; Catherine (Skirven) 284; Catherine M. 383; Catherine R. 284; E. Homer 451; Edward H. 451; Edward T. 383, 451; Fannie 437; Florence 451; Frederick 284; Hamilton Lewis 451; Harry A. 284; Helen 284; Hester Ann 383; Hettie V. 383; J. A. 383; James A. 451; Lizzie 451; Maggie 383; Margaret 628; Martha A. 451; Mary J. 751; Oscar 751; Rebecca 197, 291; Sallie S. 284; Thomas P. 437; Thondyke 451; Virginia 451; Walter D. 451; William E. 383
ROEDER Elizabeth 175; John J. 175
ROGERS Delia 733; Bartholomew 733; Edward 752; Eleanor A. 95; John 93; Mariana 752; Mary 769; Raymone 93
ROLISON Elizabeth 171; James 171; Susan 171
ROSE Adela 477; Charles H. 477; D. C. 477; Estelle 477; Harriet 477; J. H. 477; John 477; Julia E. 477
ROSEBERRY Alphonsa 147; B. S. 478; Maria E. 478
ROSEBERY Edvina 128
ROSS A. P. 583; Anna 606; Anne 437; Carrie 207; Columbus N. 552; Eugene 207; George 437; Joseph 583; Laura A. (Woodland) 583; Lulu 583; Mary A. 210; Sallie E. 552; William 210
ROUSE Sallie C. 715
ROWE Elizabeth Adeline 271; Emma 271; George T. 271; Georgia 271; Louisa E. 416; Martha 226; Monmonier 271; Samuel 271; Sarah E. 271; Sophia 108; William D. 226
ROWENCRANS Cynthia 564
ROWINS Margaret E. 296
ROWLEY Z. Ellen 585
ROWLINSON William T. 35
RUARK Alexander W. 729, 799; Amanda 79; Amanda A. 729; Cora T. 656; Ernest L. 729; Eugene Henry 656; Frederick E. 729, 799; Henry W. 468, 656; Howard 729; James 729; Laura J. 729; Lina 729; Lucy R. 656; Lucy Rebecca 656; Major T. 729; Nettie Ann 656; Oliver G. 656; Rebecca T. 656; Richard 729; Sarah 729; Susie E. 468; T. 799; Thomas 729; Thomas L. 656; W. T. 79; Wilbur 729; William 29, 729; William T. 656; William Thos 656; William W. 656
RUBELL Gen. 513
RUCKLE Miss 731
RUDESTINE Elizabeth 786; William F. 786
RUMBOLD 219; Elizabeth 219; James B. 219; John 219; Martha 219; Mary 219
RUNNELL Caroline 575; Robert 575
RURCHELL Sarah 731
RUSSELL Alger 620; Amy Claudine 122; Ann 122; Ann Tittle 122; Annie L. 177; Carmeta 58; Charlotte R. 122; Fannie

INDEX (to paragraph numbers)

G. 6; Frances George 122; Hester Ann 122; James 93; James Alexander 122; John 122; John Hamer 122; John Waters 122; Lewis L. 122; Maria 93; Mary 620; Mrs. Frances (George) 122; Sarah L. 122; T. W. 6; T. Waters 58, 122; Theophilus 122; William 122; William F. 58, 122; William F. Jr. 58; William George 122
RUSSUM George M. 20, 245; George Mitchell 20, 509; Jamor 516; Judge 389, 411; Mitchell 20; Robert Polk 20; Sarah A. (George) 20; Sydenham Thorne 20
RUTH Elizabeth 173; Grace M. 504; John F. 504; John L. 504; Robert 173; Sarah (Guessford) 504; Thomas 155
RYAN Margaret 142
RYEBOLD William 616
RYNER Sallie R. 425

SALISBURY Lord 8
SAMPSON'S railway station 10
SANDRES Maj 761; May C. 761
SAPPINTON Elizabeth 577; Samuel 577
SATTERFIELD Calvin 426; Clara 426; Daniel 426; Elizabeth 426; Ida T. 426; John 300; Lawrence 426; Lindsay 426; Mary Elizabeth 726; Mary T. 426; Minnie 92, 426 92; Phoebe 426; Rose 426; Susan P. 426; Virginia 426; William Calvin 426
Sauerhoff Charles 571; Clara 82; Harry W. 571; Henry 571; Joseph H. 82, 571; Julia C. 571; Kate 571; Lillian 571; Maggie L. 571; Sarah Ann 571; Thomas J. 571; William 571
SAULSBURY Abraham 108; Ann E. 438; Charles 108; Eli 438; Ella 245; Georgiana 108; James 108; James W. 438; John 108; Lizzie 108; Mary Jane 675; Rachel 438; Richard W. 108; Susan 424; Vashti 438; Willard 151; William 438; William E. 245, 675
SAUNDERS Sallie 417
SAXTON Clarence L. 614; Eustace P. 614; Harriet 614; James Anna 614; James Arthur 614; May 614; Thomas 614; Thomas J. 614; Wm. 614
SCARBOROUGH Castle 66; Edward 66; Harriet E. 66
SCHLEY John 771; Margaret 771; Mary 771

SCHNAUFFER Charles 152
SCHOCKLEY Mary A. 599
SCHOENEWOLF Fred 578; Victoria 578
SCHOOLFIELD Annie 694; Elijah 526; Ella 526; Emily S. 210, 526; Emma 526; George E. 526; Hattie 526; Laura 526; Mary S. 210; Samuel 210; W.M. 210; William 526 695; William M. 526;
SCHOON Ella 473
SCHUYLER C. H. 478; Rosalie M. 478
SCHWARTZE Henry 735; Melusina E. 735
SCOON Anne E. 446; Maiden Ann E. 246
SCOTT Anne 450; C. W. 432; Emily 432; Ida 198; John J. 541; Maria 165; Mary A. 650; Mrs. James 101; S. E. 541; William 124; Winfield 691
SCOTTON John A. 436
SEAMAN Catherine M. 412
SEAMANS ---- 415
SEARS Amnanda M. 308; Bessie M. 308; Charles E. 308; Elizabeth (Murdock) Sears 308; Georgia 308; Gilbert M. 308; Harry C. 308; John K. 308; Margaret E. 308; Mary E. 308; Peter Gray 120; Robert L. 308; Susie 308; William 308; William H. 308
SEARS' CHOICE 308
SEDGWICK --- 558; Dorcas 558; Elizabeth 558, 683
SEE Catherine 327; Hester S. (Shepherd) 327; John 327
SELBY Annie 705; Chas W. 705; Edna 705; Hattie Washington 705; Jas Gordon 705; John Parker 307; John T. 705; John W. 705; Mamie Ellen 705; Margaret 705; W. W. 620; Walter O. 307; Wilminia 307
SELLERS Ann 569; Charles 569; Elizabeth 569; Eva 569; George W. 569; Gertrude 569; Herman 569; James E. 569; John F. 569; Lena 569; Lulu 569; Maggie 569; Martha 569; Martin 569; Mary 569; Mary Jane 569; Nellie 569; Ollie M. 569; Stelle 569; T. C. 569; Thomas 569; Thomas C. 569
SELOVER Clarence L. 511; May 511
SENAT Isabel 562; Lewis D. 562
SETH A. H. 533; Alexander H. 189; Frank W. 189; Jacobus 189; James 189; Joseph 189; Joseph B. 189; Julia T. 189; Julian O. 189; Robert L. 189; Samuel H. 189; Sara 189; Thomas A. 189; William H. 189

SEWARD Alta 433; Anna 433; Charles H. 514; Columbus 514; Ella 433; Frances 514; Frank 433; George 514; Jane 514; John H. 514; Joshua 433; Laura 514; Levin 514; Lida 433; Mary 514; Mary R. 514; Olive 433; Richard 514; Thomas 514; William E. 514; William W. 433
SEYMOUR Ann J. 159; Levin S. 556; Matilda A (Berridge) 556; William S. 566
SHAFER Annie M.E. 175; Emma C. 175; John 175; Theresa (Roeder) 175; Tilghman 175
SHALLCROSS Catherine F. 461; Emma 461; Frances 461; Jacob 461; James 461; Jenett 461; Jennett 461; John 461; Lambert T. 461; Leonard 461; Margaret 461; Sereck 461; Thomas 461; Thomas J. 461; William 461; William G. 461
SHANAHAN Fannie R. 88; Mary E. 296; W.E. 88; W.J. 88; Emma 366; J. E. 366; Luisa 759; Wm E. 759
SHARP Mrs. A. L. 518
SHAWN Elizabeth 341
SHEHAN Anna 383
SHEPARD Benjamin 590; Matilda 591; Priscilla A. 590
SHEPHERD Caleb 579; Elizabeth Elen 579; Elizabeth Hooper 579; Frank Lockwood 579; Helen 579; Henry Pattison 579; Hester S. 327; J. Hooper Pattison 579; James Hooper 579; James Lockwood 579; James Sangston 579; Margaret Robertson 579; Mary Caroline 579; Nancy Pattison 579; Nellie 579; Priscilla Elizabeth (Pattison) 579; Robinson Cator 579; Wilsie 579
SHEPPARD Albert Cook 749; Albert Nathan 749; Amanda F. B. 323; Amanda Freeman 749; Benjamin 541, 643; Boss 581; Cave Bowen 749; David 749; Elizabeth 749; Florence Katherine 323, 749; Francis N. 323; Francis Nathan 749; Isaac Mulford 749; Isabella 75; Jonadab 749; Jos 749; Jos Cook 749; Justus Bonham 749; Leander Wm 749; Margaret 541; Maria Elizabeth 749; Martha 749; Mary Adelaide 749; Nathan 749; Nathaniel 749; Priscilla A. 643; Prudence 749; Rachel 749; Rebecca 75; Reed 749; Ruma Austin 749; Sarah (Lloyd) 643; Theodore Warren 749; William H. 75

SHERMAN Mary E. A. 84; Mary Jane 273
SHERWOOD Elizabeth 765; Hugh 765; Mary 765; Mary Anne 575; Mrs. M.M. 6; Thomas 765
SHEUBROOKS Leonard 89; Mary E. 89
SHIELDS Jane A. 36; Sallie V. 229
SHIEN Caroline 652; Wm 652
SHIP Johanna 316; John 316
SHIPLEY Celia 207; 557; Dr. 557; Laura D. 317
SHIPPLEY Susannah 768
SHIPPS anna A. 12
SHOCKLY Benjamin T. 65; Clarence L. 65; Emily J. 65; Henry B. 65; Joshua J.W. 65; Lorenzo D. 65; Nancy (Lokey) Shockly 65; Peter 65; Peter S. 65; Rebecca 65; Richard 65; Uriah D.C. 65; Uriah F. 65; William 65; William J. 65; William Sr. 65
SHOPPER Mary Ann 615
SHORES Eveline 188; Julia 596; Julia A. 280; L. L. 280, 596; Lambert 315; Sarah Jane 315; William 188
SHOWELL Ellen 275; William 275
SHRIVER, Bartlett & Co 56
SHULL R. R. 281
SHURLOCK Elizabeth 784
SHUSTER Allie E. 58
SHYROCK Ann L. 430
SIEGLER John 46
SIGLER Carrie 137
SIMKINS Maria 261; William 261
SIMMONS Elizabeth 344; Harriet R. 661; Harriet Ruth 660; Jas 643; Josias S. 270; Laura 660; Lawrence 661; Lawrence F. 661; Lawrence Fletcher 660; Leah 614; Leah C. 661; Levin 614; Webster Rebecca 614; Mary 660, 661; Rebecca 614, 643; Thomas W. 660, 661; William G. 344
SIMMS Mary 171; William 171
SIMPERS E.W.F. 273; Earle D. 273; Emma B. 273; Fannie W. 273; Frank V. 273; Henry G. 273; J. H. 691; J. Raymond 273; John B. 273; John H. 273; Mary A. H. 273, 691; Mary Jane 273; Milton S. 273; Thomas W. 273
SIMPKINS Henrietta 253
SIMPSON Nettie 552; Oliver 552
SINCLAIR Edwin 464
SINGER Henrietta 533; John M. 533
SINGLETON & TALBOT 75
SINGLETON Anna 785; John 785, 787

INDEX (to paragraph numbers)

SISK Albert W. 109, 281; Amanda 109, 281; Amanda C. 274; David 109; David F. 109; Elizabeth 109; Emma Gilbert 281; Francis A. 109; Gilbert 281; Grace 281; Herman 281; Joseph 109; Joseph F. 109, 281; Lizzie E. 281; Lucetta (Dean) 281; Lucetta 274; Mary A. 109; Minnie Grace 281; Pauline 281; Sallie 109; Susanna 109; Susie E. 109; Thomas F. 109; Thomas J. 109; 281; William 109, 274, 281
SITZER Elizabeth 564; Solmon 564
SKEGGS Capt. 427; Rosie 427
SKINNER Andrew 352; Ann 624; Elizabeth 579, 624, 733; Emma 750; Eva 750; J.K. 224; Lucy J. 266; Margaret 624; Mary Adelaide 266; Mary C. 670; Milcha 352; Rbt C. 670; Rheuelma 224; William 624
SKIRVEN Ada 24; Charles Howard 11; Edmund Howe 11; Francis 11; Frank 11; George C. 304; Harriet Lillian 73; Harry 11; J. Walter 24; James W. 331; Jennie 549; John T. 11; Lewin 24; Minnie 304; Mrs. C.V. 21; Percy Granger 11; T. Arthur 73; Thomas Arthur 11; Thomas W. 11, 24; William 549; William T. 94
SLAUGHTER Ella 89; H. B. 749; Henry 628; Margaret A. 628; Sarah E. 137; Susanna 628; Thomas 137
SLAY ---110; John O. 110; Martha 110; Mary E. 110
SLOAN Parson 462
SLUTTER Harriet 564; N. 564
SLY William L. 752
SMITH Addie 676; Albert G. 46; Albert H. 227; Alice Anita 46; Alice P. 673; Amelia 663; Angeline 57; Anna Burton 80; Anna E. 449; Anna Maria 577; Anne 733; Annie 711; Annie F. 105; Artemus 46; Asa 564; Benjamin L. 70, 196; Bertha Bayly 491; C. S. 172; Capt. 801; Charles 105, 308, 355, 491; Charles D. 105; Charles F. 46; Charles Franklin 172; Charles S. 172; Charles Sappington 577; Charles W. 135; Charlotte (Whittington) 267, 529; Charlotte A. 760; Clarence E. 611; Clement 57; Cora D. 247; Daniel 693; David 46, 693; E. O. 429; Edgar W. 618; Eliza 516; Elizabeth 70, 485, 509, 564, 577; Ella B. 429; Elsie S. 46; Emma 267, 564, 577; Emma G. 247; Emma N. 172; Ernest F. 135; Ethel M. 247; Fannie F. 196; Fannie Giles 577; Fanny 247 Frances A. 70; Frank W. 577; Frederick 105; G. J. 196; Georgia 308; Hallie Chambers 577; Harriet 564; Henry 693; Henry Earl 247; Herman K. 135; Hester A. 381; Hester Ann 227; Howard 57; Ida Orem 172; Inez 801; Ira 564; Jacob 571; James 80; James H. 46, 247, 381; James J. 80; James M. 227; Jas N. 711; Jas T. S. S. 663; John 564, 733; John A. 80; John W. 267; John Walter 529; 593; Joseph F. 564; Josias 564; Julia 80; Julia Lucinda 80; Kate 571; Katie Dodd 577; L. Q. 693; L.C. 57; Lacy 693; Larua V. 227; Laura 46; Leonard 564; Levin 485; Lewis C. 57; Lilian 564; Lillian F. 511; Lorinda 564; Lottie 577; Lurene 172; Lydia 418; M. Virginia 618; M. W. 367; Mabel 57; Magdalene (McNitt) 117; Maggie 733; Manlove 117; Margaret (Garrison) 618; Margaret A. 663; Marion de Kalb 676; Marion De Kalb 80; Marion deKalb Jr 80; Martin 245; Martin A. 227; Martin Bates 245; Mary 564; Mary A. 196; Mary E. (Cover) 105; Mary E. 51, 57, 117, 172; Mary Elizabeth 733; Mary Frances 529; Mary Louise 79; Mary M. 367; Mary Purnell 733; Mary W. 693; Matthew 227; Matthew Jr. 227; Milton 135; Minnie M. 611; Nathan 577; Nathan R. 369; 429; Owen C. 577; Philip 564; Rachel 438; Rebecca 564; Retta C. 227; Richard L. 663; Risdon L. J. 227; Robert D. 46; S. Frank 172; S. N. 663; S. S. 511; Sallie M. 80; Sally 57; Samuel 760; Samuel A. 577; Samuel F. 105; Samuel Franklin 577; Sarah 707; Sarah E. 647; Sarah Emily 245; Sophia 702; Sophia C. 754; Susan 564; Susan A. 88; Susan L. 663; Sylvester 46; T. Eugene 754; Tansy J. 355; Theopolis W. 46; Thomas A. 46; Thomas A., Jr. 46; Thomas Alexander 46; Thomas J. 80, 245; Thos B. 673; Virginia 105; W. Breckenridge 105; W. Grason 227; W. Harvey 227; Washington A. 105; Wesley T. 135; William 564, 693, 733, 770; William A. 577; William C. 57, 247, 647, 707; William D. 247; William F. 449; William G. 618; William M. 57; William T. 618; Williamima 770
SMITH, Dixon & Co. 56

SMITHERS William P. 614
SMITHMAN Thomas 558
SMOOT Melissa E. 693; Wm 693
SMYTH Blanche 181; Caroline (Stean) 181; Caroline Isabelle 299; Carrie 181; George 181; Gresham 254; Hallie C. 181; Harriet M. 21, 94; Harriett M. 181; Henry M. 120; Jefferson L. 181, 299; Lizzie M. 299; Martha Isabelle 299; Mary 181, 787; Mary C. 181; Minnie M. 299; Murray 181; Nathan R. 511; Richard 21, 94, 181, 299; Richard A. 299; Richard C. 181; Samuel 181; Sarah M. 120; William G. 299; Willie S. 181
Snow Elisha 50; Harry W. 664; James 50; James P. 50; John R. 50; Mary 664; Rachel (Pickering) 50; Rachel 50; Reuben 50; Sallie 50; Silas 50; Susan 50
SOLLAWAY Gertrude 569; Zion 569
SOMERS Dr. 651; Mamie 651; Sidonia V. 550
SPARKLIN Emma 54; Silas 54
SPARKS A. Levenia 727; Alice 789; Annie 727; Carrie V. 727; Edith 727; Edwin P. 789; Ella G. 179; Frank B. 727; George 3; Isabella 789; John F. 727; Jos B. 727; Jos B., Jr. 727; Kate 789; Lillian 789; Louisa 789; Lucy 727; Marion J. 789; Mary 727; Oliver P. 789; Robert 51; Sarah 51; Sarah Rebecca 727; Walter 789; William B. 727; Wm Dudley 727
SPEAR Edna J. 797; Edwin W. 797; Elizabeth 797; Emily E. 797; Esther 797; Franklin Lee 797; Helen 239; Jas 797; Jas Edwin 797; L. R. 797
SPEDDEN--- 70; Elizabeth (nee Taylor) 70; John 535; John L. 535, 539 Joseph Hugh 535; Levin 535; Margaret 535; Mary L. 539; Prudence 535; Prudence 70; Robert B. 535; Robert B., Jr. 535; Salley 535; Thomas 535
SPEIGHTES Charles H. 598, Clara 598
SPENCE David McClellan 520; James A. 520; James McFarland 520; John S. 674; Martha 520; Martha M. 520; Mary N. 674; Mary R. 520; Mrs. Milcah 795; Susan 520; Susie (Bennett) Graseley 520; Thomas A. 448, 555; William Wallace 520
SPENCER Anne 600; Annie 67; Catherine 687; Charlotte 672; Dr. 266; Eliza 676; Elizabeth 687; Frances E. 733; Geo W. 672; Helen 672; Henry 393; Jas 678; Jervis 672; John B. 51, 733; Laura 672; Margaret C. (Ringgold) 672; Maria 678; Maria Louisa 15; Mary 331; R. 331; Richard 15; Sophia (Gresham) 15
Spicer Annie F. 145; Annie Luda 145; James T. 145; Levin J. 145; Linden T. 145; Mattie E. 145
Spilman Carrie 96; Hattie Keen 96; Henry Pattison 96; James C.H. 96; Jeremiah P. 96; Nannie L. 96; Robert Lee 96; Robert Lee Jr. 96
SPRELL Lizzie 59; W.A. 59
SPRINGER Mary R. 757
SPRINGLE Elizabeth (Smith) 509; Elizabeth 509; John 509
SPRUANCE --- 346; Smyth William F. 346
SPRY Mary 102; Sarah Maria 686; William T. 398
SPURRY Adaline 675; George W. 675; Mary (Griffin) 675; Mary Jane 675; William 675
St. CLAIR Allie 437; Harry 437
STABLEFORD Miss 123
STACK John R. 509; Martha J. 224; Mary A. 509
STAFFORD Mary 385; Sally 57
STAKE Judge 394
STALLINGS Sophia 345
STAM Colin 202; Colin Ferguson Jr. 202; Donald Fergusan 202; Ferguson 202; John L. 202; John Rudolf 202; Lillian Roberts 202; Louis K. 202; Louisa 202; Louisa Antoinette 202; Susie Roberts 202
STAMBAUGH Della C. 45; E. Grace 45; Frederick B. 45; Jacob B. 45; Lemmon 45; Michael 45; Sarah 45; Tillie 45
STANDLEY Elizabeth 764
STANFORD Henry L. D. 397; Henry L. D., Jr. 397; Isaac W. H. 397; Marian F. 397; Marian Waller 397; Martha J. (Moore) 397; Mary A. 338; Mary S. 397; Samuel M. 397; Williamanna 397
STAPLEFORD Emily Josephine 709; Lillian 704
STAPLEFORT Annie 190; Isabella 190; John S. 190; Julia L. 190; Laura B. 190; Mary Virginia 190; Victoria 190; William T. 190
STARKEY Ellen T. 666
STAUFFER L.S. 224

INDEX (to paragraph numbers)

STAUNTON Benton 777; Elizabeth 777
STEELE Annie 674; Isabela 674; Jas B.
647; John 674; Mary Nevett 674; Miss
777; Mrs. Thomas B. 34; Thomas 674
STEINER Kate 312
STEPHENS Emma 296; Estella 73; George
258; James A. 612; John W. 612; M.
Bates 612; Martha H. 107; Mary J. 358;
Nanie B. 258; Sarah 612; Thomas C.
612; Wesley 296; Wm. B. 612
STEPHENSON Joseph 265; Lycurgus 265;
Margaret 265; Sarah 265; Sarah Anne
651
STEPLEFORTE Mary Elizabeth 5; Virginia
A. 5; William T. 5
STERLING Alger S. 488; Arintha J. 475;
Cornelia 342; Edith 342; Eveline 342;
Frederick 459; George F. 342; Jane
342; John 342, 722; John C. 342; John
E. 342; Lillie 342; Luther 342; Marhia
342; Mary 459; Mary E. 342; Sallie
488, 722; Warren 342; William 342
STEVENS A. J. W. 486; A. Levenia 727;
Alexander 53; Ann 621; Anna McKeel
770; Annie 486; B. Gootee 755;
Catherine 486; Charles 138, 404;
Charles E. 138; Eliza 414, 454;
Elizabeth 219; Flora 523; George 414;
Georgia 486; James 414; James A. 53;
James M. 621; Jane L. 53; Jennie 698;
John 138, John 414, 678, 780; John
Kemp 138; Katherine Valerie 486; Laura
514; Levi 53; Martha 198; Mary 698,
708; Mary F. 246; Mrs. Anna McKeel
770; Nancy 385; Nancy A. 469; Nannie
86; Perry G. 219; Richard 523; Samuel
198; Sarah 687; Susan E. 404; W. T.
371; W. W. 86; William 414; William
Elliot 486; William Trystram 486
STEVENSON Alula E. 399; Aurinthia a.
399; Benjamin F. 399; Benjamin T. 399;
Bessie 609; Bettie M. 609; Catherine
N. 511; Dr. 733; Harriet 399; Henry
Dr. 85; Ira E. 399; Julia 85; Lizzie
M. 399; Maria 609; Mary 609; Nancy
733; Riley M. 609; Riley P. 609;
Thomas 399; Thomas F. 609; William J.
399; Willie 609
STEVINSON Dr. 733
STEWART Arthur 237; Clara J. 722;
David 687; Elizabeth 164; Eva 237;
Henrietta Maria 687; J. S. 722; John
164; Luvenia Lucretia 131; Sarah E.
610; Thomas J. 257; William 131

STINER Dan 312
STITH Mary (Epes) 193; Mary P. 193;
Putnam 193
STOKES Catherine V. 682; Emma 242;
George E. 242; John H. 682
SJTONE--- 750
STOOPS Mr. 777; Susan Hall 777
STRAUGHN David 52; Eliza (Willis) 52;
James 52
STREET Adah L. 540; Amos R. 540;
Hattie L. 540; Isaac J. 440; Lena A.
540; Mary A. 540; Mary W. 540; Sallie
540; Thomas 540
STREETS Charles 144; Dora 144; Edward
144; Edward B. 144; George 144;
Henrietta 144; Josephine 144; Maggie
144
STRIDER Julianna 771
STRING Beld Wm 784; Harriett 784
STRONG Anna Page 305; Catherine a.
305; Charlotte A. 305; Elwood S. 305;
James P. 305; Louisa 305; Martha Edna
305; Mary Augusta 305; Thomas A. 305;
Thomas Romain 305; William 305;
William R. 305
STUART Alexander 379
STUBBS Louisa 690
STUMP Judge 496
STURETT Commodore 744
SUDLER A. D. 721; A.E. 111; Arthur
Emory 111; Carroll H. 111; Charles H.
111; Eleanor F. 164; Elizabeth 164;
Eugenia 111; Foster 111; James E. 164;
James R. 226; John M. 111; John S.
164; John Wells Emory 111; Martha
Virginia 111; Mary Morling 536; Mary
R. 111; Matilda A. 229; Morling 536;
Sallie J. 229; Sarah 164; Susan E.
164; Thomas 164; 229; Tubman 164;
Virginia 111; William 164; William J.
111; William Jackson 111
SULLIVAN Clara 355; Eliza 355; Harry
355; Howard 355; James 355; Nellie 198,
355; Peter W. 355; Tansy J. 355
SULLIVANE Clement 310; William 316
SUTHALL Anna 113
SUTHERLAND Miss 674
SUTTON Annie S. 67 B.S. 67; Carrie F.
67; George 616; George C. 193; George
W. 67; Gilpin 67; Henrietta 208; J.
Wilson 67; James N. 157; John 607;
John C. 67; John C. Jr. 67; Julia 157;
Julia 607; Leonora 699; Lewis 298;
Margaret 547; Martha (Hawks) 193; Mary

-276-

616; Susan E. 67; Thomas 563; William C. 67
SWANN Gilbert 279; Henrietta 279; James 279; Mary (Chaffinch) 279; Mary 279; Sarah Elizabeth 279; William Thomas 279
SYKES Alfred 770; Anna Matilda 770; Elizabeth 770; James 770; William 770
SYLVANIUS Grace A. 413; J. E. 413
SYLVESTER Bettie C. 215; Charles H. 215; Charles W. 215; Clementine 215; David 215; James T. 215; John T. 215; John W. 215; Martin B. 215; Sallie C. 215; Sarah E. 215; Sarah M. 215

TAGG Annie J. 431; F. T. 431
TALOR Josephine 652
TANNER Cornelius 341; Eliza 341; Elizabeth 341; Ella 341; Emma 341; Hester A. 341; John William 341; Philemon 341; Susan 341; Thomas 341; William P. 341
TARBERTON Annie G. 363; Cooper 363; Mary L. 363
TARBUTTON Addison G. 553; Annie I. 553; Charles H. 553; Edward 553; Elizabeth 553; Ella B. 707; Elma 553; Emily J. 553; George 422; George B. 553; George H. 707; George R. 553; George W. 553; James 553, 707; James C. 553; John 553; Mary 553; Mary E. 553; Mary N. 553; Mary S. 553; Nancy 553; Sarah 422; Sarah A. 707; Thomas 553; William 553
TARGERTON Hiram G. 363
TASKER Lord 697; Magdeline 697
TATE Miss 732, 733
TATEM C. P. 557; Hattie 557
TATMAN Arranna 587; Mrs. George 587
TAWES Adaline 534; Addie B. 554; Arentha C. 534; Charles L. 534; Edward 534; George W. 534; Grace (Lawson) 534; H. E. 534; Isaac H. 534, 554; James C. 534, 554; John W. 534; Julius 534; Laura A. 534; Lillian 534; Margaret 534; Noah R. 534
TAYLOR Adaline 675; Alexine 472; Alice 580; Amanda 314; Amanda B. 472; Andrew J. 439; Ann E. 595; Anna 595; Annie 472; 580, 671; Arthur W. 391; Belle Everett 4; Benjamin 458, 595; Betsey 458; C.F. 4; Calvin B. 391; Calvin M. 439; Catherine J. 581; Charles Albert 4; Charles R. 1; Colin F. 4; Ebenezer 580; Edward F. 359; Elias 439; Elisha S. 439; Eliza 516; Elizabeth 171, 472; 631; Ellen 516; Emily 198, 472; Emma 458; Esther A. 655; Fannie 580; Franklin 743; Fred 580; George 268; George W. 458; Gillis T. 458; Hester P. 439; Horatio 439; Hyland Frederick 4; Ida 472; Ida May 59; Isaac 4; Isaac T. 439; James 516; John 472; John B. 439, 580; John C. 439; John E. 580; Josiah S. 439; Kate 439; L. C. 458; Letitia E. 439; Levi 276, 458; Levi D. 458; Levin 516; Lizzie 472; Margaret Ellen (Bowen) 391; Martha 198, 458, 472; Martha R. 4; Mary 472, 580, 671; Mary A. 685; Mary E. 439, 472, 743; Mary H. 458; Mattie 391; Merrill 472; Minnie 359; Minnie Alberta 439; Miss 705; Nancy Virginia 439; Perry D. 198, 314; Perry De Rochebrune 472; Polly 439; Ralph 171; Robert P. 472, 671; Rebecca 322, 580; Robert P. 472; Sallie E. 276, 458; Sarah C. 359; Sarah E. 4, 723; Sophia 458; Sophronia 580; Susan 268; Susie C. 4; Thomas 458, 472, 671; Thomas B. 516; Thomas W. 229; Uriah 516; Walter 472; William 516, 631; William L. 458
TEACKLE Mary W. 378
TEAGLE Littleton D. 429
TEMPLE Emma V. 124; Mary 622; Mary A. 398; William 124; William G. 124
THARP Benjamin 685; Llewellyn 685; Mary 685; Mary E. (Fleming) 685
THAWLEY Addie 517; Anne 748, John W. 517; Mary F. 804; William 748,
THOMAS Ann 783; Anna Frances 51; Annie 515; Catherine 100; Charles 783; Eliza Ann 768; Elizabeth 550; Elizabeth Allen 785; Ellen Francis 783; Emily 414; Fannie 194; Frances E. 51; George Archer 396; Henrietta Maria 396, 783; James 31; Janet 113; John B. 201; Juliana 768; Kirby 515; Margaret 51, 733; Maria 393, 783; Mary 201, 687, 785; Mary A. 182; Mary Ann 768; Mary Isabella 768; Mary Morre 783; Matilda 31; Miss 468; Nicholas 786; Philip Francis 389, 733, 775, 783; Richard 51, 733;Robert T. Goldsborough 768; Samuel 113; Samuel W. 51, 100; Sarah E. Bacon 31; Sophia 733; Tristram 768, 783; Wilbur J. 194;

INDEX (to paragraph numbers)

William 31, 182, 515, 733, 785; William Dorson 781
THOMPSON --- 607; Acksah 594; Ann 13; Ann E. 196; Annie 515; Annie E. 604; Carrie 515, 701; Celia (Webster) 604; Celia 604; Celia M. 515; Charles H. 701; Charles M. 604; Charles V. 515; Chauncey 701; Chauncey H. 701; Edith May 701; Elizabeth (Ballard) 164; Elizabeth 604; Emily M. 75; George 604; George Albert 604; George F. 75; Grace 604; H. 69; Hedge 594; Howard A. 515; J. J. 518; James 75, 164; James M. 604; Jasper L. 604; John 701; Katie 75; Laura E. 701; Leila 604; Lottie 604; Mary (Woolford) 196; Mary 69, 701; Mary A. 515; Mary Ann 613; Mary R. 545, 594; Mattie 604; Miss 731; Mitchell 604; Mrs. George A. 760; Myra 604; Olevia 760; Rebecca (Johnson) 594; Rebecca 75, 594; Sarah 701; Sarah Olivia 604; Susan E. 164; Susan Emma 75; Thomas 594, 604; Thomas E. 515; Thomas J. 515; Walter 75; Walter H. 75; Walter Mills 75; William 196, 701; William E. 615; William S. 545
THORMAN Sophia 183
THORPE Gov 805
THROP Mary 613
TIDINGS Capt Lloyd 366; Mattie E. 366
TIGNER Alice 276; Thomas 276
TILDEN Catherine 548; Charles 185, 548; Dr. 189; Mary L. 185; Samuel J. 163
TILGHMAN Ann 777; Ann Maria Lloyd 767; Anna E. 1; Anna Maria 467, 687, 773, 786; Catherine 687; Catherine M. 76; Dick 678; Edward 120, 777, 782, 786; Eleanor Sarah 120, 786; Elizabeth 352, 765; Elizabeth Tench 785, 786; Frederick Boyd 134; Harriet (Tilghman) 301; Henrietta 802; Henrietta Maria 767, 774, 776, 779; Henry Cooke 352; James 134, 768; Joshua 65; Julia A. 65; Kate H. 555; Lloyd 134, 802; Margaret 768; Margaret Lloyd 773; Maria 352; Mary 687, 690, 782; Matthew 120, 134, 678; Oswald 134; Peregrine 1, 301, 688; R. 678; Richard 134, 352, 687, 765, 767, 776; Richard Cook 467; Richard Cooke 352; Richard Cooke, Jr 352; Richard, 3rd 690; Samuel O. 562; Sidell 134; Tench 120, 134, 492, 774, 785, 786; Ward 499; William 134, 773;

William B. 555; William C. 467; William G. 76
TIMANUS Fannie 317; John T. 317
TIMMONS John S. 800; Mary 800
TITTLE Ann 122
TOADVIN Amanda 555; Catherine H. 555; E. Stanley 555; Kate H. 555; Purnell 555
TOADVINE Caroline 593; Josephine A. 114; Lillian N. 283; Purnell 114
TODD Agnes 511, 757; Alonzo 803; Alonzo R. 803; Anna R. 803; Annie 511; Benjamin 203; Bennett 203; Catherine N. 511; Charles E. 203; Edwin N. 511; Elizabeth 203; Ella 647; Emma 203; Frank 203; George 511; George W. 511; H. Laird 511; H. S. 757; Harry S. 511; J. N. 647; J. W. 219; James 257; Jonathan 511; Julia A. 511; Lewis N. 203; Lillian F. 511; Lizzie 309; Lucinda H. 803; Lydia 219; Mary 287; Mary A. 257; May 511; Melvina 237; Milcah 611; Milcha 559; Minnie B. 203; Mrs. R. V. 757; Mrs. Roland 451; Mrs. William 237; Noah L. 257; Peter 803; Priscilla 257; Rose 511; Ruth 203; S. Edith 276; Samuel 548, 611; Sarah 548; Ulysses Grant 203; W. B. 287; W. C. 276; W. I. 511; Wilhelmina 203; Willard C. 203; Zebedee 257
TOLLEY Louisa 417
TOLSON Ann (Legg) 621; Ann 621; Benjamin 340, 621; Caroline 621; Eliza 409; Elizabeth 621; J. Harry 621; James Sudler 621; John H. 621; Lillie A. 709; Mary 340, 621; Minnie Lowe 621; Mrs. Thomas W. 37; Rachel Rebecca 686; Theodore 709; Victoria 621; William Denney 621
TONKIN Arthur E. 205; Catherine R. 205; Charles Henry 205; Emma 205; Henry 205; Henry Moffett 205; Howard J. 205; Jane (Thomas) 205; Mary E. 205; Rosamond 205; Rosanna 205
TOULSON Andrew 427; Catherine 427; Fannie 427; Hallie Isabella 427; James 427; James H. 427; John Milbourn 427; John Thomas 427; Joseph 427; Laura Jane 427; Mabel 427; Maria 427; Mary M. 256; Mary Maria 427; Milbourn A. 427; Nannie Rebecca 427; Philip 427; Rachael 427; Sarah Isabella 427; Susan 427; Thomas 256, 427; William Houston 427

TOWERS Albert G. 741; Curtis 741; Elijah 741; Elizabeth (Deen) 755; Henry Alpha 755; James H. 755; Lawrence B. 741; Mary A. (Garey) 741; Thomas F. 741; William F. 741
TOWNSEND Annie R. 733; Rev George W. 10; Susan L. 663
TOWSON Anne Tolly 734; William 734
TRADDER Sarah J. 84
TRAIL Josephine 772; Lewis 772
TRAVERS Adeline 298; Benjamin 79; Caroline R. 443; Catherine A. 356; Edgar Eugene 419; Eliza Jane 70; Ella G. 356; Emily 624; Eugenia 419; Harry 356; Henry 70; Hicks 356; Jane L. 105; John 356, 624; John C. 70; John Chaplin 419; Julia Ann 70; Levi D. 70, 225, 298, 419; Levi Dickinson 70; Mamie E. 225; Margaret 79; Margaret E. 356; Martha E. 105; Martha Jane 70; Mary (Dove) 70; Mary A. 150; Mary Elizabeth 298; Nanuleita 419; Philip Lee 419; Rose Anna 624; Samuel C. 356; Samuel M. 356, 624; Sophia S. 70; Thomas 150; Thomas B. 298; William C. 298, 356; William D. 70; William Dove 419; William K. 419; William M. 70
TRAVIS Hattie Keen 96; William D. 96
TRAX Annie 312; Catherine 312; Cruitt 312; Emma 312; Eurith 312; George 312; George H. 312; Henry 312; Jacob 312; John 312; Kate 312; Lola 312; Louis 312; Lydia 312; Percy 312; Rose 312
TRENCHARD Rebecca 545; Thomas W. 545
TREW Mary 37; Sallie A. 37
TRICE Ann (Willis) 509; George 296; Hester A. 509; Ida 296; Mrs. 631; Samuel 213; Sarah E. 213; William 509
TRIMBLE David C. 492; I. R. 492; Sally S. 492
TRIPP Anne 731; Arthur Sampford 731; Baron 731; Charles 731; Charles George 731; Charles Upton 731; Eliza 731; Elizabeth 731; Elizabeth Anne 731; Frances 731; Frances O. 731; Frances Upton 731; Francis 732; George 731; Harriet 731; Henry 731; Howard 731; James 731; James Upton 731; John 731; Marianne 731; Mary 731; Mary Georgina 731; Peter 731; Robert 731; Robert Henry 731; Samuel 731; Sarah 731; Sarah Caroline 731; Victor Albarnum 731; William Owen 731; William Upton 731

TRIPPE Mary Smythe 733; Amelia 733; Andrew Cross 733; Andrew Noel 733; Ann 733, 734; Anne Tolly 734; Annie R. 733; Augustus Schwartze 735; Caroline Augusta 733; Catherine D. 733; Cuthbert 733; Delia 733; Edward 732, 733, 734; Edward Jr. 732; Edward R. 730, 734, 735; Edward Richard 733; Edward Thomas 733; Eleanor 733; Eliza C. 733; Elizabeth 733; Elizabeth (Noel) 733; Elizabeth (Skinner) 733; Elizabeth 732; Elizabeth H. 733; Elizabeth Noel 733; Elizabeth Purnell 733; Elsie Caroline 733; Elvino Dickinson 735; Florence 733; Frances 733; Frederick Wright 733; Fredericka Leypold 735; Grafton Wallace 733; Hariett 733; Harriet Choirs 734; Helen 733; Hennie 733; Henrietta 732, 733; Henrietta M. 626; Henrietta Rogers 733; Henry 732, 766; Henry S. 735; Henry V. 626; Holliday 733; James 733; James McConkey 733; John 732, 733; John Fletcher 733; John H. 626; John, 3rd 733; Joseph Ennalls 733; Joseph Ennalls, Jr. 733; Joseph Everitt 733; Lavinia 733; Levin 733; Maggie 733; Margaret 733; Margaret Helen 733; Marian A. 396, 626; Marian C. 626; Marion 733; Martha 733; Mary (Ennalls) 733; Mary 732, 733, 787; Mary Emerson 766; Mary Ennalls 734; Mary Harriett 733; Mary L. 626; Mary Louisa 733; Mary Purnell 733; Mary Susannah 733; Mary Webb 734; Melusina 735; Melusina E. 735; Nancy 733; Nicholas Hammond 733; Rachel Elizabeth 733; Robert H. 733; Richard 732, 733, 734, 787; Richard Henry 733; Richard John 733; Samuel C. 626, 733; Sarah 732; Sarah Elizabeth 733, 734; Sarah Patterson 733; Sarah S. H. 733; ; Sophia 733; Sophia Elizabeth 735; Susan 733; Susannah 732; Theodore 733; Thomas Hayward 733; William 732, 733; William H. 733; William H., Jr. 733; William Jas 733; William R. 626; William Richard 733
TROUT Mary 472; Peter N. 472
TROY A. Howard 142; John 142; Julia 142; Mary L. 142; Robert 784; Rosanna 784; William D. 142
TRUE Annie 18; William G. 18
TRUETT Drusilla A. 294; John 294

INDEX (to paragraph numbers)

TRUIT --- 599
TRUITT Alice 338; Eliza M. 335; Ella (Brown) 60; Florence 338; George W. 335, 338; Henrietta 338; James G. 338; James T. 338; John 60; Laura 338; Mary 480; Mary A. (Stanford) 338; Mary V. 60; Naomi 320; Raymond King 338; Rose E. 309; Rufus K. 338; Samuel P. 335
TUBMAN Ann M. 746; Phoebe 750
TUCKER & Holland 101
TUCKER Alfred 132; Alfred Sr. 101, 132; Charles 286; Charles E. 132; Charles Edward 132; Clarence Atwell 132; Emily F. 132; George L. 132; George W. 132; John 132; John T. 132; Juliet M. 286; Mary 132; Mary A. 616; Mrs. Alfred Sr. 101; Percy 132; Richard 132; William C. 132
TULL Allen 344; Alonzo E. 218; Anice 344; Anna 606; Annie 344; Annie O. 601; Bertie 606; Bessie 606; Caroline 218; Carrie L. 218; Casie 606; Catherine 218, 376; Christiana M. 601; Clifford 218; E. James 606; E. W. 347; Edna J. 601; Edward 606; Edward W. 218; Eliza J. 232; Elizabeth 344; Elizabeth L. 222; Emeline b. (Parker) 601; Fannie B. 218; Florence 344; Frank H. 218; Franklin 344; Gertrude 606; Gordon 218, 376; Grace S. 344; Harding P. 601; Henry R. 344; Henry T. 344; J. Emory 222; Jane 377, 606; Jennie 606; Jennie F. 601; John C. 606; John E. 601; Joseph S. 601; Margaret 260; Margaret J. 601; Matilda 606; Mattie 606; Miles 601; Minnie 218; Mrs. E. W. 347; N. J. P. 232; Nathan J. P. 601; Nathan T. 601; Olive M. 218; Oscar Paul 344; Rodger; Ruth 344; S. Ashton 218, 260; Sallie Elizabeth 344; Samuel 218; Samuel L. 218, 260, 376; Samuel O. 344; Samuel Oscar 344; Samuel W. 260; Sarah Mather 260; Stella K. 218; T. H. 344; Thomas 218, 377; Thomas H. 29; Towland 218; Underwood 606; W. A. 218; William T. 601
TUNIS Helen D. 404; Joseph T. 404
TURBUTT Ann 777, 782; Anna Maria 783; Anna Maria T. 687; Bridget 766, 777, 782; Elizabeth 687, 782; Elizabeth T. 687; Foster 766, 777, 782; Greenbury 783; James Edward 783; Mary 687, 782; Mary Anne 782; Michael 687, 777;
Rachel 782; Samuel 783, 785; Sarah 777, 782; Sarah Jolly 785; Susan Loockerman 783; William 687
TURNER Ann Maria 238; Anna 576; Catherine 142; Elizabeth 576, 643; Emma C. 666; Florence A. 140; Francis 643; James 238, 738; Joseph 576; Malissa 738; Martha E. 576; Mary 608; Mrs. W. G. 666; Rachel B. 576; Richard T. 576; Richard T. Sr. 576; Richard T. Jr. 576; William B. 576
TURPIN Alfred B. 162; Aurelia 162; Clara 637; Cora V. 162; Elizabeth 162; Elizabeth B. 162; Emily 162; J. W. 637; John 162; John A. 162; Martha (Long) Mitchell 162; Sidney F. 162; Susan M. 162; Thomas W. 162; William 162
TUTHILL H. B. 693; Maggie E. 693
TWIFORD Mary 256
TWIGGS Edward 363
TWILLY Hester Ann 227
TWOMBLEY Edith C. 460; Mrs. Clifford 460
TYBOUT Harriet 678
TYLER Caroline 443; Caroline R. 443; Dinette 690; Elizabeth 443; George 443; George W. 443; Grafton 600; John G. 443; Matthew T. 443; Robert 443; Sarah Jane 443; Solomon 443;
TYLOR Jonathan 126; Jonathan Edward 126; Rebecca (Huyck) 126; Thomas 126; Wilson Moore 126

UNGLE Mary 779; Robert 779
UPSHER George M. 593
UPSHUR --- 537; Arthur 5; Sallie B. 408; Virginia 5
UPTON Anne 731; Frances A. Deborah Frederica 731; James 731; Sarah 731
URIE Frank H. 713; H. Frank 116; Helen 116; Helen E. 713; Helen Lillian 116; James 116, 652, 713; James W. 116, 713; John 713; John D. 713; John David 116; Mary 116, 652; Mary E. 713; Mary Louisa 116; Mollie 713; Thomas 116; William 116
USILTON Adaline 592; Addie L. 313; Albert 592; Alletha A. 139; Annie C. 331; Clara 592; Clarence 605; Edwin L. 592; Frances Philena 170; Francis 170, 592; Fred G. 592; Frederick G. 592; Gustavus 592; Hannah Rebecca (Lamb) 170; Harriett M. 181; Herbert 605;

Hosanna 170; Jesse 94; Jesse H. 21, 331; John Gale 605; John N. 605; Joseph 21, 139, 592; Joseph R. 21, 94; Lewin 21, 94; Lewin J. 21; Lewin M. 181; Louise 592; Lucia 605; Mary 592; Mary F. 592; Mary S. 21; Milton Earl 592; Miriam 592; Robert 592; Samuel 592; Sarah 592; Sarah M. 605; Virginia 24; William B. 592; William B. Jr. 592; William Barger 592

VALK C. D. 586; Elizabeth 586
VALLIANT Ardilla 159; E. Stevens 230; Edwin S. 230; J.J. 159; Jean 230; Mary 230; Mary C. 759; Mary T. 230; Nellie 230; Rigby 230; Thomas R. 230; William E. 230
VAN AUSDAL Emily 182
VAN DER MILLER Pieter Wonter 650
VAN DORN Gen. 674
VAN DUSER Miss 720
VAN DYKE James M. 291; Olivia 291
VAN GESEL Anna M. 252; Asbury 252; Clara 252; John 252; John H. 252; Mary M. 252; Priscilla (Furby) 252; W.T. 252
VAN HICKEL Elizabeth 179
VAN SANT Annie M. 136; George R. 136; Mary E. (Duyer) 136
VAN SAUN Jane M. 371; Samuel 372
VAN WYCK Fanny 120
VAN ZANDT J.R. 10; Samuel 372
VANDERBILT Cornelius 66
Vanderbilt farm 66
VANDERHEYDEN Ariana 30
VANE Alexander 277; Allen 277; Allen P. 277; Annie 277; Floyd B. 277; Frances 664; Henrietta 277; James G. 277; James Guy 357; Joseph 277; Joseph H. 277; Joseph T. 277; M. Estelle 357; Sarah P. 277; William A. 277; William B. 277; William S. 664
VANNORT Ezra Adams 691; Alletha A. 139; Augustus 691; Avis E. 691; Catherine D. 691; Julia Claire 139; Mary A. H. 273, 691; Samuel 139, 691; William 273; William J. 139, 691
VANSANT Benjamin 323; Cornelia 712; Edith A. 712; Ethel G. 712; George M. 712; J. Frank 712; Joshua L. 712; Julia A. 712; Martha 323; Mary J. 712; Sadie E. 712
VAUGHAN Susannah 764

VENABLE Ballard 316; Effie C. 365; Margaret 268; Rosa A. 316; Seth 365; Seth D. 442; Susan A. (Jones) 365; Susan A. 442; Susie M. 432
VENABLES Elizabeth 482; Robert 482
VICKER Louise 652
VICKERS Ann M. 207; Anne 557; Annie 171; Annie B. 665; Ellen 516; George 110; Henry 516; Henry C. 665; James C. 145; Julianna 35; Maria 171; Pattie 35; Samuel 35; Stewart 145; Thomas 171; William T. 207, 557
VICKERY Capt. 744; Josephine A. 744; Stephen Thomas 744; Thomas 744
VINCENT Annie 277, 511; Betsy 645; Beulah 593; C. L. 537; Caroline (Toadvine) 593; Clarence L. 593; Elizabeth 762; John 762; Sarah 762; Thomas 645; Thomas H. 593; Virginia L. 593
VOGEL Clayonia 249; Theodore K. 249
VOSHELL Anne 664; Frances 664; Frances F. 664; Voshell House 172; Ira S. 664; John W. 664; Levi 664; Levi T. 664; Lida R. 664; Mary 664; Obadian 664; Rebecca C. 664; Ruth A. 664; Samuel 664; Sarah E. 664; Ulysses G. 664; William 664; William H. 664
VOSS James 25; Martha J. 25

WADDELL Agnes H. 703; Alexander 703; Collison 703; Columbus 703; David F. 703; Ella 703; Ella B. 703; George 221 703; Grover S. 703; Henrietta 703; Ira s. 703; Jas M. 703; Jas W. 703; Nancy 703; Rose M. 703; Sarah 221; Thos Collison 703; Victoria 703; Walter Laing 703; Walter Scott 703; William 221 703; Winfield M. 703; Wm B. Jr. 703; Wm Bishop 703; Wm Elwood 703
WADKINS J. E. 798; Mary V. 798
WAINWRIGHT Charles W. 379; Charles W., Jr. 379; Edward B. 379; Edward J. 379; Estelle 379; Esther 351; Francis North 379; Jesse 379; Joshua 235; L. C. 379; Olivia 379; Rebecca J. 379
WAKEFIELD 204
WALDRON Margaret (Gillen) 742; Thomas F. 742; Thos J. 742
WALER Mary 240
WALKER Anna E. 97; Anna Isabel 97; Christiana (Graham) 97; Cornelia Ricaud 97; John 40; 97; John W. 97;

INDEX (to paragraph numbers)

Joseph 346; Mary 498, 580; Mary Elizabeth 97; R. Lindsay 426; Susan 40; Susan P. 426; Thomas 97, 346; William S. 97; William S. Jr. 97
WALLACE Amelia Ross 617; James 270, 570, 578; Lew 532; Mary 416; Sarah E. 271
WALLER Adeline 288; C. C. 397; Edith 570, George 240, 288; George W. 288; George W. B. 288; James 570; James A. 288; James A. Jr. 288; Jonathan 288, 332; Joseph A. 288; Julia Ann 288; Julia D. 288; Margaret C. 288; Marian F. 397; Martha I. 288; Mary A. 692; Myra 288; Richard 288; Richard Lee 288; Sarah J. 332; Thos W. 692
WALLS Arthur S. 337; Carrie 337; Charles Oscar 289; Charles R. 289; Charles W. 337; Edgar 289; Edna 289; Elizabeth 289, 337; Elwood 337; Estelle 289; Fanny 247, 289; Florence 289; Frank 289; George 337; George A. 337; Henry 337; James 337; Jennie 337; John 337; Joseph W. 337; Joshua 337, 727; Julia Ann 9; Mary C. 289; Mary E. 289; Mildred 289; Rebecca 337; Ruth 289; Sally A. 337; Samuel 289, 337; Samuel C. 289, 337; Sarah Rebecca 727; Spencer 337; Temperance A. 337; Walter 337; William L. 289
WALRAVEN Elias 522; Elizabeth 522; John 98; Mary 98
WALSTON E. 794; Lizzie 794
WALTER Bernice 684; Elizabeth (Porter) 684; Hampton B. 280, 596; Harriet 369; Margaret 684; Mary E. 684; Melissa J. 280, 596; Thomas J. 684; W A. 684; Wm 684
WALTERS Alexander 409; Annie 644; Charles H. 101; J. M. 693; Martha 693; Mary E. 409; Mary Emeline 409; Rebecca 68; W. H. 644; William H. 68
WAPLES Susan 480
WAPPINGS 375
WARD & COLLINS 474
WARD Christopher Columbus 528; Clara O. 649; Edwin E. 528; F. H. 649; Harriet 399; John B. 601; Louisa 528; Love 550; M. P. 528; Margaret J. 601; Maria 768; Sarah A. 528; Thomas 399
WARFIELD Lot 780; Miss 780
WARNER Asa 133; John L. 533; John W. 421; Lucinda 421; Margaret Ann 133; Mary J. 533; Sallie M. 751; W. M. 751

WARREN General 59; Gretha V. 418; Jabez 418; Louis E. 418; Louis Kossuth 418; Lydia 418; Margaret (Webb) 418; Mary 355; Mary Elizabeth 418; Rachel G. 303; Reuben 303; Robert Noble 418; Ruskin B. 418
WARRING Miss 772
WARRINGTON Ann E. 196
WARWICK James A. 530; James W. 530; Josiah 530; Mary G. 530; Mary J. 530; Nancy Estelle 530
WASHINGTON General 120; George 254; 581; Martha 95
WATERS Annie 532; Annie E. 375; Arnold E. 532; Arnold Elzey 532; Edward 532; Eliza 532; Eliza W. 532; Emily R. 532; Francis 263; Henry Jackson 532; John 532; Levin 532; Levin L. 375, 532; Levin Littleton 532; Lucretia 532; Mary 263; Nellie 164; Virginia L. 328, 445; William S. 362
WATKINS Anna 304; William H. 304
WATTS Charles Garfield 102; George 102; Isaac 102; Mary R. 102; William M. Jr. 102; William Maxwell 102; William Sr. 102
WEATHERLOW Eliza 725
WEATHERLY Charles S. 471; Christiana 471; Elizabeth (Lowell) 471; Elizabeth H. 471; George T. 471; James 471; Levin B. 471; Nancy 471; William James 471; Yancey W. 471
WEBB & Co. 310
WEBB Elizabeth 733; Francis H. 270; Hannah 619; Joseph W. 130; Margaret 418, 733; Mary 733; Mary A. 270; Peter 733; Samuel 619; Sarah 733
WEBSTER Ada E. 596; Andrew J. 280; Benjamin F. 280; Brazilia 315; Catherine C. 280; Celia 604; Charles 590, 643; Col. 32; David O. 280; Drusilla 280; Edward Z 596; Elizabeth 280, 643; Elizabeth E. 315; Emily J. 596; Esther 315; Ethel 315; Eugene Brown 596; Frank 590, 643; George 315; Grace 315; Guy L. 590; Helen 315; Ida A. 590 Indiana F. 315; Isabel 280, 596; Jabez 280; Jacob 596; Jacob W. 596; Jacob Wesley 280; John 590, 596, 614, 643; John B. 590; 643; John W. 596; Julia 596; Julia A. 280; Lloyd 590; 643; Luther 315; M. Augusta 643; Margaret 643; Marion 590; Mary 26, 280, 523, 643; Mary C. 188; Mary E.

-282-

280; Mary J. 280; Mary P. 596; Melissa 280; Melissa J. 280, 596; Michael 188; Nellie 590; Noah 590, 643; Oscar C. 315; Pricilla A. 643; Priscilla A. 590; Rebecca 643; Roland 590, 643; Ruth 315; Sadie V. 596; Samuel 315, 590; Samuel L. 590, 614, 643; Sarah 315, 643; Sarah F. 32; Sarah Jane 315; Shepard 590, 643; Sml 643; Sml L. 643; Thomas J. 280; Thos 643; Virginia C. 280; William C. 596; William J. 280, 596 William W. 280; Winfield 590, 643; Zachary W. 280; 596; Zack H. 315
WEEDEN Annie 760; John O. 760; Austin R. 545; Henry 545; J. H. W. G. 545; Mary A. 545; Mary R. 545; Rebecca (Legg) 545; Rebecca 545; Trystram 486
WEEKS Captain 181; Lewin 181
WELLS Tobia 764; Tobias 764
WELSH Albert 455; Albert E. 455; Annie 455; Caroline 455; Charles 455; Ella 455; Emmett 455; Ida 455; Leila B. 455; Margaret 455; Margaret H. 455; Margaret Jane 455; Mary 455; Mary E. 455; Robert 455; Sally (Harrington) 455; Sarah Augusta 466; Thomas 455; William 455; William H. 466
Wenzell Kate Gale 170
WEST Anna 634; Annie G. 421; Charles H. 634; Clara M. 2; Cora A. 421; Elijah W. 421; Ellen 421; Howard E. 421; John W. 421; Lucinda 421 Lulu E. 421; Margaret A. 634; Mary E. 421; S. Leslie 634; Simeon 634; Thomas C. 634; Thos. K. 634; Titus Irons 634; William 421, 634; Zadockely 421
WESTCOTT Edward S. 185; Elizabeth R. 185; Ellen L. 185; George B. 185; George Godfrey 185; Hallie R. 185; Hezekiah P. 206; Joseph P. 185; Mary L. 185; Nicholas G. 185; Polly 185; Polly Wickes 185; Samuel Buck 185; Simon Wickes 185; Susan 206
WESTON Anna L. 372; William E. 372
WETHERED Ann Elizabeth 349; Elizabeth 264; John L. 83; Lewis 547; Louisa Maria (Wickes) 264; Margaret Spencer 83; Peregrine 264
WHALEY Edw 800; Edward Thomas 800; Elizabeth 800; Florence 800; Hester A. 800; Jas 800; John W. 800; Maria K. 800; Mary 800; Peter 800; Seth 800; Seth M. 800

WHEATLEY 698; A.B. 6; Arthur 6; Frances George 122; J. L. 158; J.C. 6; J.F. 6; Jennie 698; Joseph N. 6, 122; Joseph N. Jr. 6; Kate 6; Mary 514; 698; T. W. Russell 6; W.A. 6; Wm 698
WHEELER Margaret 535; Miss 357
WHITE Albert 393; Alward 770, 780; Alward McKeel 770, 780; Anna M. 659; Anna Maria 780; Anna McKeel Stevens 770; Anna Mckeel Stevens Goldsborough 770; Anna McKell Goldsborough 780; Annie 261, 561; Bernard 561; Betsy M. (Wainwright) 235; Cardinal 561; Catherine 561; Chas 780; David 280; Edward 561; Elizabeth 454; Emily 235; Fannie 780; Frances 731; Frederick 561; Gladys 561; Henrietta Maria 780; Indiana F. 315; Isaac 235; James 235, 561; John 770; John Goldsborough 780; Josephine 561; Julia 561; Louisa 453; Madeline 561; Major 261; Margaret 261, 364; Margaret E. 667; Maria L. 409; Marmaduke 561; Mary 28, 62, 547; Mary E. 280; Mary G. 530; Mary Louisa 733; Olivia A. 235; Sally 780; Samuel 235, 409; Samuel C. 315; Sue 561; Thomas W. K. 561; Tubman 364; Virginia W. 476; Walter 561
WHITEFIELD Sml 750
WHITELEY Annie F. 153; Col. 750; Elizabeth 750
WHITELY, Stone & Co. 750
WHITING Emma J. 348; Isabella 92; Samuel 348; Virginia 348; William 348
WHITINGTON Judge 267
WHITMAN Louise 372; Anna L. 372; Bertram Edward 372; Frederick S. 371; Frederick William 372; George 371; Jane M. (Van Saun) 371; John 371; Samuel Edward 371; Walter 372; Walter Weston 372
WHITTINGTON Alfred 377; Alfred A. 602; Aurelia M. 642; Austin L. 602; Beulah 377; Caroline 377; Charles S. 347, 377, 602; Charlotte 529; Clara 651; Eda E. 347; Eliza 602; Elizabeth 20; 598; Emily C. 377; Emma C. 602; Isaac 642; Isaac T. 642; Jane (Tull) 602; Jane 377; Jas 642; John 377; Joseph H. 377, 602; Mary 377, 642; Mary E. 642; Mrs. William 232; Norman T. 602; Olive M. 218; R. 218; Rbt 651; Rbt H. 642; S. Frank 377, 602; Sallie 602; 642; Southey 377, 602; Stéphen 377; Stephen

INDEX (to paragraph numbers)

H. 642; Stephenson 377, 602; William
529; Wm R. 642
WHITTLE Bishop 193
WICKES --- 678; Anna Maria 467; Anna
Tilghman 467; Anne Elizabeth
(Wethered) 349; Anne Elizabeth 264;
Anne R. 264; Anne Rebecca 321; 467;
Benjamin Chambers 321, 466; Caroline
Barney 467; Charles Henry 321;
Charlotte A. 305; Elizabeth (Blake)
264; Elizabeth 321; Elizabeth C.
(Chambers) 467; Elizabeth Caroline
466, 489; Ezekiel Chambers 466; Fannie
321; Gladys 467; Gladys Robinson 467;
Hannah 321; Hester Van Bibber 466,
467; Isaac Freeman 321; Joseph 321,
466, 467, 489; Joseph A. 321, 466,
467; Josephine Rebecca 467; Lambert
678; Lewin W. 264, 349; Louisa 264;
Marie 466; Mary (Piner) 466; Mary
Elizabeth 466; Mary Freeman 321; Mary
Hamilton 321; Nancy 321; Peregrine L.
466; Polly 185, 321; Sarah Augusta
466; Sarah P. 466; Simon 185, 264,
321, 467; Simon Alexander 466; Thomas
466; Thomas Stockton 264, 321; Thomas
W. 321; William N. E. 349; William
Nichols Earle 264, 321; William
Nichols Earle, Jr. 264
WICKS Charlotte 672; Judge 128; Thos
W. 672
WIGGIN Emily 460; Timothy 460
WILCOX Henry 13; Jane 13
WILCUTT Susan 520
WILEY John 291; Olivia 291
WILIS Sallie B. 331
WILKINS B.N.S. 93; Ben N.S. 93;
Brayman Rogers 93; Edward 93, 155 178;
Edward M. 93; Edward Mifflin 178;
Fannie 178; Fannie L. 93; Frances
Olivia 93; Frank 93; Grace 178; Henen
Gray 93; Jennie 178; Julia Anna 155;
Juliana 93; Maria 93; Mary 265; Mary
A. 178; Maude 93; Maurice Gray 93;
Mrs. 178; Samuel Merritt 93; Sue C.
178
WILKINSON Addie 709; Anna De
Rauchbrune 328; Christopher 328, 563,
687; Eliza 563; Jane 581; John 244,
563, 709; Louisa 563; Molly G. 244
WILLARD Annie M. 104; Catherine R.
152; William D. 104
WILLEY E. M. 559; M. M. 282; Margaret
I. 559

WILLIAMS A. Blanche 255; Adeline 288;
Alcade 484; Alonzo L. 255; Angie L.
484; Ann 540, 671; Ann E. 671; Annie
361, 671; Arthur 470; Arthur Everett
255; Bolivan 361; Caroline 255; Carrie
484; Catherine 288, 400; Charles E.
288 Daniel 509; Eleanor 29; Eleanor W.
(Wootten) 255; Eliza C. 255; Elizabeth
(Newlee) 484; Elizabeth (Springle)
509; Elizabeth Cooke 352; Elizabeth E.
484; Ella M. 671; Emma 437; Frances
461; George N. 484; Ida G. 400; Isaac
F. 176; J. K. 461; James 671; James H.
440; James M. 255, 484; Jane L. 484;
Jay 255; John 29, 255 288, 400, 437,
509; John Henry 509; Josephine M. 425;
Julia Smith 509; Larua V. 227; Laura
E. 501; Levin P. 671; Lottie 470; Lucy
E. 255; Luther M. 255; Lydia 671;
Madison 472, 671; Margaret 671;
Margaret C. 288; Margaret M. 440;
Martha J. 255; Mary (Jackson) 509;
Mary 46, 671; Mary E. 472; Mary S.
484; Otho Holland 352; Rebecca R.
(Stuart) 176; Richard 484; Robert W.
501; Roger 614; Sarah E. 215; Sir
William 509; Thomas 425; Thomas Henry
176; William N. 484
WILLIAMSON Addie 434; Alexander 83;
Allie 434; Ann 83; Betsy 434; Carrie
278; Charles 434; Edgar 278; Elias W.
434; Elijah 278; Eliza A. 434; Ennalls
278; James 83; Manly 434; Mary 278;
Mary J. 660; May 278; Orrin 434;
Richard 83; Sarah 278; Stephen 434;
William 83; William E. 434; William W.
278
WILLIE Adeline 237
WILLIS Alexander 331; Ann 509; Annie
21; Annie C. 331; Edgar 750; Eleanor
S. 331; Elizabeth 331; Ella 613; Emily
219; Emma 750; H.F. 219; Harry C. 331;
Harry M. 219; John 331; Jonathan S.
331; Lillie 750; Margaret E. 331; Mary
219, 331, 509; 750; Mary E. 331; Mary
Elizabeth 414, 454; May L. 331; Mrs.
Harry C. 21; Nicholas 331; Peter 509;
Thomas J. 21, 331, 414, 454; Thos
Adolphus 750; Walter 613; William 331,
750; William B. 331; Willie Woolford
750
WILLOUGHBY Edward 92; Martie 666; Mary
(Cheesman) Woollen 552; Mary Ann 92;

Nettie 552; Wilhelmina 203; William 552; William M. 92
WILLSON--- 254; Ann M. 254; Anna E. 180; Anne E. (Brooke) 180; Charlotte M. 180; Eleanor 784; Henrietta M. 180; Horace A. 254; James 768; John 784; John Charles 180, 248, 793; Julia R. 254; Julia Rena 180; Maria 254; Maria Smyth 254; Mary H. 248, 793; Mary Isabella 768; Mary Jacob 768; Mary Regina 180; Maude Agnes 180; Milford M. 254; Notley O. 254; Paul Alexander 254; Peter C. 254; Richard Bennett 180; Thomas B. 254; Thomas Bennett 180; Thomas Bennett Jr. 180; Thomas Smyth 248, 793; William 254
WILLTON 707
WILMER Mary 777; Mrs. Harry 802; Perry 777
WILMOT David 372
WILSON A. 57; Agnes 302; Angeline 57; Anna D. 445; Anna De Rauchbrune 328; Annie E. 300; Ary A. 151; Aurelia V. 497; Belle C. 647; Bertha 99; C.E. 88; Capt John F. 39; Charlotte 510; Clara 300, 424; Cora V. 302; Dennis 559; Edith Jennings 302; Elennor 465; Elizabeth 497; 538; Elizabeth A. 497; Ellen E. 302; Emma 216; Ethel May 302; Everett B. 99; Ezekiel 326; Fannie 318; Fannie E. 657; farm 616; Frank 300; Frank Kennedy 300 Frederick 99; George 300; George M. 88; George Rochester 302; George T. 439; George W. 300; Hannah C. 99; Harry C. 99; Harry Eugene 302; Henry 424; Henry Beatty 302; Ida M. 424; Isabel 280, 596; J. F. 102; J. Frank 497; J. R. 10; James 300; James D. 279; Jennie 300; John 302 John A. 302; John E. 99, 424; John Nicodemus 302; John T. 318, 364, 497; Jos E. 647, 657; Joseph 216; Joseph C. 302; Judge 453; Katie 302; L. N. 318; Laurine 99; Lazarus 280; 596; Letitia J. 47, 541; Levin A. 497; Levin M. 318, 497, 541; Lizzie 318; Louis N. 497; Louisa 326; Luther Roy 302; M. H. 379; Margaret 302, 559; Mariana 88; Mary 279; Mary Ann 204; Mary Louise 302; Mary M. 99; Mary R. 102; Mrs. John E. 638; Nancy Virginia 439; Norman S. 300; Rebecca 580; Rebecca J. 379; S. Kennedy 302; Sallie E. 326; Samantha 498; Samuel D. 194; Samuel P. 300; Sarah 300; Sarah E. 194; 326; Susan 300; Susan T. 300; Thomas 204, 313, 497; W.G.G. 131; Walter Duncan 302; William 424; William E. 300; William Griffith 88; William H. 88; William T. 498; Winter L. 99
WILSON-SMALL Steamboat Co. 491
WINCHESTER Catherine 561; Julia 561
WINDER Alice 492; Charles S. 492; Levin 679
WINDSOR Brazilia 315; George W. 315; Hattie L. 540; Isaac W. 540; Langford 540; Marcellus 540; Matt 540
WINGATE Geo W. 736; J. E. 736; Laura J. 729; Laura M. 736; Virginia 736
WINSOR Philip 567; Wilhelmina 567
WINTERBOTTOM Harrison T. 127; Mamie G. 127; Mary E. 127
WIRT Elizabeth 782; Elizabeth G. 782; Wm 782
WISE Anne 731; John Henry 731
WITHERS Samuel 784
WODCOCK Rose 511
WOELFORD Mrs. Whitely 483
WOLFORD Hannah C. 750
WOOD Mary 522; Mr. 106
WOODAL A. W. 607; Alice 607
WOODALL Adele 27; Agnes L. 27; Andrew 27; 39; Andrew W. 39; Ann 808; Augustus 27; Capt Andrew 39; Catherine 39; Edward 27; Edward B. 27, 39; Edward E. 27; Edward E. Jr. 27; Elizabeth 27; Emily 39; Fannie 27; Howard 27; James E. 39; James F.M. 39; John 204; Joseph 27; Lillian 27; Louisa 27; Mary E. 27; Matilda J. 204; Sallie E. 39; Simon 39; 808; Simon R. 39
WOODFORD Anne H. 436; Elmira 436; Ida 436; J. W. W. 436; James 436; John, Wallace 436; Marion J. 436; Thomas R. 436; Walter E. 436; William J. 436; William T. 436
WOODLAND Ann 362; Cephelia 319; Emma A. 758; J. F. 758; Jas F. M. 758; Jas Freeman 758; Laura A. 583; Mary E. 758; Nellie 212
WOODLE Ann 374
WOODS Nancy 652; Thos 652
WOODSLAND Samuel H. 212
WOODSTOCK 518
WOODWARD Elizabeth 579

INDEX (to paragraph numbers)

WOOLFORD Almira 750; Amelia 733; Annie 532; Annie E. 375; Battie 750; Benjamin Whiteley 750; Charlotte 750; Clara L. 375; Eliza B. 750; Elizabeth 750; Elizabeth E. 375; Ellen 750; Emma 750; Eva 750; Frank 750; Geo 750; Geo Whitefield 750; Hiram 750; J. S. B. 750; Jas 733, 750; John 375; 750; Kate 750; Lena R. 375; Levin 375, 532, 750; Lillie 750; Lillie C. 750; Lillie Crawford 750; Lizzie V. 750; Lydia 750; Mabel 750; Mary 750; Mildred 750; Miles 750; Mollie 750; Nancy 750; Nellie 750; Roger 375, 733, 750; S. B. B. 750; S. W. 750; Sallie 750; Sarah 750; Sml W. 750; Sml W., Jr. 750; Sml Whitefield 750; Sml Whitefield, Jr. 750; Stephen 750; Stephen W. 750; Susie 750; Susie L. 750; Thos 750; Valeria 750; Willie 750
WOOLLEN George M. 552; Grace 552; John 552; Katie 552; Lillie B. 552; Lloyd 552; Mary (Cheesman) 552; Mary J. 552; May 552; Nellie H. 552; Sallie E. 552; William J. 552
WOOTERS Charles R. 445; John 612; John T. 301; Sarah 612 .
WOOTTERS Laura B. 23; Lemuel J. 186; M.L. 186; Sarah E. 186
WORRELL William Page 548; Catherine (Tilden) 548; Catherine 548; Charles 548; Elizabeth 548; Frederick 548; Maria L. 548; Mary C. 548; William 548
WORTHINGTON Achsah 772; John 719; Nicholas 719, 771; Sarah 771; Thos 719; Zachariah 719
WRIGHT & McKENNEY 132
WRIGHT Abraham 233; Abraham R. 717; Abram 406; Alcade 282; Alvin 368; Alvin W. 406; Amanda 368; Ann E. 671; Ann M. 207; Anna O. 717; Anne (Kimmey) 282; Anne 207; 557; Anne Adkins 557; Annie 472; Annie H. 243; Arah Ann 406; Arthur L. 588; Atha 469; Benjamin 588; Berkley H. 588; Bethany 406; Betsy Ann 406; C. M. 495; Carrie 207; Catherine 406; Celia (Lewis) 406; Celia 207; 406, 557; Christiana 406; Clarence E. 282; Clementine 654; Clinton 687; Constant 282; Cornelius 406; Daniel 132; Deborah 687; Dora 282; Dorcas (Nichols) 406; Dorcas 296; Edith 512; Edward 557, 588; Eleanor 296; Eliza 296; Elizabeth S. 207; Elsie 368;
Emilene 282; Emily 296; Emily F. 132; Emma 296; Ethel 368; Eva 368; Evelyn (Taylor) 1; Everett 368; Everett K. 406; Fanny 173; Fannie 296, 580; Frank 557, 580; Fred 207; Gustavus 687; Harriet 207, 296, 304; Harriet P. 557; Harry M. 207; Hattie 207, 557; Henry Annels 173; Henry M. 557; Herman 368; Hester 233, 654; Hester Ann 406; Hubert H. 512; Ida 296; Ira W. 282; Isaac 296, 557; Isaac H. 207, 557; Jabez 368, 406; Jacob 557, 588; James 296; James M. 368; James Marcus 368, 406; Jennie 588; Jesse 282, 557; Jesse A. 282; John A. 588; John N. 207, 557; John P. 282; Joseph 233, 654; Joseph W. 512; Josephus A. 588; K. A. 717; Katie 521; Katie M. 737; Kennelly 406; Kennelly J. 406; Kennely J. 368; Kinley 233, 654; Levin E. 588; Levin W. 588; Lewis 406; Lillian P. 207; Lizzie 495, 588; Louisa H. 588; Lovey 406; Lyda 557 Lydia 671; M. Rhodolph 406; Maggie 310; Maggie A. 282; Margaret A. 296, 406; Margaret Ann 406; Margaret E. 296; Martha Maude 717; Martin M. 282; Mary 296, 368; Mary C. 406; Mary E. 296; Mary F. 687; May 207, 557; Minnie E. 282; Minus 406; Mrs. Curtis A. 671; Mrs. J.M. 198; Mrs. James B. 472; Mrs. Jesse 671; Nettie V. 282; Nicholas 296; Oliver R. 282; R. T. 570; Rebecca C. 557; Rhoena V. 406; Rigsby T. 512; Riley W. 282; Robert 521; Robert Lee 557; Rodolph 368; Roland 282; Rowena 368; S. A. 717; S. M. 737; Samuel 296, 406; Samuel Jr. 296; Sarah G. 512; Sarah J. 296; Sarah P. 512; Sella 717; T. E. 310; Thomas 1; Thomas I. 296; V. Grace 717; Walter M. 282; Wilbur F. 406; William 207; William J. 282; William O. 521; William W. 557; Zed 368, 406
WRIGHTSON Ada G. 366; Albert 582; Ann 798; Anna Marie 69; Annie R. 759; Charles T. 366, 759; Edward G. 366; Eliza 582; Elizabeth (Orem) 558; Ellen J. 366, 572; Emma L. 366; Francis 69, 366, 572; Francis A. 366, 572; Frank G. 69; Frank G. Jr. 69; G. Edward 366 ,724; George D. 69; George E. 366; Helen Dawson 69; Hester 582; James 558, 798; James T. 69; James W. 69;

John 558; Johnathan, Jr. 582; Jonathan
J. 582; Joseph G. 366; Joshua G. 69;
Kirby 278; Laura B. 582; Madge S. 69;
Mary 69, 558; Mary Ann 366; Mary Anne
(Lowe 572; Mary Anne 572; Mary F. 366;
572; Mary R. 594; Mattie E. 366; May
278; 366; May Grace 366; Minnie Lowe
69; Mrs. W. O. 725; Rebecca Ann 572;
Rebecca Sherwood 765; Robert 451; Rose
G. 582; Samuel H. 582; Sarah 798;
Sarah A. 582; Sarah D. 69; Susan May
724; Thomas 582; William 582; William
J. 366; William L. 366, 69; William
V. 69
WROTEN Cora A. 788; Jos 788
WROTH Mrs. W.F. 128
WYNAN Ross 360
YAPP farm 478
YELLOT Jeremiah 61; Margaret F. 61
YERBURY Richard 769; Sarah 769; Sarah 769
YOUNG --- 403; Ann M 254; Benjamin
254; Elizabeth Ann 161; John 664;
Notley 254; Rbt E. 664; Rose 487;
William J. 487; William S. 341
YOUNGER Sidney Usilton 170

Other Heritage Books by F. Edward Wright:

Abstracts of Bucks County, Pennsylvania Wills, 1685–1785
Abstracts of Cumberland County, Pennsylvania Wills, 1750–1785
Abstracts of Cumberland County, Pennsylvania Wills, 1785–1825
Abstracts of Philadelphia County Wills, 1726–1747
Abstracts of Philadelphia County Wills, 1748–1763
Abstracts of Philadelphia County Wills, 1763–1784
Abstracts of Philadelphia County Wills, 1777–1790
Abstracts of Philadelphia County Wills, 1790–1802
Abstracts of Philadelphia County Wills, 1802–1809
Abstracts of Philadelphia County Wills, 1810–1815
Abstracts of Philadelphia County Wills, 1815–1819
Abstracts of Philadelphia County Wills, 1820–1825
Abstracts of Philadelphia County, Pennsylvania Wills, 1682–1726
Abstracts of South Central Pennsylvania Newspapers, Volume 1, 1785–1790
Abstracts of South Central Pennsylvania Newspapers, Volume 3, 1796–1800
Abstracts of the Newspapers of Georgetown and the Federal City, 1789–99
Abstracts of York County, Pennsylvania Wills, 1749–1819
Bucks County, Pennsylvania Church Records of the 17th and 18th Centuries Volume 2: Quaker Records: Falls and Middletown Monthly Meetings
Anna Miller Watring and F. Edward Wright
Caroline County, Maryland Marriages, Births and Deaths, 1850–1880
Citizens of the Eastern Shore of Maryland, 1659–1750
Cumberland County, Pennsylvania Church Records of the 18th Century
Delaware Newspaper Abstracts, Volume 1: 1786–1795
Early Charles County, Maryland Settlers, 1658–1745
Marlene Strawser Bates and F. Edward Wright
Early Church Records of Alexandria City and Fairfax County, Virginia
F. Edward Wright and Wesley E. Pippenger
Early Church Records of New Castle County, Delaware, Volume 1, 1701–1800
Frederick County Militia in the War of 1812
Sallie A. Mallick and F. Edward Wright
Inhabitants of Baltimore County, 1692–1763
Land Records of Sussex County, Delaware, 1769–1782
Land Records of Sussex County, Delaware, 1782–1789
Elaine Hastings Mason and F. Edward Wright
Marriage Licenses of Washington, District of Columbia, 1811–1830
Marriages and Deaths from the Newspapers of Allegany and Washington Counties, Maryland, 1820–1830
Marriages and Deaths from The York Recorder, 1821–1830
Marriages and Deaths in the Newspapers of Frederick and Montgomery Counties, Maryland, 1820–1830

Marriages and Deaths in the Newspapers of Lancaster County, Pennsylvania, 1821–1830
Marriages and Deaths in the Newspapers of Lancaster County, Pennsylvania, 1831–1840
Marriages and Deaths of Cumberland County, [Pennsylvania], 1821–1830
Maryland Calendar of Wills Volume 9: 1744–1749
Maryland Calendar of Wills Volume 10: 1748–1753
Maryland Calendar of Wills Volume 11: 1753–1760
Maryland Calendar of Wills Volume 12: 1759–1764
Maryland Calendar of Wills Volume 13: 1764–1767
Maryland Calendar of Wills Volume 14: 1767–1772
Maryland Calendar of Wills Volume 15: 1772–1774
Maryland Calendar of Wills Volume 16: 1774–1777
Maryland Eastern Shore Newspaper Abstracts, Volume 1: 1790–1805
Maryland Eastern Shore Newspaper Abstracts, Volume 2: 1806–1812
Maryland Eastern Shore Newspaper Abstracts, Volume 3: 1813–1818
Maryland Eastern Shore Newspaper Abstracts, Volume 4: 1819–1824
Maryland Eastern Shore Newspaper Abstracts, Volume 5: Northern Counties, 1825–1829
F. Edward Wright and Irma Harper
Maryland Eastern Shore Newspaper Abstracts, Volume 6: Southern Counties, 1825–1829
Maryland Eastern Shore Newspaper Abstracts, Volume 7: Northern Counties, 1830–1834
Irma Harper and F. Edward Wright
Maryland Eastern Shore Newspaper Abstracts, Volume 8: Southern Counties, 1830–1834
Maryland Militia in the Revolutionary War
S. Eugene Clements and F. Edward Wright
Newspaper Abstracts of Allegany and Washington Counties, Maryland, 1811–1815
Newspaper Abstracts of Cecil and Harford Counties, Maryland, 1822–1830
Newspaper Abstracts of Frederick County, Maryland, 1816–1819
Newspaper Abstracts of Frederick County, Maryland, 1811–1815
Sketches of Maryland Eastern Shoremen
Tax List of Chester County, Pennsylvania 1768
Tax List of York County, Pennsylvania 1779
Washington County Church Records of the 18th Century, 1768–1800
Western Maryland Newspaper Abstracts, Volume 1: 1786–1798
Western Maryland Newspaper Abstracts, Volume 2: 1799–1805
Western Maryland Newspaper Abstracts, Volume 3: 1806–1810
Wills of Chester County, Pennsylvania, 1766–1778

www.ingramcontent.com/pod-product-compliance
Lightning Source LLC
Chambersburg PA
CBHW070724160426
43192CB00009B/1307